# Cognitive Technologies

Managing Editors: D.M. Gabbay   J. Siekmann

Editorial Board: A. Bundy   J.G. Carbonell
M. Pinkal   H. Uszkoreit   M. Veloso   W. Wahlster
M.J. Wooldridge

Hermann Helbig

# Knowledge Representation and the Semantics of Natural Language

With 258 Figures, 23 Tables and CD-ROM

 Springer

*Author:*

Hermann Helbig
Fachbereich Informatik
FernUniversität Hagen
Postfach 940, 58084 Hagen, Germany
hermann.helbig@fernuni-hagen.de

*Managing Editors:*

Prof. Dov M. Gabbay
Augustus De Morgan Professor of Logic
Department of Computer Science, King's College London
Strand, London WC2R 2LS, UK

Prof. Dr. Jörg Siekmann
Forschungsbereich Deduktions- und Multiagentensysteme, DFKI
Stuhlsatzenweg 3, Geb. 43, 66123 Saarbrücken, Germany

ACM Computing Classification (1998): I.2.4, I.2.7, H.1.2, F.4.1

ISSN 1611-2482
ISBN-10 3-642-43999-3  Springer Berlin Heidelberg New York
ISBN-13 978-3-642-43999-5  Springer Berlin Heidelberg New York

Cover design: KünkelLopka, Heidelberg
Typesetting: Camera ready by the editors
Production: LE-TeX Jelonek, Schmidt & Vöckler GbR, Leipzig
Printed on acid-free paper    45/3142/YL - 5 4 3 2 1 0

# Preface

Natural Language is not only the most important means of communication between human beings, it is also used over historical periods for the preservation of cultural achievements and their transmission from one generation to the other. During the last few decades, the flood of digitalized information has been growing tremendously. This tendency will continue with the globalization of information societies and with the growing importance of national and international computer networks. This is one reason why the theoretical understanding and the automated treatment of communication processes based on natural language have such a decisive social and economic impact. In this context, the semantic representation of knowledge originally formulated in natural language plays a central part, because it connects all components of natural language processing systems, be they the automatic understanding of natural language (analysis), the rational reasoning over knowledge bases, or the generation of natural language expressions from formal representations.

This book presents a method for the semantic representation of natural language expressions (texts, sentences, phrases, etc.) which can be used as a universal knowledge representation paradigm in the human sciences, like linguistics, cognitive psychology, or philosophy of language, as well as in computational linguistics and in artificial intelligence. It is also an attempt to close the gap between these disciplines, which to a large extent are still working separately. It must be emphasized that many of the problems treated in this book have already been investigated from various points of view in different scientific disciplines, especially in linguistics, psychology, and artificial intelligence, but often without their taking notice of each other. One reason for this is the fast growing amount of literature, where individual results are obtained and reported by different "schools", or are embedded into different terminological systems whose translation into each other is extremely difficult. Therefore, the transfer of research results, or merely a comparison of these results, is very complicated and time consuming. Furthermore, the use of the results in systems for automatic language processing plays only a minor part (if any) in many scientific disciplines. To be fair, this can also not be expected regarding the goals of their work. Nevertheless, the comprehensive background knowledge provided by these disciplines is an important basis for automatic processing of natural language.

The representational means of **Multi**layered Extended Semantic **Net**works (abbreviated MultiNets), which are described in this book, provide a universally applicable formalism for the treatment of semantic phenomena of natural language. To this end, they offer distinct advantages over the use of the classical predicate calculus and its derivatives. The knowledge representation paradigm and semantic formalism MultiNet is used at the University of Hagen as a common backbone for all aspects of natural language processing (be they theoretical or practical ones). It is continually used for the development of intelligent information and communication systems and for natural language interfaces to the Internet. Within this framework it is subject to permanent practical evaluation and further development.

The semantic representation of natural language expressions by means of MultiNet is mainly independent of the considered language. In contrast, the syntactic constructs used in different languages to describe the same content are obviously not identical. Thus, the syntactic phenomena and their translations into MultiNet discussed in this work apply primarily to German. When we give an English translation for the natural language examples, trying to stay as close as possible to the German counterpart, we pursue a double goal: On the one hand, that the phenomena discussed be hopefully better understood by readers not familiar with German, and, on the other hand, that it be seen how similar the problems of semantic interpretation are for languages grammatically as close to each other as English and German.

If the parallelism is obvious, only the English sentence, phrase, or example is given. If the syntactic phenomena are diverging (as is often the case with negation and other language phenomena of English and German) the examples are given in both languages using the indicators "Ge:" for "German" and "En:" for "English". In graphical representations, the English and German concept labels are often separated only by a slash.

This book is concerned primarily with the description of a system or language for semantic knowledge representation, and not with the logical formalism working with this language (that will be the topic of another book). Nevertheless, we will often refer to the axiomatic underpinning and the inferential power of the expressional means, because this is important for their operational semantics in a question-answering game or question-answering system (QAS). Thus, these expressional means obtain their full meaning only in the whole framework of a QAS. By choosing a different set of axioms and inference rules assigned to specific relations or functions, different manifestations of a knowledge base can be obtained, which are technically built on the same representational means.

This book consists of two parts:

- Part I deals with the most important problems of semantic knowledge representation and with the semantic interpretation of typical natural language phenomena. The representational language explained in Part II provides the basic constructs of MultiNet to be used in this interpretation task.
- Part II contains a systematic compilation of the whole repertory of representational means, which are described according to a uniform schema facilitating their easy comparison.

The reader is recommended to first acquire a global overview of the representational means and the method of their description using Part II. This will be a good basis for the understanding of Part I. In general, Part II is designed as a kind of dictionary to enable easy access to the definitions of the representational means. In this sense, Parts I and II complement each other. To improve readability, an appendix common to both parts was added with the following structure:

**Appendix A.** List of abbreviations used throughout the book. A general reference to this appendix at the beginning avoids an interruption of the flow of reading by footnotes. Therefore, the reader is requested to have a look at Appendix A if he or she encounters a shorthand notation which has not been explained in the text.

**Appendix B.** List of relations and functions in lexicographical order with their signatures (domains and ranges, respectively) and a short mnemonically chosen description.

**Appendix C.** A compilation of semantic templates that are formulated as propositional types complementing the question patterns of Part II, Chap. 18. They elucidate the meaning of relations as well as the choices for the ordering of their arguments.

**Appendix D.** Declaration of default values concerning the assignment of a relationship R to the immanent, situational or restrictive knowledge with respect to a node N (depending on the position of N as the first or second argument of R).

**Appendix E.** List of typical axioms, which give an impression of their classification and of the inferential power of the representational means.

For the practical application of the knowledge representation methods presented in this book, it is important to know that they are supported by several software tools (among them a workbench for the knowledge engineer, Sect. 14.2, and a workbench for the computer lexicographer, Sect. 14.4). Moreover, a system for syntactic-semantic analysis was developed which automatically translates natural language expressions into their meaning representations, i.e. into multilayered extended semantic networks (see Sect. 14.3). This system is also the basis for the semantic annotation of large text corpora with millions of sentences and for automatic concept learning.

MultiNet has also been used and is still in use in different projects, e.g. in the "Virtual Knowledge Factory", as an interface between clients and the data server for natural language search in image libraries, or as semantic interlingua in the natural language interface NLI-Z39.50, which supports the Internet protocol Z39.50 (see Sect. 14.3). The most recent applications are planned in the project BenToWeb of the European Union for supporting disabled people in barrier-free access to the Web, and in the VILAB project for realizing a natural language communication between students and the automatic tutor of a virtual electronic laboratory (see Sect. 14.5).

In addition, the MultiNet approach is taught at several universities; it is also one of the cornerstones in the interactive AI laboratory VILAB for electronic distance teaching (see Sect. 14.5), where MultiNet serves as the central knowledge representation paradigm. The feedback and experience from all these applications is used for continuous improvement of MultiNet.

It is our goal to give the MultiNet paradigm a distribution as broad as possible, because we consider it an ideal tool for exchanging scientific results in semantically oriented disciplines.[1] But, even if another formalism for the semantic representation of natural language expressions should be generally accepted by the scientific community, such a semantic "interlingua" would be a great help to all disciplines engaged in research on natural language, be it linguistics, cognitive psychology, or artificial intelligence. Only on the basis of such an interlingua can the results of the scholars in different fields be easily transferred from one discipline to another, and they might even be validated by their application to technically realized systems. This book is also a contribution to overcome the present diversity in the representation of research results and the lacking degree of formalization in many language-oriented investigations.

---

[1] One should only think of the immense advantage computational linguistics could draw from existing dictionaries of the valencies and distribution of verbs, nouns, and adjectives ([105], [245], and [246]) if they had been written on the basis of a computationally useful semantic formalism like MultiNet.

A knowledge representation paradigm like MultiNet, which is used in many applications and in teaching, is continually developing in a living environment and receiving responses from all participants in the tasks involved. Therefore, I want to thank above all my colleagues and students who over many years of cooperation contributed to the present state of work through their constructive criticism, applications, and evaluations of the concepts presented in this book. Especially the above-mentioned software tools were a prerequisite to overcoming certain quantitative barriers (be they in the automatic semantic analysis of large text corpora or in the creation of large computational lexica).

Special thanks go to S. Hartrumpf, I. Glöckner, J. Leveling, R. Lütticke, and R. Osswald, whose indefatigable readiness for discussion gave many stimuli for the development of MultiNet. S. Hartrumpf and R. Osswald helped to better understand the connection between semantic analysis and knowledge representation on the one hand and between computational lexicon and language processing on the other. I. Glöckner contributed to a deeper understanding of the axiomatization and logical properties of the representational means of MultiNet, while J. Leveling and R. Lütticke gave valuable help in the use of MultiNet in different natural language interfaces and electronic teaching, respectively. Finally, Ch. Doppelbauer and C. Jenge supported the technical preparation and the proofreading of the manuscript.

Last but not least, I want to thank my American and British colleagues who facilitated sabbatical stays at the University at Buffalo (The State University of New York), the University of Edinburgh, the University of Sheffield, and King's College in London. They and other members of their universities gave valuable advice during our discussions and helped to elucidate the parallelism between German and English language phenomena. Among them I have especially to thank S. Shapiro, F. Johnson, J.-P. Koenig, W. Rapaport, and L. Talmy (University at Buffalo); M. Steedman, R. Cann, J. Lee, K. Markert, and T. Miller (University of Edinburgh); Y. Wilks (University of Sheffield); and S. Lappin and D. Gabbay (King's College, London).

I also express my gratitude to Ronan Nugent from Springer for his certainly difficult publishing work. He and an unknown copyeditor were a great help in improving the quality of the text.

Hagen, July 2005                                Hermann Helbig

# Contents

Part I

# Knowledge Representation with MultiNet

# Chapter 1

# Introduction

The problem of semantic representation of natural language information is the central topic of this work. This task is important for the following scientific disciplines:

- the theoretical foundations of artificial intelligence (AI), concerning the knowledge representation problem itself;
- linguistics, in connection with the formal description of the semantics of natural language expressions and for the formalization of lexical knowledge;
- cognitive psychology, to model conceptual structures and the processes of reasoning;
- the development of natural language processing systems, e.g. question-answering systems or machine translation systems (especially for the creation of knowledge bases and large computational lexica).

The present work describes a comprehensive repertoire of representational means, allowing for an adequate description of the semantics of natural language expressions, be it "on paper" or in a computer. At the same time, the use of these representational means for the investigation of fundamental problems of natural language semantics will be demonstrated.

In dealing with the semantics of natural languages in general, one should be aware that the term **language** (Ge: "Sprache") has a twofold meaning. On the one hand, we have to investigate language as a system, e.g. the German or English languages, with its regularities being independent of actual speech acts (this system aspect has been called "la langue" by the Swiss linguist de Saussure). In this regard, the meaning of natural language expressions can be described independently of a specific context of utterance, and, therefore, we speak of the **primary meaning** or **core meaning**. The investigation of meaning in this sense is the topic of a special branch of linguistics and computational linguistics, known as the "Semantics", which is also the main topic of this book.

On the other hand, language expressions can be investigated with regard to their use in concrete utterances (this aspect is called "la parole" by de Saus-

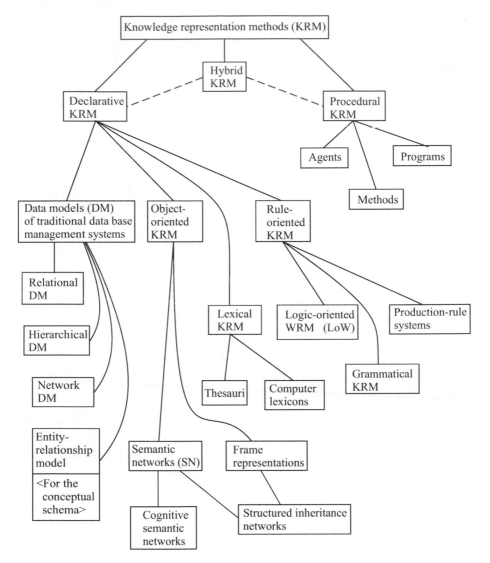

**Figure 1.1.** Overview of knowledge representation models

sure). It is connected with a specific context of utterance or a specific dialogue situation. Researching this aspect of meaning, one has to take into consideration the intentions of the speaker/writer (what the speaker/writer really means) as well as the effects on the hearer/reader (what is achieved with the hearer/reader). In general, such an utterance has various **side meanings** or **secondary meanings** apart from its primary meaning (its propositional content).

The investigation of these aspects is the subject of **pragmatics** or **speech act theories** (see [229]), which will be only touched upon in this work.

It is important to note that the representational means described in this book are language-neutral and thus provide a kind of semantic **interlingua**. The general paradigm of knowledge representation they are embedded in is the **semantic network** paradigm (see Chap. 2). Its position in the world of knowledge representation methods is shown in Fig. 1.1. **Multi**layered Extended Semantic **Net**works (acronym: **MultiNet**s) are based on the following main components (a detailed description is given in Part II; for a short description of MultiNet see [113]):

- Representatives of concepts (the nodes of the network);
- Functions and relations (providing the arcs between the nodes);
- Sorts and features representing semantic classes ("normal" labels of nodes);
- Multidimensionally organized attributes of nodes (labels of nodes which are the basis for the discrimination of different layers in the network);
- Methods of encapsulation (used for the partitioning of the network);
- Axiomatic rules (used for the inferential connection of nodes and for the formal definition of relations and functions).

Unfortunately, there is no generally accepted definition to determine the **adequacy** of a system of representational means. From a theoretical point of view, it would be very desirable to have a finite and manageable number of basic conditions or criteria from which we could "automatically" derive an appropriate set of semantically primitive representational means (e.g. the sorts, relations, functions, and semantic features proposed in this book). It would be very helpful if these criteria allowed us to decide whether certain representational elements are admissible or not, whether they are necessary or not, etc. In reality, such a complete set of criteria does not exist (at least not at this moment). In addition, no system of semantically primitive representational means can fully cope with the richness of nuances and the diversity of natural language, because it necessarily results from classification, generalization, and therefore also from coarsening. But, just as no linguistic theory can do without a classifying and coarsening concept formation, no natural language processing system that has to be realized in practice and that has to use a large knowledge base can do without a classifying and systematizing repertoire of representational means. The epistemically and cognitively fundamental relationships mirrored in the set of representational means are important for another reason as well. They are carriers of the most important inferential mechanisms connected with conceptual reasoning. To renounce them would make it necessary to interconnect all natural language constructs standing in logical relation to each other, leading to an unmanageable combinatorial explosion.

It has to be emphasized that the term **semantically primitive representational means** does not imply that every concept can be decomposed and reduced to the meaning of semantically primitive elements (as attempted in [276]). Rather, these representational means are used as irreducible concepts on a metalevel to classify the concepts on the semantic level and to describe their fundamental interrelationships and the inferential connections between them. Since every natural language is both **language** and **metalanguage** at the same time, all formally defined concepts can be described in natural language again, something that produces a complicated hierarchy of language layers. To avoid an infinite iteration, this hierarchy is closed by formal constructs, which are described by logical methods.

In the following list, we propose a set of criteria which should be fulfilled by every system of representational means in order to provide the basic elements of a formal description of natural language semantics:

a) **Principal (global) requirements**

- **Universality** – The representational means must be defined independently of a specific natural language or the application domain, and should not be "tailored" ad hoc to a special field of discourse.
- **Cognitive adequacy** – The representational means must allow for an adequate modeling of human conceptual structures (as far as they are known) and of their manifestation in the semantics of the natural language expressions describing them. These models must be **concept-centered**, i.e. every concept should have a unique representative through which all information belonging to it is accessible.[1]
- **Interoperability** – The representational means must be applicable to theoretical investigations of semantically oriented disciplines or computational linguistics, as well as to the specification of formal interfaces to the components of applied AI systems. They should be usable for the construction of a computational lexicon as well as for expressing the results of the syntactic-semantic analysis, as building blocks for the formal language used in the inference machine, and as a basis for text generation. Only in this way can the results of the above-mentioned disciplines or system components build on each other and the necessary integration be achieved.
- **Homogeneity** – It must be possible to describe the meanings of words or the meanings of sentences or texts (dialogues) with the same means used for the description of logical rules governing the formal processes of reasoning.

---

[1] In computer science, this characterization would be called **object-orientedness**.

- **Communicability** – No single person is able to construct a large knowledge base or a complex applied AI system like a question-answering system or a theoretical edifice that covers all the semantic phenomena of a natural language. To accomplish this, whole teams are required whose members cooperate effectively. This necessitates, among other things, that they have a common understanding of the representational means of a knowledge representation system to be used by all of them. Hence the requirement that the definitions also be intuitively intelligible.
- **Practicability** – Every knowledge representation system designed for a real-world application has to fulfill certain pragmatic requirements, i.e. it must be technically tractable and effectively implementable. Of what use, for instance, is the most fine-grained semantic representation if no one is able to provide the corresponding background knowledge necessary for the syntactic-semantic analysis to disambiguate the theoretically possible variants of meaning, or if the representation and processing of knowledge can not be effectively implemented or dealt with in such a highly differentiated system?
  This requirement has also a quantitative aspect. The usefulness of a KRS should be proved by applying its expressional means to the description of thousands, or tens of thousands, of concepts. It is of little use to demonstrate the functioning of a KRS with a few examples if the representational principles proposed cannot be practically maintained during the treatment of a large stock of knowledge.
- **Automatability** – The predefined repertoire of expressional means should permit automatic processing of knowledge, and especially automatic knowledge acquisition from natural language sources.

### b) Internal, structural requirements

- **Completeness** – There should be no meaning which cannot be represented with the representational means. It must be emphasized that this requirement does not concern completeness in the logical sense, i.e. that every true expression which can be formulated in the representational language should also be derivable.
- **Optimal granularity** – On the one hand, different meanings must be mapped into different structures; on the other hand, to keep a system manageable, not every fine semantic nuance can be mirrored in a KRS.
- **Consistency** – Pieces of information logically contradicting each other must not be derivable from one another. For equivalent meanings, however, it is precisely this mutual derivability that must be warranted. It follows that inference rules and the definitions of representational means (carried in Multi-

Net essentially by the R-Axioms) must be adapted to each other in such a way that the kernel of a knowledge base must be **globally consistent**. When knowledge about concrete concepts or concrete facts is added, the knowledge base must only be **locally consistent** (see Sect. 13.1). This means that knowledge pieces contradicting themselves in one part of the knowledge base must not affect other parts which are not semantically connected with it.

- **Multidimensionality** – The qualitative distinction of different aspects of knowledge (immanent vs. situational knowledge, intensional vs. extensional aspect, quality vs. quantity, etc.) must be mirrored in the assignment of concepts to different layers of representation.
- **Local interpretability** – The basic constructs should be logically interpretable by themselves, and independent of their embedding in the context of the knowledge base as a whole.

One question often arises in connection with knowledge representation: Does a **canonical meaning representation** exist, i.e. are we able to define a general function which maps semantically equivalent NL-expressions into identical meaning representations? As already stated by Woods [281], there are theoretical reasons why such a canonical representation does not exist at all, since such representations do not exist even for formal languages essentially weaker than natural languages (cf. the undecidability of the word problem or of the problem of simplification for symbolic mathematical expressions [213]). What can be achieved, however, is a certain **normalization** of the meaning structures of natural language expressions. Thus the great variety of semantic structures can be reduced by identifying the representations of semantically (nearly) equivalent sentences (e.g. active vs. passive voice), or by ignoring the differences in the topic-focus structure of sentences (see [231], [90]).

In the present work, we prefer a semiformal, content-oriented definition of the representational means. This is a necessary precondition for a completely formal treatment of their semantics; for, how could one define formally what is not completely understood conceptually? When describing the relations and functions of MultiNet, we use logical expressions which give a starting point for the inferential interlinking of meaning structures and thus provide a basis for the definition of an operational semantics (see Sect. 13.2). However, it has to be conceded that an entirely formal description of the semantics of the representational means has still to be worked out on the basis of the more content-oriented definitions in this book. Basically, three different methods can be taken into account for this purpose:

a) a **model-theoretic extensional method**, as used in logic and logic-oriented semantic theories. This approach is already problematic because many natural language concepts, and also the proposed expressional means of Multi-Net, can be interpreted extensionally only with great difficulty, if at all. What are the extensions of *"religion"*, *"illness"*, *"abstract"*, *"physical"*, *"intension"*, etc. or how do we treat modal restrictions of temporal relationships like *"possibly after the dinner"* extensionally?

b) a **procedural method**, as it is used in natural language interfaces to databases or in robotics, where meaning representations of natural language queries are mapped onto procedural expressions of the target system (e.g. onto retrieval procedures of a database management system or onto actions of a robot); this method also has only restricted applicability;

c) a **use-theoretic method**, where the meaning of concepts and semantic primitives is defined by their interrelation among themselves and by their proper use in the language game or in a question-answering game ("meaning as use").

We believe that for the foundation of meaning representation, as well as for theoretical investigations, the latter method, which dates back to Wittgenstein [279], is the most appropriate one. A purely procedural explanation of concept meanings is at best apt for restricted applications (e.g. for the above-mentioned natural language interfaces or for interpreting natural language commands to robots).[2] As a basic assumption discerning a) from b) and supporting c), we cite the following thesis:

*"Concepts essentially do not work as classificators during language understanding, thus discerning between "meant" and "non-meant" (this approach is typical of an extension-based model-theoretic semantics); they rather are connectives receiving their full potential in their mutual interconnections and enabling us to experience reality and to communicate our experiences to others."* [242]

Furthermore, the truth or falsity of sentences does not play such a central role for understanding natural language as assigned to these categories in logic-oriented (extensional) theories of semantics. Human beings are often not able to decide on the truth or falsity of a proposition or on the applicability of a concept to a real object, even if the utterance in question has been understood (see the discussion in Sect. 15.3).

On the basis of this argument, the present work prefers method c), which, according to Wittgenstein, can be described as a question-answering game (or

---

[2] This method is actually used by our research group for realizing natural language access to the Internet and natural language interfaces to traditional databases (see [115]).

**language game**) governed by its own rules and manifested in the correct interplay between question and answer. This method is most clearly realized in the paradigm of a question-answering system of artificial intelligence (see Part II and [111]). For better understanding of our concern, this paradigm can be thought of as an integrated system into which the knowledge representation methods of MultiNet are embedded. The question-answering system does not have to be an implemented AI system; it can also be imagined as an abstract functional model into which the essential processes of language understanding are integrated. Because of this double interpretability, we deliberately use the same abbreviation **QAS** throughout the book for both terms, **question-answering game** and **question-answering system**.[3] Those familiar with the methods of artificial intelligence and automatic knowledge processing may associate a question-answering system with a QAS; those approaching the problem of meaning representation from linguistics or psychology may interpret the abbreviation QAS as "language game".

It should be stated that human beings apparently have all three methods at their disposal to support the symbolic conceptual system that is closely connected with natural language. They are able to link words or concepts with objects of the world (analogously to model-theoretic/extensional semantics of formal theories where predicates are mapped into sets of individuals in an artificial "world", i.e. into a universe of a predefined algebraic structure); human beings are also able to translate language expressions (e.g. the command *"Stand up!"*) into actions, i.e. into contractions of their muscles ("procedural" semantics); finally, they are able to interconnect concepts in a dialogue in a correct way without resorting to the first two methods (use-theoretic semantics).

Although the book mainly deals with knowledge representation and not with knowledge processing, it might be useful for the understanding of the whole system to explain the embedding of the knowledge base into a QAS. The functional diagram given in Fig. 1.2 can be seen as representative of both a technical question-answering system and a "natural" question-answering process. It comprises all the components characteristic of a question-answering game where the knowledge base (which can be built using the representational means of MultiNet) plays a central role.

Information formulated in natural language and given to a computer or a person must first be analyzed to determine its meaning, which has to be ex-

---

[3] In German we coined the ambiguous abbreviation **FAS** for **QAS** after the corresponding terms **Frage-Antwort-Spiel** (En: **question-answering game**) and **Frage-Antwort-System** (En: **question-answering system**) which have the same initial letters in their components and thus better mirror this double interpretability.

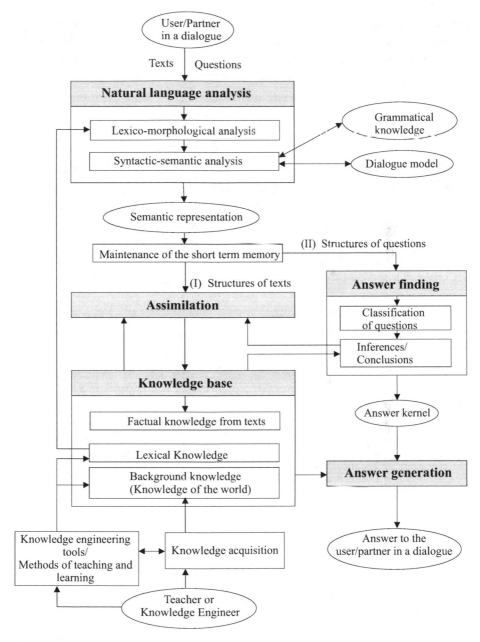

**Figure 1.2.** Overview of the most important functional components of a QAS

pressed in a convenient format for semantic representation. In this process, the **lexico-morphological analysis** is mainly based on lexical knowledge, while the **syntactic-semantic analysis** is mainly supported by grammatical knowledge and world knowledge. Furthermore, the interpretation of natural language expressions generally requires a **dialogue model** describing the situational embedding of the utterances. This is especially important for the understanding of deictic language elements (which, among other things, comprise deictic pronouns, like *"I"*, *"you"*, or deictic adverbs, like *"here"*, *"there"*, *"yesterday"*).[4]

To ensure the interaction of all components, the same representation formalism should be used for the **lexical information** (see Chap. 12) and the **background knowledge** needed for the language understanding process, as well as for the **dialogue model** (MultiNet has been used successfully in all three fields). MultiNet can also be used to a certain extent for the formalization of **grammatical knowledge**, which plays a role in the **word-class-controlled functional analysis** [116], especially in the semantic interpretation of prepositions and conjunctions [258].

The semantic structures of single sentences are stored at first in a short-term memory so that intersentential references (especially pronoun references between sentences) can be resolved. Afterward, questions and propositions (in general texts) are processed differently. While questions are subjected to logical answer finding, the information contained in texts (propositions) has to be assimilated into the knowledge base. The **assimilation process** connects incoming meaning structures with knowledge already available in the knowledge base or possibly identifies them with equivalent pieces of information to avoid double storage. In addition, the assimilation has to close apparent "semantic gaps" in texts by using background knowledge available in the knowledge base.[5]

Finding an appropriate answer to a given question is based on a process of **question classification** (see Sect. 3.2.4). The type of query does not only deter-

---

[4] The term **deixis** denotes the phenomenon that certain language expressions are related to elements of the situational context of an utterance (*"here"* denotes the location of the speaker/writer; *"today"* denotes the day comprising the moment of speaking or writing the expression, etc.).

[5] Let us take the following sentences: *"The firm NN developed a new car. The motor needs only 3 litres of gas per 100 km."* These sentences lack a semantic connection, if there is no knowledge available that a car has a motor as its part (this kind of information is called **world knowledge** instead of **linguistic knowledge**). Especially the reference induced by the definite article in the phrase *"the motor"* cannot be resolved without this knowledge. In the present case, the assimilation should be able to find the correct subordination of concepts and to supply a corresponding part-whole relation PARS between the concepts ⟨new car⟩ and motor and add it properly to the conceptual structures already stored in the knowledge base.

mine the **inference method** to be applied, but also the type of knowledge asked for (situational vs. immanent, definitional vs. assertional, etc.; see Sect. 3.2.3). Additionally, the classification of questions is relevant to the answer finding and is used as a basis for **answer generation**. Answers to decision questions are of another type (namely "*Yes*" or "*No*") than answers to supplementary questions (also called "WH-questions"). In the latter case, it is typical that a single node of the semantic network, the so-called **answer kernel**, found during the process of answer finding, has to be reformulated in natural language. With so-called "essay questions" ("*What is a Y?*", "*What do you know about X?*"*, etc.), a whole text (essay) has to be generated, stemming mainly from the immanent knowledge of the answer kernel. While the aspect of deduction, or of logical inferences in general, plays a prominent part in answer finding for decision questions and supplementary questions, the aspect of information retrieval is dominant for essay questions. In the latter case, it is the retrieval of the immanent knowledge connected with the answer kernel and its reformulation which is predominant (see Sects. 3.2.3 and 13.2).

Concluding this chapter we want to state that MultiNet and its predecessors have proved their usefulness in many applications; among them we mention the following:

- Knowledge representation in question-answering systems [107, 98]
- Semantic interlingua in natural language interfaces to databases and to the Internet [109, 159, 114]
- Semantic annotation of large text corpora and automatic knowledge acquisition [98, 79]
- Backbone for building large semantically based computational lexica [100, 192]
- Central knowledge representation formalism in the virtual electronic laboratory VILAB [166, 164].

# Chapter 2

# Historical Roots

Semantic Networks (abbreviated: SNs) already have a long tradition and are especially suitable as a knowledge representation method for investigating the semantics of natural language expressions. They can be traced back to the work of Quillian on associative networks [208] and are heavily influenced by contributions of cognitive psychology and cognitive modeling [216, 261]. In this chapter, the embedding of the MultiNet paradigm and its predecessors [108, 117, 112, 114] into this line of development will be shortly outlined (see Fig. 2.1).

An important starting point for developing a convenient repertoire of representational means for the semantic representation of natural language words and texts originated from Fillmore's work in linguistics [66]. He investigated the case systems of different languages and established a first list of so-called **deep case relations**, which are realized by different surface case marking.[1] An extension of the repertoire of DCR set up by Fillmore can be found in Sect. 5.2.1. Because of the distinction between **surface structure**[2] and **deep structure**[3] well known from linguistics and following the pattern of the DCR, we designate all relationships between meaning representatives of natural language expressions as **deep relations**.

The work of Schank and his school also had strong influence on the development of the SN [221]. This school dealt mainly with dynamic situations and tried to reduce their semantic structure to only a few (approximately a dozen) semantically fundamental deep concepts (like PTRANS – for physical transport, INGEST – for incorporation, and so on). Although this approach was not successful in the long run, it nevertheless enriched the discussion on the problem of a canonical meaning representation (see Sect. 15.2.4).

The connection between the expressional means of predicate calculus and semantic networks was tightened in the 1970s, particularly by the contribu-

---

[1] The term **deep case relations** will be abbreviated to **DCR**.

[2] The language form encountered in texts or spoken utterances.

[3] The meaning representation of the corresponding natural language text or utterance expressed in a fixed formalism.

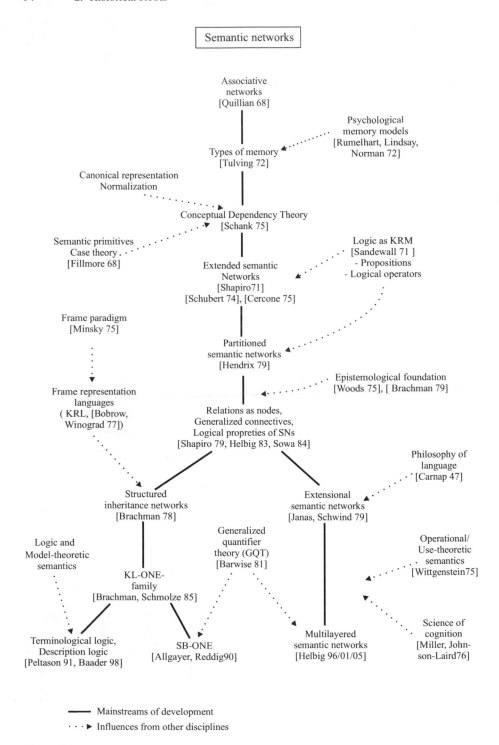

**Figure 2.1.** Stages of development of semantic network models

tions of Sandewall [219], Cercone [44], Schubert [225], Hendrix [119], and Shapiro [233, 234]. An important issue in their work was the correct representation of the scope of logical connectives and quantifiers, where partitioning of semantic networks and special expressional means for the dependencies between representatives of concepts in connection with mixed quantification had been introduced into the semantic network paradigm. Other contributions concerning the logical properties of SNs and more detailed definitions of the expressional means of an SN came from Sowa [248] and Helbig [108], respectively. It should also be mentioned that many ideas underlying the semantic representation of natural language expressions have been influenced by Wilks, who in his preference semantics [277] emphasized a more procedural aspect of semantic representation.

Fundamental questions concerning the problem of what is really represented in a semantic network (or to be more specific, in its nodes and arcs) had been discussed and to a certain degree also clarified by Woods [281] and Brachman [30]. This was necessary because in the early days of AI a clear distinction was not drawn between the logical-conceptual level and the level of implementation. The latter aspect (i.e. the implementation level of Multi-Net) cannot be discussed here, but it should be remarked that there exists a full implementation of the MultiNet paradigm in the AI language LISP. This implementation is closely tied in with a well developed workbench for the knowledge engineer, which is under continual development (see Sect. 14.2).

By the end of the 1970s, at least two lines of development could be observed in the field of semantic networks. The first line, which includes structured inheritance networks [29] and the knowledge representation system **KL-ONE** [34], is strongly influenced by the frame concept [183] and by frame-oriented knowledge representations (see, for instance, [27]). These models are also associated with logic and a model-theoretic foundation of semantics, especially in their newer manifestations such as **SB-ONE** [5], **Terminological Logics** [198], and **Description Logics** [55].

The second line comprising the MultiNet paradigm is more closely linked with the views of the cognitive sciences [182] and with a use-theoretic (operational) conception of semantics going back to Wittgenstein [279]. A special characteristic of some members of this line (e.g. [131] and [117]) is that extensional aspects of meaning, besides the intensional aspect, are explicitly included in the knowledge representation itself (see also [41]). Finally, it should be emphasized that all modern semantic networks have influenced each other and are somehow interconnected. They have also drawn from other methods of knowledge representation, especially from the logic-oriented systems (see Chap. 15). Among modern semantic theories, the **Generalized Quantifier Theory (GQT)** [15], the **File Change Theory** [103], and the **Discourse Representation Theory** [134] should also be mentioned in this context, even if they are not knowledge representation systems in the proper sense (see Sect. 15.3). Especially the insight of GQT that quantified nominal phrases (like "*very many children*", or "*almost all students*") form a semantic unit on which something can be predicated (e.g. that they "*are intelligent*") was adopted by many modern knowledge representation systems, among them SB-ONE and MultiNet (see Chap. 15).

Unfortunately, it is not possible to deal here exhaustively with the embedding of semantic networks in their scientific surroundings. We shall exemplarily list only some disciplines closely intertwined with the development of the knowledge representation paradigm "Semantic Networks" together with a few relevant citations:[4]

- Cognitive psychology [38, 132];
- Artificial intelligence [157, 249, 259, 32];
- Lexicography [206, 274, 10];
- Logics [75, 262];
- Philosophy [247, 207, 209];
- Psycholinguistics [61, 154, 155];
- Linguistics [23, 130, 56, 22, 168].
- Computer science and interdisciplinary perspectives [83]

---

[4] The literature cited does not imply valuation and should not be considered complete. It is rather an entry into the relevant specialist literature and shows links to other scientific disciplines.

# Chapter 3

# Basic Concepts

## 3.1 General Remarks

Concepts and their mutual interrelationships are essential structural elements of the cognitive apparatus and are hence also essential for the meaning representation of natural language information.

A **concept** can be generally characterized by three components:[1]

1. a word or a word group designating the concept and representing it externally, i.e. in the NL-communication (the so-called word label);
2. a collection of relations to other concepts;
3. a complex pattern of perceptual (mostly visual) origin.

Not all three features must be present with every concept. There are concepts like ⟨the car being bought by Paul yesterday⟩ which cannot be designated by a single word label. On the other hand, there are concepts where only the first two components are encountered. In these cases the third component moves almost entirely into the background, e.g. righteousness, determinism, etc. With semantic networks we try to describe just the first two components. **Neural Networks**, in contrast, are very suitable for modeling the third aspect [217, 143, 284]. However, they largely lack the inclusion of the first two components. It is hoped that essential progress in the field of knowledge representation and cognitive modeling can be achieved by the unification of both lines of development (a goal that lies still ahead of AI).

Please note that natural language expressions and the conceptual meanings underlying them have to be clearly distinguished. To differentiate between **words** or natural language phrases and the **concepts** associated with them, we use the following convention: Natural language expressions embedded in the text (like "*house*" and "*the tree in front of my house*") are set in italics and put in double quotes. If we refer to the corresponding concepts, we use a sanserif

---

[1] Strictly speaking, this characterization meets the intensional aspect only. The extensional aspect will be dealt with later on.

font and, with multiword concepts, additional pointed brackets (e.g. house
and ⟨the tree in front of my house⟩).

- A **semantic network (SN)** is the mathematical model of a conceptual structure consisting of a set of concepts and the cognitive relations between them.
  It is represented by a generalized graph where the representatives of concepts
  correspond to the nodes of the graph and the relations between concepts correspond to the arcs.

To elucidate which layers of reality correspond to the knowledge representation on a computer, we refer to Fig. 3.1. This also answers the question
brought up by Brachman [30] concerning the epistemic status of semantic networks. Figure 3.1 shows three levels: The lower two levels, Level I and Level
II, belong to the **real world**, lying outside of our mental apparatus, and to
the **cognitive level**, respectively. Level II represents the human memory structures and contents of reasoning. To what extent the state of affairs at Level I
is completely and adequately mirrored at Level II is the topic of philosophical
theories (of epistemology, to be exact) and cannot be discussed within the thematic framework of this book. Apart from philosophy, cognitive psychology
and psychology of perception are also engaged in clarifying the relationship
between Levels I and II. It is important for understanding semantic networks
that an SN at Level III is thought to model the mental Level II on a computer.
An SN is not a direct model of the real world (Level I). With regard to the
fact that the scientific community has not yet succeeded in integrating the third
component of a concept (see above) into formal knowledge representations,
there are good prospects in the near future for combining symbolic methods
of knowledge representation with subsymbolic methods manifested by neural
networks, among them the very promising Kohonen Nets [142]. It must be kept
in mind that we will use a convenient shorthand notation throughout the book,
when we speak of nodes of the SN representing "objects", "states", etc. What
we actually mean in all these cases are the representatives of mental concepts
mirroring these entities in the human brain.

By definition of an SN, every node of the semantic network represents a
concept and vice versa. For the sake of simplicity, we will label the nodes in
the graphical representation of an SN by means of natural language words, provided there is no possibility of a mistake and no ambiguity.[2] Representatives of
concepts that can be designated by a single word are **lexicalized concepts** (e.g.

---

[2] The strict observation of the above-mentioned convention concerning the distinction between
words and concepts is not necessary in graphical representations, since there we encounter
only representatives of concepts, and no words.

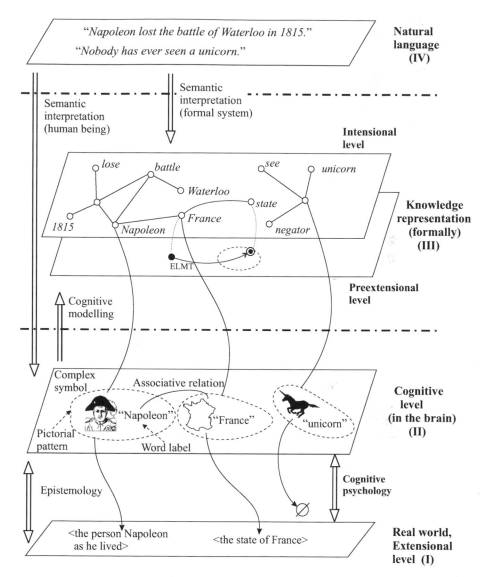

**Figure 3.1.** The embedding of the knowledge representation into different layers of the reality

house and green). All other concepts are called **nonlexicalized concepts**, e.g. ⟨the tree in front of my house⟩ and ⟨a small green leaf⟩. If a word has several meanings, and thus several meaning representatives, the corresponding nodes are marked by indexed labels (e.g. bank$_1$ monetary institution, bank$_2$ side of a river, or alternatively bank.1.1, bank.1.2, respectively). With regard to lexical ambiguity, i.e. **polysemy** and **homography**, we must refer to Chap.

12. Every node bears a unique name, which for nonlexicalized concepts can also be generated automatically by the QAS (G01, G02, G03, etc.).[3]

It has often been argued (e.g. in [31, p. 33]) that the mnemonic labeling of nodes of an SN with natural language words has no semantic value in itself. This is correct insofar as a label like bank$_1$ or school.1.2 has no more meaning in itself (especially in computer applications) than an artificially generated label like G001 or X8327. But, according to the explanations given above, in a QAS (especially in its computational realization as a question-answering system) there exists an isomorphic mapping between lexicalized representatives of concepts in an SN and the corresponding lexemes in a lexicon (unfortunately, there is no such isomorphic mapping between words and lexemes). In this way, the labels of lexicalized concepts are closely connected with natural language words in the phase of analysis as well as in the phase of language generation. At the semantic level, the connection between concepts is established by inference processes, which are governed by axioms and rules of inference where representatives of concepts (labels of nodes) and semantic relations (labels of arcs) play an important part (see Sect. 13.2 and Appendix E). For this reason, the criteria of interoperability and homogeneity mentioned at the beginning are so important, since they warrant that words, lexemes, and representatives of meaning, as well as the semantically primitive representational means, are consistently interwoven in a unified system during all phases of language processing.

As already mentioned, the arcs of the semantic network have to be considered as epistemologically and cognitively justified categories which function as fundamental semantic deep relations in the framework of meaning representation. In selecting them, the appropriate balance between the different requirements of the criteria set up in Chap. 1 has to be found (this concerns especially the demand for completeness and optimal granularity on the one hand and for universality on the other hand). Only such relations are permitted in the semantic deep structure which in any case are uniquely interpretable and which are fundamental in the sense that they represent significant classes of relationships encountered in nature or in society, or which can be pragmatically justified to warrant an effective answer finding in a QAS (i.e. to allow for effective logical conclusions). A too fine-grained differentiation of the semantically primitive representational means would overload the axiomatic apparatus of the knowledge representation to such a degree that no effective logical inferences would be possible. For that reason, words or expressions that are actu-

---

[3] With regard to **lexicalized concepts** and applications in computational linguistics, we have to take care that there is a one to one mapping between **lexemes** in the lexicon (see Chap. 12) and the representatives of the corresponding concepts in the SN (see also [226]).

ally stylistically colored paraphrases of one and the same deep relation should be mapped onto the same corresponding semantic relation or function by the analysis (e.g. *"possess"* and *"being the property of"* onto POSS; phrases with *"being the cause of"*, *"to cause"*, *"having as an effect"* onto CAUS). This does not mean that there should be no separate representatives in the SN for the concepts **property, possess** or **cause, effect**, etc. They must be connected only with the core meanings underlying them via appropriate meaning postulates or transformation rules (see Fig. 4.21 and Part II, relations SUBR and ARG1/2/3).

On the other hand, the representational means must not be so coarse that important distinctions will be lost in the semantic representation. This would be the case if all local relationships were expressed by means of only three basic relations, LOC, ORIGL, and DIRCL, representing location, local origin, and direction, respectively (see Part II), without taking into account the information contained in the local prepositions. An attempt in this direction had been made by Schank and his school ([223], [220]), who endeavored to reduce all dynamic events to a few fundamental actions (see Sect. 15.2.4).

An extreme in the opposite direction would be to use natural language itself as a knowledge representation language, on which logical processes operate during answer finding, thereby retaining all nuances characterizing natural languages. Such an attempt would be doomed to failure because of the combinatory explosion of natural language constructs that would have to be interrelated according to their semantic affinities. This is exactly why artificial (formal) knowledge representation languages have been designed, being able to attach the most important logical implications and inference rules to a finite and manageable set of fundamental semantic constructs (the semantic primitives).

The representational means presented in this book result from many years of our own work in the field of knowledge representation and automatic natural language processing, as well as from comparison of work carried out internationally on semantic networks (see http://pi7.fernuni-hagen.de/research/ and Chaps. 2 and 15). Nevertheless, a further underpinning from linguistic or psychological quarters would be very helpful.

Since a comparison with other knowledge representation formalisms and methods will be comprehensible only after an explanation of the representational means of MultiNet, this juxtaposition must be postponed to the end of this work (see Chap. 15). An overview of the representational means, which are described in full detail in Part II, is given in Fig. 3.2.

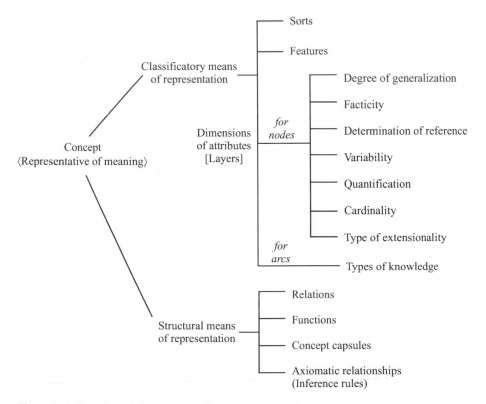

**Figure 3.2.** Overview of the representational means as a whole

## 3.2   Classificatory Knowledge

### 3.2.1   Sorts and Features

Almost all paradigms of knowledge representation are based on a so-called ontology of the entities to be represented:

- A classification of concepts from an epistemic point of view, which to a certain degree also mirrors a classification of the real world according to ontological aspects, is called an **ontology**. The classes of concepts defined by this ontology are also named **sorts** (see Part II, Sect. 17.1, in particular Fig. 17.1).

Sorts play an important role in designing the formal apparatus of meaning representation, because they are an indispensable precondition for the definition of ranges and domains for functions and relations, i.e. for the definition of their algebraic signatures. It is an essential feature of the relation CAUS (the cause-effect relationship), for instance, that it can hold only between two facts (and not, say, between two concrete objects), and that the function *COMP for the comparison of properties assigns a graded property to an object and another (nongraded) property, and does not assign an object to two other objects. The sorts also play an important part in language analysis and in the definition of lexical meanings (see Chap. 12). In this way, it is possible to recognize from the attribute [SORT = $d$] of the entity representing the grammatical object of the sentence "*The student conjugates the stone*" that this sentence is not acceptable. The verb "*conjugate*" and, thus, the underlying concept of action require at least an abstract concept with [SORT = $io$] as an object.[4] In addition to this, the sorts give a first starting point in a QAS for answer generation on the basis of a given partial network, since a correlation can be established between sorts and syntactic categories which is useful for language generation: objects (sort $o$) – nominal phrases, properties (sort $p$) – adjective groups, etc. Apart from the ontologically and algebraically motivated sorts, there are further attributes of objects (called **semantic features**), which also play a role in the classification of objects and in the syntactic-semantic analysis. These features will be explained and motivated in Chap. 12. A first short overview of sorts and features is given in Fig. 3.3. A detailed description can be found in Part II, Sect. 17.2.

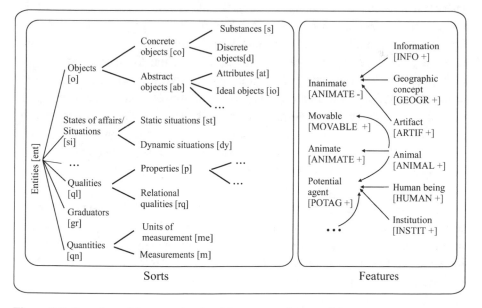

**Figure 3.3.** Overview of the upper levels of the system of sorts and features

---

[4] We will see that even the sorts are not sufficient to describe these **selectional restrictions** of verbs, nouns, and adjectives (see Chap. 12).

## 3.2.2    Multidimensional Layer Attributes

An essential characteristic of MultiNet consists of embedding all entities into a multidimensional space of attributes, one of which introduces a preextensional layer into the knowledge representation. Although the contrasting of intensional and extensional meaning belongs to the intellectual foundation of philosophical semantic theories [41], an explicit representation of extensional aspects has scarcely been considered in knowledge representation systems of AI (attempts can be found in [6] and [131]). Especially with a model-theoretic foundation of logic-oriented knowledge representations, the extension of concepts or predicates stands clearly outside of the knowledge representation language. But there is evidence that certain extensional aspects have to be integrated into the knowledge representation itself. Let us take a look at the following sentences, whose semantic representations are given in Fig. 3.4.[5]

(3.1) *"Max gave his brother several apples."*
(3.2) *"This was a generous gift."*
(3.3) *"Four of them were rotten."*

If someone reads or hears only the first two sentences, the concept C01 = ⟨several apples⟩ is considered an intensional unity, which is reinforced by the singular reference word *"This"* in Sentence (3.2). In particular, the readers/hearers of Sentences (3.1) and (3.2) do not care about the number of apples involved. However, if one reads Sentence (3.3), then the extensional aspect of concept C01, i.e. its characterization as a set with a certain number of elements (or with a certain cardinality), is explicitly emphasized. Through the phrase *"four of them"* it becomes apparent that the concept C01 represents a collection of things, which must consist of more than four elements. The meaning of the word group *"of them"* additionally causes the constitution of a subset relation at a second (the so-called "preextensional") level.

It is easy to see from the discussion above that the full meaning representation of sentences and texts, and also of single phrases (especially of quantified nominal phrases and their interrelationships), can be accomplished only by the interplay of two representational levels, called the intensional level and the preextensional level.

---

[5] To understand the graphics, we have to leap ahead to the definition of the representational means of MultiNet, which can easily be done by means of Part II. Furthermore, the representation of the net was simplified by omitting the encapsulation of concepts. It has also been made more transparent by the addition of knowledge pieces which must be inferred from the text. It is the combined effect of the intensional and preextensional level which matters here.

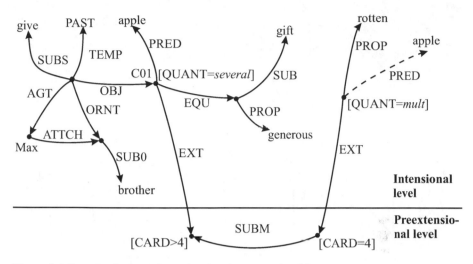

**Figure 3.4.** Interplay between intensional and preextensional layers

- The **intensional level** is characterized by nodes of predefined sorts, by cognitive roles between these nodes (the meaning representatives), and by attributes like degree of generality (**GENER**), determination of reference (**REFER**) and (intensional) quantification (**QUANT**). The elements of this level are, for short, called **intensionals**.
- The **preextensional level** by contrast is characterized by representatives of elements and sets of a different type (attribute **ETYPE**) as well as by set relations and functions. The representatives of this level are, for short, called **extensionals**. In addition to the type of extensionality (**ETYPE**), they are described by three further attributes: degree of variability (**VARIA**), facticity (**FACT**), and cardinality (**CARD**).[6]

Figure 3.5 gives an overview of the different dimensions spanned by attributes according to which the nodes of a semantic network can be categorized. The following dimensions are shown: degree of generality **GENER** (with the attribute values: generalized – *ge* and specific – *sp*), determination of reference **REFER** (with the attribute values: determined – *det* and not determined – *indet*), facticity **FACT** (with the attribute values: real – *real*, hypothetical – *hypo*, nonreal – *nonreal* or, for short, *non*), degree of variability **VARIA** (with the attribute values: variable – *var*, constant – *con*) and **CARD** (with natural numbers as values). The type of extensionality (attribute **ETYPE**) of the

---

[6] For the sake of brevity and if no mistake is possible, we sometimes attach all information belonging to layer attributes to the representatives at the intensional level.

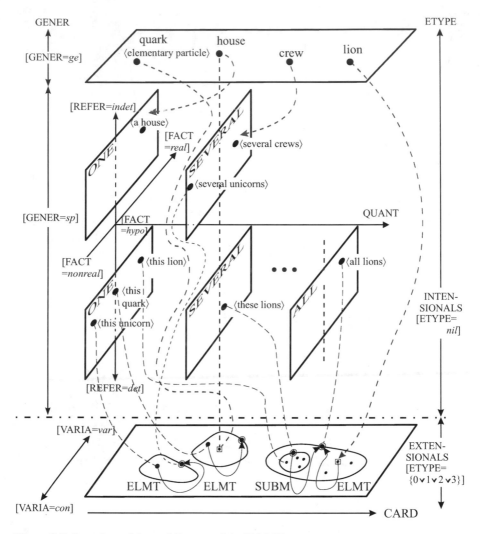

**Figure 3.5.** Overview of the multilayer model of MultiNet

preextensional level corresponds to the sorts at the intensional level. The sorts are not shown in Fig. 3.5 (see Part II, Sect. 17.1).

We speak of a **preextensional** representational level (instead of an extensional level), because the extension of a concept in the philosophical sense (i.e. parts of the real or a possible world) could never be mirrored completely in a knowledge representation (be it on a computer or in the human mind). Sets – even finite sets – are always only exemplarily modeled by some selected elements or by a prototypical representative for the whole set, a fact which is also confirmed by psychological investigations [132].

It must be stated that the intensionals as well as the extensionals are components of the knowledge representation proper, i.e. of the cognitive model. They are not immediate mappings of the real world, which has to be emphasized especially for the extensionals. In general, only the combination of an intensional with its corresponding extensional gives the full meaning representation of a concept (provided the concept in question admits an extensional component in its meaning representation). In many cases, however, it is sufficient to consider meaning representations which deal with the intensional aspect only. Such a representation corresponds to a semantic resolution as it is used by a person during the first spontaneous understanding of sentences and texts, e.g. when someone is perceiving the following sentence:

(3.4) *"Five archeologists discovered several new graves."*

The inclusion of the preextensional level in this case is necessary only, when a decision has to be made about which of the archeologists discovered how many graves; this means, whether every archeologist discovered some graves on his own (**distributive interpretation**) or whether they discovered all graves together in one act (**collective interpretation**), (see Chap. 9).

To embed the nodes of the SN into the attribute space illustrated in Fig. 3.5, every single node bears a complex attribute **LAY** (derived from "layer"), which comprises the layer attributes and their values described above (Table 3.1 gives a summarization of the subattributes of **LAY** and their values). The different conceptual layers of a network can be distinguished from each other by assigning a corresponding combination of fixed attribute values to each of them.

| Name of the attribute | Abbreviation | Possible values |
|---|---|---|
| Facticity | **FACT** | *real, hypo, nonreal (non)* |
| Degree of generalization | **GENER** | *ge, sp* |
| Intensional quantification | **QUANT** | *one, several, many, ..., all* |
| Determination of reference | **REFER** | *det, indet* |
| Variability | **VARIA** | *con, var* |
| Preextensional cardinality | **CARD** | $1, 2, 3, \ldots, n \in \mathcal{N}$ |
| Type of extensionality | **ETYPE** | *nil, 0, 1, 2, 3* |

**Table 3.1.** Overview of the layer attributes and their values

A detailed description of these attributes and the conceptual layers connected with them can be found in Part II, Sect. 3.2.2. To achieve an economical graphical representation, layer information will be attached to nodes only when absolutely necessary to facilitate understanding. A full specification can easily be derived following the explanations given in Chaps. 9 and 10. We agree upon the convention that all object nodes and all situational nodes which have no other explicit layer specification are bearing the attribute value [**FACT** = *real*].

### 3.2.3   Immanent vs. Situational Components of Meaning

An important distinction with regard to different types of knowledge, which is also relevant to language understanding and language generation, is that between immanent and situational knowledge. This distinction has a certain analogy to the contrast between definitional and assertional knowledge met in the literature on other knowledge representation models (see [34], [5]). It should be noticed, however, that the two distinctions are not identical.

- The **immanent knowledge** comprises the totality of all essential meaning components inherently attached to a conceptual entity. This information is characteristic of the concept in question and does not depend on its embedding in special situations or contexts.

Thus, the fact from a discourse domain "Vehicles" stating that a car has a motor, a chassis, and wheels, and is able to move belongs to the immanent knowledge about the concept car. The fact that Mr. NN yesterday bought a red car is not essential for the characterization of the concept car, and therefore it belongs to the situational knowledge (see below).

The immanent knowledge is often not explicitly mentioned in a discourse. In many cases it is rather tacitly supposed to be known to the reader/hearer. For a QAS to work successfully, the immanent knowledge must be provided in a teaching phase (e.g. in the form of extra definitions, generally valid propositions, etc.), should it not be provided by the normal textual input.

The immanent knowledge is important not only as the aim of potential questions. This use would actually cover only a small part of the cases (e.g. if someone is asking the QAS a definitional question). Immanent knowledge is needed in particular during the assimilation phase (see Fig. 1.2) to understand texts or discourses, because without it, semantic coherence cannot be established.

To demonstrate the text-constituting effect of immanent knowledge and its use for the disambiguation of grammatically ambiguous sentences, we consider the following example. In the sentences

(3.5) *"The price of the book is 25 Euro. Its author lives in Canada."*

we cannot decide by means of grammatical information alone (in particular, on the basis of grammatically discoverable agreements alone), whether the possessive pronoun "*Its*" in the second sentence refers to "*price*" or to "*book*". This can be done only by means of background knowledge that reads approximately as: books have prices and authors, but a price (as an attribute) is not characterized by having an author; therefore, the concept price cannot be the antecedent for the phrase "*Its author*". So the proper antecedent must be the node introduced by "*the book*".

- As a counterpart to the immanent knowledge, there is a type of knowledge which is related to the occurrence of a concept in the description of concrete states of affairs or situations. This kind of knowledge does not characterize the concept itself, but rather the use of this concept in the description of special situations, and is therefore called **situational knowledge**.

MultiNet provides special means to signify for a node N (a conceptual representative) which part of knowledge connected to N belongs to the immanent knowledge and which to the situational knowledge. Every arc incoming into N or outgoing from N is marked by the knowledge type *imman* (or one of its subtypes, see below) if the arc characterizes immanent knowledge for N, or by the label *situa*, if the arc characterizes situational knowledge for N. The immanent knowledge is further classified into **categorically valid knowledge** (label *categ*) and **prototypical knowledge** (default knowledge, label *proto*).

Furthermore, we distinctly bring out those parts of the meaning representation of a node N which have a restricting effect by limiting the range of its meaning conditionally, modally, or contextually. Arcs corresponding to this type of semantically **restrictive knowledge** are labeled *restr*. From a technical point of view, we annotate every node with information concerning the type of knowledge of its incoming or outgoing arcs. In other words, every arc is marked with regard to its first and its second arguments by a definite value of an attribute **K-TYPE** specifying the assignment of that arc to the corresponding type of knowledge (see Table 3.2). Please note that an arc connecting two nodes can have an immanent characteristic for one node (the first argument) and a situational characteristic for the other node (the second argument) at the same time. Examples are given in Figs. 3.7 of Part I and 17.8 of Part II.

A first orientation for the assignment of a certain knowledge type to an arc is given in Appendix D. There it is stated, for instance, that an arc representing the relation ($k_1$ AGT $k_2$), i.e. it is outgoing from $k_1$, normally belongs to the categorical (i.e. immanent) knowledge with regard to $k_1$, while the incoming

AGT arc at the second argument $k_2$ bears a situational character with regard to $k_2$. This means that the situation $k_1$, but not the carrier of the action $k_2$, is immanently characterized by that AGT arc.[7]

| Knowledge type (K-TYPE) | | Name of the type |
|---|---|---|
| Immanent knowledge | | *imman* |
| | Categorical knowledge | *categ* |
| | Default knowledge (Prototypical knowledge) | *proto* |
| Situational knowledge | | *situa* |
| Restrictive knowledge elements | | *restr* |

**Table 3.2.** The different knowledge types and their names

As specified in the table of Appendix D, relations such as the lexical relations, the subordination relations SUB, SUBS, or certain relations characterizing objects (among them, PARS, ORIGM, and ATTR), and the comparison relations are typical of the immanent knowledge with regard to their first arguments. The use of conceptual representatives in the description of states of affairs is characteristic of situational knowledge, as indicated by the proposed assignment of **K-TYPE** values to the second arguments of C-Roles[8], of the subordination relation and of other expressional means.

It would be possible to assume that C-Roles under certain conditions may also contribute to the immanent knowledge with regard to their second arguments. Thus, if the second argument represents the relative pronoun and its antecedent in a semantically restrictive relative clause (e.g. "*the man who married my sister*") or if they are used for the description of generic situations (as in the example "*Bees produce honey*", where the generic concept bee is undoubtedly characterized to a certain extent by this C-Role), then the AGT role must also be labeled by *imman* with regard to its second argument. Instead of classifying this knowledge as immanent knowledge, we generally consider knowledge characterized by the second argument of a C-Role as situational knowledge and classify it rather along another dimension as definitional knowledge, which is the counterpart to the so-called assertional knowledge in this classification dimension (see below). Nevertheless, the table in Appendix D can be consid-

---

[7] This statement is undoubtedly true for special states of affairs, such as, for instance, "*Max bought a bicycle.*" For generally valid situations, where only generic concepts are involved, or for information stemming from semantically restrictive relative clauses, this position cannot a priori be maintained without further justification.

[8] C-Roles technically describe cognitive roles which characterize participants of situations; for participants, see Fig. 3.3.1.

ered a heuristic help for the syntactic-semantic analysis; it cannot cover all decisions to be made, because we have to treat a complex interplay of syntax and semantics here.[9] One can generally state that the automatic discrimination between immanent and situational knowledge (and, additionally, between definitional and assertional knowledge, see below) is an unsolved problem within computational linguistics.

As an example, Figure 3.6 shows the semantic representation of a sentence taken from a larger text about geographical discoveries:

(3.6) *"The Portuguese Magalhães reached the south cape of South America in 1520 and, in a journey taking 21 days, sailed through the rocky waterway being approximately 600 km long and separating South America from Tierra del Fuego."*

This sentence demonstrates how closely interwoven immanent and situational knowledge are, and what problems arise if one has to distinguish them from each other by means of an automatic language processing system. The situations represented by the nodes C01 and C02 in Fig. 3.6 are events which belong to the situational knowledge with regard to the concepts Magalhães and ⟨southern part of South America⟩ (≙ node C04), respectively. In contrast, the situation represented by C03 and the relationships contained in the broken circle in Fig. 3.6 belong to the immanent knowledge with regard to the concept C05 (≙ ⟨the waterway separating South America from Tierra del Fuego⟩), and possibly also with regard to ⟨Tierra del Fuego⟩ and ⟨South America⟩. Thus, it has to be inferred by the language understanding process in a QAS (i.e. during analysis) that this information has to be characterized by [**K-TYPE** = *categ*] for arcs starting or ending in ⟨Tierra del Fuego⟩, ⟨South America⟩, and C05 (see Fig. 17.7), while other information possibly connected with these conceptual representatives (e.g. *"Magalhães saw Tierra del Fuego in 1520."*) has to be attached to the S-part of Tierra del Fuego (see Fig. 17.7).

As indicated at the beginning, the distinction between **immanent** and **situational knowledge** on the one hand and the distinction between **definitional** and **assertional knowledge** encountered in the AI literature (e.g. [5]) on the other hand, do not coincide in every case.

---

[9] In addition, prosodic information also plays an important part in this discrimination. It is conventional that the article in natural language descriptions of generic concepts not be stressed in a spoken sentence (if an article is used at all). This can be observed especially in German.

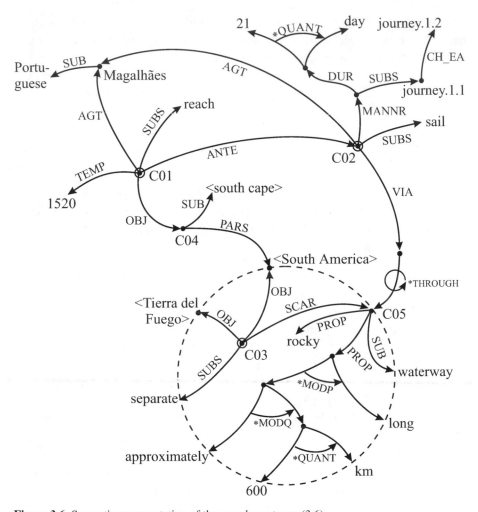

**Figure 3.6.** Semantic representation of the sample sentence (3.6)

- **Definitional knowledge** is that part of conceptual knowledge belonging to a concept node which uniquely characterizes the concept in question, and therefore also uniquely fixes its reference. All other parts of knowledge linked to this node constitute the **assertional knowledge**.

The method used in MultiNet to distinguish these two types of knowledge is the **concept capsule**. Every arc lying inside the concept capsule is part of the definitional knowledge. All other arcs connected with the corresponding concept node belong to the assertional knowledge (see Fig. 3.7). From a question-answering perspective, it is exactly the definitional knowledge that has to be reformulated for sufficiently characterizing the corresponding concept to the questioner in a QAS.

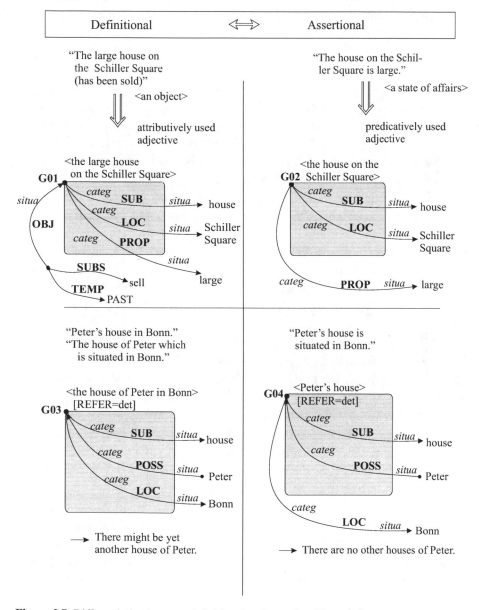

**Figure 3.7.** Differentiation between definitional and assertional knowledge

It must be emphasized that there is immanent (or even categorical) knowledge that is classified as assertional knowledge (see the lower right part of Fig. 3.7), as well as situational knowledge that defines the meaning extent of a concept, i.e. it belongs to the definitional knowledge (see the lower right part of Fig. 17.7).

The distinction between immanent and situational knowledge on the one hand and definitional and assertional knowledge on the other hand is particularly difficult with individual concepts, because there are significant events that have special importance in the human system of values and that are used for the unique characterization of an individual (this often holds for a historical personality). It is true that it is irrelevant for the characterization of ⟨Max Meyer⟩ that he spent his last holidays in the Black Forest, but it is characteristic information about ⟨Otto Hahn⟩ that he – together with Strassmann – discovered the nuclear fission. In principle, the latter information could also be classified as **situational knowledge** and as **assertional knowledge**. But in a historical perspective, this information has been raised, so to speak, by human valuation to the status of **definitional knowledge**.[10] The analogue could be stated in connection with the fact that Magalhães discovered the waterway named after him in 1520, something what is not represented in Fig. 3.6. This has generally to be taken into account with questions of the type "*{Who / What} {is / was} X?*".

For the sake of illustration, let us compare first the object description "*the large house on the Schiller Square*" (semantically represented by the concept node G01 in Fig. 3.7) with the description of the state of affairs "*the house on the Schiller Square is large*", which is represented by the arc (G02 PROP large). In the first sentence (attributive use of "*large*"), the stated property belongs to the meaning range of the concept G01 and, therefore, to its concept capsule. In the second case (predicative use of "*large*"), the object G02 is already uniquely characterized by the phrase "*the house at the Schiller Square*" with [**REFER** = *det*] for G02. The node G02 is additionally described by the assertion of a property, which is the reason why the PROP arc has not been included into the definitional capsule. Nevertheless, the PROP characterization stays an immanent property of G02 (expressed by the label *categ*). The analogue holds for G01. The situational knowledge ⟨G01 had been sold⟩ must be positioned outside the capsule of G01 from the very beginning, since an act of selling does not determine the concept G01 or a house in general (neither in the immanent sense nor in the definitional sense). The concepts G03

---

[10] Many people don't know anything else about Otto Hahn and would therefore answer the question "*Who was Otto Hahn?*" with "*The discoverer of nuclear fission*".

and G04 illustrate an analogous situation with the use of prepositional phrases or restrictive relative clauses on the one hand and predicative constructs on the other hand. It should be observed that local relationships (especially with movable objects) do not normally constitute immanent knowledge; however, with immobile objects like houses, this exactly is the case (see also the table in Appendix D, which unfortunately can only be used as a heuristic guideline, since the value assignments to the attribute **K-TYPE** are superimposed by several effects depending on the background knowledge).

To avoid overloading the graphical representations with these subtle distinctions, we largely refrain from their pictorial representation. However, it is crucial that the representational means of conceptual encapsulation, together with the labeling of arcs with values of the attribute **K-TYPE**, allow for a very fine-grained meaning representation able to express these differences.

To give an orientation with regard to the impact of the different knowledge types upon question answering (especially for so-called "Essay questions", see Sect. 3.2.4) and to show that the proposed classification into knowledge types is no end in itself, we establish a first rough connection between question patterns and types of knowledge (C stands for the concept that is asked for; the arrow '→' indicates that part of the knowledge connected with C which has to be selected as a basis for answer generation):

- *"What do you know about C?"*    →    [**K-TYPE** = *imman*]
- *"What do you know {for certain / categorically} about C?"*    →
    [**K-TYPE** = *categ*]
- *"What does (only) typically hold for C?"*    →    [**K-TYPE** = *proto*]
- *"Tell me everything about C!"*    →
    [**K-TYPE** = *imman*] and [**K-TYPE** = *situa*]
- *"What is a(n) C?"*, *"Who {is / was} C?"*    →
    Definitional knowledge (content of the capsule belonging to C)

For a practically realized NLP system not having enough background knowledge or inferential capacity to distinguish exactly between the different types of knowledge, we propose to identify in a first approximation the immanent knowledge with the definitional knowledge, and the situational knowledge with the assertional knowledge (being well aware that these categories belong to different classification criteria which should not be mixed in a strict approach).

### 3.2.4   Classification of Questions

An important basis for a QAS is the classification of questions. One may group questions according to the deep relations they are aiming at. The classes emerging from this approach are characterized by question patterns dealt with in Part II, Chap. 18, in connection with structural representational means. Another classification is governed by methods being used during logical answer finding. This classification represented in Fig. 3.8 distinguishes three classes at the top level:

- **Supplementary Questions (query type ERG-0)** – This type of question is characterized by the fact that it possesses a so-called **question focus**, a node in the meaning structure of the question which has to be considered a variable. It denotes the entity toward which the interest of the querying person is directed. Special cases of this type are count questions (query type **COUNT**) and operational questions (query type **OPERG**). To answer them, one has to perform an additional action (counting, computing an average value, etc.) after finding the substitution for the question focus. In English, questions of type **ERG-0** are often called **WH-questions**, because the corresponding interrogative pronouns generally begin with "*Wh*".
- **Decision Questions (query type ENT-0)** – This type of question in its pure form requires only the verification of the proposition indirectly specified in the question; it has to be answered with "*Yes*" or "*No*" (Yes-No questions). Note that there are also questions classified as "decision questions" from the syntactical point of view only, as is the case with questions asking for a decision and for the existence of an entity at the same time (query type **ENTEX**). In case of a positive outcome, these questions should not be answered simply with "*Yes*" with a cooperative answer strategy. They must rather be treated as supplementary questions, where the object whose existence is asked for must be described in the answer.
- **Essay Questions (query type ESS)** – This type of question has no proper question focus, i.e. there is more than one node of the network functioning as kernel of the answer. In this case, a whole text (an essay) has to be generated as an answer on the basis of a partial network retrieved during question-answering from the knowledge base.

Depending on the question type, different inference methods have to be used for knowledge extraction and also for answer generation. This is also an important distinguishing feature for the semantic and pragmatic interpretation of different questions. The semantic representation of questions will be dealt with in Sect. 13.2. It should be kept in mind that the distinction between immanent and situational knowledge discussed in Sect. 3.2.3 is crucial for answering the above-mentioned essay questions.

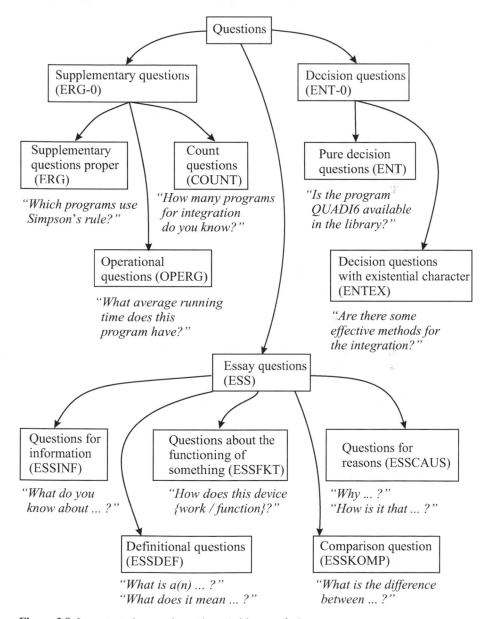

**Figure 3.8.** Important classes of questions (with examples)

It would also be thinkable to classify questions by means of logical methods or problem solving techniques that have to be used for answering these questions (deduction, analogical reasoning, numerical calculations, pure retrieval methods, etc.). Unfortunately, these decisions cannot be deduced immediately from the semantic structure of a question. This problem goes far beyond the domain of knowledge representation, the main topic of this work.

## 3.3    Structural Means of Representation

### 3.3.1    Relations and Functions

The most important representational means for describing conceptual structures, i.e. the links between nodes of semantic networks, are given by the relations and functions assembled in the global overview of Fig. 3.10. Since this repertory of relations and functions will be described in Part II, Chap. 18, only a few principal remarks shall be given here.

The functions and relations of MultiNet are associated with natural language expressions in two different ways. On the one hand, they are referred to by specific question patterns which unfortunately are not uniquely assigned to the representational means (see Part II, Sect. 18.2). On the other hand, the semantically primitive representational means can themselves be described by natural language expressions, as shown in Fig. 3.9.

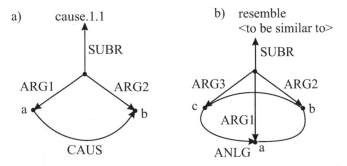

**Figure 3.9.** Connection between semantic primitives and natural language concepts

Figure 3.9a shows that the relation CAUS has two arguments (ARG1 and ARG2); it can be described in English by "*a causes b*". In contrast, Figure 3.9b states that the similarity relation ANLG, with arguments ARG1, ARG2, and ARG3, is a ternary relation, which can be described by expressions like "*a is*

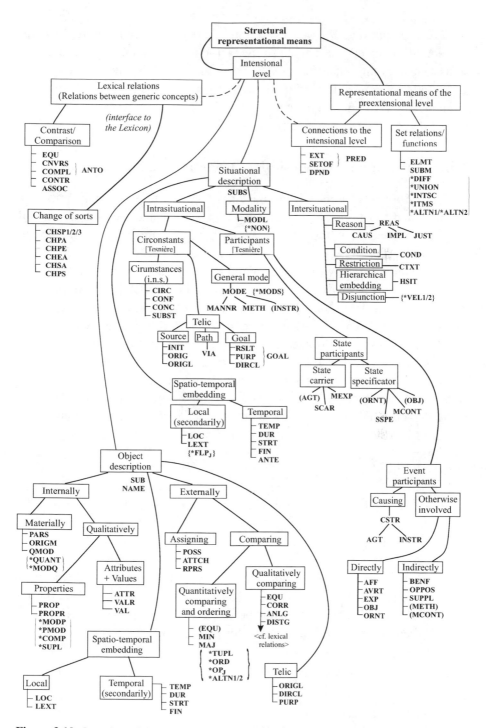

**Figure 3.10.** Overview of the structural representational means

*similar to b with regard to c"*. These interrelations are used mainly for paraphrasing the deep relations in the surface structure of natural language expressions, which is important for a QAS in the phase of language understanding (analysis phase) as well as in the phase of generating answers or texts from semantic representations (generation phase). Therefore, they are an essential part of the lexicon (see Chap. 12).

### 3.3.2    Inferential Relationships – Axiomatic Rules

Let us consider the problem why the introduction of semantically primitive relations and functions is so crucial for representing the meaning of natural language sentences and texts, and let us try to address this from the standpoint of the working of a QAS.

The relationship between question and answer, and also the connection between semantically related pieces of texts, cannot be established simply by a topological comparison of the corresponding semantic structures. In general, we need logical inferences, which often amounts to constructing whole chains of inferences based on axiomatic rules that are formalized as logical implications. What is really decisive (in the sense of economical reasoning in a human question-answering game and in a technical question-answering system, too) is the fact that a large part of these inference rules need not be connected with particular language elements, but with only a few fundamental relations or functions representing whole classes of individual relationships:[11]
Example:

- (x CAUS y) $\longrightarrow$ ¬(y ANTE x)                    (1)

Rule (1) asserts a connection between the causality relation CAUS and the temporal predecessorship ANTE; it says: If x causes y, then y cannot temporally precede x.[12]

Rules that do not contain logical constants (i.e. representatives of concepts) as arguments are called **R-Axioms**, since they define relations and functions with regard to their logical properties. These rules have a global effect during the inference process over a semantic network, as they can become active at all places where these relations are encountered in the SN.

---

[11] In all the following formulas, the widespread convention is used that free variables in logical expressions have to be considered as universally quantified.

[12] The technical term **rule** is used in a double sense, as is common in AI and computational linguistics. On the one hand, it designates inference rules like the modus ponens or the cut rule (see Sect. 13.2). On the other hand, it designates axioms written in the form of implications. There exists a close relationship between both.

There are also axioms that contain constants designating meaning representatives of natural language expressions (especially of single words), i.e. they contain names of concepts. Such axioms have to be considered as components of the meaning representation of these concepts. For this reason, they are called **B-Axioms** or **meaning postulates** (Ge: "Bedeutungspostulate"). Example:

- (v SUBS give.1.1) $\land$ (v AGT a) $\land$ (v OBJ o) $\land$ (v ORNT d) $\longrightarrow$
  $\exists$w (w SUBS receive.1.1) $\land$ (w OBJ o) $\land$ (w AVRT a) $\land$ (w EXP d)    (2)

Rule (2) establishes a link between the concepts give and receive, and at the same time characterizes the change in the deep case relations of both actions. In contrast to R-Axioms, B-Axioms have only a local effect on the inference processes over the SN. B-Axioms also describe relations between concepts, but in a somewhat more complex way than the semantically primitive relations (i.e. by using whole logical expressions instead of a single relation).

Moreover, there are axioms that introduce certain concepts or relations through defining expressions. The corresponding logical connector will be denoted by $\longleftrightarrow_{Def}$.
Example:

- $(s_1$ REAS $s_2) \longleftrightarrow_{Def} (s_1$ CAUS $s_2) \lor (s_1$ IMPL $s_2) \lor (s_1$ JUST $s_2)$    (3)

Finally, we have to agree upon the convention that, in contrast to logic, regularities specified by axioms in MultiNet may be associated with **constraints** restricting their range of validity. Thus, there are axioms which have to be considered default rules that cover typical cases which are not, however, valid without exceptions. This restriction is expressed by inserting the corresponding axiom into the D-part of the capsules representing the concepts or relations which are part of the axiom in question (see Part II, Fig. 17.7, and the explanations below).
Example:

- $(k_1$ PARS $k_2) \land (k_2$ ORIGM s) $\longrightarrow (k_1$ ORIGM s)        [Default]    (4)

This rule states the following: If $k_2$ as a whole consists of a certain material s, then this is generally also true for a part $k_1$ of $k_2$. However, this is only a plausible assumption, since a plastic car, for instance, may have wheels made of rubber.[13]

For the semantic specification of relations and functions, we can use the same techniques at the **metalevel** as those proposed for the conceptual level.

---

[13] With regard to this assumption, please compare Axiom (7) with Axioms (5) or (6) in Sect. 4.1. For them, the distinction between axioms holding strictly and axioms holding only prototypically is also relevant.

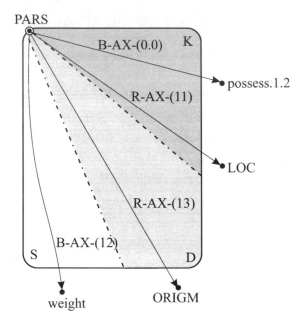

Defining B-axiom:

$$B\text{-AX-(0.0)}: \quad (x \text{ PARS } y) \longrightarrow \exists\, s \,(s \text{ SUBR possess.1.2}) \land$$
$$(s \text{ ARG1 } x) \land (s \text{ ARG2 } y)$$

**Figure 3.11.** Relations and functions as nodes (conceptual capsules) at the metalevel

In metalevel networks, the nodes represent relations and functions, which are also enclosed in capsules (Fig. 3.11). The arcs between nodes at the metalevel are defined by axioms (a kind of hyper-relations). This view is supported by the fact that all axioms written as an implication and used in an inference step during the question-answering process establish a connection between meta-concepts (i.e. relations and functions) or concepts standing on the left side of the implication and metaconcepts or concepts standing on the right side of the implication.[14]

There are also rules which are restricted to certain side conditions stating, for instance, that some arguments belong to specific subsorts that are not already predefined by the signature of the participating relations or functions (see Axiom (5) and the discussion in Sect. 4.3.2 about the properties which can be

---

[14] R-Axioms contain metaconcepts only, while in B-Axioms both metaconcepts and concepts can be found. (The latter are represented as normal nodes of the SN.)

semantically quantified). This information is annotated at the corresponding axioms as a constraint.[15]

Certain properties of relations, such as the restricted transitivity of some relations, can only with difficulty be described by pure logical means. Thus, the transitivity rule (a $\langle$REL$\rangle$ b) $\wedge$ (b $\langle$REL$\rangle$ c) $\longrightarrow$ (a $\langle$REL$\rangle$ c) cannot be applied ad infinitum to relations like ASSOC and PARS. The problem is that, on the one hand, we are intuitively inclined to assign the transitivity property to relations like PARS; on the other hand, this property does not hold unrestrictedly (see Sect. 4.2 and Part II, relation PARS). With such relations, the transitivity is therefore considered a default rule that can be refined by further constraints if necessary (e.g. constraints specifying the maximum number of rule applications in an inference chain or more complicated constraints requiring that the arguments belong to the same functional level).

It is an important task to support the generation of axioms by convenient software tools (see Sect. 14.2), or even to (semi)automatically generate meaning postulates from lexical resources or text corpora. A first successful attempt in this direction is the automatic generation of B-axioms (entailments) from glosses incorporated in the German computational lexicon GermaNet (see[79] and [149, 148]).

Concluding this chapter, we have to emphasize that the axiomatic specifications of the expressional means of MultiNet are kept strictly apart from the knowledge base describing a certain domain. Thus, it would be possible in principle to substitute axioms, or even whole groups of relations and functions, with others to establish another semantic framework. However, this step would disconnect MultiNet from the computational lexicon HaGenLex and leave the burden of redefining the semantic characterization of tens of thousands of concepts to the user.

---

[15] Constraints concerning the validity of axioms are only verbally or semiformally specified in this book. They characterize semantically restrictive knowledge at the metalevel (which is analogous to the feature [**K-TYPE** = *restr*] in the SN proper).

# Chapter 4

# Semantic Characterization of Objects

## 4.1 The Hierarchical Order of Objects

Entities, which can be thought of as objects, are called **conceptual objects** (or "objects" for short). This category comprises concrete objects as well as abstract objects (e.g. house, leg, or theory, law, respectively). Formally, all these objects belong to sort $[o \setminus (abs \cup re)]$, which is somewhat restricted with regard to the general sort $o$ (see Part II, Sect. 17.1).[1] A comparison of objects and properties can be found in Sect. 4.3.

The most important relation introducing an order between conceptual objects is the subordination relation SUB: $[o \setminus (abs \cup re)] \times [\overline{o} \setminus (\overline{abs} \cup \overline{re})]$, see Fig. 4.1. This relation may hold between two generic concepts (with layer attribute [**GENER** = $ge$], which is indicated by overlining the sort symbols) as well as between an individual concept (with attribute [**GENER** = $sp$]) and a generic concept. Both cases are often distinguished from each other in the literature, where the latter case is covered by the **IS-A relation**. Contrary to the opinion held in [31], the relations SUB (restricted to generic concepts only) and IS-A need not be separated in a QAS founded on a sorted calculus. The argumentation used in the cited paper is based mainly on first order logic (FOL) and its extensional interpretation, where individuals are usually formalized as logical constants, and generic concepts as predicates. This argumentation cannot be transferred to MultiNet, because MultiNet is not based exclusively on predicate calculus, let alone on an extensional interpretation. Even in FOL, an individual concept designated by a proper name like "*Peter*" could be for-

---

[1] The reason why we only discuss objects in a narrower sense in this section, excluding the subsorts *abs* and *re*, is the following: On the one hand, elements of the sorts *abs* and *re* are subject to other inheritance mechanisms than objects in the narrower sense, and they belong to other conceptual hierarchies built with relations SUBS and SUBR, respectively. Therefore they are excluded from the considerations in Chap. 4. On the other hand, elements from sorts *abs* and *re* can have attributes and properties like "normal" objects, e.g. a wedding can be expensive, wonderful, etc., see relations ATTR, PROP, for example. From this point of view, they also belong to sort *o*.

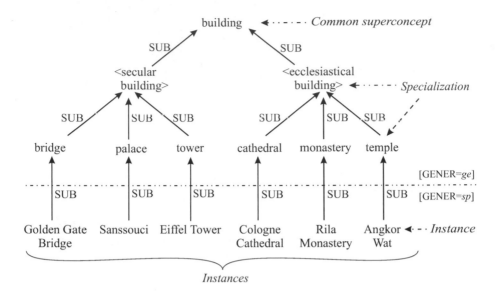

**Figure 4.1.** Part of a hierarchy of conceptual objects

malized as a predicate using a LAMBDA-expression or a simple equivalence relation: $\forall x$ PETER(x) $\leftrightarrow$ (x $\equiv$ Peter). More important, however, is the fact that the (restricted) relation SUB and the relation IS-A are associated essentially with the same axioms and inference rules. It should also be remarked that neither of these relations are reflexive. Thus, a distinction of them would lead only to a duplication of axioms. Checking the layer attributes of the arguments of the SUB relation during knowledge acquisition finally warrants that no concept (be it a generic or an individual one) is ever subordinate to an individual concept.

The relation SUB is transitive, not reflexive, and asymmetric. All concepts subordinate to a common superordinate concept form a **conceptual hierarchy**, and therefore constitute a partial tree in the SN. The top node of this hierarchy (the root) is exactly the aforementioned superconcept. The terminal (individual) concept nodes of the tree are called **instances**. All other nodes of the hierarchy, except for the root, are **specializations** of the top node. A node at a higher level in the hierarchy is called the **superconcept** (or **prototype**) of all **subconcepts** positioned below it in the hierarchy.

The SUB-hierarchy plays an outstanding role, since it is connected with **inheritance mechanisms** by means of which information from superconcepts is

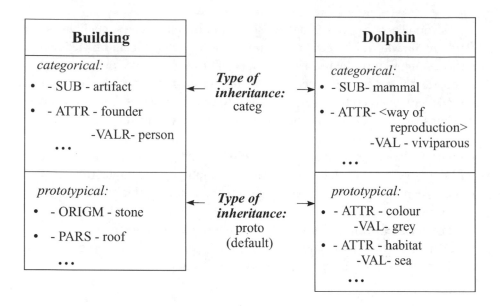

**Figure 4.2.** Different types of inheritance

transferred to the corresponding subconcepts. In this connection, two different types of inheritance have to be distinguished (Fig. 4.2).[2]

On the one hand, there is **categorical knowledge** associated with a concept and inherited without any exception by all its subconcepts, i.e. by all its specializations and instances (**monotonic reasoning**). This type of inheritance is sometimes called **leave same** in AI [280]. The information, for instance, that a building is an artificially created object (an artifact), or that a dolphin gives birth to living young, belongs to the categorical knowledge about these concepts. There are no exceptions.[3] We encounter another situation with conceptual knowledge which is typical only of a certain object, such as the information that a building is made of stone, or that it has a roof. Here, we encounter exceptions: A building can also be made of other materials (e.g. a wooden house), and it may not possess a roof (e.g. in the case of a bridge).

---

[2] The relation names included by hyphens in this figure represent the labeled arcs between the nodes indicated.

[3] The fact that actually only female animals give birth has to be taken into account by anchoring this knowledge as a constraint in the concept capsule of ⟨give birth⟩. This can be done by assigning the relationship (a PROP female) as categorical knowledge to the agent a of this concept.

In contrast to value restrictions (relation VALR), which can be specialized or "narrowed" at lower levels in an inheritance hierarchy, values specified by VAL are transferred down to the last instance of the hierarchy without any change during the inheritance process. They can be overwritten only if they are marked as default assumptions.

Nevertheless, it is very economical for a knowledge representation system (and, by the way, for human beings too) to store such **typical knowledge** as a basic assumption or **default assumption** inherited by means of special rules. In contrast to strict inheritance, it must be possible to overwrite this kind of knowledge, inherited by concept specializations or instances from their super-concepts, if there is already some contradicting information available at the lower level (e.g. that a special building is made of wood). This type of inheritance is sometimes labeled **override** in AI [280]. Prototypical knowledge will therefore be inherited as a standard assumption (i.e. as a **default**) only. It holds as long as there is no conflicting information available (**nonmonotonic reasoning**).

The transfer of information, like the inheritance of properties or the conveyance of part-whole relationships from a superconcept to its subconcepts, can be characterized formally by the following axioms:

- Transfer of properties:[4]
  $$(\text{o1 SUB o2}) \wedge (\text{o2 PROP p}) \longrightarrow (\text{o1 PROP p}) \tag{5}$$
- Inheritance of the part-whole relationship:
  $$(\text{d1 SUB d2}) \wedge (\text{d3 PARS d2}) \longrightarrow \exists \text{d4} \, [(\text{d4 SUB d3}) \wedge (\text{d4 PARS d1})] \tag{6}$$

As already stated in Sect. 3.3.2, the knowledge about relations and functions (the **metaknowledge**) is also divided into categorical knowledge and default knowledge. Thus, the transitivity axiom for the relation SUB:

- $$(\text{o1 SUB o2}) \wedge (\text{o2 SUB o3}) \longrightarrow (\text{o1 SUB o3}) \tag{7}$$

has strict validity (therefore, it belongs to the categorical knowledge). In contrast, both of the preceding axioms, (5) and (6), have to be considered prototypical knowledge. The application of these rules time and again produces only default knowledge with regard to the subconcepts in an inheritance process.

The inheritance of information from superordinate to subordinate concepts also plays an important role in the attribute-value characterization of objects by means of the ATTR relation (see Sect. 4.3.3). It should be remarked here that, contrary to the opinion held by Brachman ([31, p. 35]), the inheritance of knowledge in conceptual hierarchies is not primarily a matter of implementation. It is rather an essential characteristic of relations that produce conceptual hierarchies like SUB, SUBS, or PARS (see Sect. 4.2) that they are connected with inheritance of knowledge, while this is not true for other relations (such as the deep case relations AGT, ORNT, etc.). From the psychological point of view, inheritance of knowledge is a basic process economizing on storage

---

[4] Axiom (5) holds for semantically total properties [SORT = $tq$] only (see Sect. 4.3).

capacity of memory, and – from the aspect of knowledge representation – it is a fundamental property discerning certain relations from others by their logical properties.[5] It is certainly not the SUB relation or, in other terminology, the IS-A relation, which will be overburdened with different interpretations (prototypical inheritance of properties, interpretation with logically universally quantified expressions, etc.) if one maintains the encapsulation principle for concepts and the division of these capsules into categorical, prototypical and situational knowledge. It is rather the concept (to be accurate, the superconcept), which is connected with these different meaning components. The SUB relation merely specifies how these different facets have to be treated during the inheritance process. It must be emphasized that the SUB relation also can not be identified with the subset relation. It is primarily an aspect of the meaning of a concept, whether this concept is extensionally interpretable as a set (as with house and tiger) or not (as with charm, great, or reference).

However, it is a property of the relation SUB that the following rules hold, provided the concepts involved are extensionally interpretable:

- (a SUB b) $\longrightarrow$ ($\langle$all a$\rangle_{EXT}$ SUBM $\langle$all b$\rangle_{EXT}$) $\hspace{2cm}$ (8)
  if both a and b are generic concepts being extensionally interpretable at all;

- (a SUB b) $\longrightarrow$ (a$_{EXT}$ ELMT $\langle$all b$\rangle_{EXT}$) $\hspace{2.5cm}$ (9)
  if the extension of a is an individual element and the extension of b is a set.

With these statements, we are already addressing the problem of the meaning representation of plural constructs, dealt with in Chaps. 9 and 10.

It should be emphasized that phrases containing word groups like "*be*", "*are*", and "*to be a(n)*" must not automatically be translated into the relation SUB at the semantic level. Apart from the fact that "*to be*" can also function as a full verb in the sense of "*to be situated*" or "*to live*", as in "*Max is in Argentina*" (Relation LOC), there exist also other interpretations for the copula "*be*":

"*A bachelor is an adult unmarried man.*" (Relation EQU),
"*The cherry is red.*" (Relation PROP),
"*Peter is a teacher (by profession).*" (Relations ATTR, VAL, and SUB)
(see Sect. 4.3.3).
The last example clearly shows the importance of the correct interpretation

---

[5] Notwithstanding this thesis, nothing can be said against the statement of Brachman that a formalism with inheritance must not have more expressional power than a formalism without it (one has only to imagine that all implicitly inheritable information was a priori made explicit). Nevertheless, we had to deal with entirely different KRSs in the two cases, and also with different systems of semantically primitive relations and functions having other logical properties.

of the copula *"be"*. In MultiNet, the concept teacher has to be treated properly as a meaning molecule (see Chap. 12) with the facets $teacher_1$ [**SORT** $= co$] denoting a group of people and $teacher_2$ [**SORT** $= at$] denoting an attribute.[6] Within this approach one has to formulate (Peter SUB $teacher_1$) and ($teacher_2$ SUB profession) without creating a contradiction. The connection between the above-mentioned two meaning facets is then given by ($teacher_1$ ATTR $teacher_2$), meaning that $teacher_1$ as a person is always $teacher_2$ by profession.

If one takes into account somewhat sloppy use of language, often met in daily practice, the danger of misinterpretation caused by a wrong treatment of the concept teacher with its different facets as attribute value and superconcept for certain persons can be shown by the following example (danger of misinterpretation by equivocation):

From *"Peter is a teacher."* (Relation (Peter SUB teacher) ??) and
*"Teacher is a profession."* (Relation (teacher SUB profession) ??)
one could wrongly deduce on the basis of the transitivity of SUB that
*"Peter is a profession."* (Relation (Peter SUB profession) ??), which is clearly wrong.

The difficulty of the semantic interpretation of the English copula *"be"* or the German copula *"sein"* can be illustrated by sentences already investigated by Lakoff [151, p. 121]. They are built on the copula *"be"* and introduced by phrases like *"juridically"* (Ge: *"juristisch gesehen"*), *"loosely speaking"* (Ge: *"grob gesprochen"*), etc. Semantically, these phrases establish different views (so-called **multiple views**), which can be expressed in MultiNet by means of the relation CTXT. This relation restricts the whole conceptual capsule and its content (including the subordination relation SUB) to a certain world (world view) or a certain context (a juridical view, a rough view etc.). In a similar way, one can also deal with the so-called **folk theory**. This is a collection of rather simplifying and sometimes naive opinions, according to which, for instance, a dolphin is a fish or a slow-worm is a snake (see Fig. 4.3).

Examples (after Lakoff) with their German counterpart[7]:

(4.1)  *"Juridically, Nixon is a gangster."*
    Ge: *"Juristisch gesehen ist Nixon ein Gangster."*
    (Nixon SUB gangster) + (* CTXT ⟨juridical view⟩).

---

[6] The same could be stated of all professions or jobs, e.g. farmer, moderator, or caretaker, etc.

[7] In the following examples the star "*" characterizes the representation of the embedded situation (e.g. * = (Nixon SUB gangster) in (4.1)).

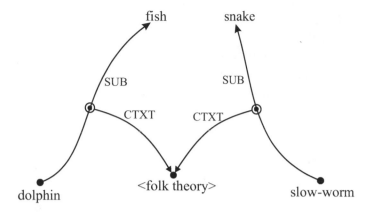

**Figure 4.3.** *Folk theory* as a contextual restriction

(4.2) *"Loosely speaking, Carter is a peanut farmer."*
    Ge: *"Grob gesprochen ist Carter ein Erdnussfarmer."*
    (Carter SUB ⟨peanut farmer⟩) + (* CTXT ⟨rough view⟩).

(4.3) *"A dolphin is a fish."*
    Ge: *"Ein Delphin ist ein Fisch."*
    (dolphin SUB fish) + (* CTXT ⟨folk theory⟩).

**But**:

(4.4) *"Mary is a real snake."*

In this case, the word group *"is a"* must not be associated with the relation SUB but rather with the relation ANLG, where the attribute with regard to which Mary is similar to a snake is not explicitly specified (it could be falseness, ⟨way of movement⟩, or something like that). The analogue can be stated for the German sentence:

(4.5) *"Maria ist eine richtige Schlange."*

Rounding off this thematic complex, we shortly have to go into the problem of **proper names**. In the foregoing discussions we assumed that all nodes of the SN can be labeled by a unique name. Unfortunately, the "natural" proper names of objects are highly ambiguous. On the one hand, there are objects (especially in their different manifestations, see Sect. 4.5) which have more than one name, e.g. Napoleon, Bonaparte or ⟨Napoleon I⟩. On the other hand, it is possible and very common that proper names (e.g. Luxembourg) denote different objects (in this case, the state and the capital of Luxembourg). In cases, where proper names have an inner structure (typically, they are partitioned into first name and last name), the semantic representative will be given an artificially generated name (as for instance G132 in Fig. 4.4), and then the relation NAME or alternatively the relations ATTR and VAL are used to attach the "natural" name(s) to the concept node. In this way, the parts of names also become nodes of the network, to whom their own semantics can be assigned (e.g. that a certain name denotes a male person, or that names can be decomposed according to the following axiom, which is graphically represented in Fig. 4.4).

- $(o \text{ NAME } n) \land (n = (*\text{TUPL } v \text{ f})) \leftrightarrow$
  $$\exists a_1 \, \exists a_2 \, (o \text{ ATTR } a_1) \land (a_1 \text{ SUB } \langle \text{first name} \rangle) \land (a_1 \text{ VAL } v) \land$$
  $$(o \text{ ATTR } a_2) \land (a_2 \text{ SUB } \langle \text{last name} \rangle) \land (a_2 \text{ VAL } f) \qquad (10)$$

The philosophical aspect of naming objects (especially with regard to changing or hypothetical worlds) and the problem of the **cross-world identity** of objects connected to the naming problem cannot be dealt with in more detail (see [147]).

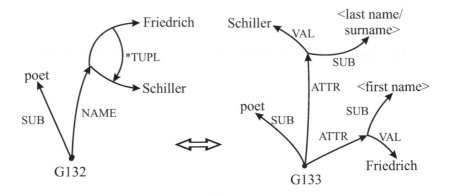

**Figure 4.4.** Representation of proper names of objects

## 4.2   Material Characterization of Objects

The material or physical structure of objects plays an important part in their conceptual characterization. For this purpose, MultiNet provides the relation PARS for the description of the part-whole relationship, the relation ORIGM for specifying the substances making up an object, and the relation QMOD for the specification of a quantity of objects (⟨3 kg of nails⟩) or of a substance (⟨3 kg of ice⟩).

The part-whole relation PARS gives rise to a hierarchy similar to that induced by the SUB relation (see Sect. 4.1). However, it is not associated with such far-reaching transfer mechanisms of properties and attribute-value combinations as the SUB relation. An example of two different PARS hierarchies is given in Fig. 4.5. The structures shown there are interlinked by the concept leg. For correctly building a PARS-hierarchy, one has to observe the proper subordination relations, apart from the part-whole relationships. In Fig. 4.5, for instance, the concept leg must not be directly connected with the concept table via the relation PARS, but indirectly via the SUB relation, since not all things which can be imagined as a leg are associated with the concept table (human beings, animals, chairs, etc. also have legs). The concepts table and ⟨human being⟩ can be characterized by two different subconcepts, each being "part of a whole". Both subconcepts are subordinate to the same superconcept leg (definable as the main part of a supporting apparatus used for locomotion or for holding up something). In German, there is even a lexicalized concept for one of the above-mentioned subconcepts: Tischbein (En: ⟨leg of a table⟩).

In contrast, the PARS hierarchy given in Fig. 4.6, which was used as a starting point for the discussion in one of the earlier works on the semantics of the part-whole relationship [20], has to be considered as a simplification that is not permitted, since the necessary subordination relations are lacking. Within such an approach, the concept leg would be immediately attached to both concepts, ⟨human being⟩ and table, by means of the PARS relation, something which is not appropriate.[8]

The part-whole relation PARS obeys the axioms of **transfer of location** (Axiom (11)), **weight restriction** (Axiom (12)), and **transfer of material** (Axiom (13)):

- $(k_1 \text{ PARS } k_2) \wedge (k_2 \text{ LOC } l) \longrightarrow (k_1 \text{ LOC } l)$     (11)     (default knowledge)

This axiom asserts that a part is located at the same place as the whole.

- $(k_1 \text{ PARS } k_2) \wedge (k_2 \text{ ATTR } m_2) \wedge (m_2 \text{ SUB weight.1.1}) \wedge (m_2 \text{ VAL } q_2) \rightarrow$
  $\exists m_1 \exists q_1 [(k_1 \text{ ATTR } m_1) \wedge (m_1 \text{ SUB weight.1.1}) \wedge$
  $(m_1 \text{ VAL } q_1) \wedge (q_1 \text{ MIN } q_2)]$     (12)

---

[8] One should be warned of speaking about the subordination of nouns by the part-whole relationship (something often done by inexperienced students); this is not allowed in connection with deep relations, which always connect concepts, not words.

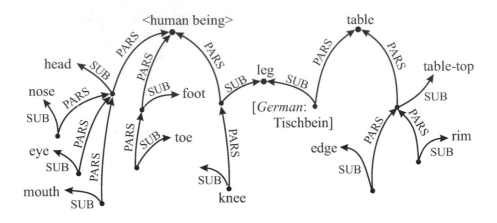

**Figure 4.5.** A correct PARS hierarchy taking into account the proper subordination relations

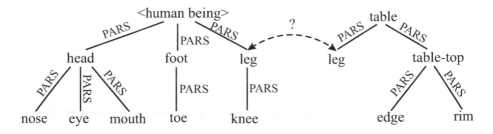

**Figure 4.6.** An inadmissibly simplified PARS hierarchy

According to this rule, the part is always lighter then the whole (i.e. it has less weight). Axiom (12) is valid without exceptions, and therefore belongs to categorical knowledge.

- $(k_1 \text{ PARS } k_2) \wedge (k_2 \text{ ORIGM } s) \longrightarrow (k_1 \text{ ORIGM } s)$  (13)

This axiom states that the part consists of the same material as the whole. Such a rule clearly can only be used to create default knowledge. It is surely typical that the arm of a golden statue also consists of gold. But it is not always true that this also holds for every detail (one can easily imagine that the eyes of a golden statue consist of jade).

The relation PARS, like the relation SUB, is transitive, asymmetric, and not reflexive. However, in contrast to SUB, the transitivity rule (14) does not hold without restrictions:

- $(k_1 \text{ PARS } k_2) \wedge (k_2 \text{ PARS } k_3) \longrightarrow (k_1 \text{ PARS } k_3)$  (14)

This rule belongs to the default knowledge about PARS. Thus, one can state that the balance spring is part of the clockwork, the clock is part of the church steeple, which is part of the church. However, no one would say that the balance spring is part of the church (even if this is true in a strictly formal sense). The example shows that the transitivity of the PARS relation seems to get lost over larger chains of PARS arcs (**fading effect**). It is important to demand additionally that a certain functional connection exist between part and whole. Furthermore, the part-whole relationships connected by transitivity should belong to the same conceptual level or framework. This also explains why the PARS relation is not usually asserted between a macro-body (e.g. a tree) and a micro-particle (e.g. a proton), even if that may be true from a purely physical point of view.

In addition to the relations already mentioned, MultiNet provides the function ∗QUANT and the relation QMOD to describe the quantitative aspect of material composition. Figure 4.7 shows the interplay of these representational means in describing a more complex material specification (see also Sect. 16.3, especially the convention associated with Fig. 16.3f).

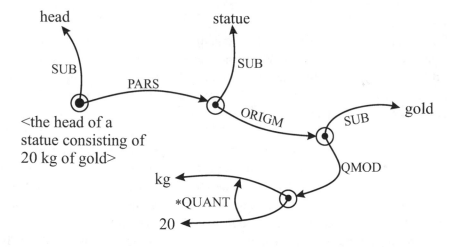

**Figure 4.7.** Material characterization of conceptual objects

The example leads to a more general connection between the quantitative characterization by means of QMOD and ∗QUANT on the one hand, and an attribute-value characterization on the other hand (see Sect. 4.3.3):[9]

---

[9] An analogous rule holds for the inverse direction.

- $(s \ QMOD \ q) \land q = (*QUANT \ x \ me) \land (a \ ATTCH \ me) \longrightarrow$
  $\exists a_1 \ (s \ ATTR \ a_1) \land (a_1 \ SUB \ a) \land (a_1 \ VAL \ q)$ \hfill (15)

One might ask whether it is sufficient to allow only for one of these characterizations to achieve a more canonical semantic representation (the representations can anyway be transformed into each other). Since this problem is encountered repeatedly, a general statement may be helpful at this point. It is possible, of course, to mark one of the representations and prefer it to the other, even if they describe the same state of affairs. In this case, the second has to be reduced to the first during analysis (i.e. during language understanding). Whether or not human beings use such a kind of normalization is not yet known. From the point of view of automatic language processing, both representational variants should be maintained, since each of them is closer to a certain language behavior and to certain intentions of the speaker/writer. In a QAS, there is always a trade-off between the effort to be expended during analysis and during the phase of answer generation. If one wants to normalize the semantic representation to a higher degree, then axioms like (15) have to be applied as transformation rules during analysis (this has to be done, so to say "in reserve"). This effort is lost, however, if a query aiming at this state of affairs is never asked in a QAS.
If one wants to simplify the syntactic-semantic analysis, then such transformational axioms have to be used as logical rules during the inference processes, and a corresponding effort has to be expended during answer finding. Experience with the development of question-answering systems indicates that the second way is preferable.

To conclude this discussion, a remark should be made on the connection between the meaning of "*to have*" and the part-whole relation PARS. It is sometimes argued in the literature ([128]) that the PARS relation used in semantic networks seems to be totally overburdened. This argumentation is often based on a hidden identification of the meaning of the polysemous words "*to have*" or "*part*" with the relation PARS, something which almost automatically leads to an unduly high number of meaning aspects of this misunderstood relation. It has to be taken into account, however, that phrases like "*to have*", "*to be part of*", etc. are highly ambiguous. The relation PARS covers only a certain segment of the meaning spectrum of these phrases (in fact, only the part-whole relationship defined in Part II). Further meanings are covered by POSS, ATTR, ATTCH, ELMT, and SUBM, among others.[10]

---

[10] Here, we meet a similar problem as with the copula "*be*" whose meaning is also not covered by the SUB relation alone.

Somewhat more problematic is the decision to extend the PARS relation to abstract concepts (as expressed in the signature of PARS). This choice was made because most inheritance rules of the PARS hierarchy and the argumentation with regard to the transitivity of PARS are also valid for abstract concepts. An illegal application of axioms not valid for abstract concepts (like Axiom (13)) can be excluded by strict observation of the restrictions imposed on the arguments by the signatures of relations and functions (the relation ORIGM can indeed hold for concrete objects only).

## 4.3 Qualitative Characterization of Objects

### 4.3.1 General Remarks on the Qualitative Characterization of Objects

Objects and their qualitative characterization form a **dialectical unity** (Fig. 4.8). No object can be conceived without its properties in the widest sense, and no properties exist without any objects. Nevertheless, the properties seem to be secondary from the cognitive point of view and the objects primary (an object "*has/possesses*" properties and not vice versa). In natural language, as well as in reasoning about our conceptual world, no difficulties arise in treating properties and objects as entities which are clearly distinguished from each other, even though they cannot be separated perceptually.

The idea of objects and their qualitative characterizations (properties) forming a unity is expressed in MultiNet by the encapsulation of conceptual representatives. The cognitive difference between the two types of entities is expressed by their representation in different nodes of the SN and in their assignment to different sorts, as well as in the explicit specification of the relations between them.

Objects can be qualitatively characterized in several ways:

1. by means of **attributes** [**SORT** = $at$] and their **values** (these will be dealt with in Sect. 4.3.3);
2. by means of **properties** in a narrower sense [**SORT** = $p$], which can be divided into **semantically relative qualities** (i.e. **gradable qualities** [SORT = $gq$]) and **semantically total qualities** [SORT = $tq$] (that cannot be graded, see Sect. 17.1). This kind of characterization of objects, which is close to predications in the logical sense, is treated in Sect. 4.3.2 (where it is contrasted with the following two types of qualification);

3. by means of **semantically functional qualities** [**SORT** $= fq$] which characterize an object by assigning another object (or a group of objects) to it;

4. by means of **semantically relational qualities** [**SORT** $= rq$] which, strictly speaking, establish relationships between different objects.

When comparing qualitative characterizations with situational characterizations of objects (i.e. with their participation in occurrences and states), one can observe a certain order with regard to the temporal stability. Qualitative characterizations, including the assignment of properties or attribute-value pairs to objects, are generally stable over a relatively long time and typically belong to the immanent knowledge about objects. In contrast, **states** [**SORT** $= st$] often have limited durations. They typically belong to situational knowledge with regard to the objects involved (as is also the case with events). States on their part have a certain stability in comparison with **events** [**SORT** $= dy$], which, by definition, represent changes in the world. The boundaries between these classes are floating, and it is often difficult to distinguish exactly between the assignment of a property and the characterization of a state on the one hand, and between a state and a process (especially a mental one) on the other hand (cf. [265]). These phenomena have not yet been investigated thoroughly, neither in psychology nor in epistemology. Figure 4.8 gives an overview of the relationships discussed so far, and shows the connection of these semantic aspects to typical natural language expressions, especially to the parts of speech.

## 4.3.2 Assignment of Properties to Objects

The great variety of qualitative characterizations (called properties in their broadest sense) finds its counterpart in the distinction between total, gradable, associative, operational, and relational qualities, described in Table 17.1. The total and gradable qualities (examples are dead and large, respectively) can be joined into one sort $p$ because of their common features. In logic, these properties in the narrower sense are usually formalized as predicates, supported somewhat by the predicative use of the adjectives designating them. This practice, however, is already questionable for gradable properties, because there are important differences between both sorts, $tq$ and $gq$. The total qualities [**SORT** $= tq$] cannot be increased step by step on a scale of possible outcomes (see the definition of the function $*$COMP in Part II). This has its counterpart in the fact that the corresponding adjectives cannot be graded. In contrast, adjectives designating properties of sort $gq$ may be graded.

The identification of properties with logical predicates, often encountered in logic-oriented KRMs with their model-theoretic foundation, is allowed at

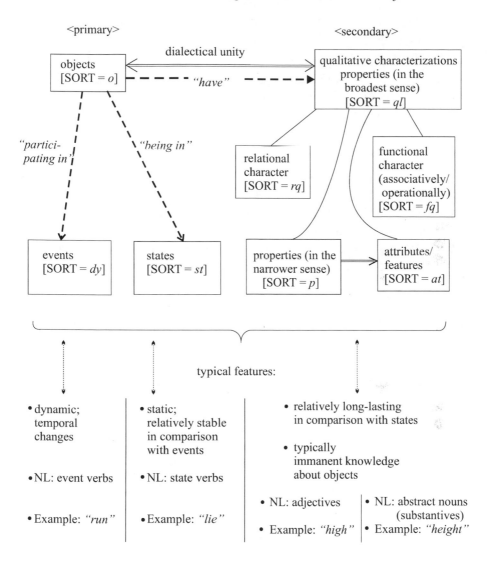

**Figure 4.8.** Semantic characterization of conceptual objects (overview)

best for semantically total properties, but not for gradable properties (at least not without restrictions). If one defines the property **large** as a predicate LARGE(x), then the extension of this predicate would be the set of all large things in the universe to be considered. However, this set does not exist in a universe underlying natural language interpretation (see the discussion in connection with Fig. 4.10 below). In contrast, the ranges of meaning of total properties and also their extensions are largely independent of the entities specified by these properties. The gradable properties [**SORT** = $gq$] can be further divided into two subsorts:

- Properties having a valuating character, i.e. they express a more or less subjective opinion and are **nonmeasurable** [**SORT** = $nq$] (examples are charming and important).
- Properties connected with some sort of scale (e.g. broad and heavy), therefore called **semantically quantifiable** or **measurable** [**SORT** = $mq$].[11]

It is characteristic of the semantically quantifiable properties that the scale associated with them (allowing for the decision whether or not the property holds) cannot be absolutely fixed. It has rather to be calibrated on the basis of the extension of the concept to be specified. Properties of this type (e.g. broad, heavy, and expensive) are additionally linked to abstract concepts (breadth, weight, and price, respectively) by means of the relation CHPA. These connections make it possible to establish logical relationships between the assignments of properties to objects and the attribute-value characterizations of these objects (see Fig. 4.9 and Sect. 4.3.3), which can be formalized by means of axioms as specified with relation CHPA in Part II.

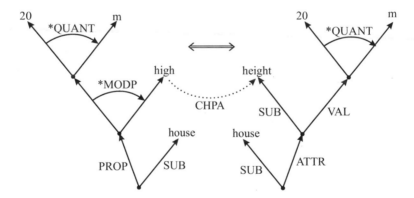

**Figure 4.9.** Relationship between the assignment of properties and attribute-value characterizations

If someone states a semantically quantifiable property of an individual, the class or frame of comparison will be defined by a conceptual object, which often can be derived only from a general context or from background knowledge (e.g. *"Gerd is small."* ⤳ Frame of comparison: class of all Europeans, all students of his age, or something similar).

---

[11] For the time being, we neglect the fact that the words *"broad"* and *"heavy"* also have nonmeasurable interpretations, such as *"a broad understanding"* and *"a heavy task"*.

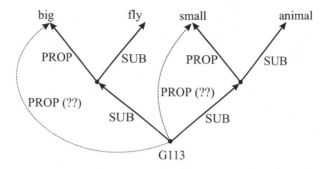

**Figure 4.10.** The relativity of semantically quantifiable properties

In contrast to the absolute or total properties [**SORT** = *tq*] like dead, empty, round, linear, green, open, etc., a gradable property (like big) is not independent of the concept specified by it. An essential characteristic of gradable properties is their **polarity**. This means that they occur in pairs of concepts (e.g. big – small) which stand in the relation CONTR to one another and are attached to a common attribute (in this case, size).

With concepts of sort *gq*, the property positioned at the positive pole (here, big) generally expresses a value of the corresponding attribute, which lies above the average of the class of comparison. Only because of this can we understand that the same object may be a "*big fly*" and a "*small animal*" at the same time. The same holds for a "*heavy letter*", which may be a "*light thing*", or a "*warm room*", which has a "*(relatively) low temperature*".

Because of the facts discussed so far, Axiom (5) of Sect. 4.1, which describes the transfer of properties under the SUB relation, is not valid for semantically quantifiable properties. Otherwise, a contradiction could be deduced if the same individual (node G113 in Fig. 4.10) had been characterized as a "*small animal*" and a "*big fly*" at the same time. With a wrong assignment of rules or axioms to the relations concerned, one could namely infer (G113 SUB animal) because of the transitivity axiom for SUB, which is doubtlessly true. From that, the process of answer finding could generate "*G113 is a big animal*" and also "*G113 is a small fly*", which is not true.[12] With the unrestricted Axiom (5) one could generally deduce that an object has the property at the positive pole and the negative pole at the same time, something avoided if the above-mentioned constraints are observed.

Finally, we have to state that not all adjectives and adverbs can be semantically interpreted as properties (in however fine-grained a manner one wants

---

[12] In contrast, a "*dead fly*" is surely also a "*dead animal*" because of Axiom (5).

to differentiate them), and not all properties can be described with PROP or with the ATTR-VAL mechanism. Thus, it should be clear that *"former"* or *"suspected"* in phrases like *"a former minister"* or *"the suspected murderer"* – even if attributively used – must not be understood as properties of the minister or the murderer, respectively. In the second case, the entity described never needs to be a murderer at all. A semantic representation with the relation PROP should therefore be excluded in all these cases. The adequate semantic representation of the above phrases using the expressional means of MultiNet is given in Fig. 4.11 and will be discussed later in greater detail.

In the considered context, the following phenomena must be taken into account:

1. **Temporal adjectives and adverbs**

   Words traditionally subcategorized as adjectives and adverbs which express temporal specifications belong to this class. Typical examples of this are *"former"*, *"future"*, *"recently"* (see Fig. 4.11a, where the phrase *"a former minister"* is represented).[13]

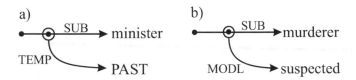

**Figure 4.11.** Modal and temporal adjectives

2. **Modal adjectives and adverbs**

   These words designate operators in the sense of the explanation given in Sect. 8.3. They comprise modal words like *"suspected"*, *"probable"*, and *"possibly"*. The semantic representation of these expressions is based mainly on the relation MODL (see Fig. 4.11b and the discussion about the treatment of manifestations in Sect. 4.5).

3. **Qualification of situations vs. properties of objects**

   Even if adverbs are normally used for the qualification of situations (see

---

[13] The temporal concepts PAST for the past time, NOW for the moment of the speech act, PRES for the current time, and FUT for the future time are deictic elements that can only be used in a semantic representation when the moment of the narration does not change. With changing moments of utterance, these concepts always have to be reinterpreted. What for one moment of utterance has to be considered FUT(URE) is PAST for the next utterance, cf. [129]. PAST, PRES, and FUT can be dealt with as special time periods belonging to sort $t$ if the moment of utterance is fixed.

Fig. 4.12a), they often describe properties of objects participating in these situations (see Fig. 4.12b). Figure 4.12 shows the following cases:

a) *"Peter drove fast with the car across the square."* (fast ↝ manner of driving); the adverb specifies the manner of the action.

b) *"Peter drove merrily with the car across the square."* (merry ↝ property of Peter); the adverb characterizes the agent rather than the manner of the action.

The decision problem, which of the two cases applies, is far from being solved in automatic language processing (see Chap. 5), since considerable background knowledge is needed for that purpose.

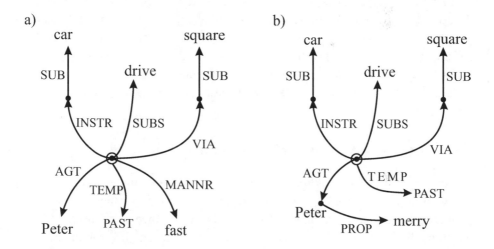

**Figure 4.12.** Manner of a situation vs property

A problem especially difficult to solve is the vagueness of adjectives and their proper treatment in a theory of semantics. An overview of this topic is given by Pinkal [200]. There are also other opinions in the literature which we choose not to share because they lack the necessary care in the semantic treatment of adjectives and properties (and also of nouns). Thus, Hamann writes in [91, p. 661]:

> *"We follow Kamp (1975) and assume that typical nouns are sharp predicates; typical adjectives, however, are inherently vague."*

Apart from the fact that neither nouns nor adjectives should be compared directly with predicates, but at best with the semantic concepts underlying them, one cannot see, why nouns should typically not be vague (or do we not have to categorize *"mountain"*, *"hill"*, *"stone"*, *"sand"*, *"child"*, *"luck"*, etc. as typical nouns?). Also the asserted vagueness of adjectives does not generally apply to them. So semantically total properties like dead, empty, etc. are relatively precise; they show at least a clear difference to gradable properties or to nouns with regard to vagueness. Also, the opinion held by Hamann that

> *"Adjectives are one-place predicates, so are intransitive verbs."* [91, Sect. 1.4],

can not be accepted in its generality. Adjectives like chemical, philosophical, etc., which are classified by us as semantically associative, should not be treated as predicates at all. Furthermore, there are adjectives (those which describe semantically relational properties) that must be interpreted as binary or ternary predicates (i.e. as relations). It should be emphasized that this discussion is not a matter of criticizing a single work (which, after all, is a contribution to the international handbook of semantics [269]). The observations should rather illustrate the complexity of the matter and the diversity of opinions.

### 4.3.3   Attribute-Value Characterizations

While properties of sort $p$ typically bear a predicative character (i.e. they can apply to an object or a collection of objects), attributes include a third element, the value, in the qualitative characterization of objects. In MultiNet (and we think from the cognitive point of view, too), there is a clear distinction between attributes (such as depth, weight, and color), which are abstract concepts, i.e. they belong to sort $at$, and properties in the narrower sense (such as deep, heavy, and blue), which themselves constitute a sort of their own. The term **value** belonging to the concept "attribute" is used not only for the specification of numerical values or for measures, but also for the description of non-numerical, qualitative attribute values. The most important relations in this context are:

| ATTR: | $[o \cup l \cup t] \times at$ | Attribute |
|---|---|---|
| VAL: | $at \times [o \cup qn \cup p \cup fe \cup t]$ | Value |
| VALR: | $\overline{at} \times [o \cup qn \cup p \cup fe \cup t]$ | Value restriction |

Apart from this, the following relations and functions are available for the quantitative characterization of objects (see also Part II):

| QMOD: | $[s \cup \ddot{d}] \times m$ | Quantitative modification |
|---|---|---|
| *QUANT: | $qf \times me \rightarrow m$ | Generation of a quantity |
| *MODQ: | $ng \times [m \cup qf] \rightarrow [m \cup qf]$ | Modification of a quantity |

together with the comparison relations

| MIN{E} / MAJ{E}: | $qn \times qn$ | Smaller-than- / Greater-than-relation |
|---|---|---|
| EQU: | $sort \times sort$ | Equality |

In MultiNet, all unique assignments of entities to attributes of other entities are conceived as values.[14]

- An **attribute** is an abstract concept that can be functionally interpreted in the sense that it assigns an entity, which is the **value** of that attribute, to each individual concept (characterized by [**GENER** = $sp$]) to which it can be applied. Correspondingly, an attribute assigns a **value restriction** to a generic concept (characterized by [**GENER** = $ge$]).

In many natural languages, such attribute-value constructions are described in the surface structure by means of genitive attributes or equivalent prepositional phrases (e.g. Ge: *"die Höhe des Turms"* or colloquially *"die Höhe vom Turm"*; En: *"the height of the tower"*; French: *"l'altitude de la tour"*, and Russian: *"высота башни"*).

### 4.3.3.1   Instances, Attributes, and Values

The method of representing the relationship between an individual entity, an attribute, and its value in MultiNet by means of the relations ATTR, SUB, and VAL is illustrated in the "triangles of paraphrasing" discussed below. These triangles describe the basic ways of expressing the above-mentioned relations by means of natural language phrases. They play an important role for the analysis phase of a QAS as well as for the generation phase. In connection with that, two main cases can be distinguished:

- **Triangle of paraphrasing for attributes with nonquantitative values**
  The attribute-value mechanism for nonquantitative values and its corresponding natural language descriptions are illustrated in Fig. 4.13. The phrases shown (to be more accurate, one should speak of patterns of phrases)

---

[14] Formally, the uniqueness of attribute-value assignments by means of the relation ATTR is warranted by a special R-Axiom (holding only for temporally unrestricted attribute-value assignments):
$(o$ ATTR $a_1) \wedge (a_1$ SUB $a) \wedge (a_1$ VAL $v_1) \wedge (o$ ATTR $a_2) \wedge (a_2$ SUB $a) \wedge (a_2$ VAL $v_2) \rightarrow$
$(v_1 = v_2)$.

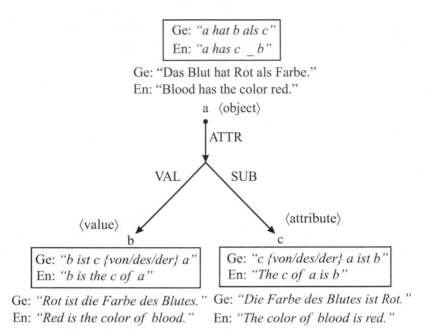

**Figure 4.13.** Triangle of paraphrasing – Type I

are of a paradigmatic character. In German and English, for instance, the value b can simply be used in an attributive position: *"Das Blut hat eine rote Farbe"* or *"Blood has a red color"*, which is more common than *"Das Blut hat Rot als Farbe"* or *"The blood has red as color"*.

- **Triangle of paraphrasing for attributes with quantitative values**
  The attribute-value mechanism for quantitative values and its correspond-ing natural language descriptions are illustrated in Fig. 4.14. The patterns at the lower left corner are not so common (they are used at best if the value of the attribute is to be emphasized, e.g. in an answer). Apart from that, the above remarks about the paradigmatic character of the paraphrases hold analogously.

The triangles of paraphrasing support the process of answer generation in a QAS. In this context, the patterns shown can be used as standard reformula-tions for deep structures which are described by means of the relations ATTR, SUB, and VAL to construct a natural language answer.

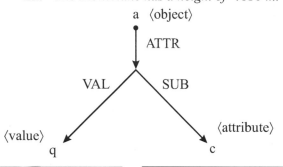

Ge: *"Der Montblanc hat eine Höhe von 4810 m."*
En: *"The Montblanc has a height of 4810 m."*

a ⟨object⟩

ATTR

VAL      SUB

⟨value⟩                      ⟨attribute⟩
q                          c

Ge: *"q beträgt {der/die/das}*
*c {des/der} a"*
En: *"q is the c of a"*

Ge: *"{der/die/das} c {des/der}*
*a beträgt q"*
En: *"The c of a {is/amounts to} q"*

Ge: *"4810 m beträgt die Höhe*
*des Montblanc."*

En: *"4810 m is the height*
*of the Montblanc."*

Ge: *"Die Höhe des Montblanc*
*beträgt 4810 m."*

En: *"The height of the*
*Montblanc is 4810 m."*

**Figure 4.14.** Triangle of paraphrasing – Type II

### 4.3.3.2 Generic Concepts, Attributes, and Value Restrictions

It has to be emphasized that attributes of generic concepts in general do not have fixed values, but **value restrictions**. Of course, there are exceptions of this rule. For instance, the relationship between tooth, color, and white can be represented as shown in Fig. 4.15. The color of typical teeth has a priori no "range" of values but a specific value, which may be assumed to be white.[15] In general, the assignment of a value restriction to an attribute of a generic object is specified by means of the relation VALR (the second argument of this relation defines the value restriction of the attribute given as the first argument).

In a SUB hierarchy of concepts, there exists a close connection between attributes and **value restrictions** at the level of a superconcept and the corre-

---

[15] This is no contradiction of the fact that, as an exception, there are also yellow or black teeth. Because of that, the information about the value of the attribute "color" is characterized as default knowledge in Fig. 4.15.

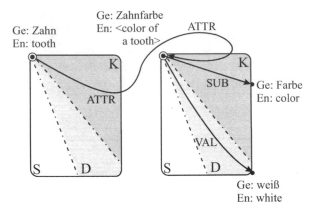

**Figure 4.15.** Example of a special value of a generic attribute

sponding attributes and values at the level of subconcepts (specializations) or instances. The inheritance mechanism working between these different levels is explained by means of Fig. 4.16.

Every attribute of a generic concept opens a so-called **slot** X (an argument place to be filled in a later specialization of the concept). The slot X is characterized by a **slot name** C (the label of the attribute) and a value restriction B. Every subconcept A' (every specialization) and every instance a of A has to have an attribute-value structure or an attribute-value restriction structure similar to that of the superconcept A. At the same time, the value restriction B' of the attribute C with the subconcept A' of A and the value b of the attribute C with an individual concept a, which is subordinate to A, depend in a well-defined way on the value restriction B. The relationships between B' and B as well as between b and B are shown in Table 4.1 for some of the most important cases. The transfer rules represented show a clear parallel with the frame-oriented KRMs (see Sect. 15.4). The node marked by z in Fig. 4.16 is the counterpart to **slot** X. In AI terminology it is called **filler**. This name is suggested by the following view on these relationships: The structure spanned by the nodes a-b-c, which can be considered a specialization of the structure A-B-C, has to fit into the general frame given by A-B-C (it has to "fill in" the slots opened by A-B-C). The filler z with the concrete value b must also fit into the slot represented by X. It has to comply with constraints and value restrictions of slot X specified by means of the relation VALR (cf. the analogous discussion regarding Fig. 15.7 in Sect. 15.4).

The slot-filler mechanism associated with the relations ATTR, VALR, and VAL is also of relevance to the analysis of natural language sentences. The

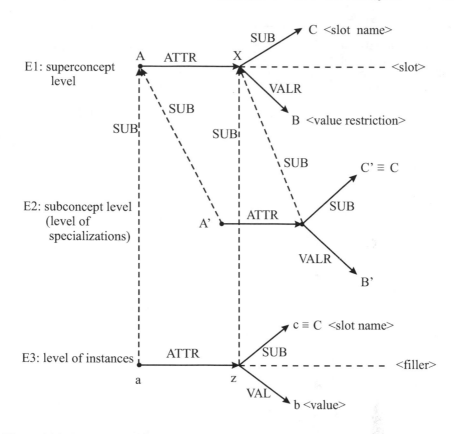

**Figure 4.16.** Transfer of attributes and values from superconcept A to subconcept A' and to instance a (this figure is complemented by Table 4.1)

slots rooted in the deep structure of concepts at the generic level can be interpreted as (obligatory or facultative) valencies of words in the surface structure which have to be saturated by certain constituents of a sentence (primarily nominal groups, genitive attributes, or special prepositional phrases). The structures shown in Fig. 4.16 at levels E1 and E2 have to be considered as part of the immanent knowledge, which is used during the semantic interpretation of the aforementioned constituents. The information contained in levels E1 and E2 constitutes indispensable background knowledge needed during the analysis of natural language descriptions that involve concepts of level E3.

To illustrate these regularities, we give three typical examples.

1. **Quantifiable attributes**

   This kind of attribute has a clear parallel in the semantically quantifiable properties [**SORT** = $mq$]:

   (4.6) *"The depth of the lake is 20 m."* ↔ *"The lake is 20 m deep."*

| B | B' | b |
|---|---|---|
| Concept characterizing the value restriction of attribute C | Value restriction belonging to the subconcept A' | Value belonging to the instance a |
| B - Generic concept | (B' = B) ∨ (B' SUB B) | (b SUB B) |
| B - Set of concepts $B = (*\text{ITMS-I } c_1, c_2, \ldots, c_n)$ | (B' = B) ∨ (B' SUBM B) | $\exists c[(c \text{ ELMT } B)$ $\land (b \text{ SUB } c)]$ |
| B - Quantity $B = (*\text{QUANT nil m})$ with $m \in me$ and (C ATTCH m) | B' = (*QUANT nil m) | $b = (*\text{QUANT n m})$ $n \in nq$ |
| B - Set of individuals or properties $B = (*\text{ITMS-I } i_1, i_2, \ldots, i_n) \vee$ $B = (*\text{ITMS-I } p_1, p_2, \ldots, p_n)$ | (B' = B) ∨ (B' SUBM B) | (b ELMT B) |

**Table 4.1.** Transfer of attributes and values from superconcept A to subconcept A′ and to instance a (this table is complement to Fig. 4.16)

In Example (4.6), the attribute **depth** has a quantitative value. For attributes of this type, connected with a gradable property through the relation CHPA, there exist corresponding synonymous surface structures that have deep structures "dual" to each other. The equivalence of these dual structures illustrated in Fig. 4.17 is warranted by Axioms (16) and (17).[16]

- (k ATTR a) ∧ (a SUB op) ∧ (a VAL q) ∧ (p CHPA op) ⟶

    (k PROP (*MODP q p))                        (16)

- (k PROP (*MODP q p)) ∧ (p CHPA op) ⟶

    ∃a [(k ATTR a) ∧ (a SUB op) ∧ (a VAL q)]         (17)

## 2. Qualifying attributes and their values

Analogously to the quantifiable attributes, there are attributes corresponding to the semantically validating properties [**SORT** = $nq$]:

(4.7) *"The color of the petal is red."* ↔ *"The petal is red (looks red)."*[17]

---

[16] It is possible to reduce the structures given in the example to a single deep structure if one takes the corresponding surface structures as fully synonymous (see the discussion in Sect. 4.2). So it would be possible to take the structure at the left side as the canonical deep structure of both surface structures (to choose the other one as the canonical deep structure would be inappropriate, since there do not exist corresponding gradable properties for many attributes as is the case for **diameter, capacity**, etc.). With this choice, the Axioms (16) and (17) have to be applied during syntactic-semantic analysis as transformation rules. To reduce the transformational apparatus of the syntactic-semantic analysis, it seems to be more appropriate to keep both deep structures in parallel, and to establish their equivalence, if necessary, in the phase of answer finding by means of Axioms (16) and (17), i.e. during the processing of a concrete query. From the point of view of a QAS, this is purely a methodological question (see the discussion about the canonical representation in Chap. 1).

[17] The deep structure of the first sentence is emphasized in Fig. 4.18 by heavy lines. The remaining parts are background knowledge or result from deductive inferences.

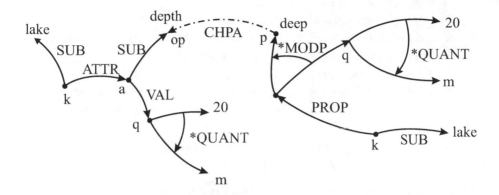

**Figure 4.17.** Relation between attribute and property

Example (4.7) shows that concepts like color, shape, etc. can be connected directly to a value restriction by means of the relation VALR (i.e. without the use of an intermediate SUB relation and without introducing a mediating node). The value restriction is an essential part of the meaning of the attribute itself. The same holds, by the way, for the concept depth, which is linked via VALR to the template of a quantity (∗QUANT *nil* m) and through that to the measurement unit m = meter, which is a typical unit of measure for length (*nil* is a placeholder for the unspecified number of measurement).

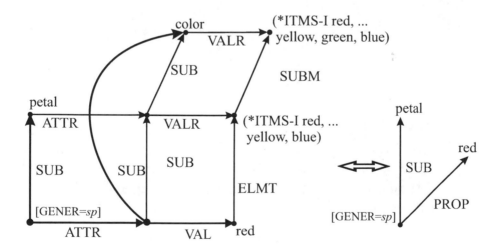

**Figure 4.18.** Semantically qualifying attribute and its value

The transfer mechanism for values and value restrictions associated with
the subordination of entities having sets of properties as value restrictions
(see the last row in Table 4.1) is illustrated in Fig. 4.18.

As with the quantifiable attributes, two surface structures and two corresponding deep structures can be opposed to each other in this case. The
deep structures can be interlinked by an axiom that holds only if the attribute values are properties (i.e. for $w \in p$):

- $(k\ \text{ATTR}\ a_1) \wedge (a_1\ \text{SUB}\ a_2) \wedge (a_1\ \text{VAL}\ w) \wedge (a_2\ \text{VALR}\ g)$
  $\wedge (w\ \text{ELMT}\ g) \longrightarrow (k\ \text{PROP}\ w)$                                 (18)

3. **Qualifying attributes which have no proper values**

   Finally, there are attributes having no proper value (e.g. charm, courage,
   and patience); they are represented by the relationship ($x$ VAL nil). The
   symbol *nil* is generally used for an underspecified or undefined value. In
   this context, we are also speaking of "improper" attributes (see Fig. 4.19).
   Example:

   (4.8)  *"Max has courage and charm." ↔ "Max is courageous and
   charming."*

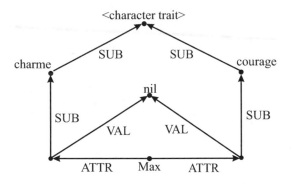

**Figure 4.19.** Improper attributes

The following axiom holds for this type of attribute:

- $(k\ \text{ATTR}\ a_1) \wedge (a_1\ \text{SUB}\ a_2) \wedge (a_1\ \text{VAL}\ \text{nil}) \wedge (p\ \text{CHPA}\ a_2) \longrightarrow$
  $(k\ \text{PROP}\ p)$                                                                    (19)

## 4.4 Possession, Attachment, and Association

### 4.4.1 Possession

The relation of possession does not help structure the world in the material sense. But it is rather important for modeling socio-economic states of affairs.[18] The relation of possession POSS: d × [co ∪ io] assigns a concrete or abstract possession to a possessor, i.e. to a natural or a legal person (see Fig. 4.20). It is important that the possessor p in a relation (p POSS b) be allowed to dispose of a possession b or to transfer it to someone else, something that can also be said of an abstract possession (a right or a claim). [19]

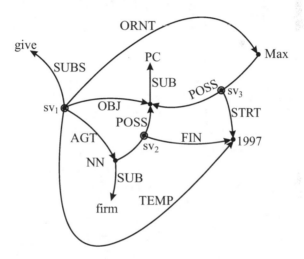

**Figure 4.20.** The representation of relationships of possession

Figure 4.20 shows three situations $sv_i$. The first situation $sv_1$ represents the fact that the firm NN gave a PC to Max in 1997. The other two situations $sv_2$ and $sv_3$ describe the change of possession induced by $sv_1$: The firm NN owns the PC until 1997 ($sv_2$), and Max owns the PC from 1997 on ($sv_3$). It should be noted that with the event lending, instead of giving, there is no change involved in the relation (p POSS b) (the possession remains with p). In the

---

[18] Which, of course, do also belong to the world in the broadest sense.

[19] We assume here a "naive" point of view, where possession (Ge: Besitz) and property (Ge: Eigentum) coincide (which is very often true). In the juridical sense, however, both concepts have to be distinguished from each other. In application fields, where this distinction is relevant, a corresponding differentiation has to be made.

case of lending, a pure change of location of the object b takes place (in this case, only the LOC relation is affected).

The conceptual field of possession relationships is additionally described by R-Axioms and B-Axioms (meaning postulates), for which the following formulas can be taken as typical examples (see also relation POSS in Part II).

- **R-Axiom:**   (a POSS b) ∧ (c PARS b) ⟶ (a POSS c)                    (20)
    This axiom states that the possessor of a whole also owns its parts.
- **B-Axiom:**   (p POSS b) ⟶ ∃sv [(sv MODL *perm*) |
                    (sv SUBS sell) ∧ (sv AGT p) ∧ (sv OBJ b)]          (21)

The B-Axiom (21) asserts that an owner or possessor p is permitted to sell his possession b.[20] The construction [⟨modality M⟩ | ⟨situation sv⟩] on the right side of the axiom involves an extension of the expressional means of FOL. In terms of MultiNet this means that the situational description standing at the second position in the pair [M | sv] must be represented as a conceptual capsule, which as a whole is restricted in its validity by the modality M (see Chap. 8). In contrast to modal logic, where the modality M can be practically expressed only as a modal operator having no inner structure, it is allowed in MultiNet to specify M itself as a complex situation, e.g. *"a person p is allowed to carry out a certain activity sv within the boundaries of her job with firm F until a specific date t"*. Using such a complex specification, references from constructs inside the semantic representation of M to the outside of it and into the inner structure of sv may also occur.

The relation POSS is lexically connected with the lexemes possess.1.1, own.1.1, and have.1.1, where the index "1.1" indicates the selection of exactly that meaning of the polysemous verbs *"possess"*, *"own"*, *"have"* which corresponds to possession in the sense of the relation POSS (see Fig. 4.21).

Figure 4.21a shows that the POSS relation between an owner o and its possession p may also be represented as a state st of possession or owning, with o as the carrier of the state and p as the object (see Sect. 5.3). There also exists a connection to the attachment of objects dealt with in the next section, which is illustrated in Fig. 4.21b. Both relationships can also be characterized by means of axioms, see Formulas (22) and (23). Here, again, it is a methodological question as to whether these axioms are used as transformation rules for the purpose of normalization during analysis or as inference rules during answer finding.

---

[20] This axiom could be generalized to an axiom schema permitting other actions which include a transfer of possession, in addition to just sell. The modality *perm* as the second argument of MODL specifies the permission (see Sect. 8.3).

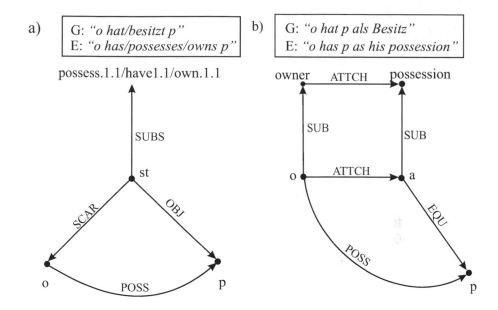

**Figure 4.21.** The connection between lexemes expressing a possession and the relation POSS

- ∃st (st SUBS possess.1.1) ∧ (st SCAR o) ∧ (st OBJ p) ↔ (o POSS p) (22)

- ∃a (o SUB owner) ∧ (o ATTCH a) ∧ (a SUB possession) ∧ (a EQU p)
  ↔ (o POSS p)                                                         (23)

### 4.4.2  Assignment of Objects to Objects (Attachment)

Objects can be assigned to each other in a situation without standing in a relationship of possession ("*the dog with the leather collar*", "*the woman with the girl*"). They may also be immanently connected with each other, where none of the relations PARS, POSS, or ORIGM holds (as is the case in "*the government of the state*"). The distinction between all these cases is not possible on the basis of natural language expressions alone; it needs rather some kind of background knowledge (see Fig. 4.22).

The attachment of objects to a given object, if unique, has a clear similarity to the assignment of attributes to an object. Because of that, these attachments represented by the relation ATTCH are called **pseudo-attributes**. Figure 4.23 demonstrates that this analogy can also be extended to the **schemata of paraphrasing**. A comparison with Fig. 4.13 shows that the relations ATTCH and EQU in the new schema play the role of the relations ATTR and VAL in the original triangle. The insertion of the relation EQU in Fig. 4.23 is necessary

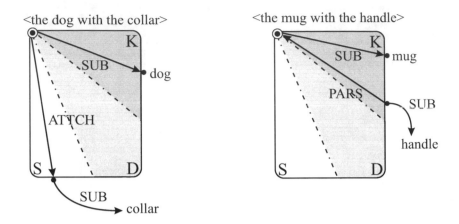

**Figure 4.22.** Situational attachment of objects in comparison with the part-whole relationship

since both argument nodes are intensionally different but extensionally identical. Someone may quite correctly speak about the capital of France, while taking Paris as a town in Spain at the same time (this speaker is apparently not aware of the connection established by the EQU relation).[21]

The templates of paraphrasing shown in the triangle of Fig. 4.23 bear only a paradigmatic character (similar to the templates in Figs. 4.13 and 4.14). Thus, the prepositional phrases at the two right vertices of the triangle (constructed with "*von*" in German or "*of*" in English) can be generally substituted by a pure genitive construction in languages like German or Russian (e.g. Ge: "*Paris ist die Hauptstadt Frankreichs*" or "*Die Hauptstadt Frankreichs ist Paris.*"). Of course, other prepositions may also be used instead of the standard ones (e.g. "*zum*", "*zur*" in German for the preposition "*als*" in the lower left box).

The application of the SUB-ATTCH-EQU combination for representing the attachment of generic and nongeneric objects, together with a temporal limitation, is shown in Fig. 4.24. Concepts like capital and ⟨head of the state⟩ are so closely related to the concept state that, as second arguments of the ATTCH relation in Figs. 4.23 and 4.24, they must not be connected via SUB with the

---

[21] In Fig. 4.23, the term **triangle of paraphrasing** is related to the triangle spanned by the three arcs on the right side below the diagonal. The concept d usually plays no part in the paraphrasing; as background knowledge, it is often not mentioned. Actually, it could be explicitly introduced in the form of an apposition "*The state of France has Paris as its capital.*"

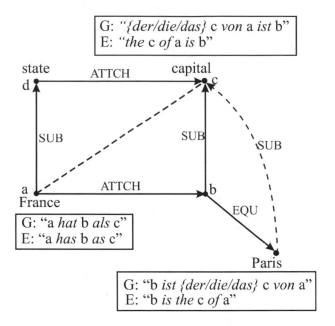

**Figure 4.23.** The triangle of paraphrasing for pseudo-attributes

first argument, since there is no concept capital outside the conceptual field of state, and also no ⟨head of the state⟩ without a state.[22]

A peculiarity of the example on the right side of Fig. 4.24 is the fact that the **value** of the pseudo-attribute ⟨head of the state⟩ for a concrete state (in this case the USA) has to be considered as temporally changing. This is independent of the fact that the concept ⟨head of the state⟩ is an immanent attribute of every state and not a situational attribute (as is the case, for instance, with the pseudo-attribute illness with regard to ⟨human being⟩). Immanent and situational assignments of values to pseudo-attributes are described with the same relations. Their representations differ only in the detail that the former are stored in the D-part or the K-part of a conceptual capsule, while the latter are attached to the S-part,[23] see the description of conceptual capsules in Part II, Sect. 17.3.

From the constellation EQU-SUB in Figs. 4.23 and 4.24, one can deduce an additional subordination relation between the outer arguments:

---

[22] The direction of the arc labeled by ATTCH in the examples is given by the triangle of paraphrasing in Figs. 4.23 and 4.24: A state **has** a political head (in this case a president) or a capital and not vice versa.

[23] According to the different types of knowledge, we distinguish in a conceptual capsule a K-part containing categorical knowledge (abbreviation K from German "kategorisch"), a D-part containing default knowledge, and an S-part containing situational knowledge.

*"The Vatican is the residence
of the pope."*

*"Bush has been the president
of the USA since 2001."*

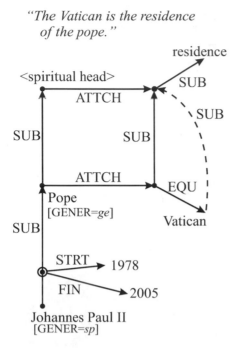

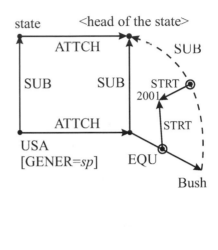

**Figure 4.24.** Pseudo-attributes for generic concepts and individual concepts (with and without temporal limitation)

- $(x\ \text{EQU}\ y) \wedge (x\ \text{SUB}\ z) \longrightarrow (y\ \text{SUB}\ z)$  (24)

This axiom does not hold for $z \in re$, which can be easily seen by looking at the signature of the relation SUB.

One must be aware that knowledge about an object o which is acquired by inferential processes using knowledge lying outside the conceptual capsule of o must not be transferred to the inside of that capsule (see Fig. 4.25). Thus, it is possible to derive from Axiom (24) and the knowledge connected with the right conceptual capsule in Fig. 4.25 that the subordination relation (h SUB domicile) represented by a broken line holds for h = ⟨Peter's houseboat⟩. This relation has to stay outside the conceptual capsule of h. Otherwise, the concept h could be paraphrased as ⟨Peter's domicile⟩, which is not correct, since Peter possibly does not live on his own houseboat. The correctly inferred and stored state of affairs can be paraphrased as *"Peter's houseboat is a domicile as well"* (which corresponds to the facts represented in Fig. 4.25).

Though attachments of concrete objects to other objects have something in common with the attribute-value formalism, the object attachment, in contrast

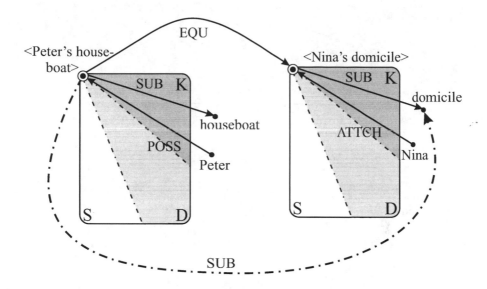

**Figure 4.25.** The role of conceptual capsules with the inclusion of inferentially acquired knowledge

to the latter, is not always unique, something that can be illustrated by the kinship relations represented in Fig. 4.26.

The figure shows that kinship relations like ⟨father (of)⟩, ⟨mother (of)⟩, ⟨spouse (of)⟩, etc. can be represented by means of the semantic relation ATTCH.[24] All these concepts have in common the fact that they represent so-called meaning molecules (see Chap. 12), which possess several facets of meaning and which can be assigned different sorts (here, [**SORT** = *co*] and [**SORT** = *re*]). For this reason, the relation SUB0 has to be used instead of SUB, since SUB0 allows for the subordination of concrete objects and the subordination of abstract relational concepts. The relationships ⟨friend (of)⟩, ⟨deputy (of)⟩ or similar cases can also be treated on the basis of this schema.

---

[24] With the word "*child*", one has to discern two sememes: child$_I$ (in the biological sense or as a kinship relation) and child$_{II}$ (defined by a certain limit of age). The concept child$_I$ also subsumes adults (everyone is a child$_I$ of someone). A simplification has been admitted with the concepts ⟨nephew (of)⟩ and ⟨uncle (of)⟩, which are not generally left-unique, as is the case, for instance, with ⟨father (of)⟩ or ⟨mother (of)⟩. For an adequate representation of nonunique kinship relations, the expressional means of the preextensional level have to be included (see relation ELMT in Part II). It must be emphasized that there are also relational concepts like friend which are not meaning molecules (see Chap. 12 for the definition of this term). Such concepts have to be connected to a network only by the relation SUBR (otherwise, a reformulation "*x is a friend*" would be possible, a reformulation permitted for the relations SUB and SUB0).

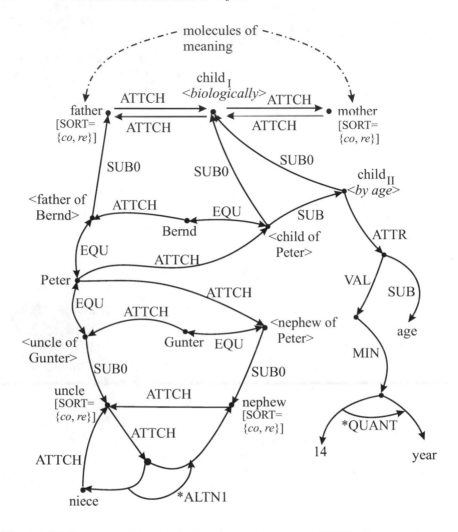

**Figure 4.26.** The representation of kinship relations by means of ATTCH

## 4.4.3   Association

To complete the assignment of concepts to other concepts, one also has to consider the associative relation ($e_1$ ASSOC $e_2$), which can hold between any two entities $e_1$ and $e_2$ with [**SORT** = *ent*] that are connected by a cognitive interrelationship. The sorts of the arguments $e_1$ and $e_2$ cannot be further restricted in comparison with the signature of ASSOC, since elements from all pairs of sorts may be associated with each other. This can be illustrated by the diversity of the following pairs of concepts connected by ASSOC:

| water | [**SORT** = $s$] | | swim | [**SORT** = $dy$], |
|-------|------------------|---|------|--------------------|
| boil | [**SORT** = $dy$] | | $\langle 100^{\circ}C \rangle$ | [**SORT** = $m$], |
| leaf | [**SORT** = $co$] | | green | [**SORT** = $tq$]. |

The fact that the ASSOC relation cannot be characterized by an unrestricted transitivity is shown by the following example:

| (4.9) | (sea ASSOC fish) | holds, |
|-------|------------------|--------|
| (4.10) | (fish ASSOC fillet) | holds, **but** |
| (4.11) | (sea ASSOC fillet) | does not hold. |

Since the ASSOC relation can be circumscribed somewhat casually by "*has to do with*", the following axiom schema holds:

- (x $\langle$REL$\rangle$ y) $\longrightarrow$ (x ASSOC y)                                  (25)

This means that for any pair of conceptual entities $e_1$ and $e_2$ standing in an arbitrary relation $\langle$REL$\rangle$ the relation ($e_1$ ASSOC $e_2$) also holds. In this sense, ASSOC is the weakest relation between two conceptual representatives. Nevertheless, such a range of meaning, which is certainly very wide, does not render this relation worthless. On the one hand, the proposition "*concept $e_1$ has to do with concept $e_2$*" conveys important information. On the other hand, it is this generalization of relations that supports the robust understanding in a QAS or the robust parsing in a system of NLP (cf. relations SOURC, MODE, and GOAL). By sharpening or loosening axioms such as (25), one can also narrow or broaden the spectrum of answers to questions of the type "*With what or whom does X have anything to do?*".

The relation ASSOC can also play an important part in connection with associatively guided answer finding and with inferences in a QAS. It permits one to restrict the search for relevant concepts to the conceptual surroundings of given nodes of the network, even if the "semantic neighborhood" or "semantic relatedness" between these nodes is sometimes only vaguely specified (see Sect. 13.2). The analogue holds for the resolution of references during assimilation. In the following two sentences, the background knowledge (car ASSOC motor), however unspecific it may be, is already sufficient to find the correct antecedent for the pronoun "*Its*":

(4.12) "*The firm bought an old car. Its motor had to be repaired.*"

Without the aforementioned background knowledge "*the firm*" would be as likely an antecedent for "*its motor*" as "*an old car*".

## 4.5   Different Manifestations of Objects

Objects may appear in different representations or in different manifestations, and they can be perceived in different "Gestalts" by different people. Typical examples are an actor in different roles, a mathematical object in different representations, and human beings in different phases of their life (e.g. ⟨the young Goethe⟩ / ⟨the later Goethe⟩) or Napoleon as Corsican, as a French general, or as emperor of France (see Fig. 4.27). The dialectic between the unity of a conceptual object on the one hand, and the difference in the manifestations of the underlying object on the other hand, is also reflected in the conceptual world. The relation RPRS was defined to cover these conceptual phenomena and to represent them formally.

In Fig. 4.27, the upper left conceptual capsule **Napoleon** represents that part of information which is independent of the different manifestations of the underlying object. The fact that each of these manifestations (Corsican, general, emperor) represents the same person is expressed by the circumstance that they all share the same extensional at the preextensional level. Moreover, we have to discern between immanent and situational knowledge in the context of manifestations as well. Thus, the general Bonaparte triumphed in the battle of Arcole, but he lost the Battle of the Nations of Leipzig as emperor of France.[25]

A typical example of different manifestations of an object is given by the physical phase transitions in nature. So, the water in a container can exist as ice or in its liquid state, it can also be transformed into vapor. In all these cases we encounter the same substance (the same entity).

The use of manifestations is an appropriate method to represent propositions containing phrases such as "*the former minister*" (see Fig. 4.11), "*the former chancellor*", etc. in a semantically noncontradictory way (one should think, for instance, of sentences such as "*the {former minister / Federal Chancellor} resigned as an honorary chairman of the party*"). As long as the persons in question were still ministers or chancellors (Manifestation I), the cited propositions did not hold; however, as soon as the restriction "*former*" becomes true (Manifestation II), the above-mentioned propositions apply to the persons involved; but then, they are not ministers or chancellors any more.

---

[25] Please remember that *a priori* there is no default knowledge with individuals (it can at best be inherited by them).

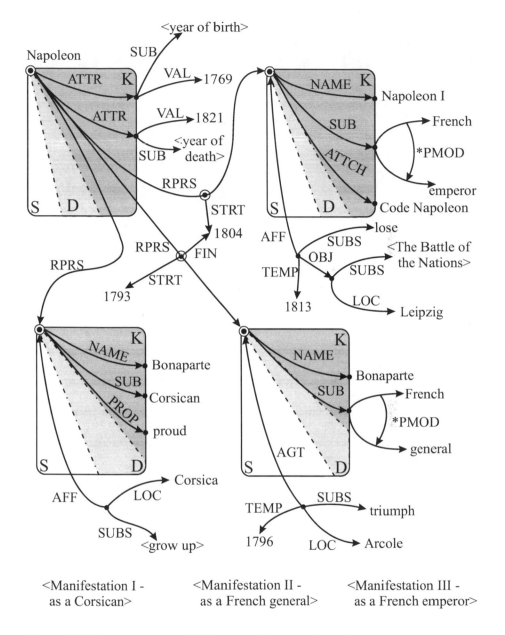

**Figure 4.27.** The representation of different manifestations of an object

# Chapter 5

# Semantic Characterization of Situations

## 5.1 The General Structure of Situations

Situations or states of affairs correspond to the meanings of sentences in a way similar to how conceptual objects are typically the semantic representatives of nouns or noun phrases.[1] The word "situation" and the phrase "state of affairs" are treated as synonymous. It must be emphasized again that both designate conceptual constructs that possibly have no correspondence in reality.

It is a well known fact that the most important carrier of semantic relations in a sentence is the verb, which therefore is the main "bracket" in a sentence keeping constituents together. To design a semantic representation language along the lines of FOL, one could try and interpret the verb as a relation taking the semantic representatives of other constituents of a sentence as its arguments, e.g.

(5.1) *"Peter gives Paul a book."* $\rightsquigarrow$ GIVE(Peter, Paul, ⟨a book⟩)

A consistent attempt in this direction was undertaken by Freundlich in his "Theory of Language" [70], who in the early 1970s tried to interpret the verbs as relational predicates which constitute sentences. Until today, this is the standard way of formalization in most logic-oriented representations. This approach, however, has several disadvantages of principal nature:

1. **Arity**: Because of the changing number of constituents which can be taken as arguments by a verb, the relators representing verbs should also have variable arity (which is not allowed in standard logic). Approaches using a situation-centered formalism (such as the one used in the LILOG system [122]) try to avoid this difficulty, but they normally have no concept of encapsulation and no clear definition of the relations connecting the central representative of a situation with the objects involved in this situation.

---

[1] For the time being, we shall restrict our discussion to propositional sentences only. The other types of sentences are dealt with in Chap. 13.

2. **Order of the logic**: Since references to contents of sentences or larger semantic units are very common in natural language, the logical meaning representations of these units should bear names which can themselves be used as arguments of relations.[2] This again would require either a logic of higher order or complicated reification techniques which are inferentially difficult to handle.

The aforementioned representational paradigms are not well suited for the reasons discussed. The observations that every state of affairs is a conceptual entity in itself and that the argument places of the verb can be semantically interpreted suggest another solution, described in this chapter.

Corresponding to the tradition of semantic networks, every situation sv is represented by a node of the network, in agreement with the demand of Chap. 3 that every conceptual entity be represented uniquely by a node of the SN. The complete information constituting a certain situation is enclosed in a conceptual capsule (see Fig. 5.1), in analogy to the representation of definitional knowledge of a conceptual object (see Sect. 3.2.3).

The node belonging to sv is generally subordinate to the representative of the meaning of the verb which semantically determines the character of the state of affairs in question. The corresponding connection is established by the SUBS relation (cf. Sect. 5.2.2).

The objects $A_i$ taking part in the situation sv (i.e. the **participants** or **actors**), whose number is not fixed a priori, are connected to sv according to their cognitive roles in that situation (an event or a state) by means of appropriate relations – called C-Roles – or (in the graphical representation) by means of corresponding arcs (see also Sects. 5.2 and 5.3).

Temporal relations play a special role in MultiNet (see Sect. 7.3). They belong to the immanent knowledge about a situation and must always be expressed, be it by an adverbial construct or by the tense of the verb, if the situation has to be reformulated in natural language.[3]

The relations SUBS, the C-Roles, and the temporal relations typically constitute the immanent knowledge about a situation sv, which must be reproduced in a question-answering game if a corresponding query is aiming at sv.

---

[2] The deficiency of most traditional logic systems having no explicit representative for situations has been considered already by the Davidsonian Logic of Actions and Events [54], which explicitly introduces situational variables for states of affairs.

[3] This is no contradiction of the fact that the relation TEMP is often omitted in the graphical representations for the sake of simplicity, since we use the convention that temporal relations absent in a representation mean TEMP + PRES (so-called **present convention**).

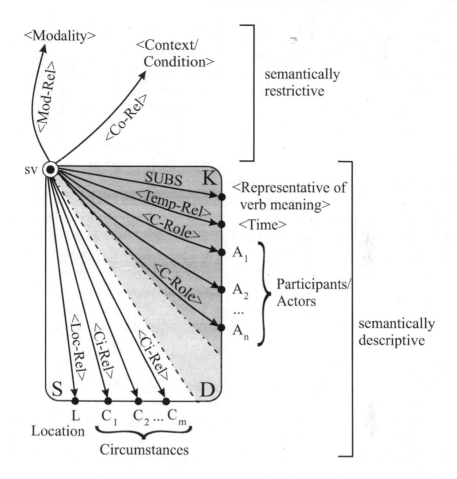

**Figure 5.1.** Typical components of the semantic representative of a situation

In contrast, the **circumstances** $C_i$ (here linked to sv via $\langle$Ci-Rel$\rangle$, see Sect. 5.2.3) describe the situational embedding of sv, which can generally be omitted in the generation of a short answer without changing its truth.[4] The meaning components described up to now, which are represented within the conceptual capsule of sv, will be called **semantically descriptive**.

Furthermore, there are also semantic components in a sentence which limit the range of validity of the corresponding situation, be it modally (see Chap. 8), contextually (see Sect. 11.4), or conditionally (see Sect. 11.2.3). These constituents of the representation are called **semantically restrictive** because they

---

[4] Only the degree of informedness of the interrogator is influenced by including situational knowledge in the answer. This is a question of the answering strategy in a QAS, which will not be discussed here.

restrict, or even negate, the validity of a situation defined by a conceptual capsule. They must not be omitted under any circumstances in the answer generation, otherwise the truth of the answer would be inadmissibly changed.[5]

The local specifications occurring in some situations play a special role (see Sect. 7.2). They mostly have to be considered purely situational information (*"Peter met his friend yesterday <u>at the railway station</u>."*). In some situations, however, local specifications have a defining function like temporal relations, and therefore constitute immanent knowledge about this situation (e.g. *"<u>In the polar zone</u>, all hunters wear fur clothing."*). Omitting a location in such a natural language sentence would result in a false proposition (in this case, *"All hunters wear fur clothing."*). At first glance, the slightly asymmetric treatment of times and locations (the former are treated as immanent and the latter as situational knowledge) seems a bit counterintuitive, since both, space and time, are essential forms of existence from an epistemic point of view. This general aspect is taken into account by considering both as definitional knowledge about a situation and including both in the capsule representing the situational concept. Characterizing the time as immanent knowledge and the locations as situational knowledge corresponds to their different treatment in natural language. Time is always involved in the grammatical form of a natural language sentence (it is often hidden in the tense of the verb), whereas locations need not be specified in a natural language sentence. This is supported by the fact that human beings interpret a missing local specification by an implicit "somewhere", which is always correct. Therefore, we use the convention in MultiNet representations that missing locations have always to be interpreted as LOC+⟨somewhere⟩.

It must be emphasized that MultiNet does not prescribe which of the semantically descriptive specifications belong to situational or immanent knowledge. MultiNet provides only the representational means for the appropriate characterizations (in that, as with objects, the attribute **K-TYPE** of arcs plays an important role). In this sense, the above explanations for semantically descriptive relations have only to be understood as an orientation. Semantically restrictive specifications, by contrast, always limit the range of validity of a state of affairs. Consequently they are always related to the entire conceptual capsule of the situation which is restricted by them. This may also be the case for temporal or local relations.

---

[5] The metasymbols labeling the arcs in Fig. 5.1 have the following meaning: ⟨Temp-Rel⟩ – temporal relation, ⟨Mod-Rel⟩ – modal relation, ⟨Co-Rel⟩ – conditional or contextual relation, ⟨C-Role⟩ – deep case relation, ⟨Ci-Rel⟩ – relation specifying circumstances, ⟨Loc-Rel⟩ – local relation. These relations are explained in the corresponding sections cited above.

In connection with the distinction between representational means constituting semantically restrictive and semantically descriptive knowledge, but also with regard to the topics of negation, modality, and quantification, which still have to be dealt with, it is important to fix the restricting power, or the **scope** of the expressional means. This scope is defined by the ordering schema given in Fig. 5.2.

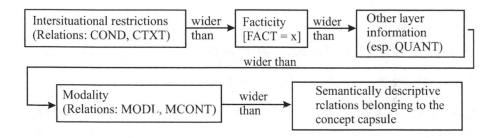

**Figure 5.2.** Scope of different representational means (strength of restriction)

All situations or states of affairs can be classified according to Fig. 5.3. This pattern corresponds largely to the semantically oriented classification of verbs which can be found in traditional grammars [133].

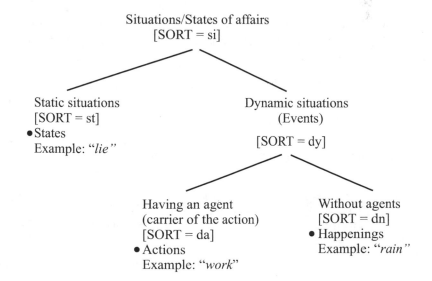

**Figure 5.3.** Classification of situations

Traditional grammars distinguish between **action verbs** (*"hit"*, *"calculate"*, *"read"*, etc.), **happening verbs**[6] (*"melt"*, *"snow"* etc.), and **state verbs** (*"contain"*, *"lie"* etc.). In Sects. 5.2 and 5.3 we shall investigate the events (comprising occurrences and actions) and the states, respectively. Since actions and happenings are distinguished only by the presence or the absence of an agent, respectively, they will be treated together in Scct. 5.2 (and are therefore also subsumed under one common sort *dy*).

## 5.2   Events [Dynamic Situations]

### 5.2.1   Participants and C-Roles [Valency Frames]

The MultiNet representation of a situation is essentially determined by the meaning of the verb that dominates the situation. After all, the semantic representative of the verb is crucial for the membership of a situation in a certain sort (events belong to sort *dy* and states to sort *st*). The objects participating in an event are divided, as has already been stated, into **participants** (possibly, also into **actors**) and **circumstances**.[7]

The participants are closely connected with the semantic structure of the verb. They represent those entities involved in an event which are required by the valencies of the verb.

- **Valencies** are understood as the argument places or expectations (**slots** in AI-terminology) which have to be completed or satisfied by other constituents (the **fillers**) to get a complete description of a situation.

Valencies are not opened by verbs alone, but also by adjectives, nouns, and prepositions. An ample compilation of such valencies can be found in [105], [245], and [246]. Since the work of Fillmore [66] (see also [36] and [214]) it has become customary to describe the semantic valencies in terms of **deep case relations** or **cognitive roles**.[8] These deep case relations were distilled from the

---

[6] Jung coined the German term "Vorgangsverben" for these verbs [133]. In English, there is unfortunately no convenient term for dynamic situations having no agent. We will use the technical term **happenings** (Ge: "Geschehen") because these kinds of events just happen, without having a cognitively recognizable causator.

[7] This distinction and terminology goes back to the French linguist Tesnière [256], who coined the terms "Actants" and "Circonstants". In our context, the term **actor** shall be restricted to usage in connection with actions only.

[8] For the elucidation of the connection between **deep case relations**, **thematic** or **cognitive roles** (**C-Roles**), and $\theta$-**roles**, we refer to [210]. Further work on this topic, putting the concept of theta-roles into the center of the investigation and setting up criteria for their definition, is reported in [130] and [56].

comparison of case systems of different languages and found by a corresponding generalization. As is apparent from the history of deep cases, this approach is mostly syntax-based, i.e. one starts with the surface cases (pure cases or prepositional cases) in different languages and tries to determine the underlying semantic relations, while at the same time generalizing and classifying the relations discovered. Such an approach has apparently been chosen also in [14], where deep case relations such as *EXCL* (**exclusion**) are postulated. Example (24) from [14]:

(5.2) *"Everybody slept [except him$_{EXCL}$]."*

In this case, there is no relation (here, *EXCL*) that semantically binds the representative of *"him"* to the situation. In MultiNet, one has to build rather a semantic construct representing the entity ⟨everybody except him⟩ using the expressional means of the preextensional level (including, especially, the function *DIFF). This construct has to be linked to the central situational node by means of the relation MEXP (see Part II). The relation *ORD* (order) proposed in Example (65) in [14]:

(5.3) *"He filed the Baker file [before the Abel file$_{ORD}$]."*

is also not an ordering relation between ⟨Abel file⟩ and the situation, but rather between the participating objects ⟨Baker file⟩ and ⟨Abel file⟩.

In MultiNet, the following relations are provided as deep case relations or C-Roles which can be used to connect a participant with a dynamic situation (i.e. with an event):

| | | |
|---|---|---|
| AFF | $[dy \cup ad] \times [o \cup si]$ | Affected object |
| AGT | $[si \cup abs] \times o$ | Carrier of an action/Agent |
| AVRT | $[dy \cup ad] \times o$ | Object from which an event is turning away |
| BENF | $[si \cup o] \times [o \setminus abs]$ | Beneficiary |
| CSTR | $[si \cup abs] \times o$ | Causator |
| EXP | $[si \cup abs] \times o$ | Experiencer |
| INIT | $[si \cup abs] \times [o \cup si]$ | Initial state |
| INSTR | $[si \cup abs] \times co$ | Instrument |
| MCONT | $[si \cup o] \times [o \cup si]$ | Mental content of an action or of an informational object |
| METH | $[si \cup abs] \times [dy \cup ad \cup io]$ | Method (with a floating transition to circumstances) |
| OBJ | $[si \cup abs] \times [o \cup si]$ | Neutral object |

| OPPOS | $[si \cup abs] \times [si \cup o]$ | Entity being opposed to a situation |
|-------|------------------------------------|--------------------------------------|
| ORNT  | $[si \cup abs] \times o$           | Orientation toward something        |
| RSLT  | $[si \cup abs] \times [o \cup si]$ | Result                              |
| SUPPL | $[si \cup abs] \times o$           | Supplement of an action             |

The deep case relations have to comply with specific criteria, which can be dealt with completely only after the treatment of the SUBS hierarchy (see Sect. 5.2.2). A detailed description of these relations can be found in Sect. 18.2, under the name **C-Role**.

Strictly speaking, one has to discern between language-dependent syntactical valencies, which have an effect only on the surface structure of a sentence, and language-independent semantic valencies, which belong to the level of semantic representations, or deep structures (see Fig. 5.4). The formal description of the first is called **subcategorization frame**, and that of the latter **(semantic) valency frame**.[9]

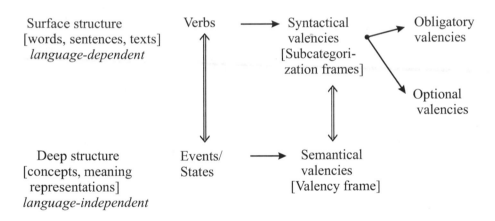

**Figure 5.4.** Syntactic and semantic valencies

There is a close interrelationship between syntactic and semantic valencies, illustrated by means of an example in Fig. 5.5.[10] The cognitive roles are rooted

---

[9] The subcategorization schemata had a purely syntactical orientation over a long period of time in grammar theory. Meanwhile, semantic aspects were also taken into consideration, as witnessed by the inclusion of so-called $\theta$-**roles** in Chomsky's Government and Binding Theory [47].

[10] In the graphical representation, the syntactic and semantic characterization of valencies are deliberately pulled apart in order to better depict the assignment of the different categories to the syntactic or the semantic level. In a computational lexicon, however, both characteri-

in the deep structure of that concept which underlies the verb meaning (this structure is labeled with the attribute SEMV in Fig. 5.5). The syntactic valencies (they are labeled with the attribute SYNV in Fig. 5.5) specify which (pure) case, prepositional case, or other surface structure corresponds to which cognitive role (C-Role or deep case relation) in a special language. At the syntactic level one has to further distinguish between obligatory and optional valencies. The first, in any case, must be realized to build a complete sentence or phrase; for the second, this is not true.

It must be emphasized that the term "optional valency" is not applicable at the semantic level. For example, it immanently belongs to the deep structure of the action show.1.1 (in the sense of prove) that it is carried out by means of a method (METH), or of the action hit.1.1 (in the sense of strike) that it is carried out by means of an instrument (INSTR). However, both specifications may, but need not be, articulated in the surface structure of a corresponding sentence.[11]

The valency frame and the subcategorization frame for two of the readings of the verb "*show*" are given in a schematic form in Fig. 5.5. The first frame for show.1.1 illustrates that the underlying concept is carried out by an object $\hat{k}_1$ bearing the feature "potential agent", which is syntactically described in a "normal" sentence by a nominal constituent $k_1$ (a **noun phrase NP**) in the nominative (case attribute [CASE 1]).[12] This constituent is obligatory, which also holds for the constituent $k_2$ having to be adjoined in the form of an object-sentence via the conjunction "*that*". The counterpart $\hat{k}_2$ to $k_2$ representing a situation at the semantic level is marked with the C-Role OBJ (i.e. $\hat{k}_2 \in si$ holds). Finally, the third component $k_3$ is optional and described in the surface structure by means of a prepositional phrase (prepositions "*with*" or "*by (means of)*"). Semantically, this constituent fills the role of a method (relation METH). Its semantic representative $\hat{k}_3$ is an abstract object (sort *ab*).

The second reading, show.1.2 (in the sense of exhibit), can be interpreted analogously. It has three obligatory valencies ($k_1$, $k_2$, and $k_3$) and no optional arguments. At the semantic level, it has an agent (relation AGT), a living ob-

---

zations are represented in a more compact way that is better adapted to the close interconnection between them (see Chap. 12).

[11] Compare, "*Max has shown (by a simple argumentation) that the formula holds.*" (METH relation) vs. "*Max hit the horse (with a whip).*" (INSTR relation).

[12] The asterisk "*" is a placeholder for the action concept functioning as a first argument. For the sake of brevity of the representation of show.1.1, the possibility was omitted that $k_2$ may also be described by a direct object in the form of a nominal phrase ⟨NP⟩: "*He showed the validity of the formula by mathematical induction.*" To cover this case, one should also allow for $\hat{k}_2 \in abs$. The description of show.1.2 has also been abbreviated for the sake of simplicity.

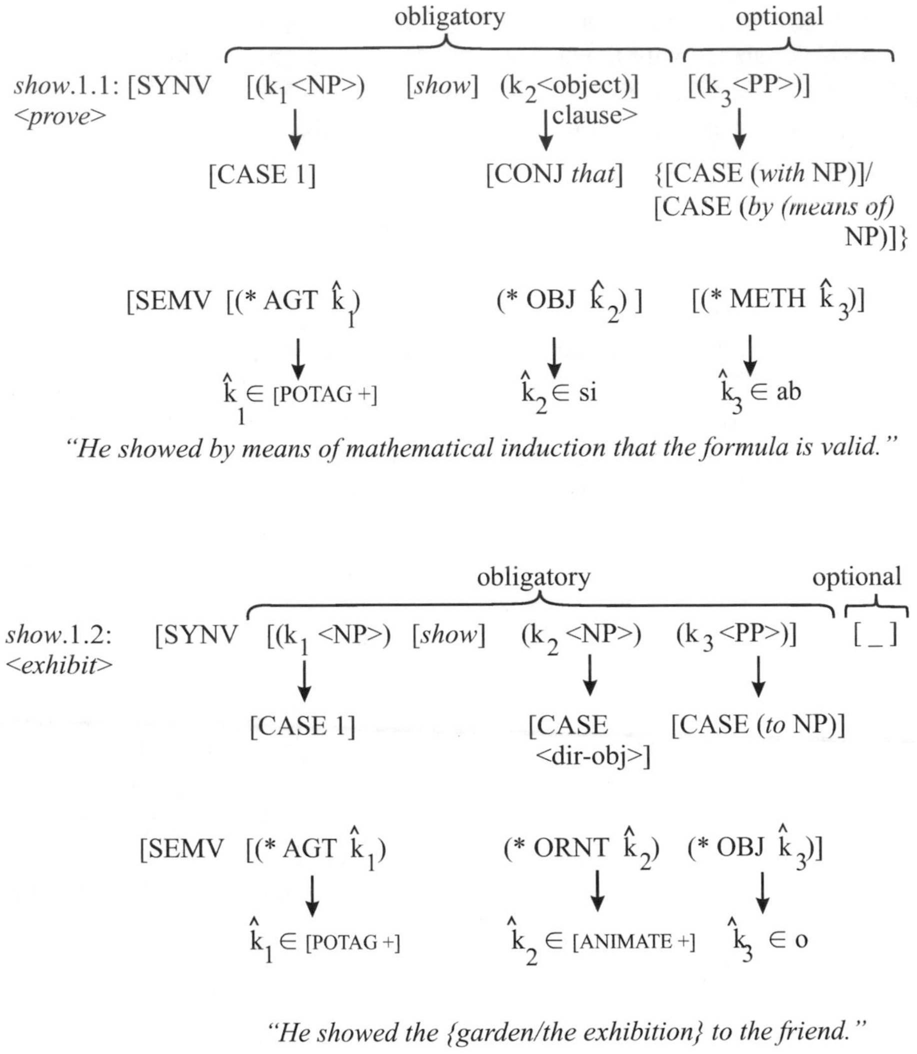

obligatory                    optional

$show$.1.1: [SYNV     [($k_1$<NP>)     [$show$]  ($k_2$<object)]     [($k_3$<PP>)]
<$prove$>                                        |clause>

                    ↓                           ↓clause>              ↓

              [CASE 1]                    [CONJ $that$]    {[CASE ($with$ NP)]/
                                                           [CASE ($by$ $(means$ $of)$
                                                                          NP)]}

       [SEMV  [(* AGT $\hat{k}_1$)              (* OBJ $\hat{k}_2$) ]    [(* METH $\hat{k}_3$)]

                    ↓                           ↓                     ↓

              $\hat{k}_1$ ∈ [POTAG +]           $\hat{k}_2$ ∈ si       $\hat{k}_3$ ∈ ab

*"He showed by means of mathematical induction that the formula is valid."*

obligatory                                      optional

$show$.1.2:     [SYNV    [($k_1$ <NP>)   [$show$]    ($k_2$ <NP>)    ($k_3$<PP>)]    [ _ ]
<$exhibit$>

                    ↓                           ↓               ↓

              [CASE 1]                    [CASE         [CASE ($to$ NP)]
                                          <dir-obj>]

       [SEMV  [(* AGT $\hat{k}_1$)              (* ORNT $\hat{k}_2$)   (* OBJ $\hat{k}_3$)]

                    ↓                           ↓               ↓

              $\hat{k}_1$ ∈ [POTAG +]           $\hat{k}_2$ ∈ [ANIMATE +]   $\hat{k}_3$ ∈ o

*"He showed the {garden/the exhibition} to the friend."*

**Figure 5.5.** Part of the subcategorization and valency frames of two senses of the verb *"show"*

ject toward which the action is oriented (relation ORNT), and a neutral object which is independent of the action (relation OBJ). The other specifications should be self-explanatory after the preceding discussion.

In contrast to the participants, the circumstances or accompanying situations, which characterize the situational embedding of states of affairs, do not belong to the semantic structure of the verb in the narrower sense. In linguistics, the natural language descriptions of circumstances are classified as free adjuncts, which can be adjoined to practically every verb in the surface structure of a sentence. The corresponding deep relations will be dealt with in Sect. 5.2.3 and are summarily shown in the situational part of the conceptual capsule in Fig. 5.1. One has to state, however, that the borderlines between free adjuncts and valencies (or, in linguistic terms, between adjuncts and complements) cannot be drawn very sharply by a classification of the participating deep relations. Thus there are verbs, like live in the sense of dwell (Ge: wohnen) that demand either a location (relation: LOC) or a manner (relation: MANNR).

Examples:  En: *"He lives in Berlin."* / Ge: *"Er wohnt in Berlin."* or

En: *"He lives very nicely."* / Ge: *"Er wohnt sehr gut."*, but not

En: *"He lives."* or Ge: *"Er wohnt."*[13]

In general, however, the relations LOC and MANNR typically characterize free adjuncts in the surface structure.

Concluding this topic, a phenomenon must be mentioned which in linguistics is called **alternation** or, to be more specific, **subject-object alternation** (see [160]). This term designates the systematic change in certain diathetic relations of the verb, especially the change from transitive to intransitive use with genuinely transitive verbs.

(5.4) *"Max moved the stone away."*                     (transitive use)

(5.5) *"The stone moved away."*                     (intransitive use)

There are two different opinions with regard to this type of alternation, both of which can properly be treated within the framework of MultiNet. The first one states that we do not actually meet two different meanings of the same verb *"move away"* since the semantic roles do not change.[14] Because of the inherent systematical character of this phenomenon, it can primarily be considered a syntactical effect, which must be dealt with in the phase of syntactic-semantic analysis in a QAS supported by convenient lexical rules.

The second opinion assumes a priori two different readings of the verb (in this case, move_away$_1$ and move_away$_2$), the first having an agent (deep case relation AGT) and the second not having an agent. If this is accepted, the two readings have to be included into the lexicon and must be interconnected by an appropriate B-Axiom (meaning postulate).

---

[13] While the German sentence *"Er wohnt."* is not acceptable in any case, the English counterpart *"He lives."* is acceptable, but with another reading of *"to live"* (meaning *"not to be dead"*).

[14] In both examples, ⟨the stone⟩ is characterized by the C-Role OBJ, and though there is only one participant mentioned in the second example, the verb semantically has an agent or causator, at least implicitly, even in the intransitive use.

## 5.2.2    Conceptual Subordination of Situations – The SUBS Hierarchy

In the same way as conceptual objects can be embedded in a hierarchical system (see Sect. 4.1), subordinations between situational concepts can also be defined. However, they are represented by another subordination relation,

SUBS: [si ∪ abs] × [si ∪ abs],

which is governed by separate laws of inheritance.

Figure 5.6 shows some verbs of change and motion with their semantic valency frames (deep case frames). The subordinate concepts in a SUBS hierarchy each inherit the valency frame of the superordinate concept (this frame is symbolized by [–]) except for the case where the slot x of the subordinate concept is explicitly characterized by a more special C-Role at a lower hierarchy level. This can be seen in Fig. 5.6, where the general concept move has only an object (relation OBJ y) which is moving. The subordinate concept ⟨move (something)⟩ has an additional valency (characterized by relation CSTR x), while its subordinate concept ⟨intentional movement⟩ in turn has the more specific valency (relation AGT x) (the corresponding slots are symbolized by the same variable x in both cases).[15]

The laws of inheritance are relatively complicated and cannot be characterized by simple axioms (but, at best, with axiom schemata). It would be more effective, however, to describe the corresponding transfer mechanisms of valency frames in a procedural way because of the variable number of valencies with the different concepts in the hierarchy. For our discussion, only two aspects are important: First, that the subordinate situational concept has the same or more specific valencies than the superordinate concept and, second, that the subconcept can have additional valencies. The fact that the specialization may grow from top to bottom in the hierarchy by adjoining further information to the valencies of a higher hierarchical level is indicated at the lowest level of Fig. 5.6 by a somewhat informal specification characterizing a possible change of possession.

Conceptual hierarchies similar to that in Fig. 5.6 can also be constructed for other dynamic situations (e.g. for working events like work ← create or ⟨work on something⟩ ← form ← plane, knead, and carve). In a complete knowledge base, one also has to consider cross-classifications, since a concept like transport does not belong only to the hierarchy of motion concepts but also to the hierarchy of working concepts.

---

[15] The asterisk "*" is used again as a placeholder for the action concept to be characterized, which serves as the first argument of the indicated relation.

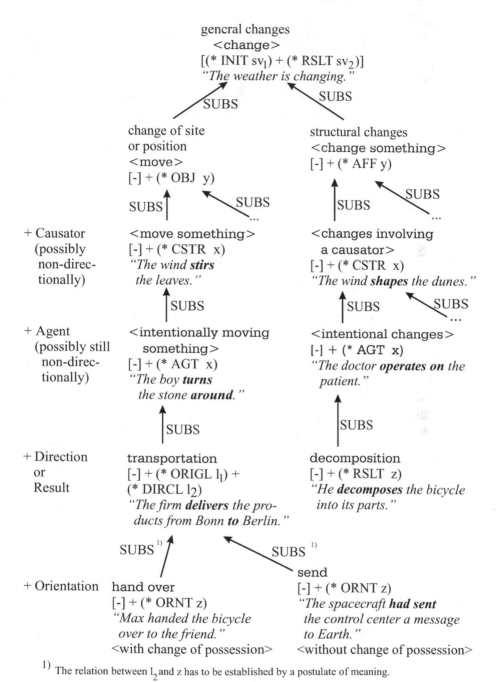

general changes
\<change\>
$[(* \text{ INIT } sv_1) + (* \text{ RSLT } sv_2)]$
*"The weather is changing."*

SUBS

change of site
or position
\<move\>
$[-] + (* \text{ OBJ } y)$

structural changes
\<change something\>
$[-] + (* \text{ AFF } y)$

SUBS

SUBS ...

SUBS

SUBS ...

+ Causator
(possibly
non-direc-
tionally)

\<move something\>
$[-] + (* \text{ CSTR } x)$
*"The wind stirs
the leaves."*

\<changes involving
a causator\>
$[-] + (* \text{ CSTR } x)$
*"The wind shapes the dunes."*

SUBS

SUBS

SUBS ...

+ Agent
(possibly still
non-direc-
tionally)

\<intentionally moving
something\>
$[-] + (* \text{ AGT } x)$
*"The boy turns
the stone around."*

\<intentional changes\>
$[-] + (* \text{ AGT } x)$
*"The doctor operates on the
patient."*

SUBS

SUBS

+ Direction
or
Result

transportation
$[-] + (* \text{ ORIGL } l_1) +$
$(* \text{ DIRCL } l_2)$
*"The firm delivers the pro-
ducts from Bonn to Berlin."*

decomposition
$[-] + (* \text{ RSLT } z)$
*"He decomposes the bicycle
into its parts."*

SUBS[1]

SUBS[1]

+ Orientation

hand over
$[-] + (* \text{ ORNT } z)$
*"Max handed the bicycle
over to the friend."*
\<with change of possession\>

send
$[-] + (* \text{ ORNT } z)$
*"The spacecraft had sent
the control center a message
to Earth."*
\<without change of possession\>

[1] The relation between $l_2$ and z has to be established by a postulate of meaning.

**Figure 5.6.** Part of a SUBS hierarchy for some concepts of change and movement

Having introduced the SUBS hierarchy, it may be useful to set up some criteria which have to be fulfilled by the deep case relations:

- **Uniqueness**
  The same cognitive role must not be represented by different deep relations, unless there exists a subordination relation between them.[16]
- **Substitution criterion**
  Constituents of a sentence paradigmatically related to each other (and, therefore, mutually exchangeable) must play the same cognitive role.[17]
- **Contrast/Differentiation**:
  Participants involved in the same situation and playing different roles must not be linked to the situational node by the same deep relation unless the difference is clarified by other means (e.g. by a differing inheritance of additional characteristics for the arguments involved).
- **Consistency**
  The valency frame of a situational concept must consistently fit in the corresponding conceptual hierarchy (SUBS hierarchy), following the rules of inheritance.

It should be emphasized that these criteria do not exclude an actor playing different roles in the same state of affairs.
Example:

(5.6) *"Peter washed himself."*

In this case **Peter** is assuming the AGT and the AFF role at the same time. On the other hand, it is also possible that two different actors are playing the same role in a situation.
Example:

(5.7) *"Max is playing chess with Peter."*

Here, Max as well as Peter are playing the role of an agent (relation AGT). If there is any difference between the constituents *"Max"* and *"Peter"* it lies in the topic-focus structure of the sentence, something that is not the subject of our discussion (see [231], [90]).

The criterion of contrast, for instance, helps to recognize that the two underlined constituents in the following sentence have to be represented by means of different deep case relations:

(5.8) *"Max writes a letter to the tax office$_{ORNT}$ for his mother$_{BENF}$."*

---

[16] Thus, every agent (relation AGT) is also a causator (relation CSTR), or every DIRCL is also GOAL, etc.

[17] *"{Max / the firm / the new student of the fifth class /...} gave a party."* → AGT

These criteria can also be extended to other deep relations (as in the following sentence, where a differentiation between VIA and DIRCL has to be taken into account):

(5.9) *"Max travels through the desert$_{VIA}$ to Ulan Bator$_{DIRCL}$."*

Finally, the subtle working of the differentiation criterion in combination with the consistency criterion is shown in Fig. 5.7 (here the contrast in meaning results from different pathes of inheritance). Let us look at the following sentences, whose meanings are contained in the representations of Fig. 5.7:

(5.10) *"Max bought a car for $3000."*
(5.11) *"Max paid $3000 for the car."*

From a deeper semantic perspective, the constituents Y = ⟨a car⟩ and Z = ⟨$3000⟩ play the role of objects in an event of exchange (expressed by two OBJ relations), where the first object is the commodity and the second object is the price (i.e. a certain amount of money). To discern these two OBJ roles, there must be a difference between both participants that has to be expressed in the representation. In this case, one gets a first clue by the observation that buy as well as pay are both subordinate to the concept exchange, as shown in Fig. 5.7. The difference between the objects of exchange Y and Z (namely that Y is in the possession of X after the exchange action, and Z is possessed by X before that action) is transferred along the SUBS and SUB paths to the corresponding participants of buy and pay by means of inheritance. With this process, the difference between the cognitive roles of Y and Z is explained, and the criterion of contrast is not violated. The nonsymmetry undoubtedly existing between the participants Y and Z in a buying event can be underlined by introducing an additional relation (Y SUBST Z), which expresses the fact that Z is replaced with Y in the event in question (with pay, the SUBST relation should be running in exactly the opposite direction between Y and Z, which is not shown in Fig. 5.7). The discussion also shows how the deficiencies in connection with the application of thematic roles mentioned in [195] can be avoided. It further shows that not all necessary differentiations in the meaning of concepts can be explained by cognitive roles alone (for that, we need additional meaning postulates and other background knowledge associated with the semantic representatives of the verbs).

There are also arguments against introducing a special deep case relation MEAS (for **measure**) for attaching objects like "*$3000*" in the sentence "*Max bought a car for $3000.*" to the semantic representative of the situation as proposed in [14]. First, one can pay with stocks or products, which are only very

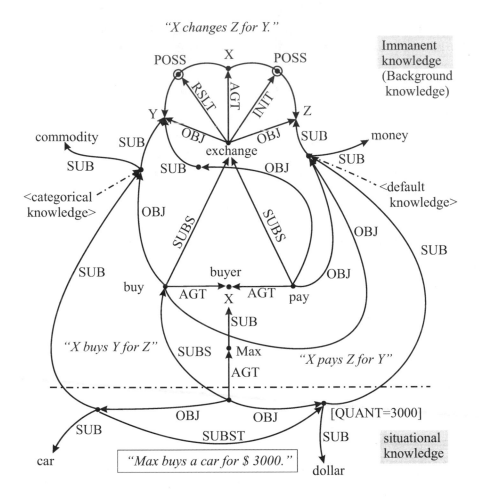

**Figure 5.7.** The inner consistency of valencies within the SUBS-hierarchy

indirectly associated with measures.[18] Second, since the specifications of the objects in question play the same role (in this case the role of means of payment), they must also be represented by the same deep relation, which is also true for the concept ⟨exchange for⟩ (Ge: ⟨(ein)tauschen für/gegen⟩) having the same configuration of cognitive roles. These roles, however, are not primarily connected with measures appropriately representable by the above-mentioned relation MEAS.

---

[18] The representation of Fig. 5.7 covers the fact that the "*$3000*" as means of payment in the paying action can be replaced with "*products*", "*stocks*", etc. without changing their cognitive role (here OBJ). This should also be expected because of the substitution criterion.

The correct (and possibly automatic) differentiation of cognitive roles or deep case relations is very difficult. In Fig. 5.8 we have compiled a group of criteria supporting this process (they should be considered only as an orientation). These criteria can be very useful to a lexicographer who has to build a (computational) lexicon on the basis of the representational means of MultiNet (see Chap. 12). They are complemented by the question patterns given in Part II for all definitions of relations and by the semantic templates presented in Appendix C. In addition to this, the different meaning postulates (B-Axioms) and R-Axioms connected with the C-Roles also warrant a different treatment of the C-Roles in the inference process, as is the case with the other relations. With regard to the correct use of C-Roles, these axioms are based (among other aspects) on the information contained in Fig. 5.8.

To explain this table, we start by paraphrasing the criteria, which are only laconically designated by a single term, using typical questions for this (SV is the situation containing the C-Role indicated at the top of the corresponding column, and O denotes the conceptual object playing this C-Role):

- Independence – "Does O exist independently of SV?"
- Change – "Is O changed by SV?"
- Beneficiary – "Does O benefit from SV?"
- Passivity – "Is O passively involved in SV but not changed?"
- Orientation (toward) – "Is SV oriented toward O?"
- Averting (from) – "Is SV averting from O?"
- Opposition – "Is SV opposed to O?"
- Causation – "Is O a causator with regard to SV?"

For further explanation we consider the relations AGT and AFF. The agent of an action (AGT) is always independent of this event (otherwise it could not give rise to the event). In connection with affected objects (relation AFF), there are cases where the independence of the object has to be negated (e.g. with **destroy** – "annihilating of the existence" or with **create** – "bringing something into existence"), as well as cases where the independence of the objects involved can be asserted (e.g. in an action ⟨color in⟩ the object is changed, but it is essentially independent of the action; it is the value of the attribute color that is changed). This is in contrast to MCONT, where the second argument typically exists only in connection with the first argument (a mental process), or where the former is even invoked by the latter (as is the case with "*think that*"). The agent (AGT) is typically not changed by the action (in contrast to the relation AFF). Exceptions are certain reflexive verbs (as, for instance, "*cut oneself*", Ge: "*sich schneiden*", or "*kill oneself*", Ge: "*sich umbringen*") where the agent has an effect on itself (this is the reason why the question about

| Type of question | AGT / CSTR | AFF | AVRT | BENF | EXP / MEXP | INSTR | MCONT | OBJ | OPPOS | ORNT |
|---|---|---|---|---|---|---|---|---|---|---|
| (1) Independence | *categ* yes | (--) | *proto* yes | *proto* yes | *categ* yes | *categ* yes | *proto* no | *categ* yes | *proto* yes | *proto* yes |
| (2) Changes | *proto* no | *categ* yes | *proto* no | *categ* no | *categ* no | *proto* no | *proto* no | *categ* no | *proto* no | *proto* no |
| (3) Beneficiary | *proto* no | (--) | (--) | *categ* yes | *proto* no | *categ* no | *proto* no | *proto* no | *proto* no | (--) |
| (4) Passively involved and not changed | *proto* no | *categ* no | (--) | *proto* yes | *proto* yes | *proto* no | *proto* yes | *categ* yes | (--) | (--) |
| (5) Orientation (toward) | *proto* no | (--) | *categ* no | *proto* no | *proto* no | *categ* no | *proto* no | *proto* no | (--) | *categ* yes |
| (6) Averting (from) | *proto* no | (--) | *categ* yes | *proto* no | *proto* no | *categ* no | *proto* no | *proto* no | (--) | *categ* no |
| (7) Opposition/ Adversary | *proto* no | (--) | (--) | *proto* no | *proto* no | *categ* no | *proto* no | *proto* no | *categ* yes | (--) |
| (8) Causator | *categ* yes | *proto* no | *proto* no | *categ* no | *proto* no | *categ* yes | *proto* no | *proto* no | *proto* no | *proto* no |

subject position (EXP / MEXP)     object position (OBJ) ┈┈▶ neutral (non-specific) C-Role

*categ*: categorical commitment;   (--) means: both cases (affirmative and negative answer) possible
*proto*: default assumption (may be overruled in the case of double characterizations)

**Figure 5.8.** Differentiation criteria for the distinction of cognitive roles

whether or not the agent is changed by the action cannot be categorically, but only prototypically, negated). With the aforementioned verbs, we have to use a semantic double characterization of the subject by means of AGT and AFF, where the information about the criterion of "change" with AGT ($no^{proto}$) is overruled by the characteristics of AFF ($yes^{categ}$). If one selects the criterion of "being passively involved but not changed", then it has to be categorically affirmed with OBJ, and it must be negated anyway in connection with AFF for the same reasons as above. The shaded fields in Fig. 5.8 indicate that the corresponding decision has to be considered as an essential characteristic of the relation in question.

## 5.2.3  Circumstances

In contrast to the participants of a situation, which are already determined by the verb governing the corresponding description, the circumstances have to be considered as accompanying situations, which give a more detailed description of the state of affairs but do not restrict its validity. Typical representational means for the description of circumstances are given by the following relations (which were summarily labeled by ⟨Ci-Rel⟩ in Fig. 5.1).[19]

| CIRC | $[si \cup abs] \times [ab \cup si]$ | Relation between situation and circumstance |
|------|-------------------------------------|---------------------------------------------|
| CONC | $[si \cup abs] \times [si \cup ab]$ | Concessive relation |
| CONF | $[si \cup abs] \times [ab \cup si]$ | Reference to an external frame, to which a situation conforms |
| DIRCL | $[si \cup o] \times l$ | Relation specifying a local aim or a direction |
| GOAL | $[si \cup o] \times [si \cup o \cup l]$ | Generalized goal |
| MANNR | $si \times [ql \cup st \cup as]$ | Relation specifying the manner of existence of a situation |
| METH | $[si \cup abs] \times [dy \cup ad \cup io]$ | Method (with a floating transition to C-Roles) |
| MODE | $[si \cup abs] \times [o \cup si \cup ql]$ | Generalized mode of a situation |

---

[19] For the time being, the list serves only as an overview. On the one hand, the distinction between circumstances and the spatio-temporal embedding of situations by means of LOC and TEMP cannot be drawn with sufficient sharpness. On the other hand, the participants and circumstances also cannot be discerned exactly: Is "method" (relation METH), for instance, a special mode of action and, thus, a circumstance, or is it a participant like "instrument" (relation INSTR)? Apparently, the transitions between the two cases are floating. Here, a certain parallelism can be observed with linguistics, where also no clear distinction between optional valencies and free adjuncts has yet been found.

| ORIG | $o \times [d \cup io]$ | Relation specifying an intellectual or informational source |
|------|------------------------|-------------------------------------------------------------|
| ORIGL | $[o \cup si] \times l$ | Local origin |
| PURP | $[si \cup o] \times [si \cup ab]$ | Relation specifying a purpose |
| SOURC | $[si \cup o] \times [si \cup o \cup l]$ | Generalized source |
| VIA | $[d \cup dy \cup ad] \times l$ | Relation specifying a path |

As a thesis we assume that circumstances normally have to be inserted into the situational part of the conceptual capsule representing a situation (see Fig. 5.1). Using a restrictive and sparing answer strategy, these specifications can be disregarded with a query aiming at the core meaning of a situation. Example:

(5.12) "*[The bad weather notwithstanding]*$_{CONC}$, *Linda went for a walk yesterday evening.*"
Query: "*What did Linda do yesterday?*"
Sparing answer: "*She went for a walk.*"
Cooperative answer: "*Notwithstanding the bad weather, she went for a walk.*"

Whether a constituent has to be semantically anchored in the situational or in the categorical part of a capsule representing a situation cannot be schematically decided on the basis of a deep relation alone; this depends rather on the meaning of the carrier verb of the sentence. Thus, the relation DIRCL immanently belongs to the meaning of directional verbs like ⟨shoot at⟩, and it cannot be considered as a peripheral circumstance.[20] In contrast, the specification of a direction with sell would certainly not be assumed to belong to the proper meaning of the verb ("*Max sold his collection [to Munich]*$_{DIRCL}$.").

Whether the approach proposed above can claim to be more than a general overview has to be decided in the treatment of answer generation and on the basis of the analytical possibilities of a QAS. The topic of this work, however, is the description of a knowledge representation system, not the problem of answer generation or natural language analysis.

## 5.3  States [Static Situations]

States and verbs describing states are treated in a stepmotherly way in semantic investigations. One reason is because of the fact that a large part of state

---

[20] Verbs demanding constituents as valencies, which typically belong to the field of circumstances, are called **circumstantially bound** in some grammars (see [133, Sect. 3.7.1]).

verbs does not denote states in the physical or psycho-physiological sense; rather, the state verbs often have a very abstract meaning. Because of this, it is considerably more difficult to semantically interpret the cognitive roles of the participants in such a strongly generalized state. In spite of these problems, we will try to establish a certain system for the state verbs. An overview of the semantic phenomena in the field of state verbs is given in Fig. 5.9; it will be discussed in greater detail shortly.

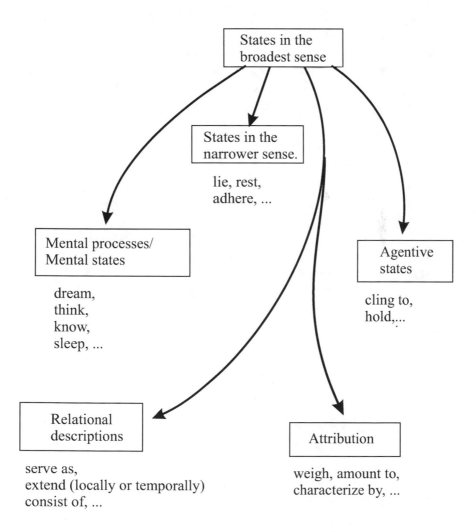

**Figure 5.9.** Systematic overview of state verbs classified by semantic aspects

It is remarkable that among the states in the widest sense one very often encounters verbs obligatorily governing prepositional phrases (so-called "prepositional verbs"), which are especially difficult to interpret semantically. Actually, the corresponding prepositions are so closely connected to the meaning of the verb that dropping or changing the preposition yields an entirely different meaning (e.g. Ge: bestehen vs. ⟨bestehen aus⟩ or ⟨bestehen auf⟩, or En: ⟨consist in⟩ vs. ⟨consist of⟩).

The representational means of MultiNet have also been used to semantically interpret 1500 German verbs obligatorily governing prepositional phrases and to distinguish their basic meanings from each other (the corresponding results are included in HaGenLex). This topic has largely been neglected in the linguistics literature. To the best of our knowledge, there has been no other systematic investigation till now which clearly shows the semantic structure of the concepts underlying these verbs. (Even the well known work of G. Helbig [105] is mainly syntactically oriented and gives no information about the cognitive roles associated with the verbs being investigated.)

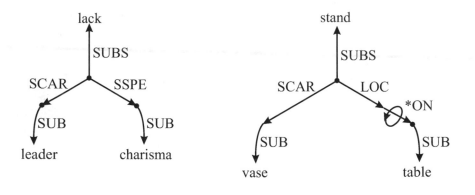

"The leader is lacking
in charisma."

"The vase stands on the table."

**Figure 5.10.** States in the narrower sense

1. **States in the narrower sense**
   These states are physical or psycho-physiological states, like rest, stand, hold, lie, etc. As typical relations for the semantic representation of these static situations, MultiNet provides the roles "carrier of the state" (relation SCAR) and "state specifier" (relation SSPE), which characterize the

participants in these states (see Fig. 5.10).[21] Moreover, circumstances and (mostly nondirected) local characterizations may also enrich the specification of these states.[22]

In general, it is typical of states that an agent is missing, but there are also exceptions (see Point 3 below). One has also to consider states which cannot be described by means of static verbs, but rather by adjectives or adverbs combined with the copula "*be*" (Ge: "*sein*"), for instance ⟨being ill⟩, ⟨being dead⟩, or ⟨to be cold⟩ (Ge: ⟨krank sein⟩, ⟨tot sein⟩, or ⟨kalt sein⟩, respectively).

The states semantically underlying these phrases are not immediately lexicalized; therefore, the connection between the property in question (e.g. cold) and the corresponding state (in this case ⟨to be cold⟩) has to be established through the relation CHPS (see Fig. 5.11).[23]

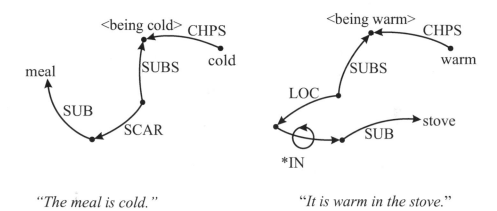

"*The meal is cold.*"                    "*It is warm in the stove.*"

**Figure 5.11.** Relationship between states and properties

---

[21] It should be remarked that the concepts of **actor** or **player** are not appropriate for verbs describing states because of the active meaning component of these terms. This is why we generally prefer the more neutral term **participants** for objects playing a cognitive role in a situation.

[22] This does not mean that the specification of local directions is entirely excluded in this context. Example: "*The tumor pressed [on the optic nerve]$_{DIRCL}$.*"

[23] The state, so to speak, must be created at first by means of an appropriate property. In reality, not all properties are usable for this purpose, which can be illustrated by phrases like "*Max is tall.*" or "*The flower is red.*" These expressions do not mean that "*Max is in a state of tallness.*" or "*The flower is in state of redness.*" (see relation PROP).

## 2. Mental processes or states

Mental states play a special role, since they also have meaning components of a process and are characterized by a dynamical aspect (e.g. think, believe, and dream). These states are preferably represented by the roles "mental experiencer" (MEXP) and "mental content" (MCONT) (see Fig. 5.12). In contrast to the cognitive role SCAR, which expresses a complete passivity of the participant, the role MEXP presupposes the ability of the participant for a mental activity.

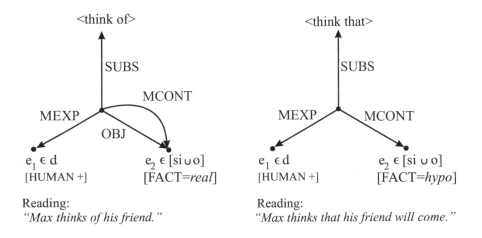

Reading:
*"Max thinks of his friend."*

Reading:
*"Max thinks that his friend will come."*

**Figure 5.12.** Mental processes and states

It is important to remember that the role $(sv_1$ MCONT $sv_2)$ bears a semantically restrictive character limiting the validity of the situation $sv_2$ to the modal context $sv_1$. Such a specification can be combined with other roles like OBJ, thus compensating and relieving the modal restriction (compare the categorical answer with OBJ, regarding the criterion of independence and the default assumption with MCONT; see Fig. 5.8). This aspect can be illustrated by the difference in meaning between ⟨think of⟩ (Ge: ⟨denken an⟩) and ⟨think that⟩ (Ge: ⟨denken, daß⟩); see Fig. 5.12. While the object $e_2 \in [si \cup o]$ of the former can be a real state of affairs or a real entity (since there exists a double characterization of the object $e_2$ by OBJ and MCONT), in the latter case, the object $e_2$, which is primarily characterized by MCONT alone, can only be assumed to have a hypothetical character, provided there is no further information about the event ⟨think that⟩ (here, the object must neither exist, in the case of $e_2 \in o$, nor be valid, in the case of $e_2 \in si$).

3. **States with an active component of meaning**

Some states can be sustained only by an active engagement of their carrier objects. This group comprises states like ⟨hold on to⟩, ans ⟨cling to⟩. Therefore, objects in such a state are carriers of an action (or agents) at the same time (see Fig. 5.13). The examples of this figure show that other C-Roles belonging to the field of event characterizations may also be involved in the description of states.

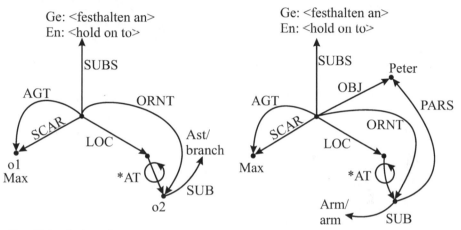

Ge: *"Max hält sich am Ast fest."*
En: *"Max holds on to the branch."*

Ge: *"Max hält Peter am Arm fest."*
En: *"Max holds on to Peter's arm."*

**Figure 5.13.** States with an active carrier

4. **Descriptions of relationships**

There are state verbs which have nothing to do with "states" in the narrower sense (they can be interpreted at best as states on a metalevel). This group includes verbs that describe relations in the sense of the representational means of MultiNet, e.g. ⟨consist of⟩ for PARS, ORIGM, or ELMT (depending on the selected sememe); ⟨stay at⟩ or ⟨be in⟩ (local meaning) for LOC; ⟨extend over⟩ for LEXT or DUR; represent for RPRS; ⟨be analogous to⟩ for ANLG. To characterize these states of affairs, the corresponding metasituation is linked to the superordinate relational concept through SUBR, the arguments of which are specified by means of ARG1, ARG2, or ARG3 (depending upon the arity of the relation). Simultaneously, the arguments whose order is fixed by convention are connected with each other by the corresponding MultiNet relations (see Fig. 5.14).

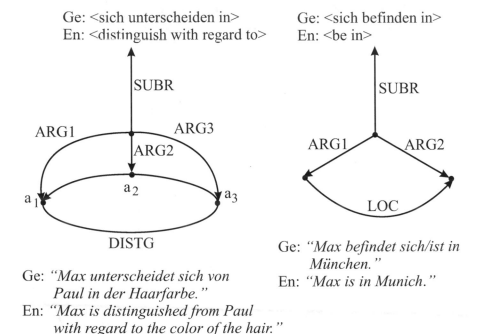

Ge: *"Max unterscheidet sich von Paul in der Haarfarbe."*
En: *"Max is distinguished from Paul with regard to the color of the hair."*

Ge: *"Max befindet sich/ist in München."*
En: *"Max is in Munich."*

**Figure 5.14.** Metastates as descriptions of relations

## 5. **Attributions**

An intermediate position between states and relational descriptions is taken by the specification of attributes (e.g. *"to weigh"*, *"to cost"*). On the one hand, they characterize the physical or psychical constitution of entities, and thus belong to states in the broadest sense (see sort *st*, Sect. 17.1); on the other hand, there exists a close connection to the description of MultiNet relations, since these verbs describe a small partial semantic network (see Fig. 5.15). Therefore, a certain compromise is proposed in MultiNet: In the lexicon and in order to support the analysis, a representation is chosen which is based on the relations SCAR, SSPE, and SUBS, as in the case of ordinary states (see Point 1 and the left side of Fig. 5.15). To achieve a deeper semantic representation of the SN, the attribute-value formalism already discussed in Sect. 4.3.3 must be employed (see the right side of Fig. 5.15).

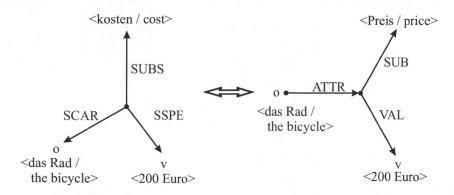

Ge: *"Das Rad kostet 200 Euro."*    Ge: *"Das Rad hat einen Preis von 200 Euro."*
En: *"The bicycle costs 200 Euro."*    En: *"The bicycle has a price of 200 Euro."*

**Figure 5.15.** Metastates as descriptions of attributions

The relationship represented in Fig. 5.15 can be expressed by a meaning postulate:

- (z SUBS cost) $\wedge$ (z SCAR o) $\wedge$ (z SSPE v) $\rightarrow$
  $\exists$ a (o ATTR a) $\wedge$ (a SUB price) $\wedge$ (a VAL v) (26)

The distinction between happenings and states in the sort of situations is also problematic. Here, we refer to investigations reported in the literature, especially with regard to the aspect of the verb (see, for instance, the classification of verbs into "states", "activities", "accomplishments" and "achievements" in [265], or the work on the distinguishing criteria between these classes in [57, Sect. 2.2.1]).

# Chapter 6

# The Comparison of Entities

## 6.1 Typical Relations of Comparison

Languages like German and English possess a whole spectrum of lexical, morphological, and syntactical means to construct statements of comparison (the analogue is true for other Indo-European languages like French or Russian[1]).

1. **Lexical means**
   - Nouns, like *"difference"* (Ge: *"Unterschied"*), *"similarity"*/*"analogy"* (Ge: *"Ähnlichkeit"*/*"Analogie"*), and *"equality"*/*"equivalence"* (Ge: *"Gleichheit"*/*"Äquivalenz"*).
   - Verbs, like *"differ (from)"* (Ge: *"sich unterscheiden"*), *"correspond to"* (Ge: *"entsprechen"*), and *"equal"* (Ge: *"gleichen"*).
   - Adjectives, like *"different"* (Ge: *"unterschiedlich"*/*"verschieden"*), *"similar"*/*"analogous"* (Ge: *"ähnlich"*/*"analog"*), *"equal"*/*"equivalent"* (Ge: *"gleich"*/*"äquivalent"*).
   - Numerals (multiplicatives), like *"twice (as)"* (Ge: *"doppelt (so)"*), *"threefold/three times"* (Ge: *"dreifach/dreimal"*).
2. **Degrees of comparison**
   - Absolute or positive, like *"as large as"* (Ge: *"so groß wie"* or *"ebenso groß wie"*).
   - Comparative, like *"larger than"* (Ge: *"größer als"*).
   - Superlative, like *"(the) largest"* (Ge: *"der größte"* or *"am größten"*).
3. **Comparative sentences**
   - expressing a real comparison with conjunctions like *"as"* and *"like"* (Ge: *"als"* and *"wie"*) and their correlates *"as"* (Ge: *"so"* or *"ebenso"*), and *"insofar"*/*"inasmuch"* (Ge: *"insofern"*).
   - expressing a counterfactual comparison with conjunctions like *"as if"* (Ge: *"als ob"* or *"als wenn"*).

---

[1] The following examples are given in English and German (in parentheses) to show the parallelism in different languages. They could easily be extended to French or Russian, too.

### 4. Sentences comparing <u>correlated gradations</u>
- Conjunctions, like "*the ... the*" (Ge: "*je ... desto*" or "*je ... umso*").

The natural language expressions listed under Point 1 (except for numerals) can be seen as paraphrases of the deep relations DISTG (for difference/distinction), ANLG (for similarity/analogy), CORR (for correspondence), and EQU (for equality), and can thus be reduced to them semantically. The following schema can be assumed as paradigmatic for the semantic representation of **multiplicatives**:

$$k_1 \; is \; \left\{ \begin{array}{c} twice/two \; times \\ three \; times \end{array} \right\} \; as \; p \; as \; k_2$$

The comparison described by this schema is represented in Fig. 6.1, where it is shown that multiplicatives are interpreted as graduators for compared properties.

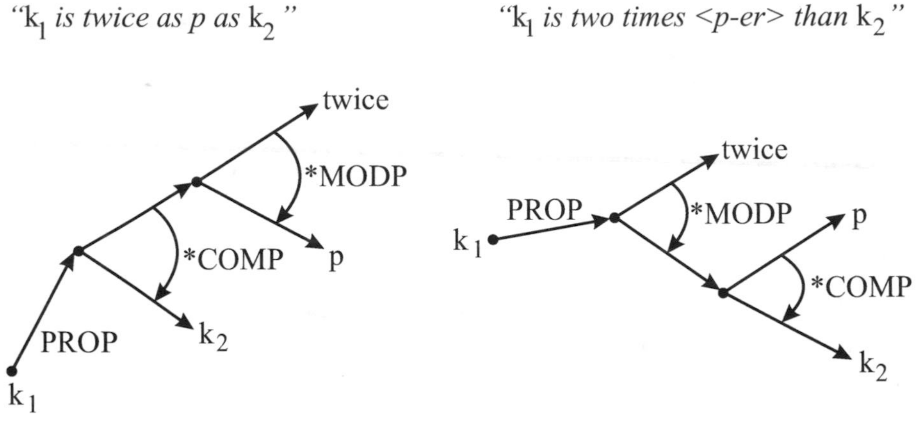

"$k_1$ is twice as p as $k_2$"                    "$k_1$ is two times <p-er> than $k_2$"

**Figure 6.1.** The semantic representation of multiplicatives

The different degrees of comparison play an important role in the comparison of objects (and also of events and states). For that reason, they will be dealt with separately in Sect. 6.2. Before going into that topic, the representations of comparative sentences (Point 3 above) and of correlative sentences (Point 4 above) will be considered first.

### Comparative sentences
With this type of comparison, one has to distinguish between sentences expressing **real comparisons** and sentences expressing **nonreal comparisons**.

Flämig speaks about "unbedingte Gleichsetzung" (unconditional comparison) with the former and "bedingte Gleichsetzung" (conditional comparison) with the latter [67, p. 95]. While the real comparison is built with the indicative mood, the subordinate clause of a counterfactual comparison is built with the subjunctive mood. Corresponding to these surface phenomena, the semantic representations of the first are characterized by [**FACT** = *real*], and the semantic representations of the second are built using pseudo-situations with [**FACT** = *hypo*] or explicitly negated states of affairs with [**FACT** = *non*].

a) Real comparison (example):

(6.1) *"The ambassador has passed the message on just as he received it."*

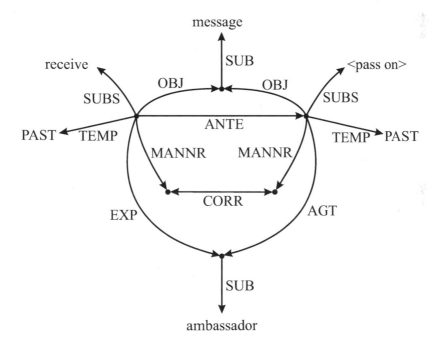

**Figure 6.2.** Representation of a real (unconditional) comparison

The representation of this real comparison can be found in Fig. 6.2, where the relation CORR is serving as the carrier of the comparison. In the graphical representation of the example, the interpretation ⟨just as⟩ ⇒ ⟨in the same way⟩ was chosen. There is also another interpretation possible: ⟨just as⟩ ⇒ unchanged. The different variants of interpretation which exist also with comparative sentences have yet to be investigated more deeply in the broader context of "semantic interpretation of conjunctions". They are not so much a problem of semantic representation but rather of syntactic-semantic analysis.

b) Counterfactual comparison (example):

(6.2) *"The machine is crunching as if sand had been thrown into the gear."*
The semantic representation of this counterfactual comparison can be found in Fig. 6.3, where the relation CORR is again the central element of the comparison.[2]

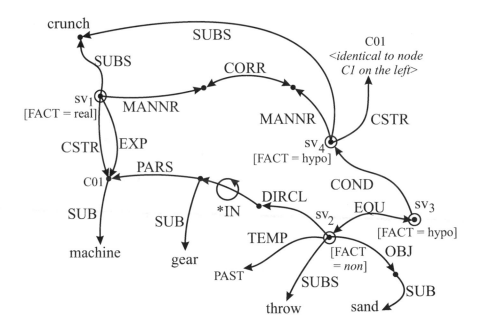

**Figure 6.3.** Semantic representation of a counterfactual (conditional) comparison

The interpretation of this example is relatively complicated: First, the sentence states that the machine is crunching, which is described by the fact $sv_1$. Second, the situation $sv_2$ can be concluded from this sentence, asserting that indeed no sand was thrown into the gear of the machine (which is expressed by [**FACT** = *non*] with $sv_2$).[3] Additionally, the sentence explicitly contains a conditional relation of the following kind: *"If someone throws sand into the*

---

[2] The relation between **gear** and **machine** (reference of the article *"the"*) can only be resolved by immanent knowledge comprising the fact (**gear** PARS **machine**).

[3] Those who find this conclusion too far-reaching and share the opinion that there could actually be sand in the gear, have to fuse the two nodes $sv_2$ and $sv_3$ and assign the attribute [**FACT** = *hypo*] to the resulting node.

*gear (of this machine or of any machine in general), it crunches in a certain way. And that corresponds to how the machine is actually crunching.*" This is described by setting up a situation $sv_3$ that is intensionally of the same kind as situation $sv_2$, but it is "timeless" and bears the characteristic [**FACT** = *hypo*]. Situation $sv_3$ stands in a conditional relation ($sv_3$ COND $sv_4$) to the hypothetical crunching process $sv_4$.[4] The latter is again connected to node C01 via the relational chain MANNR-CORR-MANNR, and is further specified by the relation CSTR.[5]

**Correlated gradations**

For the treatment of the relationship between correlated gradations (see Point 4 above) one can start from the following basic pattern built up with the two-part conjunction "*the ... the*" (Ge: "*je ... desto*" or "*je ... umso*"):

>"*the* ⟨comparative of $p_1$⟩ *the* ⟨comparative of $p_2$⟩".

>Example: "*the sooner the better*"

The semantic representation of such correlations is given by the schema in Fig. 6.4. The schema specifies that the gradation of property $p_1$ corresponds to the gradation of property $p_2$ (or, in certain cases, the latter can be inferred from the former or is causally related to it).

If the dynamic character of the comparison of two changing properties which grow or decrease in a correlated way has to be emphasized, it is expressed by the transition of sorts from properties $p_1$ and $p_2$ to events $v_1$ and $v_2$, respectively, and by the relation CHPE. The explicit specification of a comparison frame is omitted here (symbolized generally by $X or $Y in the semantic representation), since the comparison takes place at any time with each of the foregoing states of the change of the properties (which may be virtually assumed). Note that placeholders like $X or $Y are not elements of the MultiNet language in the proper sense. Rather, they are indicators for lacking pieces of information which still have to be found. A concrete example is shown in Fig. 6.5, where the relation IMPL (which is more specific than CORR) is used to express the comparison.

---

[4] If one prefers the generic interpretation for the implicit conditional relation, then the situations $sv_3$ and $sv_4$ must not be connected to the special machine (node C01) or its gear, but must be built by means of a generic machine and its part, a generic gear.

[5] The node C01 is actually represented only once. It is doubled only for the simplification of the graphical representation.

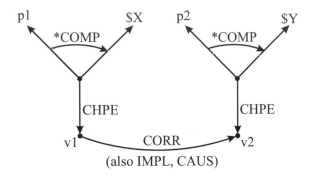

**Figure 6.4.** General schema for correlated gradations

(6.3) *"The smaller the volume of the container becomes, the higher the pressure in this container will be."*

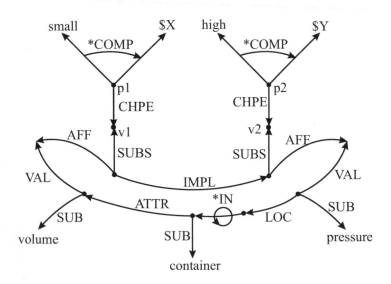

**Figure 6.5.** Relation between the change of volume and pressure as an example of correlated gradations

# 6.2   The Semantic Treatment of Comparison

## 6.2.1   The Absolute or Positive

With regard to the gradation of properties, three stages have to be distinguished at the semantic and syntactic levels: the basic stage called **absolute** (or **positive**), the **comparative**, and the **superlative**.[6]

As stated above in Sect. 4.3.2, even the absolute form of gradable properties contains an aspect of comparison. What "*big*" or "*small*" really mean can only be decided with regard to a certain class of elements that is used as a framework of comparison (in Sect. 4.3.2 we juxtaposed the phrases "*a big fly*" and "*a small animal*" with each other; see Fig. 4.10).

A positive comparison can also be expressed by means of conjunctions, like "*as ... as*" or "*in the same way as ...*". This is one of the methods by which the agreement of entities with regard to certain attributes can be stated (see Fig. 6.6).

For a better understanding of the following discussion and of the representations in Fig. 6.6, we should remember that the polarity of properties is a characteristic feature of elements of the sort $gq$ (see relations COMPL and CONTR). One can distinguish between a negative and a positive pole (which are functioning, respectively, as the first and second arguments in the following expressions).

Examples:

| | | | |
|---|---|---|---|
| En: | (short CONTR long) | Ge: | (kurz CONTR lang) |
| En: | (narrow CONTR broad) | Ge: | (schmal CONTR breit) |
| En: | (light CONTR heavy) | Ge: | (leicht CONTR schwer) |

It is typical of measurable properties that quantitative statements are always constructed by using the property at the positive pole ("*3 mm long*" but not "*3 mm short*"; Ge: "*3 mm lang*" but not "*3 mm kurz*").[7] Within such quantitatively modified adjective phrases – if they are at all allowed – the property at

---

[6] We shall restrict our investigations to gradable properties (sort $gq$) only, though comparisons of semantically total properties are also possible: "*white as snow*", "*dead as a stone*", etc. This shows that a living language allows for expressional means which cannot be considered rigidly fixed. On the one hand, the color properties in the examples have to be considered as fuzzy concepts, which open the way to their "gradations" (as in the German advertising slogan "*Weißer geht's nimmer!*", in English, literally, "*Whiter is impossible!*"); on the other hand, certain stylistic means also make properties especially vivid by using comparisons (e.g. "*quiet as a grave*"). Such fine nuances of languages cannot be considered here.

[7] This type of formulation is quite common in German but not so systematically observed in English. Compare German "*500 g schwer*" (allowed) and "*500 g leicht*" (not allowed) with the corresponding verbal translations "*500 g heavy*" and "*500 g light*", neither allowed in English.

the positive pole is unmarked and has a neutral meaning. It does not express the highest value of the corresponding property. The nature of polarity has to be taken into account when comparisons between values of properties must be semantically analyzed.[8] Figure 6.6 elucidates the difference between the following sentences:

a)  Ge: *"Das Modell ist genau so groß wie das Original."*
    En: *"The model is exactly as big as the original."*
b)  Ge: *"Das Modell ist genau so klein wie das Original."*
    En: *"The model is exactly as small as the original."*

a) *"The model is as big as the original."*

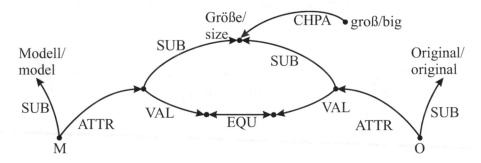

b) *"The model is as small as the original."*

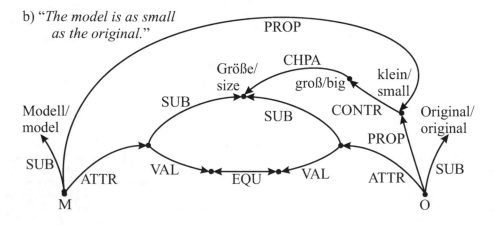

**Figure 6.6.** Positive comparisons and the polarity of properties

---

[8] The semantics of gradable adjectives and their connection to scales and degrees has also been investigated by Kennedy [138].

At first, both sentences state that the value of the attribute which can be derived from the properties big and small (in both cases it is size, or Ge: Größe) is the same. The relation between the property at the positive pole (big/groß) to the corresponding attribute (in this case size/Größe) is directly established by means of CHPA, while the connection between the property at the negative pole (small/klein) and the attribute size/Größe is mediated by the combination of the relations CONTR + CHPA (in German, the attribute corresponding to polar pairs of concepts like groß/klein – in this case the attribute Größe – is also morphologically often derived from the property at the positive pole).

We mentioned already that with measurable properties the positive pole of a pair of antonyms as well as the corresponding attribute have a neutral meaning with regard to the value of this attribute; i.e. sentence a) could also have been uttered if the model and the original were actually small. This is also true for the sentence *"The model and the original have the same size."* (Ge: *"Das Modell und das Original haben die gleiche Größe."*). A phrase like *"A is as big as B"* / *"A ist genauso groß wie B"* does not necessarily mean that A or B must be *"big"*/*"groß"*. For this reason, in representation a) of Fig. 6.6 the relation PROP to the property big/groß must not be attached to the nodes M and O. In contrast, in sentence b) it is presupposed that model and original are both small, i.e. if the property at the negative pole of a pair of antonyms (small/klein) is used, then this property itself holds and must therefore be attached via PROP to the entities being compared.

## 6.2.2    The Comparative

The comparative as the first degree of gradation of a property characterizes an inequality of properties; to be exact, it specifies a higher degree on a scale implicitly associated with the graded property. This gradation of properties is determined by a comparison with certain reference objects constituting the so-called **comparison frame**. For the semantic representation, MultiNet provides the function ∗COMP and the relations MIN and MAJ (where the relations are used for a quantitative comparison). The comparison of properties at the semantic level corresponds to the comparative form of adjectives and adverbs at the morphological level. It should be remembered that not all adjectives or adverbs are gradable (e.g. the adjectives *"dead"*, *"empty"*, *"round"*, *"angular"*, *"single"*, etc. have no comparative form), and only a few "genuine" adverbs (e.g. *"soon"* ⇒ *"sooner"*) can be graded.[9]

Colors like *"red"*, *"yellow"* or *"green"* show a special behavior with regard to

---

[9] In German there are even a few participles which have a comparative form, e.g. *"naheliegend"* (En: *"natural"*) ⇒ *"näherliegend"* (En: *"more natural"*).

comparison. On the one hand, words denoting colors can be graded ("*redder*", "*yellower*", and "*greener*"), but on the other hand, there is no scale of "*redness*", "*yellowness*", or "*greenness*" associated with them on which they are semantically shifted by gradation. We believe that either the intensity of the color is actually graded by the comparison, or the wavelength of the graded color (e.g. "*yellower*") is shifted toward the indicated color in the spectrum (i.e. toward "*yellow*").

Properties not gradable may not be used in comparative sentences, at least in principle (for exceptions showing a stylistic effect, see Sect. 6.2.1). Two examples for the semantic representation of gradations are given in Fig. 6.7. In connection with quantitative comparisons, words like "*greater*" and "*higher*" must often be understood as paraphrases of the relations MIN or MAJ, i.e., in these cases, one of the relations MIN or MAJ, but not the properties great or high, must be included in the semantic representation (see Fig. 6.7b).

a) "*Lake Baikal is  deeper*
   *than Lake Titicaca."*

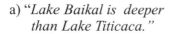

b) "*Lead has a density which is*
   *3.6 g/cm³ higher than that of iron."*

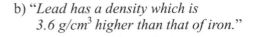

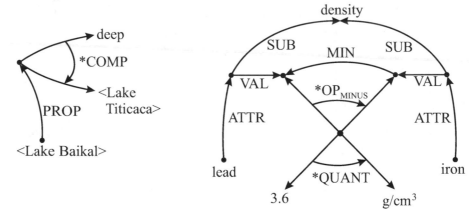

**Figure 6.7.** Qualitative and quantitative comparisons

The function ∗COMP may also be used to establish the lexical relationships between the different forms of irregularly graded adjectives. Examples:

| | | | | |
|---|---|---|---|---|
| En: | good | (positive); | better = (∗COMP good $X) | (comparative) |
| Ge: | gut | (positive); | besser = (∗COMP gut $X) | (comparative) |
| En: | much | (positive); | more = (∗COMP much $X) | (comparative) |
| Ge: | viel | (positive); | mehr = (∗COMP viel $X) | (comparative) |

The problem of presuppositions associated with comparative phrases has been dealt with by Kiefer [139]. He states that from the graded property at the positive pole of polar properties, one cannot infer the property itself in its basic form. Example:

(6.4)　　$\begin{array}{c}\textit{"Peter is \underline{taller} than John."}\\ \text{+ pole}\end{array}$　　$\left\{\begin{array}{l}\nrightarrow \textit{"Peter is tall."}\\ \nrightarrow \textit{"Bernd is tall."}\end{array}\right.$

However, according to Kiefer one may infer from the graded property lying at the negative pole that the corresponding property not graded (the positive) holds for both compared objects. Example:

(6.5)　　$\begin{array}{c}\textit{"Lena is \underline{uglier} than Julia."}\\ \text{- pole}\end{array}$　　$\left\{\begin{array}{l}\rightarrow \textit{"Lena is ugly."}\\ \rightarrow \textit{"Julia is ugly."}\end{array}\right.$

Using the representational means of MultiNet, Kiefer's postulates can be expressed by the following schemata:

- $(o_1 \text{ PROP } (*\text{COMP } p_+ \ o_2)) \nrightarrow (o_1 \text{ PROP } p_+)$ ⠀⠀⠀⠀⠀⠀⠀⠀(27)
- $(o_1 \text{ PROP } (*\text{COMP } p_+ \ o_2)) \nrightarrow (o_2 \text{ PROP } p_+)$ ⠀⠀⠀⠀⠀⠀⠀⠀(28)

with $p_+$ property at the positive pole,

- $(o_1 \text{ PROP } (*\text{COMP } p_- \ o_2)) \rightarrow (o_1 \text{ PROP } p_-)$ ⠀⠀⠀⠀⠀⠀⠀⠀(29)
- $(o_1 \text{ PROP } (*\text{COMP } p_- \ o_2)) \rightarrow (o_2 \text{ PROP } p_-)$ ⠀⠀⠀⠀⠀⠀⠀⠀(30)

with $p_-$ property at the negative pole.

While the first two statements expressed by formulas (27) and (28) are undoubtedly true, the general validity of the Formulas (29) and (30) may be questioned. It is indeed true that the last two formulas hold for properties like $p_- =$ poor, $p_- =$ ugly, $p_- =$ lazy, etc. (but one could indeed have some doubt about whether "*Peter is lazier than John.*" really means that John is also "*lazy*"). With regard to properties like $p_- =$ light, $p_- =$ small both formulas, (29) and (30), do not, in our opinion, hold unrestrictedly. It seems possible to assert of two tall persons that one of them is "*a little bit smaller*" than the other, or of two relatively heavy objects that the one is "*lighter*" than the other, and so on. In contrast (and in accordance with Kiefer), one may not assert of N. Rockefeller and P. Getty that one of them is "*poorer*" than the other, because this would imply that both of them are poor. In the axiomatic apparatus of MultiNet, it is assumed that Formulas (29) and (30) are not unrestrictedly valid (they are valid, at best, as default assumptions) for properties which can be quantitatively modified, while they are accepted for all other properties. However, further investigations are needed to empirically support this hypothesis.

A phenomenon that can only be understood in the light of the polarity of properties is the **absolute comparative** (Ge: *"ein älterer Herr"*, En: *"an older gentleman"*). This construction does not describe a comparison of two or more objects. One may also not deduce from the graded property (*"älter"* / *"older"*) that the property itself holds; *"an older gentleman"* (Ge: *"ein älterer Herr"*) is not an *"old gentleman"* (Ge: *"ein alter Herr"*). The absolute comparative describes rather a distinct shift in the value of an attribute (here, age) from its antipole (young) in the direction of the pole which is used to build the graded property (here, old), in other words, an *"older gentleman"* is not young any more, but he is not necessarily old.[10]

A further characteristic of the comparative is its **transitivity**, which can be described by the following axiom:

- $(o_1 \text{ PROP } (*\text{COMP p } o_2)) \wedge (o_2 \text{ PROP } (*\text{COMP p } o_3)) \rightarrow$
  $\quad (o_1 \text{ PROP } (*\text{COMP p } o_3))$ 
  $\hfill (31)$

Example:

|        | From       | *"Peter is taller than Bernd."*  |
| ------ | ---------- | -------------------------------- |
| (6.6)  | and        | *"Bernd is taller than Gunter."* |
|        | it follows | *"Peter is taller than Gunter."* |

It should be emphasized that axioms like (31) are valid for semantic deep structures only. They must not be applied thoughtlessly to surface structures. Otherwise this would lead to wrong conclusions, something already pointed out by Patzig [196, p. 30]. Thus, one may not infer from *"Nobody is taller than Peter."* and *"Peter is taller than Bernd."* that *"Nobody is taller than Bernd."* (this can already be seen from the fact that *"Nobody"* is indeed the grammatical subject, but semantically it is not a proper entity; see Sect. 8.2).

A special feature of comparative constructions is their **elliptical character**, i.e. they can be thought as resulting from omissions of sentence parts or from the contraction of different sentences into one sentence. Example:

(6.7) *"He is running as lightning."*

should be read as

(6.8) *"He is running as fast as a lightning flash is coming down."*

Very often, the comparison frame is omitted from the construction of a comparative or superlative phrase if it can be derived from the context of the

---

[10] Brinkmann [35, p. 120] states with regard to the absolute comparative: *"Since the comparison may orient itself at the antipole, it is possible that the first stage of comparison can denote a lower degree as the basic stage of comparison."*

utterance (from its surrounding text), from the situational embedding, or from the background knowledge. Within a QAS, a difficult problem arises in finding (automatically, in certain circumstances) the completion of the sentence parts which were omitted. This problem, in general, has not yet been solved. It still requires intense research. To illustrate the difficulties, we give the following pairs of sentences, where the first shows the context and the second the elliptical sentence. The phrase enclosed in parentheses indicates the comparison frame to be completed.

(6.9) *"In 1977 Peter was running the 100 m distance in 12.0 seconds."*
*"Now Peter is running faster."* (than in 1977)

(6.10) *"Until last year Paul always outperformed Peter in a race over the 100 m distance."*
*"Now Peter is running faster."* (than Paul)

(6.11) *"Peter never thought that he would ever run the 100 m distance in 12.0 seconds."*
*"Now Peter is running still faster."* (than he ever thought / than a time of 12.0 seconds or less)

There is also a close connection between comparison and negation (see Sect. 8.2) insofar as with every comparative or superlative form of a property, the invalidity of the graded property is stated for all entities specified in the comparison frame. Examples:

(6.12) *"It has become colder."* → *"Yesterday / a little while ago it was not as cold as now."*

(6.13) *"The algorithm A\* is the most effective."* → *"The other algorithms in question are not so effective."*

These regularities can also be formalized by means of axioms whose application, however, presupposes that the comparison frame can be either directly taken from the sentence or can be automatically inferred from the sentence.

A **growing gradation**, which is described in the surface structure by the following means:

En: • *"getting/becoming"* + ⟨comparative⟩
   • *"ever"* + ⟨comparative⟩
   • ⟨repetition of the comparative⟩
Ge: • ⟨comparative⟩ + *"werden"*
   • *"immer"* + ⟨comparative⟩
   • ⟨repetition of the comparative⟩

has to be represented in the deep structure by means of the relation CHPE and the function ∗COMP (see Fig. 6.8). The comparison frame in these cases is always the foregoing moment.
Example:

(6.14)  En: *"The motor was running faster and faster (ever faster)."*
(6.15)  Ge: *"Der Motor lief schneller und schneller (immer schneller)."*

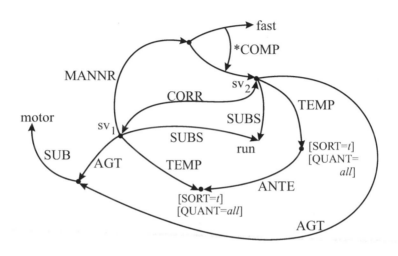

**Figure 6.8.** The growing of properties and the comparative

The **amplification of comparatives** by means of *"far"* and *"much"* (Ge: *"weit"*, *"bei weitem"*, *"weitaus"*, and *"viel"*) has to be represented by means of the functions ∗MODP and ∗COMP. The analogue holds for the amplification of superlatives with *"by far"* and *"much"* (Ge: *"bei weitem"* and *"weitaus"*). Example (see Fig. 6.9a):

(6.16)  En: *"much deeper than the Baltic Sea"*
        ↔ (∗MODP much (∗COMP deep, ⟨Baltic Sea⟩)).
(6.17)  Ge: *"viel tiefer als die Ostsee"*
        ↔ (∗MODP viel (∗COMP tief, Ostsee)).

Finally, a degree of a property **being too high** can be expressed by *"too"* and *"far too"* (Ge: *"zu"*, *"allzu"*, and *"viel zu"*), see Fig. 6.9b. The comparison frame in these cases is defined by a reference situation (relation CTXT), a purpose (relation PURP), or a beneficiary (relation BENF), the automatic discovering of which lies beyond the current possibilities of a technically realized QAS.

a) *"**much deeper** than the Baltic Sea"*

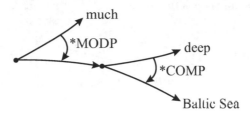

b) *"The basin is **too deep** for non-swimmers."*

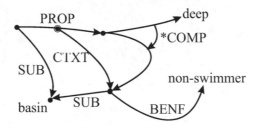

**Figure 6.9.** Modifications of the comparative

### 6.2.3   The Superlative

The superlative characterizes the highest degree of a property within a certain comparison frame. It can be built only from gradable properties (as is the case with the comparative). The superlative as a grammatical form can be found within the noun group as well as outside of it (see Fig. 6.10).

If one had to consider only the superlative within a noun group (i.e. its attributive use), it would be a natural approach to interpret the superlative as an object-generating function SUPL': $gq \times [\bar{o} \cup \ddot{o}] \rightarrow o$, which selects the element with the highest attribute value on a suitable scale from a class of objects (the collection or conceptual extension determined by the comparison frame). Such a representation would imply that constructions of the superlative in the adverbial use (as in *"This program works best."* or Ge: *"Dieses Programm arbeitet am besten."*) require a different representation. To warrant homogeneous semantic representations of all superlative constructions that are independent of their grammatical embedding in a certain surface structure, a unified interpretation of the superlative as a property-generating function is preferred: *SUPL: $gq \times [\bar{o} \cup \ddot{o}] \rightarrow tq$   (see Fig. 6.10).

This interpretation spares additional axioms and makes the semantic equivalence of the following constructions more transparent: *"The blue whale is the*

a) **within** the noun group
   (Ge: purely inflectional construction)

b) **outside** the noun group
   (Ge: prepositional construction
   preferred)

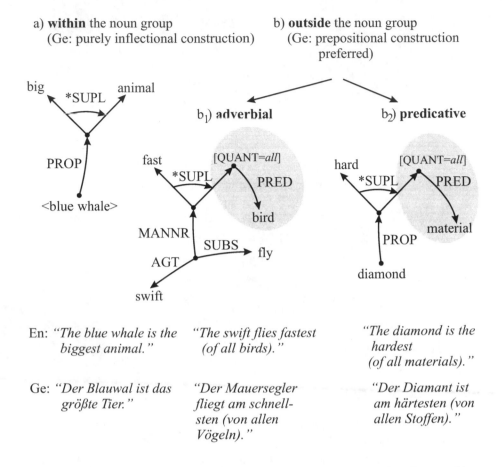

En: *"The blue whale is the*      *"The swift flies fastest*        *"The diamond is the*
    *biggest animal."*            *(of all birds)."*                *hardest*
                                                                    *(of all materials)."*

Ge: *"Der Blauwal ist das*        *"Der Mauersegler*                *"Der Diamant ist*
    *größte Tier."*               *fliegt am schnell-*              *am härtesten (von*
                                  *sten (von allen*                 *allen Stoffen)."*
                                  *Vögeln)."*

**Figure 6.10.** The semantic representation of different superlative constructions in natural language

*biggest animal."* and *"The blue whale is (the) biggest of all animals."* or *"Diamond is the hardest substance."* and *"Diamond is (the) hardest of all substances."* (Ge: *"Der Blauwal ist das größte Tier."* and *"Der Blauwal ist am größten von allen Tieren."* or *"Der Diamant ist der härteste Stoff."* and *"Der Diamant ist am härtesten von allen Stoffen."*). Apart from this advantage, the representation proposed fits more organically into the semantic representation of the series: **Positive – Comparative – Superlative** (see Fig. 6.11).

The equivalence of a comparative that is related to all elements of a collection with a superlative can be expressed by the following axiom (compare the last two examples in Fig. 6.11):

**a) Positive**

*"The blue whale
is big."*

**b) Comparative**

*"The blue whale is bigger
than all other animals."*

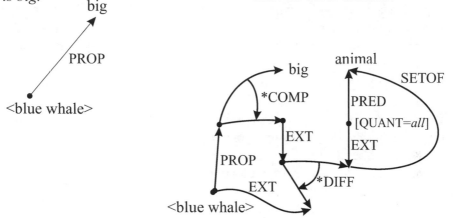

**c) Superlative**

*"The blue whale is
the biggest animal."*

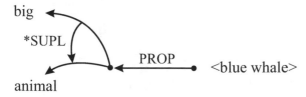

**Figure 6.11.** Positive, comparative, and superlative semantically compared

- (o PROP (∗COMP p e)) ∧ (g PRED c) ∧ [QUANT(g) = all]
  $\wedge\ [e_{EXT} = (*DIFF\ g_{EXT}\ o_{EXT})] \rightarrow$ (o PROP (∗SUPL p c))        (32)

Another phenomenon is the **absolute superlative**, which is a stage of gradation corresponding to a superlative not built by means of a comparison frame. In English, it is constructed using words like *"very"*, *"extraordinarily"*, and *"exceptionally"* and in German by means of *"sehr"*, *"überaus"*, *"äußerst"*, *"außerordentlich"*, and other graduators. The semantic representation of the absolute superlative, which expresses a very high degree of a scaled property without explicit comparison, is formed by means of the function ∗SUPL and a placeholder $X for the second argument of the superlative function (marking the lack of a comparison frame).

An analogous representation is chosen for such superlatives that actually express a comparison but whose comparison frame is not explicitly specified in the corresponding sentence (see Sect. 6.2.2 with regard to the elliptical character of comparative sentences). Thus, the parts shaded in gray in examples $b_1$ and $b_2$ of Fig. 6.10 had to be substituted by $X, if the corresponding sentence parts enclosed in parentheses were not given.

**Compositions** of the type ⟨(noun or adjective) + positive⟩ = ⟨adjective⟩, quite common morphological constructions in German, are used to specify a very high degree of gradation of a property, e.g.
Ge: todsicher = (∗MODP absolut sicher)
        (En: ⟨absolutely sure⟩),
Ge: blitzschnell = (∗MODP außerordentlich schnell)
        (En: ⟨fast as lightning⟩), and
Ge: stocktaub = (∗MODP absolut taub)
        (En: ⟨stone-deaf⟩).

# Chapter 7

# The Spatio-temporal Characterization of Entities

## 7.1 General Remarks on Space and Time

Because of the complexity of the phenomena of **space** and **time**, and the more than 2000 years of dispute about these concepts, only some of their aspects can be touched upon here. With regard to the far-reaching philosophical problems associated with space and time, we have to refer the reader to the literature. It is characteristic of the complexity of the matter that the early disputes in this field, for which the paradoxes of Zeno are typical, are still a topic in modern times (see [65, 43] and [86, 42]).

From the point of view of natural science, especially against the background of the results achieved in 20th century physics, we must assume that space and time are not absolute entities. Strictly speaking, they cannot be assigned the same ontological status as objects or events. Nevertheless, people use these concepts in a way as if locations and time intervals were objectively existing autonomous entities into which objects or events can be embedded. Examples:

(7.1) *"He hangs the lamp into the upper left corner of the room."*
(7.2) *"There exists a background radiation of 2.7 Kelvin in the universe."*
(7.3) *"The meeting of the class falls into Christmas time."*

From the epistemological point of view, and also in the intellectual development of mankind, it can be assumed that objects and events (i.e. the changes of objects) are primary, and space and time are secondary. With the growing capability for abstraction and the increasing role of temporal and spatial measurements by means of gauges, clocks, and calendars, space and time have won an ever greater autonomy. Thus, for many people time appears to be the cognitively more fundamental concept, by means of which the beginning and end of events, changes, temporal succession of events, etc. can easily be described.[1] The analogue holds for the cognitive autonomy of space, because it is seemingly possible to remove single objects from space without loosing the perception of space.[2]

Local and temporal specifications are also distinguished from objects and events, respectively, with regard to their intensional interpretation. Descriptions of locations, such as *"under the table"* (a spatial region), stimulate other conceptions and other associations than designations of objects like *"the table"* (a concrete thing). Temporal descriptions like *"in January"* / *"at Christmas"* arouse their own ideas within a human being (e.g. associations with snow or holidays) revealing the cognitive autonomy of these concepts.

Altogether, the autonomy of spatial and temporal concepts is reflected in almost all ontological systems or contemplations, be it within the framework of linguistics [52, 130], of logic [263, 69] or of artificial intelligence [158, 117].

Even Newton developed the conception of absolute space and time, which can be regarded as a proof for the above-mentioned autonomy, since this "naive" (from our modern standpoint) view is closer to the human way of thinking than the more comprehensive general theory of relativity of Einstein, which can be understood only by means of abstract mathematical descriptions. It is quite plausible that the idea of absolute space and time, being more "natural" from the point of view of the history of sciences, had been taken for granted before the contemporary perspective of natural sciences had its way. However, one has to consider the fact that there exists a great difference between the abstract conception of space and time in modern physics and the cognitive role these concepts normally play for human beings (including the reflection of these concepts within natural languages and knowledge representations). This difference is also expressed by the fact that, in cosmological or relativistic physics, one speaks of a compact **space-time** (see [102]), while from the psychological point of view space and time have to be seen rather as distinct fields of experience.

Also, the perception of spatial or temporal relationships is not identical to the conception of space and time in physics. We have only to think of perspective perception of space, of gestalt perception, of psychological dilatation of time connected with boredom, or of the subjective compression of time when we experience a high density of events, etc. (see [264] and [173]).

---

[1] Interestingly enough, even authors defining the concept of time secondarily on the basis of equivalence classes of events do not manage without the concept of simultaneity, cf. [74, p. 224].

[2] Of course, this mental experiment does not work for the removal of all objects. The analogue is true for time. If one imagines that some events from a multitude of events are canceled, time does not disappear. But in an entirely eventless world there is no place for time.

In a knowledge representation system, which has to model cognitive states of affairs and which is essentially determined by everyday experiences of human beings, space and time are seen as a **frame of reference** given by the arrangement of objects (space) and events (time). Space is extended into three directions (dimensions); it is also from the cognitive point of view homogeneous and isotropical, as postulated in classical physics. In contrast, time is extended in one direction only; it is homogeneous (like space) but not isotropical, i.e. there is a distinguished direction from the past, via the present, into the future because of the irreversibility of many processes.

From an epistemological point of view, the concepts **space** and **time** are characterized by a special dialectics of aspects contradicting each other:

- **Space**

  On the one hand, a closed conception of space is impossible without comprehending a collection of objects as a unity spanning this space (the universe, the solar system, the earth, a living room, the world of atoms, etc.).

  On the other hand, it would be impossible to define positions or measures of distance (and also volume measures) without taking apart a whole into its *spatially separated* parts or distinguishing the different elements of an ensemble of objects without a concept of space.

- **Time**

  On the one hand, the irreversibility of many processes, especially of the processes of life, is crucial for the human conception of time, and of structuring it into past, present, and future.

  On the other hand, the measurement of time is essentially based on the existence of reversible processes, and would be impossible without periodical processes (the rotation of the earth, the movement of a pendulum, the oscillations of atoms, etc.).

## 7.2  Local Relations

There are essentially two different approaches to modeling spatial concepts: A geometric method oriented to a pictorial representation and a logical symbolic method (see Table 7.1).

Human beings are apparently able to use both methods of modeling.[3] Within the range of Method I, we are able to use geometric computations as well as purely pictorial conceptions (by way of "inner viewing", so to speak)

---

[3] For example, combining the intensional symbolic interlinking of spatial concepts like near and far with estimates or measurements of distances.

to grasp and process spatial relationships.[4] The latter approach is not realized on the computer or in the field of artificial intelligence until now. In spatio-temporal databases the concept of space is essentially defined geometrically or topologically (see [1]). Because of its closeness to natural language (see Table 7.1), Method II is preferred in MultiNet, where the specifications in this table have to be understood only as a tendency, since it is also possible in MultiNet to operate with quantitative measurements (see functions $*QUANT$, $*OP_j$).

| | Method I | Method II |
|---|---|---|
| Representational form | geometrical/pictorial representation (analogous) | symbolic representation (discrete) |
| Formalism | geometry | logic |
| Aspect | quantitative aspect | qualitative aspect |
| Main operation | computation (basis: coordinate system) | inference (basis: set of formulas) |
| Advantages | efficiency of computation; completeness and exactitude of the description | relatively easy to derive from NL descriptions; the vagueness and incompleteness inherent in spatial NL descriptions need not be resolved; automatic creation of the representation is possible for very different fields of application |
| Disadvantages | relatively far from NL descriptions; complete modeling always for restricted domains only | costly deductions necessary; continuous transitions difficult to model |

**Table 7.1.** The comparison of methods for the treatment of spatial states of affairs

Miller and Johnson-Laird [182] investigated spatial concepts from a psychological point of view. They proposed an explanation of local prepositions by means of perceptual schemata described in a notation similar to the predicate calculus, albeit attached to a procedural semantics (search in spatial regions). The following schema (33) can be seen as a generic template for the definition of the semantics of a local preposition (see [182]).

- LOC-REL(x, y) with LOC-REL: local relation                    (33)
    x : Referent (**Target object**)
    y : Relatum (**Landmark**)
    ⟨Conditions over x, y⟩

---

[4] One has only to think of the manner in which a person deals with queries like *"Where is the desk in your working room?"* To answer this question, no computation or logical inference is done. The person asked evokes the room before his "inner eye" and "reads" the spatial relationships from the corresponding picture.

The conditions given by the last component in (33) are defined on the basis of perceptually elementary predicates, which comprise, for instance,

Adjcnt(x, y)    –    "x and y are touching each other",
Incl(x, y)      –    "x is spatially contained in y",
Part(x, y)      –    "x is a part of y".

The referent (**target object**) is the entity of which the spatial position has to be defined, and the relatum (**landmark**) is the object used to determine the spatial region selected by the preposition. As an example of a concrete interpretation of a preposition, the following definition of the local preposition "*in*" shall be given (loc. cit. p. 385; see also Fig. 7.4):

- IN(x, y): A referent x is "*in*" a relatum y if
  $$[Part(x, z) \& Incl(z, y)]^5 \tag{34}$$

For the concept pair "Referent – Relatum", one also uses the terms "Figure – Ground" stemming from Gestalt Psychology [121].

In MultiNet, the meaning of local prepositions is generally not taken as a relation, but more specific as a function which assigns a spatial region to a given object or a set of objects (in the case of "*between*"), using the following schema (see the description of the family of local functions *FLP$_j$ in Part II):

- *FLP$_j$*: $\langle$Object$\rangle \rightarrow \langle$Location$\rangle$ $\tag{35}$

Following this semantic conception, most local prepositions (like "*at*", "*in*", "*on*", "*under*", etc.) do not primarily establish relationships between objects, but they are interpreted rather as functions generating locations from objects.[6] Consequently, the position held is different from that of Bierwisch [22], where the local prepositions arc generally assigned an attribute Dir marking the directedness of the corresponding concept. So, the German preposition "*über*" (En: "*above*") is characterized in [22, p. 7], with reference to the Government and Binding Theory of Chomsky [47], in the following way:

- /über/: [-V, -N, -Dir] $\hat{y}$ [$\hat{x}$ [x [ABOVE y]]] $\tag{36}$

In contrast, the opinion is held that in general the attribute of directedness ($\pm$Dir in [22]) does not befit the preposition, but rather the verb or a noun selecting for this attribute.

Examples:

---

[5] This expression has to be interpreted in the following way: "*x in y*" holds if x possesses a part z that is spatially contained in y. It remains open how large this part must be (compare "*the raisin in the cake*" and "*the spoon in the cup*").

[6] The specialities of directional prepositions like "*to*" and "*from*" will be dealt with shortly.

(7.4) Ge: *"in der Stadt leben"* – *"das Leben in der Stadt"*
     En: *"to live in the town"* – *"the life in the town"*
(7.5) Ge: *"in die Stadt reisen"* – *"die Reise in die Stadt"*
     En: *"to journey into the town"* – *"the journey into the town"*
(7.6) Ge: *"in den Sessel setzen"* – *"im Sessel sitzen"*
     En: *"to sit down into the armchair"* – *"to sit in the armchair"*

One distinction between the meanings of *"leben / to live"* and *"reisen / to journey"* consists in the fact that the former is not compatible with a direction, whereas the latter is. In the first instance, the combination of *"in"* and *"town"* in Sentences (7.4) and (7.5) creates semantically a location (or cognitively a spatial region) which in itself has no inherent direction. It is only by combination with *"journey"* that the relation of directedness comes into play. Also, the selection of case in German is not determined by the preposition, but by the directedness of the verb or noun derived from a verb which governs the prepositional phrase.[7] The difference in meaning between the German verbs *"setzen"* (*"sit down"*) and *"sitzen"* (*"to sit (somewhere)"*) is defined just by the feature that the former semantically is inherently connected with a direction (expressed in MultiNet by an optional valency, relation DIRCL), whereas the latter is not compatible with a direction described by DIRCL.

Since directionality is an inherent feature of verbs and nouns, and the property of being directed or not belongs to the proper meaning of these words, an additional specification of the attribute ±Dir with prepositions would lead only to a duplication of semantic features with most of these prepositions (something, by the way, that would also contradict the principle of **Ockham's razor**[8]).

For this reason, whether or not a verb or a noun is directed is expressed in the specification of these lexemes by the following relations:

LOC      – static location, without any direction
ORIGL   – direction away from a location
DIRCL   – direction toward a location.

There are also local prepositions like *"to"*, as in *"a journey to Berlin"*, and *"from"*, as in *"he came from Berlin"*, that have to be taken as direct paraphrases of relations expressing a spatial direction (i.e. they are paraphrases of the relations DIRCL or ORIGL, respectively). For prepositions like *"into"* (Ge: *"in*

---

[7] In English or German plural constructs, even the case differentiation is of no help to determine whether *"in cups"* or *"in Tassen"* has to be characterized as directed or not. It is the verb alone which allows for this decision: *"to put it in cups"* vs. *"to be in cups"* or *"gieße es in Tassen"* vs. *"sich in Tassen befinden"*.

[8] *"Entia non sunt multiplicanda praeter necessitatem."* or *"Entities are not to be multiplied beyond necessity."* – which has to be related in this case to the attribute **Dir**.

*(hinein)")* or *"out of"* (Ge: *"aus (heraus)")*, the adequate semantic representation consists of a combination of local relations and functions, in this case of DIRCL + *IN and ORIGL + *IN, respectively (see Fig. 7.1 and Table 7.2).

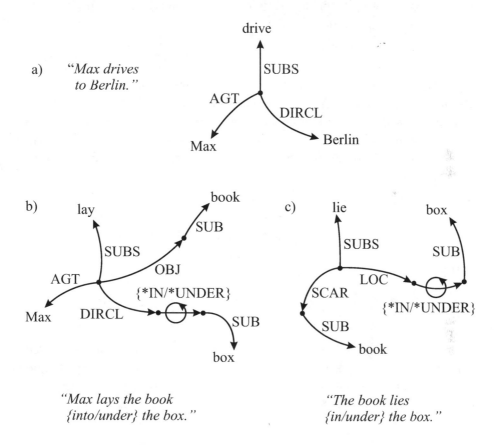

a)    *"Max drives to Berlin."*

b)    *"Max lays the book {into/under} the box."*

c)    *"The book lies {in/under} the box."*

**Figure 7.1.** The semantic representation of local prepositions

In general, spatial specifications are represented in MultiNet by means of a combination of local relations and functions[9] (or by a relation alone, in the case of a pure paraphrase of a local relationship), or to be exact:

---

[9] The fact that the phrase *"in Munich"* describes a closed cognitive entity (a location) is taken into account in the MultiNet formalism by creating a functional term (*IN Munich), which describes an entity of sort *l*. In contrast to that, the phrase *"to Munich"* seems to be somewhat incomplete (like a free radical in chemistry). It has to be described in MultiNet by the expression $\lambda x$ (x DIRCL Munich) with an open first argument (this is a relational expression which is not closed with regard to the first argument – and thus is not a conceptual entity; therefore, there is also no sort which could be attached to it).

- The meaning of prepositions as selectors of spatial regions is represented by functions generating locations which have no feature of directionality attached to it;
- The property of directionality is described by relations connecting objects or situations with locations.

Another controversial problem in the literature is related to the decision about whether a local specification expressed in a sentence has to be attached to the objects involved or to the entire situation described by the sentence. The first approach, which is certainly more appropriate from the physical point of view, is called **object localization**. The latter approach, which possibly comes closer to ordinary language use, is called **situation localization** (see [204]). For the purpose of explanation, consider the following situational descriptions. Examples:

(7.7) *"The mother bakes a cake in the kitchen."*

(7.8) *"The mother bakes a cake in the oven."*

(7.9) *"Many people have already sold their valuables at an auction in Munich."*

(7.10) *"In Munich, many people have already sold their valuables at an auction."*

(7.11) *"The policeman observed the children on the street. "*

(7.12) *"The policeman met the children on the street."*

These few examples show that a broad background knowledge is needed to infer from the sentences which objects are located in which place. Examples (7.7) and (7.8) illustrate that this decision does not depend on the verb alone (one has to know, for instance, whether or not a person can be situated in an oven or in a kitchen). Examples (7.11) and (7.12) elucidate the role of the verb meaning in the interpretation process (one may *"observe"* something form a larger distance; the policeman need not be on the street; but, *"To meet somebody"* is only possible if the participating objects are located in the same spatial region, i.e. the policeman and the children both have to be on the street). Finally, Examples (7.9) and (7.10) demonstrate the role of syntax (or to be specific, of word order) for semantic interpretation. In Example (7.9), it can be assumed that Munich has been the location of the auction, but neither the people nor the valuables need physically have been in Munich. In Example (7.10) the assignment of locations stays relatively open, thus either the people, or the auction, or both could have been located in Munich.

Because of the difficulties described, we hold the opinion that human beings do not resolve these rather complicated semantic interrelationships immediately with the first spontaneous understanding, and that they do not assign the correct locations to all objects participating in the corresponding situation right away. Therefore, it is proposed to attach local characterizations to situations as well (see the definitions of the relations LOC, DIRCL, and ORIGL), and to assign the proper locations to the objects involved by meaning postulates.[10]

If there is no location explicitly given in the natural language description of a situation sv, it is also omitted from the semantic representation of sv. Such a situational representative has to be taken as implicitly specified by means of (sv LOC ⟨somewhere⟩) (see Table 8.1 for the bundle of layer attribute-values describing the second argument).

Though, from the epistemological point of view, locations are primarily assigned to objects, situation localization is preferred from the methodological point of view. The following examples show how the location of objects can be inferred from situation localization on the basis of meaning postulates:[11]

- [(v SUBS meet) ∧ (v EXP a) ∧ (v OBJ b) ∧ (v LOC l)] →

  [(a LOC l) ∧ (b LOC l)]                                                      (37)

  *"a meets b at location l"* ⇒ *"a and b are located at l"*
- [(v SUBS observe) ∧ (v AGT a) ∧ (v OBJ b) ∧ (v ORIGL l)] →

  (a LOC l)                                                                     (38)

  *"a observes b from l"* ⇒ *"a is at l"*

  (the analogous conclusion does not hold for b in this case!)

Adverbs may also be used as expressional means to describe local regions. A special difficulty associated with local adverbs like *"left"* (Ge: *"links"*), *"right"* (Ge: *"rechts"*), *"in front of"* (Ge: *"vorn"*), *"behind"* (Ge:*"hinten"*), *"here"* (Ge: *"hier"*), *"there"* (Ge: *"dort"*), *"out"* (Ge: *"heraus"*), *"into"* (Ge: *"herein"*), *"out"* (Ge: *"hinaus"*), and *"into"* (Ge: *"hinein"*) is their deictic character. This means that a model of the dialogue situation, and especially the location of the speaker, has to be included into the semantic interpretation of these words.[12]

---

[10] It must, however, be emphasized that this methodological approach has to do with the syntactic-semantic analysis and the inferences in a QAS rather than with the representational means of MultiNet, since both **object localization** and **situation localization** are supported by MultiNet.

[11] The opinion that the equivalence of object localization and situation localization can be shown with the help of meaning postulates is also held in [283].

[12] In English, the distinction between the meanings of expressions denoting the direction "from inside to outside" (Ge: *"hinaus"* or *"heraus"*) and the direction "from outside to inside" (Ge: *"hinein"* and *"herein"*), which depend on the speaker's position, cannot be made on the basis of the preposition alone (we have here *"out"* and *"into"* for both positions of the speaker). In English one has also to include the directionality of the verb in the interpretation (e.g. *"come into"* and *"come out"* or *"go out"* and *"go into"*).

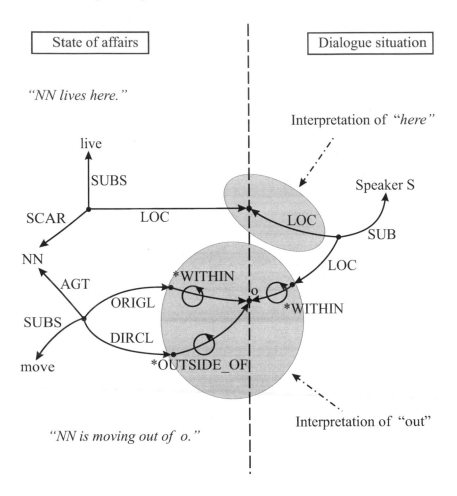

**Figure 7.2.** The inclusion of the dialogue situation (comprising the location of the speaker) into the semantic interpretation

The semantic relations involved in the interpretation of the local adverbs "*here*" (Ge: "*hier*") and "*out*" (Ge: "*hinaus*") are given in Fig. 7.2. In the sentence "*NN lives here.*" the adverb "*here*" denotes the same location as that also held by the speaker. In the sentence "*NN is moving out of o.*" (Ge: "*NN bewegt sich aus o hinaus.*") we meet a situation where the speaker is "within" the object o and the movement is directed from "within o" (ORIGL) to "outside of o" (DIRCL). The other adverbs have to be interpreted analogously, where the appropriate combinations of *WITHIN and *OUTSIDE_OF are obtained by corresponding exchanges in the semantic representation according to Table 7.2.

| | | ORIGL of NN | DIRCL of NN | Location of S |
|---|---|---|---|---|
| En: out | Ge: hinaus | (*INSIDE_OF o) | (*OUTSIDE_OF o) | (*INSIDE_OF o) |
| En: into | Ge: hinein | (*OUTSIDE_OF o) | (*INSIDE_OF o) | (*OUTSIDE_OF o) |
| En: out | Ge: heraus | (*INSIDE_OF o) | (*OUTSIDE_OF o) | (*OUTSIDE_OF o) |
| En: into | Ge: herein | (*OUTSIDE_OF o) | (*INSIDE_OF o) | (*INSIDE_OF o) |

**Table 7.2.** Combination of the locations involved with the semantic interpretation of the deictic adverbs "*into*" and "*out*" (NN = reference object, S = speaker)

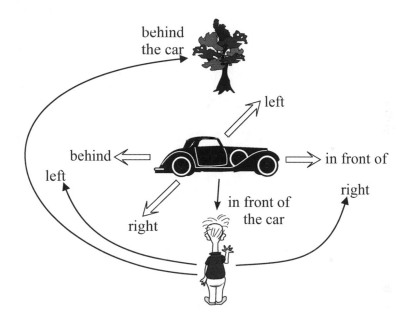

**Figure 7.3.** The deictic character of local adverbs

Adverbs like "*left*", "*right*", "*in front of*", "*behind*" (and also the corresponding prepositions) are inherently connected with two different kinds of interpretation, which depend on whether the utterance in question is interpreted from the standpoint of the speaker or with regard to a system of orientation inherent to the reference object (e.g. "*in front of*" referring to the face of someone or to the driving direction of a car, "*behind*" referring to the stern of a ship or the back of a car); see Fig. 7.3. We call the first interpretation **extrinsic interpretation** and the second the **intrinsic interpretation**. It can easily be seen from Fig. 7.3 that the phrase "*behind the car*" selects different spatial regions depending on the decision about whether one is virtually putting oneself into the coordinate system of the speaker or of the car.[13]

---

[13] The double arrows in Fig. 7.3 are related to the coordinate system fixedly connected to the car, while the single arrows are related to that of the speaker.

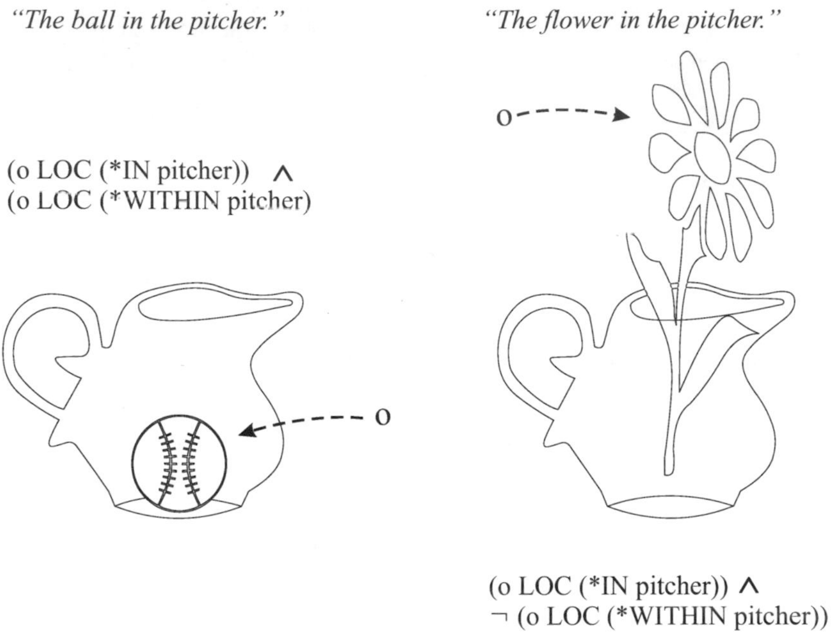

*"The ball in the pitcher."*                    *"The flower in the pitcher."*

(o LOC (*IN pitcher))  ∧
(o LOC (*WITHIN pitcher)

(o LOC (*IN pitcher)) ∧
¬ (o LOC (*WITHIN pitcher))

**Figure 7.4.** Fine differentiation of local prepositions

To specify the meaning of local prepositions, one can either choose a more constructive method by trying to explicate their meaning without falling back on the meaning of other prepositions, or one can favor a more comparative method contrasting the meaning of prepositions with each other. The first method makes use of appropriate meaning postulates; an example of this approach is given by definition (34) of IN, which can be translated with the expressional means of MultiNet as follows (*IN is the functional counterpart of MultiNet to the relation IN from (34)):

- (y LOC (*IN x)) ↔ ∃z ∃s [(z PARS y) ∧
  (s SUBS enclose) ∧ (s SCAR x) ∧ (s OBJ z)]                    (39)

The PARS term is necessary because the whole object y does not need to be enclosed by x if "*y in x*" holds (see Fig. 7.4).

The constructive specification of the meaning of prepositions reaches its limits within the framework of purely symbolic representations (see Method II in Table 7.1), since the existence of an axis with the reference object, the direction of the gravity, the concept of a perpendicular, and other factors play an important role in the definition of prepositions like "*at*", "*above*", "*under*", "*beside*", etc. Though all these concepts could be described by means of Multi-

Net, a symbolic representation alone is not adequate. In this case, geometric forms of representation (see Method I in Table 7.1) should be used as well, or at least a combination of symbolic and geometric methods. Therefore, only a semiformal approach shall be sketched here:

| | | | |
|---|---|---|---|
| above(x, o) | ↔ | [Perpendicular from x onto o in the direction of gravity meets o] | |
| on(x, o) | ↔ | [above(x, o) ∧ supports(x, o)] | (default) |
| below(x, o) | ↔ | [Perpendicular from x onto o against the direction of gravity meets o] | |
| over(x, o) | ↔ | [above(x, o) ∧ ¬ supports(x, o)] etc. | |

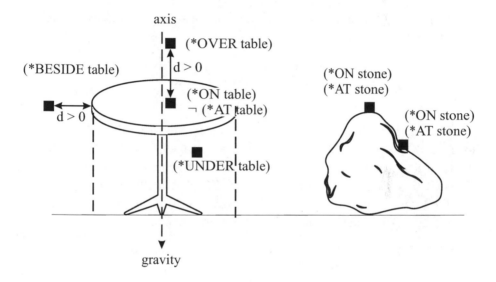

**Figure 7.5.** The role of gravity and body axes for the semantic interpretation of local prepositions

Figure 7.5 shows how complicated these relationships really are. Thus, for instance, one cannot always conclude from (o LOC (*ON m)) that (o LOC (*ABOVE m)). With a stone having no distinct axes, the phrase "*there is a colored spot / a moss cushion <u>on the stone</u>*" may be interpreted in such a way that the colored spot / the moss cushion are located on the whole visible surface of the stone. In the case of a table, however, the analogous phrase "*there is* *a colored spot / a moss cushion <u>on the table</u>*" would certainly mean that the colored spot / the moss cushion are on the tabletop.[14]

It is also possible to characterize the meaning of local prepositions axiomatically by contrasting them with the representations of other prepositions (in some cases, this approach involves even a negative explanation of concepts):[15]

- (o LOC (*ABOVE m)) → [¬(o LOC (*IN m)) ∧
  ¬ (o LOC (*UNDER m)) ∧ ¬(o LOC (*BESIDE m))]    (40)
- (o LOC (*IN m)) → [¬(o LOC (*ON m)) ∧ ¬(o LOC (*BESIDE m))
  ∧ ¬(o LOC (*ABOVE m))]    (41)
- (o LOC (*ON m)) → [¬(o LOC (*UNDER m)) ∧
  ¬(o LOC (*BESIDE m)) ∧ ¬(o LOC (*IN m))]    (42)

But there are also axioms which do not contain "negative characterizations" of local functions:

- (o LOC (*IN m))∧ (m LOC (*IN n)) → (o LOC (*IN n))    (43)
- (o LOC (*ABOVE m)) → (o LOC (*OVER m)) ∨
  (o LOC (*ON m))    (44)

With regard to the axiomatic characterization of local relationships, the following observation might be of interest: The statement that certain spatial regions exclude each other can be expressed at the metalevel by the relation CONTR.[16] At that, the relationship $(*FLP_i \text{ CONTR } *FLP_j)$ with $i \neq j$ means that the local functions $*FLP_i$ and $*FLP_j$ (see Part II, Sect. 18.3) are contrary to each other, explicated formally by the axiom schema:

- $(*FLP_i \text{ CONTR } *FLP_j) \rightarrow$
  $\forall o \forall m [(o \text{ LOC } (*FLP_i \text{ m})) \rightarrow \neg(o \text{ LOC } (*FLP_j \text{ m}))]$    (45)

Summarizing, one can state that the modeling of spatial interrelationships by means of symbolic logical methods is certainly insufficient. On the other hand, geometric representations are generally very far from natural language formulations and from meaning representations automatically generated by methods of computational linguistics. In artificial intelligence, both

---

[14] It is not only the body axis of the object serving as a landmark but also the axis of the target object which play a role in this interpretation (see Sect. 7.1). This can be seen from the example: "*A vase <u>on the stone</u>*" or "*A vase stands <u>on the stone</u>*". Here, an interpretation that the vase is at the side of the stone can be excluded.

[15] The following formulas do not claim to be complete characterizations. They are rather thought to illustrate the method in principle.

[16] It must be remembered that relations and functions are nodes at a metalevel (i.e. they are concepts of a higher order), which can again be connected by relations.

approaches for the representation of spatial interrelationships are used, where the first (i.e. Method I in Table 7.1) is preferred in natural language processing systems, and the second (i.e. Method II in Table 7.1) is preferred with robots or in spatio-temporal databases. The fusion of both of these methods is a matter of future research.

## 7.3 Temporal Relations

Every situation s, i.e. every event and every state, which is described by a writer/speaker Sp and temporally ordered by her is assigned a time interval or a point of time t(s) on a linear temporal scale for which she assumes that s holds or exists. To convey this conception to the outside (i.e. to a partner in a communication act), the writer/speaker relates this "subjective" time interval t(s) of her inner mental world to explicit temporal specifications using certain temporal relationships. These time specifications are built by means of a **temporal comparison frame**, which is attached to s in a sentence or an utterance. This comparison frame will be denoted here by tv(s) or, for short, by tv, if no mistake is possible. tv(s) need not coincide with t(s).

- A **time interval** $z = (t_1, t_2)$ is represented by a pair of points $t_1$ and $t_2$ on a temporal scale, where $t_1 = \text{begin}(z)$ and $t_2 = \text{end}(z)$ denote the beginning and the end of z, respectively.

It must be emphasized that the "subjective" time interval t(s) of the speaker Sp introduced above need not be identical with the time interval corresponding to the validity of s in reality. The latter is denoted by $\hat{t}(s)$. This time interval need not be known by Sp; it is important only if one has to decide on the validity of the proposition made by Sp about s. It is not so important in the first instance to the representation of s itself.

The levels relevant to the temporal description of situations and their embedding into the actual time are summarized in Fig. 7.6, where the term **actual time** has to be understood as the intersubjective time fixed by social consensus. The fact that the levels shown in Fig. 7.6 have to be considered as different from each other can be illustrated by means of the following observations. The speaker Sp may quite correctly associate an event with the geological era "Cambrian" (expressed in the meaning representation by the relation TEMP). At the same time, she may mistakenly put this era at a wrong position on the generally accepted time scale fixed by geologists and paleontologists ($\rightarrow$ real time). Conversely, the period of time taken by Sp as Cambrian may coincide with the generally accepted geological convention, but the event s actually taking place in the Cambrian may have been transferred by Sp to another period (e.g. into the Devonian). This means that $\hat{t}(s)$ lies at a position other than tv(s) at the time scale.

In sentences like *"In the Middle Ages, there was no general compulsory school attendance."* the situation s (the nonexistence of a general compulsory school attendance) is related only to the Middle Ages ($\hat{=}$ tv(s)). Beyond that, there is no proposition. Actually, the situation s or the actual time $\hat{t}(s)$ have a much longer duration (in Germany, for instance, until the 17th or 18th century, when cumpulsory school attendance was introduced). Finally, the time intervals t(s) and tv(s) are also different in general, as can be seen from the sentence *"In spring (→ tv), I shall visit my friend"*. Though I may possibly know how much time the visit will actually take, it may be sufficient for a certain communicational purpose to use a vague temporal specification like *"in spring"*.

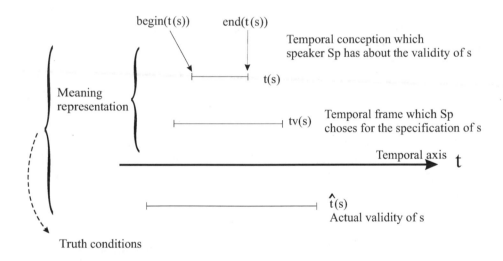

**Figure 7.6.** The different levels of observation with regard to the temporal embedding of situations

The whole descriptional situation, and together with that the knowledge representation, are complicated even more by the fact that the writer/speaker Sp need not use an explicit temporal specification tv to determine the time $t(s_1)$ of a certain situation $s_1$. They may as well use another situation $s_2$ with a corresponding $t(s_2)$ as a temporal orientation (as a **temporal landmark**, so to speak); see the following example.[17]

(7.13) "*When Max came home, the dinner was ready.*"

In natural language, time intervals are specified more or less sharply, where the "degree of fuzziness" always depends on the context, i.e. the corresponding temporal specifications are inherently vague. The precision or granularity of the time interval used often depends on the duration of the situation described. Examples:

(7.14) "*The lesson lasted from 8:30 a.m. until 10:00 a.m.*"

Granularity: With temporal specifications within a day → hours or minutes.

(7.15) "*The Assyrian empire lasted from the twentieth century B.C. until the sixth century B.C.*"

Granularity: With historical periods, centuries are often sufficiently accurate in a specification.

(7.16) "*The Paleozoic era lasted 340 million years.*"

Granularity: In geological periods of time, a hundred thousand years do not matter in general. 335 million years could also be an acceptable temporal specification in this context (but not 340,329,247 years, since this would suggest a temporal specification which is exact to a single year).

A **point of time** or a **moment** can be seen as a special case of a time interval $TP = (t_1, t_2)$ with $begin(TP) = end(TP) = t_1 = t_2$. Because of this the principle of vagueness or fuzziness stated for time intervals can also be transferred to moments. The phrase "*on January 3, 1998*" in many contexts denotes a point of time that is only roughly specified (it is then not conceived as a time interval). The phrase "*from January until December 1997*" analogously describes a time interval with very vague "points of time" as beginning and end. From the cognitive point of view and also with regard to natural language, it seems as if the human speaker/writer had a kind of "zooming" capability, so that a moment (like "*August 20*") may at one occasion be thought of as a point of time without inner extension and structure and at another occasion as a time interval into which many different singular events can be embedded (each of these variants depends on the sentence context and on the perspective of temporal resolution).

---

[17] Please note that at this stage it does not yet matter whether the sentences used as examples are true or false. It must be possible to discuss their intensional meaning and to represent it properly independent of this decision. It is only in the second step that one can decide whether a truth value can be assigned to a certain meaning representation or not, and, if this is possible, what truth value it is (see Sect. 8.2).

Examples:

(7.17) *"Goethe was born on August 20, 1749."*

(7.18) *"On August 20 there was nice weather."*

(7.19) *"In the morning of August 20 Paul attended school; then he had his lunch, and afterward he played with his friends."*

The vagueness discussed above has also been taken into consideration in the definitions of the temporal relations of MultiNet (see (46) through (51) below). Accordingly, in the expression ($s_1$ TEMP $s_2$) the time $t(s_1)$ may be identical with $t(s_2)$, but it may also be embedded into $t(s_2)$. What really holds depends essentially on the verb concept V governing $s_1$ (durative verb or not, "normal" duration of the event or state V vs. duration of $s_2$, etc.; see Sect. 7.4).

Examples:

(7.20) *"Yesterday afternoon, Peter ate a pear."*
    → Eating a pear normally does not take a whole afternoon.

(7.21) *"Yesterday afternoon, Peter relaxed at the beach."*
    → Relaxing probably took the whole afternoon.

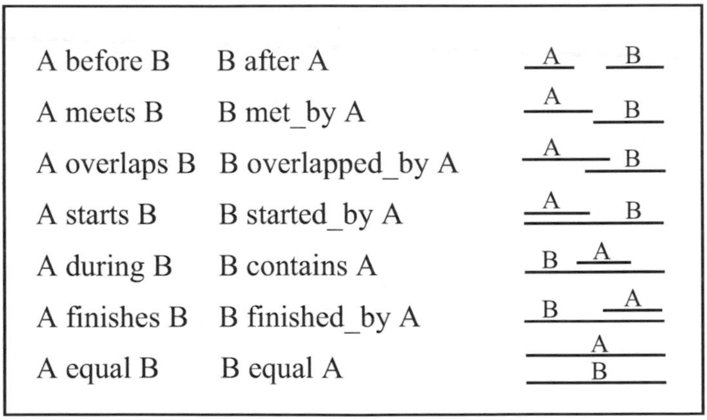

| A before B | B after A |
| A meets B | B met_by A |
| A overlaps B | B overlapped_by A |
| A starts B | B started_by A |
| A during B | B contains A |
| A finishes B | B finished_by A |
| A equal B | B equal A |

**Figure 7.7.** The relations between time intervals after [4]

In logic, time (corresponding to the model-theoretic "real time" introduced above) is often defined as a set of points densely lying on a temporal axis together with an ordering relation ≤, which is reflexive, antisymmetric, and transitive, where cycles of the kind a ≤ b ≤ c ≤ a are excluded [180]. In contrast, Allen [4] builds a time calculus on the basis of the interval conception alone. He argues that practically all **points of time** have, at least in principle, a finite extension (i.e. they are actually time intervals). Most papers on temporal logic distinguish seven (or if one is also counting the inverse relations, thirteen) possible relations between time intervals (see Fig. 7.7).

This is not the right place to investigate which logical consequences arise from the interval conception of time in contrast to the point conception, or whether the points on the temporal axis have to be considered as a continuum (like real numbers, corresponding to the prevailing time model of physics), or whether the time points lie densely in the mathematical sense everywhere on the time axis (like rational numbers). With regard to a discussion of these and other problems of temporal logic, we refer the reader to the literature (see, for instance, [263]). It is our aim here to discuss the definitions of temporal relations used in MultiNet for the modeling of cognitive relationships and for the semantic representation of natural language sentences (see the top part of Fig. 7.6). It is crucial what conclusions can be drawn in a QAS on the basis of these definitions. For instance, it is essential for an immediate understanding of a sentence like Sz = "*Until his promotion he was always short of money.*" uttered by speaker Sp, and for the semantic representation of this sentence, that Sp also accept the sentence "*Before his promotion he was always short of money.*" Knowing these relationships is more important to the understanding of Sz than is deciding on the truth value of Sz. In the following definitions of relations, only a situation $s_2$ and, together with it, the temporal point of orientation or temporal comparison frame $t(s_2)$ are used as a second argument of the time relations without loss of generality. To use an explicit temporal specification tv, the second argument has simply to be replaced by tv instead of $t(s_2)$.[18]

- **ANTE**
  Typical prepositions: "*before*" and "*after*"
  $$(s_1 \text{ ANTE } s_2) \Leftrightarrow [\text{begin}(s_1) < \text{begin}(s_2) \wedge \text{end}(s_1) \leq \text{begin}(s_2)] \qquad (46)$$
  Corresponding relations in Fig. 7.7: **before** and **after**.
  The definition (46) warrants that with a punctual event $s_1$ the time $t(s_1)$ does not lie within $t(s_2)$. In contrast to the relations **before** and **after**, it is permitted for ANTE that the intervals touch each other (cf. relation FIN).
  Example:
  (7.22) "[*Before World War I*]$^{\text{ANTE}_{arg2}}$ [*there were no cars.*]$^{\text{ANTE}_{arg1}}$"

---

[18] The superscripts $\text{REL}_{arg1}$ and $\text{REL}_{arg2}$, respectively, label the natural language paraphrase of the first and the second argument of relation REL in a sentence. The term "corresponding relation" in the definitions has to be understood as a rather loose relationship, and not as exact coincidence in meaning. This may already be seen from the fact that the corresponding definitions are related to different levels in Fig. 7.6.

- **FIN**

  Typical preposition: *"until"*               (only defined if $t(s_1)$ is an interval)

  $(s_1 \text{ FIN } s_2) \Leftrightarrow [\text{end}(s_1) = \text{begin}(s_2)]$ (47)

  Corresponding relations in Fig. 7.7: meets and met_by.

  From (47), the following implication can be inferred:

  $(s_1 \text{ FIN } s_2) \rightarrow (s_1 \text{ ANTE } s_2)$ (48),

  i.e. FIN is a special case of ANTE.

  Example:

  (7.23)  *"[Until the arrival of the police]*$^{\text{FIN}_{arg2}}$, *[all traces had been removed.]*$^{\text{FIN}_{arg1}}$*"*

- **STRT**.

  Typical preposition: *"since"*               (only defined if $t(s_1)$ is an interval)

  $(s_1 \text{ STRT } s_2) \Leftrightarrow [\text{begin}(s_1) = \text{begin}(s_2)]$ (49)

  Corresponding relations in Fig. 7.7: starts and started_by.

  Examples:

  (7.24)  *"[Since the Second World War]*$^{\text{STRT}_{arg2}}$ *[there exist jet fighters.]*$^{\text{STRT}_{arg1}}$*"* [19]

  (7.25)  *"[Since the emergence of the universe,]*$^{\text{STRT}_{arg2}}$ *[there has been space and time.]*$^{\text{STRT}_{arg1}}$*"*

  As can be seen from the second example, it would not be advantageous to add the expression $[\text{end}(s_2) < \text{end}(s_1)]$ conjunctively to the right side of the definition of STRT, otherwise the meaning of *"since"* would not be covered by STRT. In this way, the relation STRT is different from starts in Fig. 7.7.

- **TEMP**

  Typical prepositions: *"in"*, *"at"*, *"on"*

  $(s_1 \text{ TEMP } s_2) \Leftrightarrow [\text{begin}(s_1) \geq \text{begin}(s_2) \wedge \text{end}(s_1) \leq \text{end}(s_2)]$ (50)

  Corresponding relations in Fig. 7.7: during and contains.

  Axiom (50) describes that $t(s_1)$ falls into $t(s_2)$, but it may also completely fill up $t(s_2)$.

  Example:

  (7.26)  *"[At Christmas]*$^{\text{TEMP}_{arg2}}$ *[Peter got a bicycle.]*$^{\text{TEMP}_{arg1}}$*"*

  (7.27)  *"[In the Middle Ages]*$^{\text{TEMP}_{arg2}}$ *[there was no compulsory school attendance.]*$^{\text{TEMP}_{arg1}}$*"*

- **DUR**

  Typical prepositions: *"during"*, *"in the course of"*

  $(s_1 \text{ DUR } s_2) \Leftrightarrow [\text{begin}(s_1) = \text{begin}(s_2) \wedge \text{end}(s_1) = \text{end}(s_2)]$ (51)

---

[19] This example shows that a clear-cut definition of the semantic relation **STRT** is problematic. Does the sample sentence (7.24) really mean *"from the very beginning of World War I"*? How precisely the start of situation $s_1$ is specified by the assertion $(s_1 \text{ STRT } s_2)$ depends on the extent of $t(s_2)$ and the more or less sharp interpretation of the terms $\text{begin}(s_1)$ and $\text{begin}(s_2)$.

Corresponding relations in Fig. 7.7: **equal**.

Axiom (51) expresses that DUR is a special case of TEMP. Furthermore, the following equivalence holds:

$$(s \text{ DUR } z) \wedge z = (t_1, t_2) \leftrightarrow [(s \text{ STRT } t_1) \wedge (s \text{ FIN } t_2)] \tag{52}$$

Example:

(7.28)  "[*Peter slept*]$^{DUR_{arg1}}$ [*during the (whole) lesson.*]$^{DUR_{arg2}}$"

Since the functions begin(x) and end(x) are defined for both, situations and time intervals, it can be easily seen that the relations (46) through (51) can also be extended to time intervals as arguments (see the definitions of temporal relations in Part II).

The relation characterized by **overlaps** or **overlapped_by** in Fig. 7.7 has not been given a direct counterpart in MultiNet as it can be expressed by the combination FIN + TEMP (see Fig. 7.8).

a) *"Max worked on into the morning."*

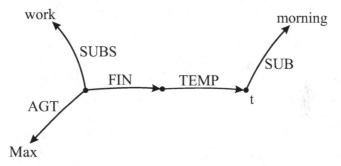

b) *"Max worked until the morning."*

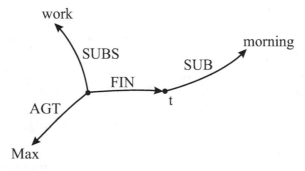

**Figure 7.8.** The overlapping of time intervals

Also, the relation denoted by finishes or finished_by in Fig. 7.8 seems not to be an elementary one with regard to its use in natural language interpretation (in its core, it is a description of end(B)=end(A)). Moreover, the vagueness of A and the above-mentioned zooming effect, as well as a certain cognitive dominance of the beginning of the situation used as a temporal landmark, play the role of a superimposing effect with regard to the semantic interpretation.[20] Finally, it must be emphasized that the specification of prepositions, together with relations corresponding to them, is only useful for a first orientation since there is no 1:1 correspondence between prepositions and semantic relations. Thus, the word *"during"* is actually a typical paraphrase of the relation DUR, but there are also sentences like *"During the event an explosion was heard."* where this preposition has to be translated by TEMP.

Reichenbach proposed a temporal model for the treatment of the grammatical category of **tense** of English [211] which is also valid for German (see Fig. 7.9). According to this model, the moment a sentence is uttered has to be considered for the embedding of the semantic representation into the temporal system as well. Altogether, three moments are necessary for a proper interpretation of the grammatical category **tense**.

With regard to MultiNet, no additional representational means are required to deal properly with the category "tense" (Ge: "Tempus"). To achieve a proper interpretation of the tense system, the embedding of the utterance into the dialogue situation has also to be considered. The complete discourse situation can be characterized as follows, where the different temporal points of reference proposed by Reichenbach and their interrelationships are explicitly shown in the semantic representation in Fig. 7.10:

(7.29)  *"Sp states / says at time point $t_s$ that the Situation $s_e$ holds at the temporal point of reference $t_r$ with the temporal restriction* ($s_e$ TEMP = $t_e$)."

The problem is not so much to represent this complex situation adequately with regard to its semantics, but rather to find the correct temporal relationships (maybe even automatically) and to use them properly during inferential answer finding in a QAS. Here, one has to reconsider that tense is a grammatical category while time is a semantic phenomenon. The translation from one layer to the other has to be done by the analysis (including the assimilation

---

[20] Thus, the relation between the semantic representatives of the sentence parts A and B in *"The economical rise of the state (B) came to an end due to Second World War (A)"* should not be expressed by Allen's relation (B finished_by A) (which could be expected because of the naming of the relation), but rather by means of the MultiNet relation FIN. The analogue holds for the German sentence: *"Der ökonomische Aufstieg des Staates (B) wurde durch den Zweiten Weltkrieg (A) beendet."*

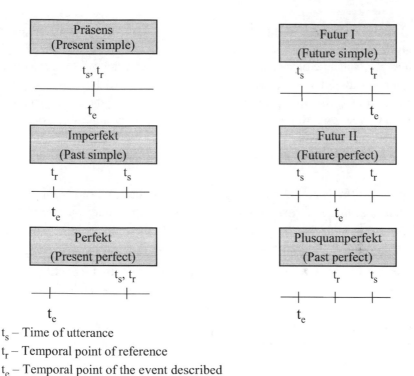

$t_s$ – Time of utterance

$t_r$ – Temporal point of reference

$t_e$ – Temporal point of the event described

**Figure 7.9.** The logical interpretation of the tense system in German and English

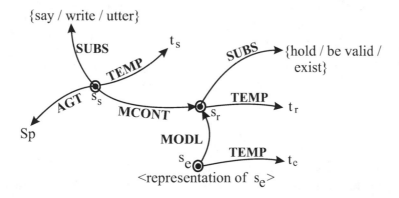

**Figure 7.10.** The embedding of a temporally specified utterance (a description of a situation) in the dialogue situation taking into account the temporal points of reference by Reichenbach

process) and, in the inverse direction, by the generation of natural language expressions in a QAS.

If there is no change of speaker, or if the time of deliverance of the information can be considered as fixed (as is generally the case with a text), the explicit representation of $s_s$ and the specification of the time $t_s$ may be relinquished.[21] The semantic representation can be reduced to the actually interesting situation $s_e$ and the time $t_e$ connected to it if one takes into account only the present, future, and past tenses, since the time specifications $t_r$ and $t_e$ coincide in these cases.

A special difficulty is associated with the semantic interpretation of the present tense, as in the German sentence *"Delphine schwimmen im Meer."* (En: *"Dolphins swim in the sea."*). There are principally three different possibilities for a semantic interpretation:[22]

a) The interpretation as an event taking place or a state actually existing at the moment the sentence is uttered (*"Just now, dolphins are swimming in the sea."*); characterized by
[**GENER**(sv) = *sp*] and (sv TEMP PRES).

b) The interpretation as a potential capability (*"Dolphins are principally able to swim in the sea."*) or as a disposition (*"Dolphins normally swim in the sea."*), characterized by
[**GENER**(sv) = *ge*] without temporal specification.

c) The interpretation as a temporally universally quantified proposition (*"Dolphins always swim in the sea."*, represented by means of
(sv TEMP always) (see Table 9.3).

In the case of special states of affairs with [**GENER**(sv) = *sp*] interpretation a) should always be assumed as default, by convention, if no temporal relations are explicitly given in the semantic representation.

## 7.4   Situations and Times

In systems of temporal logic which are model-theoretically founded, there are essentially three approaches for ascertaining the temporal validity of situations, which can be seen as alternatives with regard to their underlying assumptions:

• An approach based on **points of time** (see [179], [180]), where time is thought as a linearly ordered set of idealized temporal points;

---

[21] In this case, the situation $s_s$ and time $t_s$ of Fig. 7.10 have to be added intellectually.

[22] These interpretations strongly depend on prosodic information and do not run entirely parallel in English and German. Because of that, we only discuss the German sentence.

- An approach based on **intervals** (see [4]), where every event (however elementary it may be) is assumed to have a finite temporal extension, and where temporal points are judged to be idealizations not adequate to natural language;
- An approach based on **events** (see [74], [134]), which takes a system of events as a starting point and tries to derive the temporal structure from the ordering of these events.

Each of these approaches has its own difficulties. In this context, only the problem of the "dividing instant", which is characteristic of the first two approaches, shall be mentioned (for a more detailed discussion we refer you to the literature; see, for instance, [263], [134, Chap. 5], and [266]). This problem is illustrated in Fig. 7.11.

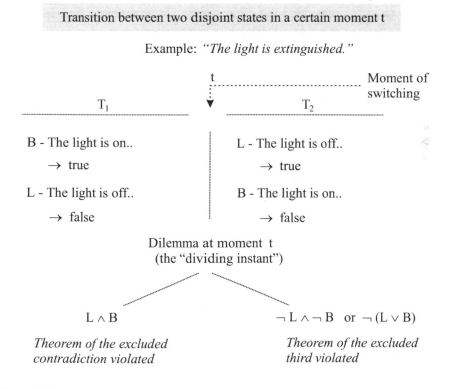

Figure 7.11. The problem of the dividing instant

The question is, which of the states shown in Fig. 7.11 holds in the instant dividing the beginning and the end of a switching process? The difficulty arises from the fact that one tries to apply natural language predicates which in their meaning already bear a two-valued aspect (like *"switched on/switched off"* or, for short, *"on/off"*) to transitional situations whose descriptions can neither be built up adequately on the basis of these natural language expressions nor by pure logical means (in any case, not on the basis of a two-valued logic).[23] A similar problem arises, by the way, with the interval-based approach, if somebody asks what truth-value has to be attached to the propositions *"The light is burning."* and *"The light is not burning."* during the whole interval $T = T_1 + T_2$ in Fig. 7.11 (see [134, Chap. 5]).

With regard to a QAS, all three approaches of temporal characterization of situations (by points of time, by time intervals, and by other situations) are relevant. But it should be emphasized once more that the conception of a "point of time" with MultiNet does not mean an idealized point on the temporal axis, but rather a more or less exactly described temporal specification which is not further resolved by the speaker. Corresponding to that, a question aiming at these specifications can be answered only more or less exactly.

The classification of situations into states [**SORT** = *st*] and events [**SORT** = *dy*] (see Sect. 3.2.1) does not capture all semantic features of verbs. Thus, an event may be finished or it may last a longer time, it may be habitually repeated, or it may occur at a singular point of time only. To describe these and other features, some languages (especially the Slavonic languages and, to a certain degree English and French) have a special means of expression called **aspect**. The semantic interpretation of the English aspect is discussed in [73].[24]

In German, the grammatical category "aspect" does not exist. However, there are equivalent expressional means like certain adverbs and different **types of action** (Ge: "Aktionsarten") for the verbs. The latter, as far as they are lexically or morphologically marked, are represented in an overview in Tables 7.3 and 7.4. For every action type there is a special row showing in an abbreviated

---

[23] An adequate description of collapsing electromagnetic fields during switching processes could at best be given by means of partial differential equations. These characterize complex physical processes which, at least in principle, could also be described by natural language, though no one would do that. The detailed inner analysis of the "dividing instant" is simply not interesting for normal human communication; there is nothing to be stated and nothing to be inferred about it at this level. For people who have to investigate these matters, physics provides the proper language, not logic.

[24] In Russian, there are still further possibilities for differentiation with regard to these features in connection with verbs of movement. Thus, the habitually repeated "going" is already lexically distinguished from a single act of going: "Он ходит в школу" (En: *"He (regularly/repeatedly) goes to school"*, Ge: *"Er geht (regelmäßig) zur Schule"*) vs. "Он идёт в школу" (En: *"He (just now) is going to the school"*, Ge: *"Er geht (gerade jetzt) zur Schule"*); see [187].

form which expressional means of MultiNet have to be used to represent the semantic specialities of the corresponding situation (named s in all rows).[25]

The interrelationships involved in the semantic representation of the above-mentioned actions can be described only by means of more detailed meaning postulates (entailments) related to the specific action. Thus, line 2 in Table 7.3 has to be read as follows:

Associated with the action s (*sleep to the end*, *eat up*), there is a situation s' (*sleep*, *eat*) which is finished by s, and a final state z (e.g. the carrier of the state is awake or the food is finished, respectively) holds as a result after the end of s'.

It should be emphasized that the above types of action cannot be sharply discriminated. For instance, there are close relationships between the action types described in rows 2 and 5, or between rows 8 and 9 of Table 7.3; also the classification of verbs into the classes of rows 11 and 15 cannot be taken as unique. Also the affixes given in column 2 of Tables 7.3 and 7.4 cannot be seen as strict criteria. Nevertheless, the tables can be used as a basic orientation, where the semiformal specifications given in the last row of every type of action delivers a first indication of the inference rules connected with these action types. The latter also have consequences on the analysis in a QAS. Thus, verbs belonging to class 12 are not compatible with the relations DUR, STRT, and FIN, which is the reason why sentences like "*The bomb has been exploding since half past six.*" are semantically excluded. Figure 7.12 gives a short impression on how to use the action types discussed so far in semantic representations (as examples, actions from classes in rows 6 and 9 are chosen). The representational elements of MultiNet that are typical of each of the action classes (marking, so to speak, the distinguishing semantic features) are emphasized in the graphic representation of Fig. 7.12 by means of heavy letters and by putting the corresponding relations into boxes.

It might be interesting for the sake of elucidation to state the differences between "*grow*" (in the sense of "*The grass is growing*") and "*enlarge*"; while in the first case the underlying concept **grow** is of sort *dn*, the concept **enlarge** is of sort *da*. Moreover, **grow** in the sense indicated has no agent, whereas **enlarge** does.

---

[25] SORT(x) in Tables 7.3 and 7.4 denotes the sort of x, and QUANT(x) denotes the intensional quantification of x expressed by the layer attribute QUANT. t(s) stands for the time attached to s by the speaker. With regard to the quantification of time, we refer to Chap. 9. s' denotes a situation associated with s which can not be generally specified since it depends on the specific event.

| Aktionsart (Aspect type) (Latin/German name) | Examples | Semantic Characteristics |
|---|---|---|
| 1. attenuativ/ diminutiv/deminutiv | *etwas schlafen* (*sleep a bit*) *etwas nachdenken* (*think a little*) | [low intensity] |
| (s MANNR $\langle$degree of intensity$\rangle$) |||
| 2. deliminativ | *ausschlafen* (*sleep to the end*) *aufessen* (*eat up*) | [temporal limitation] |
| $\exists$s' (s' FIN s) $\wedge$ (s' RSLT $\langle$specific final state$\rangle$) |||
| 3. diminutiv-iterativ | Suffix "*-eln*" *hüsteln* (*cough slightly*) *kränkeln* (*to be sickly*) | [repeating in irregular intervals with decreased intensity] |
| $\langle$like 1.$\rangle$ $\wedge$ $\exists$t (s TEMP t) $\wedge$ [QUANT(t) = repeated] |||
| 4. durativ | *lieben* (*love*), *fühlen* (*feel*) *schlafen* (*sleep*) | [longer duration] |
| $\exists$t (s DUR t) $\wedge$ [SORT(s) = $dy$] $\vee$ [SORT(s) = $st$] |||
| 5. egressiv | Prefix "*er-*"; *ersteigen* (*climb to the top*) *erobern* (*conquer*) | [Conclusion of an action emphasizing the end/the result] |
| $\exists$s' (s RSLT s') $\wedge$ [SORT(s') = $st$] |||
| 6. evolutiv | *sich entwickeln* (*develop itself*) *wachsen* (*grow*) | [not oriented toward a specific result, qualitative or quantitative change] |
| (s INIT $\langle$attribute with value $v_1$ $\rangle$) $\wedge$ (s RSLT $\langle$attribute with value $v_2$ $\rangle$) $\wedge$ (($v_1 < v_2$) $\vee$ ($v_2 < v_1$)) |||
| 7. faktitiv | *bauen* (*built*) *schreiben* (*write*) | [action with a resulting object] |
| $\exists$x (s RSLT x) $\wedge$ [SORT(x) = $o$] |||
| 8. inchoativ | *verwelken* (*wilt*) *festigen* (*strengthen*) | [gradual development] |
| $\exists$x (x CHPE s) $\wedge$ [SORT(x) = $p$] $\wedge$ [SORT(s) = $dy$] |||
| 9. ingressiv/initiv | Prefix "*auf-*"/"*los-*" *aufgehen* (*rise*) *losfahren* (*drive off*) | [starting point of an action] |
| (s AFF o) $\wedge$ (s TEMP t) $\Longrightarrow$ $\exists$s' (s' SCAR o) $\wedge$ (s' STRT t) or: (s AGT o) $\wedge$ (s TEMP t) $\Longrightarrow$ $\exists$s' (s' AGT o) $\wedge$ (s' STRT t) |||
| 10. iterativ/frequenta- tiv/multiplikativ | *schaufeln* (*shovel*) *zittern* (*tremble*) | [action repeated within itself] |
| $\exists$s',t' $\langle$s' = partial action of s (parameterized by t')$\rangle$ $\wedge$ (s DUR t) $\wedge$ [t(s') = t'] $\wedge$ (t' TEMP t) $\wedge$ [QUANT(t') = several] |||
| 11. kausativ | *töten* (*kill*) *induzieren* (*induce*) | [giving rise to an action or a state] |
| $\exists$s' (s CAUS s') at the individual level, and (s IMPL s') at the generic level |||
| 12.momentan/ punctual | *explodieren* (*explode*) *blitzen* (*flash*) | [restricted to a time moment] |
| t(s) = $\langle t_1, t_1 \rangle$ |||

**Table 7.3.** Overview of the different types of action in German after [49] (Part I)

| Aktionsart (Aspect type) (Latin/German name) | Examples | Semantic Characteristics |
|---|---|---|
| 13. mutuell | *miteinander spielen* (*play with each other*) *miteinander ringen* (*wrestle with each other*) | [actions which are carried out mutually] |
| | $\exists x,y\ (s\ AGT\ x) \wedge (s\ AGT\ y) \wedge x \neq y$ | |
| 14. resultativ/ perfektiv/effektiv | *zerreißen* (*tear apart*) *sich überarbeiten* (*overwork*) | [a resulting state is included which holds beyond the end of the action] |
| | $\exists s',t\ (s\ TEMP\ t) \wedge (s\ RSLT\ s') \wedge [SORT(s') = st] \wedge (s'\ STRT\ t)$ | |
| 15. semelfaktiv | *spalten* (*split/chop*) *zerstören* (*destroy*) | [action which can be carried out only once] |
| | $\exists t\ (s\ TEMP\ t) \wedge \neg\ [QUANT(t) = \mathsf{several}]$ | |
| 16. stativ | *liegen* (*lie*) *schweigen* (*be silent*) | [states] |
| | $t(s) = \langle t_1, t_2 \rangle \wedge t_1 \neq t_2$ | |

**Table 7.4.** Overview of the different types of action in German after [49] (Part II)

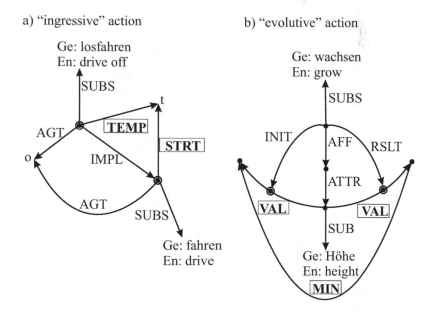

a) "ingressive" action

b) "evolutive" action

**Figure 7.12.** Example illustrating the representation of two different types of action

Allen introduces three predicates in his "Theory of action and time" [4], namely HOLDS(p, t), OCCUR(e, t) and OCCURRING(pr, t), which essentially characterize the semantics of "properties" p, of "events" e, and of "processes" pr. Unfortunately, it does not become quite clear what properties really are. Thus, he introduces a type PROPERTY by *"Terms of type PROPERTY, denoting propositions that can hold or not hold during a particular time."* (page 128), which seems to be too unspecific and which in the sort hierarchy of MultiNet would comprise the assignment of properties to objects as well as to situations (including processes and events). Also, the distinction between events and processes by means of such criteria as countability or noncountability seems not to be compulsory. Thus, after Allen, the sentence *"I'm walking."* describes a process, while *"I'm walking to the store."* is classified as an event. In MultiNet, the concept walk characterizes a "Vorgang" (the latter term is not fully equivalent to the English word "event") or, to be more specific, an action, independent of whether or not the verb is morpho-syntactically used in the progressive form. The differences in meaning between such sentences have to be expressed by other means (by temporal specifications, like duration, by repeatability, by goal-directedness expressed with meaning postulates, etc.) as discussed above in connection with action types and aspects.

In the following discussion, the three predicates mentioned above will be considered in more detail, and the parallels between them and the semantic representations of MultiNet will be investigated.

- HOLDS(p, t): This relation (according to Allen) is valid if and only if the property p holds at time t. The following axiom is postulated for this predicate[26]:

$$\text{HOLDS}(p, T) \leftrightarrow [\forall t \ \text{IN}(t, T) \rightarrow \text{HOLDS}(p, t)] \tag{53}$$

From the point of view of MultiNet, two cases have to be discerned:

a) Situation s of type: (o PROP p)          [assignment of a property in the narrower sense]

It is **categorically true** that

$$(s \ \text{DUR} \ T) \rightarrow [\forall t \ (t \ \text{TEMP} \ T) \rightarrow (s \ \text{TEMP} \ t)] \tag{54}$$

b) Situation s of type: (s SUBS z) $\wedge$ [SORT(z) = st]          [state]

In this case, an axiom analogous to (54) is not categorically valid, but valid only with exceptions.

**Default assumption**:

$$(s \ \text{DUR} \ T) \rightarrow [\forall t \ (t \ \text{TEMP} \ T) \rightarrow (s \ \text{TEMP} \ t)] \tag{55}$$

---

[26] Following Allen, the predicate IN(t, T) holds if and only if the time interval t is completely contained in the time interval T.

With a state s lasting over a longer period T, one would accept (s DUR T) even if there were a short interruption for time moments t with IN(t, T) and ¬ (s TEMP t). In this way, states differ from properties.

- OCCUR(e, T): This relation of Allen holds if and only if e occurs during T, but not in a partial interval t of T. Allen postulates the following axiom:

(OCCUR e, T) ∧ IN(t, T) → ¬ OCCUR(e,t)                    (56)

With this definition, the relation OCCUR(e, T) seems to be too sharply defined. (When exactly does the relation OCCUR(e, T) hold if e is described by e = "*Yesterday Peter got a new bicycle*"?) Such a relation neither corresponds to natural language practice, nor is it possible to determine its validity with model-theoretic methods. We rather need expressional means which allow us to specify that an event e is falling into the time period T, and this again should allow for inferences like "e does not occur before T and does not occur after T".

For this purpose, MultiNet provides the relation (e TEMP t), which is connected (among other things) to the following axiom:

(e TEMP t) → [¬(e ANTE t) ∧ ¬(t ANTE e)]                  (57)

- OCCURRING(pr, T): This relation of Allen holds if and only if the process pr is running in the interval T and in at least one partial interval t of T. From that, the following axiom can be derived:

OCCURRING(pr, T) ↔ [∃t IN(t, T) ∧ OCCURRING(pr, t)]      (58)

This axiom, at least in principle, allows for an infinite nesting of intervals, where for each of the intervals contained in another, the process pr may be meaningfully stated. However, for each process s there is a lower boundary $\bar{t}_s$ of temporal resolution below which s may not be stated. Actually, $\bar{t}_s$ is different for every s; with s = **clatter** it may be $\bar{t}_s = 0.1$ sec, and with s = **shovel** the boundary may be $\bar{t}_s = 10$ sec.

Summarizing, one may postulate for MultiNet:

Situation s of type: (s SUBS **process**)

**Default assumption**:

(s DUR T) → [∀t (t TEMP T) ∧ (length(t) ≥ $\bar{t}_s$) → (s TEMP t)]    (59)

It does not pay to formalize these interrelationships in greater detail because it is impossible to determine properly the time $\bar{t}_s$ for every process s.

A definition of temporal relations that tries to model the fuzziness of language by means of exact time intervals (on the basis of whatever approach) will run into difficulties. For this reason, the terms begin(s) and end(s) used in Formulas (46) through (51) also have to be regarded as fuzzy concepts. This is taken into consideration in a QAS, among other things, during answer generation, where the terms mentioned are translated into corresponding natural language expressions whose meanings are also defined only very vaguely (e.g. *"at the beginning"*, *"start at / in"*, *"initially"*, *"at the end"*, *"finally"*, which may be combined with fuzzy temporal specifications such as *"in the evening"*, *"in summer"*, etc.).

The differences between states, events, and processes, which are widely characterized by the fact, that states are homogeneously valid in time (i.e. they hold without interruption), events take place in a relatively short period of time, and processes are heterogeneous, will not be discussed here further. In particular the condition of heterogeneity for processes is not unchallenged (see [74]).

# Chapter 8

# Modality and Negation

## 8.1 The Modal Characterization of Situations

By modality in the broadest sense we mean the validity assigned by the speaker to his utterances (see [35, p. 345]). We call the different means a language provides for expressing modalities **modal field** or **modal system**.[1]

A comprehensive investigation of the modal system of German stems from Gerstenkorn [77]. He identifies the following phenomena within the German modal system: [2]

1. Negations (see Sect. 8.2)                                    [1. - 2. Negation]
2. Conjunctions and prepositions
   (like "*neither - nor*", "*without*", or "*except*")
3. Modal adverbs and auxiliaries
4. Nouns and adjectives
5. Mood of the verb                                              [3. - 7. Modalities in
   (especially indicative vs. subjunctive)                       the narrower sense]
6. Modal infinitive
7. Modal verbs
8. Modal particles, interjections                                [Emotional aspect]

---

[1] For the sake of terminological clarity it should be remarked that the word "*modal*" in English and German is used at least in two senses. On the one hand, "*modal*" is used in phrases like "modal conjunctions", "modal adverbial qualification", or "modal descriptions" to characterize adverbial qualifications belonging to the field of the verb and specifying the manner of an action or of a situation. This is the meaning used in Sect. 5.2.3. On the other hand, the word "*modal*" (as in "*modal verb*"or "*modal auxiliary*") is used to characterize the modification of a whole sentence or clause by specifying the attitude of the speaker (writer) with regard to the content of the sentence.

[2] Although Gerstenkorn's results apply primarily to German, a large part of them can also be applied to English. While the morphological, lexical, and semantic phenomena of both languages have a lot in common, the syntactic phenomena show larger differences. Even if emphasis is laid on the German modal system in this chapter, the striking parallelism between German and English with regard to the modal phenomena should become sufficiently clear through the English translations given in the text.

It can be seen from this summarization that negation, as well as the conjunctions and prepositions connected to them, are also included in the modal system (see Points 1 and 2). This will be dealt with separately in Sect. 8.2.[3] Also, the subjective emotional attitude of the speaker is considered as part of the modal system by some scholars. This aspect is expressed mainly by means of modal particles and interjections (see Point 8). In German, the following modal particles are typical: *"denn"*, *"doch"*, *"ja"*, *"auch"*, *"nur"*, *"bloß"*, *"eben"*, *"halt"*, *"aber"*, *"mal"*, *"etwa"*, among others.

In a QAS, the distinction between modal particles and other homonymous particles is possibly of importance, because the former may be omitted without great loss of information, but the latter may not. In German, it could be helpful for the disambiguation of the spoken language that modal particles in a sentence are never emphasized (although they have a special expressive character).

Examples:

(8.1)  Ge: *"Ist der Rechner auch billig?"*                              [modal particle]
       En: *"Is the computer really cheap?"*

(8.2)  *"Ist der Rechner auch billig?"*                                [no modal particle]
       En: *"Is this computer also cheap?"*

Modal particles play only a minor role in many fields of discourse, since the expression of emotional attitudes with factual information or in technical descriptions is not usually desired. Besides that, modal particles generally have a small informational value, which is the reason why this aspect will not be considered here further. Therefore, only the semantic representation of the phenomena summarized in Points 3 through 7 will be dealt with in Sect. 8.3.

The modal aspect hidden in many sentences in present tense is more a problem of the logical interpretation of generic situations than of the explicit semantic representation of modalities.

Example:

(8.3)  Ge: *"Peter spielt Klavier."*     En: *"Peter plays the piano."* /
                                             *"Peter is playing piano."*

This sentence has two interpretations in German:

a) an **actual** one, realized, for instance, if the sentence is serving as an answer to the question *"What is Peter doing just now?"* In this case the present tense

---

[3] The opinion that negation has to be considered part of the modal system in the broadest sense is also supported by Admoni [2, p. 33] who states that words of negation are used to express the attitude of the speaker with regard to the content of his or her speech, and thus the negation has to be classified as a "modal category". It is just this view which finds its correspondence in the representational means of MultiNet.

is used for the specification of a certain time represented by
(s TEMP now).

b) a **potential** one, realized, for instance, if the teacher is asking his or her
students about their abilities. The interpretation prevailing in this context
introduces a modal aspect, which can be paraphrased by *"Peter is able to*
*play the piano"*, i.e. he does not really carry out this activity at the moment
the query is uttered.

A similar problem can be observed with the interpretation of general proposi-
tions in the present tense that contain plural constructions or generic actants:
*"Weaverbirds build artistic nests."* or *"The weaverbird builds artistic nests."*
The semantic interpretation of such sentences is dealt with in Chap. 9.


## 8.2   Negation

There is a plenitude of carriers of negation which directly or indirectly express negated propositions in natural languages. In the following, the carriers
of negation for German, compiled by Gerstenkorn [77], Helbig/Rickens [104],
and Stickel [252], will be summarized. To illustrate the (almost) parallel language phenomena in English, translations will be given in parentheses.

A) Words of negation:
   *"nicht"*, *"nichts"*, *"kein(-e, -er, -es)"*, *"niemand"*, *"nie"*, *"niemals"*, *"nir-*
   *gends"*, *"nirgendwo"*, *"nirgendwohin"*, *"nirgendwoher"*, *"keinesfalls"*, *"kei-*
   *neswegs"*, *"nein"*, and the negated numeral *"keinerlei"*
   (En: *"no"*, *"nothing"*, *"none"*, *"nobody"*, *"never"*, *"nowhere"*, *"by no*
   *means"*, *"under no circumstances"*, and *"no … what(so)ever"*[4])

B) Affix negation:
   *"un-"*, *"a-"*, *"dis-"*, *"des-"*, *"i(n)-"*, *"miß-"*, *"-los"*, and *"nicht-"*
   (En: *"un-"*, *"a-"*, *"dis-"*, *"i(n)-"*, *"mis-"*, *"-less"*, and *"non-"*)

C) Negation by conjunctions:
   – Coordinative negation: *"weder – noch"* and *"entweder – oder"*
     (En: *"neither – nor"* and *"either – or"*)
   – Conditional negation: *"sonst"* and *"andernfalls"*
     (En: *"otherwise"*)

---

[4] The last three negations (which are not expressed by a single word in English) and the coincidence of different German negators like *"nirgendwo"* and *"nirgendwohin"* in English (we
have only *"nowhere"* for both lexemes) indicate the breaks in the general parallelism even in
such similar languages as German and English.

- Modal negation: *"ohne daß"*, *"statt daß"*, *"ohne zu"*, and *"statt zu"*
  (En: *"without"* (conj.) and *"instead of"* + gerund)

D) Negation by prepositions:
   *"außer"*, *"ohne"*, *"(an)statt"*, and *"anstelle"*
   (En: *"without"* (prep.) and *"instead of"* + NP)

E) Relationship between Negation and Limitation:
   *"nur"*, *"bloß"*, and *"lediglich"*
   (En: *"only"*, *"solely"*, and *"merely"*)

F) Relationship between comparison and negation:
   *"weniger"*, *"die meisten"*, *"mehr"*, ...
   (En: *"fewer"*, *"most"*, *"more"*, ...)

G) Verbs implying a negation:
   *"vermeiden"*, *"verhindern"*, *"verbieten"*, *"warnen"*, ...
   (En: *"avoid"*, *"prevent"*, *"forbid"*, *"warn"*, ...)

H) Counterfactuals and optative clauses.

A special problem with regard to negated utterances is connected with the decision about whether they have to be classified as "sentence negation" or as "constituent negation", i.e. whether the whole sentence or only a part of it has been negated. The opinions published in the literature differ with regard to this point. While Hartung does not accept the necessity of discrimination between sentence negation and constituent negation [101][5], other scholars like Hajičova [89] and Helbig/Rickens [104] hold the opinion that the different types of negation have to be discerned not only in the surface structure but also in the deep structure. The latter view is also assumed in MultiNet, since otherwise the presuppositions connected with negated sentences could not be inferred.

Helbig/Rickens [104] give the following rules for the distinction of sentence negation and special negation (constituent negation) based on the position of the negator *"nicht"* (En: *"not"*) in German sentences[6]:

a) *"nicht"* (*"not"*) as **special negation (constituent negation)** is positioned immediately before the negated constituent.

---

[5] Thus, on page 15 of the cited work, he writes :
"There are special arguments from generative grammar questioning the traditional distinction between sentence negation and word negation ... An alternative is given by the proposal that primarily (i.e. at the deep structure level – annotation by the author) there is only a unified negation, and that only secondarily (i.e. at the surface structure level – annotation by the author) a kind of word negation is emerging under certain contextual conditions."

[6] Because of the use of *"to do"* in negated English sentences, these rules cannot simply be transferred to English.

*"Der Mörder hat das Opfer <u>nicht</u> mit diesem Messer getötet."*

(En: *"The murderer did not kill the victim with this knife."*)

Exceptions:

– The negated constituent bears a clearly audible stress.

*"<u>Heute</u> ist mein Freund nicht gekommen."*

(En: *"<u>Today</u>, my friend did not come."*)

– With negated modal words, the negator *"nicht"* is always postponed.

*"Peter kommt <u>wahrscheinlich nicht</u>"* or *"Er <u>darf nicht</u> von zu Hause weg-bleiben."* (En: *"Peter will probably not come."* or *"He is not allowed to stay away from home."*)

b) The negator *"nicht"* as **sentence negation** is drawn to the end of a sentence and together with the verb constitutes the so-called "sentence bracket".

– *"Peter sah das Auto nicht."* (En: *"Peter did not see the car."*)

Exceptions:

– Non-finite verbs or separable verb elements displace the negator *"nicht"* from the end of the sentence.

*"Peter kam gestern <u>nicht</u> an."*

(En: *"Peter did not arrive yesterday."*)

– A predicative noun or an adjective always occupy the end of the sentence.

*"Das Auto ist <u>nicht</u> teuer."* (En: *"The car is not expensive."*)

– A negator *"nicht"* used to indicate sentence negation may also be positioned before free local adjuncts:

*"Er stellt das Buch <u>nicht</u> in den Schrank"*, but not

*"Er stellt das Buch in den Schrank <u>nicht</u>."* (??)

(En: *"He does not put the book in the bookcase."*)

The following representational means are provided by MultiNet to semantically describe the phenomena of negation:

- The family of metafunctions

$$\left.\begin{array}{ll} *NON_1 : \text{<relation>} & \longrightarrow \text{<relation>} \\ *NON_2 : \text{<md>} & \longrightarrow \text{<md>} \\ *NON_3 : & \longrightarrow \text{FALSE} \end{array}\right\} * NON$$

These functions in the above order will be named for the time being with $*NON_1$, $*NON_2$, and $*NON_3$, respectively. They will later be given the common name $*NON$ when the intended meaning uniquely follows from the context.

$*NON_1$ is preferred for representing constituent negation. It takes a relation R to the complementary relation $\overline{R} = *NON_1(R)$, which states that a and b are not in relation R if and only if (a $\overline{R}$ b) holds.

∗NON$_2$ is used to deal with negated modalities (see Sect. 8.3), while the function ∗NON$_3$ with arity zero represents the truth value FALSE.

- The relation MODL: $\tilde{si} \times md$
  This relation is used together with the function ∗NON$_3$ for the representation of sentence negation.
- The relation SUBST: [o × o] ∪ [si × si]
  This relation is used for negation by prepositions and for modal negation (see C3 on page 182).
- The functions
  ∗DIFF: $pe^{(n)} \times [pe^{(n)} \cup pe^{(n-1)}] \rightarrow pe^{(n)}$     (for negation by prepositions)
  ∗ALTN2: $o \times o \ldots \times o \rightarrow o$          (for coordinative constituent negation)
  ∗VEL2: $\tilde{si} \times \tilde{si} \times \ldots \tilde{si} \rightarrow si$          (for coordinative sentence negation)
- The layer information [**FACT** = *nonreal*] vs. [**FACT** = *real*].

On the basis of these representational means, the most important language phenomena containing the carriers of negation introduced at the beginning will be dealt with semantically in the following exposition.[7] To simplify the graphical representation of the relatively complicated encapsulation of concepts, we use the convention described in Part II, Fig. 16.3f, where the node representing a situation is enclosed in a small circle. Arcs going into this circle belong to the concept capsule, while arcs ending at the outskirts of the capsule are related to the entire situation, functioning as semantically restrictive specifications.

| | FACT | VARIA | REFER | SORT | FEAT |
|---|---|---|---|---|---|
| nichts  (En: nothing) | *non* | *varia* | *indet* | *o* | - |
| etwas  (En: something) | *real* | *con* | *indet* | *o* | - |
| kein/e/er/es  (En: no one/none) | *non* | *varia* | *indet* | *d* | - |
| (irgend)ein/e/er/es  (En: some) | *real* | *con* | *indet* | *d* | - |
| niemand  (En: nobody) | *non* | *varia* | *indet* | *d* | [HUMAN +] |
| jemand  (En: somebody) | *real* | *con* | *indet* | *d* | [HUMAN +] |
| nie(mals)  (En: never) | *non* | *varia* | *indet* | *t* | - |
| jemals/einstmals  (En: once) | *real* | *con* | *indet* | *t* | - |
| nirgend(wo)  (En: nowhere) | *non* | *varia* | *indet* | *l* | - |
| irgendwo  (En: somewhere) | *real* | *con* | *indet* | *l* | - |
| keinesfalls/keineswegs (En: under no circumstances) | *non* | *varia* | *indet* | *si* | - |
| gegebenenfalls  (En: in case of) | *hypo* | *con* | *indet* | *si* | - |

**Table 8.1.** The negators and their antonyms as bundles of attribute values

---

[7] For the sake of brevity, the temporal characterizations are dropped in the semantic representations shown in the figures; they can be easily completed by the reader (most often it is simply TEMP + PAST or TEMP + PRES; compare with the annotation on page 62).

## A) Words Expressing Negations / Negators

Most negators except "*nicht*" (En: "*not*") come as pairs of antonyms, with each pair having a negative and a positive counterpart, e.g.

(niemand ANTO jemand)          (En: "*nobody*" vs. "*somebody*") or

(nirgendwo ANTO irgendwo)      (En: "*nowhere*" vs. "*somewhere*"), etc.

The meanings of negators and their counterparts are also concepts, which can be represented in the semantic network as nodes. It is typical of negators and their antonyms that they are characterized by bundles of layer information and by sorts or features only. These specifications are summarized in Table 8.1. If a knowledge representation, for instance, contains the concept something as a marker of a node, then this has to be interpreted as a shorthand notation for the corresponding attribute-value combination from this table.

### A1) nicht (En: not)

The meaning of the negator "*nicht*" (En: "*not*") is represented by

MODL + *NON                        (in the case of sentence negation)

*NON ($\langle$Relation$\rangle$)              (in the case of constituent negation)

Examples:

(8.4)  "*Peter reparierte sein Fahrrad nicht.*"          (sentence negation)

    (En: "*Peter did not repair his bicycle.*")

(8.5)  "*Die Elbe fließt nicht in die Ostsee.*"          (constituent negation)

    (En: "*The Elbe does not flow to the Baltic Sea.*")

From Example (8.5) and Fig. 8.1b, it becomes clear that the part of the fact representing the information "*The Elbe is flowing (somewhere)*" has to be considered as a presupposition which is not negated in Sentence (8.5). This is supported by the background knowledge (Elbe SUB river) $\wedge$ (river EXP flow), according to which the concept river is immanently connected with the concept flow.

- Following Kiefer [139], a **presupposition** P is defined as follows. Let S and P be two sentences. Let P not be explicitly stated by S. If P can be inferred from S, as well as from the negated proposition $\neg$ S, then P is a presupposition of S. In other words, P is invariant with regard to the negation of S.

The immanent background knowledge is generally an important starting point for finding out what is presupposed by a certain statement. A special type of presupposition is regularly taken into account by MultiNet: The so-called **existential presupposition** (see Chap. 10). This means that objects involved in a factual proposition (except those whose existence is explicitly negated or which appear in opaque contexts) will be taken as really existing.[8] The concept of presuppositions has also been dealt with in [137] and [9]. With regard to special problems, such as presuppositions of higher order, verbs with negative presuppositions, and the transitivity of presuppositions, we have to refer the reader to the literature (see, for example, [150]).

a) Ge: *"Peter hat sein Fahrrad **nicht** repariert."*
   En: *"Peter did **not** repair his bicycle."*
      (Sentence negation)

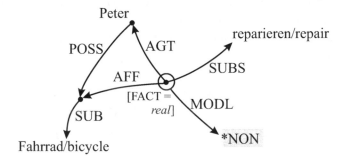

b) Ge: *"Die Elbe fließt **nicht** in die Ostsee."*
   En: *"The (river) Elbe does **not** flow to the Baltic Sea."*
      (Constituent negation)

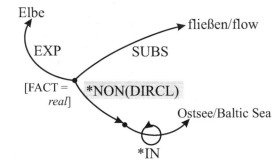

**Figure 8.1.** Sentence negation and constituent negation with *"nicht"* (En:*"not"*)

---

[8] A proposition is said to be in an opaque context if it is embedded in a modal specification, as for instance, *"Peter <u>believed</u> that he had seen a unicorn."* In this case the unicorn, of course, need not exist, in contrast to the sentence *"Peter has seen a unicorn"*, where this should be true at least from the speaker's point of view.

## A2) nichts (En: nothing) [9]

– It is morphologically similar (symbol: $\cong$) to a noun.
– Duality: nichts $\hat{=}$ nicht + etwas     (En: nothing $\hat{=}$ not + something[10])
– It is used for sentence negation.

a) Ge: *"Der Vater hat dem Kind    b) Ge: **"Es trifft nicht zu**, daß der Vater
      **nichts** mitgebracht."*           *dem Kind nichts  mitgebracht hat."*
En: *"The father has brought*     En: *"**It is not true** that the father has*
      ***nothing** for the child."*           *brought nothing for the child."*

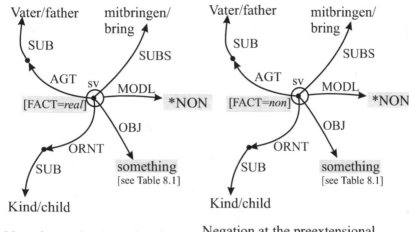

Negation at the  intensional     Negation at the preextensional
level by (MODL+*NON)     level by [FACT=non] + intensional
                                      negation with (MODL+*NON)

**Figure 8.2.** Negation at the intensional and preextensional levels

In MultiNet, the negation can be expressed at two different levels:

• at the intensional level (as inner part of the meaning of a situation, so to speak), where the above-mentioned representational means – especially the relation MODL and the metafunction *NON – are applied;

---

[9] The single lines of comment given together with the following words of negation go back in this order to Admoni [2] (first line), to rules of Bech (second line), cited after [77], and to Stickel [252] (third line). The morphological similarity indicated in the first line must be related to German only.

[10] It should be emphasized that **something** is the representative of the factually existing object defined as the corresponding bundle of layer attribute values shown in Table 8.1, which can be **semantically** combined with negation, notwithstanding the fact that **syntactically** the forms with "*any-*", in this case "*anything*", are preferably used with negation in English.

- at the preextensional level, where we use the layer attribute **FACT**; the values [**FACT** = *nonreal*] or abbreviated [**FACT** = *non*] specify that the state of affairs sv characterized in this way does not hold in reality, while the value [**FACT** = *real*] indicates that sv actually holds. The situation sv may itself contain an (intensional) negation, as shown in Fig. 8.2b, where we have a double negation. Although [**FACT** – *non*] and (sv MODL *NON) cancel each other out from the pure truth-functional point of view because of the logical law of double negation (i.e. from Fig. 8.2b one can deduce that *"the father has brought something for the child"*), it is nevertheless meaningful to preserve both kinds of negation in the representation. Taking into account the conversational maxims of Grice [84] (especially the maxim of avoiding redundancy), it must be assumed that the double negation was used on purpose (for example, to reply properly to a foregoing statement or to revise an assumption).

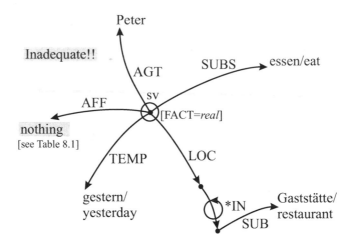

**Figure 8.3.** Semantically inadequate representation of sentence negation with "*nichts*" (En: "*nothing*")

The semantic representation of the sentence Sn = "*Peter hat gestern in der Gaststätte nichts gegessen.*" (En: "*Yesterday, Peter ate nothing in the restaurant.*") in Fig. 8.4, and the semantically inadequate representation of this sentence in Fig. 8.3 show that the "nonexisting object" (symbolized by the concept nichts (En: nothing); see Table 8.1) must not be introduced in the semantic representation of a real situation without special care.

a) Ge: *"Peter hat gestern in der Gaststätte **nichts** gegessen."*
En: *"Yesterday, Peter did **not** eat **anything** in the restaurant."*

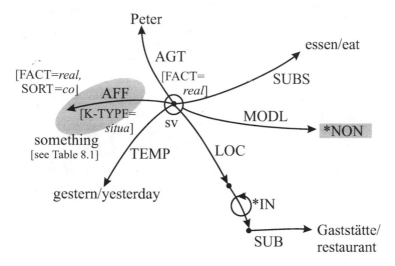

b) Ge: *"Das, was Peter gestern in der Gastsstätte*
*gegessen {hat/haben soll}, **gibt es nicht.**"*
En: *"That what Peter {has/should have} eaten*
*in the restaurant yesterday **does not exist.**"*

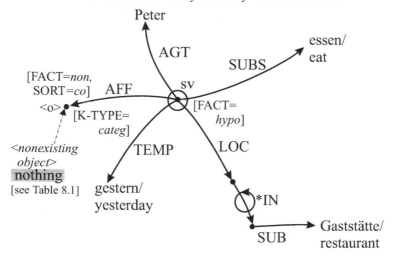

**Figure 8.4.** Semantically adequate representation of sentence negation with "*nichts*" (En: "*nothing*")

Because of the conjunction convention (see Part II, Sect. 16.3) being assumed in MultiNet, the question *"Did Peter eat in the restaurant yesterday?"* has to be answered with *"Yes"* against the background of the representation given in Fig. 8.3 (which is apparently false). The reason for this lies in the properties of the relation AFF, which – in contrast to the relation MODL – does not belong to the semantically restrictive relations.

In principle, there are two possibilities for representing the meaning of sentence Sn correctly (see Figs. 8.4a and b). On the one hand, one may first construct a state of affairs sv = *"Peter hat gestern in der Gaststätte (etwas) gegessen"* (En: *"Yesterday, Peter ate (something) in the restaurant."*), where the word *"etwas/something"* may also be dropped (in Fig. 8.4, this corresponds to the AFF arc shaded in gray). Afterward, this state of affairs has to be negated by MODL + *NON. The layer attribute [**FACT** = *real*] in Fig. 8.4a indicates that this negated fact does really hold (see also Fig. 5.2). On the other hand (see Fig. 8.4b), one may define an object o eaten by Peter by setting up a hypothetical situation sv into which o is hooked by the relation AFF[11], and then the existence of the object defined in this way has to be negated by [**FACT** = *non*]. Since the relation MODL in Fig. 8.4a and the layer information [**FACT** = *hypo*] in Fig. 8.4b restrict the validity of **all** elementary relationships involved in sv in both semantic representations of the sentence, one can not draw conclusions from them on the validity of the substructure which corresponds to the sentence *"Yesterday, Peter ate in the restaurant."* So the above-mentioned query will not be answered wrongly.

### A3) kein (En: no)

– German only: kein $\cong$ ein (indefinite article, like possessive pronoun)
– Duality: kein $\hat{=}$ nicht + eine/r/s (possibly also: nicht + jemand)
      (En: no $\hat{=}$ not + a/an)
– In German: Sentence negation, if *"keiner"* (En: *"nobody"*) takes the position of a nominal part of the sentence; constituent negation, if this negator is used attributively (i.e. it stands before a noun); the latter is often the case, if *"keiner"* is followed by *"sondern"* (En: *"but"*).

The example from Fig. 8.5 shows that the meaning representation of the sentence *"Keiner hat Peter sein Werkzeug geliehen."* (En: *"Nobody lent his tool to Peter."*) needs a semantic representative for the grammatical subject corresponding to an existentially quantified variable. Otherwise, the relationship of possession could not be described properly. The adequate representation

---

[11] I.e. the corresponding arc labeled by AFF has to be inserted into the immanent part of the conceptual capsule of o, which is indicated by [**K-TYPE** = *categ*].

therefore corresponds to the paraphrase *"Es trifft nicht zu, daß jemand Peter sein Werkzeug geliehen hat."* (En: *"It is not true that somebody has lent his tool to Peter"*).

Ge: *"**Keiner** hat Peter sein Werkzeug geliehen."*
En: *"**Nobody** lent his tool to Peter."*

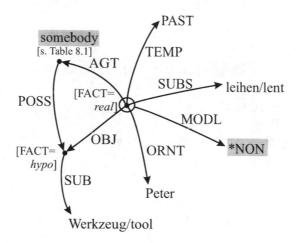

**Figure 8.5.** Sentence negation with *"kein"* (En: *"no"*)

Ge: *"Peter kauft **kein** Motorrad **sondern** ein Fahrrad."*
En: *"Peter buys **no** motorcycle **but** a bicycle."*

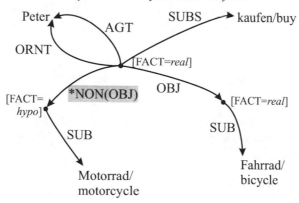

**Figure 8.6.** Constituent negation with *"kein"* (En: *"no"*)

In contrast to the negation of a whole state of affairs (semantically expressed by MODL + *NON), the next sentence, see Fig. 8.6, gives an example of the negation of a single constituent (expressed by *NON(OBJ)).

(8.6) *"Peter kauft sich kein Motorrad sondern ein Fahrrad."*
    (En: *"Peter does not buy a motorcycle but a bicycle."*)

### A4) niemand (En: nobody)

– German only: niemand ≅ jemand (nominal indefinite pronoun with a personal character)
– Duality: niemand ≙ nicht + jemand     (En: nobody ≙ not + somebody)
– Sentence negation

Example (see Fig. 8.7):

(8.7) *"Niemand hat bis jetzt ein Perpetuum mobile gebaut."*
    (En: *"Nobody has ever built a perpetual motion machine until now."*)

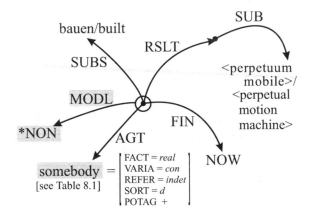

**Figure 8.7.** Sentence negation with negator *"niemand"* (En: *"nobody"*)

For the sake of illustration, the graphic representation in Fig. 8.7 explicitly shows the layer information for the indefinite pronoun *"jemand"* (En: *"somebody"*; see Table 8.1).

### A5) nie, niemals (En: never)

– Pronominal adverb, belonging to the verb group
– Duality: nie, niemals ≙ nicht + jemals     (En: never ≙ not + once)
– Sentence negation

An example of this kind of negation is given by the next sentence whose semantic representation is shown in Fig. 8.8.

(8.8) *"Der Patient ist <u>niemals</u> operiert worden."*
    (En: *"The patient had <u>never</u> been operated on."*)

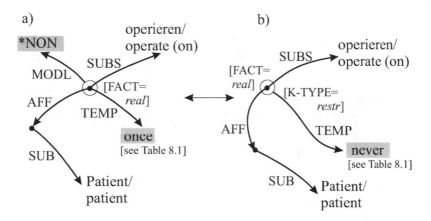

**Figure 8.8.** Sentence negation with negator *"niemals"* (En: *"never"*)

First, it has to be stated that the adequate semantic representation of the example, classified as sentence negation, is given in Fig. 8.8a. But there is also an equivalent representation which has the advantage of being built up analogously to a corresponding proposition that is not negated, as is the case in the representation for *"Der Patient wurde <u>gestern</u> operiert."* (En: *"The patient was operated on <u>yesterday</u>."*). The second representation is not in conflict with the conjunction convention (as the semantic net shown in Fig. 8.3), since TEMP connected with never, in contrast to AFF in Fig. 8.3, is marked as a semantically restrictive relation and thus influences the validity of the whole state of affairs. Using the representation in Fig. 8.8b, a common treatment of negated and non-negated propositions is possible during syntactic-semantic analysis. Additionally, the second representation allows for the same question-answering mechanism for negated and non-negated propositions, which is also appropriate for queries of the kind *"When has the patient been operated on?"* (the answer in the one case is *"Never"* and in the other case *"Yesterday"*). In any case, we have to provide transformation rules which allow for a transition between these representations:

En: (sv TEMP niemals) ↔ (sv MODL *NON) ∧ (sv TEMP jemals)
Ge: (sv TEMP never) ↔ (sv MODL *NON) ∧ (sv TEMP once)      (60)

Because of the semantically restrictive character of the relations involved, these rules of pattern substitution may not be considered as axioms in the usual sense by means of which the pattern on the right side of the implication arrow can be derived **additionally** to the relational triple on the left side (i.e. the patterns of the left side have to be canceled from the representation after applying such a rule; ⤳ nonmonotonic behavior).

The introduction of axioms as (60) does not imply higher costs in a QAS, since such axioms are needed anyway to establish the relationship between facts and questions of the type given in Fig. 8.9.[12]

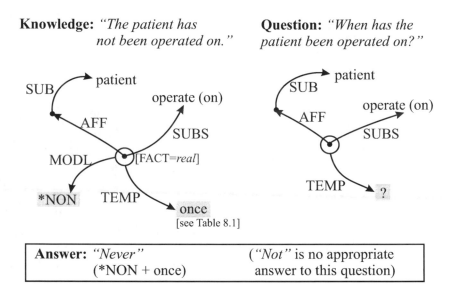

**Knowledge:** *"The patient has not been operated on."*    **Question:** *"When has the patient been operated on?"*

| Answer: *"Never"* (*NON + once) | (*"Not"* is no appropriate answer to this question) |

**Figure 8.9.** Question-answering with negated temporal specifications

## A6) nirgends, nirgendwo, nirgendwohin, nirgendwoher    (En: nowhere)

– Pronominal adverb, belonging to the verb group
– Duality: nirgends/nirgendwo ≙ nicht + irgendwo    (LOC)
  nirgendwohin ≙ nicht + irgendwohin    (DIRCL)
  nirgendwoher ≙ nicht + irgendwoher    (ORIGL)
  (En: nowhere ≙ not + somewhere)
– Sentence negation

---

[12] Also, the simplicity of the question-answering process based on the representation from Fig. 8.8b can be seen as an argument in favor of its use.

a) Ge: *"Der Lehrer findet*
     ***nirgends** einen Fehler."*
En: *"**Nowhere** did the teacher*
     *find an error."*

b) Ge: *"Peter fährt in den Ferien*
     ***nirgendwo** hin."*
En: *"Peter goes **nowhere** during*
     *the holidays:"*

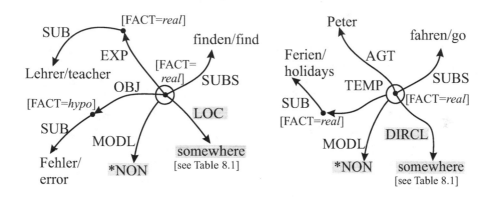

**Figure 8.10.** Sentence negation with negators having a local meaning

Examples:

(8.9)  *"Der Lehrer findet nirgends einen Fehler."*
     (En: *"The teacher did not discover an error anywhere."*)
(8.10)  *"Peter fährt in den Ferien nirgendwo hin."*
     (En: *"Peter does not go anywhere during his holidays."*)

The meaning representatives of *"nirgends"*, *"nirgendwo"*, *"nirgendwohin"*, *"nirgendwoher"* (En: *"nowhere"*) will be assigned the sort *l* (location); see Table 8.1. This kind of negation, being a sentence negation, is linked to the situational node by means of MODL + ∗NON. In addition, a direction has possibly to be taken into account, which in German can be derived from the negation word alone, while in English the verb must also be considered. In the case of German negators, the connection to the situational node is established by LOC for *"nirgends"* and *"nirgendwo"*, by DIRCL for *"nirgendwohin"*, and by ORIGL for *"nirgendwoher"*.

### A7) keinesfalls, keineswegs (En: under no circumstances)

– Sentence negation.

(8.11)  *"Peter wird dem Vorschlag keinesfalls/keineswegs zustimmen."*
     (En: *"Under no circumstances will Peter approve the proposal."*)

The condition which cannot be fulfilled (described in German by *"keines-falls/keineswegs"* and paraphrased in English by *"under no circumstances"*) is assigned the sort *si* (situation/state of affairs). Since COND is a semantically restrictive relation, there are essentially two equivalent representations, as in the case of TEMP. The first (see Fig. 8.11a) is equivalent to the situation *"Peter will not agree with the proposal"*, which possibly is connected with the loss of a small nuance in meaning. The second (see Fig. 8.11b) emphasizes that Peter **under no circumstances/conditions** will agree with the proposal, which comes closer to the original intension.

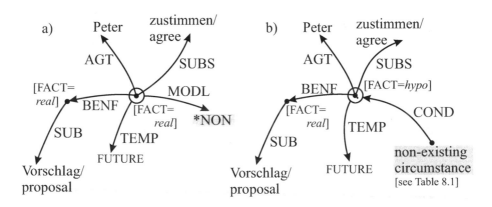

**Figure 8.11.** Sentence negation with conditional negators

### A8) nein (En: no)

This modal equivalent to a sentence appears only in a dialogue as an answer; it need not be represented in a knowledge base.

### B) Affix Negation

Adjectives, nouns, and verbs being negated by affixes (e.g. *"unfreundlich"* (En: *"unfriendly"*), *"Illegalität"* (En: *"illegality"*), *"mißverstehen"* (En: *"misunderstand"*)) will be treated as inseparable lexemes. The connection to the unnegated counterparts *"freundlich"* (En: *"friendly"*), *"Legalität"* (En: *"legality"*), and *"verstehen"* (En: *"understand"*) is established by means of the antonymy relation. Here, one has to take into consideration that a "double negation" (not + affix) does not correspond semantically to the meaning of the positive word.

Example:   ⟨not unfriendly⟩ ≠ friendly.

## C) Negation by Conjunctions
### C1) Coordinative negation
"*weder – noch*" (En: "*neither – nor*")    (with regard to "*entweder – oder*" (En: "*either – or*") see Fig. 11.5, example K1)

In this case, as with the ordinary negation, one has to discern between constituent negation (Fig. 8.12) and sentence negation (Fig. 8.13). The additional effect consists in the fact that more than one constituent or situation is simultaneously negated. In Figs. 8.12 and 8.13 the meaning of the following sentences is represented:

(8.12)  "*Der Artist arbeitet weder mit Netz noch mit Balancierstange.*"
   (En: "*The artist works neither with a net nor with a balancing pole.*")
                  (See Fig. 8.12.)

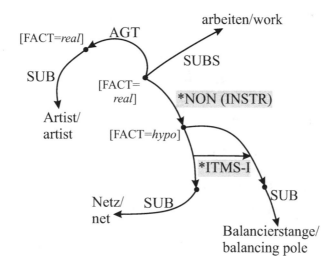

**Figure 8.12.** Constituent negation with "*weder – noch*" (En: "*neither – nor*")

(8.13)  "*Das Gerät wies weder bei der Überprüfung einen Fehler auf, noch wurde es bei der Auslieferung beschädigt.*"
   (En: "*The device neither showed a defect during the inspection nor had it been damaged during the delivery.*")    (See Fig. 8.13.)

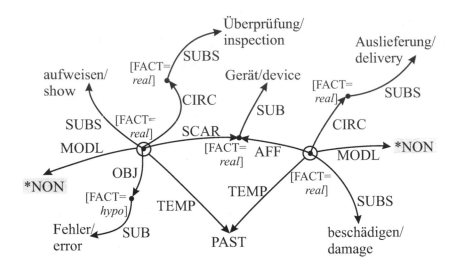

**Figure 8.13.** Sentence negation with *"weder – noch"* (En: *"neither – nor"*)

## C2) Conditional and causal negation
See Chap. 11 for a detailed treatment.

## C3) Modal negation[13]
Typical conjunctions in this context are *"ohne"* and *"statt"* (En: *"without"* and *"instead of"*).
Examples (see Figs. 8.14 and 8.15):

(8.14) *"Ohne die Sicherheitsvorschriften zu beachten, betrat der Angestellte die Werkhalle."*
(En: *"The employee entered the factory building without observing the security instructions."* (Negation + CIRC)

(8.15) *"Statt zu fragen, benutzte der Kunde eigenmächtig das Telefon."*
(En – verbally: *"Instead of asking, the customer used the telephone unauthorized."*)                    (Negation + SUBST)

The semantic interpretation of the conjunctions *"ohne"* and *"statt"* (En: *"without"* and *"instead of"*) clearly shows the necessity to distinguish between a negation at the intensional level by means of (MODL + *NON) and at the preextensional level by means of [**FACT** = *non*]. In both cases, a factual situation $sv_1$ (characterized by [**FACT** = *real*]) is contrasted with a second situation $sv_2$. In the case of *"ohne"* (En: *"without"*) (Fig. 8.14), the negation does refer to

---

[13] In this paragraph, "modal" is used in the sense of characterizing the manner in which an action is carried out or a situation holds.

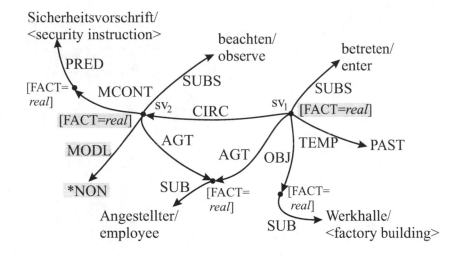

**Figure 8.14.** Negation of an accompanying circumstance with "*ohne*" (En: "*without*" )

the intensional meaning of the accompanying circumstance $sv_2$ = ⟨die Sicher-heitsvorschriften wurden nicht beachtet⟩ (En: ⟨The security instructions had not been observed⟩), which gives a more detailed specification of the situation $sv_1$ by means of the relation CIRC, and this circumstance $sv_2$ does really hold (expressed by [**FACT** = *real*]). For the decision about what has to be intensionally expressed by $sv_2$, the following question is important: "*What is the accompanying circumstance of $sv_1$?*"

In the case of "*statt*" (En: "*instead of*") (Fig. 8.15), it is the situation $sv_2$ = ⟨der Kunde fragt⟩ (En: ⟨the customer asks⟩) which is expressed by the sub-ordinate sentence and which characterizes the expectations of the speaker. This situation is explicitly substituted by $sv_1$ (described by the relation SUBST). At the same time, the meaning of "*statt*" (En: "*instead of*") comprises the fact that $sv_2$ actually does not hold (expressed by [**FACT** = *non*]). Here, it is not possible to represent the negation contained in the meaning of "*statt*" (En: "*instead of*") as a presupposition at the intensional level by means of MODL + *NON (as had been done in Fig. 8.14). This would mean that the expectations of the speaker were directed toward $s\tilde{v}_2$ = ⟨der Kunde fragt nicht⟩ (En: ⟨the customer does not ask⟩), and that this state of affairs was substituted by $sv_1$, something which is really not true. The decision about which intension must really be described by $sv_2$ can be supported by the following question: "*What situation $sv_2$ is replaced by $sv_1$?*" Based on the representation from Fig. 8.15 and on an appropriate meaning postulate for the relation SUBST, the query "*Did the customer ask?*" can be correctly answered by "*No*" and the query

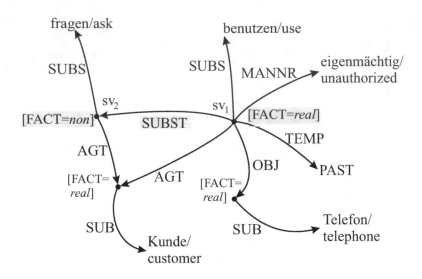

**Figure 8.15.** Replacing a situation by another one using SUBST

*"What could have been expected?"* correctly answered by *"that the customer does ask"*. On the basis of the expressional means of the predicate calculus alone, which knows only one type of negation, such a differentiation would not be possible. Analogue observations can be made with invalid causes (negation of CAUS), with an invalid manner (negation of MANNR), and so on.

The necessity of distinction between negation at the intensional level (by MODL + *NON) and at the preextensional level (by [**FACT** = *non*]) becomes even more obvious if the subordinate sentence introduced by *"statt"* (En: *"instead of"*) itself contains a negation. In the sentence *"Statt ihrer Freundin nichts zu erzählen, hat sie alles ausgeplaudert."* (En: *"Instead of telling nothing to her friend, she blurted out everything."*), we encounter an intensional negation by the negator *"nichts"* (En: *"nothing"*) in the situation to be substituted. This negation alone is relevant if one has to answer a question aiming at the expectations of the dialogue partners. Through the conjunction *"statt"* (En: *"instead of"*) a second negation comes into play compared with the foregoing example (it must be expressed by [**FACT** = *non*]), stating that the state of affairs which had been expected does not actually hold.

With questions aiming at the truth of the situation described in the subordinate sentence (e.g. *"Did she tell something to her friend?"*), both negations have to be included into the inferences. In this case, where only the propositional content of the sentence is of interest, they can be canceled following the law of double negation $A \leftrightarrow \neg(\neg A)$ , and the adequate answer to the question would be "*Yes*". However, it must be emphasized again that the law of double negation is not globally valid in a QAS (see Sect. 60 for affix negation and Sect. 13.2 for inferential answer finding).

## D) Negation by means of prepositions
### D1) außer/ohne (En: except/without)
Example:

(8.16) "*Alle Programme außer PR12 ...*"
    (En: "*All programs except PR12 ...*")

The representation is built up by means of the function *DIFF with an explicit reference to the preextensional level (as shown in Fig. 8.16).

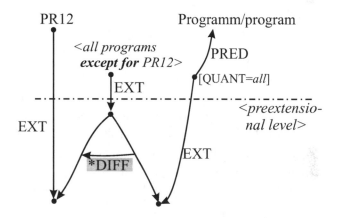

**Figure 8.16.** Exclusion of an element or a subset from a collection

## D2) anstelle/(an)statt (En: instead of)
Example (see Fig. 8.17):

(8.17) "*Peter kaufte sich ein Fahrrad anstelle eines Motorrads.*"
    (En: "*Peter bought a bike instead of a motorcycle.*")

It is typical of constructions with "*anstelle/(an)statt*" (En: "*instead of*") that a hypothetical or imagined entity (an object or a situation) characterized by the layer information [**FACT** = *hypo*] is substituted by another (real) entity which has to be specified at the semantic level by means of [**FACT** = *real*]. The network representation is carried mainly by the relation SUBST (see Fig. 8.17). The negated relation *NON(OBJ) present in the example shown in Fig. 8.6, which is almost synonymous with the example represented in Fig. 8.17,

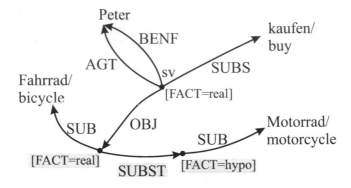

**Figure 8.17.** Substitution of a hypothetical object by a real one

can be inferred by the axiom:

$$(sv \; OBJ \; o_1) \wedge (o_1 \; SUBST \; o_2) \longrightarrow (sv \; *NON(OBJ) \; o_2) \qquad (61)$$

**E) Negation and Limitation**

The limiting particles *"nur"*, *"bloß"*, and *"lediglich"* (En: *"only"* and *"solely"*) will be suppressed for the time being in the semantic representation because of their minor informational value. To consider them in the context of quantitative specifications, the function *MODQ is provided. Altogether, these particles do not give rise to special difficulties in connection with the semantic representation, the problem consists in the automatic discovering of the expectations presupposed by them (this, however, is not the topic of this work).

**F) Negation and Comparison**

Every comparison is implicitly connected with a negation (see Sect. 6.2):

- With the assignment of the positive (or absolute) of one of two polar properties to an object, the negation of the contrary is also stated. Thus, the proposition ¬ (o PROP young) follows from the assumed fact (o PROP old), from the definition of the relation CONTR, and from the immanent knowledge (old CONTR young).
- With the comparative, the fact that o does not have the property p to the same degree as o' follows from (o' PROP p') and p' = (*COMP p o).
- With the superlative characterized by p' = (*SUPL p o) it follows from (o' PROP p') that all elements belonging to the collection determined by the comparison frame o have the property p to a lower degree than o'.

**G) Verbs Having a Negative Connotation**

Verbs implying a negative proposition (like *"mißachten"* and *"mißfallen"* (En: *"disregard"* and *"displease"*)) do not require special expressional means in comparison with other verbs. They stand in a contrary relation to corresponding positive verbs (like *"(be)achten"* and *"gefallen"* (En: *"consider/regard"* and *"please"*)). There are axiom schemata describing a direct transition from the semantic representation of a verb with negative meaning to the corresponding positive verb with an additional negation:

$$(\text{sv SUBS } \langle \text{neg-vb} \rangle) \wedge ((\langle \text{neg-vb} \rangle \text{ CONTR } \langle \text{pos-vb} \rangle) \wedge$$
$$\langle \text{participant\_structure}(\text{sv}, p_1, p_2, \ldots, p_n) \rangle$$
$$\longrightarrow \exists \text{sv' (sv' SUBS } \langle \text{pos-vb} \rangle) \wedge (\text{sv' MODL } *\text{NON} \wedge$$
$$\langle \text{participant\_structure}(\text{sv'}, p_1, p_2, \ldots, p_n) \rangle) \tag{62}$$

**H) Counterfactuals**

This language phenomenon is dealt with in Sect. 11.3.

Concluding this section, yet another remark should be made with regard to the **negation of the existence of objects**, which is described by means of phrases like *"There is no* $\langle o \rangle$ *that P(o)"*, *"A(n)* $\langle o \rangle$ *with P(o) does not exist"*, etc., where P is an appropriate predicate. In this case, the semantic representation of $\langle o \rangle$ has to be specified by means of [**FACT** = *non*], since we have a clear relationship to the preextensional level. At that, the semantic representation of the predicate P has to be anchored in the immanent part of the conceptual capsule of $\langle o \rangle$; see Fig. 9.11b (apart from the violation of signature specifications, a representation on the basis of MODL + *NON would not be adequate since the latter would express a negation at the intensional level, where the negation would be a part of the specification of $\langle o \rangle$).

It should also be mentioned that there is a rich literature in logic dealing with the problem of negation and its different aspects (an overview and starting point for further reading is given in [72]).

Summarizing, in MultiNet one may discern four possibilities to represent semantically the negation by means of a negation word. These have been compiled in Table 8.2.

| Short characterization | Field of application |
|---|---|
| MODL + *NON | Sentence negation (intensional negation) |
| *NON($\langle$Relation$\rangle$) | Constituent negation |
| [**FACT** = *non*] | Negation with regard to reality (extensional negation) |
| Employment of dual quantifiers: e.g. nobody $\hat{=}$ somebody + (MODL + *NON) | Logically equivalent to the first case (line 1) |

**Table 8.2.** Representational means for negation

## 8.3 Modalities in a Narrower Sense

To characterize modal restrictions of the validity of situations (states of affairs), two different representational forms are provided by MultiNet:

- An **abbreviated form** using the relation MODL: $\tilde{si} \times md$, where the first argument (a situation) is modally restricted by the second argument. The sort $md$ contains the semantic representatives of modal words, or, to be exact, representatives of classes of meaning representatives of modal words.[14] These sort elements each characterize groups of modalities which belong together with regard to their meaning (alethic modalities, deontic modalities, epistemic modalities, etc.; see Tables 8.3 and 8.4). Using this representation, a close parallelism to modal logical systems of philosophical and mathematical logic is given, each of which are determined by pairs of dual operators which have been investigated very thoroughly (see, for example, [18]). The advantage of the well-foundedness of these systems has to be contrasted with the disadvantage that they are not sufficient to distinguish every aspect of meaning.

- A **full form** using the relation MCONT: $[si \cup o] \times [\tilde{si} \cup \tilde{o}]$. On the one hand, this representation allows for an essentially more fine-grained differentiation (thus, it is possible to express *"Who did {believe/allow/take as possible/etc.} what at which time and which location."*). Such a fine-grained differentiation, however, goes far beyond the "terrain" well explored in modal logics. In a QAS (especially in its technical realization as a question-answering system in computational linguistics), complex modal restrictions need in many cases only be retranslated during the phase of answer-generation as verbalizations without their inferential potentiality being fully exploited for the time being.

Examples of the abbreviated form and the corresponding full form of a modal characterization are given in Figs. 8.18 and 8.19, respectively.[15] Typically, the abbreviated form is described in natural language by means of a modal adverb (in Fig. 8.18 by *"vermutlich"* (En: *"presumably"*)), and the full form is described by means of a modal verb (in Fig. 8.19 by *"vermuten"* (En: *"suspect"*)).

---

[14] In this context, by "modal words" we understand modal auxiliaries and modal adverbs only.

[15] The problem that the **belief** operator **bel** in the abbreviated form should be restricted at least to the speaker cannot be dealt with here. For this purpose, in modal logic and its application in AI, the corresponding operators are normally indexed by means of the carrier of the belief; see [76]. This problem does not exist in the full form, since the carrier of the belief is always the mental experiencer (MEXP) or the agent (AGT).

Examples:

(8.18) *"Die Firma NN entwickelt <u>vermutlich</u> einen neuen Speichertyp."*
(En: *"The company NN is <u>presumably</u> developing a new type of storage."*) (See Fig. 8.18.)

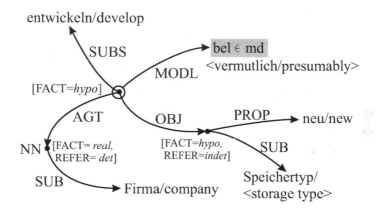

**Figure 8.18.** Abbreviated form of a modal characterization using the operator bel∈md (analogously to the operator of belief in epistemic logic)

(8.19) *"Beobachter <u>vermuten</u> seit 1997, daß die Firma NN einen neuen Speichertyp entwickelt."*
(En: *"Observers have suspected since 1997 that the company NN is developing a new storage type."*) (See Fig. 8.19.)

A special difficulty results from the necessity to decide (automatically) which value of the facticity attribute has to be assigned to objects being embedded in opaque contexts. Here, the thesis is held that the specification [**FACT** = *real*] has to be chosen as a default assumption in the case of determination of reference [**REFER** = *det*], and the specification [**FACT** = *hypo*] in the case of indetermination of reference [**REFER** = *indet*]; see Figs. 8.18 and 8.19.

In the following exposition, the modal expressions enumerated in Sect. 8.1 from Points (3) through (7) shall be investigated more closely.

## A) Modal Words – Modal Adverbs and Auxiliaries

Modal words are parts of speech like *"vermutlich"* (En: *"presumably"*), *"vielleicht"* (En: *"maybe"*), *"wahrscheinlich"* (En: *"probably"*), *"möglicherweise"* (En: *"possibly"*), *"schwerlich"* (En: *"hardly"*), *"gewiß"* (En: *"certainly"*),

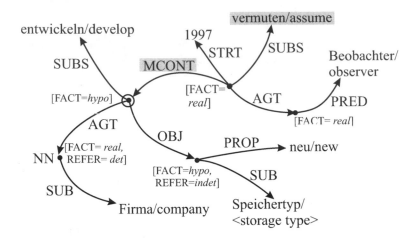

**Figure 8.19.** Full form of a modal characterization with the semantic representative of a verb

*"sicher"* (En: *"surely"*), *"leider"* (En: *"unfortunately"*), and *"glücklicherweise"* (En: *"fortunately"*).[16]

The semantic representatives of modal words are included into the sort *md* of MultiNet. They have to be linked via MODL to the situational node which is the meaning representative of the corresponding sentence containing this modal expression. Some (but not all) of these modal adverbs can be mapped in the sense of the above-mentioned classification onto standard modal operators showing a clear parallelism to the operators of modal logic.

| Modal adverb | | Modal operator ∈ md | Mnemonic |
|---|---|---|---|
| möglich(erweise) | (En: possibly) | possib | Possibility |
| notwendig(erweise) | (En: necessarily) | nec | Necessity |
| vielleicht | (En: maybe) | possib | Possibility |
| vermutlich | (En: presumably) | bel | Belief |

**Table 8.3.** The mapping of some modal adverbs onto standard modal operators

A further difficulty is connected with the task of distinguishing (automatically) between modal words and normal adverbs. In this context, Admoni gives the following delimitation [2]:

> *"Modal words do not denote properties of situations but rather the validation of the meaning of a syntactic relationship by the speaker."*

---

[16] The two modal adverbs *"fortunately"* and *"unfortunately"* belong to the emotional expressive field and ought to have minor importance for practical fields of discourse.

| Modal auxiliary | | Modal operator $\in$ md | Mnemonic |
|---|---|---|---|
| (nicht) brauchen₁ | (En: need not) | norm + *NON | Not a norm |
| brauchen₂ (benötigen) | (En: need) | intent | Intention |
| dürfen | (En: may) | perm | Permission |
| können₁ | (En: may) | perm | Permission |
| können₂ | (En: can) | possib | Possibility |
| mögen₁ | (En: want) | intent | Intention |
| mögen₂ | (En: might/must) | possib | Possibility |
| müssen | (En: must/have) | norm | Norm |
| sollen | (En: shall/be) | norm | Norm |
| wollen | (En: want) | intent | Intention |

**Table 8.4.** The mapping of modal auxiliaries onto standard modal operators

In literature, three criteria are reported supporting this distinction [77]:

a) In contrast to normal adverbs, modal words may be transformed into a superordinate sentence:
*"Peter wird wahrscheinlich kommen."* ⤳ *"Es ist wahrscheinlich, daß Peter kommt."*
(En: *"Peter will probably come."* ⤳ *"It is probable that Peter will come."*)
This transformation is not possible with *"Peter will come punctually."*

b) In connection with a decision question it is not allowed to answer with a normal adverb alone (this is important for a QAS):
*"Will Peter come?"* – *"Probably."* but not: *"Punctually."*

c) In German, the distinction is also marked by the different positions of the negator *"nicht"* (En: *"not"*):
*"Er kommt vermutlich **nicht**."* (En: *"He will probably not come."*)
but: *"Er kommt **nicht** pünktlich."* (En: *"He will not come punctually."*)

## B) Adjectives and Nouns Expressing a Modality
## B1) Adjectives

The adjectives relevant in this context are synonymous with the corresponding adverbs, if predicatively used, and thus belong to the sort of modal operators. With the attributive use, we have to take into consideration that these adjectives do not restrict the whole sentence with regard to its validity, but only a subordination relation (and, in some cases, another deep relation):
Examples:

(8.20) *"der vermutliche Mörder"*                    (See Fig. 8.20a.)
      (En: *"The suspected murderer"*)

(8.21) *"das wahrscheinliche Ergebnis"*              (See Fig. 8.20b.)
      (En: *"The probable result"*)

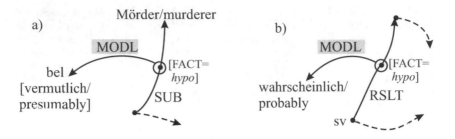

**Figure 8.20.** Modal restrictions of relationships

**B2) Nouns**

This group includes *"Gewißheit"*, *"Unsicherheit"*, *"Notwendigkeit"*, *"Möglichkeit"*, *"Glaube"*, *"Wissen"*, *"Wahrscheinlichkeit"*, etc. (En: *"certainty"*, *"uncertainty"*, *"necessity"*, *"possibility"*, *"belief"*, *"knowledge"*, *"probability"*, etc.).

With regard to the semantic representation, there exists the possibility to reduce case B2 to case A if we consider only simple nominalizations of adjectives which are not attributed.

(8.22) *"Es besteht eine gewisse Wahrscheinlichkeit, daß der Patient überlebt."* ⤳ *"Der Patient überlebt wahrscheinlich."*[17]
(En: *"There is a certain probability that the patient will survive."* ⤳ *"The patient will probably survive."*)

If the noun comprising a modality is itself attributed, or is subject to a predication, then there are propositions involved which belong to different logical levels. The treatment of these phenomena reaches far beyond the realms of contemporary logical systems.[18] Example:

(8.23) *"Die Wahrscheinlichkeit, daß der Patient überlebt, wurde immer geringer."*
(En: *"The probability that the patient survives had become ever smaller."*)

**Operator level:**     *"probability"* ⟸ *"is becoming ever smaller"*
$$\hat{=} sv_2$$
$$\Uparrow MODL$$
**Propositional level:** *"the patient survives"* $\hat{=} \widetilde{sv}_1$

---

[17] The full synonymy of these sentences may be challenged, however.
[18] It should be emphasized that the following schema is used only for illustration. It does not claim to be a detailed semantic representation. Nevertheless, the problem is not so much a lack of convenient representational means (which is a minor issue) but rather a lack of appropriate logical mechanisms to deal properly with these language phenomena in a QAS.

## C) Modal Infinitives

The German modal infinitive and the constructions containing modal participles, which can be transformed into such infinitives, are used to express normative speech acts (request to the hearer/writer or to a third party to do something). A typical example showing a corresponding semantic representation for
the German present passive participle is given in Fig. 8.21.

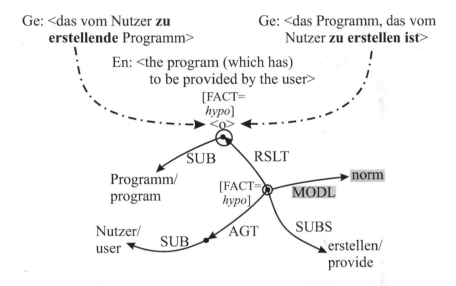

**Figure 8.21.** The semantic representation of the modal infinitive

## D) Modal Verbs

Besides the above-mentioned and already considered modal auxiliaries (see
Point A), verbs like *"vermuten"*, *"glauben"*, *"wissen"*, *"zweifeln"*, and *"verbieten"* (En: *"guess"*, *"believe"*, *"know"*, *"doubt"*, and *"forbid"*) have to be
incorporated into this group. They semantically belong to the field of mental situations or actions and also express a specific modality. They have to be
treated like other verbs characterized by certain cognitive roles. In this case,
they are obligatorily connected with the deep case relation MCONT, the second argument of which is a pseudo-situation $\widetilde{sv}$ which, by definition, has the
layer characteristic [**FACT** = *hypo*]. In impersonal expressions (such as *"man
glaubt"* (En: *"it is believed"*) and *"es ist erlaubt"* (En: *"it is allowed"*), etc.), the
meaning of modal verbs may also be represented by standard modal operators
as shown in connection with modal words dealt with under Point A). These

operators will be summarized together with the different types of systems of modal logic in the following list:

a) **Alethic modalities**:

  $a_1$) – **nec** (Abbreviation for "*necessity*")
  $a_2$) – **possib** (Abbreviation for "*possibility*")
  Examples of $a_1$) "*notwendig wahr sein*"
  　　　　　　　　(En: "*to be necessarily true*")
  Examples of $a_2$) "*können*" and "*möglich sein*"
  　　　　　　　　(En: "*can*" and "*to be possible*")

b) **Deontic modalities**:

  $b_1$) – **norm** (Abbreviation for "*norm*" or "*normative*")
  $b_2$) – **perm** (Abbreviation for "*permission*")
  Examples of $b_1$) "*müssen*", "*sollen*", and "*gefordert sein*"
  　　　　　　　　(En: "*must*", "*shall/should*", and "*to be required*")
  Examples of $b_2$) "*dürfen*" and "*erlaubt sein*"
  　　　　　　　　(En: "*may*" and "*to be allowed*")

c) **Epistemic modalities**:

  $c_1$) – **know** (stands for "*know*")
  $c_2$) – **bel** (Abbreviation for "*believe*")
  Examples of $c_1$) "*wissen*" and "*bekannt sein*"
  　　　　　　　　(En: "*know*" and "*to be known*")
  Examples of $c_2$) "*glauben*" and "*vermuten*"
  　　　　　　　　(En: "*believe*" and "*guess*")

d) **Intentional modalities**:

  $d_1$) – **intent** (für "*intent*")
  $d_2$) – **hope** (für "*hope*")
  Examples of $d_1$) "*wünschen*", "*wollen*", and "*mögen*"
  　　　　　　　　(En: "*wish*", "*want*", and "*like*")
  Examples of $d_2$) "*hoffen*" and "*erwarten*"
  　　　　　　　　(En: "*hope*" and "*expect*")

As already mentioned, the "artificial concepts" emphasized by bold types are representatives of classes of modalities that belong to the sort *md*. Thus, a connection to modal logic is established, where partial fields (alethic, deontic, epistemic, and intentional logic) are each determined by pairs of modal operators $\square$ and $\lozenge$ definable by truth conditions within the framework of Kripke Semantics (see [145] and [146]). These truth conditions have the general form:

- $[\square \text{ S is true in w}] \leftrightarrow \forall \text{w' } [(\text{w R w'}) \longrightarrow (\text{S is true in w'})]$　　　　(63)
- $[\lozenge \text{ S is true in w}] \leftrightarrow \exists \text{w' } [(\text{w R w'}) \wedge (\text{S is true in w'})]$　　　　(64)

R is a relation connecting alternative worlds w and w' among themselves (the so-called accessibility relation). If we denote the real world with $w_0$, then the truth of $\square$ S or $\diamond$ S in $w_0$ can be obtained from the foregoing formulas by inserting $w_0$ for w. These truth conditions and the properties of the accessibility relation R (deciding on whether or not R is transitive, symmetric, etc.) do essentially determine the axiom systems that define the formal properties of these operators.

Although MultiNet does not lean on a model-theoretic foundation of the semantics of the representational means, the conception of possible worlds is nevertheless relevant to a question-answering game. If, for instance, there is a state of affairs characterized by (MODL + possib), and somebody asks a question like *"Is a {situation / a state} of the world {possible / thinkable / ... } so that sv holds?"*, then this question has to be answered by *"Yes"*.

With regard to the logical treatment of modalities in a QAS, many of the axiomatic statements and rules investigated in systems of modal logic can be transferred to MultiNet because of the correspondences discussed above. Examples:[19]

- (sv MODL know) $\longrightarrow$ [**FACT** (sv) = *real*]         (65)
  corresponds to: **K** sv $\longrightarrow$ sv

However, the **axiom of negative introspection** encountered in modal logic has to be challenged:

- $\neg$ **K** sv $\longrightarrow$ **K** $\neg$ **K** sv         (66)

It states that somebody who does not know a certain situation sv, does actually know this.

From the field of deontic logic, one could transfer the axiom [20]:

- $\mathbf{P}(s_1 \vee s_2) \longrightarrow \mathbf{P}(s_1) \vee \mathbf{P}(s_2)$         (67)

into the corresponding MultiNet relationship

- sv' = (∗VEL1 $s_1$ $s_2$) $\vee$ (sv' MODL perm) $\wedge$ [**FACT** (sv') = *hypo*] $\longrightarrow$
  ($s_1$ MODL perm) $\vee$ ($s_2$ MODL perm)         (68)

The analogue axioms for the permission of a conjunction are not unproblematic, since there are cases where the conjunction of two situations is permitted, but not one of these situation alone.

---

[19] The symbol **K** of the following formulas denotes the operator of knowledge used in epistemic logic, which has to be indexed in systems with more than one agent (epistemic subject) with the name of the corresponding agent.

[20] **P** stands for the operator of permission, and sv' = (∗AND $s_1$ $s_2$) in Formulas (70) and (72) is an abbreviation for (sv' HSIT $s_1$) $\wedge$ (sv' HSIT $s_2$), a notation supported by the conjunction convention.

- $\mathbf{P}(s_1 \wedge s_2) \longrightarrow \mathbf{P}(s_1) \wedge \mathbf{P}(s_2)$ [problematic!] (69)

or, in terms of MultiNet expressions,

- sv' = (*AND $s_1$ $s_2$) $\wedge$ (sv' MODL perm) $\wedge$ [**FACT** (sv') = *hypo*] $\longrightarrow$
  ($s_1$ MODL perm) $\wedge$ ($s_2$ MODL perm) (70)

Only the following (somewhat weaker) axiom can be accepted:

- $\mathbf{P}(s_1 \wedge s_2) \longrightarrow \mathbf{P}(s_1) \vee \mathbf{P}(s_2)$ (71)

or, in terms of MultiNet expressions,

- sv' = (*AND $s_1$ $s_2$) $\wedge$ (sv' MODL perm) $\wedge$ [**FACT** (sv') = *hypo*] $\longrightarrow$
  ($s_1$ MODL perm) $\vee$ ($s_2$ MODL perm) (72)

Altogether, it is not possible to borrow too many ideas from deontic logic since some of its axioms are not unquestioned and even lead to paradoxical conclusions, like the above-mentioned postulate (70) (see [144, Sect. 5.4.5] for further discussion).

# Chapter 9

# Quantification and Pluralities

Natural language provides a plenitude of expressional means to characterize the referential determination and the range of significance of a concept that is described by a certain phrase (this applies especially to noun phrases). Specifically, these expressional means comprise **determiners**, **quantificators**[1], and **classificators**. Since the last of these plays only a minor role in Indo-European languages, we shall restrict ourselves to the first two.[2]

- **Determiners** are modifiers which, together with nouns, result in expressions whose reference is determined with regard to the referent in a more or less exact way just by these modifiers.
  Examples: "*this* house", "*a* house", "*every* house", ...
- **Quantificators** are modifiers which, together with nouns, result in expressions whose reference is determined just by these modifiers with regard to the extension of the set of individuals described or to the amount of a substance.
  Examples: "*almost all* houses", "*some* milk", "*many* houses", ...
  There are also adverbs among these quantificators which determine the referential extension of locations and times without being syntactically embedded into noun groups.
  Examples: "*always*" $\hat{=}$ "*at every time*" (Ge: "*immer*" $\hat{=}$ "*zu jeder Zeit*"), "*seldom*" $\hat{=}$ "*at a few times*" (Ge: "*selten*" $\hat{=}$ "*zu wenigen Zeiten*"), ...
  Examples: "*everywhere*" $\hat{=}$ "*at all locations*" (Ge: "*überall*" $\hat{=}$ "*an allen Orten*"), "*at some places*" $\hat{=}$ "*at a (certain) number of places*" (Ge: "*mancherorts*" $\hat{=}$ "*an einigen Orten*"), ...

---

[1] This term is used to mark the difference between expressions belonging to natural language (the **quantificators**, together with their semantic representatives) and the logical **quantifiers**, which are used in logic as operators to bind existentially or universally quantified variables. The separation of these terms will be maintained throughout this book.

[2] The definitions given below go back to Lyons [168] who, however, uses the term "quantifier" with both meanings. Classificators describe the type of the concept being quantified. They can be observed in Chinese and Mayan languages, which are called therefore **classificator languages**.

Linguistic tradition distinguishes between **definite determiners** (like Ge: "*der*" / "*dieser*"; En: "*this*" / "*that*"; Ru: "этот") and **indefinite determiners** (like Ge: "*ein*"; En:: "*a*" or "*an*"; Ru: "некоторый") or the zero article quite common in Russian or in German and English plural constructions. With regard to quantification, the predicate calculus dominating a large part of semantic theories essentially provides two quantifiers $\forall x$ and $\exists x$, a shortcoming which had been criticized already in the General Quantifier Theory of Barwise and Cooper [15]; we will deal with this in greater detail in Sect. 15.3.4.

The quantifiers can be expressed by very different natural language words, which shall be illustrated only by typical examples.[3]
Universal quantifier $\forall x$: Ge: "*alle*", "*jeder*"; En: "*each*", "*every*", "*any*", "*all*"; Ru: "все", "каждый", ...
Existential quantifier $\exists x$: Ge: "*ein*", "*einige*"; En: "*a(n)*", "*some*", "*someone*" "*something*"; Ru: "один", "некоторый"

These few examples already show that the fine differentiation of natural language expressions in the field of determination/quantification is leveled by only two quantifiers in predicate logic.[4] As we shall see, the whole repertory of layer information is required to achieve the necessary differentiation of meanings of determiners and quantificators, which cannot be covered by logical quantifiers alone. It also has to be stated that a strict classification of words with regard to their membership in the group of determiners or quantificators is not possible. Thus, the semantic representative of "*a(n)*" bears attribute values that contribute to the referential determination (or better, in this case, to the underdetermination) as well as to the quantification, which is expressed in MultiNet by means of the layer attributes **REFER** and **QUANT**; see Fig. 10.3.

Quantificators and many determiners are themselves concepts which have their correspondences in the semantic network, where the quantificators constitute a partial order under the relation MINE (see Part II and Fig. 9.1). Based on these representations, one can reason about a qualitative comparison of quan-

---

[3] The foreign language terms are given to illustrate the richness in nuances with regard to determiners/quantificators in different languages. The enumeration is far from complete, since indefinite pronouns also belong to this field. They are encountered with great richness in Russian, e.g. "некто", "ктонибудь", "ктолибо", "некоторый" for "*somebody*"

[4] There are only a few "pure" determiners which fix only the reference identity (e.g. "*the*" and "*this*"). They do not themselves represent concepts and have only an anchor in the (computer) lexicon. In contrast, quantificators like "*almost all*" and "*more than the half*" are autonomous concepts represented as nodes in the semantic network. In their descriptions, also anchored in the lexicon, the same layer attributes (but with different values) are used as with determiners; see Chap. 10.

tified concepts (e.g. ⟨many o⟩ is more than ⟨several o⟩) without knowing the exact cardinality of the extension underlying these concepts).[5]

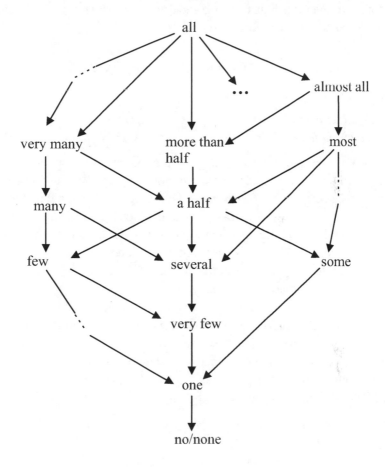

**Figure 9.1.** Detail from the partially ordered structure of quantificators

Natural numbers, of course, also belong to the quantifiers. In MultiNet we do not use only the attribute **QUANT** for their semantic characterization, but also the attribute **CARD** (see Fig. 10.3). In our approach, all natural numbers >1 are assigned the underspecified attribute value [**QUANT** = *nfquant*] (for *nonfuzzy quantification*). Only the number one is characterized by means of the concrete attribute value [**QUANT** = *one*]. These fixations are justified by the need for combinations of values for **QUANT** and **CARD** which give more

---

[5] There are also results from psychologically motivated investigations about the development of rating scales for quantifiers; see [189] and [188].

information than the attribute **QUANT** and its value alone. Moreover, there are also combinations of quantificator words that are not admissible because the values of their layer attributes are incompatible (e.g. "*many twenty*" is forbidden, while "*all twenty*" is allowed; see Chap. 10).
Example:

(9.1) "<u>*all twenty*</u> *students of class 9b*"          [**QUANT** = *all*, **CARD** = 20]

contains different information than

(9.2) "<u>*all*</u> *students of class 9b*"          [**QUANT** = *all*, **CARD** = *card*]
(9.3) "<u>*twenty*</u> *students of class 9b*"          [**QUANT** = *nfquant*, **CARD** = 20]

The determiner/quantificator "*a(n)*" is ambiguous, since it may be interpreted, on the one hand, as the logical quantifier $\exists$ in the sense of "*at least one*" (as in the sentence "*In every desert there is an oasis*"). On the other hand, the word "*a(n)*" may also be seen as a numeral which has to be characterized by [**CARD** = *1*] in the semantic representation (as in the sentence "*Last week, Paul had bought a new car*"). In this case, one surely does not mean "<u>*at least one*</u> *car*". The complete layer information for articles (including "*a(n)*") will be dealt with in Chap. 10, and is summarized in Fig. 10.3.

The following representational means are provided by MultiNet to represent semantically the determination of reference and the quantification of concepts, where the differentiation between individual concepts and collections (**pluralities**[6]) on the one hand, and between statements about generic concepts and collections on the other hand, are expressly included (with regard to the detailed definition of the following expressional means, see Part II):

- The layer Information, especially the attributes **REFER, QUANT, CARD, ETYPE, GENER,** and **VARIA**
- The relations ELMT, SUBM, EXT, SETOF, and DPND[7]
- The functions *DIFF, *UNION, *INTSC, *ITMS/*ITMS-I, *ALTN1/2, and *TUPL
- Also, the partitioning of a concept capsule into categorical and prototypical information with generic concepts is closely connected with quantification;

---

[6] Throughout this book, we use the technical term "*plurality*" for conceptual representatives of the intensional level denoting collections of entities; see also relation PRED.

[7] Please note that the use of a single DPND relation for the characterization of dependencies with mixed quantification is weaker than the concept of a Skolem function of predicate calculus. In the Skolem normal form of a predicate calculus expression, one has to introduce a special Skolem function for every existential quantified variable, which expresses the fact that this variable depends on all universally quantified variables before it in the prefix of the expression. Within a QAS it should be sufficient, however, to state (and possibly also to reproduce in an answer) which concept of a representation depends on which other concept.

see Fig. 9.2.[8] In Fig. 9.2, the relationships to the Generalized Quantifier Theory [15] and to the predicate calculus (FOL) are pointed out; alternative representations for quantification of MultiNet are shown in Fig. 9.3.

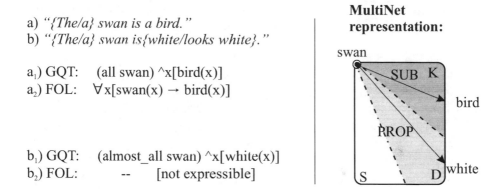

a) *"{The/a} swan is a bird."*
b) *"{The/a} swan is {white/looks white}."*

$a_1$) GQT:   (all swan) $^x[bird(x)]$
$a_2$) FOL:   $\forall x[swan(x) \to bird(x)]$

$b_1$) GQT:   (almost_all swan) $^x[white(x)]$
$b_2$) FOL:   --   [not expressible]

**MultiNet representation:**

**Figure 9.2.** Relationship between logical quantification and different types of immanent knowledge

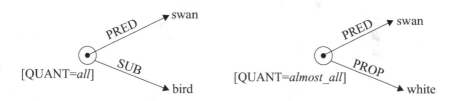

**Figure 9.3.** Reinterpretation of the components of a generic concept (see Fig. 9.2) in terms of MultiNet quantificators

Before we start a systematic treatment of the semantic representation of expressions containing determiners and quantificators, we have to go into the ambiguities which can be observed in the field of quantified noun phrases (see Figs. 9.4 and 9.5). With singular NPs introduced by the determiners *"the"* or *"a(n)"*, one has to distinguish between a generalized interpretation and a prototypical (generic) interpretation. These are shown in Fig. 9.4 for *"a(n)"* with their corresponding representations (the representation of expressions containing *"the"* is analogously built up).

---

[8] In this context, one has also to consider sort and feature restrictions, since otherwise one could derive wrong specialized statements from correct generalized ones; see Sect. 13.2.

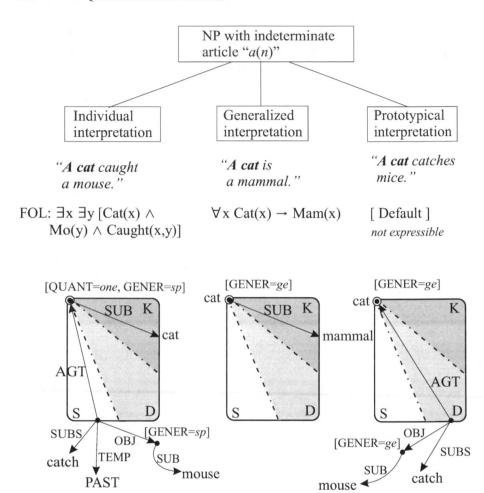

**Figure 9.4.** Possibilities for the interpretation of indeterminate NPs with the article "*a(n)*"

Special difficulties are caused by the ambiguities of plural NPs. These have basically the same interpretations as shown in Fig. 9.4 for singular NPs. Examples:

(9.4) "*The cats caught many mice.*"                    (individual/specialized)
(9.5) "*(The) cats are mammals.*"                                   (generalized)
(9.6) "*(The) cats catch mice.*"                                   (prototypical)

In addition to the aforementioned interpretations, there are further interpretations with plural NPs: a **collective interpretation**, or several individuals jointly carry out **one** action; a **cumulative interpretation**, or several individuals, jointly or one after another, produce a certain result; and a **distributive**

**interpretation**, where every member of the collection described by the subject NP carries out a separate action. These interpretations may be forced, or at least made more probable (preferable), by using certain adverbs or quantificators (see Fig. 9.5).

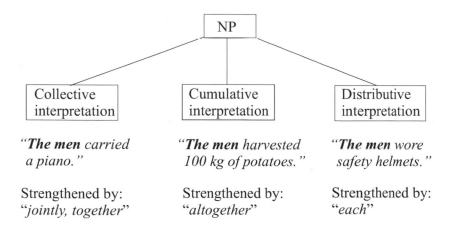

**Figure 9.5.** Different possibilities for interpreting plural NPs

In connection with the generic interpretation of NPs, another problem appears, which may analogously be observed at the right side of Fig. 9.4. In sentences like *"Cats catch mice"*, *"Bears love honey"*, and *"Trees have stems"* the prototypical interpretation is undoubtedly the only one which should be selected. In this context, the question arises whether there is also a prototypical proposition contained in these sentences for the generic concepts **mouse**, **honey**, and **stem**, respectively. On the one hand, we have to assume that the adequate semantic representative for the object NP is not the respective generic concept as a whole (in this case, **mouse**, **honey**, or **stem** with [**GENER** = *ge*]). On the other hand, these sentences do not speak of special mice, special honey or special stems (with [**GENER** = *sp*]), respectively. For this reason we propose a middle course by creating a generic intermediate node with [**GENER** = *ge*] as a representative for the object NP that is subordinate to the concept specified by the head noun of the NP (this node is characterized on the right side in Fig. 9.4 by [**GENER** = *ge*] and SUB – mouse).

The semantic representation of a sentence containing mixed quantification, and the application of MultiNet for that purpose, is illustrated in Fig. 9.6. It is typical of such sentences that quantificators and determiners come along in diverse combinations. For the sake of a better understanding of the semantic representations, it should be remembered that quantificators [**SORT** = *qn*] and quantified expressions have an inner structure in MultiNet, generally described by more than one layer attribute. They are shown for some typical representatives in abridged form in Table 9.1. A more systematic treatment of these attributes and their combinatorics together with the unification mechanisms connected with them can be found in Chap. 10.

|       | QUANT   | CARD | VARIA | REFER |
|-------|---------|------|-------|-------|
| three | *nfquant* | 3    | *varia* | *refer* |
| all   | *all*   | *card* | *con* | *det* |
| every | *one*   | 1    | *var* | *det* |

**Table 9.1.** Detail from the description of quantificators by means of layer attributes

*"**Every** student solves **an** equation."*

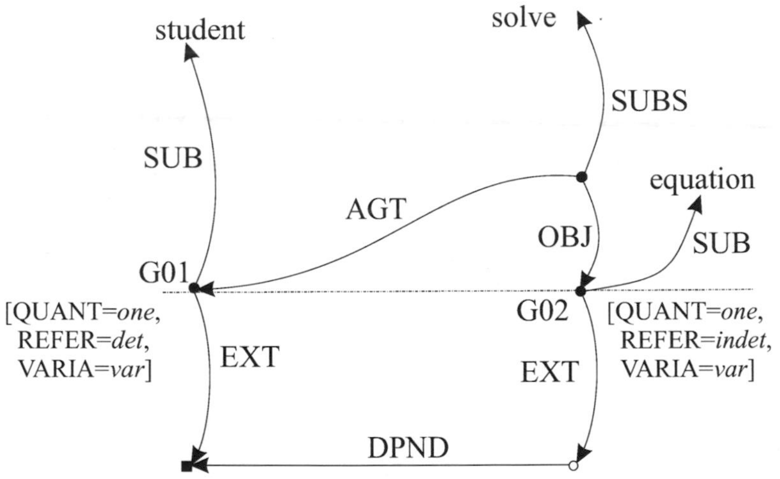

PC1:     $\forall x[\text{Student}(x) \rightarrow \exists y \, \text{Equation}(y) \wedge \text{Solve}(x,y)]$
Skolem-NF: $[\neg \text{Student}(x) \vee \text{Equation}(f(x))] \wedge$
$[\neg \text{Student}(x) \vee \text{Solve}(x,f(x))]$
*with f(x) as an arbitrarily chosen Skolem function*

**Figure 9.6.** Representation of mixed quantification by means of layer information and the DPND relation at the preextensional level

Table 9.2 shows further cases of mixed occurrences of determiners and quantificators whose semantic representations are similar to that given in Fig. 9.6. The essential difference lies in the layer information characterizing the nodes G01 and G02 in each of the examples and in the presence or absence of the DPND relation at the preextensional level (i.e. in certain dependency relationships among the nodes).

| Phrase containing two NPs | G01 and G02 | | | Dependency |
| | **REFER** | **QUANT** | **VARIA** | DPND |
|---|---|---|---|---|
| *The student* (G01), | det | one | con | – |
| who solves *every equation* (G02) | det | one | var | – |
| *The student* (G01), | det | one | con | – |
| who solves *an equation* (G02) | indet | one | con | – |
| *A student* (G01), | indet | one | con | – |
| who solves *all equations* (G02) | det | all | con | – |
| *This student* (G01), | det | one | con | – |
| who solves *that equation* (G02) | det | one | con | – |
| *All students* (G01) | det | all | con | – |
| solve *an equation* (G02). | indet | one | con | – |
| [collective interpretation] | | | | |
| *All students* (G01) | det | one | var | |
| solve *an equation* (G02). | indet | one | var | G02 → G01 |
| [distributive interpretation (analogously to "*every*")] | | | | |
| *All students* (G01) | refer | all | varia | open |
| solve *all equations* (G02). | refer | all | varia | |
| [with unresolvable ambiguity → underspecification of attribute values] | | | | |
| *Every student* (G01) | det | one | var | |
| solves *an equation* (G02). | indet | one | var | G02 → G01 |

**Table 9.2.** The representation of mixed use of determiners and quantificators

Based on Table 9.2, and in contrast to "*every*", three cases can be distinguished in the semantic interpretation of "*all*" (see Fig. 9.5):

a) collective and cumulative interpretation:
   [**REFER** = *det*, **QUANT** = *all*, **VARIA** = *con*]
b) distributive interpretation:
   [**REFER** = *det*, **QUANT**= *one*, **VARIA** = *var*]                    ($\hat{=}$ "*every*")
c) underspecified/ not resolved:
   [**REFER** = *refer*, **QUANT** = *all*, **VARIA** = *varia*],
   where the attributes of referentiality and variability remain underspecified.

Attention should be drawn to the fact that not only objects with [**SORT** = $o$], but also locations and times (with [**SORT** = $l$] and [**SORT** = $t$], respectively) may be quantified. The apparent parallelism to object quantifications is illustrated in Table 9.3. From this table we see that the corresponding quantificators differ only with regard to their sorts, but not with regard to their layer information.[9]

| **Objects** | all | almost all | ... | many | some | (a) few | no |
|---|---|---|---|---|---|---|---|
| **Locations** | every- where | almost everywhere | ... | at many places | at some places | at a few places | nowhere |
| **Times** | always | almost always | ... | often | sometimes | seldom | never |

**Table 9.3.** Parallelism between quantificators in the field of objects, locations, and times

The attribute **ETYPE** (standing for the type of extensionality) of the semantic representative AP = ⟨all N⟩ of a noun phrase specified by "*all*" has a value which is greater by 1 than that of the semantic representative of ⟨this N⟩, while ⟨every N⟩ has the same type of extensionality as ⟨this N⟩.

The type of the quantificator chosen in an expression also influences the **scope of quantification**. Thus, for English, the opinion is held [169] that "*any*" and its compounds have a wider scope than all the other operators of quantification, and negation, and the modal operators. In contrast, "*every*" always has a narrow scope, which may be paralleled to the discrimination between sentence negation and constituent negation dealt with in Sect. 8.2.
Examples:

(9.7)  En: "*I don't know anyone here.*"                      (wide scope)
   Ge: "*Ich kenne hier niemand.*"                    (sentence negation)
   $\forall x \neg \text{KNOW}(I, x)$

(9.8)  En: "*I don't know everyone here.*"                   (narrow scope)
   Ge: "*Ich kenne nicht jeden hier.*"              (constituent negation)
   $\neg \forall x \text{KNOW}(I, x)$

Since there are also counterexamples, and this problem gives rise to difficulties for syntactic-semantic analysis rather than for knowledge representation, it shall not be further considered here.

---

[9] The last column of this table indicates the transition to negation; the concepts no, nowhere, and never are characterized by [**FACT** = *non*]. The quantificators in the first, second, and third lines are related to the sorts [**SORT** = $o$], [**SORT** = $l$], and [**SORT** = $t$], respectively (see Sect. 8.2).

In the context investigated in this book, the question of **presuppositions** and **entailments** associated with different quantificators is more important. Thus, the combination "*not + everyone*" (Ge: "*nicht jeder*") is associated with presuppositions other than "*not + anyone*" (Ge: "*niemand*").[10]

(9.9) En: "*I don't know everyone with yellow lips.*"
Ge: "*Ich kenne nicht jeden mit gelben Lippen.*"
Presupposition: ↝ There are people with yellow lips.

(9.10) En: "*I don't know anyone with yellow lips.*"
Ge: "*Ich kenne niemanden mit gelben Lippen.*"
↝ Neutral, no presupposition.

Typical entailments that can be drawn from quantified expressions are summarized in Fig. 9.7. Also, the syllogisms postulated already by Aristotle belong to this context (see Sect. 13.2).

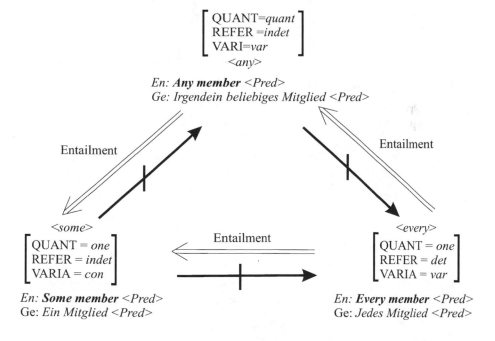

**Figure 9.7.** Entailments between expressions containing quantificators

---

[10] The following examples are taken from [169, p. 459].

a) *"Every student who owns a car lives in this house."*

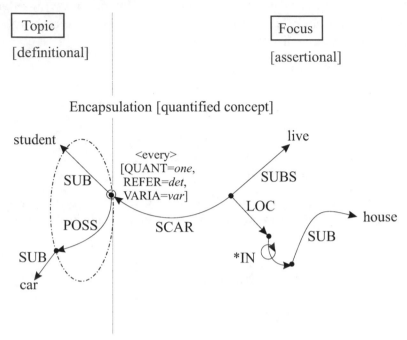

b) *"Every student who lives in this house owns a car."*

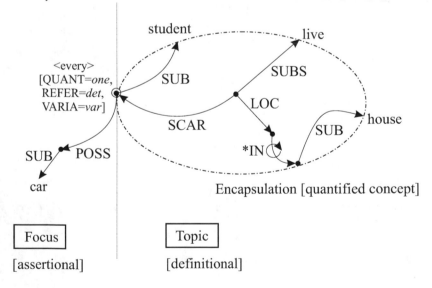

**Figure 9.8.** Topic-focus structure and the semantic range of the quantified concept

To adequately represent the meaning differences resulting from the interaction of **topic-focus** structure with the discrimination between restrictive (definitional) respective assertional parts in the meaning representation and quantification, the method of concept encapsulation has to be applied (see Fig. 9.8 and Part II, Sect. 17.3). A simple network representation which tries to avoid the encapsulation of partial networks yielding more complex, higher-order concepts (the parts being surrounded by an ellipse in Fig. 9.8) would "level" important meaning differences.

This shortcoming of simple networks has already been criticized by Woods (see [282, Sect. 7.3]), who coined the term **shared subpart fallacy**. The assignment of the same semantic representations for different sentences, such as a) and b) in Fig. 9.8, can be avoided only by the application of special means for structuring the networks as they are given by the encapsulation of concepts. This fallacy would result in Fig. 9.8, for instance, if the capsules indicated by the elliptical outlines would be omitted.[11]

Another problem arises from the combination of **quantification** and **negation**. On the one hand, there is the question of what is actually quantified or negated in a sentence (in the terminology of logic), and on the other hand, there is the question of the scope of these operators and of cognitive adequacy (the latter is not commonly taken into consideration in logic). The following discussion considers four cases characterized by typical sample sentences and concentrates on the layer attributes **FACT** and **QUANT** (characteristic phrases are printed in bold face).

**Case I** – "**There is a** *student who has received a book.*" (no negation)
We use a simple positive sentence as a starting point for the discussion; see Fig. 9.9. The phrase "*there is a(n) ⟨o⟩*" is semantically represented by marking the representative of the concept o for which the existence is stated with [**FACT** = *real*].[12]

The node o is described in Fig. 9.9 as representing a student (relation SUB) who gets a book (relation EXP). In this case, where no negation and no modal expressions are involved, all other nodes of the description of o are also assigned the attribute value [**FACT** = *real*] (compare the remarks about existential presuppositions in Sect. 8.2).

---

[11] Further effects stemming from the interaction of contextual boundedness (topic) or non-boundedness (focus) with quantification are investigated in [162] (Sect. 3.4)

[12] Correspondingly, the nonexistence has to be represented by [**FACT** = *non*] as already explained in connection with negation. The symbol ⟨o⟩ denotes a phrase describing the concept o.

Ge: *"**Es gibt einen** Schüler, der ein Buch erhalten hat."*
En: *"**There is a** student who has received a book."*

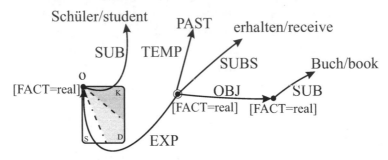

**Figure 9.9.** Non-negated sentence with existential quantification

- As a general rule with regard to the attribute of facticity, one can state that all nodes involved in factual statements that are not standing in modal or negated contexts are assigned the value [**FACT** = *real*].

  The representation given in Fig. 9.9 corresponds to the following logical expression with regard to its truth conditions:

- $\exists x \, \exists y \, \text{Student}(x) \wedge \text{Book}(y) \wedge \text{Got}(x, y)$                    (73)

**Case II** – "**Every** *student does* **not** *get a book (but a ball)."*
This case is illustrated in Fig. 9.10, where Node **G01** primarily expresses the fact that every student is involved in a situation **G02**, which itself is characterized by the description that somebody (i.e. **G01**) does not get a ball but a book.
In contrast to Case I, however, the node **G01** is *definitionally* characterized by (G01 SUB student) only, while its integration into situation **G02** by means of the relation EXP bears an **assertional** character. The situation **G02** contains a hypothetical entity **G04** representing a book. This node has to be specified by [**FACT** = *hypo*] and not by [**FACT** = *non*] as could be assumed because of the negation, since nothing is said about the existence or nonexistence of a book in this sentence.[13]

- As a second rule for the attribute of facticity, one can state that nodes in modal or negated contexts are generally assigned the value [**FACT** = *hypo*]

---

[13] One should compare the above sentence with *"He did not see a ghost but a bat."*, where also nothing is said about the existence of a ghost. The dependency relation between the nodes G03 and G01 is omitted in Fig. 9.10 for the sake of brevity; the treatment of this dependency can be easily seen from Fig. 9.6.

Ge: *"**Jeder** Schüler erhält **kein** Buch sondern einen Ball."*
En: *"**Every** student does **not** get a book but a ball."*

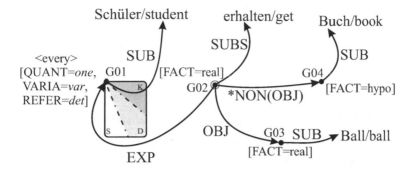

**Figure 9.10.** Universal quantification and constituent negation

if they are not determined (attribute [**REFER** = *indet*]). However, entities determined with regard to their reference (specified by the attribute [**REFER** = *det*]) are assigned the value [**FACT** = *real*] even in modal or negated contexts.

Accepting the logical expression (74) of FOL as semantically closest to the sentence from Fig. 9.10, this expression is also true if there do not exist any students or books. This is a clear indication that Formula (74) is cognitively not adequate with regard to the content of the sentence discussed as a typical example for Case II.

- $\forall x \, \forall y \, (\text{Student}(x) \land \text{Book}(y) \rightarrow$
$$\exists z \, [\text{Ball}(z) \land \text{Get}(x, z) \land \neg \text{Get}(x, y)]) \tag{74}$$

**Case III** – "**No** *student gets a book.*"
For the semantic interpretation of the sentence *"No student receives/gets a book."* (Ge: *"Kein Schüler erhält ein Buch."*), there are two dual representations which are semantically equivalent (see Fig. 9.11).
Either one considers this sentence as a statement about all students (Fig. 9.11a), where for every single student it is true that a certain state of affairs negated by MODL + *NON does hold (expressed by [**FACT** = *real*]), or the sentence is seen as a statement about the nonexistence of a student who is specified in a certain way (Fig. 9.11b). In the latter case, a node G01 has to be set up which is defined by (G01 SUB **student**) **and** by a hypothetical situation G02 representing the reception of a book (expressed by the relation EXP). The node G03 bears the attribute value [**FACT** = *hypo*] in both cases, because there is

Ge: *"**Kein** Schüler erhält ein Buch."*
En: *"**No** student gets a book."*

a)

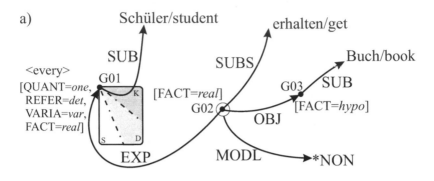

b)

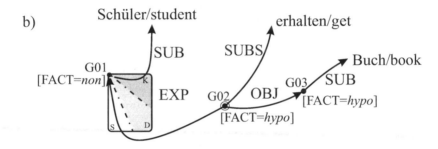

Ge: *"**Einen** Schüler, der ein Buch erhält, **gibt es nicht**."*
En: *"A student who gets a book **does not exist**."*

**Figure 9.11.** Universal quantification and sentence negation

nothing said about the existence or nonexistence with regard to this node.[14] The negator *"no"* (Ge: *"kein"*) finally corresponds to the attribute value [**FACT** = *non*] of G01 in Fig. 9.11b, where it is stated that an entity definitionally characterized in the same way as G01 does not exist.

The logically equivalent expressions (75) and (76) of FOL are possibly closest to the sentence of Case III and to the representations shown in Fig. 9.11 with regard to their truth conditions. But these formulas would be admissible (and even true) if there were no books or no students at all.[15]

---

[14] A comparison with the sentence *"Nobody has ever seen a yeti."* is recommended, where also nothing is stated about the existence of a yeti.

[15] The example sentence of Case III would not be stated if there were no students in the discourse domain (universe) considered. The logical expressions (75) and (76) do not reflect this situation.

- $\forall x \ (Student(x) \rightarrow \neg \ \exists y \ [Book(y) \wedge Get(x, y)])$           (75)
- $\neg \ \exists x \ \exists y \ Student(x) \wedge Book(y) \wedge Get(x, y)$           (76)

In contrast, in a QAS based on the representational means of MultiNet, the semantic representation a) could never be created, if it were anchored in the background knowledge that there are no students. Since in this case the concept student would be characterized by [**FACT** = *non*], an indicator for nonexistence, the creation of [**FACT** = *real*] as an entry for the subordinate concept G01 would result in a contradiction. Actually, the representations b) and (76) would be acceptable from a pure truth-theoretical point of view, if there were no students, but then both would be as redundant as the natural language sentence. Summarizing, one can state that Formula (75) is cognitively inadequate, while representation a) does most distinctly reflect the "semantic deficiency" of the example sentence with generally nonexisting students. If there were no students, representations (76) and Fig. 9.11b would be acceptable from a logical point of view, but a natural language reformulation based on them would nevertheless violate Grice's maxims of conversation [84]. Thus, both are poor candidates for a semantic representation.

**Case IV**  – "**Not all** *students get a book.*"
Taking the sentences "*Not all students receive/get a book.*" (Ge: "*Nicht alle Schüler erhalten ein Buch.*") or "*Not every student receives/gets a book.*" (Ge: "*Nicht jeder Schüler erhält ein Buch.*") as a basis, the representation in Fig. 9.12a can be accepted as semantically adequate, since the negation with [**FACT** = *non*] warrants the maximum scope of negation over the quantification (see Fig. 5.2).

The representation dual to that of Fig. 9.12a is given in Fig. 9.12b. But the latter is already an entailment with regard to the sentences taken as examples for Case IV. For the sake of comparison, another state of affairs is given in Fig. 9.12c which is equivalent **neither** to a) **nor** b). It is used to demonstrate in what way the meaning differences caused by the different scopes of the operators are reflected in the semantic representation. As one should expect, the representation of the sentence from Fig. 9.12c is identical to the semantic representation of the corresponding sentence from Fig. 9.11a except for the arrangement of the nodes.

The necessity to distinguish between representatives of concepts quantified by **all** (which allow for a cumulative or a collective interpretation during answer finding and inferencing) and by **every** (for which this does not hold) is illustrated by the sentence "*Köchel compiled a catalogue of all works which had been produced by Mozart.*" The corresponding semantic representation is

a) Ge: *"**Nicht alle** Schüler erhalten ein Buch."*/
    *"**Nicht jeder** Schüler erhält ein Buch."*
En: *"**Not every** student gets a book."*

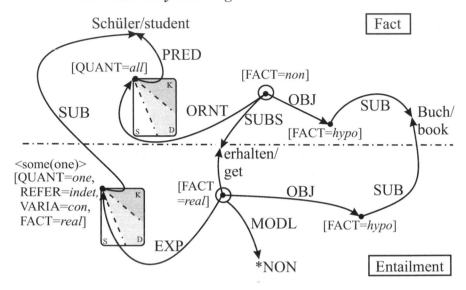

b) Ge: *"**Es gibt (mindestens) einen** Schüler, der **kein** Buch erhält."*
En: *"**There is (at least) one** student who does **not** get a book."*

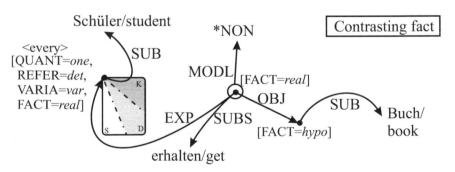

c) Ge: *"Für **jeden** Schüler gilt, daß er **kein** Buch erhält."*
En: *"It is true for **every** student that he does **not** get a book."*

**Figure 9.12.** Dual representation of the negated quantificator ⟨not all⟩ ↔ ⟨(at least) one + not⟩ (Pictures a and b) and a nonequivalent fact (Picture c) standing in contrast to a) and b)

shown in Fig. 9.13. If the quantification of the node G11 in this representation would be changed from all to every or each, the result would correspond to the sentence *"Köchel compiled a catalogue of each and every work which had been produced by Mozart."* (??) This sentence and its semantic representation[16] are not only unacceptable with regard to their truth value; they are even not admissible, since there is definitely no catalogue for a single work (such a representation, by the way, would also contradict the selectional restrictions of the lexeme ⟨catalogue (of)⟩ specified in the computational lexicon).

*"Köchel compiled **a catalogue of all works** which had been produced by Mozart."*

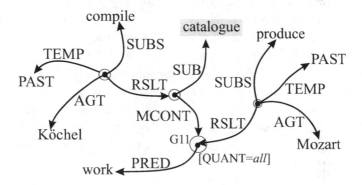

**Figure 9.13.** Concepts requiring a cumulative interpretation for [QUANT = all] for one of their complements

Concluding this chapter, a brief comment about the so-called "donkey sentences", often cited in the logic-oriented literature (see [215]), is in order. The following sentence is a characteristic one:

(9.11) **Donkey sentence**: *"Every farmer who owns a donkey beats it."*

After a generally accepted opinion, the FOL expression given below comes closest to the meaning of this sentence with regard to its truth conditions:

- $\forall x \, \forall y \, [\text{Farmer}(x) \land \text{Donkey}(y) \land \text{Owns}(x, y) \to \text{Beats}(x, y)]$  (77)

The corresponding MultiNet representation is given in Fig. 9.14.

---

[16] The node G11 represents all works produced by Mozart. It is definitionally determined by the PRED and RSLT arcs, symbolized by a capsule enclosed in a small circle.

A discussion of the problems associated with the meaning representation (77) from a logical point of view can be found in [75]. The main problem consists in the proper interplay of quantifier scope and reference identity. In our context, for the time being, we are only interested in the aspect of cognitive adequacy which is violated by Formula (77) for the following reasons:[17]

- Formula (77) contains *two universal quantifiers* and *one implication*, which are intuitively not present in the donkey sentence.
- Formula (77) is symmetric with regard to x (the farmers) and y (the donkeys). This symmetry does not hold for the donkey sentence (the latter contains a proposition about a certain class of farmers and not about donkeys). This deficiency can seemingly be remedied by using the logically equivalent formula

$$\forall x \; Farmer(x) \rightarrow \forall y \; [ \; Donkey(y) \wedge Owns(x, y) \rightarrow Beats(x, y)] \qquad (78)$$

   instead of (77). But this expression contains two implications instead of one, which is still worse with regard to cognitive adequacy.
- Formula (77) would also be true if there were no farmers at all or if the farmers did not possess any donkeys but, for instance, only horses. In contrast, the donkey sentence (9.11) does not make any statement about these cases. Thus, if Formula (77) were the correct semantic representation of (9.11), we would have the paradox that the natural language sentence would be senseless in a world where no farmers exist[18], while the corresponding Formula (77) would still be true.[19]

Considering the MultiNet representation in Fig. 9.14, one can see a representative for both concepts, F = ⟨farmer owning a donkey⟩ (quantified by every) and E = ⟨donkey being possessed by a farmer⟩ (connected with the quantificator/determiner "*a*"). Here, the proper combination of net specifications into conceptual units (each of them assigned the intuitively adequate set of layer information) is already carried out at the intensional level.[20] Also, the reference expressed in the donkey sentence by the pronoun "*it*" is correctly reflected in the representation. The proper scope of quantification is finally taken into account adequately by means of the DPND relation at the preextensional level. The fact that this dependency between farmer and donkey is not

---

[17] For further discussion see Chap. 13.

[18] Nobody would say something about farmers owning donkeys if there were no farmers at all in the world in question.

[19] This general problem observed in connection with sentences containing universal quantifications has already been discussed by Löbner in [163].

[20] Please note that node E is not quantified by all in contrast to the FOL formula. The capsule for this concept, which is essentially determined by the incoming POSS arc and the outgoing SUB arc, has only been sketched in Fig. 9.14 to avoid overloading the representation.

*"Every farmer who owns a donkey beats it."*

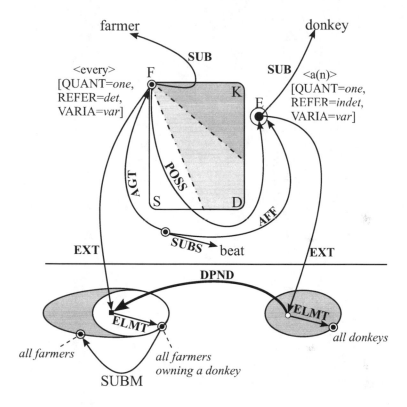

**Figure 9.14.** Semantic representation of a typical "donkey sentence"

perceived by most readers/listeners during the initial intuitive understanding of the sentence strengthens the opinion that these relationships belong to cognitively different levels. It is further important that the representation in Fig. 9.14 explicitly contains unique representatives of the objects involved (in this case, for farmers owning donkeys and for donkeys being possessed by farmers), while this is not true for (77).

The use of the knowledge representation from Fig. 9.14 in the inference process and during answer generation in a QAS, and the differences between this representation and logical representations, will be discussed from another perspective in Sect. 13.2.

# Chapter 10

# The Role of Layer Information in Semantic Representations

## 10.1 General Remarks

The embedding of entities into a multidimensional system of layer attributes and their values is most important to objects [SORT = $o$] and situations [SORT = $si$]; in some cases it is also relevant to locations [SORT = $l$] and temporal specifications [SORT = $t$]. Since layer information and its application for the semantic representation of concepts has already been dealt with in other contexts in Chaps. 3, 8, 9, and in Sect. 17.2, we shall concentrate here on special aspects associated with the origin and processing of the layer features.

In the first place, the question arises as to how the layer information of a concept described by a complex phrase can be (automatically) generated starting with the lexemes involved in the description (see Chap. 12 on lexical knowledge representation). The determiners and quantificators encountered mainly in the noun phrases of a sentence play an essential role in this. With attributes like **GENER** and **VARIA**, syntactical aspects (the position of the corresponding phrase in a sentence) or prosodic information (intonation) are also important. Finally, the values of the attribute **FACT** are more often than not determined by the modal system of the considered language (see Chap. 8).

As a basic mechanism for determining the layer information of a complex concept described by a noun phrase, the following is assumed:[1] Every lexeme is described in the lexicon by as specific as possible layer information without restricting the spectrum of interpretations that arises from combinations with other lexemes. For this purpose, the type hierarchy given in Sect. 17.2 of Part II is used. The value of the attribute **ETYPE** for lexemes representing a noun is defined as the minimal number still compatible with this lexeme. A possible increase of this value by a determiner or quantificator (mostly accompanied by plural constructs in the surface structure) is symbolized in the following exposition by + 1. With combinations of more than one determiner or quantificator,

---

[1] For the time being, we concentrate only on the basic approach; a more detailed investigation, including the unification of layer information, can be found at the end of this chapter and in [99].

only the maximum increase in the value of **ETYPE** stemming from one of these determiners or quantificators will become effective.

Examples:

|  | CARD | ETYPE | GENER | QUANT | REFER | VARIA |
|---|---|---|---|---|---|---|
| bear | *card* | 0 | *gener* | *quant* | *refer* | *varia* |
| all | > 1 | + 1 | *gener* | *all* | *det* | *con* |
| this | 1 | 0 | *sp* | *one* | *det* | *con* |
| three | 3 | + 1 | *gener* | *nfquant* | *refer* | *varia* |

The combination (or, to be exact, the unification) of the layer specifications from the above table yields the following layer characteristics, where only values from Fig. 17.4 of Part II that either are identical or stand in a subordination relation in the type hierarchy of layer attribute-values can be unified. The result of the unification process is the most specific value of both arguments of the operation.[2]

|  | CARD | ETYPE | GENER | QUANT | REFER | VARIA |
|---|---|---|---|---|---|---|
| ⟨three bears⟩ | 3 | 1 | *gener* | *nfquant* | *refer* | *varia* |
| ⟨this bear⟩ | 1 | 0 | *sp* | *one* | *det* | *con* |
| ⟨all bears⟩ | > 1 | 1 | *gener* | *all* | *det* | *con* |
| ⟨all three bears⟩ | 3 | 1 | *gener* | *all* | *det* | *con* |

# 10.2   Degree of Generalization: GENER

Though human beings are able to distinguish between a concept used in a generalized sense [**GENER** = *ge*] and one being used in a specialized sense [**GENER** = *sp*], it is difficult to formulate generally accepted rules for this problem.[3] It is possible to establish some general criteria for "*discovering*" the generic use of concepts in utterances, but, unfortunately, they have to be qualified as heuristics only.

---

[2] The value of the attribute **ETYPE** is computed by means of the indicated operation, if given in the table; otherwise it is determined by the unification rules. Thus, the value [**ETYPE** = 1] for ⟨three bears⟩ results from 0 (for bear) plus 1 from the instruction + 1 stemming from three. The value [**ETYPE** = 2] for ⟨three families⟩ is computed analogously, since family is specified by [**ETYPE** =1] in the lexicon. With ⟨all three bears⟩, the increase of the value of **ETYPE** by 1 is brought into effect only once.

[3] The formulation of such rules is critically important for automatic language processing.

- Statements about generic concepts often use the present tense.
  Example:
  (10.1) *"The grizzly loves to eat berries."*        [**GENER** = *ge*]
  Counterexample:
  (10.2) *"The tyrannosaur **was** a dangerous predator."* (in spite of past tense
  [**GENER** = *ge*])
- Determiners never bear the stress with generic concepts, something that is especially important for German.
  Example:
  (10.3) Ge: *"Der Grizzly frißt gern Beeren."*        (stress on *"Grizzly"*)
  En: *"The grizzly loves to eat berries."*        [**GENER** = *ge*]
  Determiners having a specializing effect always bear the stress (at least in subject position).
  Example:
  (10.4) Ge: *"Der (= dieser) Grizzly frißt gern Beeren."*    (stress on *"Der"*)
  En: *"This grizzly loves to eat berries."*        [**GENER** = *sp*]
- A predication about a generic concept does not in general contain any names of individuals, specializations, or strongly restricted time intervals respective locations.
  Example of generic use:
  (10.5) Ge: *"Der Bär frißt gern Honig."*        [**GENER** = *ge*]
  En: *"The bear loves to eat honey."*
  Examples of nongeneric use:
  (10.6) Ge: *"Der Bär frißt gern den Honig vom Imker Müller."*
  En: *"The bear loves to eat honey from beekeeper Miller."*
  [**GENER** = *sp*]
  (10.7) Ge: *"Der Bär frißt morgen den Honig."*
  En: *"Tomorrow, that bear will eat the honey."*        [**GENER** = *sp*]

A comprehensive investigation of the problems connected with generic concepts can be found in [40].

## 10.3   Facticity: FACT

As described in Fig. 17.2.3 of Part II, the attribute **FACT** is used with conceptual objects to represent existence [**FACT** = *real*] or nonexistence [**FACT** = *non*], or – if this distinction is not possible – it is used to specify a hypothetical object with [**FACT** = *hypo*]. The commitment to one of these attribute values leads to the problem of **existential presupposition**. The question is whether or not the objects participating in a situational description exist. As already stated in Sects. 8.2 and 8.3, it is not possible in modal contexts to infer the existence of the objects involved without further information. But even with regard to normal propositional sentences, the opinions held by logicians differ strongly, as can be illustrated by means of the following frequently cited sentence (see [247, Chap. 10], where also the dispute between Strawson and Russell concerning this matter is referred to).

Example:

(10.8)  S = *"The present king of France is bald."*

On the one hand, following Strawson, an opinion is held that the existence of a king of France now and today is a **presupposition** P of the sentence S, i.e. P is not stated in sentence S itself and follows from S as well as from ¬S. The sentence, in this opinion, is neither true nor false, but senseless if there is no actual king of France (so-called **truth-value gap**).

On the other hand, there is an opinion held by followers of Russell that the existence of a contemporary king of France is explicitly stated in S, i.e. the proposition S ↔ P ∧ S0 holds with P being a statement about the existence of the king and S0 being a statement about his baldness. Here, P can be inferred from S but not from its negation ¬S (↝ **entailment**). In this case, S is false (not senseless) if there is no current king of France.

We share the opinion of Strawson and consider implicit existential statements as presuppositions. This is supported by the rules of scope for the representational means of negation and facticity, which state that a specification [**FACT** = *real*] of an object node K involved in the representation of a situation S is invariant with regard to the negation of S by means of MODL + *NON.

A still more subtle question arises with regard to the facticity of concepts which do not stand in subject position in the natural language description of a situation.

Examples:

(10.9)   *"Peter bought a bicycle."*
(10.10)  *"Peter saw a bicycle."*
(10.11)  *"Peter dreamed that he had got a bicycle."*

While in the first sentence the corresponding bicycle must doubtlessly exist, this assumption is not so reliable in the second sentence (Peter could have been subject to a hallucination). In the third sentence, it is under no circumstance possible to derive the existence of the bicycle in question from the given information, even if the sentence is true. The differences discussed are expressed in MultiNet by means of different deep case frames of the corresponding verbs.

While the object of *"buy"* is characterized by the C-Role OBJ alone, the object of *"see"* is linked to the situational node by OBJ and MCONT, where the relation OBJ is an indication of [**FACT** = *real*].[4] In contrast, the grammatical object of *"dream (that)"*, which characterizes an imagined situation, is semantically specified by MCONT alone. On that basis, one may fix only the value [**FACT** = *hypo*] for the semantic representative of the sentence and the objects involved because of the definition of this relation.

## 10.4   Determination of Reference: REFER

Another difficult problem which has also been intensely discussed in logic is the reference problem (see [247]). If the question is asked about what the specifications [**REFER** = *det*] or [**REFER** = *indet*] for a conceptual object c (node with [**SORT** = *o*]) really mean, two cases have to be distinguished:[5]

(a) The concept c is introduced in a text/dialogue for the first time. If c is marked by [**REFER** = *det*], there must be either an existing object which is uniquely referred to by c, or c characterizes a concept commonly known to both, the speaker/writer and the hearer/reader.[6] In all other cases, only the value [**REFER** = *indet*] is admissible for c.

(b) The concept c is mentioned the second time. In this case the value [**REFER** = *det*] of c indicates a reference initiating a search for a concept which has already been introduced, and which must be identified with c. It is a task of the assimilation process in a QAS (see Fig. 1.2) to carry out the identification and to determine the overall value of referentiality of the concept for the whole text/dialogue (see case a). If c was originally labeled [**REFER** = *indet*], then we had at the beginning a newly introduced concept which can later on be referred to with [**REFER** = *det*].

---

[4] We hold the opinion that objects which are *"seen"* or *"observed"* really exist. At least, these are the fixations used in the valency frames of *"see"* and *"observe"* in the computational lexicon HaGenLex (see Chap. 12). If somebody prefers another assumption, then this can also be expressed in MultiNet, e.g. by characterizing the object of the corresponding verbs by means of MCONT alone, instead of the double characterization OBJ + MCONT actually used in HaGenLex.

[5] Please remember that the primary values of the attribute **REFER** in an isolated sentence are essentially determined by the system of quantificators and determiners involved in the description of a concept.

[6] The object $o_r$ referred to by an expression $\hat{o}_r$ can also be introduced implicitly by background knowledge associated with another object $o_p$ already mentioned (this is known as **bridging references** [177]).    Example:    *"Peter bought a new car ($\hat{o}_p$). The motor ($\hat{o}_r$)* [**REFER** = *det*] *had to be repaired."* In this case, the background knowledge consists of the hidden part-whole relationship between Peter's car $o_p$ and the motor $o_r$ of this car, a connection established by the common sense knowledge that a car has a motor.

Example:

(10.12) *"Peter bought an old car."*                    [**REFER** = *indet*]
(10.13) *"This vehicle had a very bad suspension."*     [**REFER** = *det*]

In the first sentence, a new concept c is introduced by *"an old car"* with [**REFER** = *indet*], which is typically referred to by the superordinate concept *"This vehicle"* with [**REFER** = *det*] in the second sentence. In the end, the representative for c is assigned the value [**REFER** = *indet*] by the assimilation process as it was introduced during the first mention of c.

It must be emphasized that the attribute value [**FACT** = *real*] cannot necessarily be inferred from [**REFER** = *det*] for an object representative (even if this is a good default assumption, which finds its parallel in the philosophical literature[7]).

Example:

(10.14) *"The students especially liked to speak with their teacher about
        the yeti."*                                      [**REFER** = *det*]

Although yetis do not exist according to a widely accepted opinion (expressed in the knowledge base by [**FACT** = *non*] with the concept yeti, or if one wants to be more cautious with regard to the existence of a yeti, by [**FACT** = *hypo*]), a determinate reference is quite acceptable, since the concept yeti belongs to the common background knowledge of most people.

The following dialogue shows what effects are achievable by a (deliberately) wrong use of the reference mechanism (see also the discussion in [6]).

(10.15) Speaker A: *"Why are these guys running so fast?"*     (S1)
        Speaker B: *"The winner will be awarded a prize."*     (S2)
        Speaker A: *"And why do the others run?"*              (S3)

At first, Speaker A introduces a determinate group of people in sentence S1 (see Fig. 10.1), whereas Speaker B only seemingly refers to a determinate person by means of the phrase *"the winner"* in Sentence S2. Actually, we have to take into consideration the implicit knowledge *"every race – and also this special race – will finally have a winner"* [**REFER** = *indet*]. This is the knowledge really referred to by Speaker B (he means *"the winner, whoever it may be"*). For this reason, the "winner node" in situation S2 has to be characterized by [**REFER** = *indet*]. Finally, Speaker A – in contrast to the foregoing sentence – refers to a determinate collection of people from Sentence A by using the phrase *"the others"* with [**REFER** = *det*] in a way as if it were already evident

---

[7]  Sommers, for instance, claims for "genuine reference" that the object which is referred to should also exist, see [247, p. 55].

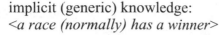

implicit (generic) knowledge:
*<a race (normally) has a winner>*

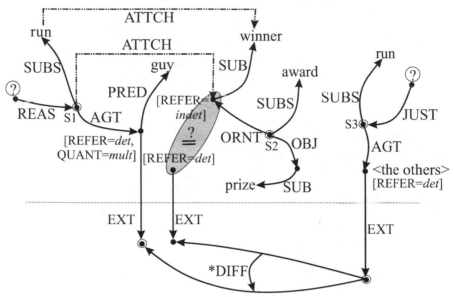

**Figure 10.1.** The effects of the violation of the consistency of values for referentiality

who need not to run. Because of the implicit construction of a set difference contained in Sentence S3, Speaker A indirectly introduces another determined object (second argument of *DIFF in Fig. 10.1 with [**REFER** = *det*]). This object, strictly speaking, is a well determined winner, i.e. Speaker A answers Speaker B in a way as if the winner were already known. Thus, the funny effect arises from a deliberate misuse of the reference mechanism.

## 10.5 Variability: VARIA

The attribute **VARIA** characterizes the variability of the representative of a concept; it must not be mixed up with the attribute **REFER** specifying whether the reference of a concept is determinate or not.

In the sentence "*There is a book which is read by every student.*" the semantic representative of "*a book*" has to be characterized by [**REFER** = *indet*] and [**VARIA** = *con*], since on the one hand it is not specified which book is exactly referred to (therefore, [**REFER** = *indet*]); on the other hand, it is clear that the underlined phrase points to a special book being independent of other entities (therefore, [**VARIA** = *con*]).

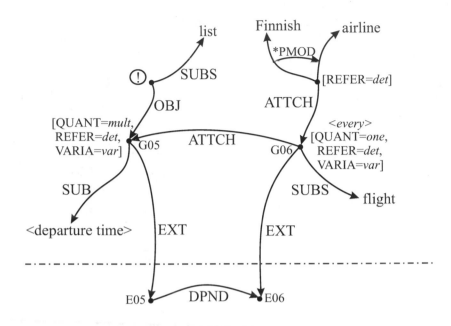

**Figure 10.2.** Interplay of the attributes REFER and VARIA

Figure 10.2 shows the representation of the sentence *"List the departure times of every flight of the Finnish airline!"* We shall concentrate on the nodes G05 and G06. On the one hand, G05 is characterized by [**VARIA** = *var*], because its extensional changes in dependence on the extensional of node G06. On the other hand, G05 must be labeled by [**REFER** = *det*], since the reference of G05 is uniquely determined given a fixed flight. A similar situation is evoked by the sentence *"List a crew member for every flight of the Finnish airline"*, whose semantic representation is built analogously to that in Fig. 10.2. The difference between the two sentences (mainly consisting in the use of the definite and indefinite article) is manifested in the node G05. In the representation of the second sentence, G05 must be subordinate to ⟨crew member⟩ and marked by [**REFER** = *indet*] and [**VARIA** = *var*]. Figure 10.2 also gives the solution to a problem which was dealt with by Woods under the heading **functional nesting and quantifier reversal** (see [282, Sect. 7.3]). The problem consists in the following: the phrase P1 = *"of every flight"* from the first example sentence is syntactically subordinate to the phrase P2 = *"the depar-*

*ture times*", while at the semantic level the representative G05 of phrase P2 depends on the representative G06 of P1 (cf. Fig. 10.2). This is also reflected by the direction of the DPND relation at the preextensional level (therefore the term "*quantifier reversal*").

As already mentioned, determiners and quantificators are the most important carriers of information about layer attributes in natural language. More specifically, determiners are words or natural language expressions that mainly specify the type of reference within an NP, while quantificators specify the extension of the described concept (see [169, Sect. 11.4]). Consequently, determiners are expressions relevant to answering questions like "*Who/what is meant?*" while quantificators contribute to answers for questions like "*How many are meant?*" or "*How much is meant?*"

Figure 10.3 shows typical determiners and quantificators together with their layer information as defined in MultiNet. The table comprises articles, demonstrative pronouns, definite numerals, and indefinite numerals. The contribution of a word to the layer attributes is often nonspecific. Thus, one cannot draw a conclusion from the article "*the*" alone to derive the exact values of **CARD**, **GENER**, **QUANT**, and **REFER** without having further information. Even if one takes into consideration the singular/plural distinction (marked by "*the$_1$*" and "*the$_2$*", respectively, in Fig. 10.3), some underspecifications still remain with regard to **GENER** and **REFER**. The table also shows, for instance, that "*all*" can be seen as neither a pure quantificator nor a pure determiner. Thus, "*all*" with [**REFER** = *det*] comprises a meaning component that describes a determinate reference (the question "*Who/what is meant?*" may be uniquely answered by "*all*"). However, the meaning of "*all*" also contains an aspect of quantification (evidenced by the fact that the question "*How many are meant?*" may also be answered uniquely with "*all*"). This meaning component is covered by the attribute value [**QUANT** = *all*].

A special characteristic of definite numerals consists in the fact that they have an explicit cardinality as a meaning component (attribute **CARD**) and, at the same time, a value for the attribute **QUANT**, which specifies whether the concept characterized by it is a plurality [**QUANT** = *mult*] or not [**QUANT** = *one*]. The definite numerals have even the same (more specific) value characteristic [**QUANT** = *nfquant*] as the quantificator "*all*", stating that they are not fuzzy quantificators. This is in contrast to "*almost all*" and "*several*" which are fuzzy quantificators (expressed by [**QUANT** = *fquant*]; see Fig. 17.4) requiring corresponding fuzzy inferences.[8]

Figure 10.3 shows clearly that one has to distinguish between words and the values of layer attributes.[9] The meaning representations of natural language determiners and quantificators are bundles of layer attributes rather than elementary representational entities. Thus, the determiner/quantificator "*all*" is specified at the same time by [**QUANT** = *all*], describing only the quantification aspect, by [**REFER** = *det*], and by [**VARIA** = *con*], describing the determination of reference and, in contrast to "*every*", the lacking variation of the corresponding extensional.[10] Unlike "*every*", the quantificator "*all*" is characterized by [**GENER** = *gener*], since "*all*" can be combined with "*these*" ("*all these animals*") and the unification associated with this combination must not result in a contradiction. (The combined value obtained by this operation is [**GENER** = *sp*].) The layer attributes for "*every*" are chosen as follows: [**QUANT** = *one*] because every single element is meant and no collective interpretation is possible (see Fig. 9.5)[11]; [**REFER** = *det*] because the reference to all elements is determined; [**VARIA** = *var*] indicating that the extensionals underlying the corresponding concepts are varying (in contrast to "*all*"); and [**GENER** = *sp*] since every single element is meant.

Based on these specifications, it can be explained why "*all these animals*" (Ge: "*alle diese Tiere*") is allowed (no contradiction during unification), whereas "*every/each these animals*" (??) (Ge: "*jede diese Tiere*" (??)) is not allowed because of the contradiction between [**VARIA** = *var*], with "*every*" (Ge: "*jede*"), and [**VARIA** = *con*], with "*these*" (Ge: "*diese*").[12]

As already mentioned, the unification of layer attributes can be used to generate the values of these attributes for more complex phrases (like "*those many*

---

[8] To avoid cross-classification, assigning the value type *nfquant* to "*one*" is renounced, since a characterization by [**QUANT** = *one*] and [**CARD** = 1] is sufficient to exclude possible "fuzziness" of the underlying concept extension.

[9] Because of that, they are always denoted by English terms in the German documentation of MultiNet. This denotation has been retained here, since a translation of the values of layer attributes into another language would result in an incompatibility of the different descriptions of the MultiNet language and also worsen the readability.

[10] The fact that some words like "*all*" have a determiner function as well as a quantificator function had been referred to already in [169].

[11] The bundle of attribute values [**QUANT** = *one*], [**REFER** = *det*], [**GENER** = *sp*], [**CARD** = 1], and [**VARIA** = *var*] is sometimes abbreviated by <*every*> (cf. Fig. 10.3).

[12] Of course, the German phrase "*jedes dieser Tiere*" (or more distinctly separated in English "*every(one)/each of these animals*") is admissible. Because of the genitive construction, we have not only one node as a semantic representative but two. These nodes have to be connected at the preextensional level by an ELMT relation. In this phrase, the two quantifiers (Ge: "*jeder*" + "*dieser*" or En: "*every(one)/each*" + "*these*") do really not cooperate to form a single concept, which is somewhat hidden in the German phrase "*jedes dieser Tiere*".

*bears*"). At the same time, this mechanism gives an indication as to which combinations of determiners and quantificators are allowed and which have to be excluded; see Fig. 10.4. Thus, row 4 of the table states that the combination "*these* + *many*" (Ge: "*diese* + *vielen*") is allowed, giving the combination of layer attributes shown in the table. Row 7, however, shows that "*every*" + "*these*" (Ge: "*jede{r/s}*" + "*diese*") is not admissible because of the conflicting information with regard to the attribute **VARIA**.

Summarizing, one can state that, on the basis of this formalism, a large part of the regularities governing the combination of determiners and quantificators with each other and with nouns modified by them in a complete noun phrase can be explained. One has to take into consideration, however, that other grammatical laws are also of relevance in this field. Therefore, not all phenomena can be explained by the unification of layer information. To be specific, the following restrictions and criteria have to be observed as well:

- Syntactical restrictions, especially those concerning the word order (thus, the combination "*these*" + "*many*" (Ge: "*diese*" + "*vielen*") may be used, but not "*many*" + "*these*" (Ge: "*viele*" + "*diese*")).
- Avoiding of redundancies; for instance, the determiners or quantificators "*a(n)*" (Ge: "*ein*") and "*some*" (Ge: "*(irgend)ein*") are actually compatible with regard to their layer information, but such a combination would be redundant.
- In some cases, the values of layer attributes cannot be restricted far enough by the unification mechanism alone (this concerns in particular the attribute **GENER**); here, prosodic aspects as well as syntactic aspects (tense) also play an important part (see the discussion in Sect. 10.2).

It has to be emphasized that, on the one hand, the consistent use of layer information opens entirely new possibilities for the explanation of the combined effects of determiners and quantificators (see [99]), but on the other hand, an exhaustive empirical validation of the methods and theses proposed here still has to be done.

| Determiner/Quantificator | | CARD | GENER | QUANT | REFER | VARIA |
|---|---|---|---|---|---|---|
| der/die₁/das | (En: the₁) | 1 | gener | one | refer | con |
| die₂ | (En: the₂) | >1 | gener | mult | refer | con |
| diese{r/s}, diese₁ | (En: this/that) | 1 | sp | one | det | con |
| diese₂ | (En: these/those) | >1 | sp | mult | det | con |
| ein₁ (numeral) | (En: one) | 1 | gener | one | refer | varia |
| ein₂ (indet. article) | (En: a(n), some₁) | 1 | gener | one | indet | varia |
| alle | (En: all) | >1 | gener | all | det | con |
| fast alle | (En: almost all) | >2 | gener | almost_all | indet | varia |
| jeder/jedes | (En: every/each) | 1 | sp | one | det | var |
| einige | (En: several/some₂) | >1 | gener | several | indet | varia |
| viele | (En: many) | >2 | gener | many | refer | varia |
| eins | (En: one) | 1 | sp | one | refer | varia |
| zwei | (En: two) | 2 | gener | nfquant | refer | varia |
| drei | (En: three) | 3 | gener | nfquant | refer | varia |
| ..... | | | | | | |
| wenige | (En: few) | >1 | gener | few | refer | varia |
| mehrere | (En: several) | >2 | gener | several | indet | varia |
| die meisten | (En: most) | >2 | sp | most | indet | con |
| irgendein | (En: any) | 1 | sp | one | indet | var |
| irgendwelche | (En: any) | >1 | sp | mult | indet | var |
| jemand | (En: someone) | 1 | sp | one | indet | con |

**Figure 10.3.** The layer information for selected determiners and quantificators

| Determiner/Quantificator | CARD | GENER | QUANT | REFER | VARIA |
|---|---|---|---|---|---|
| der/das [the₁] + ein₁ [one] | 1 | gener | one | det*) | con |
| die₂ [the₂] + viel [many] | >1 | gener | many | det*) | con |
| dieser/dieses [this] + viel [many] | reject | --- Conflict CARD/QUANT --- | | | |
| diese [these] + viel [many] | >1 | sp | many | det | con |
| ein₁/₂ [one/a(n)] + viel [many] | reject | --- Conflict CARD/QUANT --- | | | |
| alle [all] + diese [these] | >1 | sp | all | det | con |
| jeder/jedes [every/each] + diese [these] | reject | --- Conflict VARIA --- | | **) | |
| einige [several] + diese [these] | reject | --- Conflict REFER --- | | **) | |
| alle [all] + drei [three] | 3 | gener | all | det | con |
| fast alle [almost all] + diese[these] | reject | --- Conflict REFER --- | | | |
| viele [many] + alle [all] | reject | --- Conflict VARIA --- | | | |
| eins [one] + viele [many] | reject | --- Conflict CARD/QUANT--- | | | |
| zwei/drei [two/three] + viele [many] | reject | --- Conflict QUANT {nfquant/fquant} | | | |
| drei [three] + fast alle [almost all] | reject | --- Conflict QUANT {nfquant/fquant} | | | |
| irgendwelche [some₂] + alle [all] | reject | --- Conflict QUANT/REFER --- | | | |
| ein₂ [a(n)] + irgendein [some₁] | --- unifiable, but forbidden because of the redundancy rule --- | | | | |

*) Ge: Because of the synonymy with "*diese(r/s)*" in this case

**) Ge: The phrase "*{jeder/einige} dieser*" is no counterexample; results in two representatives

**Figure 10.4.** The unification of layer information for selected combinations of determiners and quantificators

# Chapter 11

# Relations Between Situations

## 11.1 Semantic Interpretation of Conjunctions

### 11.1.1 General Remarks

After verbs and prepositions, conjunctions are the most important carriers of semantic relations in (complex) sentences. While verbs and prepositions typically determine the inner structure of elementary situations, conjunctions are the carriers of the semantic relations between different situations. One has to discern between two types of conjunctions:[1]

- **Subordinating conjunctions (Subordinators)**: These words or phrases are used to introduce a subordinate clause;
- **Coordinating conjunctions (Coordinators)**: These words or phrases connect either
  - words or phrases having the same grammatical status
  - sentences of the same degree (main clauses or subordinate clauses of the same syntactic level).

Although this distinction is grammatically based, it will be used in this chapter for an overview of the conjunctions. It can be observed that both groups of conjunctions can also be discerned on the basis of the semantic phenomena described by them. Subordinators are mainly used to characterize relationships of justification and reason or situational circumstances of states of affairs. This group of conjunctions will be discussed in Sect. 11.1.2. Coordinators are mainly employed to describe logical connectives or (if they are used within an elementary sentence) to construct pluralities. Thus, the copulative

---

[1] Because, in many cases, there is no simple one-to-one translation between German and English conjunctions, we shall primarily deal with German conjunctions following roughly the classification proposed by Jung [133]. However, since the general parallelism between English and German conjunctions is apparent, the corresponding classification of English conjunctions according to the ordering criteria used for German will be given in parallel; see Figs. 11.2 and 11.4. The principal statements about conjunctions in this book hold for German as well as English.

conjunctions and the disjunctive conjunctions play the most important role in connection with coordinative sentences, and they are therefore put in the center of the discussion in Sect. 11.1.3.

## 11.1.2  Subordinating Conjunctions (Subordinators)

In this section, only a short overview can be given of a proper assignment of semantic deep relations to subordinators, since this is mainly a problem for syntactic-semantic interpretation. This assignment is partly straightforward (this holds especially for temporal and local relationships) and partly not yet understood thoroughly enough (this applies, above all, to modal and causal relationships). Here, especially in the field of automatic language processing, more profound investigations are needed. A more detailed discussion of modal and causal relationships can be found in the following sections.

The standard interpretation of subordinating conjunctions for German and English (or of groups of such conjunctions, if they have the same interpretation) is given in Figs. 11.1 and 11.2. The overviews for both languages are kept apart, since the existing parallelism between English and German conjunctions is disturbed by a diverging polysemy (e.g. Ge: "*wenn*" vs. En: "*if*" and "*when*") and by diverging grammatical correspondences (e.g. "*Indem (conjunction) er kein Geständnis ablegte, beging der Angeklagte einen schweren Fehler.*" vs. "*Making no confession (participle clause), the accused made a serious mistake*").[2] The ambiguity of conjunctions leads to difficulties especially for the syntactic-semantic analysis. Even in those cases where human beings have no difficulty in deciding which deep relation is the semantically adequate interpretation for a given conjunction, the algorithmic decision for one or the other of the possible alternatives can often be made on the basis of background knowledge only.

Example: Discrimination between causation (CAUS) and implication (IMPL) in the semantic field of reason and justification (see Sect. 11.2):

(11.1)  "*Since the number 6 can be divided by 2, it is not a
        prime number.*"     → IMPL

---

[2] The correspondence between subordinated clauses introduced by a subordinator in German and participle constructions in other languages is a phenomenon typical also of the language pair 'German – Russian'.

Another phenomenon breaking the parallelism between German and English lies in the fact that conjunctions in one language correspond to adverbs or adverbial phrases in the other language.

This example does not represent a causal relationship (at least not in the sense of the definition of relation CAUS given in Part II and in Sect. 11.2.2, but at best in the wide sense in which the term "causal sentence" is sometimes used in traditional grammars, see [133]). The correct interpretation of the relationship between the states of affairs described in the main clause and in the subordinated clause has to yield IMPL because the two partial sentences together in this case describe an analytical proposition, which is true on the basis of definitions only. In the following sentence, however, a causal relationship instead of an implication is the backbone of the semantic representation:

(11.2) *"Since the computer divided the result by zero, an error message had been created."* $\rightarrow$ CAUS

Analogous problems arise with the analysis of consecutive clauses. As semantic relations described by them, IMPL, CAUS, and RSLT have to be considered. The relation IMPL must not be used for the semantic representation of consecutive sentences connecting **factual situations** with each other. Here, only RSLT or CAUS are admissible as proper interpretations.
Example: Discrimination between RSLT and CAUS in a consecutive clause.

(11.3) *"A relief action was started, which lead to the rescue of the victims."* $\rightarrow$ RSLT[3]

In this case, the relation RSLT should be preferred to the relation CAUS. This is always recommended when the relation RSLT is involved as an immanent deep relation in the meaning structure of a connecting phrase (like *"leads to"*) or of the action dominating the main clause (a result, i.e. the deep relation RSLT, is also inherent in the semantic field of a ⟨rescue action⟩, at least implicitly). A consecutive clause is, among other things, one of the syntactic forms which may be used to express a result. In comparison with CAUS, the relation RSLT puts stronger emphasis on the goal directedness and the character as a natural outcome of the situation described by the first argument. CAUS can be deduced anyway from RSLT by means of the following axiom (which holds only if the second argument of RSLT is also a situation).

- $(sv_1 \text{ RSLT } sv_2) \rightarrow (sv_1 \text{ CAUS } sv_2)$          for $sv_1, sv_2 \in si$          (79)

CAUS may also connect two events not inherently related to each other, which is not true for RSLT. In the following example, the relation RSLT is not indicated by the meaning of the verb *"to cross"*:

---

[3] The phrase *"lead to"* in this sentence is to be seen merely as a surface description of the semantic deep relation RSLT.

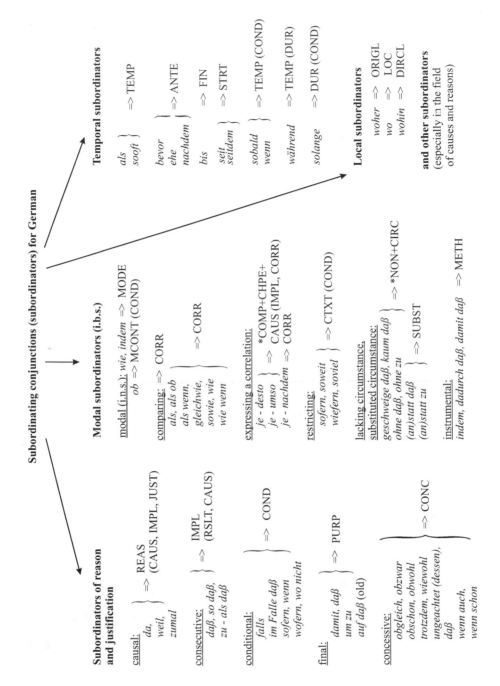

**Figure 11.1.** Overview of the standard interpretations of German subordinating conjunctions (for English, see Fig. 11.2)

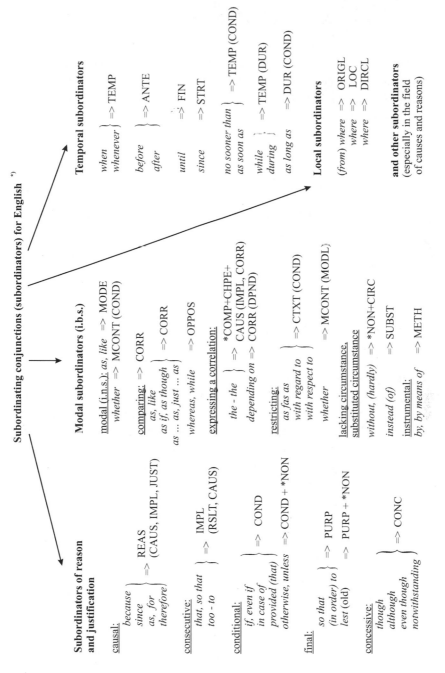

**Figure 11.2.** Overview of the standard interpretations of corresponding English subordinating conjunctions (for German, see Fig. 11.1)

(11.4) *"Peter crossed the road so carelessly, that he was hit by a motorcycle."*

$\rightarrow$ CAUS

German conjunctions in the temporal field are somewhat problematic because they are sometimes connected with two possibilities for interpretation, which often seem to coexist in one sentence. Nevertheless, it is often not necessary to decide which of these interpretations is the "correct one". Thus, *"wenn"* may express at the same time a temporal and a conditional aspect in many contexts. Example:

(11.5) Ge: *"Wenn ein Fehlerabbruch eintritt, erscheint auf dem Monitor eine Nachricht."*                                        $\rightarrow$ COND + TEMP

(En: *"When/If an interruption caused by an error happens, a message will appear on the monitor."*)

The different possibilities for expressing grammatical relations (object, subject, and attribute relations) with subordinating conjunctions cannot be dealt with here (see [133, pages 380–381]).

### 11.1.3   Coordinative Conjunctions (Coordinators)

Figure 11.3 gives an overview of the German coordinating conjunctions and their semantic interpretations (a roughly corresponding overview for English is given in Fig. 11.4). Because of the similarities in the semantic interpretation of these conjunctions compared to those in the field of subordinating conjunctions, we shall restrict ourselves in this section to the copulative, disjunctive, and adversative conjunctions.[4] When we speak about coordinations or coordinative constructions, we are dealing with relations between sentences or phrases linked together by the above-mentioned conjunctions (see the left sides of Figs. 11.3 and 11.4).

As already stated by Lang in his work "Semantik der koordinativen Verknüpfung" [152], there is actually a certain relatedness between coordinating conjunctions and logical connectives, although it is not sufficient for the modeling of general language understanding to reduce the former to the latter. In contrast to the logical connectives, the natural language conjunctions make reference to

---

[4] A deeper discrimination between nuances in the meaning of related conjunctions (if they exist at all), like between German *"denn"* (coordination) and *"weil"* (subordinator) (En: *"because"*), will be neglected here; see [120].

In general, the advances made in the semantic interpretation of coordinated clauses is comparable to that of subordinate clauses (see Sect. 11.1.2), i.e. this task is not yet completed and further investigations into that topic are necessary. The degree of semantic fine-differentiation that must be achieved will depend on the different application fields of Multi-Net.

- compatibility or incompatibility of the meaning of the conjuncts,
- dependence or independence of the meaning of the conjuncts,
- intensional distinctness or nondistinctness between the conjuncts.

In addition, the following was stated about coordinative constructions by Lang [152, p. 66]:

> "Sie haben eine operative Bedeutung, die darin besteht, daß sie Anweisungen repräsentieren, über den Konjunktbedeutungen gewisse Operationen auszuführen. Als deren Resultat wird eine **gemeinsame Einordnungsinstanz (GEI)** als eine die Konjunktbedeutung übergreifende Einheit konstituiert und innerhalb dieser Einheit werden die jeweils konjunktionsspezifischen Zusammenhänge zwischen den in den Konjunktbedeutungen repräsentierten Sachverhalten gesetzt."[5]

Since the search for a GEI requires a conclusion from the original states of affairs to this general concept, and thus belongs to the field of inferences, the GEI will not be explicitly introduced into the graphical representation.

The knowledge of these relationships is important for the semantic interpretation of coordinating conjunctions of clauses, since the latter mostly have an elliptical character. Therefore, they can be properly understood and completed only by establishing a parallelism among appropriate constituents in the single phrases of a coordinated sentence taking into consideration the abovementioned GEI. Also, the humorous effect of some coordinative constructions (especially of the so-called **zeugma**) can only be understood against this background.

Example:

(11.6) *"He plays the flute and she (plays) a real musical instrument."*

The sarcastic and provoking effect of such a sentence is caused by the fact that both objects are put into a contrast with each other and must simultaneously have a GEI, i.e. a common superconcept which is superordinated to the concepts flute and ⟨real musical instrument⟩ occurring in the sentence. Thus the speaker (willingly or not) expresses that a flute is no real musical instrument.

---

[5] En: "They have an operational meaning consisting in the fact that they represent instructions about certain operations to be carried out over the meaning of the conjuncts. As a result, a generalized concept (with Lang the so-called **gemeinsame Einordnungsinstanz** or **GEI**) is constructed as a unity superordinated to the meaning of the conjuncts; within this unity the conjunct-specific relationships are established between the situations represented in the meanings of the conjuncts."

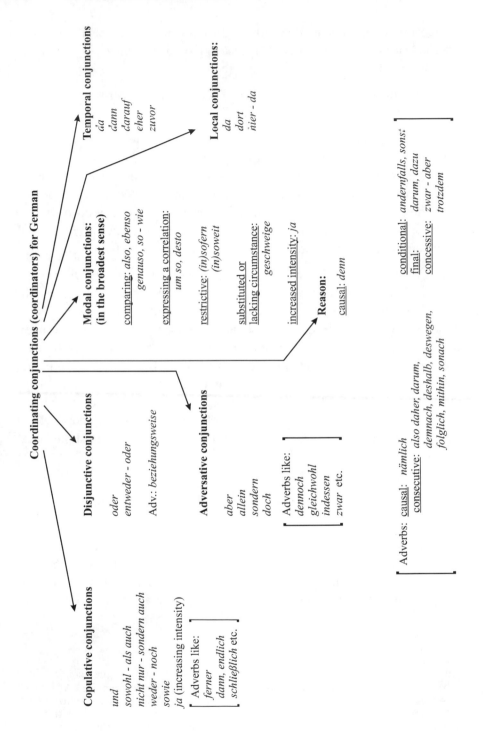

**Figure 11.3.** Overview of the standard interpretations of German coordinating conjunctions (for English, see Fig. 11.4)

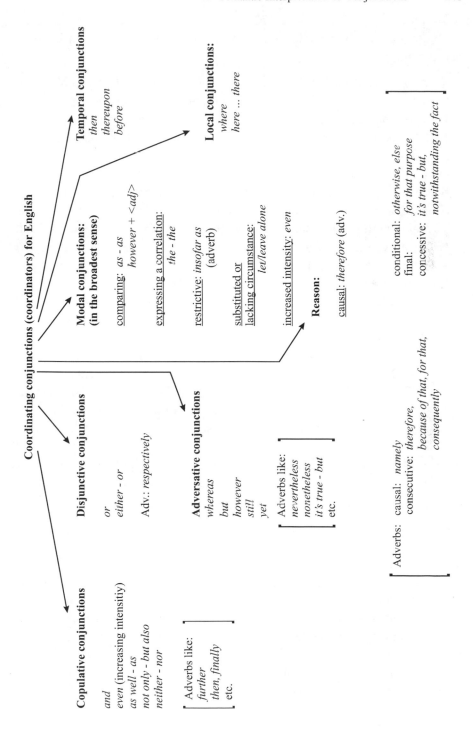

**Figure 11.4.** Overview of the standard interpretations of corresponding English coordinative conjunctions (for German, see Fig. 11.3)

In analogy to the negation, one may also discern two different types of coordinations:

- **Sentence coordination**, where, on the syntactic level, two complete sentences and, on the semantic level, two situations are coordinated;
- **Phrase coordination**, where, grammatically, two constituents of a sentence (two phrases) and, semantically, two elements of a situational description (in general two objects) are coordinated.[6] It is also possible that, from a syntactic point of view, two phrases are coordinated, whereas, from a semantic point of view, two complete situations are conjunctively or disjunctively connected.[7]

To represent the relationships expressed by coordinative constructions, Multi-Net provides the following representational means:

- Sentence coordination
  - The conjunction convention (see Part II, Sect. 16.3)
  - $*$VEL1: $si \times si \times \ldots si \to si$      for "*or*" (inclusive "*or*")
  - $*$VEL2: $si \times si \times \ldots si \to si$      for "*either–or*" (exclusive "*or*")
- Phrase coordination
  - $*$ALTN1: $sort \times sort \ldots \times sort \to sort$    for "*or*" (inclusive "*or*")
  - $*$ALTN2: $sort \times sort \ldots \times sort \to sort$    for exclusive "*or*"
  - $*$ITMS: $pe^{(n)} \times \ldots \times pe^{(n)} \to pe^{(n+1)}$    for copulative conjunctions (enumeration without considering the order)
  - $*$ITMS-I $sort \times sort \ldots \times sort \to sort$    (the analogue at the intensional level)
  - $*$TUPL: $sort \times sort \ldots \times sort \to sort$    for copulative conjunctions (enumeration with consideration of the order)

The introduction of so-called **alternative collections** as objects in the value domain of the functions $*$ALTN1 and $*$ALTN2 is only an abbreviation and auxiliary construct. Its occurrence in a representation has to be resolved during the inference process as a disjunction of different states of affairs.

Copulative conjunctions are used with phrase coordinations for an exhaustive enumeration of pluralities. $*$TUPL takes the order of the elements into consideration, whereas $*$ITMS and $*$ITMS-I disregard the order of the arguments. With respect to the logical interpretation of representations containing pluralities built up by means of $*$ITMS or $*$TUPL, the same problems as discussed with quantified pluralities (difficulty of distinction between cumulative, collective and distributive interpretations) are encountered.

---

[6] This kind of coordination is also called **constituent coordination**.

[7] This case is illustrated by Example K2) in Fig. 11.5.

In the following exposition, we discuss some semantic representations of coordinative constructions; see Figs. 11.5 through 11.7.

K1)  Ge: *"Der Patient wird **entweder** morgen entlassen,*
     ***oder** er wird am Freitag operiert."*
     En: *"**Either** the patient will be dismissed tomorrow,*
     ***or** he will be operated on on Friday."*

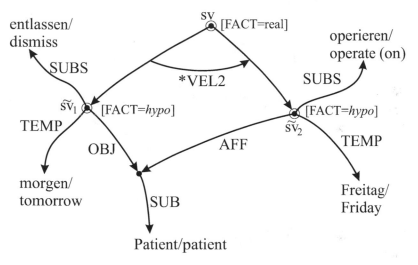

K2)  Ge: *"**Sowohl** Peter **als auch** Bernd spielen Flöte."*
     En: *"**Both** Peter **and** Bernd play flute."*

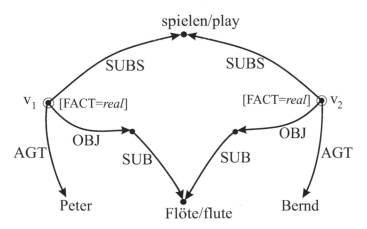

**Figure 11.5.** Coordinating conjunctions I (without collateral meaning)

K3) Ge: *"Peter reparierte sein Auto, **und**
(anschließend) fuhr (er) ins Kino."*
En: *"Peter repaired his car, **and**
(then) (he) drove to the cinema."*

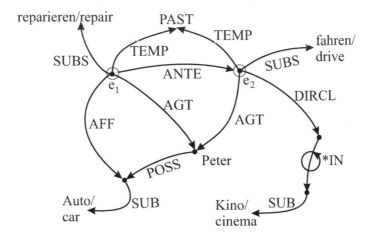

K4) Ge: *"Peter erledigte seine Hausaufgaben,
**aber** Bernd spielte auf dem Schulhof."*
En: *"Peter did his homework,
**but** Bernd played at the schoolyard."*

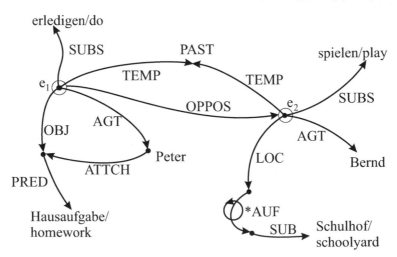

**Figure 11.6.** Coordinating conjunctions II (with collateral meaning)

K5) Ge: *"Peter **und** Bernd tragen ein Klavier."*

En: *"Peter **and** Bernd are carrying a piano."*

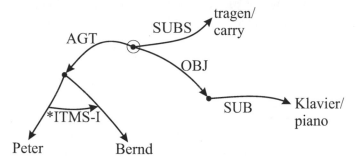

K6) Ge: *"Die Auswertung des Ausdrucks A7 ergibt notwendigerweise eine reelle **oder** eine imaginäre Zahl."*

En: *"The evaluation of expression A7 necessarily results in a real **or** in an imaginary number."*

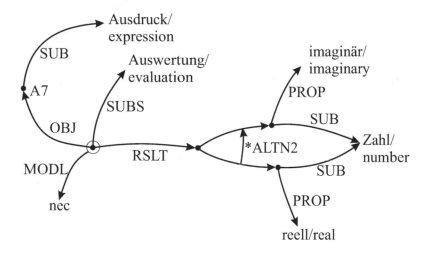

**Figure 11.7.** Coordinating conjunctions III (constituent coordination)

Examples K1), K3), and K4) are typical of sentence coordination, while Examples K2), K5), and K6) show phrase coordinations in their surface structures. In Example K3), sentence coordination is connected with a temporal ordering of the events represented by the conjuncts, often encountered in coordinations with "*and*". This temporal ordering relation ($e_1$ ANTE $e_2$) must be inferred if it is not explicitly indicated in the sentence itself (thus, the sentence "*Peter repaired his car and drove (afterward) to the cinema.*" has to be represented in the same way, whether or not the adverb "*afterward*" is present). The adversative component contained in Example K4) is expressed by the relation OPPOS. Apart from that, the semantic interpretation is the same as though the conjunction "*and*" had been used in the sentence.

To interpret Example K1) it is necessary to generate a superordinate situational node sv to which the representatives of the conjuncts are subordinated by means of the function $*$VEL2. Please note that the occurrence of the situations $\widetilde{sv}_1$ and $\widetilde{sv}_2$ as arguments of $*$VEL2 has the consequence that, without further information, neither situation $\widetilde{sv}_1$ nor situation $\widetilde{sv}_2$ needs to hold (both have to be considered hypothetical situations). This is generally true for arguments of the functions $*$VEL1 and $*$VEL2. These functions have a restricting character with regard to the facticity of their arguments in exactly the same sense as stated for the semantically restrictive relations in Sect. 5.1.

In the case of Sentence K2), two separate situational nodes $v_1$ and $v_2$ must be generated, although the construction is grammatically a phrase coordination. From our common background knowledge it should be clear that this sentence does not describe a single action which is carried out by two persons and involves only one object (in this case, a flute). This interpretation always seems to be appropriate for coordinations of subject phrases by means of "*as well as*" (Ge: "*sowohl - als auch*"), in contrast to subject coordinations by means of "*and*" (Ge: "*und*"); see Example K5). In the latter case it remains open whether one or more situational nodes have to be created to represent the described state of affairs adequately (at least if no additional knowledge is available). The decision between both types of coordination is also not straightforward for the coordination of other participants by means of "*as well as*" (Ge: "*sowohl - als auch*") or "*and*" (Ge: "*und*").

Examples of coordinated instruments or objects, respectively:

(11.7)  Ge: "*Er arbeitet sowohl mit Zirkel als auch mit Lineal.*"
    En: "*He works with dividers as well as with rulers.*"
    $\longrightarrow$ one situational node with two instruments possible

(11.8)  Ge: "*Er benutzt sowohl sein Fahrrad als auch sein Auto für die Einkäufe.*"
    En: "*He uses both his bicycle and his car for shopping.*"
    $\longrightarrow$ different situations necessary

Returning to Example K5), one may conclude from background knowledge that Peter and Bernd are jointly cooperating as agents in one and the same event. Given the normal weight of a piano, nobody would assume that either of them is carrying a piano. Under this assumption (i.e. that a piano is too heavy to be carried by one person), the subject coordination by means of "*as well as*" (Ge: "*sowohl - als auch*") instead of "*and*" (Ge: "*und*") would not be acceptable (compare Example K2).

Examples K2) and K5) illustrate the role of background knowledge with regard to the disambiguation of coordinated sentences (which is essential for the treatment of elliptical constructions in general).[8] In Example K6) we finally meet a coordination of object phrases which shows that we must not necessarily interpret the conjunction "*or*" (Ge: "*oder*") as an "inclusive or" (function *ALTN1), though this is considered the "normal" interpretation, which should always be preferred in case of existing doubts and is also not entirely wrong. Since a human hearer/reader knows that "imaginary" and "real" are mutually exclusive concepts (this should be anchored in the background knowledge by means of the relations (real COMPL imaginary)), the adequate representation of Sentence K6) should be built up with *ALTN2 rather than with *ALTN1.

To conclude this discussion, we emphasize that an exhaustive treatment of the semantic disambiguation of coordinations and the semantic reconstruction of complete situations from elliptical constructions lies still ahead.[9]

# 11.2   Conditions and Reasons

## 11.2.1   Language Phenomena and the Corresponding Representational Means

This section gives a comprehensive overview of the conditional relationship (represented by COND), the causal relationship (represented by CAUS), the relationship of logical conclusion (represented by IMPL), and the relationship of justification (represented by JUST), which expresses a reason for a state of affairs and is based on social norms or conventions. The distinction between these relations seems to be the more necessary because most knowledge representation systems still do not sufficiently differentiate between them.

To elucidate the problem, we consider Fig. 11.8 showing different bordered areas which are thought to symbolize the application domains of the corresponding relations mentioned above. Each of these areas is divided into subdomains labeled A through D for relations connecting real facts and $\tilde{A}$ through

---

[8] An entirely different question is that of automatic mastering of these difficult problems. Here, the development of computational linguistics is only at its beginning.

[9] This statement does not concern the semantic representation of these language phenomena. For this purpose, the representational means of MultiNet are sufficient.

$\tilde{E}$ for relations connecting hypothetical or nonreal facts. The indicated relations cover the following subdomains: COND – $\tilde{A}$ through $\tilde{E}$; IMPL – $\tilde{A}$, $\tilde{B}$, A, and B; CAUS – B and C; JUST – D; and REAS – A through D. Please note that this partitioning shows an overlap between COND and IMPL on the one hand, and CAUS and IMPL on the other hand. The following example sentences are typical of the application fields (or areas) associated with these relations. In Fig. 11.8, each of these areas is represented by a region and labeled by a corresponding symbol.[10]

A) Ge: *"Weil die Funktion f(x) an der Stelle x=a eine Singularität aufweist, ist sie dort nicht differenzierbar."*
En: *"Since the function f(x) has a singularity at point x=a, it is not differentiable there."*

B) Ge: *"Weil das Auto ohne Katalysator fährt, ist der Schadstoffausstoß zu hoch."*
En: *"Since the car runs without a catalytic converter, the emission of harmful substances is too high."*

C) Ge: *"Weil Peter unvorsichtig über die Straße lief, wurde er von einem Auto überfahren."*
En: *"Since Peter crossed the street so carelessly, he was hit by a car."*

D) Ge: *"Weil er die Arbeitsdisziplin wiederholt verletzte, wurde er fristlos entlassen."*
En: *"Because he repeatedly violated discipline at work, he was dismissed without notice."*

$\tilde{A}$) Ge: *"Wenn ein reelles Polynom keine reellen Nullstellen besitzt, ist es entweder positiv oder negativ definit."*
En: *"If a real polynomial has no real zero points, (then) it is either positively or negatively definite."*

$\tilde{B}$) Ge: *"Wenn das Volumen eines Behälters verringert wird, erhöht sich der Druck in diesem Behälter."*
En: *"If the volume of a container is decreased, then the pressure in this container will rise."*

---

[10] We have deliberately chosen *"because"*-compounds and *"if"*-compounds as example sentences (Ge: *"weil"*-Gefüge and *"wenn"*-Gefüge, respectively), since these are prototypical of compound sentences in the causal and conditional field. Since subordinated English causal sentences introduced by *"because"* are mostly postponed, we often use the conjunction *"since"* instead of *"because"* to introduce a causal sentence in the examples, which results in a more parallel translation between English and German sentences. Nevertheless, the English conjunction *"because"* is unique with regard to its causal meaning (in contrast to *"since"*, which has a temporal reading too), and therefore we prefer the term *"because"*-compounds as a translation for German *"weil"*-Gefüge. An overview of other synonymous constructions is given in Sects. 11.2.2 and 11.2.3.

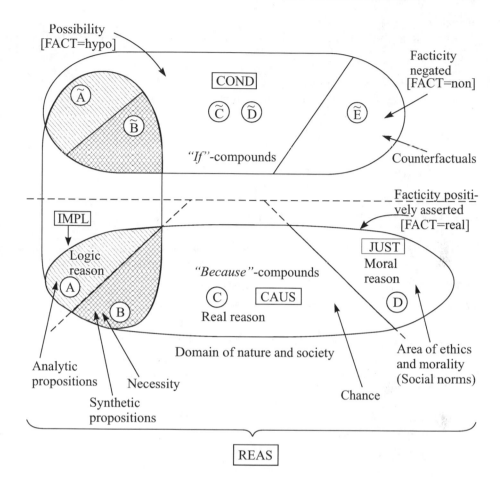

**Figure 11.8.** Relationship between causality, conditionality, and implication (after [111])

$\tilde{C}$) Ge: *"Wenn jemand unvorsichtig über die Straße läuft, gefährdet er sein Leben."*
En: *"If somebody carelessly crosses the street, (then) he endangers his life."*

$\tilde{D}$) Ge: *"Wenn das Projekt rechtzeitig abgeschlossen wird, erhalten die beteiligten Mitarbeiter eine Prämie."*
En: *"If the project is finished on time, the participating collaborators will be awarded a premium."*

$\tilde{E}$) Ge: *"Wenn die Erde einen wesentlich geringeren Abstand zur Sonne hätte, gäbe es auf unserem Planeten kein Leben."*
En: *"If Earth were a substantially smaller distance from the Sun, there would be no life on Earth."*

Looking at the overview given in Fig. 11.8 one may primarily discern two large areas:

- An area which is linguistically characterized by so-called *"because"*-compounds semantically covering relations that connect **factual** situations (lower part in Fig. 11.8).[11]
- An area which is linguistically characterized by so-called *"if"*-compounds.[12] At the semantic level, they typically connect **nonfactual** or **hypothetical** situations (top part in Fig. 11.8).

The following MultiNet relations are provided for the semantic representation of the above complex states of affairs:

| CAUS | $[si' \cup abs'] \times [si' \cup abs']$ | Causal relationship, relation between cause and effect |
| COND | $\widetilde{si} \times \widetilde{si}$ | Conditional relation |
| IMPL | $[si \cup abs] \times [si \cup abs]$ | Implication relation between states of affairs |
| JUST | $[si \cup abs] \times [si \cup abs]$ | Relationship of justification on the base of social norms |
| REAS | $[si \cup abs] \times [si \cup abs]$ | Most general relationship of reason |

- The expression $(\widetilde{sv}_1 \text{ COND } \widetilde{sv}_2)$ asserts that the hypothetical situation $\widetilde{sv}_1$ is a sufficient condition for the validity or the occurrence of a situation $\widetilde{sv}_2$.[13] This means that $\widetilde{sv}_2$ becomes valid ([**FACT** = *real*]) when $\widetilde{sv}_1$ becomes valid.

The relation COND will be dealt with more thoroughly in Sects. 11.2.3 and 11.3. Therefore, let us first consider in somewhat greater detail the relationship of reason represented by the semantic relations REAS, and its specializations CAUS, IMPL, and JUST.

- The expression $(sv'_1 \text{ REAS } sv'_2)$ states that the factual situation $sv'_1$ is the general reason for the validity or the occurrence of the factual situation $sv'_2$.

This relation is used primarily in cases where the necessary background knowledge for the fine differentiation of the semantic reason-consequence re-

---

[11] With regard to the naming of *"because"*-compounds, see the footnote on page 248.

[12] The proposed terminology is derived from the fact that the corresponding semantic phenomena are described by conditional clauses which are often (but not always) built up by means of the conjunction *"if"* (Ge: *"wenn"*).

[13] Consequently, the representatives $\widetilde{sv}_1$ and $\widetilde{sv}_2$ at first bear the attribute value [**FACT** = *hypo*].

lationship is lacking. According to Bech and Heyse-Lyon[14], one can establish the following partition of these general relationships:

- **Real reason** (cause); this relationship is covered by the application domain of relation CAUS (illustrated by the Areas B and C in Fig. 11.8);
- **Moral reason** (motive); corresponds to Area D in Fig. 11.8 and is described by the relation JUST;
- **Logical reason** (cognitive reason); corresponds to Area A in Fig. 11.8 and is semantically described by the relation IMPL.

We will return to the relation CAUS in Sect. 11.2.2. Here, we only want to state that there is a clear distinction between causal sentences in the grammatical sense and the causal relation in the semantic (or philosophical) sense. The former comprise an essentially larger range of semantic relations than the latter.

- The relation ($sv'_1$ CAUS $sv'_2$) establishes a connection between a cause $sv'_1$ (a factual situation) and an effect $sv'_2$ (also a factual situation) at the semantic level, where $sv'_2$ depends on $sv'_1$ in the sense that $sv'_2$ would not hold (or, in the case of an event, would not occur) when $sv'_1$ did not hold.

Causal sentences in the grammatical sense, of which the "*because*"-compounds are typical, cover all meaning aspects of the reason-consequence relation REAS. Hermodsson [120] distinguishes between five application domains of "*because*"-compounds:

H1 – **Causal relationships in nature**
    (belonging to Areas B or C in Fig. 11.8)
    Ge: "*Die Wellen gehen hoch, weil es sehr windig ist.*"
    En: "*The waves are high, because it is very windy.*"      → CAUS
    Ge: "*Weil das Seil stark belastet wurde, ist es plötzlich gerissen.*"
    En: "*Since too much weight had been put on the rope,*
       *it suddenly tore apart.*"      → CAUS

H2 – **Relationships of human behavior**
    (belonging to Area D in Fig. 11.8)
    Ge: "*Er geht nicht mehr ins Kino, weil er keine Lust hat.*"
    En: "*He avoids the cinema, because he does not enjoy it.*"      → JUST
    Ge: "*Weil er Angst hat, läßt man ihn nicht mehr allein ausgehen.*"
    En: "*Since he is afraid, he is not allowed to go out alone.*"      → JUST

H3 – **Ethic relationships**
    (together with group H2, they cover Area D in Fig. 11.8)

---

[14] Cited from [120].

Ge: *"Er handelte so, weil er es für richtig hielt."*
En: *"He acted in this way because he thought it was right."*    → JUST
Ge: *"Weil er unter Schweigepflicht stand, hat er kein Wort geäußert."*
En: *"Because he was bound to confidentiality,*
*he did not utter a single word."*    → JUST

### H4 – Institutional relationships

(belonging to Areas B or C, and better be named "social" or "socio-economic" relationships)

Ge: *"Die Zahl der Arbeitslosen steigt, weil gegenwärtig eine*
*wirtschaftliche Rezession herrscht."*
En: *"The number of unemployed is increasing because*
*a recession is occurring."*    → CAUS

### H5 – Logical relationships (corresponding to Area A in Fig. 11.8)

Ge: *"Weil diese Dreiecke gleichwinklig sind, sind sie auch gleichseitig."*
En: *"Since the triangles are equiangular, they are also equilateral."*

→ IMPL

Ge: *"Weil die Quersumme der Zahl nicht durch 3 teilbar ist,*
*ist die Zahl selbst auch nicht durch 3 teilbar."*
En: *"Because the sum of the digits in that number is not divisible by 3,*
*the number itself is also not divisible by 3."*    → IMPL

The following criteria can be formulated as truth conditions for "because"-compounds:

- Truth, i.e. actual validity, is required of the states of affairs described in the partial clauses;
- Validity of a general norm underlying the "because"-compound.

It is difficult to specify in general and with sufficient precision what this norm really is. This law or norm is different for every application domain and has to be considered as a presupposition which underlies these "because"-compounds. In Area H1, the norm is connected with general laws being valid in nature, where the term "nature" must be understood in a very broad sense. A relationship such as *"Since Peter carelessly crossed the street, he was hit by a car"*, which had been mentioned already, also belongs to this category. In this case, belonging to Area C in Fig. 11.8, the norm rather has the character of a correlation or a statistical law (⟨carelessly crossing the street⟩ ⟹ ⟨being hit by a car⟩) and not the character of a strictly valid natural law, as is the case in Area B of Fig. 11.8 (where we observe laws such as ⟨flowing of a current through a conductor⟩ ⟹ ⟨emergence of a magnetic field⟩).

In group H2, one meets principles, rules, and habits of human life as "norms", while moral norms are relevant to group H3. Since both groups, H2 and H3, can not so easily be separated, they are put into one area (D) in Fig. 11.8. Group H4 is characterized by economical and social laws; together with group H1 it covers Areas B and C in Fig. 11.8. Finally, Group H5 is determined by logical laws and coincides with Area A in Fig. 11.8.

Although the assignment of MultiNet deep relations to the application domains of compound sentences given by Hermodsson can be inferred from the above discussion, the corresponding relationships shall be summarized once more in Table 11.1.

| Area | H1 | H2 | H3 | H4 | H5 |
|---|---|---|---|---|---|
| Deep relation | CAUS | JUST | JUST | CAUS | IMPL |

**Table 11.1.** Assignment: Application domain – deep relation (always applicable: REAS)

Because of the important role that causal relationships and relations of reason play in human communication in general and also in human behavior and problem solving, there is a plenitude of expressional means in this area. The relationships between compounds that are at least partially synonymous with the *"because"*-compounds and the above-mentioned application domains were compiled in Tables 11.2 and 11.3 for the semantic interpretation of these compound sentences. Since there is no strict word-to-word correspondence between German and English with regard to conjunctions or other words denoting these semantic relations, separate tables are given for German and English (see Tables 11.2 and 11.3, respectively).[15]

The relationship between compounds constructed by means of a certain conjoining phrase and the corresponding deep relations can be found, respectively, by combining the information from Table 11.1 with the five middle columns from Tables 11.2 or 11.3 (for the results, see last columns of Tables 11.2 and 11.3).

It should be emphasized, however, that essentially deeper investigations into the semantic interpretation of the syntactic compounds discussed above are necessary, since the content of the clauses connected by the constructs from Tables 11.2 or 11.3 must unquestionably also be considered in this process. Thus, Tables 11.2 and 11.3 have heuristic value only. The + sign in Tables 11.2

---

[15] If two or more relations are relevant for the interpretation of a certain phrase (as in Areas D and A), then the relation that should primarily be applied in the corresponding domain is given first; other relations possibly applicable are set in brackets.

| Type of expression | Application domains | | | | | Interpretation preferred |
|---|---|---|---|---|---|---|
| | H1 | H2 | H3 | H4 | H5 | |
| *"Ursache", "verursachen"* | + | | | + | | CAUS |
| *"Begründung", "begründen"* | | (+) | (+) | | + | IMPL (JUST) |
| *"Grund"* | + | + | + | + | + | REAS |
| *"darum", "deshalb"* | + | + | + | + | + | REAS |
| *"deswegen", "daher"* | + | + | + | + | + | REAS |
| *"Folge"* | + | (+) | (+) | + | | CAUS (JUST, IMPL) |
| *"Folgerung", "folgen"* | (+) | | | (+) | + | IMPL (CAUS) |
| *"folgern", "schließen"* | + | | | + | + | IMPL |
| *"so daß"* | + | + | + | + | + | REAS |
| *"denn", "da"* | + | + | + | + | + | REAS |
| *"Wirkung", "bewirken"* | + | | | + | | CAUS |

**Table 11.2.** German constructions being (partially) synonymous with *"because"*-compounds

| Type of expression | Application domains | | | | | Interpretation preferred |
|---|---|---|---|---|---|---|
| | H1 | H2 | H3 | H4 | H5 | |
| *"cause (nom)", "cause (vb)"* | + | | | + | | CAUS |
| *"reason", "give reason"* | | (+) | (+) | | + | IMPL (JUST) |
| *"grounds"* | + | + | + | + | + | REAS |
| *"that's why",* | + | + | + | + | + | REAS |
| *"therefore",* | + | + | + | + | + | REAS |
| *"consequence"* | + | (+) | (+) | + | | CAUS (JUST, IMPL ) |
| *"conclusion", "conclude"* | (+) | | | (+) | + | IMPL |
| *"infer"* | + | | | + | + | IMPL |
| *"so that"* | + | + | + | + | + | REAS |
| *"for", "as"* | + | + | + | + | + | REAS |
| *"effect", "having as effect"* | + | | | + | | CAUS |

**Table 11.3.** English constructions being (partially) synonymous with *"because"*-compounds

and 11.3 means that the corresponding phrase is relevant to the indicated application domain. A plus sign in parentheses (+) means that the corresponding phrase is actually possible, but it is not so common in this context.[16]

Finally, some remarks should be made about the relation IMPL:

- The **implication relation** ($sv_1$ IMPL $sv_2$) establishes a relationship between two states of affairs, $sv_1$ and $sv_2$, characterized by the fact that the validity of $sv_2$ can be inferred from the validity of $sv_1$ on the basis of a general law presupposing an inner intensional coherence between $sv_1$ and $sv_2$.[17]

---

[16] Further types of expressions belonging to this field are Ge: *"kommt daher"*, *"rührt daher"*, *"beruht darauf"*, *"aus Anlaß"*, *"anläßlich"* or En: *"comes from"*, *"that is because"*, *"is based on"*, *"on the occasion of"*, etc.

[17] See also the distinction from the material implication below.

It is interesting to observe that the general law mentioned in this definition, which must be assigned to the generic level, can also be semantically represented by means of the relation IMPL. Thus, the general relationship (Area A in Fig. 11.8)

(11.9) *"If a function is differentiable, then it is also continuous."*
    (generic level)                                                  $\rightarrow$ IMPL

as well as the special relationship

(11.10) *"Since function $f_1$ is differentiable, it must also be continuous."*
    (level of instances and special concepts)                   $\rightarrow$ IMPL

are described by the deep relation IMPL.

In Area B of Fig. 11.8, the implication relation between the two states of affairs is in general mediated by physical or economic laws. In Area A, IMPL corresponds to the concept of semantically based inference of logic (Bolzano's concept of inference). In a QAS, the relation (P IMPL Q) means that somebody who states the validity of P also has to accept Q (i.e. he must not deny Q at the same time), and that there is also a semantic connection between P and Q. The Areas B and A are distinguished by the fact that the statements in the former area are **synthetic propositions**, i.e. they are found by experience and are raised to the status of a general law by abstraction, whereas the statements in the latter area are **analytical propositions** which hold on the basis of definitional relationships alone. Both areas have in common that they are open to the formulation of theories. The relations IMPL and CAUS overlap in their meaning in Area B, where, the following formula holds:

- (P REAS Q) $\rightarrow$ (P CAUS Q) $\wedge$ (P IMPL Q)    (for Area B only)    (80)

Consequently, in a QAS one may ask in this area *"What follows from P?"* or *"What is caused by P?"* In Area A, the latter would be inappropriate, and the former would at least be questionable in Area C. One should be aware that the material implication known from logic (symbol $\rightarrow$) must not be confused with the relation IMPL introduced above since the former is exclusively truth-functionally defined, which is not valid for the relation IMPL. As it is well known, the truth of the material implication (P $\rightarrow$ Q) depends only on the truth of P and Q, and not on whether or not there is an inner semantic connection between them. Thus, a sentence like

(11.11) *"If the moon is a star, then 6 is a prime number."*

could be seen from the logical point of view as the interpretation of a true implication (P → Q). Apart from the fact that such a sentence would contradict our normal use of language and be perceived as semantically deviating, the relationship between these propositions could also not be expressed by (P IMPL Q) because of the definition of the relation IMPL given above. In this case, there is actually no intensional relationship between the propositions P and Q or, as formulated by Sinovjev [244, p. 195], there is no "**Sinnzusammenhang**" (En: "**meaning connection**") between them.

## 11.2.2    Causality

Causal relations are of fundamental importance for human perception and reasoning. Since ignoring causal relationships may have fatal consequences, their knowledge plays a crucial role in daily life to ensure survival in an ever changing environment. Due to its significance, the philosophical discussion about causality has a long tradition (see, for instance, [135] and [37]). Essential traits of the causal relationship, represented in MultiNet by the relation CAUS, are

I. Asymmetry with regard to its arguments and transitivity (→ causal chains);
II. A connection to the concept of time: a cause has to precede the effect;
III. Causes either produce effects (**producing case** with Mill [181]) or are essential preconditions for the effect (**preventing case** with Mill); they provide an explanation for the effect, not vice versa; the general law underlying a causal relationship is the foundation for its explanatory power;[18]
IV. The causal relationship always connects specific factual situations (characterized by [**GENER** = $sp$, **FACT** = $real$]) with each other but never generic or hypothetical situations.

Because of the second condition, the relation CAUS is closely associated with the temporal antecedent relation ANTE. This must also be considered in the definition of these relations in Part II. From the second statement above, one could intuitively assume the validity of the following law:

- $(sv_1 \text{ CAUS } sv_2) \to (sv_1 \text{ ANTE } sv_2)$                                       (81)

The general claim expressed by this formula stating that the cause occurs strictly before the effect (i.e. $sv_1$ finishes before $sv_2$ starts) does not correspond

---

[18] The absence of a certain situation $sv_1$ (in the following example "*the lack of watchfulness*") can also be the cause of a state or event $sv_2$: "*Since the sentry had not been watchful enough, the fort was conquered.*" Nevertheless, the lacking watchfulness must not be directly connected to the activities of the enemy, which are the immediate cause for their conquering of the fort.

to our general use of language. It is a claim too strong for a formal description of causal inferences in a QAS.

Example:

(11.12) *"Since the cholera raged* ($sv_1$)*, many people left the country* ($sv_2$)*."*

In this case, the outbreak of the cholera (i.e. a partial event of $sv_1$, at best) lies before the event of many people leaving the country. Because of that, one can only claim for the causal relationship used in a QAS that the effect should never occur before the cause:[19]

- $(sv_1 \text{ CAUS } sv_2) \rightarrow \neg (sv_2 \text{ ANTE } sv_1)$ $\hspace{2cm}$ (82)

or one could formulate (81) somewhat weaker[20]:

- $(sv_1 \text{ CAUS } sv_2) \rightarrow (sv_1 \text{ ANTE } sv_2) \vee (sv_2 \text{ STRT } sv_1)$
$$\vee (sv_1 \text{ FIN } sv_2) \vee (sv_1 \text{ DUR } sv_2) \hspace{1.5cm} (83)$$

An important relationship undoubtedly exists between causal relations and **counterfactuals** (see 11.3). If somebody states ($sv_1$ CAUS $sv_2$), then he simultaneously expresses that $sv_2$ would not hold or would not have occurred without $sv_1$. The temporal and spatial coincidence of both events $sv_1$ and $sv_2$, sometimes claimed to be true by some philosophers (e.g. Hume, [58]) cannot be maintained with regard to the existence of longer causal chains or with regard to the existence of long-distance effects assumed to be certain in physics (one should think of statements like *"Since the universe originated from a big bang, one can still today observe a background radiation of a few Kelvin."*). With regard to Axiom (82) it should be noticed that sentences of the type

(11.13) *"Peter came home yesterday because his mother will celebrate her birthday tomorrow."*

are only seemingly in contradiction to (82). First, one has to realize that not every *"because"*-compound really expresses a causal relation in the sense of the definition of CAUS (see Sect. 11.2.1). Second, if somebody wants to establish a causal relationship in connection with this sentence at all, the following observation holds: The immediate cause for Peter's traveling home is his mental state before the beginning of the travel, i.e. his reasoning about a future event, the birthday of his mother (which means not the birthday itself, not yet taken

---

[19] One must also think of sentences like *"Since the skeleton was buried a long time in the earth, a distinct imprint was produced in the underground."* In this case $sv_1$ reaches temporally deeply into $sv_2$ and both events strongly overlap.

[20] The last term in the following expression is suggested by the fact that in many cases, at least for a human observer, cause and effect occur virtually simultaneously (e.g. ⟨flowing of a current⟩ and ⟨generation of a magnetic field⟩); see also [82].

place, was the immediate cause for the travel, it was the moral reason at best for the travel, → JUST).

To discover such complicated relationships automatically is beyond the capabilities of question-answering systems for the time being; it is also no trivial matter for human beings. Therefore it is sensible to semantically represent the relationship between the first and the second parts of Sentence (11.13) by means of the more general deep relation REAS, which is not necessarily connected with the temporal antecedent relation ANTE through an axiom of type (82). This proposal is additionally supported by the observation that this example can be assigned to Area D in Fig. 11.8, where the ethical norm underlying the example may be roughly formulated as ⟨mother's birthday⟩ —→ ⟨visit necessary⟩.

The deep relation CAUS comprises both, relationships which are subject to a strict regularity for which the laws of nature are typical (Area B in Fig. 11.8), as well as relationships to which elements of chance are attached (Area C). Both areas reflect objective laws of nature and society. In contrast, the relationships of Area D are rooted mainly in the field of morality and ethics, i.e. in norms given by society to itself and often fixed as juridical laws.

Some philosophers closely connect the concept of "causality" with the concept of "necessity" (see, for instance, [140]). This claim is too strong with regard to the definition of the causal relation in a QAS. For, if one understands the term "necessity" as *that which under given circumstances cannot be different from the way it is*, then one has to admit that many causal relationships, at least from the phenomenological point of view, have an element of chance in them (see Example C in Sect. 11.2.1). A necessary connection behind these cases is neither practically observable nor deducible from the natural language description of the causal relationship. For this reason, some authors (e.g. [253]) demand only that the conditional probability $P(B|A)$ connected with the situations A and B of a causal relationship (A CAUS B) must be greater than the a priori probability $P(B)$, where $P(A) > 0$ is supposed to be true. In this way, a close connection between causal reasoning and probabilistic reasoning is established [232]. This type of reasoning essentially rests on **Bayes' Theorem** and interlinks the conditional probabilities for causally connected events A and B introduced above (see [232], [253]):

- $P(B|A) = \frac{P(A|B)P(B)}{P(A)}$    (84)

Unfortunately, these formalisms (which are theoretically well founded) are only restrictedly usable in a QAS because, apart from some narrow domains, the probabilities involved (or even estimates of them) are generally not available. From the epistemological point of view, it is questionable whether statistical relationships, which are mere correlations, can be raised to the rank of real causal relationships, as done in this approach.

There is also a conflict potential in the field of causality in the philosophical sense in connection with at least three fundamental concepts, which are the topic of intense philosophical discussions, namely **causality**, **determinism**, and **free will** (see [270], [275], [257]). This problem field was made still more complicated by modern physics (especially by quantum theory). This is not the place to delve deeper into this subject. Nevertheless, the above-mentioned problems play a role for the semantics of natural language and question answering, especially with regard to the use of background knowledge for finding appropriate answers to certain questions. Thus, strictly causal relationships with their deterministic properties, as they are assumed in classical physics, may be *"known"* or *"ignored"*, but not *"changed"* or *"dismissed"* (see relation CAUS in Area B of Fig. 11.8). The same can be said about logical relationships (expressed by the relation IMPL, Area A of Fig. 11.8). In contrast, it is thinkable that causal relationships in the economic or social field (Area C of Fig. 11.8) may be *"changed"* or *"avoided"*. The latter holds especially for the general relationships of justification (relation JUST, Area D of Fig. 11.8).

As already stated in [181], the simple connection of two singular situations $sv_1$ and $sv_2$ to establish a causal relationship ($sv_1$ CAUS $sv_2$) does not, strictly speaking, cope with the actual findings. In reality, one has to take into consideration a whole complex of "positive" and "negative" conditions which produce a certain effect, whereas a speaker postulating a causal relationship generally selects only one of them.[21]

This observation can be expressed in such a way that actually either some constellation of conditions ($B_1$ and $B_2$ and $\ldots B_n$) or alternatively the constellation ($C_1$ and $C_2$ and $\ldots C_m$), each give rise to a certain effect W (i.e. every constellation is in itself a sufficient condition for W), or more formally:

- $(B_1 \wedge B_2 \wedge \ldots B_n) \vee (C_1 \wedge C_2 \wedge \ldots C_m) \stackrel{CAUS}{\longrightarrow} W$  $\qquad$ (85)

In a natural language description of this situation, the speaker generally postulates rather selectively ($B_2 \stackrel{CAUS}{\longrightarrow} W$), for instance, where $\stackrel{CAUS}{\longrightarrow}$ symbolizes

---

[21] Thus, a person might simply formulate a sentence like *"Since the driver threw away his cigarette carelessly, a forest fire broke out."* In general, he or she neglects circumstances like *"sufficient air supply by the wind"* (positive condition) or *"the lack of humidity"* (negative condition) also relevant to the outbreak of the fire.

causal inference. The emphasis on an especially prominent condition functioning in our common sense as a "general cause" is called **INUS condition**.[22]

A peculiarity in the field of causal relationships (in the grammatical sense)
are the so-called **incausal compounds**.[23] Compound sentences introduced by
"*(al)though*" (Ge: "*obwohl*") – the so-called "*although*"-compounds – are typical representatives of this type of language phenomena. They are the counterpart to the "*because*"-compounds discussed above.

> "*They characterize situations in which the normal cause-effect rela-
> tionship generally expected is not realized.*" ([120])

MultiNet provides the relation CONC together with the relations CAUS, JUST,
and COND to represent these "*although*"-compounds semantically.
Example (see Fig. 11.9):

(11.14) "*Although the construction site had been safeguarded properly, the
pedestrian fell into the ditch.*"
Underlying norm:
⟨safeguarding the construction site properly⟩ ⟹ ⟨no accident⟩,
The latter must be represented by means of COND and stored in the
knowledge base as a default assumption (not shown in Fig. 11.9).

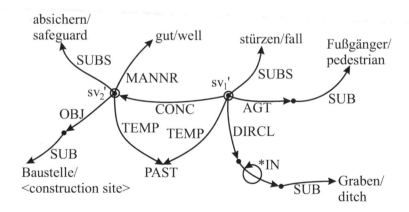

**Figure 11.9.** The semantic representation of "incausal" compound sentences

Like "*because*"-compounds, the partial sentences of an "incausal" compound sentence describe factual situations. From the example, we see that

---

[22] INUS: "insufficient but non-redundant part of an unnecessary but sufficient condition" [170]
[23] The term "incausal compounds" (Ge: "inkausale Gefüge") as well as the term "inconditional
compounds" (Ge: "inkonditionale Gefüge"), which will be used in Sect. 11.2.3, had been
coined by Hermodsson.

the presupposed norm has a more general character than the concrete situations linked together by the sentence (the same is also true for *"because"*-compounds). Therefore, the norm belongs to the generic level and connects hypothetical situations. In contrast to the *"because"*-compounds, the *"although"*-compounds have the effect of negating or rejecting just this norm in the considered situation.

For this reason, no "although"-compounds can be formulated as counterparts to the "because"-compounds in Area A of Fig. 11.8. Thus, the sentence *"Although the triangle is equiangular, it is <u>not</u> equilateral."* is semantically contradictory, and therefore not acceptable. An analogous effect makes the sentence *"Although the triangle is equiangular, it is equilateral."* sound odd. In Area B, *"although"*-compounds are normally felt deviating. However, such a deviation can be an indication that some assumptions or boundary conditions made during the formulation of a natural law are not fulfilled in the situation described. Example:

(11.15)  *"Although the temperature fell below the freezing point, the water did not freeze."*                              ($\rightarrow$ "supercooled liquid")

In the context of social or economic laws, which often have only a statistical character, the situations described by *"although"*-compounds characterize exceptions from the rule. In the remaining application domains of *"because"*-compounds, the corresponding *"although"*-compounds are acceptable without restrictions. In any case, the assertion of the relation (sv$_1$ CONC sv$_2$) means that, against the background knowledge sv$_2$, exactly the contrary of sv$_1$, i.e. its negation, should be expected (this is important for answering questions like *"What do you expect, in view of sv$_2$?"*).

In German, the following sentence types are considered constructions synonymous with the *"although"*-compounds (Ge: *"obwohl"*-compounds): sentences with the "incausal" subordinators *"obschon"*, *"obgleich"*, *"obzwar"*, *"wenn - auch"*, *"wenngleich"*, and *"trotzdem (daß)"*, compound clauses without subordinators using *"auch"* and *"doch"* (Ge: *"War er auch stark erkältet, kam er doch zur Arbeit."*; En: *"Even though he had caught a heavy cold, he still came to work."*), and coordinated clauses connected by *"doch"*, *"dennoch"*, and *"trotzdem"*. These compound sentences are semantically represented in the same way as *"although"*-compounds by using the relation CONC. The presupposed norm, which is only implicitly contained in these constructs, is formalized by means of COND.

There are several approaches for the logical treatment of causal relationships, which are discussed in an overview in [62] where further relevant citations can also be found:

- Modal approaches, which also cover counterfactuals (Burks, Lewis),
- Extensions of a logic of necessary and sufficient conditions (Mackie),
- Logic of branching time (Prior, Reichenbach),
- Probabilistic approaches (Suppes, Shafer).

Unfortunately, it cannot yet be decided which logical formalization is best for the intuitive cause-effect relation. One rather has to conclude that the causal relationship seems to escape a satisfactory definition again and again.[24] Thus, it is not quite clear what the essence of the regularity connecting cause and effect, postulated in Point III, really is. It is clear that two events co-occurring by chance (like the daily intake of breakfast at a certain hour and the regular resounding of a certain melody on the radio at the same time) do not stand in a causal relationship to each other. Also a purely statistically underpinned correlation between two events regularly co-occurring in a certain way (like the regular succession of day and night) do not establish a causal relationship. Since day and night are logically opposed, which is expressible by (day CONTR night), no causal relationship actually holds between them in spite of a clear correlative connection. It can be strongly asserted that analytical or logical relationships between two states of affairs are actually an exclusion criterion for causality (see relation IMPL).

A question discussed in psychology concerns the problem of cognitive perception of causality. Here, special aspects of the causal relationship have been investigated which are also relevant to knowledge representation (having a certain influence on B-Axioms and R-Axioms).

- Causalities in the field of human actions; they are connected with motivations, intentions, and goals
- Causalities in the field of mechanical processes (collision processes are typical of them), where cause and effect are perceived with temporal and spatial contiguity.

Piaget has drawn attention to the fact that the conception of causality is not static; rather, it undergoes a change during the development of an individual [199]. This topic cannot be discussed further in our context (an overview is given in [58]).

---

[24] Russell even goes so far as to declare the causal relation a fiction; he writes in [218]: "*The law of causality ... is a relic of bygone age, surviving, like the monarchy, only because it is erroneously supposed to do no harm.*"

MultiNet tries to model the causal relation CAUS in such a way that its use in daily language is reflected. A special problem is marked by the observation that one can find several different causal relations in natural language. Thus, causal relationships in the mechanical domain (or more generally, in the domain of classical physics) are connected with **determinism**, while cause-effect relationships in the field of voluntary actions are connected with concepts like **intention**, **goal**, and **avoidability**. The latter connections, however, do not generally hold in the field of agentive actions (e.g. in "*Because Peter inadvertently hit the table, all glasses were broken.*", Peter is actually the agent and his action causes the destruction of the glasses, but the action is not associated with Peter's intention).

### 11.2.3 Conditional Relations

The **conditional relation** ($sv_1$ COND $sv_2$) conveys that the nonfactual situation $sv_1$ (bearing the layer information [**FACT** = *hypo*]) is a **sufficient condition** for situation $sv_2$, i.e. the realization of $sv_1$ or the fact that $sv_1$ is becoming true automatically leads to the validity of the situation $sv_2$ (without further knowledge about the validity of $sv_1$, one can only conclude that $sv_2$ is possible). [25]

A **necessary condition** A for a situation B is characterized by the fact that without the validity of situation A B is not valid. This necessary condition is written as (B COND A), which is the converse to the corresponding sufficient condition. As an example of the description of a necessary and sufficient condition, we take the following natural language sentence:

*(If and) only if,*

$$A \xrightarrow{COND} B$$

$$\underbrace{\text{a programming error occurs}}_{A} \quad , \quad \underbrace{\text{an error message will appear on the terminal.}}_{B}$$

$$A \xleftarrow{COND} B$$

The conditional relation must not be reduced to the material implication of propositional logic. Here, the same reasons apply as for the implication relation of MultiNet (see Sect. 11.2.1), i.e. the conditional relation, too, cannot be reduced to a truth-value function. Even the strict implication $\Box(p \rightarrow q)$ of

---

[25] Analogously to the INUS conditions discussed in Sect. 11.2.2, this is also a simplification. Strictly speaking, the situation $sv_1$ deliberately distinguished is "sufficient" only for $sv_1$ together with a whole complex V of accompanying preconditions. Only in the case where V is stable enough and can be silently assumed as statically valid background information, can $sv_1$ alone be taken as a sufficient condition (see the work about a **defeasible logic** of the conditional relation [3]).

modal logic (see Sect. 8.3) is not an adequate semantic representation of the COND relation because the first would express that the implication p → q is true "in all possible worlds". This truth condition, however, is too strong a demand for the conditional relation COND, which must be valid only with regard to a certain norm, but may also be voluntarily postulated. The analogue is true for the relation IMPL which must also not be identified with the strict implication of modal logic, as has already been mentioned. An overview of the logic of conditionals is given in [93].

According to Sinovjev, the conditional relation may have the following origins [244, p. 294]:

S1:  empirical investigations; the conditional relation is postulated on the basis of a causal relationship underlying the corresponding situation:
    *"If a current is flowing through a conductor, a magnetic field will arise."*
S2:  logical conclusions:
    *"If A ∨ B and ¬ A are true, then B holds."*
S3:  other conditional propositions by means of inference rules (e.g. using the transitivity of the implication);
S4:  definitions; in this case, definitions having the form A $=_{def}$ B, where A and B are propositions, are written in the form (A COND B)
    *"If Max is a bachelor, (then) he is not married."*
S5:  formulation of postulates; in this case, the conditions are simply stated:
    *"If the air conditioner breaks down, the apparatus should be switched off immediately."*

Case S1 corresponds to Areas $\tilde{B}$ and $\tilde{C}$ in Fig. 11.8. Cases S2 and S4 belong to Area $\tilde{A}$. The conditional relation of type S5 corresponds to Area $\tilde{D}$. Such an "arbitrary setting of postulates" is often met in everyday use of language. Case S3 may be observed in almost all areas of Fig. 11.8. In Area $\tilde{E}$ (covering the counterfactuals), each of the five possibilities of origin is plausible.

The previous discussion also reveals that the application domains of the implication relation in the field of factual situations (Areas A and B in Fig. 11.8) have their respective counterpart in the field of possibilities (Areas $\tilde{A}$ and $\tilde{B}$). This means that the relation IMPL has an overlapping domain with the relation REAS as well as with the relation COND. This is in accordance with the definition of IMPL (see Part II), where, in contrast to REAS, no restriction was made about the facticity of the arguments. In Areas A and B of Fig. 11.8, we find implications between factual states of affairs ($sv'_1$ IMPL $sv'_2$), while Areas $\tilde{A}$ and $\tilde{B}$ are characterized by implication relations between pseudo-situations ($\widetilde{sv}_1$ IMPL $\widetilde{sv}_2$).

Finally, a remark should be made about the problem of automatic distinction between the relations COND, CAUS, IMPL, and JUST during the process of syntactic-semantic analysis. In cases where the analysis succeeds in assigning relations as specific as possible to the corresponding surface structures by using predefined heuristic rules (see Sect. 11.2, Table 11.1), the most specific relation should be inserted into the representation and preferred to the more general relation (this concerns especially the relations IMPL and CAUS, versus REAS). This demand is reasonable, since a greater number of facts can be derived from more specific relations than from general relations. Thus, the CAUS relation is connected with temporal relationships, while an inference rule corresponding to the **modus ponens** of logic is applicable to the relation IMPL. Neither statement generalizes to the relation REAS. If a splitting (disambiguation) of meanings into special relations is not possible, the more general relation REAS should be used whose distinction from COND is not as problematic.

As already mentioned, the "*because*"-compounds (Ge: "*weil*"-Gefüge) are representative of the causal domain, while the "*if*"-compounds (Ge: "*wenn*"-Gefüge) are typical of the conditional domain. In German, there are some special phenomena which are expressly excluded if we speak about "*wenn*"-Gefüge (En: "*if*"-compounds):

a) Quasiconditional "*if*"-compounds (Ge: quasikonditionale "*wenn*"-Gefüge):
"*Ich habe das Buch verbrannt, wenn Du es unbedingt wissen willst.*"
(En: "*I have burned the book, if you really want to know.*")
The subordinated clause does **not** specify a condition which influences the validity of the main clause.

b) Temporal "*if*"-compounds (Ge: temporale "*wenn*"-Gefüge):
"*Wenn die Prüfungen beendet sind, nehmen wir unseren Urlaub.*"
(En: "*When the examinations are over, we will take our holidays.*")
In German, the conjunction "*wenn*" can be substituted by "*sobald*", "*sooft*", "*sowie*", or "*indem*", if it is used temporally.

c) Topic-focus complex (Ge: Thema-Rhema-Komplex):
"*Wenn man beide Arbeiten miteinander vergleicht, so sieht man, daß sie sich in wesentlichen Punkten unterscheiden.*"
(En: "*Comparing both papers with each other, one can see that they are differing in essential points.*")

Compound clauses characterized under a) and c) play a minor role in discourse domains really relevant to practical applications, while group b) can often be observed. The latter group presents a difficult problem to the treatment in a German QAS, for these sentences must not be represented semantically by means of COND. There are also no sufficient criteria that allow for a secure distinction of these temporal relations from conditional relations (this is indeed an unsolved problem for automatic natural language processing). Also the substitution criterion sketched under b) seems to be of little value for automatic analysis.

Turning to the "*if*"-compounds proper and following Hermodsson [120], we deal at first with constructions in the indicative mood and then with "in-conditional" compounds. The "*if*"-compounds in the subjunctive mood will be discussed separately in Sect. 11.3.

**"*If*"-compounds in the indicative mood.** "*If*"-compounds have basically the same application domains as "*because*"-compounds, which can be verified by the fact that all "*if*"-sentences may be also formulated with "*because*". To illustrate the main differences between these kinds of compound sentences a schematic overview is given in Table 11.4.

| **"*Because*"-compounds** | | **"*If*"-compounds** |
|---|---|---|
| – Actuality; connection of factual situations | | – Possibility; connection of hypothetical situations |
| – Past tense is preferred in application domain C (see Fig. 11.8) | different facticity ⇔ | – Present tense is preferred (often with future meaning) |
| – Temporal adverbial qualifications are typical | | – Adverbs indicating the past tense are largely missing |

**Table 11.4.** Comparison between "*because*"-compounds and "*if*"-compounds

MultiNet provides the relation COND and the layer information of the attribute **FACT** to semantically represent the "*if*"-compounds in the indicative mood. For the distinction between causal and conditional relationships it is important to keep in mind that COND always connects so-called pseudo-situations $\widetilde{sv}$ characterized by [**FACT** = $hypo$], in contrast to the relation CAUS which connects real/factual situations characterized by [**FACT** = $real$] with each other.
Example:

(11.16) "*If a person is hurt in an accident, the police have to be called.*"

The assertion of the relationship ($\widetilde{sv}_1$ COND $\widetilde{sv}_2$) in a question-answering game has the consequence that the speaker who is stating this relationship has also to accept the validity of $sv_2$ whenever the validity of $sv_1$ is established. Using a more technical terminology, one might say that the validity of the first

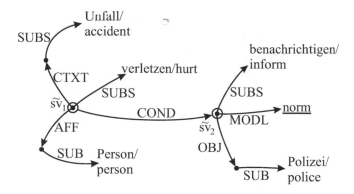

**Figure 11.10.** Semantic representation of a conditional relationship

situation $sv_1$ (now having the value [**FACT** = *real*]) triggers the validity of the second situation $sv_2$. As long as the situation $\widetilde{sv}_1$ is only hypothetically assumed, the second situation $\widetilde{sv}_2$ has also a hypothetical value because of the semantically restrictive character of the relation COND. Given a question concerning the validity of $sv_2$ in a QAS against this background, the adequate answer should roughly be like: "*Yes, but only if $sv_1$.*" The link to the properties of the conditional relation as they are investigated in logic will be discussed at the end of Sect. 11.3. For the time being, we only want to state that the relation COND, in contrast to CAUS and IMPL, cannot be characterized as being transitive. From "*If the weather is fine, Max will go fishing.*" and "*If Max goes fishing, he puts on warm clothes.*", it does not follow that "*If the weather is fine, Max puts on warm clothes.*"

The interpretation of compound clauses which are synonymous with "*if*"-compounds can be obtained analogously to the above treatment of conditional sentences. Here, above all, the following German conjunctive phrases have to be mentioned: "*falls*", "*im Falle daß*", "*insofern (als)*", "*insoweit (als)*", "*unter der Bedingung (Voraussetzung), daß*", and "*angenommen, daß*" (En: "*in (the) case of*", "*insofar (as)*", "*on the condition (assumption) that*", "*provided that*", etc.). Compound clauses without any subordinator, such as Ge: "*Ist eine Person verletzt, muß die Polizei gerufen werden.*" (En: "*If a person is hurt, the police have to be called.*") or the **imperative + propositional sentence** "*Komm her, und Du erhältst Deinen Anteil.*" (En: "*Come here, and you will get your share.*"), which also belong to this context, play a minor role in practical application domains; they are interpreted analogously to the "*if*"-compounds.

**Incondicional compounds.** In a way similar to that in which "incausal" compounds can be seen as negation or cancelation of a normally expected causal relationship, there are also **inconditional compounds** which negate a conditional relationship characterizing the "normal expectation". "Inconditional" compounds are typically introduced in German by the subordinators "*auch wenn*", "*selbst wenn*", and "*sogar wenn*" (En: "*even if*"). The German subordinator "*auch wenn*" (En: "*even if*") must not be mixed with "*wenn auch*" (En: "*although*"). While the subordinator "*auch wenn*" connects hypothetical situations (which are only assumed), the latter ("*wenn auch*") is related to real or factual situations (→ "incausal" compounds ; see Fig. 11.11).

The main difference between "inconditional" and "incausal" compound sentences lies in the facticity of the partial propositions contained in them (and therefore in the value of the attribute **FACT** of the situations described by the main and subordinate clauses). Both types of sentences – the "inconditional" as well as the "incausal" compounds – are semantically represented by means of the relation CONC. With regard to the preferred tense, the same can be stated as for causal and conditional compound sentences (see Table 11.4).

To facilitate a better comparison, Figure 11.11 shows the semantic representations of an "inconditional" sentence (Example a) and an "incausal" sentence (Example b). The networks illustrate what role the distinction between factual and nonfactual situations plays for the semantic interpretation of "inconditional" and "incausal" sentences. In Example b) we have the factual situations $sv'_1$ and $sv'_2$, while in Example a) we have hypothetical situations $\widetilde{sv}_1$ and $\widetilde{sv}_2$. The representations further show that the substitutions of CONC by COND in case a) or by CAUS in case b) yield an inadequate semantic representation (the same is true for the example in Fig. 11.9). The conditional or causal relation which can actually be inferred from an "inconditional" or "incausal" compound sentence, respectively, has to be considered a presupposition. These presuppositions express the "normally expected" conditional or causal relation and can be characterized in the following informal way:

Example a)    "normal" conditional relation (here withdrawn):

⟨the ship is heavily damaged⟩ $\overset{COND}{\longrightarrow}$ ⟨ship goes down⟩

Example b)    $b_1$) Presupposition:

⟨the ship has actually been heavily damaged⟩

$b_2$) "normal" causal relation (here rejected):

⟨the ship is heavily damaged⟩ $\overset{CAUS}{\longrightarrow}$ ⟨the ship goes down⟩

The "normal" and "expected" conditional or causal relationships which are presupposed are annulled by the "inconditional" or "incausal" sentence, respectively.

Example a): "Inconditional" compound
Ge: *"{Auch wenn/selbst wenn/sogar wenn} das Schiff schwer beschädigt wird, geht es nicht unter."*
En: *"{Even if} the ship is heavily damaged, it will not go down."*

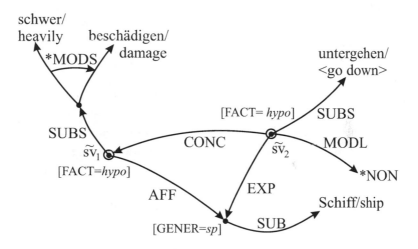

Example b): "Incausal" compound
Ge: *"{Obwohl/wenn auch} das Schiff schwer beschädigt wurde, ging es (doch) nicht unter."*
En: *"{(Al)though} the ship was heavily damaged, it did not go down."*

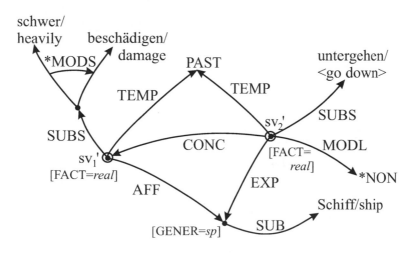

**Figure 11.11.** Semantic representation of an "inconditional" compound and a corresponding "incausal" compound having a similar semantic structure

## 11.3    Counterfactuals

"*If*"-compounds in the subjunctive mood express **counterfactuals**. In this section we shall concentrate mainly on German surface structures, because the English syntactic phenomena differ somewhat from the expressional means of German (the English translation is nevertheless given in parallel for every example). What really matters in our context is that the semantic phenomena are the same in both languages. The term "counterfactual" (Ge: "kontrafaktische Zusammenhänge") was coined because the German Subjunctive II (Ge: Konjunktiv II) characterizes a situation which is imagined only (i.e. not factual). Whether its realization is possible, dubious, improbable, or impossible depends on the specific semantic connection between the partial clauses (see [67, p. 9]). The German Subjunctive II in a conditional compound can also describe a situation in the future. It can be paraphrased by means of "*würde*", "*möchte*", "*sollte*", "*wollte*", "*könnte*", "*müßte*",and "*dürfte*" (En: "*would*", "*might*", "*should*", "*could*", etc.).

In German, one has to discern between two different phenomena in dealing with counterfactuals:

Type I:  "*Wenn die Firma das Material gestern gekauft hätte, hätte sie einen Produktionsausfall vermieden.*"
→ conditional compound with subjunctive mood in the past tense
(En: "*If the firm had bought the material yesterday, the stoppage of production could have been avoided.*")

Type II:  "*Wenn das Gerät ausfiele, würde die Anlage zerstört werden.*"
→ conditional compound with subjunctive mood in the future tense
(En: "*If the device failed, the plant would be damaged.*")

To illustrate the semantic representation of "*if*"-compounds in the subjunctive mood, the representations given in Figs. 11.12 and 11.13 shall be discussed here, since they are sufficiently representative of this kind of phenomenon.

**Type I**

If the antecedent of a conditional relationship (like the first clause in the "*if*"-compound of Fig. 11.12) is formulated in the past subjunctive, then we are dealing with a genuine counterfactual relationship. This means that in the semantic representation two pseudo-situations $\widetilde{sv}_1$ and $\widetilde{sv}_2$ have to be connected by a conditional relation where the nodes $\widetilde{sv}_1$ and $\widetilde{sv}_2$ represent the meaning of the main and subordinate clauses, and both pseudo-situations must have been possible at an earlier time. Since their validity is explicitly negated by the subjunctive, $\widetilde{sv}_1$ and $\widetilde{sv}_2$ must be associated with negated factual situations $sv'_1$ and $sv'_2$, respectively, which are essentially equivalent to $\widetilde{sv}_1$ and $\widetilde{sv}_2$ except

Ge: *"Wenn die Firma das Material gestern gekauft hätte,*
*hätte sie einen Produktionsausfall vermieden."*
En: *"If the firm had bought the material yesterday,*
*it could have avoided a stoppage of production."*

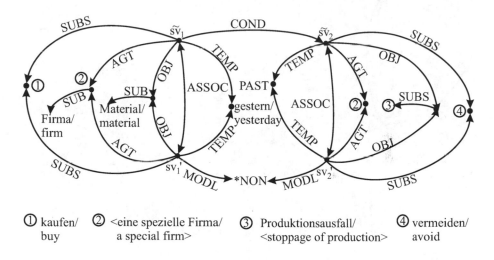

① kaufen/    ② <eine spezielle Firma/    ③ Produktionsausfall/    ④ vermeiden/
 buy          a special firm>             <stoppage of production>    avoid

**Figure 11.12.** Conditional compound in subjunctive mood with past tense

for their layer information [**FACT** = *real*] and additional negations expressed by **MODL** + *NON*. The counterfacticity of $\widetilde{sv}_1$ respective $\widetilde{sv}_2$ must not be considered as a presupposition. Rather, it belongs to the propositional kernel of the whole sentence, which is expressed explicitly in the semantic representation by including sv'$_1$ and sv'$_2$ with their respective characteristics.

## Type II

With counterfactuals in the subjunctive mood having a future meaning component (in German they are often paraphrased by means of "*würde*" or "*könnte*" – En: "*would*" or "*could*"), one cannot infer without a second thought the counterfacticity of the states of affairs described in the partial clauses.

In the example from Fig. 11.13, one cannot exclude the possibility that the device will not fail, and that the plant will nevertheless be damaged at a time to come. In general, one might at best assume a certain improbability for the occurrence of this situation. This is expressed in the semantic representation by means of the situations sv$_1$ and sv$_2$, which are essentially equivalent to $\widetilde{sv}_1$ and $\widetilde{sv}_2$, respectively, except for the characterization of facticity and modality.

Ge: *"Wenn das Gerät ausfiele, würde die Anlage beschädigt werden."*
En: *"If the device failed, the plant would be damaged."*

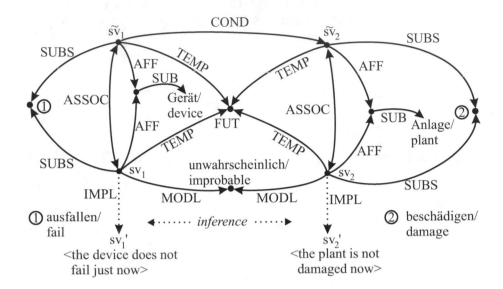

**Figure 11.13.** Conditional compound in subjunctive mood with future tense

In many cases of conditional sentences (for instance, in the example from Fig. 11.13), the counterfacticity can be assumed at least for the moment of utterance (thus, one may conclude that the device does not fail in the moment of the utterance, which is indicated by the two IMPL relations). In general, however, this presupposition does not categorically hold, as in the sentence *"If Peter would come tomorrow, he could meet Jane"*, where nothing is said about Peter possibly not coming today and entering the room at just the moment of the utterance. Therefore, in the general case, the corresponding IMPL relations linked to $sv_1$ and $sv_2$ can only be derived with the characteristics [**K-TYPE** = *proto*]. Here, we encounter complicated temporal-modal relationships which have to be further investigated. Fortunately, this is not so aggravating in a QAS (especially in its technical realization as a question-answering system), because there is no great loss of information for sentences of Type II if they are treated as normal conditional sentences in the indicative mood; i.e. the sample sentence of Fig. 11.13 may be approximately interpreted as *"If the device fails, the plant will be damaged."*

There is rich literature with regard to the logical treatment of conditionals (be they originally formulated in the indicative or in the subjunctive mood). An overview of this topic is given in [50]. In the introduction to the book cited, five kinds of conditional relationships are discerned, which partially overlap with the domains discussed in Sect. 11.2.3. However, they also introduce new aspects like activities as consequences:

C1: Causally founded conditionals:
   Schema: *"If A then causally B."*
   Example: *"If a gas is heated, it will expand."*
C2: Conditional activities
   Schema: *"If A then B is obtained."*
   Example: *"If ice is melted, water is obtained."*
C3: Conditional obligations
   Schema: *"If A then B should be the case."*
   Example: *"If he goes bankrupt, he will have to sell his property."*
C4: Generic conditions
   Schema: *"If A then normally B."*
   Example: *"Whoever holds shares is a rich person."*
C5: Counterfactuals
   Schema: *"If it were the case that A then it would be the case that B."*
   Example: *"If we had clear tax regulations, there would be fewer tax swindlers."*

To conclude this topic, we summarize a few approaches concerning the technical treatment of conditionals. According to Hansson [92], there are essentially three methods used in logic to deal with conditional relationships or **conditionals** of the kind (A COND B) :

- The derivability theory
  The proposition *"If A then B"* is true, if and only if B can be derived from A and a general law H (the background knowledge);
  $A, H \vdash B$   (with $\vdash$ denoting derivability)
- World selection analysis
  Let $W_0$ be the real (actual) world and $f(W_0, A)$ a set of possible worlds in which A is true and which are only slightly different from $W_0$. Then, the proposition *"If A then B"* is true in $W_0$, if B is true in all worlds $W_i \in f(W_0, A)$.[26]
- Belief revision[27]
  Let G be a set of beliefs inconsistent with A. The revision of G by A (symbolically: $G \otimes A$) is obtained by deleting $\neg A$ from G, adjoining A to the

---

[26] The different views in this version of conditional logic are distinguished mainly by their interpretation of the function f (is there only one world in $f(W_0, A)$, or more than one?).

[27] In modal logic and AI, **beliefs** are assumptions of an agent, which are revisable basic elements of its knowledge system.

result, and computing the closure of the derivation relation of the new set. The proposition "*If A then B*" is supported by G if $B \in G \otimes A$.

# 11.4   Contextual Restrictions and Situational Embedding

Conditional relationships have a close affinity to contextual restrictions, represented by the relation CTXT. A relationship ($sv_2$ CTXT o) restricting a situation $sv_2$ to a context o can be interpreted as a kind of "shorthand notation" for a conditional relationship ($sv_1$ COND $sv_2$), where the object o is a constituent of the condition $sv_1$, which is not explicitly described.
Example:

(11.17)  "*This workstation is entirely sufficient* ($sv_2$) *for this school* (o)."
  may be paraphrased as:
  "*This workstation is entirely sufficient* ($sv_2$), *if it is employed in this school* ($sv_1$(o))."

The relation CIRC dealt with in Sect. 5.2.3 is also used to describe the situational embedding of a state of affairs. In contrast to the relations CTXT and COND, however, CIRC is not semantically restrictive.
To illustrate the differences in applying the relations CIRC, CTXT, and COND to semantic interpretations, we take the following sentence and its possible semantic representations (see Figs. 11.14 and 11.15): Example:

(11.18)  Ge: "*Max trainiert bei schönem Wetter.*"
  En: I. "*Max is training (just now) in nice weather.*"
      II. "*Max trains in nice weather only.*"
      III. "*If there is nice weather, Max will be training.*"
  (The English translations vary depending on the different interpretations.)

This German sentence has three different meanings which are represented in Figs. 11.14 and 11.15.

Variant I:  Max is training just now. The fact that there is nice weather is mentioned only as an accompanying circumstance (factual interpretation, individualized situation). The resulting state of affairs sv remains valid even if one drops the accompanying circumstance (relation CIRC). The dotted arc labeled CTXT in Fig. 11.14 is not part of the representation of Variant I (including it would compromise the intended interpretation).

Variant I: Ge: *"Max trainiert bei schönem Wetter."*
En: *"Max is training (just now) in nice weather."*
(factual interpretation; individualized)

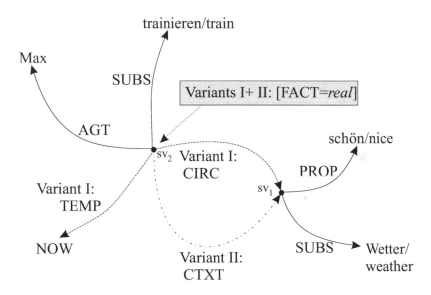

Variant II: Ge: *"Max trainiert bei schönem Wetter."*
En: *"Max  trains in nice weather only."*
(factual interpretation; generalized)

**Figure 11.14.** Contextual restrictions and situational embedding

Variant II:  Max always trains in nice weather only. The training is restricted to nice weather (factual interpretation, generalized situation). The resulting state of affairs sv loses its validity if the contextual restriction (relation CTXT) is also canceled. In this case, the broken arcs labeled by CIRC and TEMP in Fig. 11.14 are not part of the representation of Variant II.

Variant III:  Max is training under the condition that there is nice weather. In this interpretation a condition is set, which may possibly not be fulfilled (conditional interpretation, connection of hypothetical situations). The corresponding semantic representation is given in 11.15.

Let us compare the representations shown in Figs. 11.14 and 11.15. If a situation $sv_2$ is characterized by a relationship ($sv_2$ CIRC $sv_1$) as in Variant I, then the answer to a question for the validity of $sv_2$ does not depend on $sv_1$.

Variant III: Ge: *"Max trainiert, wenn schönes Wetter ist."*
En: *"If there is nice weather, Max will be training."*
(conditionally; hypothetically)

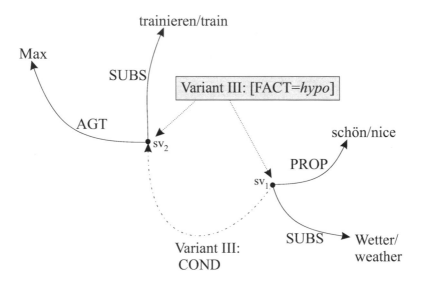

**Figure 11.15.** Situational embedding and conditional relationship

If $sv_2$ is qualified by ($sv_1$ COND $sv_2$), however, the facticity of $sv_2$ is determined ("triggered"; see Sect. 11.2.3) by that of $sv_1$. An attachment of the relation ($sv_2$ CTXT $sv_1$) to the situation $sv_2$ restricts the validity of $sv_2$ to the context $sv_1$, but one can nevertheless assume in this case that the facticity of $sv_2$ is actually defined by [**FACT** = *real*], as in the case with CIRC.[28]

The different interpretations discussed above are very difficult to disambiguate automatically (human readers/hearers, by the way, often have the same difficulties). Therefore, we propose introducing an underspecified relation CIRCOND, which comprises all three relations CIRC, CTXT, and COND, in analogy to the definition (3) of REAS in Sect. 3.3.2.

- ($sv_1$ CIRCOND $sv_2$) $\leftrightarrow_{Def}$ ($sv_1$ CIRC $sv_2$) $\lor$ ($sv_1$ CTXT $sv_2$) $\lor$
($sv_2$ COND $sv_1$)                                  (86)

Without further information, this new relation has to be interpreted as being semantically restrictive, which means that if a relationship ($sv_1$ CIRCOND

---

[28] The different properties of the relations CTXT and CIRC concerning their restrictivity are the reasons why the relation CTXT, rather than CIRC, has to be used in Fig. 11.10.

$sv_2$) is stated, and a question concerning the validity of $sv_1$ is asked, the answer should be *"Yes, but in general only if $sv_2$."*

## 11.5   The Rhetorical Structure Theory (RST)

Although the thematic spectrum of this work does not comprise the text-constituting relations in the broadest sense (which have been investigated mainly within the framework of **Rhetorical Structure Theory**, abbreviated **RST**; see [126], [175], and [174]), it is quite natural to refer to the fact that there is an organic transition from the relations discussed in this section, which establish connections between situations, to the relationships discussed in RST. It should be expected that such close connections do really exist, since the intersituational relations of MultiNet are sufficient to link the semantic representations of arbitrarily complex compound sentences. Since the corresponding situations may be described by a single complex sentence as well as by multiple sentences, i.e. by small texts, their integrated semantic representation almost automatically leads to the field of text semantics, which is a domain of RST.

On the one hand, one can find relationships in RST that are also encountered (mostly in a more differentiated manner) in MultiNet: *"Circumstance"* ($\rightsquigarrow$ CIRC, MANNR, CONC, and others); *"Cause/Result"* ($\rightsquigarrow$ CAUS, RSLT, PURP), or *"General Condition"* ($\rightsquigarrow$ COND, CTXT), etc.

On the other hand, RST goes far beyond the field of semantic relations by taking into consideration also the intention of the speaker. Typical expressional means for that are relations describing motivations, justifications, or valuations of what has been said (see, for instance, [126]). In addition, the operators for describing beliefs or intentions of the speaker, used in other text theories [85], already refer to pragmatics and illocutionary acts [229], which are not the theme of this work. With regard to them, the reader is referred to the literature cited.

# Chapter 12

# Lexicon and Knowledge Representation

## 12.1 The Relation Between Linguistic Knowledge and World Knowledge

In the context of automatic natural language processing, the available knowledge about words and concepts is usually divided into **linguistic knowledge** and **world knowledge** (both constitute the knowledge base in a broad sense). This distinction, in our opinion, has a purely methodological character, although there is undoubtedly a clear difference with regard to the relevance of the two components to the process of language understanding. It has to be stated, however, that the boundary between these kinds of knowledge cannot be sharply drawn.

Roughly speaking, "linguistic knowledge" comprises information that determines how words are "functioning" in the course of language processing, i.e. the way in which they can be combined with other words to build grammatically well-formed constructs (phrases, clauses, texts) on the basis of their morpho-syntactic properties and their meanings. In language processing systems, the parts of linguistic information which relate to single words are stored in the computational lexicon. This is the **lexical knowledge**, which is always knowledge about a special language.[1] The remaining information about concepts which constitutes the meanings of words belongs to the world knowledge (knowledge about the world and its inner structure). Since the views about the distinction between linguistic knowledge and world knowledge are diverging, and even differ from one grammar paradigm to the other, we shall only give a typical example for the sake of elucidation:

- For the proper use of the word "*granite*", it is important to know that it designates a concrete object (a substance, to be exact) which is neither an

---

[1] The general regularities of a language, which are independent of single words, are usually compiled into a grammar. They constitute so-called **grammatical knowledge**. In modern NLP systems, however, it is not possible to draw a sharp line between lexical and grammatical knowledge. Rather, a tendency can be observed to transfer more "grammatical" knowledge into the lexicon (so-called "lexicalization of the grammar").

artifact nor an animate being. Therefore, one may construct phrases like "*to see / to sell / to blow up granite*", etc., but not "*to conjugate / to teach granite*", etc. In order to describe such selectional restrictions, semantic features like concrete/abstract or animate/inanimate are normally introduced into the formal characterization of lexical entries. The fact, however, that granite consists of felspar, quartz, and mica is not relevant to the correct use of the word "*granite*" in natural language. This kind of information, therefore, is typical of world knowledge.

As already stated in Chap. 3, there is a close connection between words and concepts which are the cognitive representations of word meanings. Unfortunately, there is no bijective relationship between words and concepts in natural languages, which gives rise to **lexical ambiguities**.[2] One has to take into consideration at least two basic phenomena (a third phenomenon will be encountered later on; see Fig. 12.6 and the discussion of "meaning molecules" on page 292):

- **Homography**. By this concept we mean the phenomenon that certain words showing different morpho-syntactic behavior are identically written.[3] Examples:
  (12.1)  Ge: "*Bank*" – financial institute (plural: "*Banken*"),
               "*Bank*" – seating accommodation (plural: "*Bänke*");
          [En: "*bank$_1$*" (noun) vs. "*bench$_1$*" (noun)][4]
  (12.2)  En: "*bank*" – financial institute (noun), "*bank*" – deposit money (vb)
          In contrast to polysemous nouns (see below), these words are real homographs in our conception, since nouns and verbs have entirely different syntactical behaviors. It is just characteristic of English that the word forms of many nouns and verbs coincide.
  (12.3)  Ge: "*sein*" – possessive pronoun, "*sein*" – auxiliary;
          [En: "*his*" and "*be*"]

---

[2] This term originates from the fact that words may have different meanings, i.e. one word is in general connected with different readings in the lexicon.

[3] It should be emphasized that this definition deviates from the linguistic use, where a different etymological origin is additionally required for homographs. This criterion, however, is scarcely useful for the purposes of automatic language processing (and for human language understanding as well); it is also of little help for a practically working lexicographer.
The phenomenon of **homophony**, which is the analogue to homography in the area of spoken language will not be considered here.

[4] In English, we would consider the noun "*bank*" to be polysemous with regard to its splitting into the meanings bank$_1$ = ⟨financial institute⟩ and bank$_2$ = ⟨side of a river⟩ because of their essentially equal morpho-syntactic behavior. The fact that one can draw money from bank$_1$ and anchor at bank$_2$ (and not vice versa) is considered to belong to the world knowledge about these concepts in this view.

(12.4)  En: *"being"* – progressive form/present participle of *"be"*
        *"being"* – existence/an existing object

- **Polysemy**. Most natural language words have several meanings. The phenomenon that a word may designate different concepts, although it shows the same morpho-syntactic behavior in all its meanings, is called polysemy. The different semantic interpretations associated with a word are denoted as **semantic variants** or **sememes** or **readings**.
  Examples:
  (12.5)  Ge: *"Ball"* – dancing event, *"Ball"* – sphere;
  (12.6)  En: *"ball"* – dancing event, *"ball"* – sphere
  (12.7)  Ge: *"lesen"* – read in a book, *"lesen"* – harvest grapes
  (12.8)  En: *"read"* – read in a book, *"read"* – study
  As the examples show, the splitting of homographs and polysemes does not run entirely in parallel in different languages, which gives rise to one of the really difficult problems in language translation.

Using an index system with two indices, we achieve a unique denomination of lexical entries, which accounts for the above-mentioned ambiguities of words:
⟨Basic word⟩.⟨Index for different homographs⟩.⟨Index for different sememes⟩

Every entry into the lexicon whose name is formed according to this schema is called a **lexeme**.
Examples:

(12.9)   face.1.1 - front of the head;
(12.10) face.1.2 - surface (*"face of the earth"*);
(12.11) face.2.1 - (keenly) looking ahead to an event;
(12.12) face.2.2 - turning cards face upwards.

In these examples, the number 1 as first index specifies the nominal lexemes and the number 2 as first index marks the verbal lexemes. Based on this index system, one can establish a bijective relationship between lexical entries and lexicalized concepts in the semantic network.[5]

MultiNet offers the following representational means to describe the semantic component of lexical knowledge:

---

[5] By "lexicalized" concepts we mean concepts that can be named by a single word. Thus, the concept Hauptbahnhof is lexicalized in German (like all other compounds), while the equivalent concept ⟨main station⟩ in English is not necessarily lexicalized in this conception. But this depends on the decision about what to put into a lexicon, something which can not be discussed here further.

- **Sorts** and **features** (see Sects. 12.2 and 3.2.1), used for the semantic classification of the lexemes themselves and for the characterization of those constituents which are allowed to saturate the valencies of these lexemes.
- **Layer information** (see Sects. 3.2.2 and 17.1) for the same purpose.
- **Lexical relations** (see the top left Fig. 3.10), which directly connect different lexemes. They are also used to distinguish between different semantic variants.
- All other **relations** and **functions** as well as the **meaning postulates** or B-Axioms formulated by their means are used to anchor the lexemes in the informational background given by a MultiNet knowledge base (see the **NET attribute** in Figs. 12.2, 12.7, and 12.9 of the following section).

## 12.2   The Semantic Component of the Lexicon

To illustrate the close relationship between knowledge representation and lexical information, some typical lexical entries shall be discussed. The specifications of the lexemes discussed are actually associated with the special computational lexicon COLEX [228] and its successor HaGenLex [100], constructed with the assistance of a special workbench for the computer lexicographer (see Sect. 14.4 and [227]). Nevertheless, the descriptions of the lexemes may also be read as theory-neutral lexical characterizations, where every lexical entry is described by means of an attribute-value structure (or **feature structure**). This method is used in many grammar formalisms (see, for example, [60], [203], and [136]).

The syntax of such **attribute-value structures** (A-V-structures) can be characterized in a somewhat abbreviated BNF-like manner as follows:[6]

$$
\begin{aligned}
\langle\text{A-V-structure}\rangle &::= [\langle\text{A-V-pair}\rangle^*] \mid [\ ] \\
\langle\text{A-V-pair}\rangle &::= \langle\text{Attribute}\rangle\ \langle\text{Value}\rangle \\
\langle\text{Value}\rangle &::= \langle\text{A-V-structure}\rangle \mid <\langle\text{A-V-structure}\rangle^*> \mid \\
&\quad \{\langle\text{A-V-structure}\rangle^*\} \mid \langle\text{Atomic value}\rangle
\end{aligned}
\tag{87}
$$

An essential distinguishing feature of our approach, proposed for the description of lexical entries, is its emphasis on the semantic structure of the lexemes. This aspect manifests itself in the characterization of selectional restrictions (argument structures, valencies) controlling the admissible constituents (attribute SELECT) that can be connected with the lexeme considered, but also in

---

[6]   The star '*' symbolizes the Kleene operator, the braces '{' and '}' enclose alternatives, and the angle brackets '<' and '>' are used to enumerate sets of A-V-structures. Square brackets '[' and ']' are delimiters of A-V-structures. The admissible attributes and their values will be explained in the text.

the semantic descriptions of the lexemes themselves (attribute SEM).[7] Since we are using typed feature structures, the type of an A-V-structure is sometimes explicitly indicated at the upper left side of the square brackets enclosing this structure (see Figs. 12.2 through 12.4).

Among the representational means enumerated in Sect. 12.1, which are used to describe the semantic component of a lexicon, only the semantic features of entities are lexicon-specific. Therefore, we shall concentrate exclusively on them in this section. The basic set of features used in the lexicon conception COLEX [228] and further developed and completed in the successor system HaGenLex [100] is given in Table 12.1.

| Name | Meaning | Example values + | Example values − |
|---|---|---|---|
| ANIMAL | animal | fox | person |
| ANIMATE | living being | tree | stone |
| ARTIF | artifact | house | tree |
| AXIAL | object having a distinguished axis | pencil | sphere |
| GEOGR | geographical object | the Alps | table |
| HUMAN | human being | woman | ape |
| INFO | (carrier of) information | book | grass |
| INSTIT | institution | UNO | apple |
| INSTRU | instrument | hammer | mountain |
| LEGPER | juridical or natural person | firm | animal |
| MENTAL | mental object or situation | pleasure | length |
| METHOD | method | procedure | book |
| MOVABLE | object being movable | car | forest |
| POTAG | potential agent | motor | poster |
| SPATIAL | object having spatial extension | table | idea |
| THCONC | theoretical concept | mathematics | pleasure |

**Table 12.1.** Features for the semantic fine-characterization of objects [227]

---

[7] Other attributes used in the A-V-structures are the following (see also the examples of lexical entries in Figs. 12.2 through 12.9): The attribute MORPH comprises the specification of the basic word (BASE) of the lexeme and the corresponding root (ROOT); the inflectional categories are dropped here. The attribute SYN characterizes the syntactic properties. These have to be specified with nominal categories by the agreement attribute AGR with its sub-attributes case (CASE) and gender (GEND) (the category of number plays a minor role in a lexicon). With verbs, the attribute SYN characterizes the type of the verb, i.e. main verb (value **main**) or auxiliary verb (value **aux**), the construction of the perfect tense (in German by means of "*sein*" ("*to be*") or "*haben*" ("*to have*")), the specification of a prefix being eventually separable (SEP-PREFIX), for German only, and the control properties of the verb (attribute V-CONTROL).

This feature information allows for a description of lexeme specifications which is sufficiently differentiated for lexicographical investigations, as well as for automatic natural language processing. It must be remarked, however, that **no** predefined set of features or "semantic markers", however fine-grained it may be, is fully adequate for this purpose. In the process of language understanding, all layers (syntax, semantics, and pragmatics) cooperate in a complex way. In this interplay, the depths of semantic analysis necessary to understand the concepts involved in an utterance cannot be determined a priori. Given a fixed set of sorts and features, there are always cases where these representational means are still too coarse for the description of selectional restrictions. Sometimes, the full knowledge representation must be used for a correct description of lexical entries.
Examples:

(12.13)  mew – AGT only cats or feline animals
(12.14)  tick  – CSTR only objects having a clockwork as their part
                 (to be specified under the attribute NET with a PARS relation)
(12.15)  conjugate – AFF only verbs admissible.

Notwithstanding these limitations, no NLP system can do without such classes of sorts and features, because it is not yet possible to include the full stock of human knowledge into automatic language processing.

The set of features used in HaGenLex, summarized in Table 12.1, will be explained shortly in the following catalogue (the definitions are taken from [227]). [8]

ANIMAL characterizes animals in the narrower sense, where a distinction is made between human beings and animals. This difference is important for the German language to allow distinguishing between actions of animals and human beings, e.g. essen vs. fressen (En: eat in both cases), sterben vs. verenden (En: die in both cases), etc.

ANIMATE denotes living entities, i.e. human beings, animals, and plants. Only these objects may die, ⟨become ill⟩, or ⟨reproduce themselves⟩.

ARTIF characterizes artifacts like car or house. These entities, in contrast to entities of natural origin, can be repaired or renewed.

AXIAL indicates the possession of a distinguished axis. Entities which have the feature [AXIAL +] may ⟨stand upright⟩, ⟨tip over⟩, etc.

---

[8] The semantic features each have the value '+' if the corresponding characterization of the attribute holds and '-' if this is not true. For the sake of brevity, only the positive values are explained.

GEOGR characterizes geographical objects like ⟨the Alps⟩, Paris, France, or ⟨the Equator⟩. This feature supports the analysis of natural language sentences, especially the disambiguation of prepositional phrases in finding or excluding local interpretations.

HUMAN characterizes human beings. This feature is relevant to the subcategorization restrictions of activities which can be done only by human beings, e.g. discuss or explain; it is also used for the specification of the compatibility of certain properties, like kind or honest, with appropriate objects.

INFO signifies (abstract) sources of information like message, lesson, and performance as well as (concrete) carriers of information like newspaper, book, and picture. The corresponding nouns mostly have an optional complement described by MCONT (informational content). In most cases these words are meaning molecules (see page 292) whose semantic spectrum comprises concrete as well as abstract facets of meaning.

INSTIT characterizes institutions like university or court. The natural language denominations of institutions are often also meaning molecules. To be precise, the feature INSTIT captures that semantic facet of an institution which is able to act (as in the sentence "*The court sentenced the accused to a long term imprisonment*").

INSTRU is the feature of a typical instrument like hammer, violin, or scales; this characterization supports the disambiguation of prepositional phrases (analogously to GEOGR for geographic concepts).

LEGPER comprises natural and legal persons like firms, to which certain groups of persons and institutions (but not, for instance, babies) belong. Such objects are able to negotiate, protest, and ⟨give advice⟩.

MENTAL, in contrast to THCONC, applies to abstract mental states and events like pleasure, anxiety, and anger, which may be experienced or felt.

METHOD is the counterpart to INSTRU for abstract methods like pasteurization, freeze-drying, and ⟨smoking (of fishes)⟩.

MOVABLE characterizes objects that can be moved. These entities may be used as objects of transport activities or motions like throw, lift, deliver, bring, and ⟨carry away⟩.

POTAG is the feature of potential agents that possess an "inner power" enabling them to carry out activities on their own. Potential agents need not necessarily be animate. Apart from living beings, this feature also characterizes the concepts **wind, motor,** and **robot,** but not **stone, house,** and **road sign.**[9]

SPATIAL characterizes objects which have a spatial extension. They are suitable to be **seen** or **deformed.**

THCONC specifies theoretical concepts, like **linguistics** or **transitivity,** which are mental constructs of human beings. These may be defined, explained, or disputed.

There are regularities in the relationships between features and sorts which can be anchored in the type hierarchies of an inheritance-based lexicon ( see [227] and [96]). In this way, a succinct representation can be achieved from which all possible combinations of sorts and features can be derived (see Part II, Fig. 17.2).

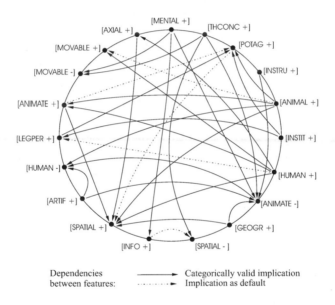

**Figure 12.1.** Selected dependencies between the values of typical semantic features

A part of the dependencies between the feature values is shown in Fig. 12.1. To give some examples, human beings [HUMAN +] and animals [ANIMAL +] are always living beings [ANIMATE +]. All living objects [ANIMATE +] are of natural origin specified by [ARTIF -]. Human beings are (in general)

---

[9] The latter may also cause an activity, as in the sentence *"The road sign warned him to drive slowly."* However, this is not associated with a genuine activity of the road sign (→ CSTR instead of AGT). The feature POTAG plays an important role for characterizing the potentially active carriers of an action.

able to act in the juridical sense [LEGPER +] (which is a somewhat simplifying default assumption, see the exception of "*babies*" above). This property
is shared by human beings and institutions [INSTIT +]. Animals and objects
characterized by [LEGPER +] are potential agents [POTAG +]. Human beings
and animals are generally movable [MOVABLE +], and so on. There are still
other dependencies which cannot be discussed here (see [193] and [191]). In
this chapter, we restrict ourselves to the semantic features.

As typical examples, three meaning variants of the verb "*schicken*" (En:
"*send*") will be discussed, whose specifications are given in Figs. 12.2 through
12.4.[10] For the sake of brevity, the semantic characterization of the arguments
of C-Roles (see the attribute SEM under ... | SELECT | SEL | SEMSEL) has
occasionally been dropped if it simply results from the signature of the corresponding deep case relation. The lexeme schicken.1.1 (En: send.1.1) designates a nonmental transport activity [**SORT** *da*, MENTAL -] that can be
considered synonymous with convey/transport (represented by the attribute
**NET**). The layer attribute **LAY** with value *si-lay* is not further restricted, compared with other situations. It is assigned its final value by inheritance (see
[96]). The lexeme schicken.1.1 (En: send.1.1) requires three arguments,
each of them being characterized by a C-Role, where the first and third arguments are obligatory, and the second is optional.

- AGT – a noun phrase in the nominative, which must have the sort d and the
feature value [LEGPER +];
- ORNT – a noun phrase in the dative case or a prepositional phrase with "*an*"
(En: prepositional phrase with "*to*" or direct object), whose semantic head must
be of sort *o* required by the signature of ORNT ("*to send something to a friend
/ to a conference*");
- OBJ – a noun phrase in the accusative which semantically designates a non-
restricted object.

The attribute **COMPAT-R** indicates those relations which are semantically
compatible with a given lexeme. In contrast to schicken.1.2/send.1.2, the
lexeme schicken.1.1/send.1.1 is compatible with INSTR or METH ("*to send
by post*" or "*to send by electronic transmission*").

---

[10] It is not the task of a knowledge representation framework to decide how many different se-
mememes are associated with a single word like "*schicken*" (En: "*send*") (thus, the three meaning variants discussed here are partially merged in [273]). In our context, it is important
that the KRS which is to be used provides the lexicographer with appropriate expressional
means to represent his intentions if he decides in favor of a certain distinction of lexemes (se-
mememes). The necessity to differentiate between several sememes associated with "*schicken*"
(En: "*send*") can be easily seen through the different semantic implications connected with
them (see attributes NET and ENTAIL in Figs. 12.2 through 12.4).

**schicken.1.1** – (En: **send.1.1**) → [concept: convey]

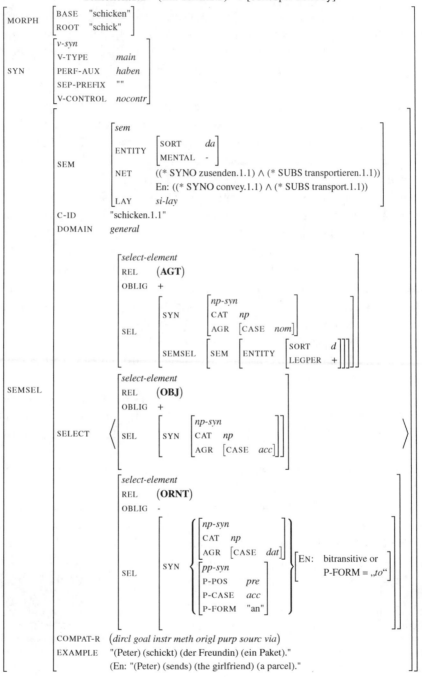

**Figure 12.2.** Lexical specification of the German word "*schicken*" (En: "*send*") with the meaning "*convey*"

**schicken.1.2** – (En: **send.1.2**) → [concept: ⟨order to go somewhere⟩]

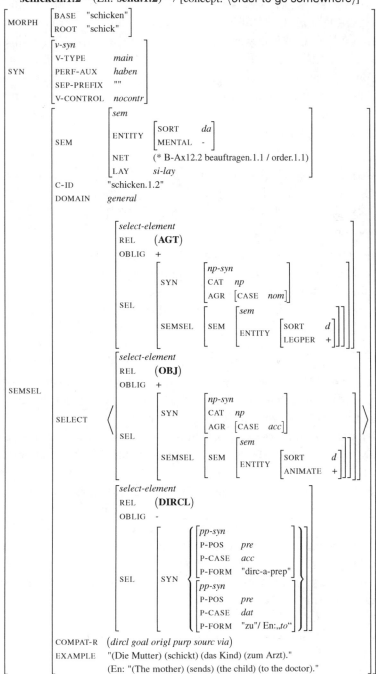

**Figure 12.3.** Lexical specification of the German word "*schicken*" (En: "*send*") with the meaning "*order to go*"

The lexeme schicken.1.2/send.1.2 also characterizes a nonmental activity with [**SORT** = $da$] and [MENTAL -]. This lexeme must be separated from schicken.1.1/ send.1.1, however, because it is not a transport activity. schicken.1.2/send.1.2 nevertheless has an associated "mental component" (in spite of its feature value [MENTAL -]), because it is connected to the verbal concept ⟨to order⟩ (Ge: beauftragen) by means of the meaning postulate (88). This axiom asserts that a person who is sent somewhere (in the sense of send.1.2) is at the same time ordered to go there.

- B-Ax12.2:

  $(s_1$ SUBS ⟨schicken.1.2/send.1.2⟩$) \land (s_1$ AGT $o_1) \land (s_1$ OBJ $o_2) \land$
  $(s_1$ GOAL $o_3) \to \exists s_2 s_3 [(s_2$ SUBS ⟨beauftragen/order⟩$) \land (s_2$ AGT $o_1)$
  $\land (s_2$ OBJ $o_2) \land (s_2$ MCONT $s_3) \land (s_3$ SUBS ⟨sich begeben/to go⟩$) \land$
  $(s_3$ AGT $o_2) \land (s_3$ DIRCL $o_3)]$ $\hspace{3cm}$ (88)

There are other differences between the lexemes schicken.1.1/send.1.1 and schicken.1.2/send.1.2 which are not so apparent at first glance. While the object of schicken.1.1/send.1.1 is not restricted beyond the specification given by the signature of OBJ, the argument of OBJ must be an animate object for schicken.1.2/send.1.2. In contrast to schicken.1.1/send.1.1, the concept schicken.1.2/send.1.2 is not compatible with INSTR or METH (see attribute COMPAT-R). The sentence "*Die Mutter schickt das Kind mit dem Fahrrad zum Arzt.*" (En: "*The mother sends the child to the doctor by bicycle.*") only seemingly contradicts this observation, since the bicycle is not the instrument of the sending act but of the movement of the child.

To demonstrate the potential of MultiNet for fine-differentiation of lexical readings, we consider the third concept schicken.1.3/send.1.3; see Fig. 12.4. In this case, we encounter the specialty that there is an argument x3 syntactically attached to the main verb by a prepositional phrase "*senden nach dem Arzt*" (En: "*to send for the doctor*"), which, however, is semantically not directly attached to the central situational node governed by the lexeme (in contrast to the object of schicken.1.2/send.1.2). This is indicated by **empty_rel** in the feature structure of Fig. 12.4. In the correct semantic representation of schicken.1.3/send.1.3 there is rather an implicit (hypothetical) situation N1 (see attribute NET) defined as the goal of the schicken.1.3/send.1.3 act ($\to$ relation GOAL), asserting that the argument x3 of schicken.1.3/send.1.3 is the desired object which is to come to x1. The corresponding semantic network is shown in Fig. 12.5. It is situation N1 to which the argument x3 is really attached. To complete the semantic description of schicken.1.3/send.1.3, an additional entailment is attached to this lexeme asserting: "*If x1 sends x2 for x3, then x2 is to bring x3 to x1.*"

**schicken.1.3** – (En: **send.1.3**) → [concept: ⟨send sb to bring sth or sb⟩]

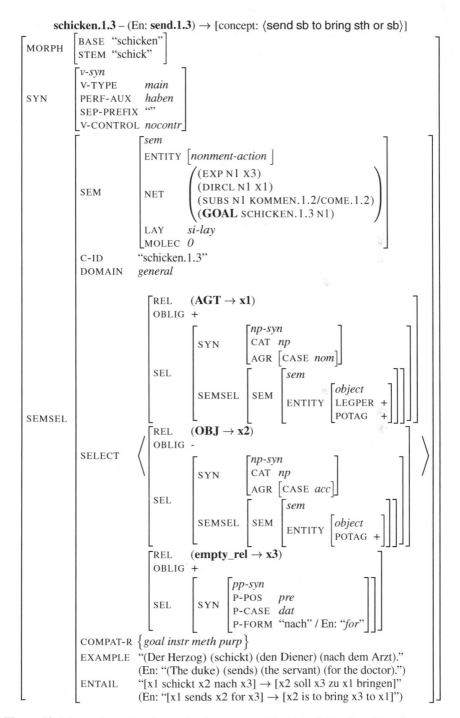

**Figure 12.4.** Lexical specification of the German word "*schicken*" (En: "*send*") with the meaning "*send somebody to bring something or somebody*"

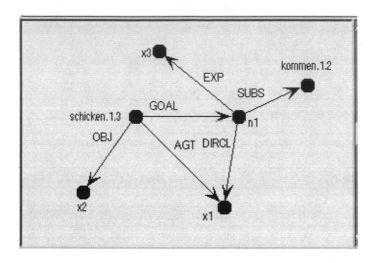

**Figure 12.5.** The NET structure of schicken.1.3 as an example for semantic fine-differentiation

There is another lexical phenomenon significant for the analysis of noun semantics, especially in the context of lexical ambiguity. This phenomenon has already been investigated in linguistics, where the term **concept family** is used [21]. Here, we will discuss this phenomenon within the framework of knowledge representation, proposing the term **meaning molecule** for it. The word "*Schule*" (En: "*school*") will be used to explain the notion of a meaning molecule.

- **Meaning molecule** (or **molecule** for short). Under this concept, we subsume words having several meanings (similar to polysemes). But in contrast to genuine polysemes, the different meanings of a molecule (denoted here as **semantic facets**) may change in the same sentence and with regard to the same word. The individual meaning facets are typically interconnected by metonymic transference (**systematic metonymy**).

Examples:

(12.16)  Schule$_I$/school$_I$ – as a building ("*the school at the corner*")

(12.17)  Schule$_{II}$/school$_{II}$ – as an institution ("*the school protested*")

(12.18)  Schule$_{III}$/school$_{III}$ – as lessons/process of teaching ("*We met him after school.*")

Example for a change of meaning allowed only for molecules:

(12.19)  "*The school* [school$_I$] *at the corner contributed $1000.*"
       (the school as subject of contribute $\rightarrow$ school$_{II}$)

A change in the meaning of a word occurring repeatedly in a sentence and referring to the same object is not allowed with "normal" polysemes:

(12.20)  *"He sat down on the bank (i.e. on the side of a river) and withdrew his money from it (i.e. from this bank)."* (??)      [semantically defective]

An overview of the semantic phenomena in the area of lexical ambiguities is given in Fig. 12.6.

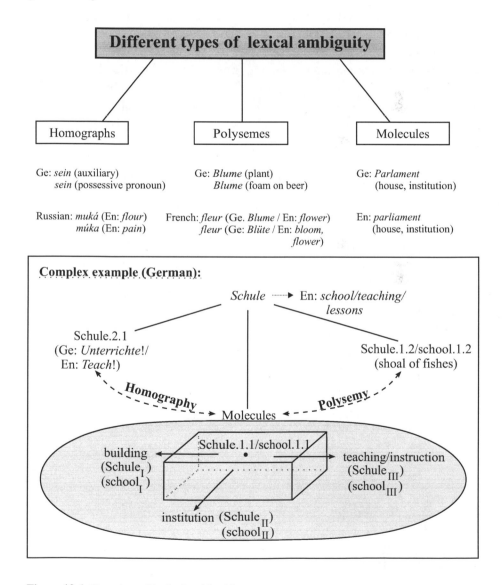

**Figure 12.6.** Overview of lexical ambiguities

The diagram shows that the types of ambiguity discussed occur also in other languages. To some extent, these phenomena overlap in different languages (see, for instance the molecules German "*Parlament*", English "*parliament*", and French "*parlement*" or German "*Schule*", English "*school*", and French "*école*"). In general, however, these phenomena cannot be arranged in parallel so easily (see, for instance the diverging polysemy of German "*Blume*" and French "*fleur*"). In Fig. 12.6, the lexeme Schule.1.1 (En: school.1.1) is shown as a meaning molecule that is simultaneously a sememe which, together with other meaning variants – like Schule.1.2 (En: school.1.2) as a shoal of fishes – underlies the word "*Schule*" (En: "*school*") as one of its different meanings.[11] In German, the homographic form Schule.2.1 (imperative of the verb "*schulen*" – in the sense of "*Teach . . . !*" – at the beginning of a sentence) can be opposed to Schule.1.1 and Schule.1.2. The latter phenomenon will not be further treated here because it plays a role only in connection with morphological analysis, but not with regard to the lexicon.

The lexical entry for Schule.1.1 is given in Fig. 12.7. (The specification of the English lexeme school.1.1 is entirely analogous to that of Schule.1.1.)

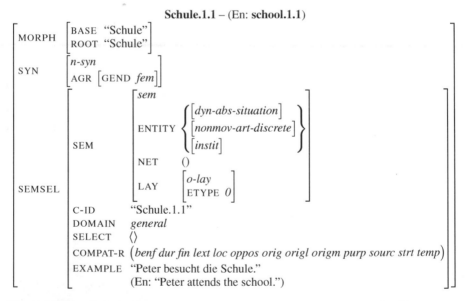

**Figure 12.7.** Lexical specification of the meaning molecule "*Schule*" (En: "*school*")

---

[11] There are still other meaning variants of the word "*school*", like ⟨school of painters⟩ or ⟨scientific school⟩, which will not be considered here.

It is typical of such meaning molecules that they generally belong to several disjunctively conjoined sorts and have several mutually exclusive features (see attribute ENTITY in Fig. 12.6). In our example, the type **dyn-abs-situation** denotes an abstract situation (in this case a process of teaching) with [SORT abs, LEGPER -] ($\rightarrow$ Schule$_{III}$/school$_{III}$). The type **nonmov-art-discrete** denotes a concrete object with [SORT co, MOVABLE -, ARTIF +] ($\rightarrow$ Schule$_I$/school$_I$). Finally, the type **instit** characterizes the lexeme in the sense of Schule$_{II}$/school$_{II}$ with [SORT io, LEGPER +]. It is these different characterizations by means of the attribute ENTITY that correspond to the different meaning facets of the molecule. This approach shows clearly the advantage of having meaning molecules in an NLP system: They relieve the syntactic-semantic analysis from the necessity of disambiguating between the different meaning facets of these molecules, which is not easy (neither for AI systems nor for human beings).

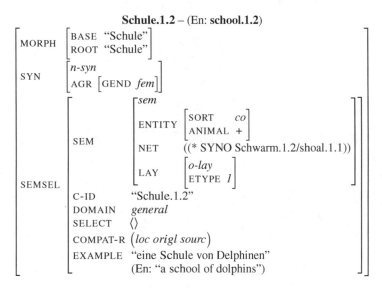

**Schule.1.2** – (En: **school.1.2**)

**Figure 12.8.** Lexical specification of the word "*Schule*" (En: "*shoal*") in the sense "*a shoal of fishes*"

In contrast to Schule.1.1/school.1.1, the lexeme Schule.1.2/school.1.2 characterizing a shoal of fishes is described by exactly one sort and by one semantic feature (see Fig. 12.8). While the lexeme Schule.1.1/school.1.1 is compatible with a temporal beginning (relation STRT) and a temporal end (relation FIN) because of its meaning facet Schule$_{III}$/school$_{III}$ (see attribute COMPAT-R in Fig. 12.7), the lexeme Schule.1.2/school.1.2 is compati-

ble neither with temporal relations nor with a purpose represented by relation PURP (see attribute COMPAT-R in Fig. 12.8). An important specialty of
Schule.1.2/school.1.2 compared with Schule.1.1/school.1.1 is expressed
by the attribute **ETYPE**. The value [**ETYPE** 1] for Schule.1.2 indicates that
the concept belonging to this lexeme is represented at the preextensional level
by a set of individuals.

It is also possible that nouns open valencies (see [246]), something that
has to be specified in the lexical entry of the corresponding noun by means
of the attribute SELECT. As an example, let us consider the German word
"*Schulung*" (En: "*training*") instead of "*Schule*" (En: "*school*"). In this case,
we have to specify two optional arguments for the attribute SELECT: AGT,
for the teacher (to be connected to the NP by the German preposition "*durch*",
English "*by*") and AFF, for the student, described by a genitive attribute in
German ("*die Schulung des Managers durch die Firma*"), which in English
must be expressed by the preposition "*of*" ("*the training of the manager by the
firm*").

As an example of the third open word class (the adjectives), the lexical
entry for "*behilflich*" (En: "*helpful*") is given; see Fig. 12.9.

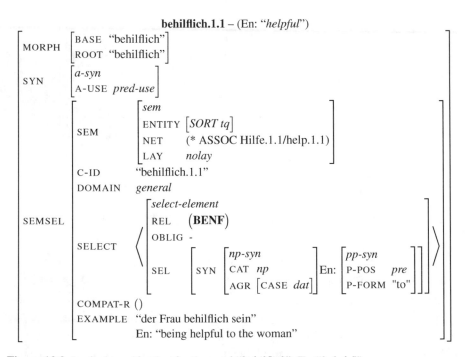

**Figure 12.9.** Lexical specification for the word "*behilflich*" (En:"*helpful*")

The attribute A-USE specifies that the German lexeme behilflich.1.1 may be used only predicatively (in contrast to English "*helpful*", as in "*a helpful example*", which is closer in this context to the German adjective "*hilfreich*"). The lexeme is further characterized as having sort tq (attribute SORT) and being associated with the lexeme Hilfe (En: help); see attribute NET. Please note that adjectives may also have valencies [245], expressed in our example by the optional argument BENF with attribute [OBLIG -] on the path SEMSEL | SELECT. The syntactic restriction for the constituent describing the only argument is given by the attribute SYN, and the semantic restriction is obtained from the signature of BENF.

The semantically oriented lexicon conception presented here, which is based on the representational means of MultiNet, has been realized in the computational lexicon HaGenLex [100]. This approach also has advantages for building multilingual (computer) lexica, because the "semantic skeleton" of a lexeme, which is basically the description of a concept, does not vary over different languages.[12] What is different is the morpho-syntactic characterization of the lexemes, evident from the following example, where special attention is paid to the description of the valencies.

For the sake of illustration, we shall use the lexeme schreiben.1.1 in German, English, and Russian (see Fig. 12.10). All three lexemes – schreiben.1.1 in German, write.1.1 in English, and писать.1.1 in Russian – have the same valency structure, consisting of an agent ("*Who is writing?*" – AGT) and four additional optional participants (**C-Roles**). These roles are: the object of orientation ("*To whom does somebody write?*" – ORNT), the result of the action ("*What is written?*" – RSLT), the transported content ("*About what does somebody write?*" – MCONT), and the beneficiary of the action ("*For whom does somebody write?*" – BENF). The status of the participants and their semantic characterization (the latter is reduced here to the description of sorts) is the same in all three languages. Only the syntactic characterizations of the participants (of the verb complements) differ across these languages. In English, the ORNT role is connected to the verb by means of the preposition "*to*" or as a direct object (in German and Russian, we have an object in the dative case for that; in German, a prepositional phrase with ⟨"*an*" + accusative⟩ may also be used). The result (relation RSLT) is described in all three languages by means of an accusative object (in English, one should better say, by a direct object). The MCONT role is expressed quite differently in each of the languages: In German, a prepositional phrase with ⟨"*über*" + accusative⟩ or an

---

[12] At least as long as one is considering languages of the same cultural sphere, and the concepts in question are lexicalized in the languages to be compared.

**schreiben.1.1/write.1.1/писать.1.1** (Valency frame only)

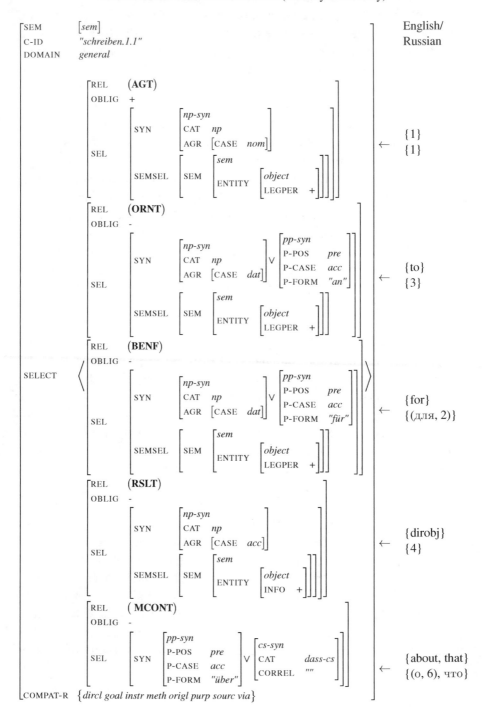

**Figure 12.10.** Multilingual characterization of the lexeme schreiben.1.1 in German, English, and Russian

object sentence introduced by the conjunction "*daß*" are acceptable[13]; in English, a prepositional phrase with "*about*" or an object sentence may be used in an analogous construction; in Russian, the corresponding constituent is connected to the verb by means of a prepositional phrase with $\langle$o + prepositive (sixth case)$\rangle$. The example clearly shows the basically analogous structure of the lexeme specifications which differ mainly in their syntactical description (attribute SYN).

**The semantic interpretation of prepositions.** It is possibly instructive to go further into the semantic interpretation of **prepositions** and their characterization in the lexicon. The following lexical specifications for the German preposition "*in*" (which is to some extent analogous to the English preposition "*in*") can be seen from the linguistic point of view as a characterization of the different meaning variants of "*in*". From a functional perspective of an NLP system, they can also be used immediately for the semantic interpretation of this preposition to automatically generate the corresponding MultiNet structures. The viability of this approach is proved by the WCFA system for syntactic semantic analysis [95].

The argument structure of prepositions and conjunctions, together with the valency structures of the lexemes belonging to the "open" word classes (verbs, nouns, adjectives) are in general the main source for the automatic determination of the relations (arcs) in a semantic network by means of an NLP system.

The following schemata show the principal approach to the interpretation of prepositional phrases of type $\langle$constituent$_1\rangle$ $\langle$preposition$\rangle$ $\langle$constituent$_2\rangle$, where $\langle$preposition$\rangle$ = "*in*". The variables c1 and c2 in the schemata denote the semantic representatives of the constituents $\langle$constituent$_1\rangle$ and $\langle$constituent$_2\rangle$, respectively, together with their syntactic-semantic characterizations. The result of the interpretation is shown in each case under the indicator **net**. c3 designates an intermediate node which is needed in certain cases (e.g. for the generation of a location in the spatial interpretation of in.loc).

The side condition **ic** (an **interconstituent constraint**) within the interpretation rule of in.elmt states that c1 and c2 must differ in the value of the layer attribute **ETYPE** by 1.

---

[13] A possible paraphrasing of the MCONT role by means of "*von*" + dative in German was ignored for the sake of brevity.

## The semantic interpretation of the German preposition "*in*"

### in.loc

"*Urlaub in Wien*" (En: "*holidays in Vienna*"),
"*die Milch im Glas*" (En: "*the milk in the glass*"),
"*die Temperatur in New York*" (En: "*the temperature in New York*")

| c1 | (sort ((o ∪ si) \ (at ∪ ta))) | | net | (LOC c1 c3) (*IN c3 c2) |
|----|-------------------------------|---|-----|-------------------------|
| c2 | (case 3) | $\Longrightarrow$ | c3 | (sort l) |
|    | (sort d) | | | |

| c1 | (sort ((o ∪ si) \ (at ∪ ta))) | | net | (LOC c1 c3) (*IN c3 c2) |
|----|-------------------------------|---|-----|-------------------------|
| c2 | (case 3) | $\Longrightarrow$ | c3 | (sort l) |
|    | (geogr +) | | | |

### in.dircl

"*eine Reise in den Regenwald*" (En: "*a travel into the rain forest*"),
"*ein Schuß ins Auge*" (En: "*a shot into the eye*"),
"*wir gehen ins Stadion*" (En: "*we are going into the stadium*"),
"*ins Grüne fahren*" (En: "*go to the countryside*")
(only in the context of "directional events", i.e. DIRCL ∈ COMPAT-R(c1))

| c1 | (sort (ad ∪ dy)) | | net | (DIRCL c1 c3) |
|----|------------------|---|-----|---------------|
| c2 | (case 4) | | | (*IN c3 c2) |
|    | (sort d) | $\Longrightarrow$ | c3 | (sort l) |
| ic | (c1 COMPAT-R DIRCL) | | | |

### in.elmt

"*Mitglied im Verein XY*" (En: "*member of the club XY*"),
"*Minister in der Regierung*" (En: "*minister in the government*")

| c1 | (sort (o \ at)) | | | |
|----|------------------|---|-----|---------------|
| c2 | (case 3) | | | |
|    | (sort (o \ at)) | $\Longrightarrow$ | net | (ELMT c1 c2) |
| ic | (= (+ (etype c1) 1) | | | |
|    | (etype c2)) | | | |

**in.ctxt**

"*Beweise in der Mathematik*" (En: "*proofs in mathematics*"),
"*Weltmeister im Biathlon*" (En: "*world champion in biathlon*"),
"*die Grammatikregeln im Deutschen*" (En: "*the grammar rules of German (language)*")

| $c_1$ | (sort (abs $\cup$ si)) | | | |
|-------|------------------------|---|---|---|
| $c_2$ | (case 3) | $\Longrightarrow$ | **net** | (CTXT $c_1$ $c_2$ ) |
| | (sort (abs $\cup$ io $\cup$ si)) | | | |

**in.temp**

"*der Angriff im Morgengrauen*" (En: "*the attack at dawn*"),
"*die Ritter im Mittelalter*" (En: "*the knights in the Middle Ages*"),
"*der Gewinn im Jahr 1995*" (En: "*the profit in 1995*"),
"*das Verhalten in der Kindheit*" (En: "*the behavior in childhood*")

| $c_1$ | (sort (o $\cup$ si)) | | | |
|-------|----------------------|---|---|---|
| $c_2$ | (case 3) | | | |
| | (sort (t $\cup$ ta)) | $\Longrightarrow$ | **net** | (TEMP $c_1$ $c_2$) |
| ic | $\neg$(**$c_2$ SUB** $\langle$temporal distance$\rangle$) | | | |

**in.temp_op**

"*die Besprechung in 3 Tagen*" (En: "*the meeting in three days*"),
"*der Termin in 2 Stunden*" (En: "*the appointment in two hours*"),
"*in einer Woche*" (En: "*two weeks from today*")[14]

| $c_1$ | (sort (o $\cup$ si)) | | **net** | (TEMP $c_1$ $c_3$) |
|-------|----------------------|---|---------|-------------------|
| $c_2$ | (case 3) | | | (*OP$_+$ $c_3$ now $c_2$) |
| | (sort (t $\cup$ ta)) | $\Longrightarrow$ | $c_3$ | (sort t) |
| ic | (**$c_2$ SUB** $\langle$temporal distance$\rangle$) | | | |

---

[14] The function *OP$_+$ used in the rule for **in.temp_op** determines the period $c_3$ by adding $c_2$ to the moment characterized by now. The other denotations should be self-explanatory. The function $c_3 = $ *IN($c_2$) used in the interpretation rules is written in its relational form, i.e. as (*IN $c_3$ $c_2$).

Concluding this chapter we shall briefly discuss the **lexical relations**, called sort-change relations in Fig. 3.10. It is characteristic of these relations that they express relationships between semantically closely associated concepts to which particular pairs of sorts may be assigned in a systematic way (see Table 12.2). These connections run parallel to certain derivational phenomena in the field of morphology. They are of special interest, since they are associated with characteristic regularities playing an important role in the lexical area as well as in the general background knowledge. So the nominalization of verbs is connected with an (almost) literal transfer of valency frames at the semantic level carried by the relation CHEA (see [194]). The syntactic characterizations of the arguments and their status (obligatory/optional) are generally not transferred identically. These changes are governed by special rules at the syntactic level.

Example (for German, with a close analogy to English):

(12.21)  befreien.1.1 (En: free.1.1 / liberate.1.1):

  AGT    –    subject,
  OBJ    –    object with accusative (En: direct object),
  AVRT   –    prepositional object with "*von*" (En: preposition "*from*")

  Ge: "*Die Regierung befreite die Menschen von hohen Steuern.*"
  En: "*The government freed people from high taxes.*"

(12.22)  Befreiung.1.1 (En: freeing.1.1 / liberation.1.1):

  AGT    –    prepositional object with "*durch*" (En: "*by*"),
  OBJ    –    genitivus obiectivus (En: preposition "*of*")
  AVRT   –    prepositional object with "*von*" (En: preposition "*from*")

  Ge: "*Die Befreiung der Menschen von hohen Steuern durch die Regierung.*"
  En: "*The freeing of people from high taxes by the government.*"

Analogue inheritance principles hold for the relations CHSP1 and CHSP2. The relation CHPA is characterized by meaning postulates connecting properties with corresponding attribute-value pairs (see Part II, relation CHPA). The relations CHPS and CHSA link properties with corresponding states or connect equivalent states with each other. Finally, the relation CHPE is typically used for the semantic description of inchoative verbs, since its first argument characterizes a situation that is obtained as a result of the event given as its second argument.

Example:

(12.23) Ge: (rot CHPE erröten) or En: (red CHPE redden)

Ge: rot {sein/aussehen} or En: {to be/look} red is the final state of the event Ge: erröten or En: redden.

| Relation | Sort Arg1 | Sort Arg2 | Parallelism in derivation (Morphology) | Example |
|----------|-----------|-----------|----------------------------------------|---------|
| CHEA | dy | ad | Nominalization of verbs | Ge: befreien – Befreiung<br>En: liberate – liberation |
| CHPA | ql | at | Nominalization of adjectives | Ge: lang – Länge<br>En: long – length |
| CHPE | ql | dy | Deriving verbs from adjectives | Ge: rot - erröten<br>En: red – redden/ turn red |
| CHPS | p | as | Nominalization of adjectives | Ge: reich – Reichtum<br>En: rich – richness |
| CHSA | st | as | Deverbalization | Ge: ruhen – Ruhe<br>En: rest (*vb*) – rest (*noun*) |
| CHSP1 | si | p | Present participle (Participle I) | Ge: schlafen – schlafend<br>En: sleep – sleeping |
| CHSP2 | si | p | Past participle (Participle II) | Ge: retten – gerettet<br>En: save – saved |

**Table 12.2.** Lexical relations indicating the change of sorts

The discussion of Chap. 12 shows that the lexical approach underlying Ha-GenLex is clearly semantically based, having MultiNet as its backbone. To the best of our knowledge, there are not so many semantically oriented lexical approaches. Other work in this direction is the SALSA project [59], closely connected to FrameNet [13, 26] and having a strong bias toward lexical analysis and corpus annotation with lexical frames.

# Chapter 13

# Question Answering and Inferences

## 13.1 Logical Principles

Notwithstanding the fact that the main topic of this work is the description of the knowledge representation language MultiNet and not knowledge processing in the broadest sense (which should include the inferences over multilayered extended semantic networks), the treatment of the representational means would be incomplete without taking a look at their use during the inferential answer finding in a QAS. For this reason, we will briefly sketch out how one should deal with MultiNet representations in connection with a formalized "rational reasoning".[1] It should be emphasized that a lot of work has still to be done in this field, and that a unified logic in the broadest sense comprising all aspects of rational reasoning simply does not exist (neither with us nor in the international community). Therefore, the discussion of the topic *"Inferences over MultiNet"* in this chapter has to be seen as a program rather than a collection of final results. A thorough treatment of inferential answer finding over MultiNet knowledge bases combining all kinds of logical inferences and the process of answer generation into a more general approach will be published in a separate volume.

Actually, there exist very good foundations for this work, since the different logical systems have produced significant insights which can be used as a basis for further work. However, one can observe an unresolved dilemma which shall be illustrated by means of classical logic.

On the one hand, very sophisticated inference systems were developed (realized, among other things, as theorem provers in AI), and deep results were obtained with regard to the formal properties of classical logical systems (e.g. with regard to completeness, decidability, computability, etc.). Unfortunately,

---

[1] The somewhat broader term "rational reasoning" is used instead of the term "logical reasoning" to express the necessity that knowledge representation systems designed for meaning representation of natural language texts and dialogues require a more comprehensive spectrum of reasoning methods than those used in classical logic (where the most far-reaching results were achieved in the field of purely deductive inferences).

these results are often applicable only for relatively restricted domains of facts, compared with what can be described in natural language, because of the specific construction of the predicate calculus and other logical systems. Nevertheless, these insights and experiences are also a valuable foundation for the inferential answer finding over a MultiNet knowledge base, especially if we think of the domain of categorically valid states of affairs and axioms.

On the other hand, most knowledge representation systems based on the predicate calculus in its standard form have substantial deficiencies with regard to the treatment of natural language meaning:

1. the purely extensional (model-theoretic) foundation of most logically oriented systems (theory of reference)
2. the reduction of the meaning of sentences to truth-conditions, which are mostly based on two categories only: truth and falsity
3. the purely truth-functional interpretation of logical connectors
4. the lack of cognitive adequacy and encapsulation of conceptual knowledge
5. the global effect of contradictions in logical knowledge bases
6. the rigidity of logical rule systems and the diversity of expressional means in different logical systems.

Before entering into the discussion of these aspects, the basic problem of natural language understanding shall be illustrated by means of some examples:

(13.1) *"A child went across the street."*
(13.2) *"Go across the street!"*
(13.3) *"Jesus was a Jewish itinerant preacher."*

Considering these sentences, it should become clear that a complete treatment of the semantics of natural language has to be supported by three methods (all of them are available to human beings):

- an extensional interpretation
- an operational (procedural) interpretation
- an intensional interpretation.[2]

---

[2] In the philosophy of language, one distinguishes between **intension** and **extension** (see [41]), mirrored in the distinction between *"Sinn"* and *"Bedeutung"*, going back to Frege, or between *"meaning"* and *"sense"* in the English philosophy of language. One can also view the correspondence between a dynamic concept and a real action as a kind of extensional interpretation. From a methodological point of view, however, the so-called *"procedural interpretation"* should be considered a separate case, since this type of interpretation has a different ontological status and must be treated separately in technical NLP systems.

In a declarative sentence like (13.1), which is used only for the conveyance of information, understanding the sentence becomes manifest mainly in the correct embedding of the semantic structure, which in the communication process is transferred into the already existing network of concepts (intensional interpretation). Nobody will include an extensional interpretation of the concepts involved into the first understanding of the sentence "*A child went across the street*", which would anyway be difficult with everyday concepts like child or go.[3] Nevertheless, given the necessity to decide on the truth or falsity of the sentence (but only then), a connection to the reality has to be established (extensional interpretation).

In Sentence (13.2), a complete comprehension of the meaning is not thinkable without a translation of the concept go into a corresponding action of movement (procedural interpretation, in the broadest sense). But, an extensional interpretation of the concept street is also important for the understanding of the command, because Sentence (13.2) would not be understood correctly (or its meaning would be disregarded) if the addressee of the command would go across the lawn.

Finally, Sentence (13.3) illustrates the problematic nature of a pure extensional interpretation in general. The word "*Jesus*" has several meaning facets and connotations associated with it, which are all present during the understanding of (13.3) (this phenomenon should not be confused with polysemy; rather it belongs to the field of different manifestations of one and the same entity; see Sect. 4.5). On the one hand, we are facing a "historical" (Ge: "historische") person which is subject to historical investigations. In this context, one can reflect, for instance, on the existence or nonexistence of the entity in question. On the other hand, one has to consider the "historic" (Ge: "geschichtliche") person manifested by the meaningfulness assigned to this person by man (enriched possibly by two thousand years of legends).[4] Both components interact and cannot be reduced extensionally to decidable sets or set operations (see Sect. 15.3). So, it could be imagined that the "historical" Jesus had actually not lived (or at least not in the same way as it is described in the Gospel), while the "historic" Jesus as a cognitive concept would still maintain its importance. In this sense, Sentence (13.3) would not do justice to the historic person Jesus for a Christian believer, since it does not express

---

[3] What are the criteria discerning a child from a youth or the concept go from the concepts walk or run?

[4] Following Trilling [260], we use the distinction between "historisch" (En: "historical") and "geschichtlich" (En: "historic") to discern between the different meaning facets of persons. One should be aware, however, that the distinction discussed here does not immediately follow from the meanings of the aforementioned terms, be they in German or in English.

the important historic role of the concept Jesus (for many people this sentence would even bear a derogative meaning "*Jesus was (nothing but) a Jewish itinerant preacher*").

One must also state in this context that a human hearer understands even sentences that contain concepts whose applicability or validity in a certain context cannot be decided by him or her immediately. This can be illustrated already by common concepts, like gold in the sentence "*The ring consists of pure gold.*" Although this sentence will be understood by everyone, only certain experts (like jewelers or chemists) have the ability of an extensional interpretation of this sentence, i.e. to discern gold from non-gold, or gold alloys from pure gold (constitution of meaning as a social phenomenon).

Let us return to the six difficulties mentioned initially, which are connected with the standard way the predicate calculus is applied to the meaning representation of natural language sentences:

Ad 1). Logic calculi generally use a kind of surrogate for an **extensional semantics** in the philosophical sense, mapping logical expressions not immediately into the real word, but rather into a formal structure which is the basis of this model-theoretic interpretation (see also Sect. 15.3). Because of the model-theoretic foundation of the predicate calculus and of most other logic-oriented KRS, every formal construct of the logic language must be extensionally interpretable. Such a model-theoretic interpretation, however, is not unrestrictedly possible for natural language concepts, as was indicated in Chap. 1. For certain concepts, like reference, it even leads to contradictions (see [151, p. 239], "*What does the expression "refer" refer to?*") Also the fixed **arity** of predicates, required for their interpretation as sets of tuples over a given universe (see Sect. 15.3) is a genuine obstacle for their application to the meaning representation of natural language concepts.[5] The aforementioned difficulty concerns above all the area of verb meanings, because every verb can be connected with differing numbers of participants and circumstances (see also Sect. 5.2). Even such relatively simple verbs like "*roll*" would have to be interpreted semantically by predicates of different arity because of their transitive and intransitive uses ("*Max rolled the stone down the hill*" vs. "*The stone rolled down the hill*"). This distinction is, in our opinion, a grammatical phenomenon with a systematic character (change in certain diathetic relationships, called **alternations**) and not a semantic phenomenon.[6] In logic-oriented approaches, these

---

[5] For logic-oriented approaches which try to avoid this problem, see the discussion of the LILOG system on p. 383 and the remarks on the Davidsonian logic on p. 86.

[6] The other opinion assuming different sememes underlying such alternating verbs can also be expressed by means of MultiNet. This approach, however, has the disadvantage of multiplying the number of meaning postulates.

and other similar phenomena give rise to complicated type changing operations (see, for instance, [250] with a grammatical view, and [205] with a lexical view).

Some principles concerning the semantic foundation of representational means and marking the interface between intensional and extensional levels were formulated by Loebner (see [162, p. 2]).

- The semantic description of natural language expressions should be generally separated from a theory of reference (the former is a precondition for the latter).
- The meaning of a sentence can not be adequately described in terms of truth conditions alone.
- Only an appropriate semantic description, together with a theory of reference, can be a basis for correct truth conditions.

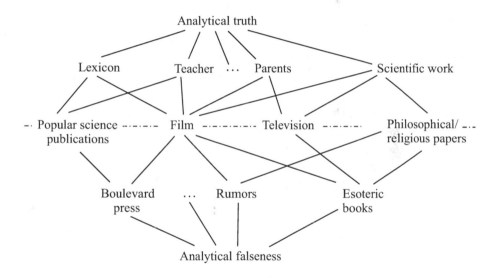

**Figure 13.1.** Possible structure of degrees of trustworthiness (detail)

Ad 2). Truth conditions are only one aspect of meaning (and not the most important one).[7] A sentence will be understood even in those cases where the hearer/reader is not able to decide on the truth or falsity of it. Indeed, the first (i.e. the understanding) is a precondition for the second (i.e. the decision). In

---

[7] It is interesting that already Wittgenstein substituted the concept of truth conditions in his semantic theory with conditions of assertion and justification; see [251, Vol. IV, "*Kripkes Wittgenstein*"].

other words, regardless of which method for verifying a sentence one takes into account (cf. [28]), understanding comes first. Furthermore, the assignment of only two categories, true and false, to a proposition has to be considered as too much a simplification. It should rather be assumed that human beings use a kind of "degree of **trustworthiness**" in validating propositional sentences and/or their source. The different degrees of trustworthiness form a **partial order** with the analytical truth as an upper bound and the analytical falsity as a lower bound (see Fig. 13.1).[8]

It must be stated, however, that a comprehensive logical system with a formal description of propositions having different degrees of trustworthiness and with a qualitative weighing of them in the process of logical reasoning is still needed.

Provided a text stems from a single source, then one and the same degree of trustworthiness can be attached to all statements so that the normal laws of logic are valid in this area. We will restrict our considerations to this case throughout the book.

Loebner has also taken issue with the role of truth conditions in logic-oriented semantics. He states in [163] that logic-oriented semantic theories formulate truth conditions that properly apply only to the truth of a sentence (and not to its falsity). A sentence is false in that conception, which leans on the law of the excluded middle, if and only if it is not true. Loebner [163] also gives examples showing the problems caused by this approach.[9] He correctly demands that an adequate definition of truth conditions for natural language sentences should not only specify when such a sentence is "true", but it should also explicitly define under what conditions this sentence is "false" (see [162, p. 20]).

Ad 3). A further handicap concerning the application of the predicate calculus for the semantic representation of natural language sentences is the purely truth-functional interpretation of its connectors, which is clearly related to the extensional interpretation of logical expressions in general, and in particular to the fact that the extension of a proposition is simply a truth value. This has,

---

[8] Even this partial order differs individually. Thus, a religious fundamentalist might assign a higher degree of trustworthiness to the statements of his dogmas than to the "analytical truth" (which includes the logical truth). An esoteric person, too, may assign a higher degree of validity to a parapsychological explanation than to a natural law. Also, the valuation of the trustworthiness of single sources has to be carried out in a more sophisticated way, since a documentary report on television certainly has a higher degree of trustworthiness than a science fiction film (the same can be said of one's comparing "instruction" with "own experience").

[9] As expected, the difficulties are rooted in the two-valuedness of traditional logic and in the assumption of the aforementioned law of the excluded middle.

among other things, the consequence that a logical implication A → B has the truth value F (false) only if A is assigned the truth value T (true) and B is assigned the value F. The implication results in the value T in all other cases of assignment of truth values to the propositional variables. As a consequence, there arise two properties of the implication which are counterintuitive:

- The implication A → B is always true if A is false, which (together with the next property) makes the implication an unsuitable candidate for the semantic representation of natural language conditionals.
- A logical implication A → B can be true also in cases where there is no inner semantic connection (no meaning connection) between A and B.

Against the background of this discussion, the question arises as to how the axioms of MultiNet, written in the form of an implication A → B, have to be interpreted:

- One is only licensed to write an axiom of the form A → B if one simultaneously wants to postulate a meaning connection between A and B.[10]
- Those who accept the implication A → B as admissible must accept B in the language game if they accept A ("commitment principle"). The implication makes no assertion in any other case (i.e. it is not applicable during the language game).[11]

In addition, asserting such an implication one has to specify whether the rule holds categorically, as Formula (89), or only prototypically, as Formula (90). This specification determines whether the respective rule has to be used within the framework of strict (monotonic) reasoning or within the framework of default logic (nonmonotonic reasoning).

$$(v \text{ SUBS buy}) \wedge (v \text{ AGT a}) \wedge (v \text{ OBJ o}) \wedge (v \text{ AVRT d}) \rightarrow$$
$$\exists w \ (w \text{ SUBS sell}) \wedge (w \text{ OBJ o}) \wedge (w \text{ AGT d}) \wedge (w \text{ ORNT a}) \qquad (89)$$

$$(k_1 \text{ PARS } k_2) \wedge (k_2 \text{ ORIGM s}) \rightarrow (k_1 \text{ ORIGM s}) \qquad (90)$$

Ad 4) Another point speaking against the cognitive adequacy of logical expressional means is the absence of concept centeredness (see Chap. 1) and the extensional underpinning (see Point 1 above). Many logical expressions used

---

[10] A rule A → B violating this condition is inadmissible, i.e. it is senseless (and not simply false).

[11] The contraposition ¬A → ¬B cannot be derived from A → B. This is possible only in a two-valued logic. Given that somebody accepts the implication A → B and ¬B simultaneously, one can only state that he or she must not accept A at the same time.

as a semantic representation for a sentence are also connected with a counterintuitive aspect. This can be shown by means of formula (91), which corresponds to the sentence "*All ravens are black.*" with regard to its truth conditions.

$$\forall x \; raven(x) \rightarrow black(x) \tag{91}$$

This formula contains a (material) implication which is cognitively not perceived during the understanding of the cited sentence. Moreover, this expression makes also an assertion about objects which are no ravens (indeed, if Formula (91) were the proper semantic representation of "*All ravens are black.*", this sentence would also be true if there were no ravens at all, which seems odd).

The second aspect is emphasized by the contraposed form (92) of (91):

$$\forall x \; \neg black(x) \rightarrow \neg raven(x) \tag{92}$$

Formula (92) asserts that all nonblack objects (green or red cars, snow, etc.) are not ravens. Notwithstanding the fact that this proposition is true, it is not the content of the above sentence, which shows once more that meaning cannot be reduced to the formulation of truth conditions.

Ad 5) A property of the predicate calculus relatively seldom discussed in the context of knowledge representation, but nevertheless important to the applicability of FOL rules to a cognitively adequate meaning representation, is the global effect of these rules on a knowledge base. This means that arbitrary expressions (even expressions that semantically have nothing to do with each other) can be connected logically under certain circumstances. This shall be illustrated by means of the following logical theorems, which are assumed in most logical systems either as axioms or as expressions which can easily be deduced from the axiom system (and, by the way, also from each other).

$$A \rightarrow A \lor B \qquad \text{(Extension rule)} \tag{93}$$
$$A \land \neg A \rightarrow B \qquad \text{(Ex falso quodlibet sequitur)} \tag{94}$$

The extension rule (93) allows us to combine concepts from different parts of a knowledge base which have semantically nothing in common (e.g. "*If a square has four right angles, then it has four right angles or the moon is {a / not a} fixed star*"). Such a rule should not be allowed in a comprehensive knowledge representation system because of its global influence and because of its cognitive inadequacy (see also Sect. 15.2.2).

A still more dangerous effect is immediately visible from Rule (94) because it requires that a knowledge base be globally consistent. Otherwise, such a knowledge base would be useless, since any arbitrary proposition could be deduced from it. With human beings, however, we almost always observe "wrong knowledge", which does not hold, and their knowledge base is seldom free of contradictions. Nevertheless, if for instance, a student has mathematical knowledge full of contradictions, then he does normally not mix up a spoon with a fork or left with right because of this circumstance. The reason for this is the fact that he applies his inference rules locally, connecting only such concepts with each other that stand in a meaningful relationship (see Point 3 above).

These difficulties can be removed if one observes a **locality principle** for the applicability of rules, which (together with the criteria formulated in Point 3 above) warrants that contradictions in one part of a knowledge base do not produce wrong entailments in another part not semantically connected with the first. In MultiNet, this principle is taken into account by means of an associatively guided application of inference rules (see Sect. 13.3).[12]

Ad 6). Considering the two thousand years of tradition in logic (or – if one counts from Frege – more than one hundred years of tradition in formal logic), one meets a plenitude of logical systems which try to formalize different types of human rational reasoning on the basis of very heterogeneous expressional means. In spite of the impressive results and experiences gathered so far, we still do not have a closed logical edifice comprising all this knowledge on the basis of a unified set of expressional means. There might yet be a long way for reaching this ambitious goal. Because of this, there seems to be no other possibility but to use a kind of **opportunistic logic** for a knowledge representation system applicable to the meaning representation of natural language information and to a QAS which has to be built on top of that. Such an apparatus has to borrow from different logical systems. It thus uses all logical laws that were discovered in the different logic schools and are significant for answering certain types of questions on the basis of the concrete knowledge relevant to the question-answering process. We believe that Gabbay's idea of **fibring logics** [71] comes very close to this demand.

If, for instance, a decision question of the type *"Did Real Madrid lose the championship yesterday?"* has to be answered, and the information *"Max knows that Real Madrid won its game yesterday."* is stored in the knowledge base, then the question must be answered with NO on the basis of modal-logical rules (to be specific, on the basis of law (65) of epistemic logic given in Sect. 8.3) and on the basis of the relationship between win and lose. If the knowledge base contained only the information *"The last game of the championship with Real Madrid was postponed to the next week."* then the question has to be answered again with NO, but in this case by including laws of tem-

---

[12] One proposal to overcome these difficulties within the framework of logic had been made in the form of a **defeasible logic** [171].

poral logic (expressing, among other things, the fact that the result of an action cannot precede the beginning of the action). Analogously, the applicability of the methods of default reasoning is determined by the decision about whether one has to include prototypical or categorical knowledge (see Sect. 3.2.3).

Altogether, we hold the opinion that organizing the cooperation of a broad spectrum of logical methods is more important to the modeling of human reasoning than achieving a very deep succession of single reasoning steps or long deduction chains (with regard to the latter point, the existing theorem provers which were developed for the classical predicate calculus, and especially for Horn clauses, outperform human beings anyway; see also [19] and [24]).

The traditional construction of the predicate calculus yields a collection of basic laws (axioms or theorems) which are problematic with regard to their use for the meaning representation of natural language. Among them

- the **law of double negation**:    $\neg(\neg A) \leftrightarrow A$    (95)

- the **law of the excluded middle**:    $\neg A \vee A$    (96)

- the **contraposition principle**:    $(A \rightarrow B) \leftrightarrow (\neg B \rightarrow \neg A)$    (97)

This does not mean that these laws are principally not valid; they are only applicable in well-defined contexts. For instance, the intensional negation of a state of affairs sv by means of (MODL + *NON) is canceled by a characterization of sv with [**FACT** = *non*] if only the truth of sv has to be decided upon, but not if the expectations presupposed by sv have to be found (see Sect. 8.3). Also, the negation of a gradable property $P_1$ having a counterpart $P_2$ contrary to $P_1$ (as, for instance, friendly and unfriendly) does not necessarily result in $P_2$ (see also Sect. 8.2).

The law of the excluded middle is problematic in those cases where one has to deal with more than two truth values or with truth value gaps (there are good reasons for both cases[13]). The contraposition principle, finally, is closely connected with the law of double negation, and is therefore problematic in the same sense.

The most important types of reasoning and inference rules essential for deductive reasoning and abductive reasoning, and important also to MultiNet, are the "modus ponens" (Rule (98)) and the schema of abductive reasoning (Rule (99)):

---

[13] Thus, some authors propose a priori a many-valued logic for the semantics of natural language; see, for instance, [25]. The law of double negation is also questioned by the intuitionistic logic; see [123].

| A | **modus ponens** | B | **abduction** |
|---|---|---|---|
| $A \rightarrow B$ | (98) | $A \rightarrow B$ | (99) |
| B | | A (more trustworthy) | |

The inference rule (98) preserves the truth value of the premises or (if one is working with degrees of trustworthiness and is assuming the strict validity of the implication) transfers the degree of trustworthiness of the premise A to B.[14] In contrast, the rule of abduction (99) does not transfer the truth value or trustworthiness of B to A, even if one has perfect knowledge about B and $A \rightarrow B$. Instead, the trustworthiness of A is only somewhat increased, compared to that of the a priori knowledge about A before carrying out the abductive inference (how much it is increased remains undetermined to some extent). However, if there are estimations or statistical knowledge about the a priori probabilities $P(A)$ and $P(B)$ and about the conditional probability $P(B|A)$ corresponding to the implication $A \rightarrow B$, then the increase of the trustworthiness of A resulting from an abductive inference can be quantitatively expressed by means of **Bayes' Theorem**[15] (see for instance [197]):

$$P(A|B) = \frac{P(B|A)P(A)}{P(B)} \qquad (100)$$

With this, a bridge is built between abductive reasoning and probabilistic reasoning. The abductive inference method shows especially that the introduction of trustworthiness as a basic concept (instead of truth values) is more adequate for qualitative reasoning processes. There are also other types of inference, like inductive reasoning (see [8]), analogous reasoning (see [118]), approximate reasoning (see [87]), temporal reasoning (see [266]), spatial reasoning (see [69]), and causal reasoning (see [232]), which cannot be dealt with here.

Naturally, all inference rules known from predicate calculus (see [241]), including the classical laws investigated already by Aristotle, the so-called **syllogisms**, can also be used as a basis for reasoning in a QAS. As an example of a syllogism, the inferential figure *"ferio"* is given; it has the following form:

---

[14] In case there are two different values $Tw_A(B)$ and $Tw_C(B)$ for the trustworthiness of B resulting from the implications $A \rightarrow B$ and $C \rightarrow B$, respectively, the overall trustworthiness $Tw_\Sigma(B)$ is defined as $Tw_\Sigma(B) = Max[Tw_A(B), Tw_C(B)]$.

[15] The term $P(A|B)$ denotes the probability of the event A provided event B has already been observed.

| | | |
|---|---|---|
| $\forall x\ R(x) \rightarrow \neg F(x)$ | | *"All robbers are unfriendly."* |
| $\exists x\ P(x) \wedge R(x)$ | (101) | *"There are persons who are robbers."* |

$\exists x\ P(x) \wedge \neg F(x)$          *"There are unfriendly persons."*

To model human reasoning processes important to natural language understanding, one has also to consider Grice's **maxims of conversation** [84]. The inference rules corresponding to these important laws are called **implicatures**. To illustrate their effect, we consider the following maxim:

- A contribution to a discourse should be as informative as necessary, but not more informative than necessary ($\rightarrow$ the demand to avoid redundancies).

One conclusion (implicature) which can be drawn from observing this maxim can be illustrated by means of the following situation:

- Somebody is entering a room where the windows are widely open and says: *"It's cold here."* Another person sitting in that room infers on the basis of the aforementioned utterance: The newcomer does not want to tell me something that is known to me and can anyway be felt by me; his remark is actually a request to close the windows.

As shown by this example, the maxims of conversation, and the implicatures based on them, open an access to indirect speech acts (a field which is still insufficiently mastered in automatic natural language processing and something beyond the scope of this work; see [229]).

The inference rules of MultiNet and the inference methods associated with them have to be shaped in such a way that they – together with the analysis processes and the generation of natural language expressions – represent the formal operations which describe the actions in a question-answering game and correctly combine questions and answers in this game. Thereby, the admissible inferences are characterized by the general inference rules provided by MultiNet and by the **axioms** written as implications (the latter possibly restricted by certain **constraints**; see Sect. 3.3).

The requirements to be met by the inference system of MultiNet can be summarized as follows:

- It must have a local effect only, i.e. possible contradictions in one part of the knowledge base do not necessarily infest the whole knowledge base.
- It is true that the inference methods to be applied share a deductive kernel. In general, however, they have to be opportunistically adapted to the question type and the type of the knowledge involved (categorical knowledge, prototypical knowledge, and situational knowledge).

- The inferences are associatively guided, i.e. only such units of knowledge which are semantically connected can be related to each other in the reasoning process.
- Logical/analytical truth and falsity are indeed important basic categories, but they are only special cases in a larger structure (a partial order or a lattice of degrees of trustworthiness).

## 13.2  Classes of Questions and Inferential Answer Finding

For the main types of questions proposed in Sect. 3.2.4 (i.e. supplementary questions, decision questions, and essay questions; see Fig. 3.8), it was the nature of the answer that provided the main classification criterion. But in connection with the subtypes, like counting questions, operational questions, or questions for reasons, the characteristic of the answer-finding process itself comes into play. It would be desirable to develop a more elaborate system of question classes based on a cross classification where one set of criteria characterizes the aspect of answer generation (the type of the answer) and the other set the method used for answer finding (deductive, abductive, inductive reasoning, computational approaches, or methods of problem solving, etc.). However, the second aspect is especially difficult to qualify, because the same question type found according to the first classification has to be treated with different techniques for answer finding, depending on the nature of the information provided. Thus, simple decision questions can in most cases be treated with purely deductive inference techniques (this is the case, for instance, with "*Are there any motors with 100 hp?*" on a sufficiently large knowledge base about motors). It might also be that a very similar decision question (like "*Are there any motors with a degree of effectiveness over 98%?*") can only be answered by means of an entire research program.[16]

We shall restrict ourselves to purely deductive methods of answer finding and demonstrate the interplay of answer finding and answer generation by means of some examples. For this purpose, we assume that, for each question, the information stemming from one of the Sentences (S1), (S2), and (S3), was the only information present in the knowledge base (see Figs. 13.2 through 13.4).

---

[16] The problem that this question is ambiguous shall be set aside here. It can be meant in a principal sense "*Are there such motors at all?*" or in the sense "*Do you know such a motor?*"

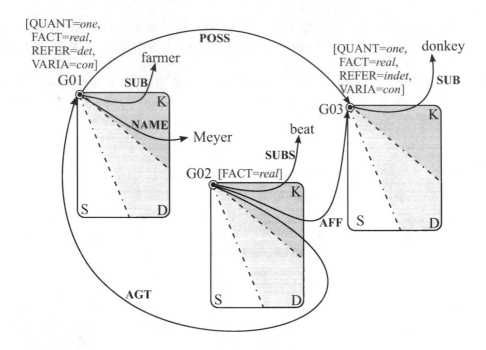

**Figure 13.2. Representation of (S1):** *"Farmer Meyer owns a donkey and beats it."*

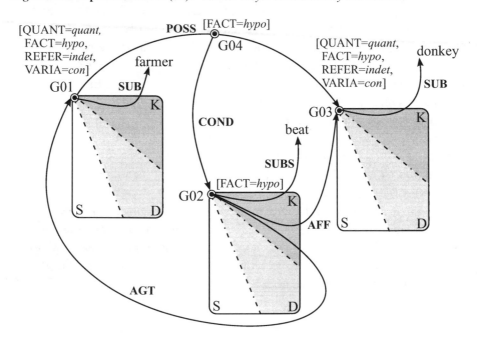

**Figure 13.3. Representation of (S2):** *"If farmers own donkeys they beat them."*

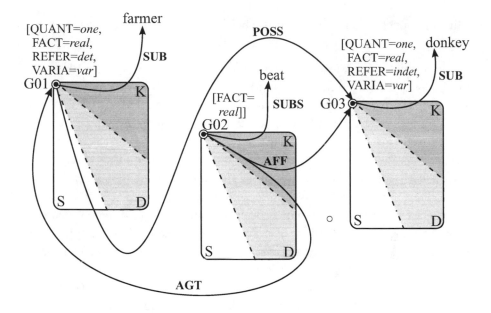

**Figure 13.4. Representation of (S3):** *"Every farmer who owns a donkey beats it."*

The questions (F1), (F2), and (F3), together with the answers obtained on the basis of the above sentences, are shown in Figs. 13.5 through 13.7. There, the first answer for every question-answer pair results from a rigid answer strategy and the second from a more cooperative ("soft") answer strategy.

To facilitate the understanding of logical answer finding, a few remarks are necessary about the meaning representation of questions:

- The question type found by the analysis (see Sect. 3.2.4) is attached to the semantic representative of the query sentence using the attribute FTYPE.
- Nodes of the semantic representatives of objects with [**SORT** = *o*] automatically obtain underspecified values for the layer attributes **QUANT, REFER,** and **VARIA** in cases where the corresponding NP does not contain determiners or quantificators that are different from the indefinite article or the zero article.[17]
- Supplementary questions ([FTYPE=*erg*]) and decision questions with existential character ([FTYPE=*entex*]) have a **question focus**, which is the entity

---

[17] This leads to a representation where the farmer and donkey nodes in Figs. 13.5 and 13.6 are maximally underspecified, while the farmer node in Fig. 13.7 bears the attribute values [**QUANT** = *all*], [**REFER** = *det*], and [**VARIA** = *con*] because of the explicit determiner / quantificator "*all*".

the questioner is interested in. It is labeled by a question mark in the graphical representations.

The second point is justified by the observation that in both cases the questioner has apparently the same intention independent of whether the underspecified NPs in the original sentence are formulated in singular or plural, or of whether or not the indefinite article is used. This is formally supported in MultiNet by the supposition that maximally underspecified values of layer attributes can be unified with all other values of the hierarchy belonging to this attribute (this does not hold for more specific values). If somebody asks whether there is a farmer who possesses a donkey (or whether there are farmers who possess donkeys), then he expects a positive answer if there is a farmer possessing an arbitrary number of donkeys (except zero). However, if somebody asks, whether a farmer possesses "three" or "all" donkeys, then he in fact means "three" or "all". To illustrate the basic principle of the question-answering process, queries (F1) through (F3) are constructed in such a way that there is no need to include axioms or further background knowledge in addition to that given by sentences (S1) to (S3). (The application of axioms and additional background knowledge is dealt with in Sect. 13.3.)

The answer finding is characterized by the following main steps:

- **ANSW1:** In the first step, the answering process tries to verify the basic meaning structure of the query against the background knowledge, temporarily neglecting the layer attributes of the nodes involved and especially of the question focus. Any differences or mismatches detected are stored, however, with every node for potential use in a later step ("rough verification"; see also Sect. 13.3 and [80]). The analogue is done with semantically restrictive relations, not be considered further in our abbreviated explanation.

- **ANSW2:** In the second step, layer information is included ("fine verification"). If the layer attributes of corresponding nodes of query and answer can be completely unified, then the query is answered by "Yes" in the case of a decision question. For supplementary questions, the node of the semantic network substituted for the **question focus** is transferred to the answer generation (natural language reformulation). If the layer attributes are not unifiable, the third step is carried out.

- **ANSW3:** The third step includes the predefined types of **answer strategy**: *rigid* – all relevant information pieces must exactly match or be derivable; *cooperative* – agreement must be warranted except for the layer information, and additional information concerning the disagreement must be given to the questioner;

*robust* – certain predefined types of disagreement between query and net structure are admissible (for example, the query may contain a CAUS relation while the knowledge base contains only the less specific REAS relation at the corresponding position).

Under a rigid answer strategy, the process is finished with step ANSW2, while in the other cases a kind of overanswering in a cooperative answer strategy takes place, illustrated here only by examples; see the cooperative answers shown in Figs. 13.5 through 13.7.

Let us firstly consider Query (F1) against knowledge background (S1). In this constellation, the query structure can be verified not only roughly (step ANSW1), but also with explicit inclusion of the layer information (step ANSW2). In this elementary case, the query structure is isomorphic to the net structure represented by the real situation (G02), and the layer attributes of corresponding nodes can be unified. Since node G01 is substituted for the question focus during the deductive answering process, only G01 must be reformulated

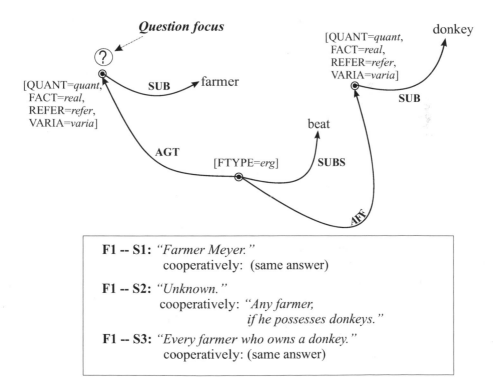

**F1 -- S1:** *"Farmer Meyer."*
            cooperatively: (same answer)

**F1 -- S2:** *"Unknown."*
            cooperatively: *"Any farmer,*
                         *if he possesses donkeys."*

**F1 -- S3:** *"Every farmer who owns a donkey."*
            cooperatively: (same answer)

**Figure 13.5. Representation of (F1):** *"Which farmer beats a donkey?"* or with the same intention: *"Which farmers beat donkeys?"*

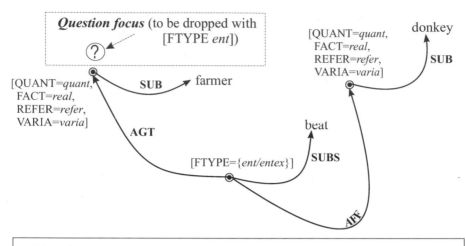

F2 -- S1: *"Yes!"*
cooperatively: *"Yes, Farmer Meyer."*

F2 -- S2: *"Unknown."*
cooperatively: *"Yes, if there are farmers who own donkeys."*

F2 -- S3: *"Yes."*
cooperatively: *"Yes - every farmer who owns a donkey."*

**Figure 13.6. Representation of (F2):** *"Is there a farmer who beats donkeys?"* or with the same intention, *"Are there any farmers who beat a donkey?"*

by the answer generator; thereby only the immanent knowledge about G01 is included in the reformulation process (which would be sufficient even for a cooperative answer). The reformulation of the situational knowledge represented by the POSS arc and by the AGT arc would be thought as redundant.

When answering Query (F1) against the background knowledge (S2), the rough verification can be carried out successfully, and thus the correspondence "question focus – G01" will be found. But the fine verification (step ANSW2) will discover a discrepancy with regard to the layer attribute **FACT**. For this reason, the answer *"Unknown"* has to be generated. Since step ANSW2 discovers the conditional restriction (G04 COND G02) as reason for the discrepancy in the values of the layer attribute **FACT** manifesting itself in the specification [**FACT** = *hypo*] of G01, G02, and G03, the answer *"Any farmer"* can be output under a cooperative answer strategy if this answer is restricted to *"If he possesses donkeys."*

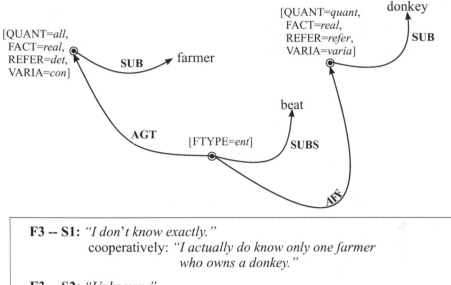

F3 -- S1: *"I don't know exactly."*
cooperatively: *"I actually do know only one farmer
who owns a donkey."*

F3 -- S2: *"Unknown."*
cooperatively: *"Yes, if they do own donkeys."*

F3 -- S3: *"No."*
cooperatively: *"This does hold at least
for those farmers who own a donkey."*

**Figure 13.7. Representation of (F3):** *"Do all farmers beat donkeys?"*

The answering process for Query (F1) against the background knowledge (S3) is carried out in the same way as in the first case, with the exception that the node G01 in (S2) is differently characterized with regard to the immanent knowledge (see the POSS arc) and that the attribute-value bundle [**QUANT** = *one*, **FACT** = *real*, **REFER** = *det*, **VARIA** = *var*] has to be taken into account during answer generation. This gives *"Every farmer who owns a donkey"* as an answer (please note that the POSS arc in Fig. 13.4 belongs to the definitional knowledge of G01 and must be included in the answer generation).

Since the other cases illustrated in Figs. 13.6 and 13.7 are dealt with analogously, only some special aspects are mentioned here. Query (F2) can be interpreted as a decision question with [FTYPE=ent] which has to be answered simply with *"Yes"* or *"No"* (this case was chosen for question answering in Fig. 13.6). It can also be interpreted as a decision question with existential character with [FTYPE=entex], which must be treated in the same way as Query (F1). It should finally be remarked that not only the content of the answer, but also its form is influenced by the respective question (illustrated by the answers to Queries (F2) and (F3)). This aspect also affects the appropriate pronominalizations during answer generation.[18]

## 13.3 Associatively Controlled Logical Question Answering

In the foregoing section, only the elementary case, where the whole question structure is isomorphic to a partial network of the knowledge base, was considered. Although this case very seldom applies to a whole question structure, it is nevertheless the final goal which must be achieved, at least for partial structures, during the inference process. Even if query and network do not immediately match each other, the query structure has to be deductively reduced, step by step, to elementary facts of the knowledge base using axiomatic rules and background knowledge in order to eventually determine the proper answer.

To illustrate the associatively guided inference method applied in Multi-Net, which is called **question centering** and whose foundations are described in [106], we consider the following example.

Information that is textually given:

(**S4**) *"The travel agency T-Serv bought a PC from CompuTex in 1998."*

Query: (**F4**) *"To which firm did CompuTex sell a computer?"*

Taking into consideration the conjunction convention (see Sect. 16.3), this query has the following linearized form:

$$\text{QP:} \quad [(\text{FOCUS ?}) \mid (\text{s SUBS sell}) \wedge (\text{s AGT CompuTex}) \wedge (\text{s OBJ o})$$
$$\wedge\ (\text{o SUB computer}) \wedge (\text{s ORNT ?}) \wedge (\text{? SUB firm})] \tag{102}$$

All arguments in QP, except for the labels of lexicalized concepts, must be considered variables. Since (F4) is interpreted as a supplementary question, the corresponding semantic structure contains a special variable "?" marking the **question focus** (see also Sect. 3.2.4). The final goal of question-answering consists in the verification of this question structure, which is called **question pattern** (QP) because special assignments of nodes to variables must be found through pattern matching during the application of **inference rules** and **axioms** involved in the verification process.

---

[18] The production of correct pronoun references in generating a "fluent" answer is a task of the reformulation process, which cannot be further discussed here.

The verification procedure works backward in the sense that the relational triples of the question pattern are deductively reduced to elements of the knowledge base. In this process, all triples or groups of triples which have been verified are removed from QP. The end of a successful search is thus marked by the empty question pattern. For supplementary questions, the node K of the SN substituted for the question focus during the verification process represents the solution. K also marks the **answer kernel**, which provides the basis for generating a natural language answer to the question.

The associative control of the logical derivation steps is based on the following idea. The inference process tries to build a path from every terminal (i.e. lexicalized) node of the SN that is simultaneously an element of the question pattern QP to all other terminal nodes of QP. Thereby, the search is associatively guided by the question pattern. Such paths between the terminal nodes of QP must exist in the semantic network, otherwise these nodes would be isolated in the SN and the question could not be answered over this network. However, it is quite normal for the relational triples of QP not to have a direct correspondence in the SN. In general, axioms must be used to build bridges between nodes not otherwise connected, and the question pattern has to be transformed partially or as a whole into another pattern by means of these axioms and corresponding inference rules. A basic idea important for the whole method consists in the endeavor to focus the "attention" of the search process on those nodes of the SN which can be reached through different paths. Such nodes are called **question centers**, since the probability of having reached a part of the SN relevant to the question-answering is significantly increased if a node lying on different search paths has been discovered.[19]

The logical-associative search described above can be modeled by a method which will be explained for the question-sentence pair (F4) – (S4); see Fig. 13.8.

At the beginning a search graph SG, which is superimposed on the semantic network SN, is initialized. The graph SG contains the information forming the basis for question answering. In the start phase, SG consists only of its root W and one successor node of W for every terminal node of the investigated question (every node of SG corresponds to one node of the SN, so that there is a homomorphic mapping from SG into the SN).

---

[19] Proposals to valuate this situation by using an appropriate heuristic evaluation function for controlling the search in the SN were made in [106].

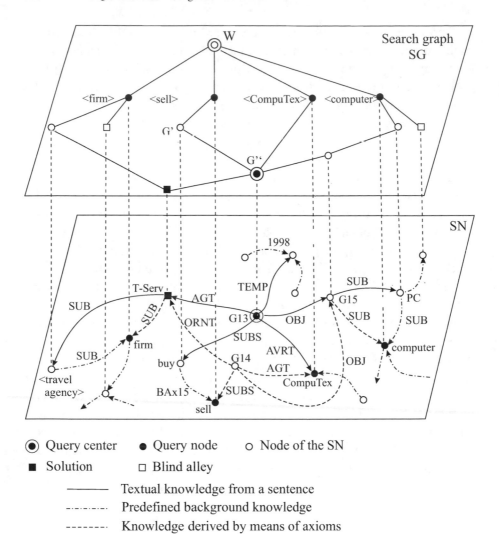

**Figure 13.8.** The method of question focusing

Generally, the nodes of SG have the following form:

⟨SG-node⟩ ::= (⟨node of the SN⟩
                ⟨valuation⟩
                ⟨part of the question pattern still to be verified⟩
                ⟨list of predecessor nodes on the search path⟩
                ⟨list of substitutions carried out during the search⟩
                ⟨list of restrictions/deviations found during the search⟩) (103)

The root W contains as its third component the whole question pattern QP (Formula (102)), because nothing has been verified yet. All other components are empty. The first component of every node of SG is called **head node**, since it marks the position in the SN to which the search has been driven starting from a certain terminal question node. It is the goal of the search process to verify every single relational triple of QP by following appropriate arcs of the SN and finding suitable substitutions for the variables of QP.

Let us assume a search starting from an arbitrary node $G_1 \in SG$ with the head node $k_1$. If a triple $Tr = (k_1 \langle Rel \rangle x)$ of QP matches an arc of the SN, i.e. there is an arc of the SN labeled by $\langle Rel \rangle$ and leading from $k_1$ to $k_2$, then a new node $G_2$ of SG is constructed. This node has the head node $k_2$, a question pattern built from QP by removing Tr from it and applying the substitution $\sigma = \{k_2/x\}$ to the result. The predecessor list of $G_1$ completed by $k_1$ is added to $G_2$ as its fourth component. The fifth component of $G_2$ is a substitution list built from that of $G_1$ by adding the new substitution $\sigma = \{k_2/x\}$. The sixth component of $G_2$ generally contains the restrictions and deviations found during the trial to derive the question pattern. These can be, for instance, modal restrictions, conditional restrictions, or deviations concerning the layer structure of nodes (in this example, this component remains empty). With regard to the valuation of a node $G \in SG$ (second component of G) we state here only that it should be chosen to be a function of the number of the arcs entering or leaving the head node, of the length of the question pattern still to be verified, and of an additional bonus for reaching a question center (for further details see [106]).

For the purpose of illustration, we look at the situation represented in Fig. 13.8 and assume temporarily that all arcs of the SN drawn with dashed lines without intermittent points are neglected (these arcs, which lack the original SN, will be derived only during the deduction process). Under this assumption, only three nodes of the search graph SG must be considered as starting points for the search in the SN; these are the nodes with the heads firm, sell, and computer.[20]

If one generally continues the search with the node having the fewest incoming and outgoing arcs, then the node sell is the best candidate in our case. It is connected with buy in the SN via the following B-Axiom (this meaning

---

[20] The node CompuTex comes into play only in a later step, since – after the assumption – there is, for the moment, no AGT arc in the SN leading to CompuTex, and there is also no axiom connecting the AGT relation to the AVRT relation directly.

postulate was named BAx15, as the corresponding arc in Fig. 13.8).[21]

**BAx15:**   (x SUBS buy) $\wedge$ (x AGT y) $\wedge$ (x OBJ z) $\wedge$ (x AVRT u) $\rightarrow$
(sk(x) SUBS sell) $\wedge$ (sk(x) OBJ z)
$\wedge$ (sk(x) AGT u) $\wedge$ (sk(x) ORNT y)                                            (104)

By applying this axiom and matching the conclusion of (104) with QP, a bridge can be built from the (otherwise isolated) node sell to the node buy giving rise to a new node G' $\in$ SG. The latter contains the head node buy, a new question pattern, obtained from the application of the axiom by pattern transformation,

[(x SUBS buy) $\wedge$ (x AGT ?) $\wedge$ (? SUB firm)
$\wedge$ (x OBJ o) $\wedge$ (o SUB computer) $\wedge$ (x AVRT CompuTex)]   (105),

the list of substitutions $\Sigma_1$ = {sk(x)/s, ?/y, CompuTex/u, o/z}, and a predecessor list enlarged by sell.

After the application of the axiom to the original question pattern, the possibility arises to continue the search from the new node G' with the head node buy by matching the triple (x SUBS buy) of the remaining question pattern (105) with the arc (G13 SUBS buy) of the SN. This leads to a further node G" $\in$ SG with the head node G13. A peculiarity of this step consists in the fact that one can verify two further triples of the question pattern (105) simultaneously, namely (x SUBS buy) and (x AVRT CompuTex), using the substitution $\Sigma_2$ = {G13/x} and thus creating a shortened question pattern:

[(G13 AGT ?) $\wedge$ (? SUB firm) $\wedge$ (G13 OBJ o) $\wedge$ (o SUB computer)]  (106)

The result of this step is as if the knowledge implicitly contained in Axiom (104) had been explicitly added to the SN (see the dashed lines outgoing from G14 in Fig. 13.8) and the node G13 had been reached in this enhanced network on two different paths starting from sell and CompuTex, respectively. Because of this, node G13 has to be considered a **question center** from which the solution can be found in a few steps.

---

[21] The term sk(x) in Formula (104) is a so-called Skolem term, which is somewhat abbreviated. It represents an existentially quantified variable v and should in a more precise formulation depend on all free variables standing before v, i.e. the term should be written as sk(x, y, z, u); see Axiom (89) which, apart from the existential quantifier explicitly contained in it, has an analogous structure.

To see this, one has only to follow two separate deduction steps, the OBJ arc from G13 using the substitution {G15/o} and the AGT arc using the substitution $\Sigma_4$ = {T-Serv/?}. After these two steps, only the remaining pattern

$$[(\text{T-Serv SUB firm}) \wedge (\text{G15 SUB computer})] \tag{107},$$

has to be verified. This can be done by means of a double application of the transitivity axiom for the SUB relation including the nodes ⟨travel agency⟩ and PC. For our investigation, the decisive effect is the substitution $\Sigma_4$ = {T-Serv/?} delivering the **answer kernel** corresponding to the supplementary question (F4). This is the node whose semantic content has to be reformulated as a natural language phrase during answer generation. In our case, where the answer kernel is simply labeled by a proper name, the phrase "*To T-Serv*" should be sufficient as a laconic answer; or, if one chooses a somewhat more cooperative answer, "*To the travel agency T-Serv*" or "*To the firm T-Serv*" should be acceptable.

In general, the inferences do not so smoothly lead from the knowledge base to the question, which is seen as a theorem to be proved. Along the derivation path, we often meet semantic restrictions or slight deviations from the question pattern which nevertheless can be tolerated or eventually made explicit in a cooperative answer. These deviations and restrictions are stored in a special pattern, RESTR = (⟨R-type⟩ ⟨R-node⟩), part of the sixth component of certain nodes in the search graph SG.

To illustrate, we discuss here only a few simple cases:
RESTR = (((⟨LAY-DIFF⟩ ⟨L-attr⟩) ⟨R-node⟩) signals deviations in the layer attribute L-attr of the node R-node.
RESTR = PROTO indicates that default knowledge or prototypical knowledge was involved in finding the proof.
RESTR = (⟨R-rel⟩ ⟨R-node⟩) states that the validity of the proof is restricted to a state of affairs described by node R-node, where R-rel stands for COND indicating a precondition; CTXT, pointing to a restricting context; and MODL, specifying a modal embedding.
Let $\tilde{\Pi}_{cat}(N)$ and $\tilde{\Pi}_{def}(N)$ denote the natural language reformulation of the categorical and definitional knowledge, respectively, connected with node N. Then a cooperative answer strategy for decision questions could produce an appropriate answer roughly following the schema:

[CASE R-type:
        COND $\rightarrow$ "Yes,if $\tilde{\Pi}_{cat}$(R-node)"
        CTXT $\rightarrow$ "Yes, but only for $\tilde{\Pi}_{def}$(R-node)"
        MODL $\rightarrow$ [CASE R-node:
                        possib $\rightarrow$ "Possibly"
                        nec $\rightarrow$ "Necessarily"
                        ...]
        MCONT $\rightarrow$ "Yes, but at least $\tilde{\Pi}_{def}$(R-node)"
        PROTO $\rightarrow$ "Yes, this is {normally/typically} the case."
        (LAY-DIFF L-attr) $\rightarrow$ "Yes, with the exception of the attribute
                        $\tilde{\Pi}_{def}$(L-attr) of $\tilde{\Pi}_{def}$(R-node)."
        ...]

Even this very sketchy discussion should show that the question-answering process as a whole can not be reduced to logical derivations alone. However, logical deduction is always the core of this process. It is also needed in the case of essay questions to spot the node of interest in the knowledge base by means of its description.

With this short explanation, which gives only an overview of the role of MultiNet knowledge bases in the phase of logical answer finding, the treatment of the most important elements of the question-answering process concludes here. In the next chapter, an overview of the software tools belonging to this knowledge representation paradigm will be given.

**Chapter 14**

# Software Tools for the Knowledge Engineer and Sample Applications

## 14.1 Knowledge Management as an Engineering Task

The treatment of knowledge with engineering methods has been especially promoted in the field of artificial intelligence. It is subsumed there under the heading "**knowledge engineering**". This new field finds its material expression in the development of software tools for **knowledge acquisition**, for **knowledge management**, and for the manipulation of knowledge (graphically oriented **knowledge editors**). Building such tools is all the more important as the knowledge needed for real-world applications is quantitatively and qualitatively so complex that it cannot be handled without the help of computational techniques.

Perhaps the largest software package for technical support of knowledge management and knowledge acquisition has been developed in the CYC project [158], but even there a large deficiency seems to exist in the automatic acquisition of knowledge from textual information.[1]

For the knowledge representation paradigm MultiNet, four complementary software tools have so far been developed which support different aspects of computer-assisted working with knowledge bases:

**MWR**, the workbench for the knowledge engineer, with its emphasis on the manipulation of knowledge by means of graphical editors and on the assimilation or accumulation of large stocks of knowledge. This system has been developed by Gnörlich [81], and the work is now continued by Glöckner [80].

**NatLink**, a system for translating natural language expressions into MultiNet knowledge representations. It is based on the conception of word-class-controlled functional analysis of Helbig [110] and has been further developed and significantly extended by Hartrumpf [116, 97].

---

[1] This impression is strengthened, among other things, by the fact that in CYC even special people, called **knowledge enterers**, are employed for gathering and inputting knowledge (see also Sect. 15.4.3).

**LIA**, a workbench for the computer lexicographer, used for the computer-aided specification of lexemes, including their morpho-syntactic and semantic characteristics. This system was originally designed and implemented by Schulz [227] under the name LIA, and has now been redesigned and newly developed by Osswald under the name LIA+ [192] (in the following text, only the abbreviated name LIA is used).

**VILAB**, a virtual tutor which can be used (as one of its applications) to teach students the essentials of MultiNet and to train new members of the MultiNet group to get familiar with the knowledge representation paradigm and its use in different applications. This interactive laboratory was developed by Gnörlich and Lütticke [166].

## 14.2    MWR – the Workbench for the Knowledge Engineer

The workbench **MWR** for the knowledge engineer (abbreviated from the German **M**ultiNet **W**issens-**R**epräsentation; En: MultiNet Knowledge Representation) was designed to permit computer-aided work with the knowledge representation paradigm MultiNet. It can be used, in addition to having other applications, by AI experts (especially by computational linguists), by linguists in general (e.g. for describing the meaning of natural language expressions), and by psychologists (for cognitive modeling tasks). At present, MultiNet is mainly used as a knowledge representation language and semantic interlingua for natural language interfaces to databases and intelligent information systems. In these applications, MWR is also used to provide the necessary background knowledge, comprising, among other things, common sense knowledge in a QAS, metaknowledge about the target databases, and the dialogue model of an NLI (see [115]), as well as language-specific knowledge which has to be included in the computational lexicon (see Sects. 12.2 and 14.4).

The workbench MWR currently consists of the following components (this enumeration is not complete, since MWR is continually extended by additional functionalities):

- A user-friendly graphical interface for the presentation of semantic networks (including a comprehensive help system).
- A graphical network editor for the manipulation of semantic networks with export functions to external formats (.dvi, .eps, .pdf, etc.). This tool is able to discover and highlight formal errors in the SN (e.g. violation of signatures of relations and functions).

- A module supporting the provision of axioms and inference rules.
- Pattern matchers and inference components supporting, among other things, the answering of queries to MultiNet networks.
- Interfaces to databases and to the Internet, together with transformation mechanisms translating MultiNet expressions into formal target languages.

Figure 14.1 shows a network "manually" created by means of MWR. It represents the meaning of the sentence *"Every robot going into room K7 takes a tool there."* An analogous network can also be produced automatically when the corresponding German sentence *"Jeder Roboter, der in den Raum K7 geht, holt dort ein Werkzeug."* is handed over to the NatLink system (see Sect. 14.3).

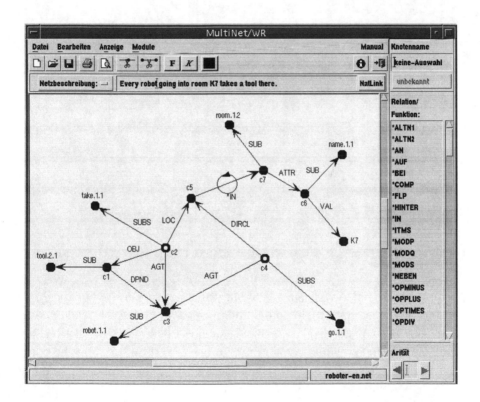

**Figure 14.1.** The graphical user interface of MWR

Through a close coupling of MWR and NatLink, it is possible to manipulate and edit the automatically created network by means of MWR for further processing. For example, one can ask for a presentation of the layer information (Chap. 10), and one can also change and manipulate this information if necessary (see Fig. 14.2, which shows the values of the layer attributes for the nodes c1 and c3 in Fig. 14.1).

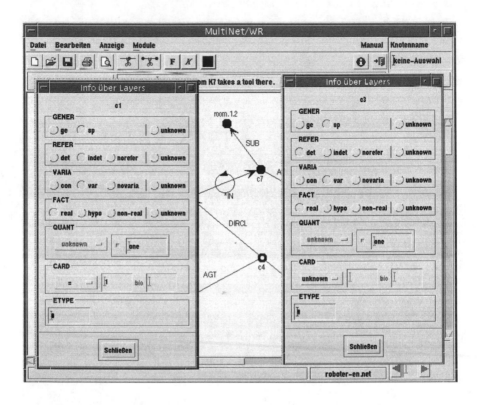

**Figure 14.2.** The representation of detailed layer information for the nodes c1 and c3 of the SN

It is also possible to change the layout of the network in the graphical user interface by "dragging and dropping" the nodes with the mouse. The labels of nodes and arcs can be changed manually, and the definitions of relations and functions associated with a certain arc can be viewed by selecting the corresponding functions of a pop-up menu accessed by a mouse button (see Fig. 14.3). It is obvious that very large semantic networks cannot be dealt with effectively without graphical user interfaces and graphical tools for the presentation of these networks; therefore it is important that networks of virtually unlimited size be presented in such a way that they can be scrolled over the working panel and that nodes or arcs relevant to a special processing step can be kept in the center of the screen (realization of a virtual semantic network). This function is supported by special MWR methods searching for specific nodes and their immediate neighbors in the network. To avoid an overloading of the screen with different types of information, the fine structure of nodes, and especially the layer information belonging to every node, are normally presented in special pop-up menus (see Fig. 14.2, an analogous menu exists for the presentation of the sorts of nodes).

It is important to the knowledge engineer to have the documentation of the representational means of MultiNet at his disposal at any time. This documentation is essentially Part II of this work as a hypertext document with an appropriate link structure that can be browsed off-line or navigated online from MWR with the help of a mouse (Fig. 14.3). The same help system, by the way, is also used in other software tools based on MultiNet (see Sects. 14.3 and 14.4).

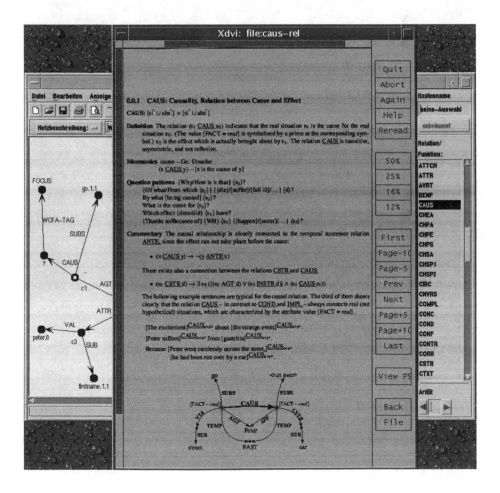

**Figure 14.3.** The help system of MWR

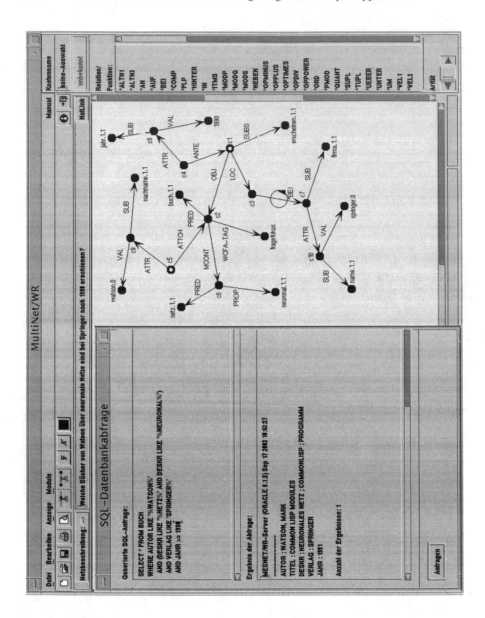

**Figure 14.4.** The interface of MWR to relational databases (the SQL interface)

Query Ge: *"Welche Bücher von Watson über neuronale Netze sind bei Springer nach 1990 erschienen?"*

Query En: *"Which books of Watson about neural networks have been published by Springer after 1990?"*

As a further aid to the knowledge engineer, who has to build large knowledge bases, the most important basic functions supporting the assimilation process and question-answering are integrated into the MWR tool. Among them are:

- Pattern-matching routines for recognizing the equivalence or similarity of (partial) semantic networks; they also support inferences (Sect. 13.2) which have to be carried out for establishing the semantic coherence of text information.
- Inference procedures, in particular methods for associatively guided deductive answer finding described in Sect. 13.3.
- Procedures for testing the intensional equality of nodes and the subordination of conceptual representatives.

Especially important for practical applications is the provision of interfaces and transformation modules translating MultiNet expressions into other formal target languages. Thus, MWR provides an interface for translating MultiNet query structures into SQL, used, among other things, for the implementation of natural language interfaces to relational databases [115]. The corresponding Z39.50 gateway will be dealt with shortly in Sect. 14.3.

Figure 14.4 shows a natural language query to the relational library database of HBZ [2], the semantic structure of this query, and the window presenting the transformation of the query into an SQL expression, as well as the answer to this query delivered by the library.

Together with the modules translating natural language expressions into MultiNet structures, dealt with in the following section, the transformation techniques described are the cornerstones for building natural language interfaces to other information systems, such as database management systems, e-business systems, or information retrieval systems on the Internet.

## 14.3    NatLink – A Semantic Interpreter for MultiNet

The tools for creating and graphical editing of MultiNet structures are helpful instruments for the provision of basic knowledge and for embedding semantic net structures in the computational lexicon (see also Sect. 14.4). However, for the acquisition of large stocks of knowledge more advanced methods are

---

[2] HBZ (**H**ochschul-**B**ibliotheks-**Z**entrum): The Cologne center for all university libraries of the German state Nordrhein-Westfalen. Since NatLink is working for German only (at least at the time of this publication), the MWR representation and the expressions of the other partial windows are also presented in German.

required. For that purpose, an automatic translation of natural language information into MultiNet knowledge bases is needed. The module supplying this functionality is called **NatLink** (or, in its latest version, **WOCADI**). It is based on a word-class-controlled syntactic semantic analysis. The basic ideas of this method, described in [110] and [116], consist in the following:

The word and its meaning play a central role in natural language understanding, and therefore also in automatic language processing. In this process, two types of knowledge connected with every word are involved: the lexical knowledge, dealt with in Chap. 12, and the grammatical knowledge, explained here. Human beings probably use their full knowledge (including their world knowledge) in all stages of language process. This can be illustrated by the semantic abnormality of the sentence

(14.1) *"The baby found an error in the computation of the integral."*

The discovery of such a semantic deviation, as well as the treatment of metaphors and metonyms, are considered **second order effects** in natural language understanding. These effects cannot be treated within the scope of this investigation.[3]

There are generally two phases during the functional interpretation of a word while processing a sentence:

**Opening phase.** As soon as a word is included in the process of language processing, certain syntactic and semantic expectations are evoked which are determined by the valencies of that word (see Chap. 12). In general, these valencies ("slots" in AI terminology) cannot be satisfied immediately, but only at a later time (i.e. they must be stored).

---

[3] Second order effects are phenomena in natural language processing that require a preliminary syntactic semantic analysis in the first step which is the precondition for a full understanding in the second step.

The example sentence (14.1) will be understood at first "quite normally", since all selectional restrictions (especially those for the agent) are formally met. Only in the second step of the analysis where world knowledge is included can it be discovered that the given example sentence has a semantic defect, since babies do not normally master integration.

With metaphors and metonymic constructs the situation is in some sense the other way around, as can be seen from the sentence *"The Angus steak wants to pay"*, uttered in a communication between two waitresses in a restaurant. In this case, the sentence had to be refuted in the first analysis step from a purely formal point of view, because the selectional restrictions of the verbs *"to want"* and *"to pay"* require an agent with the semantic feature [POTAG +], which is not the case for the concept ⟨Angus steak⟩. Only in the second step of the interpretation, which involves background knowledge, can the metonymic transfer *"Angus steak"* → *"Guest who ordered the Angus steak"* be carried out, recognizing that not the steak but a person who ate the steak is meant. Without discovering the violation of the selectional restriction of the two verbs *"to want"* and *"to pay"* in the first interpretation step, there would be no need for a metonymic reinterpretation of the concept ⟨Angus steak⟩.

**Complete phase.** When sufficient information has been gathered, i.e. when more words have been included into the language analysis and new constituents have been semantically analyzed that "match" the expectations (valencies or slots) spanned during the opening phase, then these expectations can be satisfied, and appropriate syntactic and semantic structures can be built.

Thus, a word is generally activated twice during the language understanding process: first, while opening the slots, and second, while completing (filling) the slots. With regard to the algorithmic modeling of the process described, this means that every word is generally associated with two functions which are called OPEN-ACT and COMPLETE-ACT. They represent the whole grammatical function of the word. These functions are also activated at different times during the processing of natural language expressions.

Since certain groups of words have a great deal in common, there is no need to connect every single word with such a pair of functions. One can rather find classes of words whose elements are characterized by the same grammatical behavior. It is quite instructive that word classes found on the basis of these considerations come very close to those found in traditional grammars using semantic classification criteria (see [2]). For the time being, NatLink uses 25 word-class functions, including those shown in Table 14.1.

| Name of the function | Word class |
|---|---|
| *ADJ | Adjective |
| *ART | Article |
| *CONJC | Coordinating conjunction |
| *CONJS | Subordinating conjunction |
| *FPATTR | Attributively used interrogative pronoun |
| *FPNOM | Interrogative pronoun with nominal use |
| *COMMA | Punctuation mark ',' (comma) |
| *NEG | Negator (except for no – Ge: kein) |
| *NOM | Noun / Substantive |
| *PERSPRO | Personal pronoun |
| *POSSDET | Possessive pronoun |
| *PREP | Preposition |
| *RELPRO | Relative pronoun |
| *VB | Verb (main verb) |
| . . . | . . . |

**Table 14.1.** Examples of word-class functions

It is typical of the analysis strategy used in NatLink that no intermediate syntactic structures are created. The processing is organized in such a way that

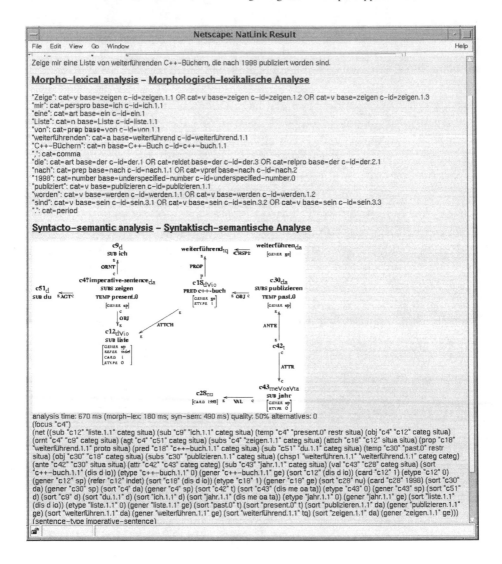

**Figure 14.5.** The working panel of the natural language interpreter NatLink showing the translation of the German form of the sentence "*Show me a list of advanced C++ books which have been published after 1998.*"

a semantic representative (a **semantic kernel**) is built immediately after finishing a COMPLETE-ACT of a word-class function. Figure 14.5 shows the window system of NatLink during the analysis of the imperative German sentence "*Zeige mir eine Liste von weiterführenden C++-Büchern, die nach 1998 publiziert worden sind*" (En: "*Show me a list of advanced C++ books which have been published after 1998*").[4]

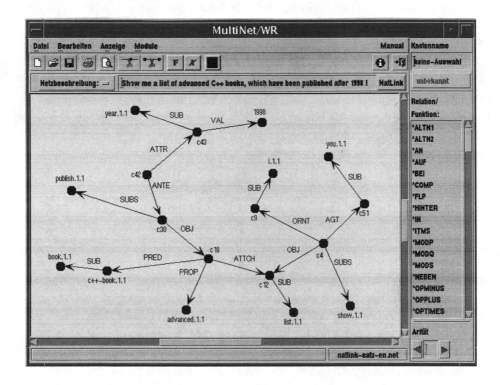

**Figure 14.6.** English counterpart of the German analysis result shown in Fig. 14.5 (created by means of MWR)

The English version of the semantic structure of this sentence is given in Fig. 14.6. It was generated by automatically analyzing the German sentence with NatLink and manually transcribing the labels of the terminal nodes of the

---

[4] To simplify the graphs and to improve the readability of analysis results, the SUB, PRED, and SUBS arcs have occasionally been included in the description of the nodes. Please note that the node c4 in Fig. 14.5, which semantically represents the whole imperative sentence, is not a question focus in the sense of Sect. 13.2. Imperative sentences require a further pragmatic interpretation which transforms them into questions to a QAS. In this step, the focus (now in the sense of question focus introduced in Sect. 13.2) is shifted from node c4 in Fig. 14.5 to node c12 in Fig. 14.6.

SN into English.[5] By aligning the lexicon HaGenLex with English computer-readable lexica like Wordnet [64], this translation process will soon be automated.

Apart from the results of the morphological-lexical analysis, Figure 14.5 also shows the results of the semantic interpretation represented in a linearized form (which is used for further processing) and as a graph (for better readability). Node $c12$ in the middle of the window, for instance, represents the semantic kernel corresponding to the complex noun phrase *"Liste von weiterführenden C++-Büchern"* (En: *"List of advanced C++ books"*).

The result of the analysis in linearized form (lower part of Fig. 14.5) also shows the characterization of the arcs by values of the attribute **K-TYPE** (see Sect. 3.2.3). In addition, the concept names which arise as a consequence of the disambiguation in the lexical analysis can be recognized from the attached indices (these indices have been suppressed in the graphical representation of Fig. 14.5).

The application of NatLink and its word-class controlled functional analysis in a natural language interface for information retrieval on the Internet using the international standard protocol **Z39.50** [190] is illustrated in Figs. 14.7 and 14.8. Many information providers, among them important libraries and providers of special information all over the world, can be reached via this protocol.

Figures 14.7 and 14.8 also show some selected processing steps for a natural language query in the interface **NLI-Z39.50** to libraries on the Internet. The first screenshot (Fig. 14.7) presents the result of the query analysis as an intermediate step of the NLI-Z39.50 (see the above discussion of NatLink). The second screenshot (Fig. 14.8) shows the input mask of NLI-Z39.50 with a retrieval result returned from the German library association GBV.

The most important recent applications of NatLink can be summarized as follows:

- NatLink as kernel of natural language interfaces, independent of special target systems
- NatLink as an instrument supporting the process of knowledge acquisition and knowledge assimilation
- NatLink as a tool for corpus analysis, used for concept learning
- NatLink as an instrument for evaluating special linguistic theories

---

[5] For a better understanding, the automatically generated labels of the nonterminal nodes of the SN have also been changed to achieve a clear parallelism in the labeling of the nodes in Figs. 14.5 and 14.6.

- NatLink as the analysis component of question-answering systems [98]
- NatLink as a component of electronic education systems in computational linguistics (part of the virtual AI laboratory at the University Hagen [165]).

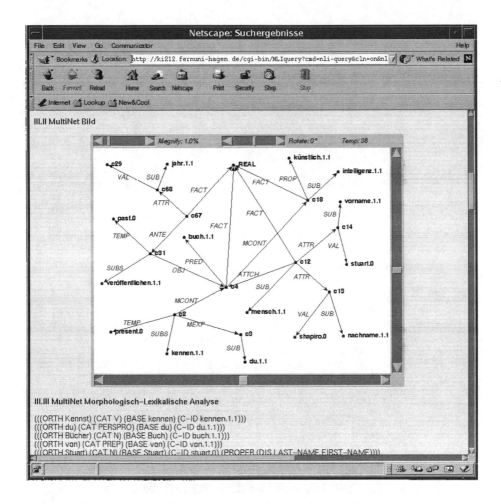

**Figure 14.7.** The application of NatLink in the natural language interface NLI-Z39.50 (I) (the German equivalent to the query "*Do you know books by Stuart Shapiro about artificial intelligence which have been published after 1982?*" and its semantic structure in graphical form)

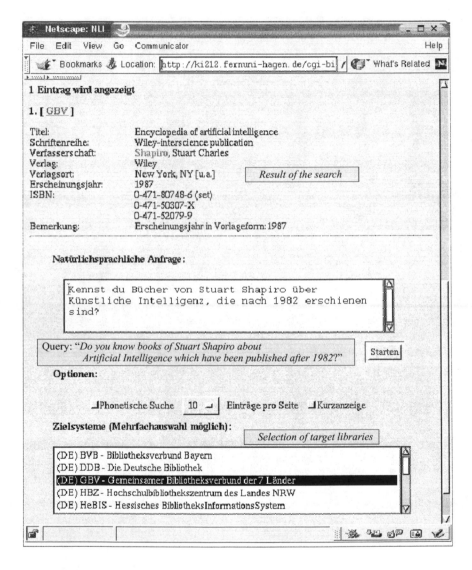

**Figure 14.8.** The application of NatLink in the natural language interface NLI-Z39.50 (II), with query (middle of the window) and retrieval result (at the top)

## 14.4  LIA – the Workbench for the Computer Lexicographer

The creation of large computational lexica is an extremely expensive and error-prone task which is a prerequisite for the functioning of every natural language processing system (Sect. 14.3). This was the reason for developing a workbench **LIA** ("**l**exicon **i**n **a**ction") for computer-assisted construction of semantically based computational lexica, which enables even nonspecialists to specify complex lexical entries after a short training period.

LIA is based on the lexicon conception HaGenLex (formerly COLEX [227]; see also [100] and Chap. 12), on the principles of an inheritance-based computational lexicon, or to be specific, on the IBL concept of Hartrumpf [94], and on the MultiNet paradigm described in the foregoing chapters. The connection between MultiNet and the computational lexicon has already been described in Chap. 12 in detail. Here, we shall concentrate on the main functionalities of the lexicographer's workbench. The lexical information characterizing a concrete lexeme has to be input with LIA by answering specific questions through an interactive interface, while generic knowledge being relevant to whole groups of lexemes is derived from classes and rules predefined in the inheritance-based lexicon.

The system of windows and menus of LIA is designed in such a way that the questions to be answered by the user (lexicographer) are presented in as comprehensible a form as possible. The user has mostly to reply by clicking the mouse and selecting from predefined sets of choices. The admissible choices are continually narrowed down during the answering process until the final specification of the lexeme under consideration has been determined. In this way, the workbench warrants the inner consistency of the lexicon, the agreement of the specifications of the lexemes with the MultiNet conventions, and integrity with regard to the formal structural definitions of lexical entries.[6]

To give an impression of the interactive work with the workbench LIA, the process of specifying the lexical entry for the German verb "*schicken*" (En: "*send*"), in the sense "*jemanden beauftragen etwas zu holen*" (En: "*send somebody to bring something or somebody*"), shall be illustrated by means of some selected screenshots in Figs. 14.9 through 14.11.

---

[6] It should not be concealed that, even with the most sophisticated lexicon technology, final editing processes are sometimes necessary (especially if semantic specifications are involved). A formal apparatus that manages with a justifiable expenditure of time can only approximately cope with the richness of nuances of a natural language. However, the experiences with LIA show that this workbench provides indispensable support to the lexicographer. It is an important tool for improving the effectiveness of his work.

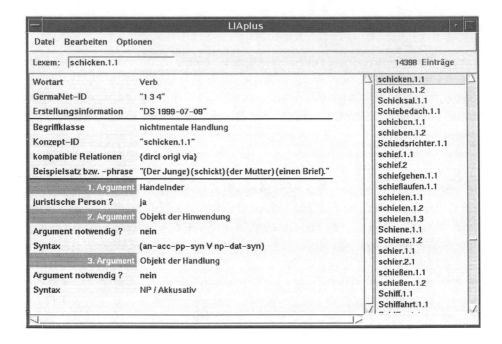

**Figure 14.9.** Lookup in the computational lexicon and search for already existing readings

The first step should be to check whether some sememes belonging to the word "*schicken*" (En: "*send*") are already present in the lexicon. This can be helpful for contrasting different readings associated with one word.[7]

Looking up the lexical entries, one sees that two readings belonging to the verb in question are already contained in the lexicon: the first is schicken.1.1/ send.1.1 (Ge: "*(Der Junge) (schickt) (der Mutter) (einen Brief)*"; En: "*(The boy) (sends) (the mother) (a letter)*"), whose full specification is shown in Fig. 12.2. The start window of LIA for creating this entry is partially shown in Fig. 14.9.

The second entry, already contained in the lexicon, is schicken.1.2/send.1.2 in the sense: "*(Die Mutter) (schickt) (das Kind) (zum Arzt)*" (En: "*(The mother) (sends) (the child) (to the doctor)*"). The corresponding lexical specification was also created by means of LIA and is shown in Fig. 12.3.

---

[7] Possibly, the intended reading (sememe) had been included in the lexicon in an earlier session. Then, this step gives the opportunity to edit the existing entry. It also warrants that no work is done twice.

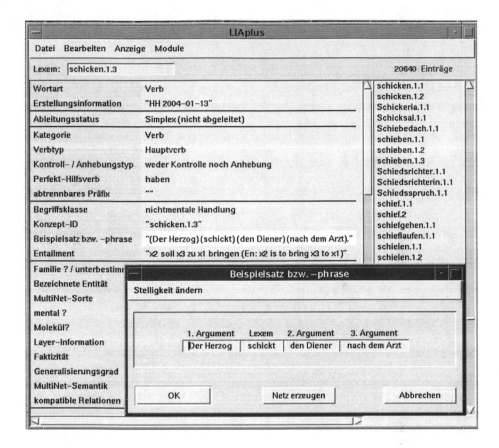

**Figure 14.10.** Determination of syntactic and other formal characteristics including the sorts of verbs

After this preliminary step, the lexical entry for schicken.1.3 is built by deciding at first on the syntactic and other formal properties of the lexeme in an initial window (Fig. 14.10).[8]

The attributes shown on the left side and their values have the following meanings (the numbers refer to the rows in the window). (1) lexeme: schicken.1.3/send.1.3; (2) word class in the functional analysis (see Sect. 14.3): verb; (3) information about the origin: encoded author name and date of

---

[8] It is important for understanding the screenshots that, by convention, the arguments of the lexemes are always labeled x1, x2, ... x3, in order from left to right in the example sentences, and top-down in the background windows. This convention also establishes a connection between the argument specifications on the left of the window in Fig. 14.11 and the templates of the entailment entries on the one hand, and the node labels of the semantic networks described under attribute NET in the full lexeme specification (or under "Multinet-Semantik" in the windows) on the other hand.

entry; (4) status of derivation: no derivation; (5) syntactic category: verb; (6) subtype: main verb; (7) control or raising property: none; (8) German perfect construction: with the auxiliary verb *"haben"*; (9) separable prefix: none; (10) conceptual class: nonmental action; (11) unique concept ID: schicken.1.3; (12) sample sentence with argument structure;[9] (13) entailment: the entailment given in the window represents a meaning postulate that has to be read as the conclusion of an implication whose premise is given by the valency structure of the considered lexeme. In this case, it is specified in a semiformal way and establishes a semantic connection between the concepts senden/send and bringen/bring.[10]

While the attributes are predefined, the answers determining their values have to be either explicitly specified (e.g. in (1), (9), (12), and (13)), or selected from predefined choices (e.g. in (2), (4), (5), (6), (7), (8), and (10)). In some cases, they can also be automatically generated (e.g. in (3) and (11)).[11]

The most important step, which also involves the largest part of LIA's intelligence, concerns the syntactic and semantic specification of the arguments (valencies) of the lexeme. Figure 14.11 shows the specification of the first argument x1 (relation AGT), second argument x2 (relation OBJ) and third argument x3 (which is not a direct argument role) of schicken.1.3. Having determined the cognitive role (i.e. the MultiNet relation) assumed by the arguments (they are indicated immediately below the gray bars on the left side of the figure), the lexicographer is asked whether the arguments are obligatory or optional. In this case, the answer to the question *"Argument notwendig?"* (En: *"Argument necessary?"*), which is not shown in the figure, would be *"ja"* (En: *"yes"*) for arguments x1 and x3 and *"nein"* (En: *"no"*) for x2. The attributes below the gray bar are used to specify the arguments syntactically and semantically by MultiNet sorts and features. Each of these attributes is actually associated with a set of subqueries, which are also not shown in the window.

---

[9] This information is entered via the pop-up menu shown in the lower right corner of Fig. 14.10. The sentence exemplifying the argument structure of the lexeme schicken.1.3 is:
Ge: *"(Der Herzog) (schickt) (den Diener) (nach dem Arzt)."*
En: *"(The duke) (sends) (the servant) (for the doctor)."*

[10] There are other attribute specifications not shown in the window, like the attribute "Domäne/domain", used to structure the stock of lexemes. The lexicon is subdivided into domains by using a so-called "club model" (Ge: "Keulenmodell"), which can be roughly characterized as follows: The general or common vocabulary which, among other things, includes the functional words (like prepositions) and those content words relevant to virtually all domains (like know.1.1, book.1.1, large.1.1, etc.) constitutes a basic sphere from which (to stay in the picture) partial lexica grow like clubs representing the special vocabulary of certain domains (e.g. bill.1.5, draw.1.3, or insolvent.1.1 in the banking domain).

[11] It should be remarked that some of the choices (normally to be selected intellectually) can be automatically settled because of the dependencies between them; see Fig. 12.1.

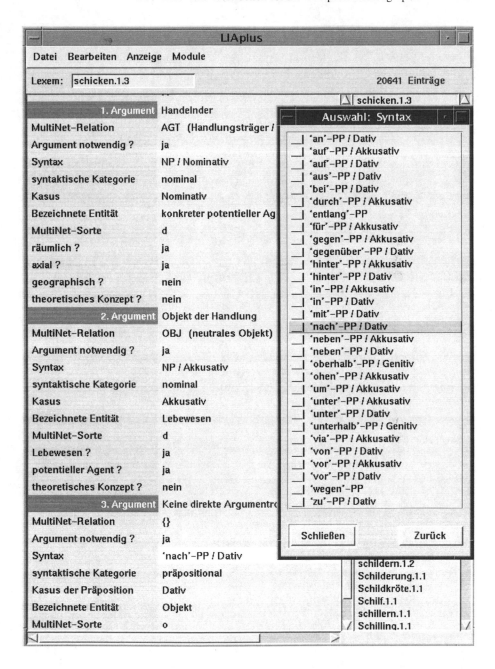

**Figure 14.11.** The window for defining the syntactic and semantic characteristics of a verb's arguments

The pop-up menu on the right of Fig. 14.11 shows the situation where the syntactic pattern for the third argument x3 of the sending act is specified. As indicated, the correct choice is a prepositional phrase with the German preposition "*nach*" (En: "*for*"). This choice is realized in the example sentence:

(14.2)  Ge: "*(Der Herzog) (schickt) (den Diener) (nach dem Arzt)*."
    En: "*(The duke) (sends) (the servant) (for the doctor)*."

As a final result, the lexical entry shown in Fig. 14.12 is obtained in a compressed IBL format (IBL is an abbreviation of "inheritance-based lexicon"). The expanded form has already been discussed in Chap. 12 in connection with Fig. 12.3.

---

"schicken.1.3"                    En: "send.1.3"
    [
    verb
    semsel [
    v-nonment-action
    sem [
            [entity sort da]
            [ net (goal c N1) (sub N1 "kommen.1.2")
                (exp N1 x3) (agt N1 x2) (dircl N1 x1)]]
    select <
            [ rel AGT
            agt-select
            sel
            [ syn np-nom-syn
            semsel sem entity con-potag]]
            [
            rel OBJ
            obj-action-select
            sel [
            syn np-acc-syn
            semsel sem entity animate-object]]
            [
            empty-select
            sel syn nach-dat-pp-syn]] >
    compat-r {purp dircl origl via}
    example [Ge: "(Der Herzog)(schickt)(den Diener)(nach dem Arzt)."
            En: "(The duke)(sends)(the servant)(for the doctor)."]
    entail ["x2 soll x3 zu x1 bringen" - En: "x2 is to bring x3 to x1"]
    ]

---

**Figure 14.12.** Sample entry of the inheritance-based lexicon for the lexeme schicken.1.3 using the IBL format

The classes used in the compressed form have the following meanings:

- v-nonment-action – general characterization of the properties of nonmental actions;
- agt-select – characterization of the AGT role of an action verb (which comprises, among other things, the feature requirement [**POTAG** +] for the corresponding argument);
  syntactic class: "np-nom-syn" – noun phrase in the nominative;
- obj-action-select – description of the C-Role OBJ with its syntactic class "np-acc-syn", i.e. noun phrase in the accusative;
- empty-select – indicates that the semantic role of the corresponding argument (here x3) is defined by the entry under the path sem | net, i.e. by a small semantic network. This means that x3 is not directly attached to the central situational node c, as is typically the case for genuine cognitive roles, but rather through the intermediate node N1 characterizing the goal of schicken.1.3;
  syntactic class: "nach-dat-pp-syn" – prepositional phrase with "*nach*" in the dative case.[12]

The full benefit of MultiNet tools becomes apparent in their close interaction. One scenario could be to specify a lexical entry with LIA using NatLink and/or MWR as supporting tools. In Fig. 14.13 we started with the lexeme beginnen.1.2 (En: begin.1.2) in the sense of "*The researcher begins the investigation at 8 pm.*" After finishing the entry, the example sentence (menu item 1 on the left of Fig. 14.13) can be parsed with NatLink simply by clicking on this item, which results in the network shown in the upper right window, also labeled 1. If there is something wrong in the resulting structure, the lexical specification can be accordingly changed. It is also possible to investigate the semantics of the lexeme more closely by clicking on the menu item "MultiNet-Semantik" (see box 2 in Fig. 14.13) corresponding to the value of the attribute NET in the formal specification of the lexeme (see the full lexical entry of schicken.1.3 in Fig. 12.4). A new window is immediately opened by the MWR tool (lower right window in Fig. 14.13). It shows the connection between the two alternations[13] beginnen.1.1 (En: begin.1.1), having two arguments ("*The investigation begins at 8 pm*"), and beginnen.1.2, (En: begin.1.2) having three arguments ("*The researcher begins the investigation at 8 pm*").

---

[12] In English, this entry would have to be substituted by another one specifying a prepositional phrase with "*for*".

[13] With regard to the term "alternation" see page 95.

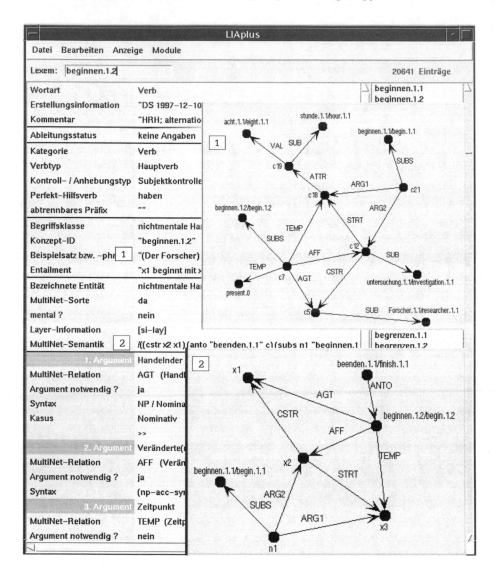

**Figure 14.13.** The integration of MultiNet tools (a screenshot illustrating the connection between LIA, MWR, and Natlink)

The figure also shows the antonymy relation between beginnen.1.2 (En: begin.1.2) and beenden.1.1 (En: finish.1.1).[14] The semantic structure shown in the window marked by 2 can be changed within MWR, if necessary, and the

---

[14] The incongruency in the indices between beginnen.1.2 (transitive) and beenden.1.1 (transitive) in the antonymy relation (beginnen.1.2 ANTO beenden.1.1) results from the fact that in German there is only a transitive reading for "*beenden*".

result can be written back to the lexicon by leaving MWR and re-entering LIA. In this way, we do not only enhance the interactivity of LIA; we also provide LIA with access to background information (definition of MultiNet relations and functions, specification of axioms, etc.) accessible via MWR. Furthermore, we enable LIA to automatically check the violation of formal constraints (e.g. of signatures) in lexical descriptions by using the functionalities of MWR.

## 14.5   VILAB – The Virtual Laboratory for E-Learning in Artificial Intelligence

The University at Hagen has a comparatively long tradition in distance teaching and e-learning. It is a declared goal of the MultiNet group as member of this university to use its latest research results for teaching in a "Virtual University". Within this framework, a virtual laboratory VILAB was created, giving students the opportunity to solve specific tasks on their own, or to experiment in predefined fields of computer science as is common in laboratories with researchers in the natural sciences. The kernel of this electronic laboratory is an intelligent tutor guiding the students through their work. It controls the different laboratory stations (each corresponding to a specific learning area or teaching module), formulates the tasks and the goals of the learners, checks the results obtained by the students, and gives advice if necessary.

One of the teaching modules of VILAB is dedicated to the MultiNet paradigm and its tools.[15] Figure 14.14 shows the start page of the laboratory station "MultiNet and MWR" displaying in the right window the didactic goals and giving hints what tools should be used, while the left window shows the tasks to be solved within the station, ordered by the difficulty of the solution. In the window displayed, three tasks are included:

(1) Experimenting with MultiNet and introduction to the application of MWR (manual creation of semantic networks; understanding the interface to LIA and NatLink, etc.);

(2) Assimilation of semantic networks stemming from different sentences into a larger knowledge base;

(3) Application of MWR for translating MultiNet expressions representing the meaning of questions into SQL expressions.

---

[15] Other modules are: Programming Languages, Databases, Natural Language Interfaces, Neural Networks, and so on.

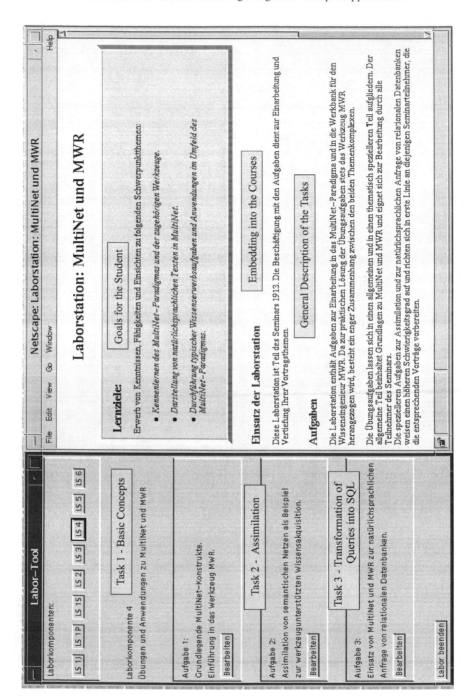

**Figure 14.14.** The VILAB window describing the laboratory station for experimenting with MultiNet and MWR

In Fig. 14.15 we see a snapshot from task (2), Assimilation. The window on the left shows the meaning structure of the sentence *"Das Verfahren wurde von einem Informatiker entwickelt."* (En: *"The method was developed by a computer scientist."*) that is assumed to constitute the information contained in the already existing knowledge base. The left part on the background window represents the meaning of the sentence *"Das macht den Informatiker zu einer gesuchten Fachkraft."* (En (verbally): *"This makes the computer scientist a specialist searched after."*), which has to be integrated (assimilated) into the existing knowledge base. The result of the assimilation process is the full network shown on the right side of the background window. In this simple case, the assimilation amounts to connecting the partial networks by the common node informatiker.1.1 (En: ⟨computer scientist⟩). In more complicated cases, however, it can be necessary to include background knowledge, axioms (meaning postulates), and inference mechanisms in order to assimilate new information into a larger preexisting stock of knowledge. During task (2) the tutor checks the correctness of networks, gives advice if signatures of relations and functions are violated, and compares the solution of the student with a predefined sample solution.

By using this laboratory station, students can acquire new skills and familiarize themselves with the following methods:

- Getting acquainted with the MultiNet paradigm and learning to properly apply its representational means in all their details;
- Creating semantic networks manually with MWR and automatically by using the interface of MWR to NatLink;
- Building larger networks from smaller partial networks (assimilation);
- Providing background knowledge and logical axioms (meaning postulates) for the assimilation process;
- Using inference mechanisms for knowledge assimilation and answer finding over semantic networks;
- Specifying transformation rules for translating meaning structures of questions (expressed in the MultiNet formalism) into SQL expressions;
- Understanding the relationship between knowledge bases and traditional databases.

All these facilities render VILAB an ideal tool for training people in the proper use of MultiNet and giving them quick access to the fundamentals of this knowledge representation paradigm.[16]

---

[16] Thus, there is direct access from VILAB via MWR to the definitions of relations and functions specified in this book.

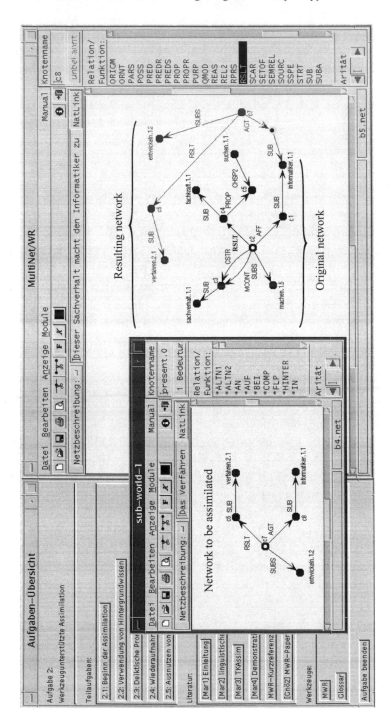

**Figure 14.15.** The VILAB window offering the tasks for the assimilation of semantic networks

# Chapter 15

# Comparison Between MultiNet and Other Semantic Formalisms or Knowledge Representation Paradigms

## 15.1 Introductory Remarks

No comprehensive work on semantic knowledge representation or knowledge processing should remain without comparison to other approaches in this field. Taking into consideration the plenitude of existing knowledge representation systems (KRS), this is no simple task, since, on the one hand, it is hard to choose the most representative paradigms and, on the other hand, a systematic comparison of different KRS has not yet been carried out by any researcher in the field.[1] In addition, one has to state that a unique catalogue of generally accepted evaluation criteria simply does not exist. It is also aggravating that many projects in this field pursue very different goals. Nevertheless, a first and admittedly rudimentary attempt shall be risked here. To this end, some typical contributions will be selected which belong to the three most important knowledge representation paradigms:

- Network-oriented KRS
- Logic-oriented KRS
- Frame-oriented KRS

It is inevitable for such a classification to have some arbitrary traits; nevertheless, these terms mirror some basic characteristics of the corresponding KRS. Moreover, the question concerning the fairness of such a comparison arises. For, how is it possible to compare more theoretically oriented work with application-oriented approaches, or how can one weigh up the better (in our opinion) cognitive and linguistic foundation of MultiNet with the deeper formal understanding of logic-oriented systems, especially since the latter do

---

[1] To simplify matters, we take here a somewhat broader view of KRS in subsuming all formalisms convenient to represent the meaning of natural language expressions under this term, even if some of the formalisms discussed have never been used in practice to represent a larger stock of knowledge.

not have such a broad coverage of natural language phenomena and are mostly not oriented toward natural language processing.

To round off the comparison, some earlier work has also been included in the discussion supplementing more recent developments. This provides the opportunity to illustrate characteristic problems of knowledge representation by means of concrete systems.

If the following sections, in spite of their singling out certain aspects, are not understood as a one-sided criticism but rather as a stimulus for discussion and, thus, for further development of knowledge representation methods, then their intended purpose has been served.

## 15.2    Comparison Between MultiNet and Other Network Representations

Semantic networks have a long tradition, as already stated in Chap. 2. Therefore, only a few samples of every knowledge representation paradigm can be discussed here, which permits the investigation and discussion of typical features. In this section, we will go deeper into the following KRS and representational formalisms in order to elucidate their characteristics:

- Structured Inheritance Networks [268, 34]
- The Semantic Network Processing System [237, 239]
- Sowa's Conceptual Structures [248, 249]
- Conceptual Dependency Theory [221]

### 15.2.1    Structured Inheritance Networks

**Structured Inheritance Networks** (**SIN**s) are an approach to describing conceptual knowledge in a way different from the methods of cognitively oriented semantic networks (abbreviated **CSN**s), which are represented by MultiNet. SINs whose most typical representative is KL-ONE are essentially based on the work of Brachman and Schmolze [29, 34].[2] They use two basic constructs, **concepts** and **roles**[3], and take essentially the conception of defining attributes (the "roles") as a starting point for structuring the conceptual world (see relation ATTR in Sect. 4.3.3). In SINs, the hierarchical relations between concepts (the **subsumption** of concepts) play a prominent role in the investigations.

---

[2] The more recent work on Description Logics will be dealt with in Sect. 15.3.3.

[3] Please note that in this section and also in KL-ONE the term "concept" is used in its technical sense. As we shall see, it must not be identified with the term "concept" in the cognitive sense. The latter will be called "mental concept" in this section.

We shall only concentrate on KL-ONE (whose successors comprise KL-TWO [267], CLASSIC [33], BACK [198], and SB-ONE [6]).These KRSs have been successfully applied to the representation of taxonomic conceptual systems and to modeling the inheritance mechanisms connected with them (this is also the justification of their name 'Structured Inheritance Networks', originating with Brachman). All these systems have in common that they use the following categories for structuring a knowledge base: concepts (individual and generic ones), roles or defining attributes, role restrictions and role differentiation, subsumption, and classification. It is characteristic of this line of development that a model-theoretic extensional interpretation of concepts and roles are used, which establishes a closeness of SIN to logic-oriented KRS.[4] Because of the clear analogy between roles of SINs and slots in frame representations on the one hand and role descriptions and filler specifications on the other hand, there is a close relationship between the technical concepts of KL-ONE and frames (see Sect. 15.4). Since the network structure of concepts also plays an important part in KL-ONE, the SINs may be seen as hybrid systems positioned between frame representations, logic-oriented KRSs, and semantic networks. In the last years, the paradigm of SIN has been worked out to a great extent, so that there are now graphical representational means for the knowledge representation [16], as well as more "linearized" formal description languages with a model-theoretic foundation of their semantics [198].

In the following discussion, some essential differences between structured inheritance networks and cognitively oriented networks shall be elucidated by using the illustration in Fig. 15.1:

**Cognitive adequacy.** An important difference is marked by the fact that in a CSN every mental concept is represented by a node, while in a SIN mental concepts are represented by nodes (concepts) as well as by arcs (roles). Because of this, there is no clear borderline in a SIN like KL-ONE between the mental concepts that should be represented by a role and those that should be modeled by a concept node. This ad hoc choice of nodes and arcs gives rise not only to problems for the computational lexicon (one should think, for instance, of the definition of roles for the representation of verb valencies), but it is also cognitively inadequate. In addition, the seemingly large degree of freedom in this choice is a serious hindrance with regard to the criterion of communicability (see Chap. 1). For, how should one warrant in a team of computer lexicographers or knowledge engineers that all of them have the same understanding in using the basic constructs of the KRS for solving a certain task, if there is

---

[4] This is also documented by the development of Terminological Logics [198] and Description Logics [55, 12] akin to SINs.

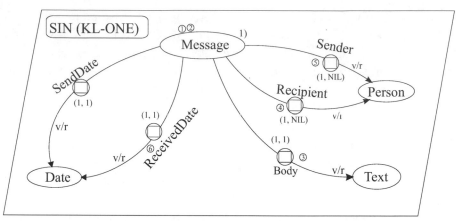

1) following [Brachman, Schmolze 1985, Fig. 2]
   (*The subordination of KL-ONE concepts under the most general concept 'Thing'
   has been dropped here; it corresponds to the assignment of sort 'entity' [SORT=ent]
   to an arbitrary node of MultiNet.*)

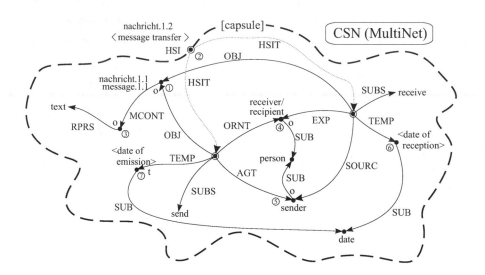

HSI= Hypersituation,  HSIT= Pointer to a constituent of a HSI

ⓝ Constructs of the two representations having the same label
   correspond to each other (without being indentical)

**Figure 15.1.** Comparison of SIN (KL-ONE) and CSN (MultiNet) using the concept
nachricht.1.2 (En: ⟨message transfer⟩)

no commitment to a fundamental and well motivated choice of roles (not to speak of the difficulties in automatically supporting the knowledge acquisition by powerful software tools or help systems). Thus, it is not clear at all in Fig. 15.1 why sender or recipient should be roles (relations), while person is represented as a concept.[5] It is sometimes argued by proponents of SIN that the roles named sender or recipient should rather be better read as sender_of or recipient_of, respectively. If this is true, then the question arises firstly as to why this is not annotated in exactly that way, and secondly, as to how should one correctly specify the connection between the semantically composed relations sender_of and recipient_of on the one hand and the simpler concepts sender and recipient on the other hand.[6] The model-theoretic approach that concepts have to be interpreted extensionally as sets of individuals of the universe U and roles as sets of pairs from U × U is also of little use, since virtually any concept can be reinterpreted as a binary relation by (mentally) adding an "*of*" to the name of that concept (name to name_of, door to door_of, etc.). In a CSN (lower part of Fig. 15.1), concepts and relations are clearly distinguished from each other, where the latter always stem from a metalanguage different from the world of natural language concepts.[7] The relations are elementary constituents of a semantic interlingua which is independent of the concepts of the discourse field under consideration and of the language investigated. In a MultiNet representation, all three concepts, sender, recipient, and person, are nodes belonging to the same sort, and the first two are subordinate to the third. This means that in a CSN, sender and recipient inherit all properties from person, while in KL-ONE there is no inheritance between concepts and roles (something that would also not be reasonable).

**Structural granularity.** The representation in a CSN is generally more differentiated with regard to the structural resolution of facts compared to a SIN. In KL-ONE, most states of affairs are practically reduced to an ATTR-VAL/VALR mechanism on the semantic level (the analogue can be stated for frame representations; see Sect. 15.4). So, it is a typical KL-ONE approach (upper part of the figure) to represent ⟨Date of sending⟩, ⟨Date of recep-

---

[5] This ad hoc use of role names is not a singular case, it is encountered throughout the KL-ONE literature. Such usage can also be found in many frame-oriented and logical KRS, see Sects. 15.4 and 15.3. It is possible, of course, to use in KL-ONE or other representation formalisms concepts and relations analogous to those proposed in MultiNet. The resulting representations would come closer to MultiNet in some aspects. As a consequence, the model-theoretic foundation of these representations would have to be given up (possibly with some exceptions concerning the characterization of concrete objects).

[6] See the discussion of the **representation trap** problem in Sect. 15.4.

[7] This is no contradiction of the fact that relations themselves can be connected with natural language concepts in a second stage (see relations ARG1/2/3 in Sect. 18.2), since NL is language and metalanguage at the same time.

tion⟩, and ⟨Message body⟩ in the same way as a defining attribute or role of the concept **Message** as it is done with **Sender** or **Recipient**. However, the relationships involved are qualitatively quite different. They are represented in a CSN (lower part of the figure) by relations like TEMP, MCONT, AGT, and ORNT. In addition, node 4 in the CSN (lower part of the figure) automatically expresses that the person to whom the message is sent (ORNT arc leading to node 4) is the same as the one who receives the message (EXP arc leading to node 4). In contrast, the concept (the node) **Person** in the upper part of the figure does not represent the sender or the recipient of the message (since both should in general be different from each other). This node specifies rather the value restriction of the corresponding roles. To get a more fine-grained representation, an essentially finer differentiation of roles would have to be used in the KL-ONE figure (the coincidence of roles could be specified by so-called "role-value maps"). It is exactly this variety of representational options and the arbitrariness in KL-ONE-like representations which are a problem: it is impossible to "nail them down" and generalize from specific representations to the approach as a whole. In contrast, MultiNet representations can always be judged whether or not they are semantically adequate (in general, there is only one way to express things on a given level of semantic resolution).

**Conceptual differentiation.** In SIN, one is often confronted with quite a simplified representation of concepts that actually comprise several meaning facets (see Chap. 12 for "meaning molecules"). How easily different concepts can be confused in an undifferentiated treatment shall be illustrated by means of the concepts labeled with the word "*Nachricht*" in German, or "*message*" in English (it corresponds in one reading to the concept **Message** shown in the upper part of Fig. 15.1).[8] Upon closer inspection, one recognizes two components of the concept nachricht.1.1 (En: message.1.1), which is actually a meaning molecule with at least two different semantic facets: $\text{nachricht}_I$ (En: $\text{message}_I$) with [**SORT** = $io$] is the piece of information conveyed ("*The message worried him*") and $\text{nachricht}_{II}$ (En: $\text{message}_{II}$) corresponds to the material carrier of information (a text, a signal, etc.) with [**SORT** = $co$] ("*He put the message on the table*"). The fact that the concept nachricht.1.1 (similar to the concept letter) is really a meaning molecule is proved by the test "*The message which had been handed over by the boy shocked him.*" (see the definition of the term **meaning molecule** on page 292).

Apart from this, we encounter yet another reading nachricht.1.2 with [**SORT** = $abs$] of the German word "*Nachrichten*" (En: "*news*", in this sense it is used only in plural). nachricht.1.2 or the synonymous concept Nachrich-

---

[8] Unfortunately, nothing has been said in the cited paper about exactly which reading is meant.

tenübertragung (En: ⟨message transfer⟩) denote a complex communication act consisting of (at least) a send act and a receive act with their corresponding actants and the special relations between them (bottom of Fig. 15.1). To be precise, only the concept nachricht.1.2 can be directly assigned a send date and a receive date. The concept nachricht.1.1, be it in its facets $nachricht_{II}$ as a material object or $nachricht_I$ as an informational object, has a priori no such temporal characteristics directly associated with it (indirectly, at best, over the communication act as a relatively undifferentiated attribute associatively attached to these objects). If necessary, the concept nachricht.1.1 could primarily be assigned only the temporal specification "duration of existence" (defined possibly by the times of creation and destruction), but these times are in general different from the above-mentioned times of sending and receiving the message.

**Cardinalities.** It must be acknowledged that cardinality restrictions of roles (or role sets) have been introduced first with a certain consequence in KL-ONE. These specifications are almost entirely wanting in traditional CSN. This must be judged all the more positively, because these expressional means of KL-ONE and its variants have been investigated very carefully, yielding useful classification algorithms and results on decidability. Sets of similar roles for one and the same concept, like the "part-of-whole" role set in "*the table has four legs*" with respect to the concept table, can be characterized very compactly with specifications of cardinalities, something that could have been expressed only very awkwardly with most traditional semantic networks. Only through the layer information of MultiNet (to be specific, through the attributes **CARD** and **QUANT**, see Chap. 10) are cognitively oriented semantic networks also provided with the corresponding expressional means.

**Semantic foundation.** SINs have an elaborate model-theoretic semantics, which, however, is subject to the same restrictions that will be discussed in Sect. 15.3 in connection with logic-oriented KRSs. Within these limitations, KL-ONE and its successors have a good mathematical basis for dealing with decidability of the subsumption problem or other theoretical issues. This advantage, however, is essentially based on the fact that, the KL-ONE literature deals almost exclusively with examples of conceptual objects which (sometimes with reservations) can be extensionally interpreted. But, this is questionable for many concepts (like semantically non-total properties, most abstract concepts, temporal and modal concepts, etc.). In cases where the set-theoretic denotational semantics is not so apparent, the model-theoretic foundations have scarcely yet been worked out. One of the primary obstacles in this context is the semantic representation of verbs as relators with variable arity and the adjunction of adverbial constructs. Also, a temporal concept like date (top of Fig. 15.1) cannot, for ontological reasons, be assigned a set of time moments in the same way in which a set of individuals (single persons) is assigned to the generic concept person. Points of time should rather be considered as indices of possible worlds or spatio-temporal world partitions. Therefore, time is more akin to modal concepts (like possibility or necessity) than to extensionally interpretable concepts (house, tree, etc.); see [161].

Altogether, one can state that CSNs are distinguished from SINs by a higher degree of cognitive adequacy and better coverage of natural language phenomena. In contrast, SINs, represented by KL-ONE and its successors, have hitherto been more thoroughly investigated with regard to their logical properties than the more cognitively oriented KRSs. This holds especially with regard to decidability results and theoretical questions concerning the complexity of classification problems. The treatment of such formal issues is facilitated by the model-theoretic foundation of SINs, something that, however, means a considerable restriction to their universal applicability.

## 15.2.2    The Semantic Network Processing System (SNePS)

The knowledge representation system SNePS resembles MultiNet in several ways and is a very useful tool for building knowledge bases (see [235, 239, 238]):

- From the very beginning it was designed for automatic knowledge acquisition and computer-assisted knowledge management (see Fig. 15.2).
- Each concept is uniquely represented by a single node of the SN.
- Relations (which correspond to the arcs of the SN) are constructs belonging to a metalevel with regard to the representatives of concepts. They are described by logical means.
- While the concepts constitute an open set (which is potentially infinite), the relations have to be chosen from a finite repertory of predefined representational means which, however, are not as strongly regulated as with MultiNet.

Apart from these similarities, the two systems, SNePS and MultiNet, are different in essential features. Thus, there is no counterpart to the layer model of MultiNet in SNePS. In particular, there is no distinction between the intensional and preextensional layers, which has the consequence that set-theoretical relationships obtain the same status as intensional relationships. Compared to SNePS, the nodes of MultiNet have a richer inner structure, described by sorts and layer attributes as well as by the partition of the node specifications into immanent and situational knowledge, an inherent feature expressed by the encapsulation of concepts.

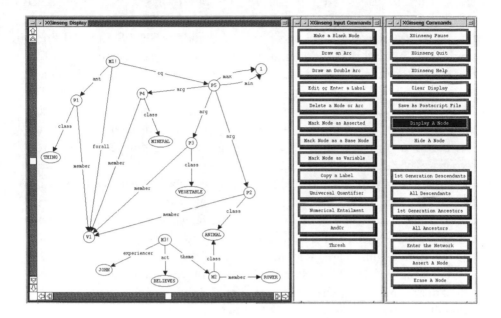

**Figure 15.2.** Screenshot from the graphical user interface of SNePS (by courtesy of S. Shapiro)

A representational method which has consequently been used in SNePS is concerned with the modeling of relations. In SNePS, every relationship between concepts is uniformly represented as a node subordinate to the dominating relation and connected to the arguments of this relation by special metarelations which have a mnemonically chosen name (in this respect, SNePS is similar to the SUBR-ARG1/2/3 constructs of MultiNet).

The relations of SNePS are only sparingly described (roughly comparable with the semantic templates in Appendix C, with some examples), and therefore the interconnection between SNePS and NLP is less tight than desirable. With regard to the restrictions imposed upon the expressional means, SNePS is positioned somewhere between FOL and MultiNet. While no restrictions concerning the interpretation of relations and functions are made in FOL, MultiNet uses a fixed repertory of these expressional means. In contrast, the SNePS group gives only some recommendations or guidelines with regard to the relations to be used in a semantic network. But the non-commitment of these proposals exhibit the problem if the expressional means were to be used for

natural language processing.[9] The relations discussed in the SNePS literature
have a quite different epistemological status and belong to quite heterogeneous
areas. Thus the part-whole relationship (introduced in SNePS as PARTSHIP
with the arguments PART and WHOLE) is discussed along with the relations
interconnecting persons in a kinship system (called in SNePS KINSHIP relations) or with relations describing the structure of sentences. But even relations
that can be found in almost all knowledge representation systems such as those
denoting the carrier of an action (called AGT in MultiNet and AGNT/ACT in
SNePS[10]) remain relatively unclear, since – besides "genuine" actions – mental processes such as sleep are also characterized by this deep case relation.
But sleep is not an action with an active agent in the same sense as throw
(compare the relations MEXP and AGT in MultiNet).

This short discussion shows that relaxing the commitment with regard to
the expressional means (as preferred with SNePS) leaves their exact specification to the user. This also loosens the bond between a potentially available
computational lexicon (where this commitment is necessary) and the knowledge base modeling a certain application domain.

A specialty of SNePS consists in a feature allowing connectives and quantifiers in its semantic representation which are strongly generalized in comparison with the standard operators of FOL.

Examples (see [237]):
• An expression qualified by the connective andor(i, j) $(P_1, P_2, \ldots P_n)$ is true
if and only if at least i and not more than j of the expressions $P_k$ $(1 \leq k \leq n)$
are true. This construct can be used to express the "exclusive OR" by means
of andor(1, 1), the "inclusive OR" by means of andor(1, n), and the NOR by
means of andor(0, 0).
• An expression constructed from the numerical quantifier
nexists(i, j, k)(x) $[P_1(x), P_2, \ldots P_n(x))]$:Q(x) means that there are k individuals
for which $(P_1(x) \wedge P_2(x) \wedge \ldots P_n(x))$ holds, and of which at least i and not more
than j also satisfy Q(x).

As illustrated by these examples, the logical connectives and quantifiers of
SNePS are rather generally defined.[11] It is also very difficult to obtain these
operators and their appropriate parameter settings by means of automatic analysis from the corresponding natural language constructs.

---

[9] It should be remarked, however, that the main application of SNePS lies in the modeling of
robot worlds and not in the construction of large-scale NLP systems.

[10] The bipartition results from the convention that every relation of SNePS (in this case, the
agent relation) is described as a node with arcs leading to the arguments of this relation
(here, AGNT and ACT).

[11] With regard to the natural language use of the quantificators expressing these logical quantifiers, one may even speak of an "overgeneralization".

With regard to the logical properties of SNePs, the proposal seems to be interesting to introduce a kind of "disjunctive modus ponens" instead of the extension rule (93), which was already criticized in Sect. 13.1:

$$A, (A \lor B) \rightarrow C \vdash C \tag{108}$$

Another strong feature of SNePS from the logical point of view is the treatment of contexts within the framework of a "belief-revision" system where, however, an ontological characterization of nodes comparable to the facticity attribute of MultiNet seems to be wanting. In other words, the facticity of assertions cannot be expressed in the object language. With regard to the demand for locality of logical derivations, which prevents the global effects of local contradictions, the same opinion is held in SNePS as in MultiNet. To deal with this problem, SNePS uses a variation of **relevance logic** [236], where the rule "Ex falso quodlibet" does not hold (see Formula (94) in Sect. 13.1).

Until the moment of this writing, SNePS still seems more elaborate with regard to its logical properties than MultiNet (see [238]), while the latter seems superior with regard to its usability in automatic natural language processing and its rootedness in the computational lexicon.

Last but not least, it should be mentioned that SNePS, like MultiNet, is supported by graphical tools for the maintenance and manipulation of network structures (see Fig. 15.2), an important feature lacking in many other systems.

### 15.2.3  Sowa's Conceptual Structures (SCS)

The paradigm of **conceptual structures** is based on the work of Sowa [248]. To give a critical valuation of this work is not easy, since on the one hand a whole scientific community has arisen around this paradigm, with its own conferences (see, for instance, [255]) and commendable results that lie, among other fields, in the area of relationships between graph-theoretical concepts and semantic networks [46] or between FOL and conceptual structures [243], and in the representation of dynamic knowledge [51]. On the other hand, the seminal work cited above contains already a number of problematic points, typical of the description of knowledge representation methods in many respects, and the topic of our discussion. Four problem areas are discussed:

 (1) *The sketchy introduction of the representational means conveying no clear idea of their exact meaning.*

Taking a look at Fig. 15.3, which shows the semantic representation of the sentence "*A monkey eats a walnut with a spoon made out of that walnut's shell*", it is not clear what the relations AGNT, OBJ, INST, and MATR in the figure mean exactly, since only a few lines are devoted to their explanation (one may guess at best what they could mean). But even then doubts arise about whether,

Conceptual graph

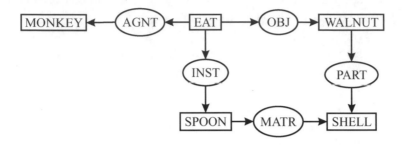

Linearized form:

[EAT] — (AGNT) ⟶ [MONKEY]
        (OBJ)   ⟶ [WALNUT:*x]
        (INST)  ⟶ [SPOON]⟶(MATR)⟶[SHELL]⟵(PART)⟵[WALNUT:*x]

**Figure 15.3.** Semantic representation of the sentence *"A monkey eats a walnut with a spoon made out of that walnut's shell"* (from [248, p. 78])

for instance, the relation OBJ linked to **eat** has the same meaning as in the case of **read** (see Fig. 4.9 in [248]), where it can also be found. If so, what is their common semantic kernel? (Compare also the relations AFF and OBJ of Multi-Net.)

The analogue holds for the relation STAT in the semantic representation of the sentence *"A cat sits on a mat"*:

$$[CAT] \rightarrow (STAT) \rightarrow [SIT] \rightarrow (LOC) \rightarrow [MAT] \tag{109}$$

In this case, especially the meaning of the relation (STAT) remains unclear. Does it denote the same role that should be used for the semantic characterization of the subject of *"to dream"* (Ge: *"träumen"*) or *"to hold"* (Ge: *"halten"*)? In our opinion, this is not the case (see the relation MEXP and the double characterization of syntactic roles by AGT and SCAR in MultiNet).[12]

Comparing the two representation forms of Fig. 15.3, it is not clear why the concept **WALNUT** should be treated differently from other concepts in the linearized form. Only in a later section, it is explained that all these nodes have to be considered as existentially quantified variables, and the special construction with the variable **WALNUT**:*x is needed to indicate referential identity. Since

---

[12] Also, cognitive roles encountered in almost every network representation, like the agent role (Sowa's AGNT) stay rather vague, since they are used in connection with **eat** (which has a genuine agent in MultiNet; see relation AGT) as well as with **sleep** (which actually has a mental experiencer and no agent; see the MultiNet relation MEXP). Whatever set of cognitive roles is used, these two roles should be different.

not every mention of a concept gives rise to an existentially quantified variable, the general representational principle cannot be recognized from these examples.

The distinction between "*word*", "*concept*", and "*type*", described by Sowa referring to Peirce (American logician, 1839 – 1914), stays rather vague:
*"The word 'cat' is a type, and every utterance of 'cat' is a new token. Similarly, each occurrence of a concept is a separate token, but the tokens are classified by a set T of basic types."* [248, p. 79].
The use of the terms "*type*" and "*token*" should not be connected with the "occurrence" of concepts. If at all, a parallel could be drawn at best between type and token on the one hand, and generic concept and specific concept on the other hand.[13]

In the graphical representations, a clear distinction is generally lacking between the different meanings discerned in MultiNet by layer attributes and their values. Here, the attributes **GENER**, **FACT**, **REFER**, and **VARIA** are especially relevant. Thus, it is not understandable on the basis of the explanations given in [248] what a "generic concept" should be, because every occurrence of such a concept is brought into connection with an existentially quantified variable by Sowa (loc. cit. p. 86). A generic concept, characterized in MultiNet by [**GENER** = *ge*], as in "*Cats eat mice*", can be adequately represented neither with a universal nor with an existential quantifier (see Chap. 9).

The problem of lexical ambiguity and of meaning molecules is also not dealt with properly, as can be seen in Fig. 15.4 with the concepts child and mother used there. Why should child be a relation, while mother is a "normal" concept? (Compare Fig. 15.4, taken from Sowa's book, with Fig. 4.26 and the discussion at the end of Sect. 4.4.2.)

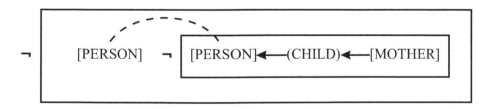

**Figure 15.4.** Conceptual structure for the sentence *"Every person has a mother."* (after [248, p. 141])

---

[13] In a natural language sentence, also generic concepts can be characterized, as in "*The bear likes honey*". Does this "occurrence" of the generic concept bear mark a "type" or a "token"?

**(2)** *Inconsistency with regard to the semantic foundations of the representational means.*

On the one hand, the exclusively extensional interpretation of the predicate calculus is rightfully criticized [248, p. 18]; on the other hand, the denotation $\delta t$ of a type t is introduced (on p. 80) as the set of all entities which are "instances of an arbitrary concept of this type", where instances are expressly seen as things of the real world. Since there is no indication that the function $\delta$ should eventually be conceived as partially defined, one has to assume that every concept has a denotation (which is in itself questionable, see Sect. 15.3). There is also a contradiction to the statement (p. 80) that the set of type UNICORN is empty. Even if one takes the hint at possible worlds seriously (p. 83), the function $\delta$ should be defined as at least a binary function taking a concept (an intension) and a possible world as its arguments and assigning an extension to every such pair.

**(3)** *Seemingly exact formal work with unclearly defined concepts.*

It is of little use to work with formal constructs, with theorems and proofs, if the basic concepts of a KRS to be formalized remain vague as to their actual meanings. This problem had been mentioned already in Point (1) in connection with the intension of the representational means (especially of relations). In order to support the extensional interpretation of the representational means, the concept of a "referent" is introduced as a function referent(c) (see [248, p. 85]), which assigns an element $i \in IM \cup C$, with $IM = \{\sharp 1, \sharp 2, \sharp 3 \ldots \}$ and $C = \{*\}$, to every concept c. The elements of IM are called "individual markers". They are used as "*surrogates*" for individuals of the real world. '*' is the referent of an (arbitrary) generic concept. Considering the first part of the definition, it is doubtful whether every individual concept can be assigned an individual of the real world, while in the second part it is not clear what "referent(c)" really means if c is a generic concept and every generic concept has the same referent. These definitions, in our opinion, are not sufficient to build a foundation for a knowledge representation formalism appropriate for investigations into the semantics of natural language (see also the discussion in Sect. 15.3.1).

**(4)** *Ignoring its own basic principles.*

The theory of Conceptual Structures claims to be committed to the principle of cognitive adequacy, which can be deduced from the positions formulated at the beginning of [248], where it is stated that SCS leans heavily on psychological evidence. But the cognitive adequacy is destroyed by choosing a representation formalism which is strictly oriented toward Peirce's representational conventions for a first-order language.

Let us consider the conceptual structure proposed for the sentence "*Every person has a mother*", shown in Fig. 15.4. It can be explained by starting from the following logical expression (which, by the way, only approximately corresponds to the meaning of this sentence; see also the remarks under Point (1) concerning the concepts child and mother):

$$\forall x \ [\text{person}(x) \rightarrow \exists y \ \text{mother}(y) \wedge \text{child}(x, y)] \tag{110}$$

From this formula, one obtains by equivalence transformations and elimination of the universal quantifier:

$$\neg \exists x \ [\text{person}(x) \wedge \neg[\exists y \ \text{mother}(y) \wedge \text{child}(x, y)]] \tag{111}$$

In this case, the cognitive adequacy was sacrificed because of a predefined goal (elimination of universal quantifiers from the representation by using the rule: $\neg \forall x \ P \leftrightarrow \exists x \ \neg P$). This transformation leads to a proliferation of negators not present in the original sentences. Thus, there exist two negators in the conceptual structure shown in Fig. 15.4, while the corresponding sentence does not contain a negation.[14] If one takes into account the requirements stipulated by the generation of semantic representations during the analysis or by the generation of natural language sentences from such representations, then Grice's conversational maxims are also violated (see Sect. 13.2). Since, if a representation is assumed to contain two negators, there should be a "natural" (not technical) reason for this (see the discussion about the double negation in Sect. 8.2); and, vice versa, there should be no redoubling of representational elements in a semantic representation if the original sentence does not give rise to it (this would also violate the simplicity principle formulated by Ockham, called **Ockham's razor**[15]).

To sum up, the conceptual structures developed by Sowa are a kind of graphical notation for a typed predicate calculus of first order (in Peirce's notation). Because of that, they are closely related to the logic-oriented KRSs discussed in Sect. 15.3.

## 15.2.4   Scripts and the Conceptual Dependency Theory

The relationship between network representations and frames had been touched upon when discussing the defining attributes in Sect. 4.3. There, we concentrated mainly on static states of affairs. But frames also play an important role in modeling dynamic situations (actions, happenings). Such "dynamic frames" are often denoted as "scripts" or "scenarios" in AI (the general definition of a

---

[14] Not to mention that the concept PERSON occurs twice in this representation, which is inappropriate.

[15] See the corresponding remark on page 136.

frame is given in Sect. 15.3). We shall restrict ourselves here to scripts, introduced by Schank and his group [222].

- A **script** is the composition of a sequence of actions that are repeated in a regular way in similar situations and represented as a standardized schema (frame).

Mental contents described by such scripts essentially determine the behavior of human beings. They help them cope with situations recurring time and again in their daily life (buying a ticket, using a telephone booth, visiting a restaurant, using the subway, etc.). The **Conceptual Dependency Theory** (**CDT**) reduces all actions occurring in the description of a script to a few basic concepts. Altogether, there are about a dozen of such fundamental actions. Thus, the following opinion is held:

- Two natural language sentences having the same meaning must be represented by the same semantic structure. A representation having this property is called a **canonical meaning representation**.
- Information implicitly contained in a natural language description of a state of affairs must be explicitly expressed in the semantic representation.

These requirements led the authors to an approach where all meanings of declarative sentences had to be represented by conceptualizations built from a few basic concepts. They distinguished active conceptualizations (comparable to the events in Sect. 5.2) with the representation

$$[\langle Actor \rangle \langle Action \rangle \langle Object \rangle \langle Direction \rangle \{\langle Instrument \rangle\}] \qquad (112)$$

and static conceptualizations (comparable to states in Sect. 5.3) with the representation

$$[\langle Object \rangle \langle State \rangle \{\langle Value \rangle\}] \qquad (113).$$

The expressions in braces are optional. The term "actor" used in CDT corresponds to the concept "agent" used in linguistics (see relation AGT). The term "participant", familiar from linguistic theories, covers the "actors" as well as the "objects" of CDT. The main focus of CDT was the investigation of active conceptualizations, which were represented by a handful of semantically primitive actions not further reducible in their meaning.

Examples:

- ATRANS (o1, a, o2) – An object o1 transfers an abstract category a (a possession, a right etc.) to another object o2.
- INGEST (o1, o2) – An object o1, which must be a living being, is incorporating an object o2 (the direction, in this case, is o1 itself).
- MTRANS (o1, f, o2) – Transfer of an information f from a living being o1 to another living being o2.

- PTRANS (o1, o2, o3) – The object o1 transfers the object o2 physically to an object o3, where o2 experiences a change in its location.

According to the principles of CDT, intensionally different situations like "a receives b from c" and "c gives b to a" are reduced to the same deep concept PTRANS(c, b, a) (provided that an exchange of possession does not occur; otherwise, ATRANS should also be included in the representation).[16]

In our opinion, the reduction of natural language meanings to a few primitive concepts results in a coarsening of the semantics of natural language expressions, and thus violates the criterion of granularity (Chap. 1). Nevertheless, the theory of conceptual dependencies certainly has its merits:

- Attention was drawn to the problem of canonical meaning representations and to the "necessary depth" of the semantic interpretation of natural language expressions. CDT also opened a way to construct meaning representations which come closer to a "more normalized" form.
- The relationship between knowledge explicitly or implicitly contained in a text was elucidated, and solutions for its treatment were proposed.
- In the investigations of CDT, the importance of relations constituting the meaning of textual descriptions of larger situations was emphasized ("story understanding"). In this way, first results were obtained in a field not yet sufficiently understood in AI and linguistics.

In spite of these unquestionable merits, some of the basic theoretical positions of CDT have to be challenged for the following reasons:

- There are serious arguments (see [281]) that a canonical representation for the meaning of natural language sentences in the strong sense does not exist.
- With regard to the technical realization of a QAS, one should have the following in mind: Even if there were such a canonical representation, it would still be doubtful whether it should actually be generated in AI systems because of the high costs of obtaining such a representation in the analysis phase (i.e. during knowledge acquisition). The alternative is to work with a "flatter" knowledge representation, which is somewhat closer to the surface structure of natural language. In this case, one must accept the necessity for carrying out certain transformations of semantically equivalent structures during logical interpretation in the question-answering process. Therefore, one has to find a reasonable compromise.
- The proposals for the more or less normalized representations discussed so far mostly involve a loss of richness in meaning nuances (not to speak of the

---

[16] Note that the concepts **give** and **receive** are eliminated from the semantic representation in CDT.

rather artificial meaning elements sometimes encountered in these representations).

With regard to the last point, it should be emphasized that intensionally well distinguished concepts like give and receive should also have different meaning representations. This follows from the criterion of granularity, which demands a sufficient resolution of the semantic description. Therefore, the representations of give and receive should not be reduced in the first instance to one and the same deep concept (in this case to PTRANS, and possibly to ATRANS). This does not exclude the possibility that behind give and receive still deeper concepts can be discovered, constituting a common semantic kernel that may be described using the above-mentioned primitive actions. These deeper relationships are mirrored in MultiNet by axiom schemata for meaning postulates containing representatives of whole classes of actions (see Appendix E.7). By defining such classes (e.g. by grouping together all transport actions or all actions involving an exchange of possession), the logical inference rules can be described far more economically.

## 15.3    MultiNet and Logic-Oriented Semantic Formalisms

### 15.3.1    General Remarks

With regard to logic-oriented knowledge representation methods (LoKs), we shall restrict ourselves to three paradigms, although many other systems could also be classified into this group, as, for instance, Terminological Logic [198], which can be seen as a "linearized" formal language variant of KL-ONE, or File Change Theory [103]. To reveal the interesting problems, the following work will be considered (where the last paradigm is not a KRS in the proper sense, and the first deals with dialogues rather than stocks of knowledge):

- Discourse Representation Theory (DRT) [134]
- Description Logics (DL) [55, 33, 11]
- Generalized Quantifier Theory (GQT) [15].

All LoKs have in common that the semantics of the representational means is founded on an extensional model-theoretic interpretation. This means that one normally starts from a formal structure $\Sigma = \langle U, \Pi \rangle$ consisting of a universe (a set) U of individuals and a system $\Pi$ of predicates, where for every n-ary predicate $\tilde{P}_n \in \Pi$ we have $\tilde{P}_n \subseteq U^n$. An interpretation of the formal language

expressions of a LoK is defined by a mapping I, which assigns elements of U to constant symbols of the LoK and a set of n-tuples (an n-ary predicate) $\tilde{P}_n \in \Pi$, the extension of $P_n$, to every predicate symbol $P_n$ of that LoK.[17]
For our discussion it is important to emphasize that every predicate symbol of an LoK is purely extensionally interpreted as a subset of some Cartesian product over U.

Let S be an elementary expression of a LoK, and the symbol $\tilde{S}$ marked by a tilde shall denote the element I(S) of the structure $\Sigma$ assigned to S under the interpretation I. Then the truth conditions for LoK can be formulated as follows: $P_n(a_1, \ldots, a_n)$ is true if and only if $\langle \tilde{a}_1, \ldots, \tilde{a}_n \rangle \in \tilde{P}_n$ holds for the argument tuple of $P_n$, where $\tilde{P}_n = I(P_n) \in \Pi$. The further compositional definition of the semantics of LoK expressions can only be sketched here:
$\exists x\, P(x)$ is true, if and only if there is at least one $\tilde{a} \in U$ for which $\tilde{a} \in \tilde{P}$. Let G and H be expressions of the LoK that have already been assigned truth values by the interpretation I; then $\neg\, G$ is true if and only if G does not hold under the interpretation I, while $G \wedge H$ is true if and only if both of the expressions G and H are true.

This is not the place here to set out the model-theoretic semantics of a LoK in every detail. A decisive fact is that formal language constructs of the LoK (meaningless in themselves) obtain a "meaning" by being mapped to another formal structure that also bears no meaning. This approach has already been criticized for being inadequate from linguistic quarters by Lakoff [151] and from the viewpoint of philosophy by Putnam [207]. Also the argument that the elements of $\Sigma$ are to be taken only as labels for things of a certain world is of no real help. One has to ask, which world? The real world is not directly available for such a mapping process; it also cannot be described by decidable sets and simple set operations (as is presupposed for the structure $\Sigma$). Another option to choose a domain (a basic structure) for building a model could be our cognitive or conceptual system. Apart from the fact that this choice would also be a part of the world in the broadest sense, the structures normally used as the basis for an interpretation in logic are much too simple to permit an appropriate description of the semantics of natural language (they would also be cognitively inadequate as we shall see). According to the explanations given in Chaps. 1 through 11, the structure $\Sigma$ needed as a basis for adequate modeling of our conceptual world requires a formal description at least as complex as Multi-Net (if not more complex). The reiteration of the question "*What again is the meaning of that?*" for every modeling step would lead to an infinite regress,

---

[17] n-ary functions need not be considered separately, since every n-ary function can be seen as an (n+1)-ary predicate.

which can be avoided only by means of use-theoretic methods, discussed in Sect. 13.1, or by proof-theoretical methods [254, 202].

Discussing logic-oriented semantic formalisms, one should also mention the linguistically motivated semantics along the lines of **Montague**, which is based on some form of intensional type theory (see [185], [156], or [201] for a short overview). In this theory, every expression of the semantic formalism is assigned a certain type. There are two elementary types: e for "entity" and t for "truth value", from which more complex types are built. If $t_1$ and $t_2$ are types already defined, then a complex type $(t_1 \rightarrow t_2)$ can be constructed with the meaning that expressions of this type take arguments of type $t_1$ and map them into expressions of type $t_2$. So, the individual constant Max can be assigned the type e, while the unary predicates human or alive are of type (e $\rightarrow$ t), since the application of these predicates to arguments of type e, like Max, gives expressions having a certain truth value (in this case alive(Max) or human(Max), respectively). This approach has the advantage that semantically total properties, like dead, alive, or empty (in MultiNet sort [tq]), which have the type (e $\rightarrow$ t), and semantically relative properties, like large, fast, or heavy (in MultiNet sort [gq]), which have the type ((e $\rightarrow$ t) $\rightarrow$ (e $\rightarrow$ t)), can be clearly distinguished in contrast to many other logical theories. Apart from the fact, that this approach seems to be too complicated, it is associated with the same problems as other logic-oriented formalisms (model-theoretic interpretation, fixed arity of predicates, truth-functional definition of connectors, etc.).[18] Semantic formalisms based on these ideas are used in linguistics as standard means to investigate different semantic phenomena (see, for instance, [68] and [39]), since in this formalisms there is a theoretical sound and straightforward way leading from syntactical structures to semantic structures on the basis of a compositional semantics (at least for certain fragments of natural language). But, to the best of our knowledge, there is no large-scale NLP application using this approach.

## 15.3.2   The Discourse Representation Theory

Let us now look at another concrete LoK, the **Discourse Representation Theory (DRT,** see [134]). Compared with FOL, the DRT language has the advantage of explicitly introducing discourse referents, which can be used as target points for coreference mechanisms. These referents, however, are not used in

---

[18] Moreover, to harmonize the treatment of quantified expressions like ⟨every student⟩ and individual constants like Peter, proper names are assigned the same type as quantified nominal expressions by "*type raising*", namely ((e $\rightarrow$ t) $\rightarrow$ t). This is counterintuitive and not cognitively adequate.

the sense of an object- or a concept-oriented representation, where the entire information about an entity can be accessed via one single representative. It is evident from the semantic representation of the donkey sentence shown in Fig. 15.5 that even for referentially identical entities (here, u and y) different discourse referents are at first introduced that have afterward to be connected by an equality relation. In addition, the total information belonging to one reference object is distributed over different discourse representations in a knowledge base and over different predications (as in logic).

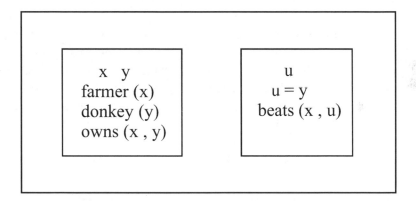

**Figure 15.5.** Representation of the donkey sentence "*Every farmer who owns a donkey beats it.*" in DRT (from [134, p. 168])

Since the interpretation of DRT is based on the predicate calculus, the representation of the donkey sentence "*Every farmer who owns a donkey beats it.*", shown in Fig. 15.5, is equivalent to the expression:

$$\forall x \forall y \; [\text{farmer}(x) \wedge \text{donkey}(y) \wedge \text{owns}(x, y) \rightarrow \text{beats}(x, y)] \tag{114}$$

This interpretation shows clearly that it is impossible to reduce the meaning of natural language sentences exclusively to truth conditions for reasons already discussed in Sect. 13.1 in connection with Formula (77). It also illustrates that the given interpretation is cognitively inadequate for the above-mentioned reasons.

It is also remarkable with regard to the semantic representation of DRT propositions containing universal quantifiers (like the donkey sentences) that they have essentially the same composition as the discourse representation structures of corresponding conditional sentences (in our case, "*If a farmer owns a donkey, then he beats it.*"). This is certainly not adequate from a cognitive point of view. Because of that, different representations are used in Multi-Net for both types of expressions (see Figs. 13.4 and 13.3).

The missing concept centeredness of DRT is also illustrated in Fig. 15.5. In contrast to the MultiNet representation of Fig. 9.14, it does not contain an explicit representative of the concept F = ⟨farmer who owns a donkey⟩ in the sense of a concept-centered representation. While exactly one representative exists in Fig. 9.14 for each of the concepts F and farmer, which are embedded in the general inheritance mechanism by means of the relation SUB, the discourse referent x introduced in Fig. 15.5 is not a central representative of the concept F in this sense. It is rather playing the role of a logical variable which is contained in several predicative expressions jointly characterizing the concept F.

The treatment of natural language quantificators in DRT as relations over sets [134, p. 315] is also counterintuitive, because quantificators are inner characterizations of pluralities (cf. Chap. 9) rather than relations between sets.[19] With regard to this aspect DRT follows an approach similar to GQT (see Sect. 15.3.4). Moreover, no distinction can be recognized in the semantic representation of "*every N*" and "*all N*" in DRT. But there is a clear difference, because "*all N*" permits a collective reading in sentences like "*All students built a snowman*", while "*every N*" in "*Every student built a snowman*" admits only a distributive reading.

Summarizing, one has to state that, notwithstanding the efforts for generalizing FOL, DRT stays too closely attached to it. This can also be seen from the main topics of the basic work [134], which in large parts is dedicated to themes like quantification, logical connectors, and conditionals. An adequate treatment of lexical semantics, especially of the complicated semantics of verbs, coping with the homogeneity criterion formulated in Chap. 1 is not recognizable. It should be positively remarked, however, that DRT had been used as a starting point for the definition of the semantic intermediate language VIT (Verbmobil Interface Terms) of the project **VERBMOBIL** [271].

### 15.3.3  Description Logics

In recent years, a class of logical formalisms known as **Description Logics**, abbreviated **DL**, has been established [55, 125, 11]. All types of DL have in common that they are decidable subsets of FOL distinguished only by their admitting different types of constructors. Because of this, DL are subject to all points of criticism that apply to FOL (see Sect. 15.3.1).

---

[19] Apart from that, it is not easy to see why all, ⟨most⟩, and ⟨almost all⟩ should require different representational principles; see Figs 2.44 and 4.22 in [134].

Typical constructors introduced in DL are given in Table 15.1. Taking again the structure $\Sigma = \langle U, \Pi \rangle$ introduced in Sect. 15.3.1 as a basis for the interpretation function I, and denoting by $\tilde{S}$ the interpretation I(S) assigned to an expression S of DL by I, one gets the semantic interpretations of the constructors shown in the last column of this table.

| Constructor | Syntax | Examples | Interpretation |
|---|---|---|---|
| (1) Atomic concept | A | Person, Male, Rich | $\tilde{A} \subseteq U$ |
| NL Transcription: | \multicolumn{3}{}{The predicate: *"X is {a person / male / rich}."*} | | |
| (2) Atomic role | R | hits, likes, sees | $\tilde{R} \subseteq U \times U$ |
| NL Transcription: | The relation: *"X {hits / likes / sees} Y."* | | |
| (3) Conjunction | $C_1 \sqcap C_2$ | Person $\sqcap$ Male | $\tilde{C}_1 \cap \tilde{C}_2$ |
|  |  | $C_1$, $C_2$, and C are used for arbitrary (atomic or complex) concepts. | |
| NL Transcription: | The predicate: *"X is a male person."* | | |
| (4) Negation | $\neg\, C$ | $\neg$ Male | $U \setminus \tilde{C}$ |
| NL Transcription: | The predicate: *"X is not male."* | | |
| (5) Exists restriction | $\exists\, R.C$ | $\exists$ has_child.Male | $\{x \mid \exists y[\langle x, y \rangle \in \tilde{R} \wedge$ $y \in \tilde{C}]\}$ |
| NL Transcription: | The predicate: *"X has a male child (i.e. a son)."* | | |
| (6) Value restriction | $\forall\, R.C$ | $\forall$ has_child.Female | $\{x \mid \forall y[\langle x, y \rangle \in \tilde{R} \rightarrow$ $y \in \tilde{C}]\}$ |
| NL Transcription: | The predicate: *"X has only female childs (i.e. daughters)."* | | |
| \multicolumn{4}{}{Expressional means of the T-box (terminological knowledge)} | | | |
| (7) Concept definition | $D \doteq C$ | Man $\doteq$ Male $\sqcap$ Person $\sqcap$ Adult | $D \doteq C$ iff $\tilde{D} = \tilde{C}$ |
| NL Transcription: | The concept D is defined by the (known) complex concept C. *"A man is a male adult person."* | | |
| (8) Axioms | $C_1 \sqsubseteq C_2$ | $\exists$ has_child.Male $\sqsubseteq$ $\exists$ likes.Football | $C_1 \sqsubseteq C_2$ iff $\tilde{C}_1 \subseteq \tilde{C}_2$ |
| NL Transcription: | All $C_1$ are $C_2$. Example: *"Those who have sons like football."* | | |
| \multicolumn{4}{}{Expressional means of the A-box (assertional knowledge)} | | | |
| (9) Concept assertion | b : C | John : (Male $\sqcap$ Person) | b : C iff $\tilde{b} \in \tilde{C}$ |
| NL Transcription: | The individual b is a C. Example: *"John is a male person."* | | |

**Table 15.1.** Typical constructors of DL

All constructors of this table are semantically defined only in those cases where the concepts and roles involved can be given an extensional interpretation. Line (1) in particular shows that entities representing objects and entities representing properties are generally not distinguished in DL. What is more dangerous from a logical point of view is the fact that semantically total properties (like male) and semantically relative properties (like rich) are uniformly represented in DL as concepts with subsets from U as an interpretation. This approach can be traced through the whole DL literature and is clearly falling back behind the insights of Montague semantics (see Sect. 15.3.1).

Line (2) illustrates the problem already discussed in connection with the fixed arity of predicates in LoK, or here, with regard to the fixed arity n=2 of roles. How should one consistently represent the fact *"The farmer hits the donkey with a rod."* using the role hits defined in Line (2)?

As it can be seen from Line (4), a DL constructed with the expressional means of Table 15.1 uses a kind of complementary principle which is generally not adequate for the global domain that natural language is concerned with. Such a DL also lacks a type concept. This has, inter alia, the consequence that all things which cannot be characterized by the concept Male (e.g. umbrellas, snowflakes, etc.) automatically belong to the extension of ¬ Male. But this would make no sense in a sound language game. Moreover, one would like to infer from the fact that the predicate "not male" holds (when it can be applied at all) that also the predicate "female" holds, as stated by Axiom (189) in Appendix E. This again is not warranted in DL using the "extensional definition of negation" given above, since one cannot conclude Female from ¬ Male. An umbrella should be neither ¬ Male (which holds in the above DL), nor Male or Female. These predicates are simply not applicable to umbrellas. Also, the construction of a "disjunctive closure" of the form [Male ⊔ Female = Animal] is not a solution since this, together with the extensional, set-theoretical definition of negation and the knowledge background discussed above, leads eventually to the conclusion that umbrellas are animals. (Remark: The union ⊔ of concepts is defined analogously to the conjunction in Line (3) but, in this case, by means of set union.)

Lines (5) and (6) show the only forms of quantification in DL, which makes it a weak candidate for the semantic treatment of noun phrases in general. For example, there are no expressional means corresponding to **fuzzy quantificators** like *"a few"*, *"most of"*, and *"almost all"*. It is also not possible to deal with the interaction of quantification and reference, as encountered in the "donkey sentences" discussed in Sect. 13.2.

The distinction between T-Box and A-Box indicated in Lines (7) and (8) on the one hand and (9) on the other hand vaguely resembles the distinction of MultiNet between the generic layer (concepts with [**GENER** = *ge*]) and the nongeneric layer (concepts with [**GENER** = *sp*]), but DL has not the possibilities for fine-differentiation of MultiNet which are given by the other layer attributes. There is especially no discrimination of immanent and situational knowledge in DL, which is characteristic of MultiNet (where the first type of knowledge is further subdivided into categorical and prototypical knowledge).[20]

An apparent strength of DL is its application to taxonomic systems [124]; for this purpose there also exist software tools supporting the management of ontologies and taxonomies [16]. Therefore, this technology is used in the German project SmartWeb [272]. Since DL has a still weaker expressive power than FOL, it is not able to cover the meaning of a large part of natural language expressions, and therefore is not an appropriate candidate for meaning representation in a fully developed QAS.

### 15.3.4   The Generalized Quantifier Theory

A representational formalism that is more general than FOL with regard to quantification was proposed by the Generalized Quantifier Theory (abbreviated GQT); see [15].[21] The great merit of this theory has been to overcome the restriction of predicate logic to the two quantifiers $\forall$ and $\exists$ and to characterize the role of quantifiers and determiners correctly as a qualification of the semantic representative of a noun phrase, rather than as operators over propositional forms, as in predicate calculus. Contrasting with MultiNet, in sentences like *"All swans are birds"* (see Fig. 9.3), GQT views the whole NP as a quantifier, which was criticized already in [162]. The quantificator *"all"* (in MultiNet terminology) is seen in GQT as a determiner interpreted as a function assigning a family of sets to a set. The GQT view on determiners and quantifiers shall be explained by means of the schema shown in Fig. 15.6.

If we denote by $\|Q\|$ the extension of a quantifier Q and, corresponding to that, $\|A\|$ the extension of an arbitrary predicate A[22], then, in GQT, $\|Q\|$ is the family of those sets for which $\|A\| \in \|Q\|$ holds if and only if Q A is true. This means that the family of sets $\|\langle$all swans$\rangle\|$ has the set $\|Ws\|$ of all white things as an element, where $\|Ws\|$ also contains snowflakes and blankets. This

---

[20] The distinction between "definitional" and "assertional" knowledge encountered in DL does not correspond to the distinction between immanent and situational knowledge (see the discussion in Sect. 3.2.3). The first distinction can be expressed in MultiNet by the encapsulation of concepts and the second by using the layer attribute **K-TYPE** with its different values.

[21] GQT is not a KRS and not a knowledge representation language in the proper sense. It is included in the discussion because it had a considerable influence on the treatment of the quantification problem in the field of knowledge representation.

[22] We deliberately keep the notation $\|S\|$ from the original literature of GQT for the extension of S. It corresponds to the notation $\tilde{S}$ in Sect. 15.3.1.

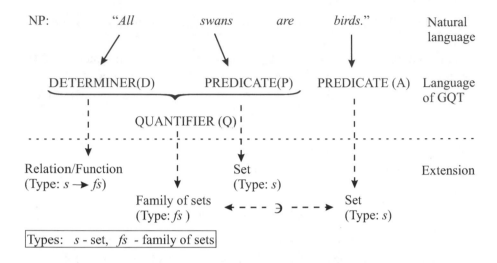

**Figure 15.6.** Schematic overview of the quantifier conception of GQT

conception of "extension" and "denotation" of a quantifier is counterintuitive and has to be considered as a purely mathematical or formal construction.[23]

It must be emphasized, however, that within the framework of GQT, interesting properties of quantifiers and determiners were found on the basis of a model-theoretic interpretation, on which also MultiNet can draw. One example of that is the **monotonicity property** .

- A quantifier Q is **monotone increasing** (symbol: mon↑) if for two predicates A and B with $\|A\| \subseteq \|B\|$ the predication Q B follows from Q A.

- A quantifier Q is **monotone decreasing** (Symbol: mon↓) if for two predicates A and B with $\|B\| \subseteq \|A\|$ the predication Q B follows from Q A.

The monotonicity property of a quantifier Q is essentially determined by the determiner D contained in Q, therefore one is also speaking of mon↑- or mon↓-determiners (depending on the property of the quantifier constructed by means of this determiner).

---

[23] This objection had been recognized by Barwise and Cooper themselves [15], but unfortunately without a convincing counterargument.

Examples: mon↑: **several, many, all, most**[24];
  mon↓: **no (Ge: kein), few**[25]**, nobody.**

The quantifier conception of GQT does not properly take into account the different contributions of the corresponding natural language constructs to the determination of reference of an NP and to the quantitative meaning aspect of the plurality described by it. This distinction is important from the linguistic point of view [169] and also from the angle of knowledge representation, which is expressed in MultiNet by the different layer attributes (see Chaps. 9 and 10). Notwithstanding its limitations, GQT gives valuable suggestions for the treatment of quantificators in MultiNet, too.

Concluding the section about logic-oriented KRS, let us briefly consider the German project **LILOG** [122], which also used a knowledge representation formalism oriented toward FOL. Although the LILOG project is now history, it can be taken as a witness for the difficulties encountered in real-world applications of logic-oriented KRS. LILOG was characterized by the addition of an extensive type system to the representational means of FOL [17], which, however, did not cope with the universality criterion formulated in Chap. 1. This is documented by the fact that more than 80% of the several hundred types (or "sorts" in MultiNet terminology) of LILOG (and also of the knowledge base in the second prototype LEU/2 of its experimental environment) were dependent on the chosen application domain (see [141, p. 218]). The heterogeneity of the LILOG ontology of sorts has already been criticized by Lang [153]. The LILOG group tried to solve the problem of variable arity of verbs contrasting with the fixed arity of predicates by introducing predicates with "maximal" arity, which, however, leads to considerable problems in creating large computational lexica. This approach was given up in LEU/2 and substituted by a more event-centered approach, which came closer to MultiNet in some respects, whereas a systematic treatment of cognitive roles (thematic roles) was still lacking. Since, in addition, the knowledge representation of

---

[24] The monotonicity of logical operators should not be applied without care in the language game. This can be seen by means of the determiner most, which is classified in GQT as being monotone increasing. So, if *"Most students eat hamburgers."* is valid, the sentence *"Most students eat sandwiches."* also holds because of *"eat hamburgers"* → *"eat sandwiches"*. But although *"eat sandwiches"* → *"take food"*, the sentence *"Most students take food."* does not have the same acceptability as the foregoing sentences, because a property holding for all elements of a certain set cannot meaningfully be restricted to a subset by ⟨most⟩.

[25] The quantification ⟨a few⟩ is somewhat problematic. If it is interpreted in the sense ⟨not many, but at least one⟩, then the property mon↓ does not hold. However, if ⟨a few⟩ is interpreted as ⟨at most a few⟩, which does not exclude no/none, then the property mon↓ holds.

LILOG showed many of the properties already discussed in connection with other LoK, the argumentation will not be repeated here (see Sect. 15.3.1).

# 15.4    Comparison Between MultiNet and Frame Representations

## 15.4.1    General Remarks

The term "frame" was coined by Minsky [183]. It denotes one of the central concepts of AI and is closely associated with the view that cognition is based on a process of recognition, where newly received memory contents are compared with a collection of prototypical components of knowledge or **conceptual schemata**, which are stored in the memory and essentially determine the expectations of an intelligent system.

- A **frame** is a schema for knowledge representation describing a certain entity (an object, a fact, or an event) or a class of entities within a hierarchy of such schemata by means of attribute-value pairs. A frame is a descriptional pattern which is encountered over and over in a stereotypical way in different situations. The attributes, called **slots**, are seen as open positions having the character of a variable that can be assigned appropriate values, or **fillers**, depending on the entity to be described.

For comparison, the following systems will be used as typical examples of frame-based languages or KRSs:

- the **K**nowledge **R**epresentation **L**anguage KRL [27]
- the knowledge representation system CYC [158].

## 15.4.2    The Knowledge Representation Language KRL

Although **KRL** belongs to the older KRS, it is an interesting candidate for comparison, since it realized the frame concept in its original form, and since the relationships which can be observed between MultiNet and KRL are also valid for other frame representations. The technical term for a frame in KRL is the "unit" (denoting a distinguished piece of knowledge in a hierarchy of such units). The top of Fig. 15.7 shows on the right side a generic KRL unit called travel, a **prototype** in KRL terminology, corresponding to the generic concept travel represented with the ATTR-VALR formalism of MultiNet (on the left of the figure). On the far left, the connection between the attributes/values

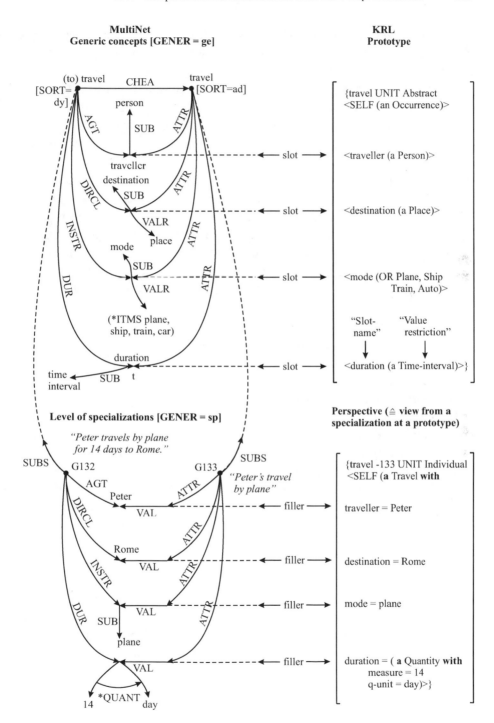

**Figure 15.7.** Comparison between the attribute-value mechanism of MultiNet and frame representations

(slots/fillers) and the C-Roles of MultiNet is indicated (the subordination relations existing between corresponding attributes are omitted for the sake of transparency).

At the bottom of the figure, the corresponding specializations for the individual event ⟨Peter traveled for 14 days by plane to Rome⟩, which can be paraphrased as ⟨Peter's travel by plane to Rome lasting 14 days⟩, are shown in the MultiNet representation (left) and in the KRL representation (right). This comparison demonstrates that the slots in KRL correspond to the attribute specifications in MultiNet (see Sect. 4.3), where the names of the KRL slots are attached to the attribute nodes in MultiNet by means of SUB. The value restrictions of KRL are specified by means of the relation VALR in MultiNet. What is not so easy to model in KRL is the connection to the C-Roles of the corresponding action travel, not to mention the lack of an axiomatic apparatus for the semantic definition of these roles in KRL. In principle, the representational means of KRL mentioned above can be expressed completely in terms of the MultiNet relations SUB, ATTR, VALR, and VAL. Thus MultiNet has a higher expressive power than KRL with reference to the means of knowledge structuring (see Sect. 3.3).

On the other hand, KRL possesses expressional means which are normally found neither in semantic networks nor in logic-oriented KRSs. Here, we have in mind the embedding of procedural knowledge parts. Every slot and every KRL unit can be connected with procedures (called "triggers" and "traps") that are waiting like **demons** (another technical term of AI) in the knowledge base to be activated by certain triggering events, e.g. by the introduction of a new piece of information into the knowledge base.

A crucial idea of frame-oriented KRSs is the embedding of conceptual entities (the units of KRL) into inheritance hierarchies, where subordinate objects (instances in KRL) inherit information from superordinate objects (the KRL prototypes). In MultiNet, this inheritance mechanism is carried by the relations building hierarchies (i.e. mainly by the relations SUB and SUBS); see Sects. 4.3 and 5.2. The idea of organizing informational objects in hierarchies of classes and instances together with the embedding of procedural elements into the representation of such objects has found its expression in the object-oriented programming languages, from SMALLTALK [7] and FLAVORS [186] to $C^{++}$ [224] and JAVA [127] (within this context, the procedural elements are called **methods**).

### 15.4.3   The Knowledge Base Project CYC

Possibly the most ambitious and vast project for acquiring a really useful
knowledge base, the project **CYC** [158], which is still alive, was originally also
based on the frame concept. Strictly speaking, the knowledge base of CYC, at
least in its form described in [158], is a frame system (similar to that of KRL)
combined with **constraints** (restricting conditions) for the slots formulated in
a predicate calculus style. In the first version of CYC (as in KRL) a frame is
called a unit, whereas (in contrast to KRL) there are not only units describing
"normal" concepts but also units describing slots.

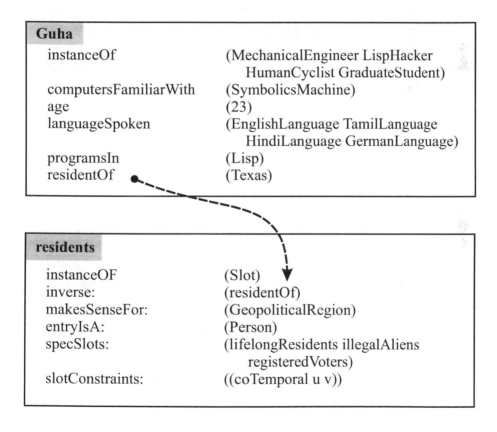

**Figure 15.8.** Frame representations with CYC units (after [158])

Figure 15.8 shows two CYC units where, in comparison to [158], the first
one (upper part of the figure) was supplemented by the slot "residentOf" to
emphasize the connection between a normal unit and a unit characterizing a
slot (residentOf is the inverse relation of residents, which should be better

called has_residents). Even if the pure frame-oriented conception of the original CYC formalism is changed now to the more logic-based formalism of the CycL language (http://www.opencyc.org/doc/), it still has a frame orientation in its background. What could be said about units, slots, and fillers in the frame representation can now be stated about predicates and their arguments in the new formalism.[26]

A core problem of CYC and many other frame-oriented KRSs is the relatively large distance to natural language and the absence of cognitive adequacy with regard to the slot descriptions (or predicate descriptions). Slots are arbitrarily labeled with artificial names (as, for instance, computersFamiliarWith or memberOfPoliticalParty; see [158, Sect. 3.2.1.1 and Fig. 2-1], or object-FoundInLocation as discussed in the context of CycL and OpenCyc). Such names suggest a meaning to a human reader, but their embedding in the entire world of concepts is not apparent. This makes the construction of natural language interfaces to CYC knowledge bases a cumbersome task (especially with regard to the creation of a linguistically well founded computational lexicon). This circumstance is all the more astonishing as this problem had been identified already in the CYC description [158, Sect. 1.5] under the heading **representation trap** as an obstacle to be avoided. If one follows the mental experiment proposed in the cited work, which has been suggested often in connection with frame representations,[27] and substitutes all concepts in Fig. 15.8 not immediately rooted in natural language by artificial names (such as X001, X002, ...), then a unit is obtained from the Guha frame which is represented by the structure shown in Fig. 15.9.[28]

Since in MultiNet labels of nodes and arcs are anchored in the computational lexicon and in the axioms of the logical background knowledge (both are crucial for organizing the language game), this representation trap can be avoided there. Even if one would optimistically assume for CYC that all proper names (like Guha, LISP, and Texas), natural numbers (like 23) or lexicalized concepts (like age) were correctly embedded through the computational lexicon and the NLP components (syntactic-semantic analysis, inferences, and generation) into the world of natural language concepts, then the tremendous problem of providing all "artificial names" with meanings would still persist. This problem must ultimately be solved by connecting the artificial names with

---

[26] Therefore, the same restrictions discussed already in Sect. 15.3 with regard to logic representations apply to the CycL formalism.

[27] This test, by the way, would also be useful for other knowledge representation systems, among them KL-ONE.

[28] The reader is invited to carry out the same experiment with the artificial predicate and argument names in CycL.

| Guha | |
|------|--------|
| X001 | (X002 X003 X004 X005) |
| X006 | (X007) |
| age | (23) |
| X008 | (X009 X010 X011 X012) |
| X013 | (Lisp) |
| X014 | (Texas) |

**Figure 15.9.** Mental experiment illustrating the representation trap

natural language concepts through meaning postulates (see Appendix E.5). This would require of us, for instance, to specify what X006 has to do with computer and ⟨familiar with⟩, or how X008 is connected with language and speak, since all these units must also be present as representatives of natural language concepts in a complete knowledge base.[29]

In order to use a CYC knowledge base in natural language AI systems, slots with a complex meaning – if they are assigned a meaning at all – have to be connected via axiomatic rules (see Sect. 3.3.2) with the surrounding world of concepts, something that is very expensive and can barely be automated. For this reason, we deem the approach of MultiNet important; it makes it possible to ultimately derive all concepts of a knowledge base, including the relationships between these concepts, from the lexicon and from natural language information during the process of morphological-lexical analysis and syntactic-semantic analysis (here, again, the homogeneity criterion formulated in Chap. 1 shows its significance).

It is worth mentioning that there are workbenches for the CYC knowledge engineer. They are used mainly for entering the knowledge and for enabling cooperative work in building large knowledge bases. Without such technological support (lacking in many KRS) a project of this size with hundred thousands of facts could never have been handled successfully.

The inference system of CYC is also interesting because it combines monotone and nonmonotone types of reasoning and thus involves certain elements of

---

[29] Of course, labels of concept nodes like Texas, age, etc. have per se as little meaning as X001, X002, etc. for any technical AI system. However, provided that the above-mentioned assumptions hold, the former labels have a fundamentally different status than the latter, since the former are anchored in the question-answering game via the lexicon, analysis, inference rules, and answer generation in an entirely different way than the latter, which are not rooted in the lexicon.

an "opportunistic" logic, as proposed in Sect. 13.2. Moreover, the distinction of more than two truth values departs from the principle of strict two-valuedness in classical logic and shows a similarity with the valuation of propositions by means of degrees of trustworthiness proposed in 13.1.

In spite of the tremendous expenditure invested in the CYC project for the accumulation of a large stock of "common sense knowledge", it remains difficult to use this knowledge for automatic processing of natural language (something confirmed by a study of the New Mexico State University; see [172]). This disadvantage has been amplified in recent years by the exchanging of the original frame-based representation with a more logic-oriented representation, which has led to an abandonment of concept-centering and to an unstructured "sea of assertions" in the knowledge representation of CYC ([172]).

**Concluding remarks.** A central problem of many knowledge representation methods oriented to the semantics of natural language seems to be that the basic constructs are not sufficiently cognitively motivated. Logic-oriented KRSs, in particular, often lack concept-centering, which is especially aggravating for situational concepts and the relations between them.[30]

Even in cognitively oriented representations, the basic constructs are seldom underpinned with a detailed description, not to mention a validation that is based on predefined criteria, like those formulated in Chap. 1 (in this context, the homogeneity and interoperability criteria should play a prominent role). This holds in particular for the definition of cognitive roles in semantic networks.

As far as logic-oriented KRSs are concerned, it is easily stated and formulated in a first-order language that intransitive verbs like "*sleep*" have to be described semantically by unary predicates and transitive verbs like "*hit*" by binary predicates or relations. This position, which can be encountered throughout the logic literature, cannot be maintained in every stage of natural language processing if one considers the words with their varying arguments in different contexts. This also leads to a quantitative aspect: It is of little practical use if a certain semantic theory is illustrated only by means of a few examples. The real usefulness with regard to NLP can only be proved by describing many thousands of concepts or analyzing millions of sentences with their different

---

[30] The need for representatives of situations had been felt already very early in AI; one example is the Situational Calculus proposed by McCarthy [178], another example from philosophical quarters are logical approaches in the Davidsonian style [53]. The use of variables for situations comes close to the MultiNet representation with regard to the outstanding position of situational nodes which can be used as arguments of relations. Nevertheless, the representative of a situation in the aforementioned proposals does not bear the character of a central encapsulated unit through which all knowledge about this situation can be accessed.

meanings (including the meanings of prepositional verbs or phrasal verbs and the difficult semantics of sentences formulated with them).[31] Such a challenging task cannot be carried out without appropriate computational tools (see Chap. 14).

A semantic formalism for natural language understanding, which covers word meaning as well as text meaning, should work in all stages of this process and in all components of an NLP system. This concerns, among other things, the lexical semantics of words (i.c. the specification of lexemes), the analysis of texts, the semantic representation of different situations involving these lexemes, the meaning postulates connecting different concepts, and the inferences based on these postulates (the latter are needed also for answer finding and for resolution of references in a question-answering game, see [176]).

Judging from the experience gained in the development of MultiNet, one should first define all representational means of a KRS verbally as exactly and in as much detail as possible. It is only in the second step that the formalization of the descriptions obtained in the first step can be dealt with; for, how could somebody define something formally (e.g. write down the axioms characterizing a certain cognitive role), if the meaning of the construct in question is not fully understood intensionally (e.g. by having only a three-line definition for the meaning of the role as a basis). After having built this foundation, the formally defined constructs should be used and tested in as many as possible different components of an applied NLP system (including the syntactic-semantic analysis, the inference system, and the computational lexicon).

An important role is played by the technological environment of a KRS in the task of validating the representational means. The workbenches for the knowledge engineer and the computer lexicographer are especially indispensable for cross-checking and cross-evaluating the definitions, and for the automatic testing of formal restrictions (such as the constraints given by signatures). Finally, the definitions and characterizations originally laid down should be revised on the basis of newly obtained insights and systematic evaluations of practical applications before the whole process can be iterated at a higher level.

With this short methodological note, the comparison of MultiNet with other KRSs is for the time being brought to a close. The issue, however, is not settled; it must be resumed at every new stage in the development of the MultiNet paradigm.

---

[31] To be fair, this is definitely not the goal of most logic theories.

Part II

# The Representational Means of MultiNet

# Chapter 16

# Overview and Representational Principles

## 16.1 Embedding of the Representational Means of MultiNet in the Context of Knowledge Processing

Part II of this book deals with the formal description and systematic compilation of the representational means of MultiNet, thus permitting a semantically adequate representation of natural language texts or dialogues on computers. The comprehension (the "understanding") of meanings of natural language expressions (words, phrases, sentences, etc.) manifests itself in the correct embedding of the semantic representatives assigned to these expressions (i.e. of conceptual objects, events, states of affairs, etc.) into the whole relational structure of all conceptual representatives. The representational means of MultiNet defined here serve the purpose of describing this entire framework of conceptual relationships in terms of a generalized semantic net. The representational means are the elementary constituents of a formal semantic language, and every surface structure of a natural language expression is assigned an expression of this semantic language (called a deep structure) by means of the syntactic-semantic analysis.[1] In other words, the natural language constructs are assigned meanings by translating them into a semantic language which can be considered a kind of metalanguage (see [184, p. 3] and [230]).

If we speak of "understanding" natural language in a question-answering game (see Chap. 1) or in a technically realized question-answering system (see below), both abbreviated as QAS, then we mean the correct embedding of the semantic representatives into the whole conceptual structure described above. What "correct" embedding precisely means is finally decided by an operational criterion judging whether the natural language questions a QAS is asked can be answered properly and adequately on the basis of the semantic representations obtained in this way (there exists a clear analogy to the Turing test known from artificial intelligence, see [63]).

---

[1] With regard to the semantic language, we hold the view that it satisfies the conditions already formulated earlier by Hajičova in [88] (similar requirements can be found in [230]).

Knowledge representation is not an end in itself; it is always embedded in a larger context. Possibly the most comprehensive conception of a natural language AI system where all aspects of knowledge representation and natural language processing are involved is the question-answering system.

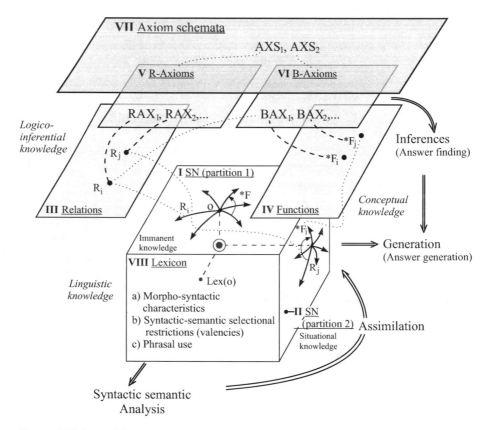

**Figure 16.1.** Embedding of the representational means into the knowledge processing components

- A **question-answering system (QAS)** is an intelligent system able to translate natural language queries and texts into their semantic representations, to answer questions by means of logico-inferential processes over this knowledge representation, and to reformulate the semantic representations of the answers in their natural language form.

It is recommended (but not mandatory) that we consider the representational means described in the following sections as being integrated into such an application context in order to be able to judge their usefulness for the different tasks of natural language processing. This aspect is emphasized because there are many different paradigms of knowledge representation but only few satisfy the criteria given in Chap. 1 (this is true especially for the criteria of cognitive adequacy, homogeneity, and interoperability). The paradigm of **Multi**layered Extended Semantic **Net**works (**MultiNet**), described in this book, was designed and developed along the lines marked by these criteria. Prior to our detailed explanation of the representational means, we would like to discuss the main building blocks of this knowledge representation paradigm and their relationships to the language and knowledge processing modules (see Fig. 16.1).

The kernel of the **knowledge base** (KB) is the **semantic network** (SN) whose nodes represent concepts and whose arcs represent the relations between these concepts (the relations and functions, to be specific). The nodes are classified into **sorts** of a predefined classification system, called **ontology of concepts**, and they are assigned values of **attributes** corresponding to certain semantic dimensions (see Chap. 17).

Every concept is connected with **immanent knowledge** (Partition I of KB) defining the meaning of the concept and with **situational knowledge** (Partition II of KB) reflecting the use of the concept in the characterizations of certain situations. The **relations** (Partition III of KB, see Sect. 18.2) and **functions** (Partition IV of KB, see Sect. 18.3) can themselves be considered nodes of a conceptual network at an abstract level. Their meaning is fixed by means of axioms. We distinguish between **R-Axioms** (Partition V of KB), which do not contain representatives of natural language concepts, and **B-Axioms** or **meaning postulates** (Partition VI of KB), which contain representatives of natural language concepts as extralogical constants. In addition, **axiom schemata** are introduced to reduce the extent of the axiomatic apparatus (see Partition VII of KB). These describe whole classes of axioms of Partitions V and VI and also use expressional means of a second order calculus (see, for instance, the characterization of *NON). The distinction between immanent and situational knowledge is technically supported by the methods of **stratification** (or **layering**) and **encapsulation**, described in Sects. 17.2 and 17.3, respectively.

It is important for knowledge representation systems of AI whose informational contents are to be acquired from natural language texts that there exists a connection between the conceptual representatives of the knowledge base (nodes of the semantic network) and natural language words (the analogue holds for human language understanding). The proper interface for this connection is the dictionary or **lexicon** (Partition VIII of the KB in Fig. 16.1), the semantic components of which (among them the valencies of verbs, nouns, and adjectives) are also specified with the representational means of the SN (see Chap. 12). In this way, the homogeneity principle is properly taken into account (Chap. 1).

The approach illustrated in Fig. 16.1 warrants that the central components of a language processing system are all founded on the same representational means. This applies to the computational lexicon, the **syntactic-semantic analysis**, the representation of the information collected in the knowledge base by the so-called **assimilation process**, the **inferential answer finding**, and the **answer generation** (see the interoperability criterion in Chap. 1). With this conception, an **operational criterion** is also gained, permitting us to judge the suitability and adequacy of the chosen knowledge representation paradigm in general and of the concrete representational means associated with it in particular. The basic idea is to check with a formal **question-answering system** or **question-answering game** to what extent the application of the representational means really yields the expected results and thus correctly links the query, the available knowledge, and the possible answers. This view shows an apparent parallelism to Wittgenstein's explanation of natural language semantics with his concept of **meaning as use** [279].

The operational criterion mentioned above is supported by the following consideration. In the way a human being is said to correctly understand a concept, if he is able to use it correctly, one can also speak of an adequate knowledge representation and a correct use of concepts in an AI system if these concepts are connected by the operations of knowledge processing in such a way that one obtains proper answers to all questions over a given knowledge base.

## 16.2 The Paradigm of Multilayered Extended Semantic Networks

As already mentioned in the foregoing sections, we are using **Multilayered Extended Semantic Networks** (abbreviated as MultiNets) as a model for the semantic representation of knowledge given in natural language. The historical roots of this approach and its development were discussed in Chap. 2. For a comprehensive description of the essential components of the MultiNet paradigm we start once more with a simple semantic network:

- A **simple semantic network** (SN) is the mathematical model of a conceptual structure consisting of a set of concepts and the cognitive relations holding between them. It is represented by a labeled oriented graph, where the nodes of the graph correspond to the representatives of the concepts and the arcs correspond to binary relations between these conceptual representatives. Every node bears a unique name as a first label. The labeling of the nodes depends further on the partition of all conceptual representatives into **sorts**, which is based on a corresponding ontology of concepts (see Sect. 17.1). The most specific sort of a node in the conceptual hierarchy given by this ontology is assigned to this node as a second label.

Starting from simple semantic networks, one obtains **extended** networks by adjoining further representational means:

- Admission of **n-ary relations** and **functional terms**. Functional terms are built by applying semantic primitive functions to elementary entities or to other terms used as arguments (see Sects. 18.2 and 18.3).
- Introduction of so-called **parameterized entities** (which correspond to nodes of the net having the character of a variable) and the expressional means connected with them. The latter allow for the representation of dependencies between conceptual nodes (see Sect. 17.2.4).
- Use of **axiomatic relationships** or **axioms**, for short, to connect the representatives of relations and functions with each other on a higher level, or to link them with natural language concepts (see Chap. 18 and Appendix E).

The additional generalization of an extended SN to a **multilayered** extended SN is based on the introduction of expressional means for **stratification** (or **layering**) and **partitioning** (or **encapsulation**) of semantic networks:

- Introduction of conceptual **attributes** corresponding to certain semantic dimensions representing the degree of generalization, the facticity, the determination of reference, the quantification, and the distinction between intensional and extensional meaning components of a concept (see Sect. 17.2).
- **Encapsulation** of partial networks, which are represented as a conceptual unit (a conceptual capsule). Within every conceptual capsule, an immanent and a situational meaning component is distinguished (see Sect. 17.3).

Altogether, every conceptual node is classified according to the sortal hierarchy and the stratificational means (see Chap. 17), and it is linked to other representatives of concepts by means of relations and functions (see Chap. 18). These relationships are schematically illustrated in Fig. 16.2.

Fixing one of the classificatory meaning components to a particular choice of a parameter value (e.g. fixing a certain sort, the value of a certain attribute, or the markers for the immanent meaning components), one obtains a corresponding layer of the semantic network (e.g. the set of all situations or concrete

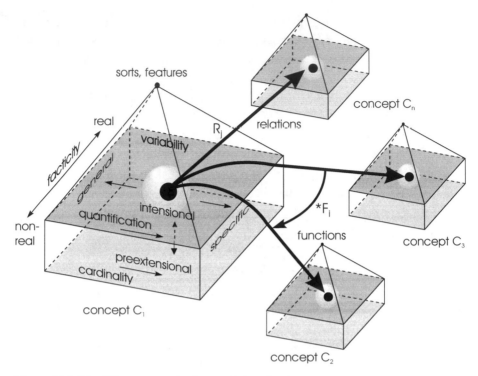

**Figure 16.2.** The different semantic characteristics of nodes

objects, the layer of all generic or all individual conceptual entities, the layer of categorical vs. the layer of prototypical knowledge, and so on). It is this view that justifies the denotation **layer model** for MultiNet (see also Chap. 17).

## 16.3   Conventions of Description

To guarantee a uniform and consistent specification of the meaning of relations and functions in the catalogue of representational means, each of these relations and functions is described by six characteristic components:

(1) An appropriate expressive **name** and a short headline as concise as possible with regard to the meaning of the relationship;
(2) The specification of a **signature**, i.e. characterization of the domains on which the relation or function is defined, and (for functions) of the range of the result; for this purpose the sorts defined in Sect. 17.1 are used;
(3) A **verbal definition**, which characterizes the relation or function intensionally;

(4) A **mnemonic indication** as to the origin of the name from English or Latin[2]; for relations, an assertional pattern (semantic template) is also given, showing one typical paraphrase of the relation in the language game.

(5) Specification of typical **question patterns** aiming at the intension of a relation or used to enquire about the validity of that relation;

(6) An **explanation** for clarifying and illustrating the meaning of the relation or function beyond the definition given in (3). In this context, relationships to functions or relations with similar or contrasting meanings are also discussed. These connections and delimitations to other representational means are formally described by logical axioms. A compilation of typical axioms can be found in Appendix E. Moreover, suggestive example sentences and pertinent natural language phenomena are presented, together with their semantic representation, and the application of the relation or function in question is illustrated.

Special conventions are used in the description of relations and functions, enumerated in the following:

Ad (1): Conventions of **naming**:

- In general, names are derived from English or Latin denotations by abbreviation (often accompanied by dropping of vowels).
- Names of functions are especially marked with a preceding asterisk "$*$".

Ad (2): For the specification of **domains** and **ranges** of relations and functions (i.e., for the specification of their respective signatures), the abbreviations and symbols for sorts introduced in Sect. 17.1 are used (see Fig. 17.1).

In these signatures, the expression REL: sort1 $\times$ sort2 has the same meaning as REL $\subset$ sort1 $\times$ sort2. An expression sort1\sort2 (set difference) appearing in the definition of domains of relations or functions is used for the specification of exceptions; it means "sort1 but not sort2 is admitted as domain where the relation or function is defined".

Sometimes the notation REL: *sort* $\times$ *sort* is used to indicate that both arguments of the relation REL must be taken from the same most specific sort in the hierarchy of sorts. Apart from this restriction, '*sort*' can be chosen arbitrarily from this hierarchy.

Ad (3): In elementary relational expressions, the name REL of a relation is written in **infix notation** at the second position, e.g. (a REL b) for a binary relation and (a REL b c) for a ternary relation. In contrast, function names are

---

[2] Since the MultiNet documents were originally published in German and have mainly been used in a German-speaking environment, we have taken the names of most of the expressional means from English or Latin to emphasize that they do not belong to the level of natural language concepts but to a metalanguage.

written in **prefix notation**, where the name of the function is included into the parentheses, e.g. (∗FNAM a b) = c for a binary function ∗FNAM.

Names of variables are generally chosen mnemonically, e.g. o, $o_1$, $o_2$, ..., for objects, e or v for events (Ge: "Vorgänge"), p for properties, and so on. Even if sorts and variables, by chance, have the same abbreviated name, there is no danger of confusion, because only names of variables and constants can be placed at argument positions of relations and functions, not names of sorts. It should be clear that only elements belonging to the sorts specified by the signatures in (2) can be inserted as arguments of relations and functions (the analogue holds for the values of functions). This must be taken into account especially in those cases where x or y are used as names of arguments that give no direct indication with regard to the assignment of values to these variables.[3]

Ad (4): The names of relations and functions have also been chosen in a mnemonically appropriate way and in general do not coincide with German or English words in order to avoid a confusion of language and metalanguage (the only exceptions are NAME, MODE, JUST). Mnemonic explanations of relations are supplemented by a natural language pattern (language template), which also shows the direction of the arcs representing these relations (i.e. the succession of their arguments).

Ad (5): No semantic deep relation can be characterized adequately alone by a few typical questions. Such a description requires rather a whole class of queries aiming semantically at the corresponding relation. For this reason, and with the aim of showing a possible way for the classification of questions in a QAS (including a method for the description of such question classes), we specify characteristic **question patterns** for every relation. These patterns are part of the definition of the described relation in the sense that they characterize just that class of questions that apply to the relation in a question-answering game.

In this context, the following **description conventions** will be used:

- ⟨symbol⟩ – Symbols enclosed in angular brackets, which occur in a question pattern, coincide either with a variable symbol of the relation definition given under (3) or with a sort symbol of the signature. In both cases, ⟨symbol⟩ stands for a natural language paraphrase of an element of the sort that is determined by the corresponding argument position;

- [ ] indicates that an appropriately inflected form of the word enclosed in square brackets has to be inserted;

---

[3] The use of mnemonically appropriate variable names has no semantic consequences. They are chosen only for better readability of the formulas.

- $\{M_1 \,/\, M_2 \,/\, M_3 \dots\}$ is used to describe alternative partial patterns $M_i$ (i = 1, 2, 3, ... );
- $\langle WH \rangle$, $\langle WS \rangle$, $\langle WM \rangle$, $\langle WMF \rangle$, $\langle WMT \rangle$, and $\langle WHA \rangle$ are symbols belonging to the description language (metalanguage) for question classes; they indicate that one of the interrogative pronouns (or phrases introduced by such pronouns) that are marked by a cross in the corresponding column of Table 16.1 has to be inserted to obtain a concrete query from the question pattern (the interrogative pronoun can also be combined with a corresponding restriction $\langle o \rangle$ on the admissible superconcept). The classes $\langle WH \rangle$ (derived from "*what*"), $\langle WS \rangle$ (derived from "*whose*"), and $\langle WHA \rangle$ (derived from "*what*" as a direct object, which is associated with the accusative in German) roughly correspond to Winograd's classification markers of English pronouns *subjective*, *possessive*, and *objective* [278], while the class $\langle WM \rangle$ (derived from "*whom*") is described in English by another direct object or a prepositional phrase with the preposition "*to*". The classes $\langle WMF \rangle$ and $\langle WMT \rangle$ (derived from "*from whom*" and "*to whom*", respectively) describe prepositional objects marked by the prepositions "*from*" and "*to*", respectively.[4]

As mentioned, the natural language paraphrase denoted by $\langle o \rangle$ in Table 16.1 specifies a restriction of the entity asked for by the interrogative pronoun. In this context, (PLUR $\langle o \rangle$) indicates the plural form corresponding to $\langle o \rangle$. So, $\langle WH \rangle$ can mean "*Who*", "*What program*", "*Which firms*", etc.; $\langle WMT \rangle$ can mean "*To whom*", "*Whom ... to*", or "*To which {program / firm}*", where "*program*" and "*firm*" characterize the restriction $\langle o \rangle$ combined with an interrogative pronoun.

---

[4] In German, only four classes $\langle WR \rangle$, $\langle WS \rangle$, $\langle WM \rangle$, and $\langle WN \rangle$ of interrogative pronouns are used; the names are derived from the German terms "*Wer*" (for nominative), "*Wessen*" (for genitive), "*Wem*" (for dative), and "*Wen*" (for accusative). In English, with its rudimentary case system, we had to adapt the classes in a certain way. It should be kept in mind, however, that the German case "dative" can be expressed in English either by a direct object (without preposition), e.g. "*He wrote the teacher a letter.*" or by a prepositional phrase, "*He wrote a letter to the teacher.*"

In Russian, where we encounter still more cases indicative of certain deep relations or C-Roles, such as the fifth case for INSTR or the sixth case for MCONT, we could define more classes of interrogative pronouns.

In all languages, there are clues hidden in the case system or in other syntactic categories that can be used as indicators for what a question is aiming at. The analogue could be said about the templates listed in Appendix C. While question patterns show the way specific relationships are asked for, templates indicate how semantic relationships are paraphrased in NL.

| German cases: | nominative | genitive | dative | | | accusative |
|---|---|---|---|---|---|---|
| English analogy: (after Winograd) | subjective | possessive | (1st) direct object or prepositional object | | | (2nd) direct object |
| | ⟨WH⟩ | ⟨WS⟩ | ⟨WM⟩ | ⟨WMF⟩ | ⟨WMT⟩ | ⟨WHA⟩ |
| who | X | | | | | |
| what | X | | | | | X |
| whom | | | X | | | X |
| to whom | | | | | X | |
| from whom | | | | X | | |
| whose | | X | | | | |
| whose + ⟨o⟩ | X | | | | | X |
| which + ⟨o⟩ | X | | | | | X |
| to which + ⟨o⟩ | | | | | X | |
| from which + ⟨o⟩ | | | | X | | |
| what + ⟨o⟩ | X | | | | | X |
| to what + ⟨o⟩ | | | | | X | |
| from what + ⟨o⟩ | | | | X | | |
| which + (PLUR ⟨o⟩) | X | | | | | X |
| what + (PLUR ⟨o⟩) | X | | | | | X |
| how many + (PLUR ⟨o⟩) | X | | | | | X |

**Table 16.1.** Classes of interrogative pronouns

Example using the question patterns of the relation AGT (see also Table 16.1):

- Let the expression $(e_1 \text{ AGT } o_1)$ be given as background knowledge, where $e_1$ and $o_1$ denote the concepts ⟨smashing the window⟩ and ⟨the student Peter⟩, respectively. In this case, the following questions can be derived from the question patterns aiming at the relation AGT or one of its arguments in the knowledge base:
  "*{Who / Which student / Which boy} broke the window?*"
  "*By whom had the window been smashed?*"
  "*What did {Peter / the student / the boy} do?*"

Ad (6): In connection with the explanations, the following additional agreement should be observed:

- To circumvent drawing of partial networks of example sentences, the phrases of a sentence describing the arguments of the relation in question are often set in square brackets, instead of elaborating their full semantic representation. The role played by the representatives of these phrases in the situation described and their positions as first or second argument of the discussed relation are indicated by superscripts. If only one argument is given for the sake of abbreviation then the whole situation described by the example sentence has to be taken as the lacking argument.

A function name attached to a bracketed phrase (without specification of arguments) indicates that the semantic representative of this phrase is to be seen as the value of the function.

- Arrows in the graphical representations drawn with bold lines are used to highlight the relation or function just explained in this section.
- Axioms are formulated in a predicate calculus style where free variables occurring in a formula have to be taken as universally quantified (with the ∀-quantifiers at the beginning of the formula).

Finally, some conventions are needed, which are used for the graphical representation of semantic networks (see Fig. 16.3).

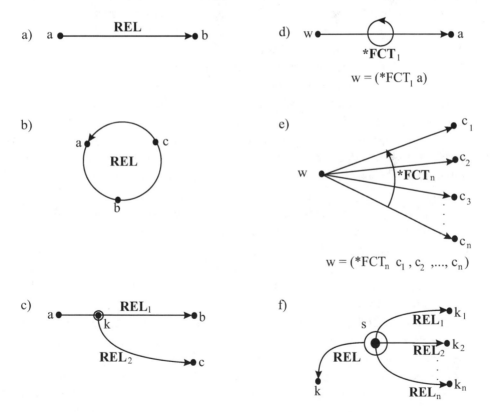

**Figure 16.3.** Conventions for the representation of relations and functions

Figure 16.3a: An oriented arc between nodes a and b labeled with a relation name (here, REL) represents the relational triple (a REL b) which is also an "elementary" state of affairs.

Figure 16.3b: This graphical element represents a ternary relation REL between nodes a, b, and c, and has to be read as (a REL b c). The arrow in this construct always points to the first argument.

Figure 16.3c: An arc between nodes a and b labeled by an encircled node k (called "node on arc") means that the elementary state of affairs (a $REL_1$ b) is represented by a special node k, which is related to node c by (k $REL_2$ c). (Here, we encounter a second order construct in the logical sense.)

Figure 16.3d: This graphical element describes the value w = (∗FCT1 a) of a unary function ∗FCT1.

Figure 16.3e: A sequence of arcs starting from node w and ending in nodes $c_1, \ldots, c_n$ and connected by a curve labeled with a function name (here: $\ast FCT_n$) depicts the value w = ($\ast FCT_n$ $c_1 \ldots c_n$) of an n-ary function $\ast FCT_n$.

Figure 16.3f: This structure is analogous to Fig. 17.7 and is used for the simplification of the complicated representation of a conceptual capsule (see Sect. 17.3). The partial network consisting of the arcs (s $REL_1$ $k_1$), (s $REL_2$ $k_2$), ..., (s $REL_n$ $k_n$) and their nodes is united in a situational capsule represented by a special node s. In this construction, the arcs $REL_1$ through $REL_n$ starting immediately from the inner node s belong to the meaning proper of s (i.e. to the immanent knowledge of s), while the relation REL starting from the border of the circle does not belong to the capsule but rather to its conceptual embedding or to a semantic restriction of the validity of s.

In addition, it is assumed that all objects and situations have to be taken as objects that really exist or as events and states actually taking place or actually holding, provided they are not expressly marked as hypothetical objects $\tilde{o}$ or situations $\tilde{sv}$, i.e. they do not bear the attribute-value specification [**FACT** = *hypo*] or, as nonexisting entities, [**FACT** = *non*] (see Sect. 17.2.5). For the sake of brevity, the assignment of sorts to nodes is indicated only when necessary for a better understanding (see also Convention (2) and the corresponding commentary). In all other cases, the sort of a node can be easily derived from the context (especially from the signatures of relations and functions).

If there is no danger of misinterpretation because of a possible ambiguity of names, proper names (designators of individual objects) are in general used directly as labels of the corresponding semantic representatives. If a node k of the network is labeled with a proper name N, then this has to be read as an abbreviation of (k NAME N).

Finally, the following **conjunction convention** is used in the net representations: All elementary relationships of the type (a REL b), (a REL b c), etc. in a network have to be taken as conjunctively connected and each of them is assumed to be true except for those where the relationships are enclosed in a capsule that is explicitly restricted in its validity by temporal, local, contextual, conditional, or modal relations, or when the capsule is marked by [**FACT** = *non*] or [**FACT** = *hypo*].

# Chapter 17

# Means for Expressing Classification and Stratification

## 17.1 Sorts and Features

For a proper definition of the semantically primitive relations and functions, one needs a classification of conceptual entities that allows one to decide whether a given relationship may be asserted about two given concepts or whether this can be excluded a priori or, in other words, for formal reasons. Such a classification is given by the conceptual ontology shown in Fig. 17.1.

A difficult problem with the construction of a knowledge representation system on the basis of semantic networks consists of adapting the ontology of conceptual representatives and the fundamental relationships of the SN (i.e. the relations and functions) to each other in such a way that both of them are cognitively adequate. At the same time the classes of concepts given by this ontology must be appropriate for characterizing the domains and the value ranges of the relations and functions that are needed to build the SN (Chap. 18). From the standpoint of modern ontological systems (see, for instance, [45]), the proposed ontology of sorts is only the upper part of the whole conceptual hierarchy in a semantic network. The latter is essentially established by the SUB and SUBS relation.

It must be emphasized that, in a knowledge representation system, one is always dealing with representatives of concepts, and not directly with objects of the real world. If we are speaking briefly of "objects", "substances", etc. in connection with such an ontology, then we do not actually mean objects, substances, etc. of the real world but rather their conceptual representatives. In the following, the sorts of MultiNet used in the meaning representations and attached to the nodes of the SN by the attribute SORT will be explained in greater detail. For the sake of illustration, typical examples are included for each of the terminal sorts of the hierarchy (see Fig. 17.1 for an overview).

**Entities [*ent*]:** The most general sort is given by the class of **conceptual entities**, which comprises all things about which something can be stated. They are represented by nodes of the SN and are different from all relations and functions defined in Chap. 18. The latter are represented by arcs of the SN.

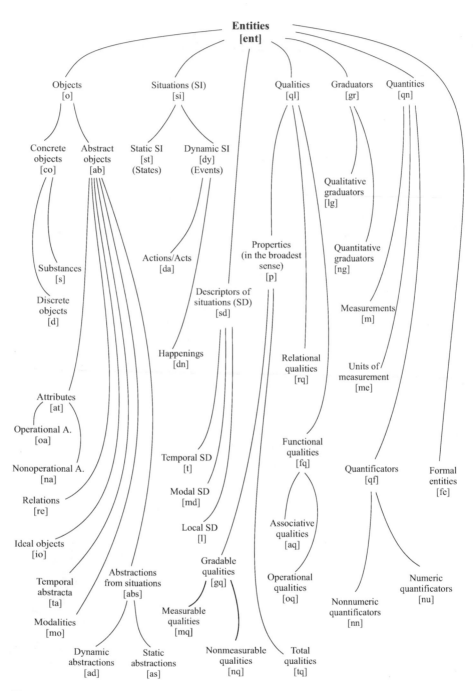

**Figure 17.1.** The ontology of sorts

At the highest level of the hierarchy shown in Fig. 17.1, there are seven main sorts of entities: objects [*o*]; situations or states of affairs [*si*]; situational descriptors [*sd*], which restrict the validity of situations or characterize their spatio-temporal embedding; qualities [*ql*] characterizing the properties of objects and situations more closely; quantities [*qn*] expressing the quantitative aspect of a concept in terms of measurements or quantifications; graduators [*gr*] determining the degree or intensity of properties or of quantitative characterizations; and formal entities [*fe*], often described by extralingual means (formulas, drawings, tables, etc.) although they are also important for practically relevant natural language texts and discourses (especially if one bears in mind that textual references often point to these formal constructs or pictures).

(1) **Objects [*o*]:** There are two types of objects, **concrete objects**, which can be sensually perceived, **abstract objects**, for which this is not true.
  - **Concrete objects [*co*]:** Among these we distinguish substances and discrete objects (things).
    - **Substances [*s*]:** These have a quasi-continuous extension; they are divisible but not countable.
      Examples: milk, honey, iron, ⟨300 g uranium⟩.
    - **Discrete objects [*d*]:** These are countable but not divisible.
      Examples: house, cherries, ⟨the Leaning Tower of Pisa⟩
  - **Abstract objects [*ab*]:** They are products of human reasoning (of an abstracting thought process, to be exact). We distinguish between the following:
    - **Situational objects [*abs*]:** They represent situations elevated by abstraction to the cognitive status of objects. They are divided into
      - **Abstractions from dynamic situations [*ad*]** – race, robbery, integration, ⟨knowledge acquisition⟩, movement, . . .
      - **Abstractions from static situations [*as*]** – calmness, equilibrium, awareness, sleep, illness, . . .
    - **Attributes [*at*]:** Here, we have to distinguish between measurable, operationally definable attributes like height, weight, average, . . . (sort [*oa*]), and attributes for which this does not hold, like form, ⟨character trait⟩, flexibility, . . . (sort [*na*]).
    - **Relationships [*re*]:** causality, similarity, difference, relationship, synonymy, contradiction, . . .
    - **Ideal objects [*io*]:** religion, mercy, justice, criterion, category, . . .
    - **Abstract temporal objects [*ta*]:** Renaissance, ⟨Middle Ages⟩, Easter, holidays, ⟨Paleozoic Era⟩, . . .
    - **Modalities [*mo*]:** probability, necessity, intention, permission, . . .

The classification of abstract concepts proposed here should be taken only as a first attempt. A complete and systematic investigation based on clear criteria for the delimitation between the different classes of abstract concepts does not yet exist, either in linguistics or in cognitive psychology.

(2) **Situations/States of affairs [si]:** Situations or states of affairs mirror the constellation of objects, their modes of being, or the changes they are undergoing. Accordingly, we distinguish between static situations (**states**) and dynamic situations (**events**).

- **Static situations (states) [st]:** This sort comprises physical states as well as psychic states. In the surface structure of natural language sentences they may be expressed by means of nouns (Ge: ⟨Hunger haben⟩, ⟨eine Temperatur haben von … ⟩, ⟨eine schwere Krankheit haben⟩; En: ⟨being pale with hunger⟩, ⟨having a temperature of … ⟩, ⟨having a serious illness⟩[1]) as well as by state verbs or constructions involving passive participles (Ge: hungern, gefroren sein, ⟨erkrankt sein⟩ – En: starve, ⟨being frozen⟩, ⟨being diseased⟩), or by means of predicatively used adjectives (Ge: ⟨ist hungrig⟩, ⟨ist warm⟩, ⟨ist krank⟩ – En: ⟨is hungry⟩, ⟨is warm⟩, ⟨is ill⟩).
  The assignment of attributes or the descriptions of relationships are also taken as abstract states belonging to the sort [st] (see Part I, Sect. 5.3).
- **Dynamic situations (events) [dy]:** These situations, also called **events**, are further classified into actions and happenings, which is important for NLP systems.[2]
  - **Actions [da]:** This term denotes dynamic situations (events) which are actively carried out by an agent (the carrier of the action)
    Examples: work, write, sing, go, sell, drive, …
  - **Happenings [dn]:** Happenings, like events, have causes but are not associated with an agent actively sustaining the event in question. (There is nothing like an active carrier of a happening.)
    Examples: rain, decay, shine, explode, ⟨turn pale⟩, …

---

[1] The use of predicative nouns for the description of states is different in German and English. While clauses like *"Er hat Hunger"*, *"Er hat Durst"*, etc. are quite common in German, the corresponding predicative use of the nouns is not so often encountered in English, or is uncommon as in *"He has hunger"*[(*)] or *"He has thirst"*[(*)].

[2] Unfortunately, there are no appropriate words for a sufficiently clear terminological discrimination of the different classes of dynamic situations (this statement holds for English and German). Because of this, we shall use the following convention, dropping all possible connotations of the chosen terms: The whole class is denoted by the term "**event**" (Ge: "Ereignis/Vorgang"), while the subclasses explained below will be denoted by "**action**" (Ge: "Handlung") and "**happening**" (Ge: "Geschehen"), respectively. **Incidents**, by contrast, are individual events (sort [dy]) with attribute [**GENER** = sp]; see Sect. 17.2.2.

(3) **Situational descriptors [*sd*]:** Situations or states of affairs can also be described with regard to their spatio-temporal embedding (local or temporal specifications) or with regard to their validity (modal specifications), yielding a more detailed or an even more restricted characterization.

- **Temporal situational descriptors [*t*]:** These comprise temporal specifications in the form of moments or periods of time, called **times** for short. Time is closely connected to dynamic changes in the world, not only from an epistemological point of view, but it is also conceptually perceived primarily through events or sequences of events.[3]
  Examples: ⟨yesterday morning 7 o'clock⟩, ⟨on Mondays⟩, ⟨Xmas 1945⟩, ⟨on holidays⟩, ...

- **Local situational descriptors [*l*]:** Locations are primarily connected to objects; if the existence and the manner of being of objects, including their mutual constellation, is assumed to constitute situations in the broadest sense, then locations are the spatial characterizations of these situations. In this way, locations are cognitively and linguistically perceived as being different from objects.
  Examples: ⟨on the roof⟩, ⟨under the table⟩, ⟨between the lines⟩, ...

- **Modalities [*md*]:**
  These comprise concepts which express the position of the speaker or the common (i.e. social) opinion with regard to the validity of states of affairs or situations.
  Examples: probably, impossible, necessary, desirable, ...

(4) **Qualities [*ql*]:** Qualities or specifications of properties can be best classified by an opposing comparison (see Table 17.1).
  At the top level of the hierarchy we discern:

- **Properties in the narrower sense [*p*]:** They comprise semantically total qualities [*tq*] and gradable qualities [*gq*], which can be assigned to certain entities as a characteristic. The latter may again be divided into measurable or quantifiable properties like tall, heavy, ... (sort [*mq*]) and into properties which cannot be measured but express rather a judgement or a validation, as with friendly, sleepy, cruel, ... (sort [*nq*]).

- **Relational qualities [*rq*]:** They establish relationships between entities and may be assigned only to pluralities with at least two elements.
  Examples: equivalent, inverse, congruent, ....

- **Functional qualities [*fq*]:** These qualities obtain their full meaning only in connection with other entities. Combined with the latter, they form a conceptual unit. Here again, we discern semantically associative proper-

---

[3] In a static world there is no place for time.

ties (sort [*aq*]) like philosophical, chemical, ... and operational properties (sort [*oq*]) like ⟨on average⟩ (Ge: durchschnittlich), latter, third, ... .

| Qualities (in general) [*ql*] | |
|---|---|
| total qualities [*tq*] | associative qualities [*aq*] |
| • are extensionally interpretable; <br> • can be predicatively used in natural language; <br> Ex.: dead, empty, rectangular, ... | • establish associations to other objects; <br> • no predicative use in natural language; <br> Ex.: chemical, philosophical, ... |
| gradable qualities [*gq*] | operational qualities [*oq*] |
| • obtain their full meaning only in connection with other conceptual objects; <br> • they cannot be extensionally interpreted directly; <br> • predicative use allowed for the corresponding natural language terms; <br> Ex.: small, good, expensive, ... | • they describe the position in a sequence or are operationally defined; <br> • they are only defined over generic concepts or pluralities; <br> Ex.: fourth, last, next, ... ⟨on average⟩, middle, ... |
| Relational qualities [*rq*] | |
| • they have to be interpreted as relations; <br> • they are only usable in connection with pluralities and collective concepts <br> Ex.: inverse, equivalent, similar, estranged, ... | |

**Table 17.1.** Classification of qualities

(5) **Quantities [*qn*]:** As the name suggests, these express the quantitative aspect of concepts. Among them one finds mainly numbers and measurements.

- **Quantificators [*qf*]:** These are described by numerical quantificators (one, two, ..., five, ...) and non-numerical quantificators[4] (all, ⟨more than the half⟩, ⟨very few⟩, ...). Accordingly, the quantificators are divided into the sorts [*nu*] (numerical quantificators) and [*nn*] (non-numerical quantificators). The former are associated with an explicit cardinality ([**CARD** = 1], [**CARD** = 2], ...), while the latter not. Non-numerical quantificators, except for all, generally describe fuzzy concepts.

- **Units of measurement [*me*]** and **Measurements [*m*]:** Units of measurement (like kg, mm, °C), together with numbers and quantificators are used for the specification of measurements.
  Examples: ⟨3 kg⟩, ⟨a few meters⟩, ⟨many hours⟩, ⟨30°C⟩

---

[4] It should be emphasized once more that the term "quantificator" for the language expressions explained here was deliberately introduced in contrast to the logical "quantifiers" because it also contributes semantically to the layer attributes **REFER** and **VARIA** (apart from **QUANT** and **CARD**).

(6) **Graduators [*gr*]:** Graduators arc used for a more detailed specification of properties and quantities. We distinguish:
- **Qualitative graduators [*lg*]:** These are used for a more specific and graded description of properties (very, ⟨a little (bit)⟩, especially, rather, quite, … ).
- **Quantitative graduators [*ng*]:** These are used (mostly) for fuzzy qualification of quantities (almost, nearly, approximately, ⟨more than⟩, ⟨less than⟩, … ).

Unfortunately, the two groups of graduators do not have disjoint natural language descriptions.

(7) **Formal entities [*fe*]:** These represent extralingual objects (formulas, drawings, pictures, etc.), which play an important role in multimedia documents. In many knowledge sources, the information associated with them is usually not isolated from textual information. Such entities are often linked to textually described objects by means of references and pointers (one may think, for instance, of graphical or pictorial representations of operating instructions, and of parts of texts referring to them with special natural language expressions like *"in the upper half of the figure"*, *"the components in the left corner"*, etc.).

**Features.** It has already been stated that for building large computational lexica it is useful to introduce additional (more fine-grained) classes of entities which facilitate the formulation of selectional restrictions of the lexemes. This kind of classification (i.e. the fine-differentiation of entities), which goes beyond the partitioning of concepts into sorts, can be achieved by an additional labeling of the conceptual representatives using special **features**. In contrast to sorts, the features or **semantic markers**, which comprise, for example, ⟨potential agent⟩ [POTAG +] and ⟨no potential agent⟩ [POTAG -] (see Part I, Table 12.1), do not lead to a hierarchical ordering of entities but rather to a cross-classification with multiple inheritance (see Part I, Fig. 12.1). Together with the sorts, the features essentially determine the valency frames of verbs, adjectives, and nouns, as well as those of the conceptual representatives underlying them.

A motivation for the introduction of semantic features and an explanation regarding their use in lexical specifications is given in Chap. 12. From the MultiNet point of view, a characterization of concepts or lexemes could actually do without features, since a specification of a node k with [ANIMATE+] can be also expressed by (k PROP animate), or [HUMAN+] can be transformed into (k SUB ⟨human being⟩). However, as already mentioned elsewhere, it is advantageous for reasons of effectiveness to represent the information describing

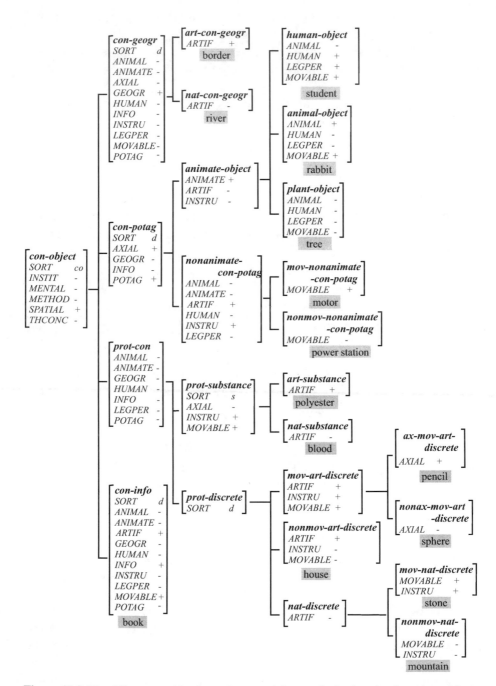

**Figure 17.2.** The different combinations of sorts and features in the domain of concrete objects

selectional restrictions and subcategorizations of lexical units by more compact specifications based on features. With their help, lexical entries can be formed with greater perspicuity and better readability, and selectional restrictions can be described with much better differentiation than with sorts alone. In that way, the semantic agreement tests of the syntactic-semantic analysis can be considerably simplified. Also, the lexicon can be kept sufficiently independent of the background knowledge (world knowledge). Since these considerations touch already upon the effective realization of computational lexica and NLP systems, they will not be pursued further here. With regard to the role of features for the construction and application of computational lexica, we refer you to [228] and [227].

It should also be noted that sorts and features are not entirely independent. Fig. 17.2 shows the partial classes (subtypes) of the sort *co*, which are defined within an inheritance hierarchy of attribute-value structures. The attributes (they correspond to the features) and their values are inherited (from left to right in the picture) by a unification operation for feature structures (see [240]). The consistency is warranted in this inheritance process by the fact that subtypes or terminal types (such as + or -) can be unified with superordinate nonterminal types (such as **boolean**). The embedding of a concept into such an inheritance hierarchy spares the specification of many individual attribute-value pairs. Moreover, many specifications exclude each other, for instance, [SORT = *co*] and [THCONC+] or [SORT = *ab*] and [SPATIAL+]. In other words, this hierarchy determines what combinations of sorts and attribute-value pairs are admissible.

In [191, Sect. 10.2] it is shown how such a classificational hierarchy can be automatically generated from a given set of dependencies between feature values (see Fig. 12.1).

## 17.2  Multidimensional Layer Information

### 17.2.1  General Remarks on the Typology of Layer Attributes (Attribute LAY)

To embed objects, situations, locations, and times into a multidimensional space of **layer attributes**[5], the complex feature **LAY** (from "layers"), whose values are shown in Figs. 17.3 and 17.4, is used. The type hierarchy (Fig. 17.3) with the type *osi-tl-lay* reveals that the layer attributes **FACT** and **GENER** are

---

[5] The layer characteristics dealt with do not apply to other sorts.

relevant to each of the sorts *o*, *si*, *t*, *l*. These attributes are the only layer characteristics of elements of sort *si*; subtype *si-lay* inherits its attribute values from *osi-tl-lay*. Elements of the sorts *o*, *t*, *l* can in principle bear all layer attributes (including those explicitly specified with subtype *o-tl-lay* and those inherited from supertype *osi-tl-lay*).

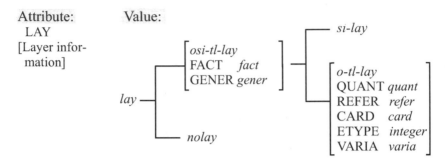

**Figure 17.3.** The value types of the complex feature LAY

The idea of "layers" is derived from an analogy to the n-dimensional Euclidean space. By fixing a certain value along an axis (e.g. the value of the coordinate z in a three-dimensional space of coordinates x, y, z), one obtains an (n-1)-dimensional hyperplane (or, in the example, a plane parallel to the x-y-plane). Similarly the "plane" (or layer) of all generic concepts is obtained by fixing the attribute value [**GENER** = *ge*], or the "plane" (layer) of hypothetical entities is obtained by fixing the value [**FACT** = *hypo*].

An overview of the value types admissible for the layers **CARD**, **FACT**, **GENER**, **QUANT**, **REFER**, and **VARIA** is given in Fig. 17.4. These attributes and their values[6] are described in Sects. 17.2.2 through 17.2.7. The convention will be used that *maximally underspecified values* of attributes are denoted by a type whose name is derived from that of the attribute by writing it in lower case.

## 17.2.2   Degree of Generality (Attribute GENER)

The distinction between generic concepts (like imperator and tower) and individual concepts (like Caesar and ⟨Eiffel Tower⟩) is encountered in almost

---

[6] The value types **integer** and **boolean** should be self-explanatory. For this reason the attribute **ETYPE** has not been further explained in Fig. 17.4. The subtypes **fquant** and **nfquant** of the attribute **QUANT** denote fuzzy and nonfuzzy quantificators, respectively.

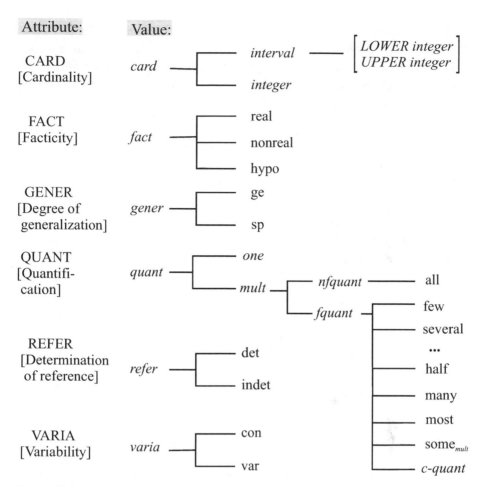

**Figure 17.4.** The layer attributes of MultiNet and their value types

all knowledge representation systems. However, it is mostly restricted to conceptual objects (MultiNet sort [*o*]). But, this distinction is also relevant to other sorts. Compare the following examples:

(17.1)  "*on trees*" – "*on the tree before my house*" (sort: [*l*])
(17.2)  "*in the morning*" – "*yesterday morning*" (sort: [*t*])
(17.3)  "*lying in the bed*" – "*Peter lay in the bed*" (sort: [*st*])
(17.4)  "*chase*" – "*the hunter chased the wolf*" (sort: [*dy*])

In MultiNet it is assumed that the pair of characterizations generic – individual is not the sole distinction, but, rather, that concepts (be they individual concepts or generalized concepts, situations or concrete objects) have to be characterized by a whole bundle of layer attributes. The **degree of generaliza-tion** (attribute: GENER) is only one of them. With this feature we distinguish two values [**GENER = ge**], meaning **generalized**, and [**GENER = sp**], mean-ing **individualized/specialized**. On the base of this distinction the following readings of noun phrases can be differentiated:

(17.5)  *"Peter met four men.* [**GENER** = *sp*]" –
         *"Four men* [**GENER** = *ge*] *are sufficient for playing Bridge."*
(17.6)  *"Max has a car.* [**GENER** = *sp*]" –
         *"A car* [**GENER** = *ge*] *warrants maximal mobility."*
(17.7)  *"These dogs* [**GENER** = *sp*] *are dangerous."* –
         *"Barking dogs* [**GENER** = *ge*] *don't bite."*

The attribute value [**GENER** = *ge*] specifies only that the concept in question has the aspect of generalization as a meaning component and thus, in contrast to concepts characterized by [**GENER** = *sp*], such a concept does not apply to a special element or a special group of elements. On the one hand, the aspect of meaning expressed by [**GENER** = *ge*] should be shared by the concepts dog and ⟨all dogs⟩. On the other hand, generic concepts and universally quantified concepts have of course to be semantically distinguished, which is not possible in logic-oriented representations.[7]

As shown below, the traditional characterization of a concept like dog as "generic" is not sufficient. For an adequate description, a combination of attribute-value pairs including [**GENER** = *ge*] is needed. A generic concept like dog is also characterized by the fact that the determination of reference is underspecified, something that clearly contrasts with a universally quantified concept like ⟨all dogs⟩, which is described by [**REFER** = *det*], [**QUANT** = *all*], [**ETYPE** = *1*], and [**VARIA** = *con*]. But this is only the aspect of knowl-edge representation. Possibly more important is the aspect of logical inferences connected with these representations. While generic concepts are associated with nonmonotonic inferences and inheritance processes, for universally quan-tified concepts categorical conclusions can be drawn by strictly monotonic in-ferences. For this reason, the first of the following sentences is true while the second is undoubtedly false; this observation is tantamount to postulating a difference of meaning between these two sentences.

---

[7] This view is justified by the fact that a statement about *"all dogs"* is equivalent to a *categor-ical* statement about the generic concept dog. Conversely, the information from the categor-ical part of a conceptual capsule is interpreted as a universally quantified logical expression (see Sect. 17.3). In spite of this consideration, the quantificator *all* is connected to the un-derspecified attribute value [**GENER** = *gener*] as it allows for a specialization by means of *"these"* (as in *"all these boys"*), which contrasts with *every* (where *"every these boys"* is not admissible; see Chap. 9).

(17.8) *"Bears are dangerous animals."*
(17.9) *"All bears are dangerous animals."*

Sentence 17.8 is true because the typical bear, or a large part of all bears, with a few exceptions, is dangerous (**prototypical inference** or **default reasoning**). Sentence 17.9 is false because the predication is extended to all bears, but bears being deathly ill and circus bears are not necessarily dangerous. While generic concepts have a prototypical element as an extensional (symbolized as a point in a square in the graphical representation), universally quantified concepts are extended to a whole set of elements at the preextensional level.

### 17.2.3   Determination of Reference (Attribute REFER)

REFER is an attribute defining the degree to which a concept determines the entity referred to (**determination of reference**). This attribute can have only a specific value for nongeneric concepts.[8] The following cases have to be distinguished:

**Determinate reference [REFER = det]**: The intensional description uniquely applies to the object referred to and presents it demonstratively.
    Examples:

(17.10) *"the last Inca ruler"* → *"Atahualpa"*
(17.11) *"the most famous tower of Paris"* → *"Eiffel Tower"*

**Indeterminate reference [REFER = indet]**: The entity denoted by the concept is not uniquely determined. The uncertainty characteristic of such a reference can be caused by the fact that the entity in question is actually fixed but cognitively unknown (see Example 17.12 below). In this case, yet another characteristic is needed for the representation, viz the attribute of variability **VARIA**, which, in this case, must be set to [**VARIA** = *con*] (see Sect. 17.2.4).[9] The indeterminacy of reference can also be caused by the fact that the extensional of a concept depends on a second concept (see Example 17.13 below). In this case, the attribute of variability for the extensional of the corresponding indeterminate concept obtains the value [**VARIA** = *var*].
    Examples:

(17.12) *"Peter bought a new cap."* – [**REFER** = *indet*], [**VARIA** = *con*]
(17.13) *"Every boy wore a new cap."* – [**REFER** = *indet*], [**VARIA** = *var*]

---

[8] For generic concepts the value of this attribute remains underspecified, i.e. [**REFER** = *refer*].
[9] It will soon become clear that, strictly speaking, this attribute applies only to the extensional of the concept in question.

In the first example, we have an indeterminate but fixed cap (whose interpretation does not depend on the sentential context); therefore, the value of the variability attribute is set to [**VARIA** = *con*]. In the second example, the cap referred to changes depending on every single boy, because each of the boys certainly wore another cap; therefore, the attribute value is [**VARIA** = *var*].

It must be emphasized that the linguistic degree of determination in the article system of German and English (corresponding to the distinction between definite and indefinite articles) does not coincide with the determination of reference introduced in this section; see the following example and the argumentation in Sect. 10.4:

(17.14)  Ge: *"Der Künstler malte im Urlaub ein neues Bild."*
       En: *"The artist painted a new picture during the holidays."*
       Ge: *"Das Bild wurde in einer Galerie ausgestellt."*
       En: *"The picture was exhibited in a gallery."*

In the first sentence, the concept B1 = {⟨ein neues Bild⟩/⟨a new picture⟩} obtains the attribute value [**REFER** = *indet*] as expected. Because of the definite article in the description of B2 = {⟨Das Bild⟩/⟨the picture⟩} in the second sentence, one might expect the attribute value [**REFER** = *det*]. However, since B2 arises only from repeated mentioning of the concept B1 of the first sentence, both conceptual representatives have to be identified, and the resulting node obtains the attribute value [**REFER** = *indet*]. It inherits, so to speak, the degree of reference determination from the first node B1. After having found the antecedent B1 and after carrying out the identification of nodes in the process of reference resolution, the task of the specification [**REFER** = *det*] of B2 is fulfilled and the characterization of B1 by [**REFER** = *indet*] dominates.

The use of the indefinite article when introducing a new concept and of the definite article when mentioning the concept again is a general regularity of German and English. If only non-composed isolated sentences are considered, the linguistic degree of determination in the article system and the determination of reference do really coincide. It is important that two concepts, which both bear the specification [**REFER** = *indet*] and which are described by different occurrences of the same natural language phrase, **not** be identified with each other.[10] Example:

(17.15)  Ge: *"Ein Kandidat [**REFER** = indet] unterstützte den Präsidenten*
          *und ein Kandidat [**REFER** = indet] unterstützte ihn nicht."*
     En: *"One candidate [**REFER** = indet] supported the president*
          *and one candidate [**REFER** = indet] did not support him."*

---

[10] Danger of wrong identification by "equivocation".

### 17.2.4    Variability (Attribute VARIA)

As already mentioned in the foregoing section, some differences in the readings of natural language expressions have to be represented by the distinction in whether a node at the preextensional level is considered a variable or a constant. This distinction is specified by means of the attribute **variability** (or VARIA). Its values have the following meanings:

[**VARIA** = con] – The node represents a fixed element of the preextensional level that does not change depending on the variation of other conceptual representatives.

[**VARIA** = var] – The node represents an element of the preextensional level that has to be considered a variable (a so-called **parameterized entity**). Such a node represents either every single element of a set (it runs, so to speak, over all elements of the set analogously to the interpretation of a universally quantified variable in logic), or the node represents an element of the set that changes depending on the extensional interpretation of another concept (analogously to an existentially quantified variable in logic whose interpretation depends on that of a universally quantified variable).

[**VARIA** = *varia*] – In the lexicon, generic concepts obtain the value [**VARIA** = *varia*] as their primary specification (underspecification of the attribute). This value is preserved with a pure plural description of a generic concept (line 7 in Table 17.2), but is instantiated to [**VARIA** = *con*] when describing a prototypical element of the extension of a generic concept (line 8 in Table 17.2).[11]

To illustrate the above definitions we consider the following sentences (Figure 17.5 shows the corresponding semantic representations):

(17.16)  *"There is <u>a book</u> [**VARIA** = con], which has been read by every student. [**VARIA** = var]"*

(17.17)  *"<u>Every student</u> [**VARIA** = var] bought <u>a new suit</u>." [**VARIA** = var]*

(17.18)  *"<u>Students</u> [**VARIA** = varia] read <u>books</u>." [**VARIA** = varia]*

The extensional of the node $k_1 = \langle$a book$\rangle$ in the representation of Sentence (17.16) is a fixed representative with [**VARIA** = *con*] which is independent of the student doing the reading. In contrast, the extensional of the node $k_2 = \langle$every student$\rangle$ is a parameterized individual running over the set of all students [**VARIA** = *var*], albeit independent of other nodes. Compared to that, the extensional of the node $k_3 = \langle$a new suit$\rangle$ depends on the student buying

---

[11] This assumption is based on the consideration that, on the one hand, a prototypical element is actually not fixed in its reference [**REFER** = *refer*] but, on the other hand, does not vary, i.e. [**VARIA** = *con*].

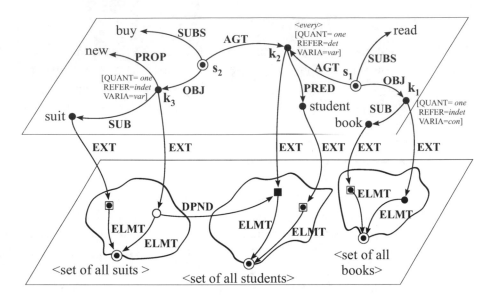

## Explanation of the symbols for nodes at the preextensional level

⊙  Representative of a set with [VARIA=*con*] (*Attention: At the intensional level, this symbol represents a situation (see Fig. 16.3); a mistake ought to be excluded, however, because the appropriate meaning can always be derived from the context*)

■  Node which definitely represents every element of a set [VARIA=*var*], [REFER=*det*] (*independently varying entity*)

○  Node which represents an indeterminate dependent element [VARIA=*var*], [REFER=*indet*] (*parameterized entity*)

●  Node representing a fixed (constant) entity [VARIA=*con*] which may be determinate [REFER=*det*] or indeterminate [REFER=*indet*]

◙  Node representing a prototypical element [VARIA=*varia*], [REFER=*refer*] (*extensional of a generic concept with* [GENER=*ge*])

**Figure 17.5.** Constant and variable elements at the preextensional level

the suit. In addition to the value of variability, this dependence is expressed by the nonsymmetric relation DPND at the preextensional level of MultiNet. Since every student buys another suit, the extensional of this concept (node $k_3$ in Fig. 17.5) bears the attribute value [**VARIA** = *var*] and is connected by the DPND relation to the extensional of node $k_2$ representing every single student.

To complete the illustration, the prototypical extensionals belonging to the generic concepts book, student, and suit are also represented in Fig. 17.5. These nodes (like the extensionals of the nodes $k_1$, $k_2$, and $k_3$) are elements of the set of all books, all students, or all suits, respectively. In contrast to the nodes $k_1$, $k_2$, and $k_3$, however, they bear the attribute value [**VARIA** = *varia*].

## 17.2.5   Facticity (Attribute FACT)

In natural language, one can explicitly or implicitly refer to the truth of states of affairs or to the existence of objects and thus also to the extensional interpretation of concepts or states of affairs in the philosophical sense. Since the content of a sentence may directly or indirectly refer to the real world or to possible worlds, this relationship must be taken into account in the knowledge representation itself (not outside of it, but at the preextensional level). For this end, a further attribute, the **facticity** (abbreviation FACT), has been introduced.

In the area of conceptual objects, existential statements like ⟨there is a(n)⟩, ⟨there is possibly a(n)⟩, ⟨there is no⟩, etc. require representational means such as those provided by the facticity attribute of MultiNet. Also the state of our world knowledge demands expressional means to distinguish objects by the information about whether they really exist (⟨Peter's car⟩, ⟨the Eiffel Tower⟩, ⟨New York⟩, ...), whether they are hypothetically assumed (quarks, ⟨black holes⟩, ...), or whether they are nonexisting imaginary objects (yetis, unicorns, ...); this can be expressed with the facticity attribute by selecting the following values: [**FACT** = real], [**FACT** = hypo], and [**FACT** = nonreal], respectively (the last is also written as [**FACT** = non]).[12]

The facticity attribute is also relevant to the treatment of **existential presuppositions** (implicit existential statements).[13] To elucidate, the following example sentences are used:

(17.19) *"The boy has got a new bicycle."*
(17.20) *"The tourist claimed that he had seen a UFO."*

The first sentence contains implicitly the statements (i.e. they can be derived) that the concepts ⟨the boy⟩ as well as ⟨a new bicycle⟩ correspond to existing

---

[12] We do not comment here on the existence of yetis. It is only shown in the examples that if yetis are taken as nonexistent objects or quarks as hypothetical ones, then this has to be represented in a MultiNet knowledge base by [**FACT** = *non*] or [**FACT** = *hypo*], respectively. The use of only three values for the attribute **FACT**, where distinctions are made between a real, a possible, and a nonexisting world, is of course a simplification. In general, this attribute could be used to distinguish and to index arbitrarily many possible worlds.

[13] A **presupposition** of a sentence S is a statement not explicitly expressed in S but following from S as well as from the negation of S.

objects. Both concepts obtain the values [**FACT** = *real*] in a MultiNet representation. Similar considerations apply to the concept ⟨the tourist⟩ in the second sentence. The situation is entirely different for the concept ⟨a UFO⟩, however, which is embedded in a modal context "*the tourist claimed*" (a so-called **opaque context**). From Sentence (17.20) one cannot conclude without further information that the UFO really exists (the tourist may lie or err). For this reason, this concept is assigned the attribute value [**FACT** − *hypo*], provided there is no additional knowledge source justifying the specification [**FACT** = *non*] or [**FACT** = *real*]. The attribute values *real*, *hypo*, and *nonreal* (abbreviated *non*) correspond respectively to the truth values **true**, **unknown**, and **false** of a three-valued logic. They characterize not only the existence or nonexistence of objects, but also the status of situations in general.[14]

Analogously to the existence of objects, natural language sentences also convey information about the validity or nonvalidity of arbitrary states of affairs ("*it holds*", "*it does not hold*", etc.). There are also means to express directly or indirectly that a situation is only imagined, only hypothetically assumed, or merely alleged, which suggests to the hearer/reader that the validity of the corresponding statement is at least uncertain ("*it is possibly the case that*", "*it is assumed that*", etc.). This information must also be reflected in the meaning representation of the corresponding sentences, thus requiring a characteristic like the attribute of facticity.

The attribute **FACT** is also important for the semantic representation of whole situations, such as those described by Sentences (17.19) and (17.20). While the representatives of the main clauses have to be characterized by [**FACT** = *real*] in both cases[15], the subordinate clause of Sentence (17.20), "*the tourist had seen a UFO*", must be assigned the attribute value [**FACT** = *hypo*]. This is justified by the observation that the content of an indirect propositional sentence generally has to be assigned an uncertain truth value in the absence of further information (cf. the relation MCONT). The semantic representation of conditional sentences or counterfactuals, which is also important for automatic language processing, can be adequately described only by explicitly including the attribute of facticity (see Sect. 11.2.3 and the relation COND).

Strictly speaking, the attribute **FACT** should be related not only to the real world and to that what is classified in this world as being valid/true, hypotheti-

---

[14] Although there seems to be a difference between the layer specification [**FACT** = *hypo*] and the truth value "unknown" from an epistemological point of view, the two characterizations are equivalent from the perspective of a language game. Thus, if we ask for the truth of a state of affairs whose specification is used to describe the premise of a condition (characterized by [**FACT** = *hypo*] in MultiNet), then the proper answer should be UNKNOWN.

[15] At least if one assumes that the speaker is telling the truth.

cally assumed, or invalid/not true following the common knowledge about the general state of affairs (at least for a certain moment). In a more general approach, one should rather specify with each fact or conceptual object in what world (in the real world or in the mental worlds of speakers $A_1, \ldots, A_n$) this fact or this conceptual object is assigned a certain degree of facticity (according to the conception of possible worlds in modal logic [146]). For such a fine-differentiation, the relation MCONT is provided in MultiNet, permitting the specification of different epistemic contexts.

### 17.2.6 Intensional Quantification (Attribute QUANT) and Preextensional Cardinality (Attribute CARD)

Articles, definite and indefinite numerals within a noun phrase, and determinative pronouns all contribute to two further aspects of the semantic representation (apart from the degree of generalization and determination of reference): firstly, they have a quantifying aspect which affects the intensional level of concept representations whose NL descriptions involve the linguistic expressions listed above; secondly, they specify the extension (cardinality) of such concepts by means of sets at the preextensional level.

Accordingly, the attribute of **quantification** (abbreviated QUANT) is introduced at the intensional level, and the attribute **cardinality** (abbreviated CARD) is introduced at the preextensional level. These two attributes are interrelated but not exchangeable. The following sentences shall be considered for illustration:

(17.21) *"Several students of class 9 made an excursion."*
(17.22) *"Seven of them came by bicycle."*

The intensionally quantifying term several is characterized by a certain vagueness so that it is not possible a priori to tell the number of students that ⟨several students of class 9⟩ refers to at the preextensional level. In general, however, it is possible to assume a certain ranking already at the intensional level, which gives a basis for the ordering of quantificators by increasing magnitude (in the sense that the extension of ⟨few XYZ⟩ is in any case smaller than ⟨almost all XYZ⟩). A first (admittedly rough) ranking could be

no → one → two → few → several → many → most → almost all → all.

These quantificators represent only one detail of the whole spectrum of possible values of the attribute **QUANT** (see Fig. 9.1).[16]

---

[16] It was remarked already in Chap. 9 that the values of the attribute **QUANT**, strictly speaking, cannot be linearly ordered in a total ordering (rather, they constitute a partial ordering). So the concepts some and few are not comparable in contrast to few and many; few ≤ many.

All terminal values of the attribute **QUANT** except for *one* and *all* are fuzzy. This is the reason they are grouped into the type *fquant* (see Fig. 17.4); correspondingly, the quantificator *all* is assigned the type *nfquant* (the abbreviations stand for "fuzzy" and "nonfuzzy" quantificators). This distinction has consequences also for the inference processes in a QAS. A very thorough investigation of NL quantificators considering their fuzziness and their logical properties stems from Glöckner [78].[17]

It must be emphasized that quantificators, in contrast to all other terminal values of layer attributes, are themselves concepts represented by nodes of the SN with sort *qf*. They may even be modified by means of the function *MODQ, resulting in more complex quantificators assigned the special type **c-quant**. Quantificators are subject to special meaning postulates expressing their ordering.

As already mentioned, the values of the attribute **QUANT** at the intensional level have their counterparts (at least in principle) in the cardinalities of sets (attribute **CARD**) at the preextensional level. These cardinalities are often not given explicitly; they can usually be deduced or bounded only by means of background knowledge. While the values of the attribute **QUANT** are concepts of sort *qf*, the values of **CARD** are natural numbers n or m, or intervals of natural numbers (written n .. m, $\leq$ n, $\geq$ n, etc.).

The following conclusions can be drawn, for instance, from the Sentences (17.21) and (17.22). The description of the concept $B_1$ = ⟨several students of class 9⟩ means certainly that, for the extension of $B_1$, [**CARD** $\leq$ 40]. This cardinality can be deduced on the basis of background knowledge about the number of students in a typical class of a school. From the information given in the second sentence, the value [**CARD** $\geq$ 8] for the extensional of node $B_1$ can be derived. Thus, the value of **CARD** can be restricted at least to the interval 8 .. 40 (or, if we assume that, by default, several means ⟨less than the half⟩, we can even further restrict this interval to 8 .. 20. Similar considerations apply to the concept $B_2$ = ⟨most students of class 9⟩ (see Fig. 17.6).

In natural language, the values of the attribute **QUANT** are often paraphrased by complex phrases like *"very few"*, *"more than the half"*, etc., whereas the values of the attribute **CARD** are always described by means of natural numbers, possibly modified by graduators like *"greater/more than"* or *"smaller/less than"*.

---

Quantificators and negators overlap in the concept no (Ge: kein; used attributively in NL), where no is normally represented as negator (see Sect. 8.2).

[17] Note that the non-fuzziness of quantificators like *"two / three / four / ..."* (i.e. of **natural numbers**) is warranted by the combined characterization [**QUANT** = *mult*], neutral with regard to fuzziness, and the crisp characterization [**CARD** = {2 / 3 / 4 / ... }].

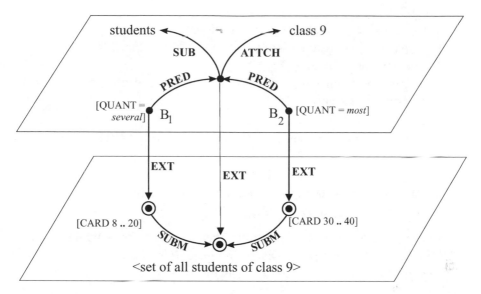

**Figure 17.6.** The cooperation of (intensional) quantification and cardinality at the preextensional level

Since cardinalities of extensionals can in general be derived only by inference processes (except for cases where they are immediately recognizable by the quantificators), they are omitted in the following discussion and especially in Table 17.2. In addition, the convention will be used that attributes not applicable to a certain concept are also disregarded there.

### 17.2.7  Type of Extensionality (Attribute ETYPE)

In the same way as sorts and features are used in signatures to specify at the intensional level which MultiNet relations and functions can in principle describe certain relationships between conceptual representatives, a classification of nodes is needed to achieve the analogue at the preextensional level. Thus, the element relation ELMT can hold only between an individual extensional which is not a set and a proper set, or between a set and a family of sets, and so on (see the definition of the relation ELMT). Similarly, a subset relation can hold only between two sets of the same type (see the definition of the relation SUBM). To formulate these regularities, the attribute **type of extensionality** (abbreviation ETYPE) is used whose values are summarily described in the following (**[ETYPE=nil]** characterizes concepts like intention, religiosity, etc., which have no extension):

**0** – Representative of an elementary extensional which is itself not a set.
Examples: the extensionals of ⟨the house⟩, Max, ⟨this school⟩, . . .

**1** – Set of elements of type 0
Examples: the extensionals of ⟨several children⟩, ⟨three cars⟩,
⟨the crew⟩, ⟨a family⟩, . . .

**2** – Set of elements of type 1
Examples: the extensionals of ⟨three crews⟩, ⟨many organizations⟩, . . .

**3** – Set of elements of type 2
Example: the extensional of ⟨two umbrella organizations⟩, where
⟨umbrella organization⟩ is a concept already denoting a group of organi-
zations (characterized by type 2).

It must be remarked with regard to cardinalities that the corresponding attribute
**CARD** is not applicable to extensionals of type 0. For an extensional E of type
n, the cardinality is the number of the elements of E with type (n-1).

### 17.2.8   The Classification of Nominal Concepts

An adequate classification of quantified noun phrases is a particularly difficult
problem (especially if it has to be solved automatically). On the one hand, it
should correctly reflect the differences in the meaning of noun phrases and,
on the other hand, it should also be a sound basis for inference and generation
processes. An approach in this direction, which was developed within a logical
framework, is the Generalized Quantifier Theory [15] (see Sect. 15.3.4) which,
to the best of our knowledge, has never been used in a large-scale NLP application. We propose a subcategorization of nominal concepts that includes all
attributes dealt with in Sects. 17.2.2 through 17.2.7 and is adapted more to the
needs of natural language processing. This approach has the advantage that the
values of the layer attributes for concepts described by complex noun phrases
can be derived from elementary constituents (i.e. from determiners, quantificators, and nouns) by means of layer unification based on information stemming
from the lexicon [99].

Table 17.2 shows the values of the semantic attributes **GENER** (degree of
generality), **REFER** (determination of reference), **VARIA** (variability), **FACT**
(facticity), **QUANT** (intensional quantification), and **ETYPE** (type of extensionality) for typical nominal concepts described by noun phrases with determiners and quantificators.[18]

---

[18] The attribute **CARD** is left out for the sake of brevity though, in many cases, its values can
easily be derived from the description of the concept.

| No. | GENER | REFER | VARIA | FACT | QUANT | ETYPE |
|-----|-------|-------|-------|------|-------|-------|
| 1 | *sp* | *det* | *con* | *real* | *one* | *0* |
| | Example: "*This bear* has a thick fur." | | | | | |
| 2 | *sp* | *det* | *con* | *non* | *one* | *0* |
| | Example: "*This unicorn* is harmless." | | | | | |
| 3 | *sp* | *indet* | *con* | *hypo* | *one* | *0* |
| | Example: "He believed that he had discovered *a new planet* ." | | | | | |
| 4 | *sp* | *indet* | *var* | *real* | *one* | *0* |
| | Example: "Everybody has already seen *a plane*." | | | | | |
| 5 | *sp* | *det* | *con* | *real* | *one* | *1* |
| | Example: "*The Alps* are the natural habitat of the ibex." | | | | | |
| 6 | *sp* | *det* | *con* | *real* | *mult* | *1* |
| | Example: "*The bears in the zoo of XX* are especially aggressive." | | | | | |
| 7 | *ge* | *refer* | *varia* | *real* | *mult* | *1* |
| | Example: "*Bears* are aggressive animals." | | | | | |
| 8 | *ge* | *refer* | *con* | *real* | *one* | *0* |
| | Example: {The / A} "*bear* is an aggressive animal." | | | | | |
| 9 | *gener* | *det* | *con* | *real* | *all* | *1* |
| | Example: "*All bears* are dangerous." | | | | | |
| 10 | *sp* | *det* | *var* | *real* | *one* | *0* |
| | Example: "*Every bear* has its own sleeping place." | | | | | |
| 11 | *sp* | *indet* | *con* | *real* | *one* | *0* |
| | Example: "All boys entered *one boat*". | | | | | |
| 12 | *sp* | *indet* | *var* | *real* | *one* | *0* |
| | Example: "Every boy entered *another boat*." | | | | | |
| 13 | *ge* | *indet* | *var* | *real* | *mult* | *1* + [**CARD**=2] |
| | Example: "*Two dogs* are easier to keep than one." | | | | | |
| 14 | *ge* | *indet* | *var* | *real* | *one* | *0* + [**CARD**=1] |
| | Example: "*One parrot* is more difficult to keep than two." | | | | | |
| 15 | *ge* | *refer* | *con* | *real* | *one* | *1* |
| | Example: "The behavior of *a crowd* is sometimes difficult to foresee." | | | | | |
| 16 | *sp* | *det* | *con* | *real* | *one* | *1* |
| | Example: "The police scattered *the crowd*." | | | | | |
| 17 | *sp* | *indet* | *con* | *real* | *many* | *2* |
| | Example:"The police have already scattered *many crowds*." | | | | | |
| 18 | *ge* | *refer* | *varia* | *real* | *several* | *2* |
| | Example: "*An umbrella organization* consists of several organizations." | | | | | |
| 19 | *gener* | *det* | *con* | *real* | *all* | *3* |
| | Example: "The president visited *all umbrella organizations*." | | | | | |

**Table 17.2.** Subcategorization of nominal concepts

Every bundle of layer information in the table is illustrated by a typical concept. The noun phrase describing the concept in question is underlined in the corresponding sample sentence.

It should be remembered that the layer specification of lexical entries is in general different from that of concepts. Lexemes are characterized by values of layer attributes that are as specific as possible but as underspecified as necessary to allow for correct layer unification in every admissible combination with determiners and quantificators (see Chap. 10 and [99] for an explanation of the unification process).

In the following, some important phenomena in the field of noun phrases and their classificatory embedding into the layer system shall be discussed on the basis of the attributes described above (see Table 17.2).

- **Individual concepts**: Concepts designating elementary individuals with a fixed identity are characterized by means of the attribute values [**GENER** = *sp*], [**VARIA** = *con*], and [**ETYPE** = *0*] (Examples: lines 1 through 3 and 11). In this context we speak of "elementary" individuals because the foregoing characterization (except for the attribute **ETYPE**) is also encountered with collective nouns, which often denote individuals of higher order (see below).
- **Generic concepts**: Ordinary generalized concepts (generic concepts) are specified by [**GENER** = *ge*], [**REFER** = *refer*], and [**VARIA** = *con*]. The type of extensionality is generally [**ETYPE** = *0*] because the extensional of a normal generic concept B is a prototypical element of the set ⟨all B⟩ (Exceptions are collective concepts, like crowd, where the attribute **ETYPE** has a value > *0*; see line 15). The attribute values [**REFER** = *refer*] and [**VARIA** = *con*] have been chosen because a generic concept does not determine the reference; it is related rather to an underspecified prototypical element which does not vary (Example: line 8). Generic concepts play an important role in knowledge representations because they are connected with different methods of inheritance governing the transfer of knowledge from superordinate entities to subordinate, more specific, entities (see relations SUB and SUBS in Part II and Sect. 3.1).
- **Collective concepts**: Concepts characterized as individual concepts at the intensional level but having an extensionality type greater than zero are called "collective concepts" (Examples: lines 5, 15, and 16). Thus, concepts like ⟨a crew⟩ or ⟨the family⟩ are treated in the first instance as normal individuals at the intensional level. They permit, however, a contextual embedding, e.g. the application of predicates that are otherwise admissible only for pluralities, e.g. zerstritten (En: ⟨being in quarrel with⟩) or ausrotten/ausgerottet (En: extinguish/⟨be extinct⟩); the analogue holds for generic collective concepts. The increase of the order of extensionality by 1 leads naturally to the effect that a concept described by a collective noun used in plural form (except for plural nouns, like "*police*", that have no plural form) is of type [**ETYPE** = 2] (Example: line 17) or, in rare cases, of type [**ETYPE** = 3] (Example: line 19).

- **Parameterized entities**: Concepts bearing the attribute value [**VARIA** = *var*] are called "parameterized entities" because they play a role similar to quantified variables in logic-oriented knowledge representations (Examples: lines 4, 10, and 12). Thereby we have to distinguish between independent and dependent parameterized entities at the preextensional level, which are respectively characterized by the lack or presence of an additional DPND relation in their specification. The latter is typical of an existentially quantified concept depending on a universally quantified concept specified by the quantificators "*all*" or "*every*" (Examples: lines 4 and 12).
- **Generalized pluralities**: Concepts described by a generalized plural construction (Example: line 13) have scarcely been taken into account in the literature. However, there is a clear distinction in the meaning of the phrase "*two dogs*" in the sentences:

  (17.23) "*Two dogs are easier to keep than one.*"
  (17.24) "*Max owns two dogs*".

The semantic difference is essentially expressed by the degree of generalization [**GENER** = *ge*] vs. [**GENER** = *sp*]. The specialty that the "collection" consists of only one element (Example: line 14) can be considered a borderline case which organically fits into this distinction. These concepts should nevertheless be distinguished from classical generic concepts because, in this case, there is cognitively no prototypical element connected with corresponding methods of default reasoning (see Sect. 17.3). Here, the values of the attributes **REFER**, **VARIA**, and **QUANT** are different from *refer*, *con*, and *one*, which characterize classical generic concepts. The choice of [**REFER** = *indet*] and [**VARIA** = *var*] in lines 13 and 14 expresses that the corresponding concepts stand for any two dogs or any parrot, respectively.

# 17.3 The Encapsulation of Concepts (Immanent vs. Situational Knowledge)

To represent the **scope of meaning** of a concept within a knowledge representation, specific expressional means are needed, since otherwise it would be impossible to specify which relational links (arcs) actually define a certain concept and which are mere pointers to the concept in question.[19] In MultiNet, the limitation of the scope of meaning is specified by means of **encapsulation** of concepts. The different components contained in such a conceptual capsule

---

[19] Purely logical representations do not in general have such expressional means.

are shown in Fig. 17.7a. A conceptual capsule is graphically represented as a rectangle divided into several parts corresponding to different meaning components.

In the first instance, there are two different parts which have to be distinguished:

- **Immanent knowledge**: This comprises the portion of knowledge which is essential for the scope of meaning of a concept, and which is independent of the situational embedding or the more or less contingent use of the concept in the description of a special situation (the immanent knowledge is represented by means of dark or light shading in the graphical representation).
- **Situational knowledge**: This comprises the portion of knowledge which specifies how a certain concept is involved in the description of special situations (the situational knowledge is represented by a field showing no shading in the graphical representation).

For the sake of elucidation, we take the concept house of Fig. 17.7b: The opinion that a house always consists of parts like roof, windows, etc. is considered immanent knowledge. The facts that Peter has bought a house or that the prices of houses in Munich are growing do not belong to the immanent knowledge about houses, but to the situational knowledge, i.e. to those parts of the knowledge base where the concept house is only used in the description of specific situations.

Within the immanent knowledge one has to distinguish again between two different parts, namely a **categorical part** (this component is darkly shaded in the graphical representation and is labeled K) and a **prototypical part**, also called **default knowledge** and is met a priori with generic concepts only (this component is lightly shaded in the graphical representation and is labeled by a $D$[20]). The essential distinction between these components is related to the inferential processes connected with these knowledge parts.

The **categorical part** of the scope of a generic concept is strictly inherited by all subordinate concepts and specializations without any exception (see relation SUB). From a logical point of view, the predications expressed in the categorical part are connected to a universal quantification. Given the specification of the concept house of Fig. 17.7b, this means that every special house (⟨a villa⟩, ⟨a storehouse⟩, ⟨Paul's new house⟩, etc.) is a building, has a roof, and can be characterized by a certain year of erection.

---

[20] The term **default knowledge** also explains the abbreviation D for prototypical knowledge. The label K is derived from the German term "kategorisch".

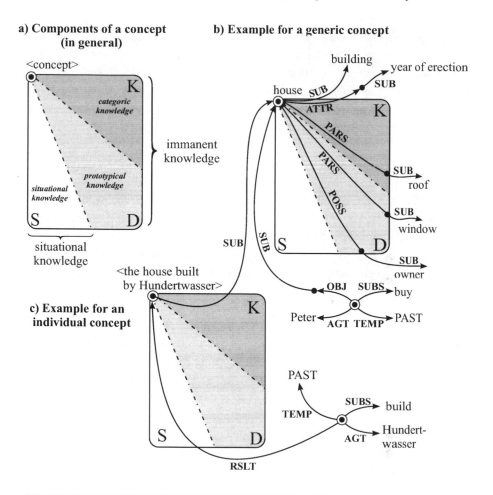

**a) Components of a concept (in general)**

**b) Example for a generic concept**

**c) Example for an individual concept**

| **K** immanent (categorical): | A house is a building; it always has a roof and is characterized by its year of erection. |
|---|---|
| **D** immanent (prototypical): | A house (usually) has windows and (in general) an owner. |
| **S** situational & assertional: | Peter has bought a house. [OBJ+SUB outside upper capsule b)] |
| situational & definitional: | The house built by Hundertwasser [RSLT inside lower capsule c)] |

**Figure 17.7.** Value types of the attribute K-TYPE for assigning different knowledge types to the arcs of an SN

In contrast, the **prototypical part** of a generic concept is inherited only as default knowledge in the conceptual hierarchy from top to bottom.[21] Thereby, a **default** is a basic assumption holding as long as there is no other information available. Unlike categorical knowledge, it can be overwritten or revised (because of that, one sometimes speaks of an inheritance mechanism **override** in AI; see the inheritance types of KEE [280]). So it is reasonable to assume for a house, for instance, that it has windows and doors or that it is owned by somebody. But one may also think of houses having no windows or no doors (a storehouse without windows, a Pueblo house without a door but with a hatch in the ceiling, etc.); a house may also have been abandoned, i.e. it may have lost its owner, etc. It should be clear that categorical knowledge is connected with **strictly monotonic** inferences, which are typical of the classical predicate calculus, while prototypical knowledge is characterized by **nonmonotonic** inferences, which can be described by the methods of **default reasoning** [212].

Immanent and situational knowledge are categorized as **semantically descriptive knowledge** because they are used to describe objects and situations. In contrast, there are also parts of knowledge (conditions, modal restrictions, contextual specifications) that do not describe objects and situations in the proper sense; rather, they restrict the conditions for their existence (in the case of objects) or the range of their validity (in the case of situations). This type of knowledge is called **semantically restrictive knowledge**.

For an adequate representation of these differences, the arcs of the SN are classified separately with regard to their start and end nodes according to the different knowledge types. This information is expressed by means of the attribute **K-TYPE** (an acronym for *"knowledge type"*). For this purpose, the types of incoming and outgoing arcs are specified for each node in the network. The admissible values of **K-TYPE**, which are subtypes of the general type *k-type*, are summarized in Fig. 17.8. The terminal values correspond to the four basic types of knowledge already explained above.

It must be emphasized that every arc ($k_1$ REL $k_2$) labeled by a relation REL and leading from a node $k_1$ to a node $k_2$ is in general characterized by different values of the attribute **K-TYPE** with regard to the two nodes $k_1$ and $k_2$ (see Part I, Table 3.2).

Examples:

- (⟨this flea⟩ SUB insect)
  The SUB arc is of type *categ* with regard to the concept ⟨this flea⟩ because it is an intrinsic part of the description of this concept that it is an insect.

---

[21] An individual concept can also obtain default knowledge by inheritance, which may be overruled by the acquisition of new, more specific knowledge.

On the other hand, the concept insect is not immanently characterized by including individual fleas in its description. Because of this, the SUB arc is of type *situa* with regard to the node insect.

- (⟨grass⟩ PROP green)
This PROP arc is of type *proto* with regard to grass, since the color of grass is typically green (there is also yellow, dried grass). The concept green is not inherently determined in its meaning by including the concept grass. Therefore, the PROP arc is of type *situa* with regard to the end node green.

Values of the attribute
K-TYPE

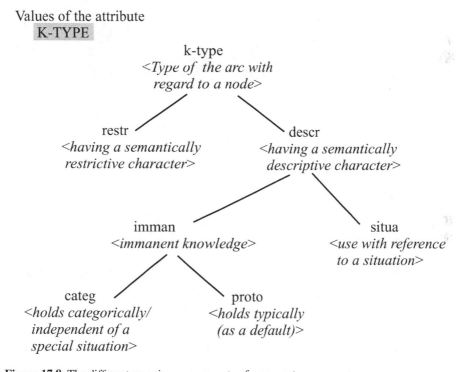

**Figure 17.8.** The different meaning components of a concept

The distinction between immanent and situational knowledge on the one hand, and definitional and assertional knowledge on the other hand, was explained already in Sect. 3.2.3. As the examples of Fig. 17.7 show, there is situational knowledge that belongs to the definitional part of a concept (i.e. it is included in the concept capsule) as well as situational knowledge that is considered assertional knowledge (staying outside of the capsule). There is also immanent knowledge that belongs to the assertional part, as well as immanent knowledge that belongs to the definitional part of knowledge (see Fig. 3.7).

# Chapter 18

# Relational and Functional Means of Representation

## 18.1 Overview

Relationships between conceptual entities (and therefore also between the nodes of a semantic network) are represented in MultiNet by means of semantically primitive relations and functions chosen from a fixed repository of representational means. To provide a better overview of the more than 140 relations and functions of MultiNet, a survey organized by thematic areas is presented in Figs. 18.1 through 18.4. The illustration should not be taken as a classification in the strict sense[1]; they should rather allow for quick access to the corresponding expressional means if one has to decide which of the representational elements should be used for a certain semantic phenomenon of interest.

In the introductory overview (Fig. 18.1), the representational means are divided at the top according to their association with the intensional or the preextensional level. While the relations and functions of the intensional level are used mainly to describe conceptual objects and situations (states of affairs), the representational means of the preextensional level are employed mainly for the description of set relations and for the interlinking of intensionals and extensionals. A special role is played by the lexical relations, which connect the meanings of words with each other. They are therefore used in applied NLP systems for the specification of entries in the computational lexicon. Since lexical relations always establish semantic connections between generic concepts, they have to be associated with the intensional level.

With regard to the description of conceptual objects, one can roughly distinguish representational means for the inner, structural, or qualitative description of objects (intraobjective description) from representational means establishing relationships between different objects (interobjective description).[2]

---

[1] This can be recognized by the fact that certain relations are grouped into different branches. In this case, the second (less typical) use is marked by use of parentheses.

[2] It should be observed that the term "object" is used as a shorthand for concrete and abstract conceptual objects.

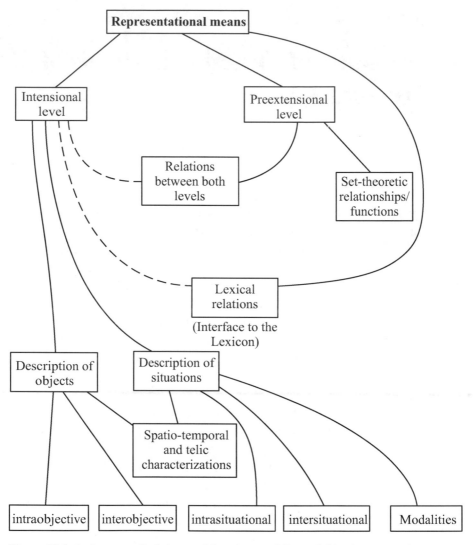

**Figure 18.1.** Assignment of relations and functions to different fields of representation

In addition, there are the descriptional means for the spatio-temporal characterizations of objects and for the telic characterizations concerning the origins, the purposes, or the aims of objects. Strictly speaking, the relations and functions of these two groups should be clearly distinguished from the spatio-temporal and telic representational means for situations (see Fig. 18.3). For this reason, the names of the corresponding relations are marked with a prefix "O-" for the time being. Since the spatio-temporal and telic characterization in the area of objects can be seen as a shorthand notation of the corresponding descriptions in the situational area (relations without the "O-" prefix), we have decided to omit this distinction and to use the same names (without the prefix) in both areas. This decision is justified by the strict classification of nodes into sorts and by the following systematic relationships making the proper distinction visible again:

(18.1) "[the natives]$^{\text{O-LOC}_{arg1}}$ [in Borneo]$^{\text{O-LOC}_{arg2}}$" –
     "the natives [living]$^{\text{LOC}_{arg1}}$ [in Borneo]$^{\text{LOC}_{arg2}}$"

(18.2) "[books]$^{\text{O-TEMP}_{arg1}}$ [from the Middle Ages]$^{\text{O-TEMP}_{arg2}}$" –
     "books which were [written]$^{\text{TEMP}_{arg1}}$
                    [in the Middle Ages]$^{\text{TEMP}_{arg2}}$"

(18.3) "[the train]$^{\text{O-DIRCL}_{arg1}}$ [to Hamburg]$^{\text{O-DIRCL}_{arg2}}$" –
     "the train [going]$^{\text{DIRCL}_{arg1}}$ [to Hamburg]$^{\text{DIRCL}_{arg2}}$"

(18.4) "[a device]$^{\text{O-PURP}_{arg1}}$ [for welding]$^{\text{O-PURP}_{arg2}}$" –
     "a device which [is used]$^{\text{PURP}_{arg1}}$ [for welding]$^{\text{PURP}_{arg2}}$" etc.

The most important relation in the area of object descriptions is the subordination relation SUB, which establishes a hierarchical structure of conceptual objects connected to certain inheritance mechanisms, whereby specializations and subconcepts inherit information from their superconcepts (see Sect. 4.1).

Analogously to objects, the descriptional means for situations can be classified at the upper level into intrasituational and intersituational relations (see Fig. 18.3). For a further characterization of situations, spatio-temporal, telic and modal specifications are included. The intrasituational representational means are differentiated according to Tesnière [256] into roles describing the embedding of situations in their environment (called **circonstants** or **circumstances**) and roles characterizing objects participating in these situations (called **participants**). Objects participating in states generally fill other roles than participants of events. But there are also certain kinds of states (like ⟨hold on to⟩ and ⟨cling to⟩) actively maintained by an agent, which is normally the carrier of an action. For that reason, the corresponding participant must additionally be linked to the representative of such a state through AGT.

Also, one can define hierarchies of concepts for situations or states of affairs. These are specified with the relation SUBS, which is connected to the inheritance of valency frames. However, the inheritance mechanism of SUBS is more complex than that of SUB (see Sect. 5.2.2) and must be described by axiom schemata.

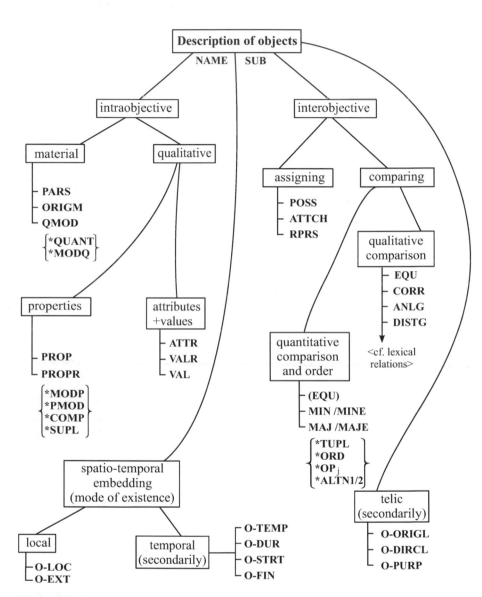

**Figure 18.2.** Semantic characterization of objects

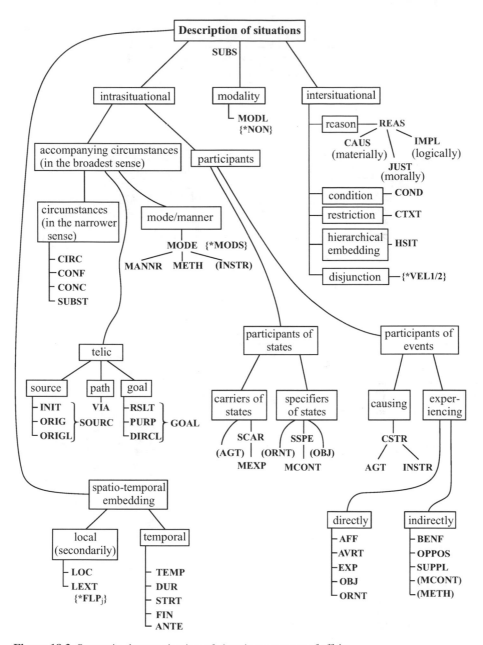

**Figure 18.3.** Semantic characterization of situations or states of affairs

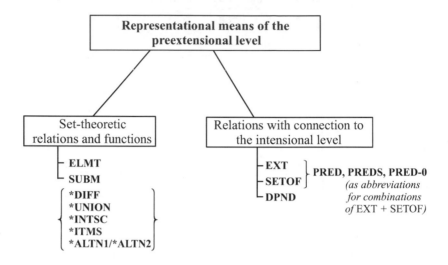

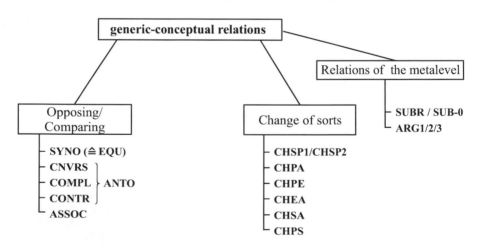

**Figure 18.4.** Representational means of the preextensional level and of the lexicon

The representational means of the preextensional level are essentially those of naive set theory, carried mainly by element and subset relations and by set operations. A specialty is the relation DPND describing the dependence of one extensional on another (see Sect. 17.2.4). The fact that this relation has to be associated with the preextensional level can be seen from an example. In the first spontaneous understanding of the sentence

*"Every student bought a new suit."* (cf. Sentence 17.17 and Fig. 17.5),

the semantic representatives of the two noun groups each constitute a separate unit, and the hearer is generally not reflecting any deeper on the exact dependencies between them. However, one may ask (upon closer inspection of the sentence) which students bought which suit. In this case, we inquire about what this sentence asserts about every student and suit bought by them, thus asking for the precise relation between the elements in the corresponding sets of students and suits. It is then, and only then, that the dependency between particular students and suits becomes relevant. It is exactly by this mental resolution of concepts into elements of their extension during a deeper semantic analysis of the sentence, that the transition to the extensional level is carried out.

A further group of representational means is given by the relations connecting the representatives of the intensional level (called "intensionals") with their corresponding counterpart at the preextensional level (called "extensionals"). Finally, one has to mention lexical relations, which are associated with terms like "synonymy" and "antonymy" or with the possibilities of changes between different sorts of concepts. The relations indicating a change of sorts find their counterpart in natural language in the phenomenon of a change in part of speech, typically induced in German by the use of productive suffixes in derivational processes at the word level.

Having explained the organization of the representational means in general, we shall consider now the basic relations and functions proposed in MultiNet.

## 18.2    Relations

### 18.2.1    AFF: C-Role – Affected Object

**AFF:** $[dy \cup ad] \times [o \cup si]$

**Definition:** (e AFF o) expresses the relation between an event e and an object o affected by e in such a way that o is changed. o is immediately acted upon by e.

**Mnemonics:** En: affect (Ge: affizieren / beeinflussen)
    (e AFF o) – [e affects / changes o]

**Question pattern:** ⟨WH⟩ {[change] / [be changed] by} ⟨si⟩?
Upon which ⟨o⟩ is ⟨dy⟩ acting?
⟨WH⟩ [be] {influenced / impaired / affected / destroyed ... } by ⟨si⟩?
By what event is ⟨o⟩ affected?
What did happen to ⟨o⟩?

**Explanation:** The relation AFF is closely associated wit the concept change $\in ad$, which is formally expressed by the B-Axioms:

- (e AFF o) → (e SUBS change)                                                    (115)
- (e SUBS change) → ∃ o (e AFF o)                                               (116)

The concept change can be considered the semantic representative of the class of all verbs whose valency frame contains AFF. The relation AFF is also characterized by a transition from an initial situation to a final situation which are different from each other, where the former holds before execution and the latter holds after execution of the action designated by e (see relations INIT and RSLT, respectively). Typical representatives of actions having AFF in their valency frame are: increase, transform, destroy, melt, ...

The extension of the domain of the second argument of AFF to situations (i.e. to events and states) is motivated by "meta-actions" like ⟨give rise to⟩, ⟨interfere with⟩, accelerate, ⟨slow down⟩, finish, etc., which do affect events or states. An example of a representation involving such a "meta-action" is shown in Fig. 18.5.

The decision about whether a certain cognitive role has to be classified as AFF is not unproblematic. Especially the boundary to the C-Role OBJ cannot be drawn sharply because the criteria for discerning C-Roles, summarized in Fig. 5.8, include fuzzy concepts (*"When is an object really changed by an event?"* or *"When is an object directly involved in an event?"*). This decision obviously cannot be made on the basis of the verbal concept alone. In many cases, the meaning of adverbial adjuncts plays also an important role ("*He was {violently / terribly} hit on the head*" → AFF vs. "*He was slightly hit on the head*" → OBJ). Because of that, the B-Axioms assigned to AFF have to be qualified as default knowledge.

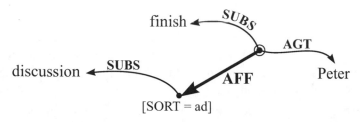

**Figure 18.5.** Example of a "meta-action" (here, finish) affecting a situation

The following example contrasts the relation AFF with OBJ:

(18.5) "*The smoker* [*bites*]$^{AFF+OBJ_{arg1}}$ [*the tip*]$^{OBJ_{arg2}}$ *off* [*the cigar*]$^{AFF_{arg2}}$."

It should be remarked that states cannot be connected through the relation AFF with other concepts because of the meaning postulate (115). From a state s characterized by the C-Role AFF we could infer that s is subordinate to the concept change, which contradicts the concept of a state.

## 18.2.2   AGT: C-Role – Agent

**AGT:** $[si \cup abs] \times o$

**Definition:** In its standard interpretation, the expression (e AGT o) with e ∈ $[da \cup ad] \subset [si \cup abs]$ characterizes the relation between an event e or, to be specific, an action e and a conceptual object o which actively causes e (i.e. o is originating/sustaining/giving rise to e). In other words, o is the active object (the agent or carrier of the action).

   The relation AGT was extended to states, where (s AGT o) with s ∈ $[st \cup as] \subset [si \cup abs]$ means that the object o actively sustains the state s.

**Mnemonics:** En: agent (Ge: Agent / Handlungsträger)
      (e AGT o) – [e is carried out by o]

**Question pattern:** $\langle WH \rangle \langle da \rangle$?
$\langle WH \rangle$ [do] {carry out / push forward / give rise to / ... } $\langle da \rangle$?
What [do] $\langle o \rangle$ do?
$\langle WH \rangle$ [do] {actively carry out the action / actively sustain the state}?
By $\langle WM \rangle \langle pass\text{-}act \rangle$?
  ($\langle pass\text{-}act \rangle$ denotes the class of all actions which are described by passive constructions.)

**Explanation:** If an action is described by a natural language sentence in the active mood, the agent of this action (if there is an agent) is normally described by the subject in the surface structure of the sentence. However, the subject of a sentence need not always be the agent.

In contrast to opinions sometimes held in the literature, the agent need not necessarily be animated. So objects like $\langle \textsf{a firm} \rangle$, $\langle \textsf{an institution} \rangle$, or $\langle \textsf{legal persons} \rangle$ may in general also function as agents. Even inanimate objects, like $\langle \textsf{a motor} \rangle$ or $\langle \textsf{a turbine} \rangle$, which inherently possess an inner power, are admissible as agents.

To characterize whether or not a certain object may become an active agent, a special feature POTAG (for **potential agent**) with boolean values [POTAG$\pm$] was introduced; see Sect. 17.1. This feature also helps distinguish general causators (see relation CSTR) from autonomously and actively working agents.

This characteristic can be expressed by the following B-Axiom:

- (e AGT o) $\rightarrow$ (e SUBS act) $\wedge$ (o PROP $\langle \textsf{capable of acting} \rangle$) $\wedge$
$$\exists s \, [s = (o \text{ PROP } \textsf{active})] \wedge (s \text{ DUR } e) \tag{117}$$

The relation AGT is a specialization of the relation CSTR, i.e. the following holds:

- (e AGT o) $\rightarrow$ (e CSTR o) $\tag{118}$

Examples:
Event having an agent:

(18.6) "$[Max]^{\text{AGT}_{arg2}}$ $[is\ playing]^{\text{AGT}_{arg1}}$ guitar."

State having an agent:

(18.7) "$[The\ ape]^{\text{AGT}_{arg2}}$ $[keeps\ a\ firm\ hold]^{\text{AGT}_{arg1}}$ of the branch."

Event with a causator which is not an agent:

(18.8) "$[The\ sand]^{\text{CSTR}_{arg2}}$ $[slowed\ down]^{\text{CSTR}_{arg1}}$ the vehicle."

### 18.2.3  ANLG2/3: Similarity Between Entities

**ANLG2/3:**  Binary and ternary variant of the similarity relation.

| | |
|---|---|
| ANLG/2: $[\ddot{si} \cup \ddot{o}] \times at$ | (binary) |
| ANLG/3: $([si \times si] \cup [o \times o]) \times at$ | (ternary) |

**Definition:** The ternary relationship $(o_1 \; \text{ANLG/3} \; o_2 \; a)$ states the similarity of the objects or situations $o_1$ and $o_2$ with regard to the attribute a. The relation ANLG/3 is symmetric with regard to the first two arguments.

**Annotation:** Since similarities of the same kind may be observed between more than two objects, the binary relation ANLG/2: $[\ddot{si} \cup \ddot{o}] \times at$ with a plurality as its first argument is introduced to achieve a more compact representation and generalization. The relationship $(\ddot{g} \; \text{ANLG/2} \; a)$ expresses the similarity of the elements of a whole class $\ddot{g}$ of objects with regard to the attribute a and, in this way, replaces a whole collection of ternary similarity relations between the elements of $\ddot{g}$ (see Axiom (119)).

**Mnemonics:** En: analogue (Ge: analog)
$(\ddot{g} \; \text{ANLG/2} \; a)$ – [the elements of $\ddot{g}$ are similar to each other with regard to a]
$(o_1 \; \text{ANLG/3} \; o_2 \; a)$ – [$o_1$ is similar to $o_2$ with regard to the attribute a]

**Question pattern:**
In {which attribute / what way} are $\langle o_1 \, / \, si_1 \rangle$ and $\langle o_2 \, / \, si_2 \rangle$ similar?
Which $\langle o_1 \, / \, si_1 \rangle$ [do] resemble $\langle o_2 \, / \, si_2 \rangle$ with regard to the attribute a?

**Explanation:** The connection between the ternary relation ANLG/3 and the binary relation ANLG/2 is described by the following axiom:

- $(\ddot{g} \; \text{ANLG/2} \; a) \leftrightarrow \forall x \, \forall y \; [(x \; \text{ELMT} \; \ddot{g}_{EXT}) \wedge (y \; \text{ELMT} \; \ddot{g}_{EXT}) \wedge (x \neq y)$
$$\rightarrow (x \; \text{ANLG/3} \; y \; a)] \qquad\qquad (119)$$

The term "similarity" designates a *fuzzy concept* and can therefore be described only with difficulties by axiomatic means, since entities x and y in the relation (x ANLG2/3 y a) need not completely conform to each other with regard to the value of the specified attribute, but conform only in a more or less determined degree. For the similarity of objects, the following axiomatic relationship can be stated:[3]

---

[3] Since the number of arguments uniquely shows which of the two relations is used in a certain context, the explicit indication of the arity in the name of the relation may be omitted (see the corresponding convention used in logical programming languages [48]). Thus, (g ANLG a) means (g ANLG/2 a), and (x ANLG y a) means (x ANLG/3 y a).

- $(o_1 \text{ ATTR } a_1) \wedge (o_2 \text{ ATTR } a_2) \wedge (a_1 \text{ SUB } a) \wedge (a_2 \text{ SUB } a) \wedge (o_1 \neq o_2) \wedge$
  $(a_1 \text{ VAL } v_1) \wedge (a_2 \text{ VAL } v_2) \wedge [(v_1 \text{ CORR } v_2) \vee (v_1 \text{ EQU } v_2)]$
  $$\rightarrow (o_1 \text{ ANLG } o_2 \text{ a}) \tag{120}$$

Corresponding to the verbal definition given above one can further state

- $(o_1 \text{ ANLG } o_2 \text{ a}) \leftrightarrow (o_2 \text{ ANLG } o_1 \text{ a}) \tag{121}$

If a similarity (not an equality) is postulated between two objects x and y, then there is at least one attribute with regard to which x and y are different (otherwise they would be equal):

- $(o_1 \text{ ANLG } o_2 \text{ a}) \rightarrow \exists d \ (d \neq a) \wedge (o_1 \text{ DISTG } o_2 \text{ d}) \tag{122}$


### 18.2.4   ANTE: Relation of Temporal Succession

**ANTE:** tp × tp                    with tp = $[t \cup ta \cup si \cup abs]$

**Definition:** In the case of $t_1$ and $t_2$ being temporal moments or periods (or, in technical terms, $t_1, t_2 \in t$), the expression $(t_1 \text{ ANTE } t_2)$ states that $t_1$ lies temporally before $t_2$ or is preceding $t_2$.

The relation ANTE is extended to sort *si* by the definition that (x ANTE y) for x, y $\in$ *si* holds if and only if $(t_x \text{ ANTE } t_y)$ is true for the moments or periods $t_x, t_y \in t$ assigned to the situations x and y. The analogue holds, if only one argument of ANTE is a situation. The relation ANTE is transitive, not reflexive and asymmetric.[4]

**Mnemonics:** Lat: ante (En: before / Ge: vor)
       $(t_1 \text{ ANTE } t_2)$ – [$t_1$ lies temporally before $t_2$]

**Question pattern:**
{Before / After} which {event / moment} [do] ⟨si⟩ {occur / happen}?
What [do] {happen / hold} {before / after} ⟨si⟩?
When [do] ⟨si⟩ {occur / happen}?
In what temporal succession [do] ⟨$si_1$⟩ and ⟨$si_2$⟩ happen?

**Explanation:** The relation POST as the converse to ANTE is not separately defined. It is simply obtained by exchanging the arguments of ANTE:

---

[4]  The definition of the relation ANTE by means of the relative position of the temporal intervals corresponding to the arguments is given in Sect. 7.3.

- $(x \text{ POST } y) \langle \rangle_{Def} (y \text{ ANTE } x)$       (123)

The relation ANTE is closely associated with the concept of causality (relation CAUS) and to the relations INIT and RSLT. In order to illustrate the succession of states and events, as well as that of abstract situations, let us consider the following examples:

(18.9) "[*Peter slept a while*]$\text{ANTE}_{arg1}$ *before* [*he went away*]$\text{ANTE}_{arg2}$."
(18.10) "*After* [*the stoppage of the production*]$\text{ANTE}_{arg1}$ [*many workers were dismissed*]$\text{ANTE}_{arg2}$."

Sometimes concrete objects are also seemingly admitted as first arguments in the natural language description of the relation ANTE:

(18.11) "*After Potsdam the relations between the Allied Forces changed rapidly.*"

In this case, the relationship expressed by ANTE does not really hold between objects, but rather between situations or events in which the indicated objects are or were involved. Sentences of this kind are characterized by a metonymic use of words. The actual meaning of the example sentence may be paraphrased approximately by:
"*After the end of the Potsdam Conference ...*"       (see also FIN and STRT).
 But, ANTE can connect temporal intervals determined by the duration of existence of given objects.

## 18.2.5   ANTO: Antonymy Relation

**ANTO:** sort × sort       with **sort** as an arbitrary, but most specific sort which must be the same for both arguments[5]

**Definition:** The statement $(s_1 \text{ ANTO } s_2)$ connects two concepts of the same sort which represent a pair of opposites belonging to the same conceptual field. The relation ANTO is superordinate to the relations: COMPL, CONTR and CNVRS. It is symmetric and not reflexive (and therefore also not transitive).

**Mnemonics:** En: antonymy (Ge: Antonymie / Gegensatz)
       $(s_1 \text{ ANTO } s_2) - [s_1 \text{ is antonym of } s_2]$

---

[5] The characterization "the same most specific sort" in the signature of a relation has to be understood as follows: If the relations $(s_1 \text{ ANTO } s_2)$ and $s_1 \in co$ hold, then it is not sufficient, that $s_2 \in o$ (even if $s_1, s_2 \in o$ were true in this case); rather, it is required that $s_2$ also must belong to the more specific sort $co$.

**Question pattern:**
What is {the contrary / the opposite / the counterpart} of $\langle s_1 \rangle$ / $\langle s_2 \rangle$?

**Explanation:** The relation ANTO is used to connect pairs of lexemes in the lexicon which are antonyms. It is the counterpart to the synonymy relation SYNO (see pages 491 and 556). It has to be stated that there is no uniform opinion held in the linguistic literature with regard to the antonymy relation[6] (see Lyons [167], who proposes the superconcept "oppositeness" for all pairs of concepts standing in the relation ANTO defined above).

   The possible specializations of ANTO are shown in a survey in Fig. 18.6.

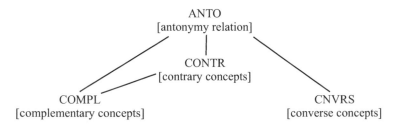

**Figure 18.6.** Specializations of the antonymy relation

### 18.2.6    ARG1/2/3: Argument Specification at the Metalevel

**ARG1/2/3:** $[re \cup si] \times ent$

**Definition:** The assertions (r ARG1 e), (r ARG2 e), and (r ARG3 e) connect a relational concept r, which is a state of affairs at the metalevel subordinate to another relational concept c, with the first, second, and third argument required by c, respectively (see Fig. 18.7 and relation SUBR).

**Mnemonics:** En: argument (Ge: Argument)
          (r ARG1/2/3 e) – [the relational concept r has e as its
                          first, second, and third argument, respectively]

**Question pattern:** Which is the first, second, and third argument of $\langle re \rangle$?

---

[6] The analogue holds for the synonymy relation.

**Explanation:** The relations ARG1, ARG2, and ARG3[7], together with SUBR, are used to define the argument structure of relational concepts corresponding to certain relations of MultiNet that can be described or paraphrased by single verbs[8]; see Fig. 18.7. Typical examples are:

Ge: *"ähneln"* or En: *"resemble"* (corresponding to ANLG2/3),

Ge: *"sich unterscheiden"* or En: *"distinguish in"* (corresponding to DISTG),

Ge: *"gleichen"* or En: *"being equal"* (corresponding to EQU).

The meanings of such verbs cannot be described with the normal structure of participants (C-Roles). In some cases their meanings include a combination of MultiNet relations and their arguments; see Fig. 18.7 (middle part). Apart from that, many of the verbs classified in traditional grammars as "state verbs" (like the above examples) do not really characterize states in the physical sense, but rather characterize relational expressions.

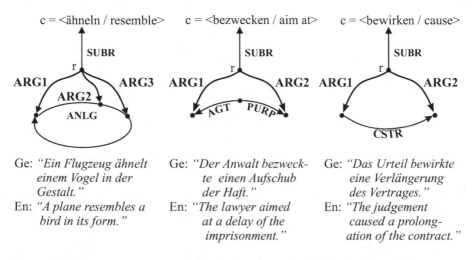

Ge: *"Ein Flugzeug ähnelt einem Vogel in der Gestalt."*

En: *"A plane resembles a bird in its form."*

Ge: *"Der Anwalt bezweck-te einen Aufschub der Haft."*

En: *"The lawyer aimed at a delay of the imprisonment."*

Ge: *"Das Urteil bewirkte eine Verlängerung des Vertrages."*

En: *"The judgement caused a prolong-ation of the contract."*

**Figure 18.7.** The argument structure of verbs denoting semantically primitive relations

Even relations denoting cognitive roles of event verbs can be described again at the metalevel by natural language concepts whose semantics, however, cannot be characterized by a participant structure. This class comprises verbs like:

---

[7] If the ternary relations ANLG/3 and DISTG/3 were eliminated, the relation ARG3 could also be omitted.

[8] It is easily seen that there are such words, since all highly developed natural languages are language and metalanguage at the same time, i.e. they allow us to speak about language, and they have sufficient expressive power to describe the semantic primitives of a representation language as well.

Ge: *"veranlassen"* / *"bewirken"* or En: *"cause"* / *"effect"* (AGT, CSTR),
Ge: *"sich ergeben"* or En: *"result in"* (RSLT),
Ge: *"dienen zu"* or En: *"serve for"* (PURP).

## 18.2.7   ASSOC: Association

**ASSOC:** *ent* × *ent*

**Definition:** The expression ($e_1$ ASSOC $e_2$) states that there is a cognitive connection (an association) between the two arguments $e_1$ and $e_2$ which is not further specified. It originates, at least in principle, from a deeper semantic relationship (even if this connection is not resolved and explicitly represented in the SN). The relation ASSOC is symmetric[9], reflexive, and restrictedly transitive.

**Mnemonics:** En: association (Ge: Assoziation)
      ($e_1$ ASSOC $e_2$) − [$e_1$ is associated with $e_2$]

**Question pattern:** Which concept has something to do with $\langle e_1 \rangle$ / $\langle e_2 \rangle$?
What can be associated with $\langle e_1 \rangle$ / $\langle e_2 \rangle$?
Are $\langle e_1 \rangle$ and $\langle e_2 \rangle$ cognitively related to each other?

**Explanation:** It is difficult to specify the relation ASSOC formally as the progression of associative links in the network cannot be defined in a strictly axiomatic way. ASSOC should be used only for the description of relationships between concepts that are semantically so closely connected that emphasizing their relationship is cognitively justified.

   On the one hand, it seems natural to assume that the relation ASSOC is transitive:

- ($e_1$ ASSOC $e_2$) ∧ ($e_2$ ASSOC $e_3$) → ($e_1$ ASSOC $e_3$)         (124)

On the other hand, associative chains cannot be continued ad infinitum because the strength of association decreases with a growing number of arcs between the entities $e_1$ and $e_3$. Unfortunately, a numerical limit for the **semantic distance** between two entities which can still be taken as associatively connected

---

[9] From a cognitive point of view there are serious reasons for doubting the symmetry of the ASSOC relation. If, for instance, someone takes the connection (shark ASSOC dangerous) as a "natural" association, then the inverse direction dangerous → shark of the association need not necessarily be observable (at least, the strength of association should be different in both cases). If this conjecture turns out to be true, then the symmetry property must be dropped.

(e.g. the number of arcs lying between them) cannot be given a priori (see Sect. 4.4.3). Nevertheless, the relation ASSOC has its heuristic value, since it can be very helpful in an associatively guided inference process to know whether or not two concepts are cognitively connected, see Sect. 13.3.

### 18.2.8   ATTCH: Attachment of Objects

**ATTCH:** $[o \setminus at] \times [o \setminus at]$

**Definition:** The assertion ($o_1$ ATTCH $o_2$) indicates that the object $o_1$ is immanently or situationally attached to the object $o_2$. A specific connection ATTCH between two objects may, but need not necessarily be symmetric.

**Mnemonics:** En: attachment (Ge: Zuordnung, Verbindung)
　　　　(x ATTCH y) – [the object y is attached to the object x]

**Question pattern:** {By what (object)} [be] $\langle o_1 \rangle$ or $\langle o_2 \rangle$ characterized?
$\langle$WHA$\rangle$ [do] $\langle o_1 \rangle$ {possess / have}?
$\langle$WH$\rangle$ {[be] attached / [do] belong to} to $\langle o_1 \rangle$?
$\langle$WH$\rangle$ [have] $\langle o_2 \rangle$?

**Explanation:**
The specification ($o_1$ ATTCH $o_2$) allows for the characterization of an object $o_1$ by means of attachment to another object $o_2$. Kinship relations are typical of an immanent attachment, and relations of friendship are typical for situational attachments.
For unique attachments, the combination of the relations ATTCH - SUB - EQU plays a role similar to the combination ATTR - SUB - VAL for the assignment of attributes (see ATTR and VAL). As the examples in Fig. 18.8 demonstrate, the relation ATTCH is not expressible by ATTR since, apart from the violation of sortal restrictions, the concepts mother and friend are not attributes of the individual concept Paul, but rather immanently or situationally attached (relational) objects.

If no unique attachment of objects is possible by combining the relations ATTCH - SUB or ATTCH - SUB0 with an appropriate superconcept (e.g. in the case that, in contrast to the picture, Paul is not the only son of Lisa), then an adequate meaning representation cannot be constructed by using the relation EQU. For this purpose, the relation ELMT and the expressional means of the preextensional level must be utilized (see the example in Fig. 18.23b).

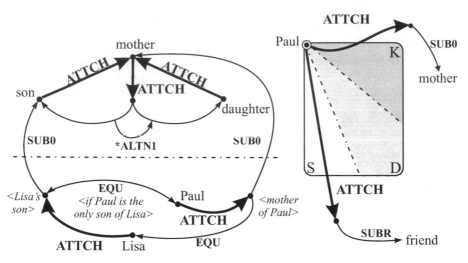

**Figure 18.8.** Examples of object attachments

## 18.2.9   ATTR: Assignment of Attributes to Objects

**ATTR:** $[o \cup l \cup t] \times at$

**Definition:** The relationship (o ATTR m) specifies that m is a characteristic attribute or a particular trait of o.

**Mnemonics:** En: attribute (Ge: Attribut / Merkmal)
(o ATTR m) – [o has the attribute m]

**Question pattern:** Which attribute(s) [do] ⟨o⟩ have?
Which object is characterized by the attribute ⟨at⟩?
{What is typical / characteristic} of ⟨o⟩?

**Explanation:** The relation ATTR is typical of the representation of general background knowledge not specific to a certain situation. Since ATTR is normally used for the specification of defining components of the meaning structure of a concept, the latter belong to the immanent part of the corresponding conceptual capsule. It should be noted that also attributes (like height, weight, etc.) whose values may vary in time must generally be considered as bearing a definitional/immanent character (only their values are situationally changing; see Fig. 18.9).

For values $w \in p$, the following relationship between ATTR and PROP holds:

- $(o_1 \text{ ATTR } o_2) \wedge (o_2 \text{ VAL } w) \rightarrow (o_1 \text{ PROP } w)$     | $w \in p$     (125)

If occasional or situational components of the meaning of a concept B have to be specified by ATTR and VAL, these components must be placed in the situational part of the meaning structure (conceptual capsule) of B as shown in Fig. 18.9.

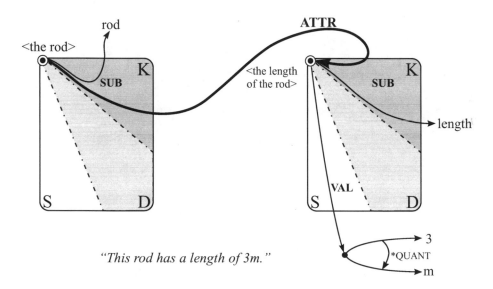

**Figure 18.9.** Attributes and their values

## 18.2.10 AVRT: C-Role – Averting from an Object

**AVRT:** $[dy \cup ad] \times o$

**Definition:** The expression (e AVRT o) specifies the relation between an event e and an object o participating in e from which the action dominating e is averting or turning away.

**Mnemonics:** En: avert (Ge: weg- / abwenden)
(x AVRT y) – [e is averting from o]

**Question pattern:** ⟨WMF⟩ is the action averting?
⟨WHA⟩ [do] somebody {renounce / repudiate / ... }?

⟨WMF⟩ [be] ⟨o⟩ {withdrawn / removed / ... }?
⟨WMF⟩ [do] somebody ⟨P-transfer-act⟩ something?
        (with ⟨P-transfer-act⟩ ∈ {take away, buy, steal, extract, ... })

**Explanation:** The C-Role AVRT is very often encountered in connection with verbs describing a transfer of a material or immaterial possession (a thing, some information, a title, etc.), which is expressed in the last two question patterns. Thereby the action is directed away from the object of the verb or diverts from it.

Examples:

(18.12)  En: *"The title was withdrawn from [the team]*$^{\text{AVRT}_{arg2}}$.*"*
            Ge: *"Der Titel ist [der Mannschaft]*$^{\text{AVRT}_{arg2}}$ *aberkannt worden."*
(18.13)  En: *"The privilege will be taken away from [the manager]*$^{\text{AVRT}_{arg2}}$.*"*
            Ge: *"Das Privileg wird [dem Manager]*$^{\text{AVRT}_{arg2}}$ *entzogen werden."*
(18.14)  En: *"The thief stole the money from [the customer]*$^{\text{AVRT}_{arg2}}$.*"*
            Ge: *"Der Dieb hat [dem Kunden]*$^{\text{AVRT}_{arg2}}$ *das Geld gestohlen."*

Typical prepositions for describing the relation AVRT are *"from"* in English or *"von"* in German. Although AVRT is often expressed by the dative in German or by a prepositional object in English (see the examples above), it is not always associated with this surface case.

(18.15)  En: *"The player [left]*$^{\text{AVRT}_{arg1}}$ *[the field]*$^{\text{AVRT}_{arg2}}$.*"*
            Ge: *"Der Spieler [verließ]*$^{\text{AVRT}_{arg1}}$ *[das Spielfeld]*$^{\text{AVRT}_{arg2}}$.*"*

It should be mentioned that there is also the possibility of double characterizations by different C-Roles in connection with movements which are directed *"**away** from something"*. This can be seen by means of the following example, where the object *"hare"* is linked to the event node by means of AFF and AVRT:

(18.16)  *"The hunter [stripped]*$^{\text{AFF+AVRT}_{arg1}}$ *[the fur]*$^{\text{OBJ}_{arg2}}$ *off [the hare]*$^{\text{AFF+AVRT}_{arg2}}$.*"*

If o is a concrete object, the relation AVRT can be seen as a specialization of the generalized origin (relation SOURC). Thus, AVRT is in a way the counterpart of the relation ORNT.

## 18.2.11   BENF: C-Role – Beneficiary

**BENF:** $[si \cup o] \times [o \setminus abs]$

**Definition:** The assertion (s BENF b) allows for a specification of the beneficiary b of a situation s ∈ si or of an object s ∈ o. In the case s ∈ si, b is usually not immediately participating in s (which is typically an event) and is also not changed by s. It must be emphasized that the term "beneficiary" has a neutral meaning in this context, because there are events s and objects b involved in these events that have a negative connotation; see Example (18.19).[10]

**Mnemonics:** En: beneficiary (Ge: Nutznießer / Bedachter)
  (s BENF b) – [b benefits from s]

**Question pattern:** For the sake of ⟨WHA⟩ [be] ⟨si⟩ donc?
In favor of ⟨WHA⟩ is ⟨si⟩ done? – For whom ⟨si⟩?
⟨WH⟩ {[be] beneficiary of / [benefit] from} ⟨si⟩?
⟨WH⟩ {[do] profit / [have] an advantage / [have] a disadvantage} from ⟨si⟩?

**Explanation:**
The relation BENF has to be well distinguished from the relation ORNT:

(18.17)  *"He [wrote]$^{BENF_{arg1}}$ a letter [for his friend]$^{BENF_{arg2}}$."*   But,

(18.18)  *"He [wrote ]$^{ORNT_{arg1}}$ a letter [to his friend]$^{ORNT_{arg2}}$."*

Object on which a *"negative"* effect is bestowed:

(18.19)  *"The warden [prepared]$^{BENF_{arg1}}$ a poisoned meal [for the prisoner]$^{BENF_{arg2}}$."*

Both relations, BENF and ORNT, can also be met in one sentence:

(18.20)  *"The sponsor [sent]$^{BENF+ORNT_{arg1}}$ [the town]$^{ORNT_{arg2}}$ a check [for the new sports hall]$^{BENF_{arg2}}$."*

There are also examples involving states rather than events:

(18.21)  *"The club [serves]$^{BENF_{arg1}}$ [the natives]$^{BENF_{arg2}}$ as a weapon."*
(18.22)  *"The evidence [speaks]$^{BENF_{arg1}}$ for [the defendant]$^{BENF_{arg2}}$."*
(18.23)  *"The apprentice [is very useful]$^{BENF_{arg1}}$ [to the master]$^{BENF_{arg2}}$."*

---

[10] In this case, it is clear that the object b is not a *"beneficiary"* (Ge: *"Nutznießer"*) in the narrower sense but there is an intention associated with the action s to exert a certain *"negative"* effect on the corresponding object b (Ge: *"dem b wird durch s etwas zugedacht"*).

The cooperation of all three relations BENF, ORNT, and OBJ is illustrated by the following event (the first argument is in each case the representative of the whole event):

(18.24)  "[*The pal*]$^{AGT}{}_{arg2}$ *gave* [*the police*]$^{ORNT}{}_{arg2}$ [*a wrong tip*]$^{OBJ}{}_{arg2}$
    *for the sake of* [*the suspect*]$^{BENF}{}_{arg2}$."

The second argument of BENF must be a concrete object. The counterpart of BENF in the area of abstract concepts is PURP.
The first argument of BENF can also be a concrete object:

(18.25)  "[*The medicine*]$^{BENF}{}_{arg1}$ *for* [*the patient*]$^{BENF}{}_{arg2}$".

Here, the purpose of the medicine is the healing process (PURP) and the patient is the beneficiary (BENF).

## 18.2.12  CAUS: Causality, Relation Between Cause and Effect

**CAUS:** [si' ∪ abs'] × [si' ∪ abs']

**Definition:** The statement ($s_1$ CAUS $s_2$) indicates that the situation $s_1$ (which must be real) is the cause for the situation $s_2$ (which must also be real). The value [FACT = *real*] for $s_1$ and $s_2$ is symbolized by a prime at the corresponding symbols. $s_2$ is the effect actually brought about by $s_1$. The relation CAUS is transitive, asymmetric, and not reflexive.

**Mnemonics:** En: cause (Ge: Ursache / Kausalität)
    ($s_1$ CAUS $s_2$) – [$s_1$ is the cause of $s_2$]

**Question pattern:** {Why / How} is it that $\langle s_2 \rangle$?
By $\langle WHA \rangle$ [be] $\langle s_2 \rangle$ caused? – What is the cause of $\langle s_2 \rangle$?
Which effect [do] $\langle s_1 \rangle$ have?
{Thanks to / Because of} $\langle WHA \rangle$ [do] $\langle s_2 \rangle$ {happen / occur / ... }?
{Of what / From which $\langle s_1 \rangle$} [do] $\langle somebody \rangle$ {die / fall ill / suffer / ... }?

**Explanation:** The causal relationship is closely connected to the temporal successor relation ANTE, since the effect cannot take place before the cause:

- ($x$ CAUS $y$) → ¬($y$ ANTE $x$)

There also exists a connection between the relations CSTR and CAUS that has in general to be described by means of axiom schemata. A typical axiom which holds for events $s_1$ subordinate to causative actions like **break**, **destroy**, and **kill**, among others, is the following:

- $(s_1 \text{ CSTR } d) \leftrightarrow \exists s_2 ([(s_2 \text{ AGT } d) \lor (s_2 \text{ INSTR } d)] \land (s_2 \text{ CAUS } s_1))$

The following example sentences are characteristic of the causal relation. The first of them shows clearly that the relation CAUS, in contrast to COND and IMPL, always connects real (not hypothetical) situations, which are characterized by the attribute value [FACT = *real*] .

(18.26) *"Since [Peter went carelessly across the street,]*CAUS$_{arg1}$
        *[he was run over by a car]*CAUS$_{arg2}$*."*

(18.27) *"[The excitement]*CAUS$_{arg2}$ *about [the strange event]*CAUS$_{arg1}$*."*

(18.28) *" [Peter suffers]*CAUS$_{arg2}$ *from [gastritis]*CAUS$_{arg1}$*."*

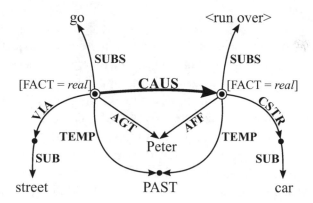

**Figure 18.10.** Situational description with causality and causator

The close connection between causal relationships and counterfactuals is discussed in Sect. 11.2.2. It can be illustrated by the following counterfactual corresponding to the causal relationship expressed in Sentence (18.26).

(18.29) *"If Peter had not carelessly gone across the street, he would not have been run over by a car".*

## 18.2.13    CHEA: Sortal Change: Event – Abstract Concept

**CHEA:** $dy \times ad$

**Definition:** The statement (e CHEA a) expresses the connection between an event $e \in dy$ and an abstract concept $a \in ad$ which agree, at least partially, in their meaning. Concepts connected by CHEA correspond to each other in a systematic way.

**Mnemonics:** En: change of event to abstract entity (Ge: Wechsel von Ereignis zu Abstraktum)

**Question pattern:** –

**Explanation:** The relation CHEA is used to represent the lexical background knowledge. It enhances the semantic repertory by representational means that model the nominalization in the surface structure at the semantic level. CHEA establishes the connection between lexemes like produce (Ge: produzieren) and $production_1$ (Ge: $Produktion_1$), investigate (Ge: untersuchen) and investigation (Ge: Untersuchung), enter (Ge: eintreten) and $entry_1$ (Ge: $Eintritt_1$), $work_3$ (Ge: arbeiten) and $work_1$ (Ge: $Arbeit_1$), etc. In contrast to the original verbs, many of the nominalized verbs have a double meaning – they denote an action indicated by index 1 (e.g. $production_1$, $work_1$, etc.) and the result of that action indicated by index 2 (e.g. $production_2$, $work_2$, etc.). It is not possible in general to equate the meanings of the verb with that of the nominalized verb. From a cognitive point of view, NL descriptions using the verb describe a situation from the inside, so to speak, while NL expressions using a nominalized verb raise the situation to an abstract (mental) object looking at the situation from the outside.

The relation CHEA plays a crucial role within the mechanism of transferring deep case frames from the verb to the nominalized verb. This mechanism is especially important for expressing lexical knowledge.

The somewhat simplified transfer schema for cognitive roles given in the following picture has this interpretation: The relations AGT and RSLT are inherited by $production_1$ (Ge: Herstellung) from produce (Ge: herstellen). The agent of $production_1$ (Ge: Herstellung) is described in the surface structure of an English sentence by means of the preposition "*by*" (Ge: "*durch*").[11]

---

[11] The syntactic characterization sketched in Fig. 18.11 is stored in the computational lexicon, not in the semantic network. The specification used in the lexicon HaGenLex [100] is indeed differentiated far more than the schematic representation given in the figure.

The result of the action (relation RSLT) is normally connected to the verb phrase by means of the preposition "*of*" (Ge: preposition "*von*", or pure genitive attribute). It can be stated that the deep relations connected with a node of sort [*ad*] in general bear the characteristic [OBLIG-] even in those cases where the relations with the corresponding node marked by sort [*dy*] have an obligatory character (symbol [OBLIG+]).

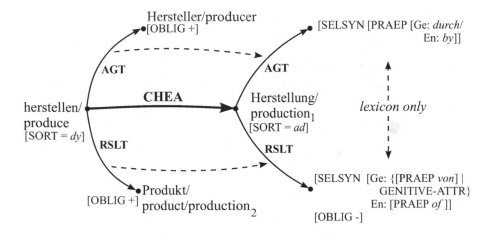

**Figure 18.11.** Transfer of valencies for nominalized concepts

## 18.2.14 CHPA: Sortal Change: Property – Abstract Concept

**CHPA:** $[(p \cup aq) \times at] \cup [rq \times re]$

**Definition:** The statement (p CHPA c) establishes a connection between a property p and an abstract concept (an abstract property or attribute) c which is semantically close to p and whose meaning is systematically related to p.

**Mnemonics:** change of property to an abstract object (Ge: Wechsel von Eigenschaft zu Abstraktum)

**Question pattern:** –

**Explanation:** This relation is important for building the lexical background knowledge and for specifying the connection between a property and the abstract concept (mostly an attribute) derived from it. Please note that the connection between philosophical and philosophy, or chemical and chemistry, is not established by CHPA but rather by ASSOC with [**K-TYPE** = *categ*] with regard to both arguments.

Examples:

| | |
|---|---|
| En: (long CHPA length) | Sorts: $[p \times at]$ |
| Ge: (lang CHPΛ Länge) | |
| En: (heavy CHPA weight) | Sorts: $[p \times at]$ |
| Ge: (schwer CHPA Gewicht) | |
| En: (equal CHPA equality) | Sorts: $[rq \times re]$ |
| Ge: (gleich CHPA Gleichheit) | |
| En: (collective CHPA collectivity) | Sorts: $[aq \times at]$ |
| Ge: (kollektiv CHPA Kollektivität) | |

Although one is scarcely asking for the relation CHPA directly, it is nevertheless important for the transformation of questions[12]

"*How* [*deep*]$\text{CHPA}_{arg1}$ *is the lake?*" $\rightarrow$
   "*What* [*depth*]$\text{CHPA}_{arg2}$ *does the lake have?*"
"*How* [*long*]$\text{CHPA}_{arg1}$ *is X?*" $\rightarrow$
   "*What* [*length*]$\text{CHPA}_{arg2}$ *does X have?*"

The relation between the assignment of a property to a concrete object and the characterization of this object by a corresponding attribute can be expressed by means of CHPA :

- (c PROP p) $\land$ (p CHPA $a_1$) $\rightarrow$ $\exists\, a_2$ (c ATTR $a_2$) $\land$ ($a_2$ SUB $a_1$)    (126)

For quantitatively modified properties, it can even be stated that

- (c PROP (∗MODP q p))$\land$ (p CHPA $a_1$)
   $\rightarrow$ $\exists\, a_2$ (c ATTR $a_2$) $\land$ ($a_2$ SUB $a_1$) $\land$ ($a_2$ VAL q)    (127)

---

[12] This regularity can be observed in German and in English as well, because one can almost always ask for the degree of a property $p \in gq$ using the corresponding property $p_+$ at the positive pole "*How $p_+$ is X?*" (see Sect. 6.2) or by using a noun $n(p_+)$ which is derived from $p_+$ to form an equivalent question "*What $n(p_+)$ does X have?*"
Example: En: "*How high is the tower?*" or Ge: "*Wie hoch ist der Turm?*"
From these sentences one can derive the equivalent questions "*What height does the tower have?*" or "*Welche Höhe hat der Turm?*"
Please note that the inverse transformation is not always possible, since an appropriate adjective need not exist for every measurable concept m $\in$ *oa*.

## 18.2.15   CHPE: Sortal Change: Property – Event

**CHPE:** $[p \cup rq] \times [ad \cup dy]$

**Definition:** The relation (p CHPE v) establishes a connection between a property p in the broadest sense and an event v, where v is a process characterizing the emergence of p.

**Mnemonics:** change property to event (Ge: Wechsel von Eigenschaft zu Vorgang)

**Question pattern:** –

**Explanation:** The relation CHPE is used to establish a connection between the semantics of certain adjectives and inchoative verbs:

En: (cool CHPE ⟨cool down⟩)     Ge: (kühl CHPE abkühlen)
En: (deep CHPE deepen)          Ge: (tief CHPE vertiefen)
En: (equal CHPE equate)         Ge: (gleich CHPE gleichsetzen)
En: (black CHPE blacken)        Ge: (schwarz CHPE schwärzen)
En: (inverse CHPE invert)       Ge: (invers CHPE invertieren)

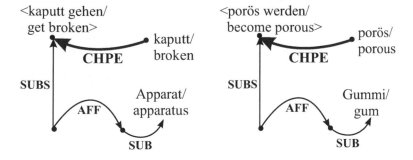

**Figure 18.12.** The change from properties to events

Correspondingly, the relation CHPE is used for the specification of lexical knowledge as well as for the representation of general background knowledge. The relation CHPE is additionally used for the representation of nonlexicalized events, which are described in English and German by means of predicatively used adjectives in connection with an auxiliary (En: *"get"* / *"become"* or Ge: *"werden"* / *"gehen"*); see Fig. 18.12.

(18.30)  En: *"The CD-ROM got [broken]*$^{CHPE_{arg1}}$ *yesterday."*
    Ge: *"Das CD-ROM ging gestern [kaputt]*$^{CHPE_{arg1}}$*."*
(18.31)  En: *"The gum [becomes porous]*$^{CHPE_{arg2}}$*."*
    Ge: *"Der Gummi [wird porös]*$^{CHPE_{arg2}}$*."*

## 18.2.16  CHPS: Sortal Change: Property – State

**CHPS:** $[p \cup rq] \times [as \cup st]$

**Definition:** The relationship (p CHPS s) is used for the characterization of a state, expressing that the state s is determined essentially by the property p.

**Mnemonics:** En: change of property to state (Ge: Wechsel von Eigenschaft in Zustand)

**Question pattern:** –

**Explanation:** The relation CHPS is intended for the semantic representation of states described by adjectival predicative phrases (it also plays a role in the representation of lexical knowledge, as in Ge: (gleich CHPS sich_gleichen)). As in the case of other relations denoting a change of sorts, it makes no sense to ask for the relation CHPS.

   States described by NL phrases such as *"it is p ..."* (Ge: *"es ist p ..."*) in the surface structure can be semantically represented by the relation CHPS.

(18.32)  En: *"It is cold at the North Pole."*          → (state: ⟨being cold⟩)
    Ge: *"Am Nordpol ist es kalt."*          → (state: ⟨kalt sein⟩)
(18.33)  En: *"It is dangerous in a dynamite plant."*     → ⟨being dangerous⟩
    Ge: *"In einer Dynamitfabrik ist es gefährlich."*   → ⟨gefährlich sein⟩
    (see Fig. 18.13).

   From the epistemological point of view, it is not yet quite clear how states and properties have to be distinguished exactly (the most important criterion for their distinction might be their persistence, but even this is not sharply defined). It is also not certain whether such nuances are needed in a QAS. If this distinction were not to be maintained in the deep structure of sentences, the relation CHPS would nevertheless provide a good starting point in the lexicon for normalization of the representation (by helping eliminate one of the two aspects, "state" or "property assignment").

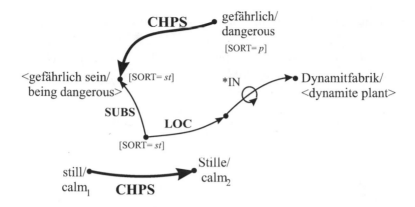

**Figure 18.13.** The change from properties to states

## 18.2.17   CHSA: Sortal Change: State – Abstract State

**CHSA:** $st \times ab$

**Definition:** The assertion ($s_1$ CHSA $s_2$) connects a state $s_1$ with an abstract conceptual object $s_2$; the meanings of these states are systematically interrelated and partially overlapping, although both concepts are designated differently in the surface structure. Specifically, $s_1$ is typically described by a state verb in the surface structure, and $s_2$ by a corresponding abstract noun.

**Mnemonics:** En: change of state to abstract object (Ge: Zustandsabstraktion)

**Question pattern:** –

**Explanation:** In this relation, the lexical character of all relations of sortal change is most clearly expressed:

| En:<br>Ge: | (thirst$_1$ CHSA thirst$_2$)<br>(dürsten CHSA Durst) | (*"P. is thirsting / P. has thirst."*)<br>(*"P. dürstet / P. hat Durst"*) |
|---|---|---|
| En:<br><br>Ge: | (hunger$_1$ CHSA hunger$_2$)<br><br>(hungern CHSA Hunger) | (*"P. is hungering"* (old)<br>*"P. has hunger / P. is hungry."*)<br>(*"P. hungert / P. hat Hunger"*) |
| En:<br><br>Ge: | (contain CHSA content)<br><br>(enthalten CHSA Inhalt) | (*"The field contains a number"* /<br>*"has a number as its content"*)<br>(*"Das Feld enthält eine Zahl"* /<br>*"hat eine Zahl zum Inhalt"*) |

The relation CHSA also mediates a transformation between roles of states like SCAR, SSPE, or OBJ, having sort [*st*] for their first arguments, on the one hand, and attribute-value specifications with ATTR and VAL (which are centered around a node of sort [*io*]) on the other hand (see Fig. 18.14).

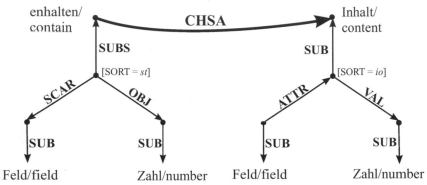

Ge: *"Das Feld enthält eine Zahl."*    Ge: *"Der Inhalt des Feldes ist eine Zahl."*
En: *"The field contains a number."*    En: *"The content of the field is a number."*

**Figure 18.14.** The change from states to corresponding abstract objects

### 18.2.18    CHSP1/2/3: Sortal Change Between Situational Concepts and Properties

**CHSP1/2/3:** *si* × p

**Definition:** The sortal changes (s CHSP1 p), (s CHSP2 p), and (s CHSP3 p) represent at the semantic level the relations holding between a situational concept s and that property p which is respectively described in NL by the present active participle, past participle, and present passive participle of the verb dominating s.[13]

**Mnemonics:** En: change of situation to property (Ge: Wechsel von Situation zu Eigenschaft)

---

[13] It must be emphasized that we do not hold the view that forming a participle is primarily a semantic phenomenon (otherwise this mechanism could be observed in almost all languages). Rather, the opinion held is the following: In languages showing the morpho-syntactic phenomenon of participle formation, the participle expresses exactly this change in sorts between a situation and a property.

**Question pattern:** –

**Explanation:** The relations CHSP1 and CHSP2 allow for a representation of the lexical connection between the meaning of a participle and that of the corresponding verb on the semantic level. They also provide the means to deal with attributively used participles in some kind of shorthand (or compressed) notation; see Fig. 18.15.

**a)** Ge: *"Eine arbeitende Maschine"*
En: *"A working machine"*

**b)** Ge: *"Der geheilte Patient"*
En: *"The healed patient"*

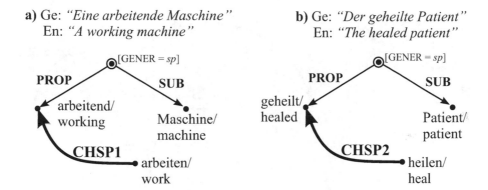

**Figure 18.15.** Compressed representation of participle constructions

**c)** Ge: *"Die mit einem Dieselmotor arbeitende Maschine"*
En: *"The machine working with a diesel."*

**d)** Ge: *"Der von Dr. M. 1975 mit Hilfe einer Schocktherapie geheilte Patient"*
En: *"The patient being healed by Dr. M. by means of a shock therapy in 1975."*

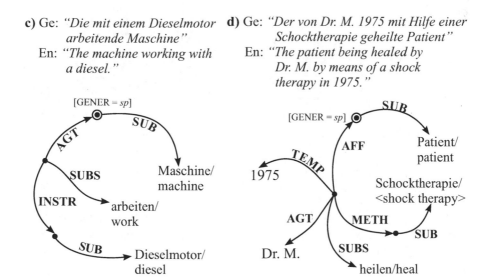

**Figure 18.16.** Semantic representation of an extended participle construction

In Examples a) through c) (Figs. 18.15 and 18.16), we have at first deliberately chosen the specializing interpretation for the main node represented by an encircled point, which is expressed by the attribute [**GENER** = *sp*].

**e)** Ge: *"**Ein brütender Vogel** (darf nicht gestört werden)."*
En: *"**A brooding bird** (must not be disturbed)."*

**f)** Ge: *"**Ein im Nest brütender Vogel** (ist leicht zu fangen)."*
En: *"**A bird brooding in its nest** (is easy to catch)."*

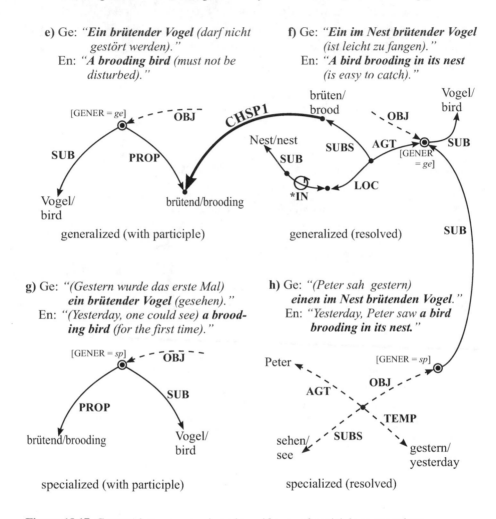

**g)** Ge: *"(Gestern wurde das erste Mal) **ein brütender Vogel** (gesehen)."*
En: *"(Yesterday, one could see) **a brooding bird** (for the first time)."*

**h)** Ge: *"(Peter sah gestern) **einen im Nest brütenden Vogel**."*
En: *"Yesterday, Peter saw **a bird brooding in its nest**."*

**Figure 18.17.** Contrast between generic and specific use of participle constructions

In the case of extended participle constructions containing one or more participants, the lexical relations CHSP1 and CHSP2 open access to the valency frames of the corresponding verbs, which can be used to resolve (expand) the participle construction into a full-fledged event. In this case, the relations CHSP1 and CHSP2 are used only to find the basic concept in the lexicon (described by the verb). Here, neither the relations CHSP1 nor the representative of the participle are part of the semantic representation of the extended participle construction; see Fig. 18.16. It should not be overlooked that phrases like a) or b) also have a generalizing interpretation. The semantic difference between both interpretations can be expressed by distinguishing the values of the attribute **GENER** in the semantic representation of a fully expanded event as well as in the compressed representation keeping the semantic representative of the participle as a node. This difference is illustrated by Examples e) through h) in Fig. 18.17.

The relation CHSP3 is used as an additional means to connect the semantic representative of a present passive participle of a certain verb (not lexicalized of course) with the representative of the verb itself. The modal aspect inherent in such representations is not described in the network proper but by means of axiom schemata.

It is possible, however, to make the modal character of such a participle construction explicit by using the schema:

⟨meaning of the participle⟩ → ⟨meaning of the basic verb⟩ + ⟨modal expression⟩

By this rule, the relation CHSP3 could be spared.

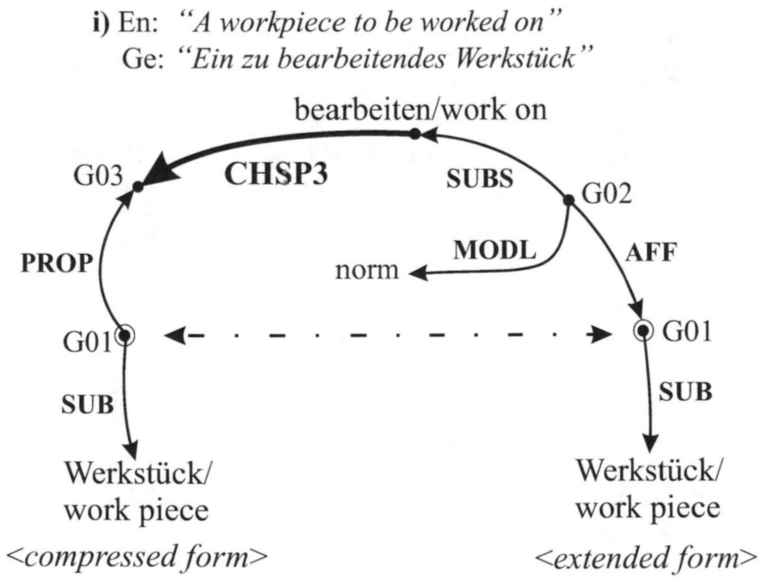

**i)** En:  *"A workpiece to be worked on"*
    Ge:  *"Ein zu bearbeitendes Werkstück"*

bearbeiten/work on

G03   **CHSP3**        **SUBS**    G02

**PROP**        norm ←  **MODL**    **AFF**

G01 ← – · – – · – – · → G01

**SUB**                **SUB**

Werkstück/                Werkstück/
work piece                work piece

*<compressed form>*            *<extended form>*

**Figure 18.18.** Participle constructions with a modal aspect

## 18.2.19  CIRC: Relation Between a Situation and a Concomitant Situation

**CIRC:** $[si \cup abs] \times [ab \cup si]$

**Definition:** The relation ($s_1$ CIRC $s_2$) specifies the connection between a situation $s_1$ and an accompanying circumstance or concomitant situation $s_2$.

**Mnemonics:** En: circumstance (Ge: Begleitumstand)
   ($s_1$ CIRC $s_2$) – [$s_1$ has $s_2$ as an accompanying circumstance]

**Question pattern:** Under which circumstances $\langle s_1 \rangle$?
{How [do] $\langle si \rangle$ {happen / occur / persist / ... }?

**Explanation:** The accompanying circumstance can be given by an event, by a state, or by an abstract situation. In English and Russian, a participle construction is often used as the grammatical form to express the relation CIRC. Examples:

(18.34) "[*Strolling through the forest without paying special attention*]CIRC$_{arg2}$, *he found a big mushroom.*"

(18.35) "*The mountaineers had a wonderful view with* [*an uncommon visibility of 50 km*]CIRC$_{arg2}$."

(18.36) "*The melting furnace was repaired with* [*a temperature of 80 degrees Celsius*]CIRC$_{arg2}$."

In contrast to the relations CTXT and COND, the relation CIRC is not semantically restrictive, i.e. it gives only additional information, neglecting which does not change the validity of the remaining state of affairs.

In German, the preferred means to express the relation CIRC in the surface structure of a sentence are prepositional phrases with "*bei*" (En: "*in*" or "*with*") and participle constructions, among others. However, there are also prepositional phrases constructed with "*bei*" (especially those which have to be interpreted as "*nur bei*" (En: "*only if*")) which must not be represented with CIRC, but rather with COND:

(18.37) Ge: "*(Nur) bei* [*Auftreten eines Programmfehlers*]COND$_{arg1}$ *werden die Fehlerbehandlungsroutinen aufgerufen.*"
   En: "*(Only) if* [*a programming error occurs*]COND$_{arg1}$ *are the routines for error handling called.*"

(18.38) Ge: *"(Nur) beim [Aufenthalt im Gefahrenbereich]*$^{COND}_{arg1}$ *ist erhöhte Vorsicht geboten."*

En: *"(Only) in case of [staying in the dangerous zone]*$^{COND}_{arg1}$ *is increased attention required."*

The test for whether or not the clause describing situation $s_1$ also holds without the supplementary situation $s_2$ can be used as a criterion to decide which of the relations CIRC, COND, or CTXT should be used to connect the situation $s_1$ with the second situation $s_2$.

## 18.2.20    CNVRS: Lexical Relation Between Converse Concepts

**CNVRS:** sort × sort        with **sort** as an arbitrary, but most specific sort
                              which must be the same for both arguments

**Definition:** The relationship ($s_1$ CNVRS $s_2$) is used to juxtapose semantically converse concepts $s_1$ and $s_2$. Such concepts can be interpreted as (mostly binary) relations where an exchange of arguments in the expression (x $s_1$ y) results in an equivalent expression (y $s_2$ x) built on the converse concept and vice versa. According to this definition, the relation CNVRS is symmetric. The relation CNVRS is generalized to relational concepts with more than two arguments (see below).

**Mnemonics:** En: converse (Ge: konvers / umgekehrt)
        ($s_1$ CNVRS $s_2$) – [$s_1$ is the converse concept of $s_2$]

**Question pattern:** What [be] the [counterpart] of $\langle s_1 \rangle$ / $\langle s_2 \rangle$?

**Explanation:** The relation CNVRS is a special case of the antonymy relation important for the computational lexicon of an NLP system, as well as for its inferences. Typical converse concepts are given by the following examples[14]:

| En: (spouse CNVRS wife) | Ge: (Ehemann CNVRS Ehefrau) |
|---|---|
| En: (give CNVRS receive) | Ge: (geben CNVRS erhalten) |
| En: (⟨cousin$_{fem}$⟩ CNVRS ⟨cousin$_{masc}$⟩) | Ge: (Cousine CNVRS Cousin) |

---

[14] The German concepts Cousine (En: ⟨cousin (fem)⟩) and Cousin (En: ⟨cousin (masc)⟩) are only restrictedly converse, i.e. only in those cases where the relations ⟨Cousine von⟩ (En: ⟨cousin of⟩) and ⟨Cousin von⟩ (En: ⟨cousin of⟩) really connect persons of different sex with each other.

The exact relations between the arguments of n-ary converses like give and receive must be described in MultiNet by special meaning postulates (B-Axioms). In this case, the relation CNVRS specified in the lexicon indicates only a change in the assignment of arguments which is generally accompanied in MultiNet by a change of the role distribution.

The exact meaning of the relation (give CNVRS receive) is specified by the following B-Axiom:

- $(v_1$ SUBS give$) \wedge (v_1$ AGT a$) \wedge (v_1$ ORNT b$) \wedge (v_1$ OBJ c$) \rightarrow$
  $\exists v_2 (v_2$ SUBS receive$) \wedge (v_2$ AVRT a$) \wedge (v_2$ EXP b$) \wedge (v_2$ OBJ c$)$     (128)
- $(v_2$ SUBS receive$) \wedge (v_2$ AVRT a$) \wedge (v_2$ EXP b$) \wedge (v_2$ OBJ c$) \rightarrow$
  $\exists v_1 (v_1$ SUBS give$) \wedge (v_1$ AGT a$) \wedge (v_1$ ORNT b$) \wedge (v_1$ OBJ c$)$     (129)

The last Axiom (129) is applicable only if the argument a bears the feature [POTAG +] (see Sect. 17.1).

## 18.2.21   COMPL: Complementarity

**COMPL:** $[p \times p] \cup [ab \times ab] \cup [si \times si]$

**Definition:** The relation COMPL describes the complementarity of properties, abstract concepts, and situations. If the arguments of COMPL are properties, the following holds: Given the relationship $(p_1$ COMPL $p_2)$, an object o which can be assigned the properties $p_1$ or $p_2$ at all must actually have exactly one of these properties (the analogue holds for abstract concepts; see Axioms (133) and (134)). The relation COMPL is symmetric.

**Mnemonics:** En: complement / complementary (Ge: Komplement / komplementär)
$(p_1$ COMPL $p_2) - [p_1$ is complementary to $p_2]$

**Question pattern:** Which property is the exact counterpart to $\langle p \rangle$?
Which concept is {opposed / complimentary} to $\langle p \rangle$?

**Explanation:** The relation COMPL connects complementary properties or values belonging to one and the same attribute with each other:

| En: (rational$_1$ COMPL irrational$_1$)     Ge: (rational$_1$ COMPL irrational$_1$) |
|---|
| [only for numbers] |
| En: (rational$_2$ COMPL irrational$_2$)     Ge: (rational$_2$ COMPL irrational$_2$) |
| [only for mental processes like inferences or thoughts] |
| En: (legal COMPL illegal)          Ge: (legal COMPL illegal) |
| [only for juridically relevant situations] |

The following defining axioms can be specified:[15]

- $(o\ PROP\ p_1) \wedge (p_1\ COMPL\ p_2) \rightarrow \neg\ (o\ PROP\ p_2)$         (130)
- $\neg(o\ PROP\ p_1) \wedge (p_1\ COMPL\ p_2) \rightarrow (o\ PROP\ p_2)$         (131)
- $(p_1\ COMPL\ p_2) \leftrightarrow (p_2\ COMPL\ p_1)$         (132)

The relation COMPL is a specialization of the relation CONTR. Examples for the complementarity of abstract concepts (sort [*ab*]) are:

| En: (day COMPL night) | Ge: (Tag COMPL Nacht) |
|---|---|
| En: (death COMPL life) | Ge: (Tod COMPL Leben) |
| En: (war COMPL peace) | Ge: (Krieg COMPL Frieden) |

Here, the following axioms are valid:

- $(a\ SUB\ c_1) \wedge (c_1\ COMPL\ c_2) \rightarrow \neg(a\ SUB\ c_2)$         (133)
- $(a\ SUBS\ c_1) \wedge (c_1\ COMPL\ c_2) \rightarrow \neg(a\ SUBS\ c_2)$         (134)

Axioms analogous to (131) can also be obtained for negated subordinations.

## 18.2.22 CONC: Relation Expressing a Concession

**CONC:** $[si \cup abs] \times [si \cup ab]$

**Definition:** The assertion $(s_1\ CONC\ s_2)$ indicates that the situation $s_1$ holds in spite of the circumstance $s_2$, which seemingly opposes $s_1$.

**Mnemonics:** En: concessive (Ge: konzessiv / einräumend)
       $(s_1\ CONC\ s_2)$ – [$s_1$ holds / takes place in spite of $s_2$]

**Question pattern:** {In spite of / Despite of} which circumstance $\langle s_1 \rangle$?
What is {hindering / hampering / opposing ... } $\langle s_1 \rangle$?

---

[15] The rule (131) is valid only if $p_1$ may at least principally be a property of o.

**Explanation:** The relation CONC is used to represent the meaning of concessive sentences introduced by conjunctions like "*although*" or "*(even) though*" (Ge: "*obwohl*", "*obgleich*", "*wenn auch*", "*selbst wenn*", etc.) It is also used for representing the meaning of prepositions like "*in spite of*", "*despite*", and "*notwithstanding*" (Ge: "*trotz*", "*ungeachtet*", etc.).

(18.39)  En: "*Notwithstanding* [*the high prices,*]CONC$_{arg2}$ [*many people buy this article*]CONC$_{arg1}$."

   Ge: "*Ungeachtet* [*des hohen Preises*]CONC$_{arg2}$ [*kaufen viele Leute den Artikel*]CONC$_{arg1}$."

One can assume by default that, normally, the negation of $s_2$ is a reason or justification for $s_1$. In this regard, CONC and REAS may be seen as complementary relations.

   The relation CONC is not transitive, as the following example shows:

(18.40)  En: "*Although* [*the weather forecast turned out to be fine*]CONC$_{arg2}$, [*it rained*]CONC$_{arg1}$."

   Ge: "*Obwohl* [*der Wetterbericht gut ausfiel*]CONC$_{arg2}$, [*regnete es*]CONC$_{arg1}$."

(18.41)  En: "*Although* [*it rained*]CONC$_{arg2}$, [*Max went on a walk*]CONC$_{arg1}$."

   Ge: "*Obwohl* [*es regnete*]CONC$_{arg2}$, [*unternahm Max eine Wanderung*]CONC$_{arg1}$."

However, the following does not hold:

(18.42)  En: "*Although* [*the weather forecast turned out to be fine*]CONC$_{arg2}$, [*Max went on a walk*]CONC$_{arg1}$."

   Ge: "*Obwohl* [*der Wetterbericht gut ausfiel*]CONC$_{arg2}$, [*unternahm Max eine Wanderung*]CONC$_{arg1}$."

### 18.2.23   COND: Conditional Relation

**COND:** $\tilde{si} \times \tilde{si}$

**Definition:** The relation ($s_1$ COND $s_2$) specifies that $s_1$ is a sufficient condition for situation $s_2$. If $s_2$ is an event, then $s_1$ activates the occurrence of $s_2$. In contrast to the relation IMPL, the relation COND is not transitive.[16]

---

[16] Though the transitivity of COND seems to be suggested by the definition of this relation, the postulation of this property in a QAS would lead to a semantic connection between situations lying intensionally far apart and having no perceivable relationship in their meanings.

**Mnemonics:** En: condition (Ge: Bedingung / Kondition)

$(s_1$ COND $s_2)$ – $[s_1$ is a (sufficient) condition for $s_2]$

**Question pattern:**

{On which condition / Under which circumstances} {$\langle s_2 \rangle$ / [do] $\langle s_2 \rangle$ hold}?

What are the {conditions / prerequisites} for $\langle s_2 \rangle$?

When {[can] / [may]} $\langle s_2 \rangle$ take place?

On what {situation / circumstance / condition} does $\langle s_2 \rangle$ depend?

**Explanation:** In contrast to the relation $(s_1$ CAUS $s_2)$, the arguments of the relation $(s_1$ COND $s_2)$ are not considered as actual or factual situations but rather as hypothetical situations that potentially hold and whose facticity has yet to be confirmed.[17] The situation $s_1$ is not a cause for $s_2$ (see relation CAUS); it may even be a condition that was arbitrarily attached to $s_2$:

(18.43) En: *"If [he comes tomorrow]*$^{\mathrm{COND}_{arg1}}$, *[he will get his money]*$^{\mathrm{COND}_{arg2}}$*."*

Ge: *"Wenn [er morgen kommt]*$^{\mathrm{COND}_{arg1}}$, *[wird er sein Geld bekommen]*$^{\mathrm{COND}_{arg2}}$*."*

Often, a deeper regularity underlies a conditional relationship which can, but need not necessarily, be of causal origin.

(18.44) En: *"If [Peter does not clean his teeth]*$^{\mathrm{COND}_{arg1}}$, *[he will have to visit the dentist more often]*$^{\mathrm{COND}_{arg2}}$*."*

Ge: *"Wenn [Peter nicht die Zähne putzt]*$^{\mathrm{COND}_{arg1}}$, *[wird er häufiger zum Zahnarzt gehen müssen]*$^{\mathrm{COND}_{arg2}}$*."*

The second argument $s_2$ of the relation COND has to be seen as the situation whose scope of validity, or period over which it persists, is determined or restricted by the first argument $s_1$ (in the same sense as the duration or range of validity of a real situation may be restricted by temporal, local, and other specifications). The validity of the second state of affairs or situation $s_2$ is "triggered", so to speak, by the first situation $s_1$.

In the case of nonreal conditionals (called **counterfactuals**), there is always an "ordinary" conditional relation $(\tilde{s}_1$ COND $\tilde{s}_2)$ connecting two analogous hypothetical situations $\tilde{s}_1$ and $\tilde{s}_2$, which are opposed to two real or factual situations $\neg s_1'$ and $\neg s_2'$; these are negated in comparison to $\tilde{s}_1$ and $\tilde{s}_2$ (see Sect. 11.2.3 on the treatment of counterfactuals).

---

[17] This characteristic is indicated by a tilde over the sort symbol standing for [**FACT**=*hypo*].

(18.45)  Example:

"*If he had not come ($\tilde{s}_1$), he would not have got his money ($\tilde{s}_2$).*"

$\qquad\qquad\Downarrow\qquad\qquad\qquad\qquad\qquad\qquad\qquad\Downarrow$

"*(he came)*" ($\neg\ s_1'$)          "*(he got his money)*" ($\neg\ s_2'$)

The same example in German:

"*Wenn er nicht gekommen wäre ($\tilde{s}_1$), hätte er sein Geld nicht bekommen ($\tilde{s}_2$).*"

$\qquad\qquad\Downarrow\qquad\qquad\qquad\qquad\qquad\qquad\qquad\Downarrow$

"*(Er ist gekommen)*" ($\neg\ s_1'$)          "*(er hat sein Geld bekommen)*" ($\neg\ s_2'$)

## 18.2.24   CONF: Relation Expressing the Conformity with an Abstract Frame

**CONF:** $[si \cup abs] \times [ab \cup si]$

**Definition:** The assertion (s CONF f) specifies an outer abstract frame f to which the situation s conforms, or according to which an event proceeds. This frame may be a plan, a rule, a law, an agreement, a general situation, etc.

**Mnemonics:** En: conform (Ge: übereinstimmen)
(s CONF f) – [s holds / takes place according to f]

**Question pattern:** {On the basis of / By virtue of} ⟨WHA⟩ ⟨si⟩?
{According to / After / In accordance with} which ⟨frame⟩ ⟨si⟩?
with ⟨frame⟩ ∈ {law, plan, treaty, regulation, legal authority, algorithm, state of affairs ... }

**Explanation:** The relation CONF plays a role in connection with texts containing normative regulations (typical of juridical domains):

(18.46)  En: "*According to* [*the law of nations*]$\mathrm{CONF}_{arg2}$, *an interference in the inner affairs of foreign countries is forbidden.*"
Ge: "*Nach* [*dem Völkerrecht*]$\mathrm{CONF}_{arg2}$ *sind Einmischungen in die inneren Angelegenheiten fremder Länder untersagt.*"
(18.47)  En: "*The planning was carried out* [*on the basis of the last annual balance*]$\mathrm{CONF}_{arg2}$.*"
Ge: "*Die Planungen wurden* [*auf der Grundlage der letzten Jahresbilanz*]$\mathrm{CONF}_{arg2}$ *durchgeführt.*"

(18.48) En: *"In accordance with [the new regulations]*$^{CONF_{arg2}}$*, smoking in the working rooms is forbidden."*

Ge: *"Gemäß [der neuen Anordnungen]*$^{CONF_{arg2}}$ *ist das Rauchen in den Arbeitsräumen verboten."*

The relation CONF is also often encountered in mathematical texts or in texts of natural science:

(18.49) En: *"According to [Newton's Law]*$^{CONF_{arg2}}$ *the body is falling ever faster."*

Ge: *"Nach [dem Newtonschen Gesetz]*$^{CONF_{arg2}}$ *fällt der Körper immer schneller."*

## 18.2.25   CONTR: Relation of Contrast

**CONTR:** $[p \times p] \cup [ab \times ab] \cup [si \times si]$

**Definition:** The relationship ($p_1$ CONTR $p_2$) with $p_1 \in p$ states that the properties $p_1$ and $p_2$ are excluding each other. The relation CONTR is extended to abstract situations *abs* because they may also stand in contrast to each other. CONTR is symmetric.

**Mnemonics:** En: contrary (Ge: konträr)
   ($p_1$ CONTR $p_2$) – [$p_1$ is standing in contrast to $p_2$]

**Question pattern:** Which property contrasts with ⟨p⟩?
Which property does exclude ⟨p⟩?

**Explanation:** The relation CONTR connects properties that cannot simultaneously be observed with one and the same object.

- (o PROP $p_1$) $\wedge$ ($p_1$ CONTR $p_2$) $\rightarrow \neg$ (o PROP $p_2$)          (135)
- ($p_1$ CONTR $p_2$) $\leftrightarrow$ ($p_2$ CONTR $p_1$)                              (136)

Stating the relation ($p_1$ CONTR $p_2$) is somewhat weaker than asserting the corresponding relation ($p_1$ COMPL $p_2$). In contrast to the relation COMPL, it cannot be concluded that if $p_1$ does not hold then $p_2$ must hold (see Axiom (131)). The relations CONTR and COMPL can both be extended to non-properties (abstract objects, situational descriptors, etc.), which, however, require rather complicated interpretations, technically expressed by meaning postulates.

| | | |
|---|---|---|
| En: (luck CONTR ⟨bad luck⟩) | – | Ge: (Glück CONTR Pech) |
| En: (love CONTR hatred) | – | not simply reducible to properties |
| Ge: (Liebe CONTR Haß) | – | analogously to English |
| En: (heat CONTR ⟨cool down⟩) | $\hat{=}$ | (hot CONTR cold) |
| Ge: (erwärmen CONTR abkühlen) | $\hat{=}$ | (heiß CONTR kalt) |
| En: (life CONTR death) | $\hat{=}$ | (living CONTR dead) |
| Ge: (Leben CONTR Tod) | $\hat{=}$ | (lebendig CONTR tot) |
| In the last case even (living COMPL dead) is true. | | |

## 18.2.26   CORR: Qualitative or Quantitative Correspondence

**CORR:** sort × sort     with **sort** as an arbitrary, but most specific sort which must be the same for both arguments

**Definition:** The expression ($e_1$ CORR $e_2$) is used to specify a qualitative or quantitative correspondence of two entities, $e_1$ and $e_2$, or a mutual assignment in a more general framework comprising both of these entities. The relation CORR is symmetric.

**Mnemonics:** En: correspondence (Ge: Korrespondenz / Entsprechung)
    (($e_1$ CORR $e_2$) – [($e_1$ corresponds to $e_2$]

**Question pattern:** ⟨WH⟩ [do] ⟨$e_1$ / $e_2$⟩ correspond to?
⟨WH⟩ [be] as ⟨p⟩ as ⟨c⟩?

**Explanation:** The different possibilities for mutual assignment of entities to each other by means of the relation CORR is illustrated by the following examples:

(18.50)  qualitative correspondence
    "[*The Bible*]$^{CORR_{arg1}}$ *of the Christian religion corresponds to the* [*Koran*]$^{CORR_{arg2}}$ *of Islam.*"
(18.51)  quantitative correspondence
    "[*The height of a giraffe*]$^{CORR_{arg1}}$ *corresponds approximately to that of* [*a house*]$^{CORR_{arg2}}$."
(18.52)  correspondence within two ordered systems
    "[*The fields* $F_1$, $F_2$, $F_3$]$^{CORR_{arg1}}$ *correspond to* [*the attributes* $A_1$, $A_2$, $A_3$]$^{CORR_{arg2}}$, *respectively.*"

Together with the function *TUPL, the relation CORR allows for a description of the mutual assignment of the elements of pluralities under the consideration of an existing ordering. These constructions correspond to NL surface structures built with "*each*" ... "*respectively*" (Ge: "*jeweils*" or "*beziehungsweise*"). The concept of correspondence which is reflected in the relation CORR is a "fuzzy concept". Even in the case of quantitative correspondences (Example (18.51)) one cannot say that the two corresponding quantities have to be "exactly equal". This finds its expression in the fact that no equality may be inferred from a correspondence, or in other terms:

- (x CORR y) $\not\vdash$ (x EQU y)  (137)

There are also connections between correspondence (relation CORR) and similarity (relations ANLG2/3) on the one hand, and comparison (relation PROP + function *COMP) on the other hand, which have yet to be investigated more thoroughly in connection with the ongoing axiomatization.

## 18.2.27  CSTR: C-Role – Causator

**CSTR:** $[si \cup abs] \times o$

**Definition:** (s CSTR o) expresses the relationship between a situation s (typically an event) and that object o which gives rise to s or which has to be seen as the causator (originator) of s.

**Mnemonics:** En: causator (Ge: Kausator / Verursacher)
(s CSTR o) – [s has the causator o]

**Question pattern:** By whom [be] $\langle si \rangle$ caused?
$\langle WMF \rangle$ [do] $\langle si \rangle$ originate?
$\langle WH \rangle$ [do] {cause / give rise to ... } $\langle si \rangle$?

**Explanation:** All objects characterized as an agent (relation AGT) also have to be classified as causators, i.e. AGT is a special case of the relation CSTR (as is INSTR). The roles of causators (but not of agents) can also be played by substances and abstract concepts like ice and wrath or by concrete objects which have no inner power and thus cannot be agents. The latter include hammer and signpost, as the following examples show:

(18.53)  "[*The ice*]$^{\text{CSTR}_{arg2}}$ *destroyed the rock.*"
(18.54)  "[*The signpost*]$^{\text{CSTR}_{arg2}}$ *reminds the driver to slow down.*"

(18.55)  "[*The hammer*]$^{CSTR_{arg2}}$ *destroyed the window.*"

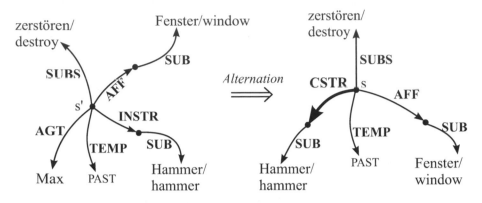

Ge: *"Max zerstörte das Fenster mit einem Hammer."*
→         *"Der Hammer zerstörte das Fenster."*
En: *"Max destroyed the window with a hammer."*
→         *"The hammer destroyed the window."*

**Figure 18.19.** The alternation of roles involving causators

A deeper analysis of such clauses always leads to an underlying causality relation. A closer inspection of the examples reveals that the causator c of an event e specified by the relation (e CSTR c) is often an agent or an instrument of another event e' causing e. In Example (18.54), the causal chain extends over several stages: The signpost shows symbols (signs); these are read by someone. The interpretation and understanding of the symbols then causes a certain effect (e.g. a warning or a reminder).

## 18.2.28   CTXT: Relation Specifying a Restricting Context

**CTXT:** $[si \cup abs] \times [o \cup si]$

**Definition:** The expression (s CTXT c) is used to restrict the persistence or validity of a situation s to a certain context $c \in \{o \cup si\}$. In contrast to CIRC, the relation CTXT has a semantically restrictive character.

**Mnemonics:** En: context (Ge: Kontext)
(s CTXT c) – [s is restricted to the context c]

**Question pattern:** In what context [be] ⟨si⟩ valid?
{With regard to / In connection with} ⟨WHA⟩ [do] ⟨si⟩ hold?
For which ⟨o⟩ [do] ⟨si⟩ hold?

**Explanation:** The relation CTXT belongs to the class of relations which describe the situational embedding of a certain state of affairs. This class includes, among other relations, LOC, TEMP, and CIRC. The assertion (s CTXT c) restricts the validity or persistence of s to a certain context c, i.e. it defines a delimiting domain of validity for s. For the specification of the context c (second argument of CTXT), the indication of a single concept can in some cases be sufficient.

To illustrate the restricting effect of the relation CTXT, the following examples are used:

(18.56) *"The price is much too high for* [*a workstation*]$^{CTXT_{arg2}}$*."*

(18.57) *"The partners in the negotiation agree (only) with regard to* [*the working time regulations*]$^{CTXT_{arg2}}$*."*

(18.58) *"The new product is a genuine innovation regarding* [*its effect on the protection of the environment*]$^{CTXT_{arg2}}$*."*

(18.59) *"The applicability of the regulation is restricted to* [*minors*]$^{CTXT_{arg2}}$*."*

The restriction of a property by the relation CTXT is illustrated in Fig. 18.20.

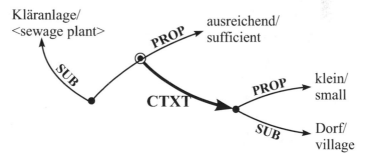

Ge: *"Die Kläranlage ist für ein kleines Dorf ausreichend."*
En: *"The sewage plant is sufficient for a small village."*

**Figure 18.20.** Contextual restriction of the assignment of a property

## 18.2.29    DIRCL: Local Destination or Direction

**DIRCL:** $[si \cup o] \times l$

**Definition:** The relation (e DIRCL l) is used primarily to specify a local goal l, or the direction l of an event e, or of its carrier action, where the goal is marked by a location or by the position of an object. In a broader sense, it is also possible to specify local goals or spatial directions for objects and for states or physical quantities (see below). Thus, the sorts $o$ and $st \subset si$ are also admitted as the first argument of DIRCL.

**Mnemonics:**
En: (local / spatial) direction (Ge: lokales Ziel / räumliche Richtung)
    (e DIRCL l) – [e is spatially directed to l]

**Question pattern:** What destination [do] $\langle si \rangle$ have?
{Where / In what direction / Through $\langle WHA \rangle$ / $\langle WMT \rangle$} [do] {somebody / something} {go / move / drive / fly / ... } ?
{{At / On} $\langle WHA \rangle$ / Where} [do] {somebody / something} {press / look ... }?

**Explanation:** Typical examples of the NL description of directions are:

(18.60)  *"The ship is going [to New York]*$^{DIRCL_{arg2}}$*."*
(18.61)  *"The message was put [into the box]*$^{DIRCL_{arg2}}$*."*
(18.62)  *"The team moved [forward]*$^{DIRCL_{arg2}}$*."*
(18.63)  *"The expedition left [for the Orient]*$^{DIRCL_{arg2}}$*."*

In analogy to the relation ORIGL, things or abstract objects may also be secondarily associated with directions. The expression (c DIRCL l), with $c \in o$ as a first argument, has to be taken as a shorthand notation, just like the corresponding linguistic construction, which is also elliptical:

(18.64)  *"The [train]*$^{DIRCL_{arg1}}$* to [Munich]*$^{DIRCL_{arg2}}$*"* $\leftrightarrow$
    *"The train that [is going]*$^{DIRCL_{arg1}}$* to [Munich]*$^{DIRCL_{arg2}}$*."*
(18.65)  *"[The message]*$^{DIRCL_{arg1}}$* to [New Nork]*$^{DIRCL_{arg2}}$*"* $\leftrightarrow$
    *"The message [sent]*$^{DIRCL_{arg1}}$* to [New Nork]*$^{DIRCL_{arg2}}$*."*
(18.66)  *"The [pressure]*$^{DIRCL_{arg1}}$* onto [the eye]*$^{DIRCL_{arg2}}$*"* $\leftrightarrow$
    *"The pressure which [is exerted]*$^{DIRCL_{arg1}}$* onto [the eye]*$^{DIRCL_{arg2}}$*."*

The first two examples above show, the specification of directions and the local goals do not primarily belong to concrete objects but rather to events inherently connected with these objects or events in which these objects are participating.

The statement (c DIRCL l) with c $\in$ o has to be interpreted by assuming the existence of a directed event where c is playing the role of an agent (AGT) or object (OBJ). In contrast, the assumption of a direction for abstract objects representing directed events (e.g. journey, $\langle$a look$\rangle$, etc.) or directed physical quantities (e.g. pressure, field strength, etc.) is quite natural.

## 18.2.30 DISTG/2/3: Relations Specifying a Difference

**DISTG/2/3:** Binary and ternary relation for characterizing differences.

$$DISTG/2: [\ddot{si} \cup \ddot{o}] \times at \qquad \qquad \text{(binary)}$$
$$DISTG/3: ([si \times si] \cup [o \times o]) \times at \qquad \text{(ternary)}$$

**Definition:** The ternary relationship ($o_1$ DISTG/3 $o_2$ a) expresses that the situations or objects $o_1$ and $o_2$ differ with regard to the attribute a. The relation DISTG/3 is symmetric with regard to the first two arguments.

**Annotation:** Since it is necessary to express also differences between more than two objects with regard to a given attribute, we introduce the binary relation DISTG/2: $[\ddot{si} \cup \ddot{o}] \times at$ as a generalization and a more compact representation admitting a plurality as its first argument. The assertion ($\ddot{g}$ DISTG/2 a) specifies the distinctness of a whole class $\ddot{g}$ of objects with regard to the attribute a. In this way, it represents a multitude of ternary relations, each stating a distinction between another pair of elements of $\ddot{g}$ (see also Axiom (138)).

**Mnemonics:** En: distinguish (Ge: unterscheiden)

($\ddot{g}$ DISTG/2 a) – [the members of $\ddot{g}$ are distinguished with regard to a]
($o_1$ DISTG/3 $o_2$ a) – [$o_1$ is distinguished from $o_2$ by feature a]

**Question pattern:** {How / In what feature} [do] $\langle o_1$ / $si_1\rangle$ and $\langle o_2$ / $si_2\rangle$ differ?
$\langle$WH$\rangle$ [differ] from $\langle o$ / si$\rangle$ in $\langle at\rangle$?
By $\langle$WHA$\rangle$ [do] $\langle o_1$ / $si_1\rangle$ stand out against $\langle o_2$ / $si_2\rangle$?

**Explanation:** The connection between the ternary relation DISTG/3 and the binary relation DISTG/2 is described by the following axiom:

- ($\ddot{g}$ DISTG/2 a) $\leftrightarrow$ $\forall$x $\forall$y [(x ELMT $\ddot{g}_{EXT}$) $\wedge$ (y ELMT $\ddot{g}_{EXT}$) $\wedge$ (x $\neq$ y)
$$\rightarrow (x_{INT} \text{ DISTG/3 } y_{INT} \text{ a)]} \qquad (138)$$

The relation DISTG2/3 is the counterpart to the similarity relation. This also concerns the conventions with regard to the arity (see relations ANLG2/3). There are connections between the relation DISTG and the relations EQU and ANLG emphasizing the differences between these relations:

- $(o_1 \text{ DISTG } o_2 \text{ a }) \rightarrow \neg (o_1 \text{ EQU } o_2)$                     (139)
- $(o_1 \text{ DISTG } o_2 \text{ a}) \rightarrow \neg (o_1 \text{ ANLG } o_2 \text{ a})$              (140)

It is also possible to conclude with a certain heuristic value from the relationship $(o_1 \text{ DISTG } o_2 \text{ a}_1)$ that there exists at least one attribute $a_2 \neq a_1$ with regard to which $o_1$ and $o_2$ are similar, or whose values are equal for $o_1$ and $o_2$ (otherwise, it would not be reasonable to emphasize a difference between $o_1$ and $o_2$ in one attribute a; this opinion can be justified by Grice's **maxims of conversation** [84]).

- $(x \text{ DISTG } y \text{ a}_1) \rightarrow \exists a_2 (a_1 \neq a_2) \wedge (x \text{ ANLG } y \text{ a}_2)$       (141)

An exception to this rule is given when $o_1$ and $o_2$ are "*entirely*" different, i.e. if they really differ with regard to all attributes (therefore, the above-mentioned rule specifies default knowledge only).
Because of the definition of DISTG the following rule holds, too:

- $(o_1 \text{ DISTG } o_2 \text{ a}) \leftrightarrow (o_2 \text{ DISTG } o_1 \text{ a})$                   (142)

### 18.2.31  DPND: Dependency Relation

**DPND:** $ent_{EXT} \times ent_{EXT}$

**Definition:** The relation $(e_1 \text{ DPND } e_2)$ characterizes the extensional $e_1$ as dependent on the extensional $e_2$. The relation DPND is not symmetric and not reflexive.

**Mnemonics:** En: depend (Ge: abhängen)
   $(e_1 \text{ DPND } e_2) - [e_1 \text{ depends on } e_2]$

**Question pattern:** What entity does ⟨ent⟩ depend on?

**Explanation:** The relation DPND shows a parallelism to the Skolem function used in predicate calculus. Both of them are used to represent the extensional dependencies in the semantic interpretations of constructs subject to mixed quantifications; it is here that the relation DPND plays an important part.
   The graphical representation of Fig. 18.21 shows that the extension of G01 with [**QUANT** = *one*] and [**VARIA** = *var*] and of the concept G03 with [**QUANT** = *all*] and [**VARIA** = *con*] clearly differ in their layer attributes. While the former represents a single element [**ETYPE** = 0], the extension of

node G03 is a set with [**ETYPE** = 1].[18] In addition, the relation DPND specifies that the extensional of G02 varies over the set of essays if the extensional
belonging to G01 also varies. Therefore, G02 is labeled by [**REFER** = *indet*]
and [**VARIA** = *var*].

Ge: *"Jeder Schüler schreibt einen Aufsatz."*
En: *"Every student writes an essay."*

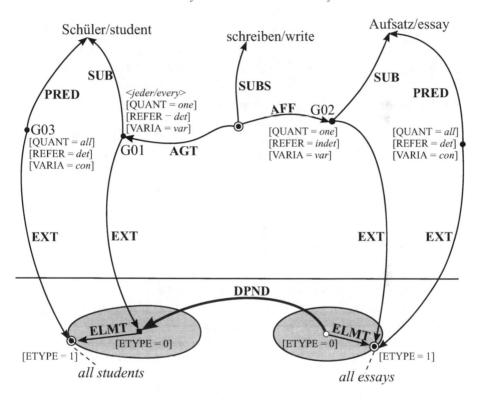

**Figure 18.21.** Dependence between the extensionals of quantified concepts

---

[18] See also the annotation (footnote) for EXT on p. 494.

## 18.2.32   DUR: Relation Specifying a Temporal Extension

**DUR:** $[si \cup o] \times [t \cup si \cup abs \cup ta \cup qn]$

**Definition:** The expression (s DUR t) specifies the duration t or temporal continuance of an event s, or the period of time t when a state s persists. In connection with objects, it is used to specify the duration of existence.

**Mnemonics:** En: duration (Ge: Dauer)
     (s DUR t) – [s holds / takes place during t]

**Question pattern:** How long [do] $\langle si \rangle$ {last / hold / persist … }?
During which period [do] {$\langle si \rangle$ / $\langle o \rangle$} exist?
In what {period / time} [do] {$\langle si \rangle$ / take place $\langle si \rangle$}?

**Explanation:** The distinction between the relations DUR and TEMP is necessary, because the specification of a time span within which an event takes place and the specification of its duration can be simultaneously met in a situation description:

(18.67)   *"In [1909]*$^{TEMP}_{arg2}$ *the Frenchman Bleriot crossed the English
     Channel in [about 35 minutes]*$^{DUR}_{arg2}$ *for the first time."*
(18.68)   *"P. waited [yesterday]*$^{TEMP}_{arg2}$ *for [3 hours]*$^{DUR}_{arg2}$
     *at the railway station."*
(18.69)   *"P. saw the Alps during [the whole flight]*$^{DUR}_{arg2}$.*"
(18.70)   *"In [the 17th century]*$^{TEMP}_{arg2}$ *a journey from Dresden to Leipzig
     took [24 hours]*$^{DUR}_{arg2}$.*"         (see Fig. 18.22).

In contrast, the following example shows an explicit specification of the beginning and end of an event (which is not directly expressed by DUR, but which, of course, is connected by axioms with this relation).

(18.71)   *"The expedition lasted [from August 1831]*$^{STRT}_{arg2}$ *until [May
     1832]*$^{FIN}_{arg2}$.*"

The first argument of the relation DUR can also be an object. In this case, the time span t in the relationship (k DUR t) with $k \in o$ has to be interpreted as the *"lifetime"* of object k.

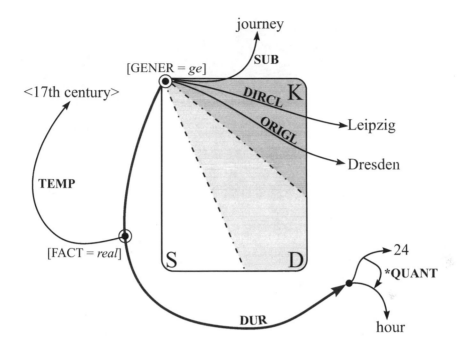

**Figure 18.22.** Temporal restriction of a duration

## 18.2.33   ELMT: Element Relation

**ELMT:** $\text{pe}^{(n)} \times \text{pe}^{(n+1)}$   with $n \geq 0$     ($\text{pe}^{(n)}$ is explained in Appendix A.)

**Definition:**
The statement (e ELMT g) indicates that the entity e is a member of the collection g, i.e. ELMT corresponds to the element relation of naive set theory. Consequently, $g \in \text{pe}^{(n+1)}$ must be a set (preextensional entity) of order n+1 compared to the element $e \in \text{pe}^{(n)}$, which is of order n. In particular, if e is an individual (or a set) then g has to be a set (or a family of sets).[19]

---

[19] Because of this definition, the relation ELMT is not transitive (in contrast to SUBM).

**Mnemonics:** En: element (Ge: Element)
   (e ELMT g) – [e is element of g]

**Question pattern:** Where [do] $\langle e \rangle$ belong to?
Which {set / collection / tuple / ... } is $\langle e \rangle$ an element of?
Which elements [do] $\langle g \rangle$ contain?
$\langle WH \rangle$ [do] belong to $\langle g \rangle$?

**Explanation:** The relation ELMT is used to express the containment of an element in a collection. This relationship is described in the surface structure of NL sentences by phrases like *"including"*, *"belong to"*, and *"is one of ..."* (Ge: *"einschließlich"*, *"gehört zu"*, *"ist eine(r) von"*).

(18.72)  *"[Several teachers]*$ELMT_{arg2}$ *including [the director]*$ELMT_{arg1}$
   *(went on an excursion). "*
(18.73)  *"[Peter]*$ELMT_{arg1}$ *is one of [Lisa's sons]*$ELMT_{arg2}$. *"*

The relationships described in Sentences (18.72) and (18.73) are represented in Fig. 18.23.

By means of the following axiom the relationship between **Peter** and $\langle$**son of Lisa**$\rangle$ may also be expressed with SUB0:

- $(c_1 \text{ EXT } e) \land (e \text{ ELMT } g) \land (g \text{ SETOF } c_2) \rightarrow (c_1 \text{ SUB0 } c_2)$          (143)

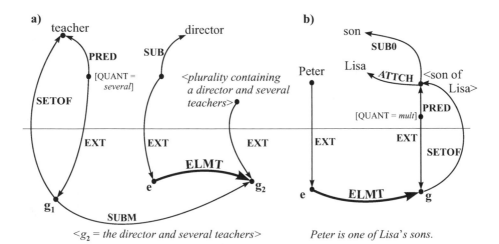

**Figure 18.23.** The use of the element relation in semantic representations

## 18.2.34    EQU: Equivalence Relation

**EQU:** sort × sort      with **sort** as an arbitrary, but most specific sort
which must be the same for both arguments

**Definition:** The expression ($e_1$ EQU $e_2$) states that the entities $e_1$ and $e_2$ are intensionally equal. The relation is symmetric, reflexive and transitive (i.e. it is an equivalence relation).

**Mnemonics:** En: equality (Ge: Gleichheit)
($e_1$ EQU $e_2$) – [$e_1$ has the same meaning as $e_1$]

**Question pattern:** ⟨WMT⟩ [be] ⟨e⟩ equal?
⟨WH⟩ [be] equal to ⟨e⟩?

**Explanation:** Strictly speaking, the relation EQU stands for a whole family of equivalence relations, where every relation is indexed by the sorts on which it is defined.

$EQU_{nu}$: $nu$ × $nu$
This is the equality of numbers defined in algebra.

$EQU_{fe}$: $fe$ × $fe$
This relation is defined as the identity relation for character strings and for elementary symbolic expressions. For symbolic mathematical expressions, it states the equivalence of the values obtained by assigning arbitrary numbers to the variables (according to the signatures of the operators) and evaluating these expressions.

$EQU_{qn}$: $qn$ × $qn$
The meaning of this relation is reduced to the meaning of $EQU_{nu}$ and $EQU_{fe}$, respectively (see function *QUANT and relations MIN/MAJ).

$EQU_{o}$: $o$ × $o$      (corresponds to SYNO; see page 556)
The semantic representatives $o_1$ and $o_2$ of two objects that are extensionally interpretable stand in relation ($o_1$ EQU $o_2$) if and only if $o_1$ and $o_2$ have the same extension, or if (with abstract concepts) the intensional definitions of these concepts can be mutually inferred from each other (this relation corresponds to the synonymy relation in the lexical area, see also the remarks on ANTO p. 452).

$EQU_{si}$: $si$ × $si$      (defined analogously to $EQU_{o}$)

For all other sorts, the equality of semantic structures (i.e. the cases when they describe the same entity) must be defined by means of axioms:

- $((*\text{MODP exceedingly p}) \text{ EQU } (*\text{MODP extremely p}))$    (144)
- $(\text{bachelor}_1 \text{ EQU } r) \leftrightarrow$

$$(r \text{ SUB man}) \wedge \neg (r \text{ PROP married}) \wedge (r \text{ SUB adult}) \quad (145)$$

The following relation holds between EQU and CORR:

- $(e_1 \text{ EQU } e_2) \to (e_1 \text{ CORR } e_2)$    (146)

It is important for the question-answering game that semantic representatives $o_1$ and $o_2$ satisfying the relation ($o_1$ EQU $o_2$) can be substituted for each other in *nonmodal* contexts.

Example:

(Einstein EQU ⟨discoverer of relativity theory ⟩)

*"Einstein lived temporarily in Caputh."* ↔

*"The discoverer of relativity theory lived temporarily in Caputh."*

Counterexample (with modal context):

*"Max knows where Einstein lived."* ↮

*"Max knows where the discoverer of relativity theory lived."*

### 18.2.35   EXP: C-Role – Experiencer of an Event

**EXP:** $[si \cup abs] \times o$

**Definition:** The expression (s EXP o) states that the object o experiences the situation s (usually an event), where o does not actively carry out s. Although o is directly involved in the situation s, it is not physically changed by s.

**Mnemonics:** En: experiencer (Ge: derjenige, der etwas erfährt /

dem etwas widerfährt)

(s EXP o) – [s is experienced by o]

**Question pattern:** ⟨WH⟩ [do] happen with ⟨o⟩?
⟨WH⟩ [be] directly involved in ⟨si⟩ without changing {itself / himself / ... }?
⟨WM⟩ [do] ⟨si⟩ {befall / happen to}?
⟨WH⟩ {[experience] / [endure] / ... } ⟨si⟩ ?

**Explanation:** The "experiencer" is typically described in the surface structure of NL expressions as the subject of such verbs which semantically have neither an agent nor a causator in their deep case frame. Examples:

(18.74)   "$[Max]^{\text{EXP}_{arg2}}$ $[found]^{\text{EXP}_{arg1}}$ *a jewel.*"

(18.75) "$[The\ stone]^{EXP_{arg2}}\ [sank]^{EXP_{arg1}}\ into\ the\ water$."
(18.76) "$[The\ water]^{EXP_{arg2}}\ [is\ flowing]^{EXP_{arg1}}\ through\ the\ channel$."

The relation MEXP is a special case of EXP:

- (s MEXP o) → (s EXP o)                                          (147)

A distinction is made between (s MEXP o) and (s EXP o) because certain mental changes are associated with MEXP, which is not the case for the C-Role EXP. (So, a gain in information can be observed in the memory of the mental experiencer (relation MEXP) of activities like **see** and **hear**.) Moreover, the participant o of the role MEXP is characterized by a certain mental activity. This is different from the relation EXP, where the participant o remains entirely passive (see also relation AGT).

To elucidate the difference between EXP and AGT, the following pairs of concepts shall be given. The C-Roles in parenthesis are each described in English and German by the subject of the corresponding verb in a normal active sentence (with the exception of **einfallen**$_1$, where EXP is described as a dative object in German).

| | | |
|---|---|---|
| Ge: **untergehen** (EXP) | – | **tauchen** (AGT) |
| En: **drown** (EXP) | – | **dive** (AGT) |
| Ge: **finden** (EXP) | – | **suchen** (AGT) |
| En: **find** (EXP) | – | **search** (AGT) |
| Or as a German example which is relevant to the lexical disambiguation: | | |
| Ge: **einfallen**$_1$ (MEXP) [mental] | – | **nachdenken** (AGT) |
| En: **occur**$_1$ (EXP) [mental] | – | **think about** (AGT) |
| But:  Ge: **einfallen**$_2$ (AFF) | [einstürzen] | |
| En: **collapse**$_2$ (AFF) | | |
| Ge: **einfallen**$_3$ (AGT) | [eindringen] | |
| En: **invade**$_3$ (AGT) | | |

## 18.2.36    EXT: Relation Between Intension and Extension

**EXT:** $ent_{INT} \times ent_{EXT}$    with $ent_{INT}$ as an intensional and $ent_{EXT}$ as an extensional

**Definition:** The assertion ($e_1$ EXT $e_2$) establishes the connection between a conceptual representative at the intensional level (the "intensional") $e_1$ and the corresponding meaning component at the preextensional level (the "extensional") $e_2$.

**Mnemonics:** En: extension (Ge: Extension)
  ($e_1$ EXT $e_2$) – [$e_1$ has the extension $e_2$]

**Question pattern:**
What {extensional / intensional} corresponds to {$e_1$ / $e_2$}, respectively?

**Explanation:** The relations EXT, together with SETOF, link the representatives of the intensional level with those of the preextensional level. The first relation is always used if an explicit reference has to be made to the extensional interpretation of concepts.[20]

The example in Fig. 18.24 demonstrates the use of EXT for the semantic representation of collective nouns.

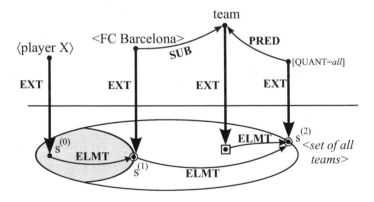

**Figure 18.24.** The extension of concepts described by collective nouns

---

[20] It must be pointed out that the intensional and preextensional levels are clearly distinguished in the graphical representation for the sake of clarity. In the implementation of MultiNet, a more compact representation is preferred where the association to the different levels is encoded in the sorts, layer attributes, and relations. At the implementation level, the relations EXT and SETOF can be omitted.

## 18.2.37   FIN: Temporal End

**FIN:** $[t \cup o \cup si] \times [t \cup ta \cup abs \cup si]$

**Definition:** The expression (s FIN e) states that e marks the temporal end of s. If the second argument e of (s FIN e) represents a situation (i.e. e $\in$ *si*), then the temporal end of s is identified with the beginning of the time interval $t_e$ assigned to e ($t_e$ = period of time e holds). The relation FIN is defined only if the first argument is temporally extended (i.e. $t_s$ is not an exact point in time). If s $\in$ *o* is an object, then e marks the end of the existence of s.

**Mnemonics:** En: final (Ge: Ende / Finale)
   (s FIN e) – [s is finished by e / s has e as temporal end]

**Question pattern:** Until when $\langle si \rangle$?
Until when [do] $\langle o \rangle$ {exist / live / ... }?
Until when [do] $\langle si \rangle$ {hold / last / persist / exist / ... }?
When [do] $\langle si \rangle$ {end / finish / stop / come to an end / ... }?

**Explanation:** The relations ANTE and FIN are connected by the following axiom provided that s, e $\in$ [$t \cup ta \cup abs \cup si$]:

- (s FIN e) $\rightarrow$ (s ANTE e)                                      (148)

The following sentences serve as examples for the temporal termination of an event by a situation (a final state in the first example) and by an ordinary temporal specification:

(18.77)  "[*The division is continued*]$^{\text{FIN}_{arg1}}$ *until*
   [*the remainder is smaller than* $\epsilon$]$^{\text{FIN}_{arg2}}$"
(18.78)  " [*The negotiations {dragged on / lasted}*]$^{\text{FIN}_{arg1}}$
   *until* [*the morning*]$^{\text{FIN}_{arg2}}$."

With regard to the elliptical and metonymic character of sentences pointing seemingly to a concrete object as a **second** argument of the relation FIN (e.g. "[*Until Potsdam*]$^{\text{FIN}_{arg2}}$ *the Allies had quite normal relations with each other.*"), we refer to the remarks on ANTE (see page 451). In this case, the relation FIN does not hold between the state of affairs ⟨the Allies had quite normal relations with each other⟩ and the object Potsdam (this is already forbidden by the signature of FIN).

   Rather than admitting concrete objects as second arguments, it is quite reasonable to extend the domain of the **first** argument of FIN to concrete objects.

In the case k ∈ *co*, (k FIN t) means that t specifies the temporal end of the existence of k ("*k existed / lived until t*").

With regard to the fuzziness of the end of the time interval marked by FIN, the same remarks as for STRT apply.

## 18.2.38    GOAL: Generalized Goal

**GOAL:** $[si \cup o] \times [si \cup o \cup l]$

**Definition:** The expression (s GOAL g) specifies that the object g is the general aim or goal of s, where s is typically a situation. The relation GOAL is superordinate to the relations DIRCL, PURP, and – to a certain extent – to the relation RSLT. The relation GOAL is extended to sort *o* with regard to the first argument, since also objects (e.g. persons) can have goals.

**Mnemonics:** En: goal (Ge: Ziel)
(s GOAL g) – [s has the generalized goal g]

**Question pattern:** What [do] ⟨si⟩ {aim at / lead to ... }?
What is {intended by / the goal of / ... } ⟨si⟩?
Annotation: Corresponding to its definition, further question patterns aiming at the specializations of GOAL are admissible.

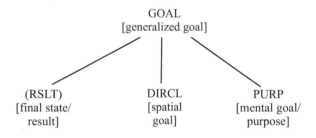

**Figure 18.25.** A relation for representing generalized goals

**Explanation:** The relation GOAL is especially useful for the meaning representation of natural language sentences, if the necessary background knowledge for a finer differentiation between the relations DIRCL, PURP, and RSLT is not available (e.g. in the computational lexicon of NLP systems).

## 18.2.39   HSIT: Constituents of a Hypersituation

**HSIT:** $si \times si$

**Definition:** The expression ($s_1$ HSIT $s_2$) states that the situation $s_2$ is a constituent of the hypersituation $s_1$. The more comprehensive situation $s_1$ is just defined by the fact that it is composed of more than one elementary situation, among them $s_2$.

**Mnemonics:** En: hypersituation (Ge: Hypersituation / globaler Sachverhalt)
  ($s_1$ HSIT $s_2$) – [$s_1$ comprises $s_2$ as a partial situation]

**Question pattern:** –

**Explanation:** The main reason for introducing the relation HSIT consists in the necessity to build global situations (generally described by whole texts) from more elementary ones (generally described by single sentences or phrases). The global situations can be assigned their own names, which can be used as arguments of further relations. Thus, hypersituations can describe causes or conditions, and they may be modified by temporal or modal restrictions. In this way, the relation HSIT is already building a bridge to the text-constituting relations, investigated in the "Rhetorical Structure Theory" [175], and which combine several semantically represented situations into one higher unit having a certain inner structure. Typical hypersituations consisting of more than one elementary situation are, for example, ⟨a wedding⟩, ⟨a horse race⟩, ⟨a visit to a concert⟩, etc.

Another reason for the introduction of the relation HSIT arises from the necessity to make propositions about a complex situation sv composed of n partial situations $sv_1, \ldots, sv_n$, which are connected to sv by means of HSIT. For example, one might want to state that the configuration sv of the situations $sv_1, \ldots, sv_n$ is believed, or gives rise to another state of affairs. If we take the concept ⟨Peter's wedding⟩ as hypersituation sv, the partial situations could be $sv_1 = $ ⟨the reception of the guests⟩, $sv_2 = $ ⟨the wedding ceremony⟩, $sv_3 = $ ⟨the wedding party⟩, etc. Having defined sv in such a way by means of HSIT, and encapsulating the partial situations $sv_1, \ldots, sv_n$ into the unit sv, one could state that sv took place before another situation sv' (e.g. the honeymoon or an accident), expressing this fact by (sv ANTE sv').

With semantically unrestricted complex situations sv composed of two or more situations, there is a connection to the conjunction convention (p. 407), since the partial situations are conjunctively connected.

Thus, the joint task of HSIT and the mechanism of encapsulation is the combination of selected situations into one unit (a hypersituation) that consists of components logically connected by a conjunction.

## 18.2.40   IMPL: Implication Relation Between Situations

**IMPL:** $([si \sqcup abs] \times [si \sqcup abs]) \cup [p \times p] \cup [rq \times rq]$

**Definition:** The assertion ($s_1$ IMPL $s_2$) expresses that the situation or concept $s_1$ implies the situation or the concept $s_2$ on a purely conceptual level, i.e. IMPL represents an analytical relation of conclusion based only on the intensional meaning of the arguments indicated. The connection between the cognitive roles of the concepts participating in the description of the arguments $s_1$ and $s_2$ is established by the entities shared by the conceptual capsules representing the situations $s_1$ and $s_2$ (see Fig. 18.26). The relation IMPL is transitive.

**Mnemonics:** En: implication (Ge: Implikation)
     ($s_1$ IMPL $s_2$) – [$s_1$ implies $s_2$]

**Question pattern:** Which {state of affairs / situation} implies ⟨si⟩?
What {follows / can be concluded} from ⟨si⟩?

**Explanation:** The relation IMPL is typically used for building and representing the immanent knowledge. It permits a compact representation of logical relations between situations or between properties.

In the case of properties, there is a rather straightforward interpretation of the relation IMPL:

- (p1 IMPL p2) –> ((o PROP p1) –> (o PROP p2))                    (149)

This means that, given the relationship (lesbian IMPL homosexual), we can state that a person who is lesbian is also homosexual. The analogue holds for the German concepts (verwandt IMPL ähnlich) (En: (akin IMPL similar)), which are examples of relational properties.
Implications between situations (e.g. between a "giving-event" and a "receiving-event") should better be described by predicate calculus expressions because of the complexities of the argument relations involved (see the B-Axioms in Appendix E.5, Axiom (215)).
The semantic structure of causative verbs can also be easily described by means of the relations IMPL and RSLT. Figure 18.26 shows a detail from the logical connection between the meanings of the verbs kill and die.

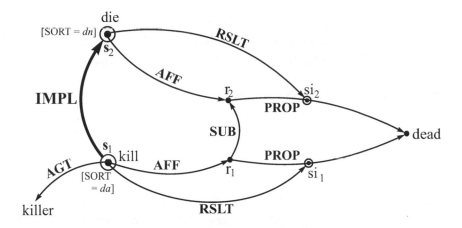

**Figure 18.26.** The implication relation between the concepts kill and die

The example also illustrates the difference between the relations IMPL and SUBS. In the partial network of Fig. 18.26, the IMPL arc expresses that die is always a logical consequence of kill; it also indicates which relationship holds between the affected objects of these events. By contrast, a supposed relation SUBS between kill and die would mean that the first action is a special case of the latter event (i.e. killing would be a kind of "⟨dying action⟩") which undoubtedly is not true. The valency frame of die must not be inherited by kill, which should be the case, however, with SUBS (kill as an action with sort *da* has an active agent, while die as a happening with sort *dn* expressly excludes an agent).

The causal relation CAUS is also not an adequate connection between kill and die, because the concepts dead and die already belong to the semantic field of kill. This can be seen from the fact that sentences of the following type are semantically deviating: *"Since Max killed him, he is dead/he died."*, which is a pleonasm. This can also be shown by the so-called **But-test**, stating that propositions contradicting each other must not be connected by the conjunction *"but"*, because *"but"* is essentially an *"and"* expressing a contrast.
Example: *"Max had killed him, but he did not die."* (??)
The But-test is not violated in the case of causality relations, which can be seen from the following examples:
*"Since Max had hit him with the club, he died."*
*"Max had hit him with the club, but he did not die."*
Also the correspondence between causal sentences and their "incausal" counterparts has no parallel for sentences describing implications.
The following transformation leads from one acceptable sentence to another:

*"Since Max had hit him with the club, he died."* (Relation: CAUS)
*"Although Max had hit him with the club, he did not die."* → acceptable
The corresponding transformation is not possible for IMPL sentences:
*"Since Max had killed him, he died."* (??) (Relation: IMPL) → not acceptable
*"Although Max had killed him, he did not die."* (??) → not acceptable.

## 18.2.41    INIT: Initial Situation or Entity

**INIT:** $[si \cup abs] \times [o \cup si]$

**Definition:** The assertion (e INIT s) establishes a connection between an event e and an initial situation (typically a state) s which is encountered immediately before e starts. The initial situation s can also be characterized, for short, by an object if this object is changed by e.

**Mnemonics:** En: initial (Ge: Initial- / Anfangs-Zustand)
(e INIT s) – [e has s as initial situation / starting point]

**Question pattern:** ⟨WHF⟩ [do] ⟨si⟩ produce the result?
From which {initial situation / initial state / ... } [do] ⟨si⟩ start?
⟨WH⟩ {can be observed / does hold} at the beginning of ⟨si⟩?

**Explanation:** The relation INIT is the counterpart of RSLT. It is closely associated to AFF and ORIGM, which can be expressed by convenient axioms.

- (e AFF $o_1$) $\land$ ($o_1$ ORIGM $o_2$) → (e INIT $o_2$)                    (150)

The use of the relations INIT and RSLT is typical of the semantic representation of events expressing changes or transformations in the broadest sense (see Example (18.79) below).
The following relationship holds between RSLT, ORIGM, and INIT:

- (e RSLT $d_1$) $\land$ ($d_1$ ORIGM $d_2$) → (e INIT $d_2$)                    (151),

If the second argument of INIT is a situation $s \in si$, then the following relationship can be formulated:

- (e INIT s) → (s FIN e) $\land$ (s ANTE e)                    (152)

i.e., the situation s is finished by e.[21]

---

[21] The term containing ANTE in (152) is in principle redundant because of the rule (s FIN e) → (s ANTE e).

(18.79) *"The program [transforms]*$^{INIT}_{arg1}$ *[the matrix]*$^{AFF}_{arg2}$ *from [its
original representation]*$^{INIT}_{arg2}$ *into [its diagonal form]*$^{RSLT}_{arg2}$*."*

(18.80) *"Starting with [a low pressure]*$^{INIT}_{arg2}$ *[the gas]*$^{AFF}_{arg2}$ *[is ever
more compressed]*$^{INIT}_{arg1}$*."*

The following example shows very clearly the elliptical character of most
of the sentences describing INIT / RSLT relationships:

(18.81) *"The scholar [translates]*$^{INIT}_{arg1}$ *[the article]*$^{AFF}_{arg2}$ *from
[English]*$^{INIT}_{arg2}$ *(i.e. from its English form) into [Russian]*$^{RSLT}_{arg2}$
*(i.e. into its Russian form)."*

## 18.2.42 INSTR: C-Role – Instrument

**INSTR:** $[si \cup abs] \times co$

**Definition:** The statement (s INSTR o) establishes a connection between a situation s (typically an action) and the instrument o, which is used to carry out s
(in the case of an event) or to sustain s (in the case of a state).

**Mnemonics:** En: instrument (Ge: Instrument)
  (s INSTR o) – [s is carried out / sustained with o]

**Question pattern:** What instrument or tool is used for ⟨s⟩?
{By / By means of} ⟨WHA⟩ is ⟨s⟩ {carried out / sustained}?
Through what medium [be] ⟨o⟩ {transferred / conveyed / ... }?

**Explanation:** As required by the definition, instruments are always concrete
objects. Strictly speaking, they should be inanimate [66]. To represent the abstract means by which an action is carried out or a state is sustained, the relation
METH is provided in MultiNet.

(18.82) *"Peter [drives]*$^{INSTR}_{arg1}$ *with [his car]*$^{INSTR}_{arg2}$ *through the
town."*

(18.83) *"Max [draws]*$^{INSTR}_{arg1}$ *the figure with [the computer]*$^{INSTR}_{arg2}$*."*

An example showing the parallel and contrasting use of MANNR and INSTR
is given in the sentence: [22]

---

[22] The distinction between MANNR and INSTR is actually not so difficult as that between
MANNR and METH. It is nevertheless not unproblematic, since both relations may be asked
for with *"How?"*, and both relations are specializations of a generalized mode; see relation
MODE.

(18.84) *"He [holds]*$^{\text{INSTR}_{arg1}}$ *the vessel [carefully]*$^{\text{MANNR}_{arg2}}$ *with [both hands]*$^{\text{INSTR}_{arg2}}$ *[over his head]*$^{\text{LOC}_{arg2}}$*."*

The simultaneous occurrence of INSTR and METH in one and the same situation is shown by the following example:

(18.85) *"The results were obtained very effectively with [a PASCAL program]*$^{\text{INSTR}_{arg2}}$ *after the [method of Cooley-Tucker]*$^{\text{METH}_{arg2}}$*."*

The following connection can be established between the relation INSTR and the relation PURP representing a purpose:

- $(v_1 \text{ SUBS s}) \land (v_1 \text{ AGT } k_1) \land (v_1 \text{ INSTR } k_2) \rightarrow$
  $\exists v_2 (v_2 \text{ SUBS use}) \land (v_2 \text{ AGT } k_1) \land (v_2 \text{ OBJ } k_2) \land (v_2 \text{ PURP } v_1)$    (153)

### 18.2.43   JUST: Justification of a Situation

**JUST:** $[si \cup abs] \times [si \cup abs]$

**Definition:** The relationship ($s_1$ JUST $s_2$) states that $s_1$ is an ethical justification or a socially conventionalized reason for the situation (state of affairs) $s_2$. In other words, $s_1$ is the social justification for $s_2$.

**Mnemonics:** En: justification (Ge: Begründung / Rechtfertigung)
       ($s_1$ JUST $s_2$) – [$s_1$ is justified by $s_2$]

**Question pattern:** {Why / For what reason} $\langle s_2 \rangle$?
Because of $\langle \text{WHA} \rangle$ $\langle si_2 \rangle$?

**Explanation:** The relation JUST represents socially postulated relationships of reason that cannot be expressed by CAUS or IMPL. The relation JUST, establishing a connection between (real) situations/states of affairs, is the complement of CAUS and IMPL in the field of moral or social reasons. All three relations, JUST, CAUS, and IMPL, are subordinate to REAS (see page 534). The order of the arguments of JUST, and thus the direction of the corresponding arc in the SN was chosen in such a way that the reason (justification) is given first, and the situation justified by the first argument follows as the second argument. With this convention, a parallelism with the argument order of CAUS and IMPL is warranted.

(18.86) *"[Since Peter is a Baptist]*$^{\text{JUST}_{arg1}}$*, [ he was baptized as an adult]*$^{\text{JUST}_{arg2}}$*."*

(18.87) "*[Nobody is smoking in this room]*$^{\text{JUST}_{arg2}}$, *because [it is forbidden]*$^{\text{JUST}_{arg1}}$."

## 18.2.44   LEXT: Relation Specifying a Local Extent

**LEXT:** $[si \cup o] \times [l \cup m]$

**Definition:** The assertion (o LEXT l) specifies the local/spatial extent y of a situation or of an object x without referring to a local origin or local end.

**Mnemonics:** En: local extent (Ge: lokale Erstreckung / Ausdehnung)
  (o LEXT l) – [o has the local extension l]

**Question pattern:** How far [do] ⟨si / o⟩ extend ?
Over what {distance / area / range} {⟨si⟩ / [do] ⟨abs⟩ extend}?
What {size / spatial extent} [do] ⟨o⟩ have?

**Explanation:** A separate definition of the relation LEXT apart from LOC is necessary because the specifications of a local restriction and a local extension have to sometimes be used in parallel (see example Sentence (18.88)).

(18.88) *"P. traveled [in Spain]*$^{\text{LOC}_{arg2}}$ *[over 30 km]*$^{\text{LEXT}_{arg2}}$ *with defective tires."*
(18.89) *"The oil pollution extended [over the whole coast]*$^{\text{LEXT}_{arg2}}$."*
(18.90) *"The cars got jammed [from Cologne to Bonn]*$^{\text{LEXT}_{arg2}}$. "*

Annotation:  In the last example, "*Cologne*" is not a local origin (ORIGL), and
    "*Bonn*" not a local goal (DIRCL).

The last example (18.90) also shows that an interval described by means of the function *TUPL can be used to specify a local extension. The relation LEXT has to be connected with a group of meaning postulates by means of which the different representational forms of local extensions can be transformed into each other. As an example illustrating the different variants for semantically equivalent representations of a local extension, the description of an object o = ⟨a dam being 3 km long⟩ shall be used [23]:

---

[23] These equivalence relations can be generalized to an axiom schema by substituting appropriate variables for **dam** and ⟨3 km⟩.

(18.91)  (o SUB dam) ∧ (o LEXT (∗QUANT ⟨3 km⟩)) ↔
         (o SUB dam) ∧ (o PROP (∗MODP long (∗QUANT ⟨3 km⟩))) ↔
         ∃x (o SUB dam) ∧ (o ATTR x) ∧ (x SUB length) ∧
                                    (x VAL (∗QUANT ⟨3 km⟩))

## 18.2.45   LOC: Location of a Situation

**LOC:** $[o \cup si] \times l$

**Definition:** The assertion (s LOC l) specifies that the object s ∈ o is at place l, or that the situation s ∈ si holds at location l, or – if the situation is an event – it is taking place at l.

**Mnemonics:** En: location (Ge: Lokation)
          (s LOC l) – [s is located at l / takes place at l]

**Question pattern:** Where ⟨si⟩?
Where [do] ⟨si⟩ {take place / persist / pertain / hold}?
Where [be] ⟨o⟩ {located / situated}?
{⟨loc-praep⟩ ⟨WHA⟩} ⟨si⟩?
          where ⟨loc-praep⟩ ∈ {at, beside, before, behind, below, between, in, next_to, on, over, out_of, under, within, ... };
          see also the groups of functions ∗FLIP and ∗FLOP on page 570.

**Explanation:** In contrast to directions, nondirected locations are primarily assigned to objects. In this case, (x LOC l), with x ∈ o, has to be interpreted as the specification of the spatial area l occupied by the object x. The relation LOC is applicable not only to concrete objects but also to abstract objects. It has to be emphasized, however, that local relationships involving abstract objects as arguments have to be especially interpreted by meaning postulates, i.e. on the basis of background knowledge (see also the remarks on abstract locations in connection with the relation SITU on page 541).

(18.92)  *"The religion [in India]*$^{\text{LOC}_{arg2}}$ ... "
(18.93)  *"The pressure [in the boiler]*$^{\text{LOC}_{arg2}}$ ... "

The relation LOC can be used for the local characterization of events (Examples 18.94 and 18.95) as well as for the spatial restriction of the validity of states (Examples 18.96 and 18.97):

(18.94)  *"The shares were sold by the broker
          [at the stock exchange]*$^{\text{LOC}_{arg2}}$."

(18.95) *"The work [in the disaster area]*$\text{LOC}_{arg2}$ *... "*
(18.96) *"Electrons are freely movable [in conductors]*$\text{LOC}_{arg2}$ *(only). "*
(18.97) *"Peter is waiting [at the station]*$\text{LOC}_{arg2}$ *."*

Example (18.94) shows that the correspondence between locations of situations and locations of participating objects can be rather complicated. In this case, neither the shares nor the broker must have been at the place of selling, i.e. at the stock exchange. Therefore, it is quite reasonable to assign the specified location in the first instance to the situation (not to the participants). It is only in the second step that one can figure out where every participating object is located. In the semantic representation of sentence (18.96), the relation LOC has to be positioned outside the conceptual capsule of the situation as a semantically restrictive modification (see Sect. 17.7). This relation, therefore, has to be characterized by [**K-TYPE** = *restr*] with regard to its first argument, which is often the case with LOC relations in generic situations.

### 18.2.46  MAJ/MAJE: 'Greater than (or Equal to)'-Relation

**MAJ/MAJE:** $qn \times qn$

**Definition:** The statement ($q_1$ MAJ $q_2$) expresses that the number or quantity $q_1$ exceeds the number or quantity $q_2$. The relation MAJE, expressing the relationship "greater than or equal to" is defined analogously to the relation MAJ .

**Mnemonics:** Latin: maior (Ge: majorisieren)
$\quad$ ($q_1$ MAJ $q_2$) – [$q_1$ is greater than $q_2$]

**Question pattern:** Is $\langle qn_1 \rangle$ more than $\langle qn_2 \rangle$?
$\langle$WH$\rangle$ [be] greater than $\langle qn \rangle$?
$\langle$WH$\rangle$ [have] a greater value of the attribute $\langle at \rangle$ than $\langle qn \rangle$?
$\quad$ The last question is only indirectly aiming at MAJ.

**Explanation:** The comparison of quantities with regard to their amount is reduced to that of numbers by defining that, for $q_1 = (*\text{QUANT } n_1 \text{ me}_1)$ and $q_2 = (*\text{QUANT } n_2 \text{ me}_2)$, the following holds:

- ($q_1$ MAJ $q_2$) $\wedge$ (me$_1$ EQU me$_2$) $\leftrightarrow$ ($n_1$ MAJ $n_2$) $\wedge$ (me$_1$ EQU me$_2$)   (154)

In certain cases a function for the transformation of measurement units (to kilometers from miles, for instance) must be used to warrant the compatibility of these entities (if they can be compared at all). It should further be noticed that the relations MAJ / MAJE are also defined for non-numerical quantifications. In this way, comparisons between meaning representatives of quantificators like few, several, many, most, etc. can be expressed; for example:

(18.98)  (most MAJ few) – most {is greater/is more than} few      (Default)
(18.99)  (many MAJ several) – many {is greater/is more than} several

## 18.2.47   MANNR: Relation Specifying the Manner

**MANNR:** $si \times [ql \cup st \cup as]$

**Definition:** The expression (s MANNR m) is used for a more detailed characterization or qualitative specification of an event or a state s by defining the manner m in which the event is carried out or the state persists.

**Mnemonics:** En: manner (Ge: Art und Weise)
(s MANNR m) – [s is carried out / persists in the manner m]

**Question pattern:** {How / In which way} [be] $\langle s \rangle$ carried out?
{How / In which way} [be] $\langle s \rangle$ {upheld / kept / maintained}?
How is $\langle s \rangle$ {qualified / characterized}?

**Explanation:** To qualify a situation more closely, entities belonging to different sorts can be used:

(18.100)  *"P. drives [fast]*$^{MANNR_{arg2}}$*."*
(18.101)  *"...positioning the numbers [in a decreasing order]*$^{MANNR_{arg2}}$*."*
(18.102)  *"...arrange things in such a way that [every piece is larger than its right neighbor]*$^{MANNR_{arg2}}$*."*
(18.103)  *"P. is hanging [upside down]*$^{MANNR_{arg2}}$ *from the horizontal bar."*

The relation MANNR is a specialization of the relation MODE. The semantic distinction from the relation METH is somewhat problematic if the second argument m is a situation $m \in si$. As a simplified criterion, it is assumed that the relation MANNR holds if m is a static situation (i.e. $m \in st$ or $m \in as$), and that relation METH holds if m is a dynamic situation (i.e. $m \in dy$ or $m \in ad$).

## 18.2.48   MCONT: C-Role – Relation Between a Mental Process and Its Content

**MCONT:** $[si \cup o] \times [o \cup si]$

**Definition:** The expression (s MCONT c) permits a specification of the informational or mental content c of a mental or informational process s. The relation MCONT is also used to represent the informational or mental content of the *result* of such a process (e.g. a writing process), see Example (18.107), which motivates this shorthand notation. By default, the second argument c is assumed to be a hypothetical object or situation (i.e. $c \in [\tilde{o} \cup \tilde{si}]$).

**Mnemonics:** En: mental content (Ge: mentaler Inhalt / Gehalt)
     (s MCONT o) – [s is characterized by the informational
                    or mental content o]

**Question pattern:**
⟨WHA⟩ [do] somebody {think / reason / dream / assume / ... } ?
What [do] somebody {say / convey / contain / hear / tell / ... }?
What [do] somebody {learn / come to know / experience / ... }?
What [do] somebody {believe / remember / ... } ?
{About what / Of what} [do] [carrier of the action] ⟨inform-proc⟩?
               (with ⟨inform-proc⟩ ∈ {speak, write, think, ... })

**Explanation:** It is characteristic of the relation MCONT that nothing can be said a priori (i.e. without additional information) about the validity or truth value of the second argument (in case it is a situation) or about its existence (in case it is an object). This is often expressed in the German surface structure of a clause by setting the second argument in the conjunctive mood (see Example 18.104). For that reason, the second argument c of the relation MCONT has at first to be considered a hypothetical entity with the attribute [**FACT** = *hypo*]. But, the corresponding situation can be qualified later on by additional information as being real. In contrast to the relation OBJ, the default assumption holds that the second argument c of MCONT is not independent of the validity or existence of the first argument.[24]

---

[24] But the simultaneous characterization of an entity as the second argument of the relations OBJ and MCONT explicitly expresses the independence of this entity from the first argument of these relations, see also the distinction between ⟨think that⟩ and ⟨think of⟩ on page 511.

The relation MCONT is often used to connect representatives of main clauses (i.e. sentence nodes) with the semantic representatives of "that-clauses" (Ge: "daß-Sätze") expressing the content of mental processes.

(18.104)  En: *"The mathematician believed that [he had found a proof]*MCONT$_{arg2}$.*"*

Ge: *"Der Mathematiker glaubte, daß [er einen Beweis gefunden habe]*MCONT$_{arg2}$.*"*

(18.105)  En: *"The boy dreams of [his girlfriend]*MCONT+OBJ$_{arg2}$.*"*

Ge: *"Der Junge träumt von [seiner Freundin]*MCONT+OBJ$_{arg2}$.*"*

(18.106)  En: *"P. is engrossed with the idea of [going on a holiday trip]*MCONT$_{arg2}$.*"*

Ge: *"P. trägt sich mit der Idee, [in den Urlaub zu fahren]*MCONT$_{arg2}$.*"*

(18.107)  En: *"A book about [the mammoth cave]*MCONT$_{arg2}$...*"*

Ge: *"Ein Buch über [die Mammuthöhle]*MCONT$_{arg2}$...*"*

(18.108)  En: *"The negotiations about [disarmament]*MCONT$_{arg2}$...*"*

Ge: *"Die Verhandlungen über [Abrüstung]*MCONT$_{arg2}$...*"*

(18.109)  En: *"The notification of [his friend's death]*MCONT+OBJ$_{arg2}$"*

Ge: *"Die Mitteilung über [den Tod seines Freundes]*MCONT+OBJ$_{arg2}$"*

## 18.2.49   MERO: Meronymy Relation

**MERO:** $[o \times o] \cup [l \times l] \cup [t \times t]$

**Definition:** The expression ($o_1$ MERO $o_2$) states that $o_1$ is a part of $o_2$ in a very general sense. MERO is defined as a generalization of the relations PARS, ORIGM, ELMT, SUBM, and TEMP comprising all partonymic relationships.

**Mnemonics:** En: meronymy (Ge: Meronymie)
      ($o_1$ MERO $o_1$) – [$o_1$ is (a generalized) part of $o_2$]

**Question pattern:** $\langle WH \rangle$ [be] {part / component / member / . . . } of $\langle o \rangle$? Which {parts / components / members / . . . } [do] $\langle o \rangle$ have?

**Explanation:** The relation MERO was introduced since the borderline between different part-whole relations is very difficult to draw from an analytical point of view. They comprise such different semantic phenomena as "a part of a thing", "a member of a collection", "a part of a time interval", "a constituent of an abstract object", "a component of a tuple", etc.

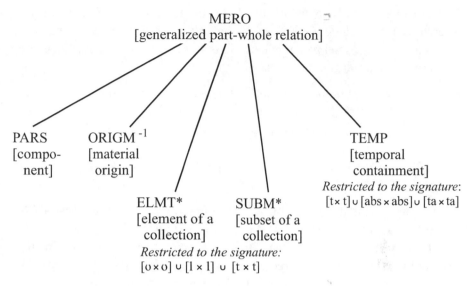

The star '*' indicates an abbreviation:
$$(x \text{ ELMT*/SUBM* } y) \leftrightarrow \exists\, x_e\, \exists\, y_e\, (x \text{ EXT } x_e) \wedge (y \text{ EXT } y_e) \wedge (x_e \text{ ELMT/SUBM } y_e)$$

**Figure 18.27.** The generalized part-whole relation (meronymy relation)

## 18.2.50   METH: C-Role – Method

**METH:** $[si \cup abs] \times [dy \cup ad \cup io]$

**Definition:** The expression (s METH m) describes the connection between a situation s (typically an event) and an abstract object or event m representing the method by which s is carried out (in the case of an event s) or by which s is sustained (in the case of a state s).

**Mnemonics:** En: method (Ge: Methode)
          (s METH m) – [s is carried out / sustained by method m]

**Question pattern:** {According to / By} which method [do] ⟨o⟩ work?
How [do] ⟨o⟩ {produce / find / proceed / ... / sit / stand / lie / ... }?
{According to / By} which method [be] ⟨s⟩ {carried out / sustained}?
By what means [be] ⟨o⟩ {discovered / proved / brought about / ... } ?

**Explanation:** To characterize the method by which an event is carried out or a state is sustained, one can not only specify an abstract concept (the designation of the method), but also explicitly use an event or a sequence of events to characterize just the method in question. In the first two of the following examples events are characterized by a method, and in the last example a method is used to characterize a state:

(18.110) *"The integration is carried out by means of [Simpson's Rule]*$\mathrm{METH}_{arg2}$*."*

(18.111) *"The students arranged themselves in such a way that [the girls came first and then the boys]*$\mathrm{METH}_{arg2}$*."*

(18.112) *"The artist keeps his balance [by using a large balance pole]*$\mathrm{METH}_{arg2}$*."*

With regard to the distinction between the relations METH and MANNR it has to be stated that a method m is generally specified by an event (m $\subset$ [*dy* $\cup$ *ad*]) or by explicitly giving the name of a known method (m $\subset$ *io*), while a manner in the narrower sense, represented by the relation MANNR, is typically described by a quality or a state. METH, like MANNR, is a specialization of the relation MODE, which describes a more generalized kind of modus operandi. The relation PURP, characterizing a purpose, and the relation METH are connected by the following axiom:

- $(v_1 \text{ SUBS } v) \wedge (v_1 \text{ AGT } k) \wedge (v_1 \text{ METH } m)$
  $\rightarrow \exists\, v_2\, (v_2 \text{ SUBS use}) \wedge (v_2 \text{ AGT } k) \wedge (v_2 \text{ OBJ } m) \wedge (v_2 \text{ PURP } v)$    (155)

## 18.2.51    MEXP: C-Role – Mental Experiencer

**MEXP:** [*si* $\cup$ *abs*] $\times$ *d*

**Definition:** (s MEXP o) specifies the relationship between a mental process or state s bearing the attribute value [MENTAL+] and an animate object o with [ANIMATE+] which is experiencing s.

**Mnemonics:** En: mental experiencer (Ge: mentaler Träger)
       (s MEXP o) – [s is mentally experienced by o]

**Question pattern:** In what mental state [be] $\langle o \rangle$?
$\langle WH \rangle$ [do] something [$\langle$ment_state_proc$\rangle$]?
       (with $\langle$ment_state_proc$\rangle$ $\in$ {believe, know, think, hope, ... })

**Explanation:** The relation MEXP is used to connect mental states or processes with their carriers. MEXP is a special case of the relation EXP; see page 492.

(18.113) "[*Max*]<sup>MEXP</sup>ₐᵣg₂ [*is convinced*]<sup>MEXP</sup>ₐᵣg₁ *that Susan will come.*"

(18.114) "[*The hunter*]<sup>MEXP</sup>ₐᵣg₂ [*saw*]<sup>MEXP</sup>ₐᵣg₁ *a black-tailed deer.*"

The relation MEXP also makes it possible to differentiate semantically between certain kinds of verbs (between their subject roles, to be specific):

see → MEXP,      observe → AGT

hear → MEXP,      ⟨listen to⟩ → AGT      etc.

A state whose semantic representation involves the relation MEXP is in general also associated with the relation MCONT, or with the relation OBJ, or possibly even with both. Exceptions are meaning representations of intransitive verbs denoting mental states (like sleep) which do not admit an object.

Example:

On the basis of this conception, the difference between ⟨think of⟩ (Ge: ⟨denken an⟩) and ⟨think that⟩ (Ge: ⟨denken, daß⟩) can be explained.

The valency frame of ⟨think that⟩ (⟨denken daß⟩) contains only MCONT apart from MEXP; or more formally expressed:

[⟨think that⟩ (MEXP x) + (MCONT y)]

In contrast, the second argument of ⟨think of⟩ (⟨denken an⟩) is characterized by both relations, MCONT and OBJ:

[⟨think of⟩ (MEXP x) + (MCONT y) + (OBJ y)]

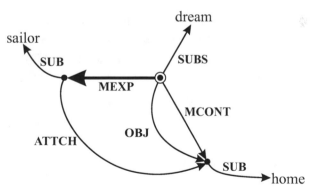

*"The sailor is dreaming of his home."*

**Figure 18.28.** Double characterization of a participant as both a neutral object and mental content

## 18.2.52    MIN/MINE: 'Smaller than (or Equal to)'-Relation

**MIN/MINE:** $qn \times qn$

**Definition:** The statement ($q_1$ MIN $q_2$) expresses that the number or quantity $q_1$ is smaller than the number or quantity $q_2$. The relation MINE denoting the relationship "smaller than or equal to" is defined analogously.

**Mnemonics:** Latin: minor (Ge: minorisieren)
    ($q_1$ MIN $q_2$) – [$q_1$ is less than $q_2$]

**Question pattern:** Is $\langle qn_1 \rangle$ smaller than $\langle qn_2 \rangle$?
$\langle WH \rangle$ [have] a smaller value of the attribute $\langle at \rangle$ than $\langle qn \rangle$?

**Explanation:** The comparison of quantities with regard to their amount is reduced to that of numbers by defining that, for $q_1 = (*\text{QUANT } n_1 \ m_1)$ and $q_2 = (*\text{QUANT } n_2 \ m_2)$, the following holds:

- $(q_1 \text{ MIN } q_2) \wedge (m_1 \text{ EQU } m_2) \leftrightarrow (n_1 \text{ MIN } n_2) \wedge (m_1 \text{ EQU } m_2)$            (156)

As the case may be, the agreement of the measurement units $m_1$ and $m_2$ (if they can at all be compared) has to be brought about by using special transformation functions for quantities and measurement units (e.g. for transforming \$US to Euro).

It must be emphasized that the relations MIN / MINE are also defined for non-numerical quantificators. On that basis, comparisons between meaning representatives of quantificators like very few, several, many, most, all, etc. can also be formulated:

(18.115)  (two MIN several) means: two is smaller than several.
(18.116)  (several MIN all) means: several is smaller than all.

## 18.2.53    MODE: Generalized Mode of a Situation

**MODE:** $[si \cup abs] \times [o \cup si \cup ql]$

**Definition:** The expression (s MODE m) specifies a generalized manner m after which an event s is carried out or a state s is sustained. It comprises the relations MANNR, METH, and INSTR.

**Mnemonics:** En: mode (Ge: Modus)
(s MODE m) – [s is carried out / is sustained by m]

**Question pattern:** {How / In which way} [be] ⟨si⟩ {carried out / sustained}?
How does the agent of ⟨si⟩ {work / move / ... } ?

**Explanation:** It is sensible to introduce the relation MODE of a generalized manner in addition to the already existing relations. On the one hand, it comprises those relations for which one can ask by means of the interrogative pronoun *"How?"*; on the other hand, this relation can be used during the automatic generation of meaning representations whenever there is insufficient background knowledge for disambiguation into the more specific relations.

(18.117) *"How did he fell the tree?"*
     ⇒ *"with [a motor saw]*$MODE_{arg2}$*"*.          (INSTR)
(18.118) *"How did he prove it?"*
     ⇒ *"by the method of [diagonalization]*$MODE_{arg2}$*"*.
                                                      (METH)
(18.119) *"How does the program work?"*
     ⇒ *"[extremely reliably]*$MODE_{arg2}$*"*          (MANNR)

The relation INSTR characterizes an action through a concrete object by means of which the action is carried out; METH characterizes an event by a method (an abstract concept which, in some sense, comprises a certain dynamic aspect); and MANNR describes the manner of existence of a situation by means of an abstract static concept.

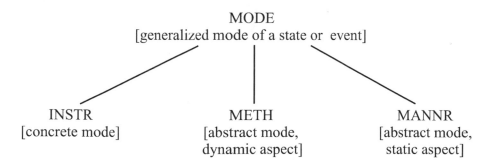

MODE
[generalized mode of a state or  event]

INSTR
[concrete mode]

METH
[abstract mode,
dynamic aspect]

MANNR
[abstract mode,
static aspect]

**Figure 18.29.** Generalized mode of a situation

## 18.2.54  MODL: Relation Specifying the Modality of a Situation

**MODL:** $[si \cup abs] \times md$

**Definition:** The expression (s MODL m) is used to restrict the meaning of a situation s by means of a modal operator m from a finite set *md*. It represents the attitude of a speaker or author of a situational description with regard to the validity of the sentences formulated by him or her.[25] By default, the first argument s is assumed to be a hypothetical situation (s $\in \tilde{si}$).

**Mnemonics:** En: modality (Ge: Modalität)
   (s MODL m) – [s is restricted by the modality m]

**Question pattern:** Which degree of validity can be assigned to $\langle si \rangle$?
Is $\langle si \rangle$ {possible / allowed / necessary / believed / ... }?

**Explanation:** The relation MODL is used (possibly in combination with the function ∗NON) to deal with modal aspects contained in natural language expressions; these include:

- modal auxiliaries: can, shall, may, must, want, desire, ...
- modal adverbs: likely, possibly, necessarily, maybe, absolutely, ...
- the mood of verbs: imperative and conjunctive
- infinitive constructs bearing a modal character: $\langle$has to keep silence$\rangle$ (Ge: $\langle$hat zu schweigen$\rangle$), $\langle$is to be proved$\rangle$ (Ge: $\langle$ist zu beweisen$\rangle$), ...

The relation MODL has to be distinguished qualitatively from other relations insofar as the modal expressions m $\in$ [*md*] (in contrast to other entities) have to be interpreted as modal operators which restrict the meaning of a situation without being part of the semantic representation of the situation. Therefore, a situation s which is possible has primarily to be assigned the facticity [**FACT**=*hypo*], i.e. s $\in \tilde{si}$. However, this characterization can be overwritten by [**FACT**=*real*] or [**FACT**=*non*] if additional information is acquired that in reality s is true or not true.

With regard to the representation of a situation as a capsule, the relation MODL is generally related to the whole capsule (see Fig. 18.30a). Exceptions

---

[25] It should be remarked that even in cases where the provider of the information (the speaker or author) is not explicitly modeled, his or her attitude with regard to the validity of the sentences uttered is nevertheless present in the corresponding natural language expressions. In many texts, it is simply the opinion prevalent in society which is expressed by the modal system.

are cases where the modality is expressly connected with only a single constituent of a sentence (see Fig. 18.30b; here, possib, standing for possibility, restricts only the relation INSTR).

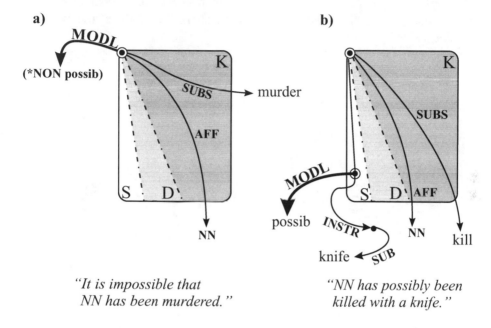

a)

b)

*"It is impossible that
NN has been murdered."*

*"NN has possibly been
killed with a knife."*

**Figure 18.30.** Modalities restricting a whole situation or a cognitive role alone

### 18.2.55 NAME: Assignment of a Name to an Object

**NAME:** *ent × fe*

**Definition:** The notation (e NAME n) assigns a proper name n to a conceptual entity.

**Mnemonics:** En: name (Ge: Name)
(e NAME n) – [e has the name / the denotation n]

**Question pattern:** {How / What} [be] ⟨e⟩ {called / named / denoted ... }?
⟨WH⟩ [be] {called / named / labeled / denoted ... } by ⟨n⟩?

**Explanation:** The relation NAME is used to connect a concept with a name. This relation is needed because proper names are generally not unique (otherwise the representative of the name could itself be used as the node representing the concept). So, one and the same proper name, e.g. **Amerika**, can be used in German for a whole continent, for the United States, or for a village in Saxony. It is also possible that different proper names are associated with the same concept, e.g. **Napoleon I** or **Bonaparte** for the victor of the Battle of Austerlitz.

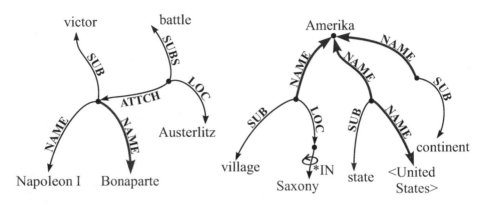

**Figure 18.31.** The ambiguity of names

**Annotation:** The classification of proper names into the sort [*fe*] of formal entities is justified since on the one hand a proper name is a character string (i.e. a formal construct), and on the other hand it is itself an entity related to other conceptual representatives, i.e. it must be represented by its own node.[26] So it is a valuable piece of knowledge that **Caroline** is a first name (not a surname) attached to the node **Caroline** by relation SUB, and that this name in general belongs to a female person (relation ATTCH).

The relation NAME is an abbreviation for a specific ATTR-VAL combination (the latter permits for a more fine-grained differentiation between first names, surnames, nicknames, etc.).

---

[26] The names discussed here, used as word labels for concepts in natural language and not necessarily unique, must not be mixed with the technical labels of nodes, like G01, G02, ..., which are always bijectively attached to nodes.

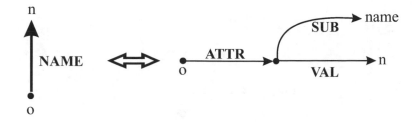

**Figure 18.32.** Names and attribute-value characterizations

### 18.2.56    OBJ: C-Role – Neutral Object as Participant

**OBJ:** $[si \cup abs] \times [o \cup si]$

**Definition:** The assertion (s OBJ b) represents the connection between a situation s and an object b that is independent of s. b is actually involved in the situation s (generally an event), but it is neither physically changed (in contrast to AFF) nor is it a beneficiary of s (in contrast to BENF). It is important for a demarcation between OBJ and MCONT that b exist independently of s in the case of OBJ (or, if s is a situation, that b persist independently of s). For perceptual events or states also elements of sort *si* can be used as the second argument of OBJ.

**Mnemonics:** En: object (Ge: Objekt)
(s OBJ b) – [the object b participates (passively) in s]

**Question pattern:** $\langle$WHA$\rangle$ [do] the carrier of the action $\langle$transitive-act$\rangle$?
(with $\langle$transitive-act$\rangle$ ∈ <actions which are described by transitive verbs>)
{About / Of / In} { $\langle$WHA$\rangle$ / $\langle$WHM$\rangle$ } [do] somebody
{think / speak / trust / . . . }?
$\langle$WHA$\rangle$ [do] somebody {see / observe / hear / meet / . . . }?

**Explanation:** The second argument of the relation OBJ is typically an object only passively involved in the given situation or action specified by the first argument of OBJ:

(18.120)  "*P. observed* [*the moon*]$^{OBJ_{arg2}}$ *through a telescope.*"

The second argument is also often the object of a transfer act:

(18.121)  "*P. gave* [*the program*]$^{OBJ_{arg2}}$ *to the operator.*"

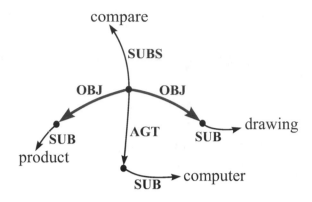

**Figure 18.33.** Two different objects symmetrically participating in an event

The deep case relation OBJ does not directly correspond to the German surface case of accusative (or to the direct object in English). Though it is indeed very often described by these syntactical constructions, it can also be marked in the surface structure by the dative (in German) or by a prepositional object (in English).[27]

(18.122)
  En: "*NN [listened]*$^{OBJ+ORNT}$$_{arg1}$ *to [the speaker]*$^{OBJ+ORNT}$$_{arg2}$."
  Ge: "*NN [hörte]*$^{OBJ+ORNT}$$_{arg1}$ *[dem Sprecher]*$^{OBJ+ORNT}$$_{arg2}$" zu.
(18.123)  En: "*NN obeys [the speaker]*$^{OBJ}$$_{arg2}$."
    Ge: "*NN hört [auf den Sprecher]*$^{OBJ}$$_{arg2}$."
(18.124)  En: "*The computer compares [the product]*$^{OBJ}$$_{arg2}$
      *with [the drawing]*$^{OBJ}$$_{arg2}$."          (see Fig. 18.33)
    Compare with: "*The computer compares product and drawing
        with each other.*"
    Ge: "*Der Rechner vergleicht [das Produkt]*$^{OBJ}$$_{arg2}$
      *mit [der Zeichnung]*$^{OBJ}$$_{arg2}$."
    Compare with: "*Der Computer vergleicht Produkt und Zeichnung
        miteinander.*"

---

[27] In contrast to EXP, AGT, and CSTR, the C-Role OBJ is generally not described by the subject in a normal active sentence (exceptions from this rule are "subject-object alternations"; see page 95).

## 18.2.57     OPPOS: C-Role – Relation Specifying an Opposition

**OPPOS:** $[si \cup o] \times [si \cup o]$

**Definition:** The statement (s OPPOS e) describes an antagonism between s and e, an opposition of s to e, or a force s conflicting with e, i.e. the situation s (generally an event) or the corresponding carrier of s (generally an agent) opposes e in a certain way.

**Mnemonics:** En: oppose (Ge: sich entgegensetzen)
        (s OPPOS e) – [s is opposed to e]

**Question pattern:** Against $\{\langle WHA \rangle / \langle WHM \rangle\}$ [be] $\langle s \rangle$ directed?
Against $\{\langle WHA \rangle / \langle WHM \rangle\}$ [do] $\langle s \rangle$ {fight / vote / polemicize / plot / ... }?

**Explanation:** The relation OPPOS can in a certain sense be considered the counterpart of BENF, which is similar to the pair of opposites "*antagonist/protagonist*".

While BENF is often described in the surface structure of German sentences with a prepositional phrase headed by "*für*" (En: "*for*"), the preposition preferred to describe OPPOS is "*gegen*" (En: "*against*"):

(18.125) En: "[*Fighting*]$^{OPPOS_{arg1}}$ *against* [*the war*]$^{OPPOS_{arg2}}$"
        Ge: "[*Kämpfen*]$^{OPPOS_{arg1}}$ *gegen* [*den Krieg*]$^{OPPOS_{arg2}}$"
        versus En: "[*Fighting*]$^{BENF_{arg1}}$ *for* [*freedom*]$^{BENF_{arg2}}$"
        Ge: "[*Kämpfen*]$^{BENF_{arg1}}$ *für* [*die Freiheit*]$^{BENF_{arg2}}$"
(18.126) En: "[*Voting*]$^{OPPOS_{arg1}}$ *against* [*the law*]$^{OPPOS_{arg2}}$"
        Ge: "[*Stimmen*]$^{OPPOS_{arg1}}$ *gegen* [*das Gesetz*]$^{OPPOS_{arg2}}$"
        versus En: "[*Voting*]$^{BENF_{arg1}}$ *for* [*the candidate*]$^{BENF_{arg2}}$"
        GE: "[*Stimmen*]$^{BENF_{arg1}}$ *für* [*den Kandidaten*]$^{BENF_{arg2}}$"
(18.127) En: "[*He polemicizes*]$^{OPPOS_{arg1}}$ *against* [*the efforts to change the closing hours of shops*]$^{OPPOS_{arg2}}$."
        Ge: "[*Er polemisiert*]$^{OPPOS_{arg1}}$ *gegen* [*die Bestrebungen die Ladenschlußzeiten zu ändern*]$^{OPPOS_{arg2}}$."

The relation OPPOS is also used to represent the meaning of adversative conjunctions. This group includes the German conjunctions "*aber*", "*sondern*", "*doch*" (En: "*but*", "*however*", "*though*").

## 18.2.58    ORIG: Mental or Informational Origin

**ORIG:** $o \times [d \cup io]$

**Definition:** The statement ($o_1$ ORIG $o_2$) is used to represent the connection between an object $o_1$ and its informational or mental source $o_2$.

**Mnemonics:** En: origin (Ge: Herkunft)
  ($o_1$ ORIG $o_2$) – [$o_1$ has the mental / informational origin $o_2$]

**Question pattern:** $\langle$WHA$\rangle$ [do] $\langle o_1 \rangle$ {stem / come / originate / . . . } from?
$\langle$WH$\rangle$ [be] {the source / the origin / . . . } of $\langle o_1 \rangle$?
$\langle$WH$\rangle$ [do] $\langle o_2 \rangle$ {produce / write / create / . . . }?

**Explanation:** The relation ORIG is used for the meaning representation of phrases such as:

(18.128)  "[*The algorithm*]$^{\text{ORIG}_{arg1}}$ *of* [*Cooley-Tucker*]$^{\text{ORIG}_{arg2}}$ . . . "
(18.129)  "[*A book*]$^{\text{ORIG}_{arg1}}$ *of* [*Thomas Mann*]$^{\text{ORIG}_{arg2}}$ . . . "
(18.130)  "*NN heard* [*the news*]$^{\text{ORIG}_{arg1}}$ *from* [*television*]$^{\text{ORIG}_{arg2}}$."
(18.131)  "*He used* [*a method*]$^{\text{ORIG}_{arg1}}$ *from* [*linear algebra*]$^{\text{ORIG}_{arg2}}$."

A clear borderline between ORIG and ORIGL can only be drawn by means of background knowledge. Since this is seldom available in practical knowledge representation systems, a more general relation SOURC is provided by Multi-Net (see page 542). It comprises, among others, the two relations ORIGL and ORIG. The following sentence gives a negative example where ORIG is not applicable if the book mentioned was lent from Max Meyer. In this case, the relation ORIGL has to be used:

(18.132)  "[*The book*]$^{\text{ORIGL}_{arg1}}$ *from* [*Max Meyer*]$^{\text{ORIGL}_{arg2}}$."

Figure 18.34 shows a situation where the relations ORIG and ORIGL coexist in the semantic representation of the following sentence (provided the painter Monet is the creator and not the owner of the picture):

(18.133)  Ge: "*Der Sammler hat ein Bild von Monet aus Paris mitgebracht.*"
      En: "*The collector brought a Monet picture from Paris.*"

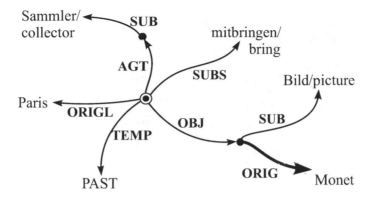

*"The collector brought a Monet picture from Paris."*

**Figure 18.34.**  The contrast between ORIG and ORIGL

## 18.2.59  ORIGL: Relation Specifying the Local Origin

**ORIGL:** $[o \cup si] \times l$

**Definition:** For e $\in$ *si* the assertion (e ORIGL l) specifies the local origin or starting point l of the event e. It is also used for the specification of the local origin of a conceptual object if the latter has a direction as a meaning component, or if it is "implicitly" associated with a directed event.

**Mnemonics:** En: origin, local (Ge: lokale Herkunft / lokaler Ursprung)
(e ORIGL l) – [e is characterized by the local origin l]

**Question pattern:** Where [do] $\langle$si$\rangle$ {come / arise / ... } from?
Where [do] $\langle$o$\rangle$ {come / stem / originate / ... } from?
{From / Out of} $\langle$WHA$\rangle$ [do] $\langle$o$\rangle$ $\langle$dir-act$\rangle$?
         with $\langle$dir-act$\rangle$ $\in$ {move, drive, run, fly, ... }
From which direction [do] $\langle$o$\rangle$ come?

**Explanation:**
The relation ORIGL is typically associated with directed events:

(18.134) *"The cat crept from [under the bed]*$^{ORIGL_{arg2}}$.*"*
(18.135) *"Birds migrate in autumn from [north]*$^{ORIGL_{arg2}}$ *to*
    *[south]*$^{DIRCL_{arg2}}$.*"*

It makes sense to connect also concrete and abstract objects with a local origin in a kind of shorthand notation (cf. DIRCL):

(18.136)  *"The train from [Berlin]*$\text{ORIGL}_{arg2}$ *..."*
(18.137)  *"The cargo from [the main station]*$\text{ORIGL}_{arg2}$ *..."*
(18.138)  *"The wine from [the cellar]*$\text{ORIGL}_{arg2}$ *..."*
(18.139)  *"A message from [Switzerland]*$\text{ORIGL}_{arg2}$ *..."*

The above-mentioned phrases are considered ellipses derived from sentences (phrases) that originally contained a verb compatible with ORIGL:

(18.140)  *"The train which came from Berlin ..."*
(18.141)  *"The cargo which had been sent from the main station ..."*
(18.142)  *"The wine being delivered from the cellar ..."*
(18.143)  *"A message coming from Switzerland ..."*

From a strict point of view, a relation (k ORIGL l) with $k \in d$ must be considered an abbreviated representational form which has to be interpreted in the following way (where $\langle$dir-act$\rangle$ again denotes the class of directed actions):

- (k ORIGL l) $\leftrightarrow$
    $\exists\, v_1\, \exists v\, [(v_1\ \text{SUBS}\ v) \wedge (v \in \langle\text{dir-act}\rangle) \wedge (v_1\ \text{ORIGL}\ l) \wedge$
    $((v_1\ \text{AGT}\ k) \vee (v_1\ \text{OBJ}\ k))]$ (157)

## 18.2.60  ORIGM: Relation Specifying the Material Origin

**ORIGM:** $co \times co$

**Definition:** The expression ($o_1$ ORIGM $o_2$) specifies the material origin of $o_1$ from $o_2$, i.e. $o_1$ has partially or wholly been created by a process of transformation or production from $o_2$. The relation ORIGM is restrictedly transitive (cf. relation PARS).

**Mnemonics:** En: origin, material (Ge: materielle Herkunft)
    (x ORIGM y) – [x originated materially of y]

**Question pattern:**
{$\langle$WMF$\rangle$ [be] $\langle$co$\rangle$ {created / produced / made ... }
{Out of / Of} $\langle$WHA$\rangle$ [be] $\langle$co$\rangle$ {made / created / produced / ... }
$\langle$WH$\rangle$ [be used] as initial {material / stuff / substance ... } for $\langle$co$\rangle$?

**Explanation:** The second argument $o_2$ of ORIGM is typically a substance, i.e. $o_2 \in s$. However, the second argument of ORIGM can also be another concrete object (e.g. a discrete thing $o_2 \in d$).

(18.144) "[A ring]$\mathrm{ORIGM}_{arg1}$ of [gold]$\mathrm{ORIGM}_{arg2}$."

(18.145) "Peter [made]$\mathrm{INIT+RSLT}_{arg1}$ [a medal]$\mathrm{ORIGM}_{arg1}+\mathrm{RSLT}_{arg2}$
from [the ring]$\mathrm{ORIGM}_{arg1}+\mathrm{INIT}_{arg2}$"

The relation ORIGM can also be deduced as a connection between the result of an action (relation RSLT) and its initial object (relation INIT); consider the following sentence, whose semantic representation is shown in Fig. 18.35:

(18.146) "The firm makes [this part]$\mathrm{RSLT}_{arg2}+\mathrm{ORIGM}_{arg1}$
of [aluminum]$\mathrm{INIT}_{arg2}+\mathrm{ORIGM}_{arg2}$"

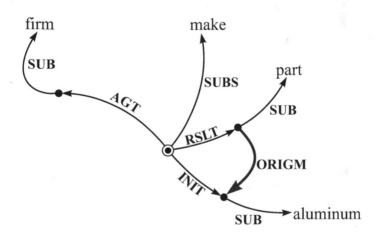

**Figure 18.35.** ORIGM as a link between INIT and RSLT

The initial material processed in an event or in a productive action is not immediately attached to the node representing the event or action. It is rather attached to the result of the action (relation RSLT) or to the affected object (relation AFF) by means of the relation ORIGM. On the basis of this conception, natural language expressions containing propositions about the material origin of something can be dealt with in a uniform way:

(18.147) Ge: "P. schnitzt [eine Figur]$\mathrm{ORIGM}_{arg1}+\mathrm{RSLT}_{arg2}$
aus [Holz.]$\mathrm{ORIGM}_{arg2}+\mathrm{INIT}_{arg2}$"
En: "P. carves [a figure]$\mathrm{ORIGM}_{arg1}+\mathrm{RSLT}_{arg2}$
from [wood.]$\mathrm{ORIGM}_{arg2}+\mathrm{INIT}_{arg2}$"

(18.148)  Ge: "*P. schnitzt* **an** [*einer Figur*]$\mathrm{ORIGM}_{arg1}$ +$\mathrm{AFF}_{arg2}$
*aus* [*Holz.*]$\mathrm{ORIGM}_{arg2}$+$\mathrm{INIT}_{arg2}$"
Free translation – En: "*P. carves* **away** **at** [*a figure*]$\mathrm{ORIGM}_{arg1}$+$\mathrm{AFF}_{arg2}$
*of* [*wood.*]$\mathrm{ORIGM}_{arg2}$+$\mathrm{INIT}_{arg2}$"

### 18.2.61   ORNT: C-Role – Orientation to an Object

**ORNT:** [$si \cup abs$] $\times o$

**Definition:** The expression (s ORNT o) specifies the connection between a situation s (typically an event) and an object o directly involved in the situation s and toward which the situation is directed. The object o is not changed.

**Mnemonics:** En: orientation (Ge: Orientierung)
(s ORNT o) – [s is oriented toward o]

**Question pattern:** ⟨WMT⟩ [do] somebody ⟨O-transfer-act⟩ something?
with ⟨O-transfer-act⟩ = {give, sell, lent, convey, communicate, ... }
Toward ⟨WM⟩ is the action oriented?
{⟨WMT⟩ / ⟨WM⟩} [do] somebody {listen / believe / adhere / swear /... }?

**Explanation:** The C-Role ORNT is often met with verbs denoting the transfer of a material or an immaterial possession (a thing, a piece of information, a title), which is expressed in the question patterns. In this context, the action is directed toward the object syntactically marked in German by the dative and in English by a direct object or a prepositional phrase with "*to*", as shown by the first three of the following examples. Examples (18.152) and (18.153) illustrate that the relation ORNT can also be marked by a prepositional phrase with "*an*" in German (corresponding to the English preposition "*to*").

(18.149)  Ge: "*Das Mädchen leiht* [*seiner Freundin*]$\mathrm{ORNT}_{arg2}$ *eine Puppe.* "
En: "*The girl lends* [*her friend*]$\mathrm{ORNT}_{arg2}$ *a doll.*"
(18.150)  Ge: "[*Dem Mitarbeiter*]$\mathrm{ORNT}_{arg2}$ *wurde mehrfach Unterstützung angeboten.*"
En: "[*The coworker*]$\mathrm{ORNT}_{arg2}$ *was offered support several times.*"
(18.151)  Ge: "*Der Minister gab* [*dem Besucher*]$\mathrm{ORNT}_{arg2}$ *ein Geschenk.* "
En: "*The minister gave* [*the visitor*]$\mathrm{ORNT}_{arg2}$ *a gift.*"
(18.152)  Ge: "*Der Programmcode wird an* [*den Compiler*]$\mathrm{ORNT}_{arg2}$ *übergeben.*"
Ge: "*The programming code is transferred to* [*the compiler*]$\mathrm{ORNT}_{arg2}$."

Although the deep semantic relation ORNT is often expressed by the **dative** in German and in other languages (see Examples (18.149) through (18.151)); it should not be mixed up with this surface case. The dative may also be a case marker for the C-Roles BENF or AFF.

(18.153) Ge: "*Der Anwalt schrieb [dem Mandanten]*$^{BENF_{arg2}}$ *einen Brief an [den Richter]*$^{ORNT_{arg2}}$."
En: "*The lawyer wrote a letter for [the client]*$^{BENF_{arg2}}$ *to [the judge]*$^{ORNT_{arg2}}$."

(18.154) Ge: "*Der Zollbeamte nahm [dem Touristen]*$^{AVRT+AFF_{arg2}}$ *das Geld weg.*"
En: "*The customs officer took the money away from [the tourist]*$^{AVRT+AFF_{arg2}}$".

The relation ORNT is the counterpart to the relation AVRT.

## 18.2.62 PARS: Relation Between Part and Whole

**PARS:** $[co \times co] \cup [io \times io] \cup [l \times l]$

**Definition:** The expression ($o_1$ PARS $o_2$) specifies that $o_1$ is a part of $o_2$; in other words, $o_2$ is the whole which contains $o_1$ as its component. The relation PARS is restrictedly transitive, asymmetric, and not reflexive; see Sect. 4.2.

**Mnemonics:** Latin: pars – En: part; Ge: Teil
($o_1$ PARS $o_2$) – [$o_1$ is a part of $o_2$]

**Question pattern:** What [do] ⟨o⟩ consist of?
Which parts [do] ⟨o⟩ {possess / have / consist of / ... }?
To ⟨WM⟩ [do] ⟨o⟩ belong? – What are the parts of ⟨o⟩?
From which object [be] ⟨o⟩ a {part / component}?

**Explanation:** For concrete objects, PARS is used to specify the physical components which constitute these objects. The relation may also be used to characterize that an abstract object contains another object with sort *ab* (this holds, for instance, for parts of a plan), or that locations are contained in each other. Because of the formal properties of PARS, this relation – like SUB and SUBS – gives also rise to hierarchies of conceptual representatives within a semantic network. The inheritance mechanisms connected with them can be described by axioms of the following kind:

- $(o_1 \text{ PARS } o_2) \wedge (o_2 \text{ ORIGM } s) \rightarrow (o_1 \text{ ORIGM } s)$      [Default]      (158)

Postulating an unrestricted transitivity for PARS would be problematic. Even if it were formally correct to propagate the transitivity of the PARS relation without restrictions, this would not conform to a normal natural language use where limits exist in this regard.

Examples:

(18.155) *"The spring is part of the lock."*
(18.156) *"The lock is part of the door."*
(18.157) *"The door is part of the castle."*

It is doubtful whether somebody would say

(18.158) *"The spring is part of the castle."* (??)

In this context, one should also think of queries like

(18.159) *"Can you tell me all parts of the castle?"*[28]

The inheritance of the part-whole relation in a SUB hierarchy is described by the following axiom (see Sect. 4.2 for motivation):

- $(o_1 \text{ SUB } o_2) \wedge (o_3 \text{ PARS } o_2) \rightarrow \exists o_4 \, [(o_4 \text{ SUB } o_3) \wedge (o_4 \text{ PARS } o_1)]$   (159)

The question patterns show that the deep relation PARS can be expressed by a multitude of paraphrases in the surface structure of NL (in this respect, it is similar to POSS and PROP). So, PARS can be described by ⟨bestehen aus⟩, besitzen, haben₁ (als Teil), ⟨Teil / Bestandteil sein von⟩, and ⟨enthalten sein⟩ (En: ⟨consist of⟩, possess, have₁ (as part), ⟨be part of⟩, and contain).

As already mentioned, ideal objects (sort [*io*]) can also be contained within each other (e.g. the scene in a theater play). The same is true for locations (sort [*l*]). So, the location ⟨at the Times Square⟩ lies in ⟨in London⟩. Please note that we did not introduce an extra relation for spatial inclusion. Because of the closeness of the inclusion of regions in one another to the part-whole relationship of objects, the relation PARS has also been extended to locations. Example: ((*IN ⟨the drawer⟩) PARS (*IN ⟨the cupboard⟩)),
i.e. the interior of the drawer is part of the interior of the cupboard.

---

[28] Here, functional aspects and aspects concerning the level or observational frame assumed by the speaker play also an important role. In the present example, the question is crucial as to whether or not the spring is an essential functional part of the castle.

### 18.2.63   POSS: Relation of Possession

**POSS:** $[co \cup io] \times [co \cup io]$

**Definition:** The statement ($o_1$ POSS $o_2$) expresses the connection between an owner $o_1$, who is usually a human or a legal person, and its possession $o_2$, which $o_1$ has at his disposal.

**Mnemonics:** En: possession (Ge: Besitz)

($o_1$ POSS $o_2$) – [$o_1$ is the possessor / owner of $o_2$]

**Question pattern:** $\langle$WH$\rangle$ {[possess] / [have] / [own] / [hold] ... } $\langle$o$\rangle$?
$\langle$WMT$\rangle$ [do] $\langle$o$\rangle$ belong?
$\langle$WHS$\rangle$ {[property] / [possession] ... } [be] $\langle$o$\rangle$?
$\langle$WH$\rangle$ [have] $\langle$o$\rangle$ at his disposal?

**Explanation:** Typical examples for paraphrasing the relation POSS in the surface structure of natural language are the following:

(18.160) "[*The state*]$^{POSS_{arg1}}$ *owns* [*large gold reserves*]$^{POSS_{arg2}}$."
(18.161) "[*MGM*]$^{POSS_{arg1}}$ *holds* [*the rights to this film.*]$^{POSS_{arg2}}$"
(18.162) "[*The house*]$^{POSS_{arg2}}$ *{belongs to / is owned by}* [*the lawyer*]$^{POSS_{arg1}}$."

The relation POSS is closely related to transfer actions ending or creating a relationship of possession. Let $s_1$ be the situation ($o_1$ POSS o) and $s_2$ the situation ($o_2$ POSS o); then, it holds:[29]

- $\exists s \, [(s \text{ SUBS } \langle\text{give-act}\rangle) \wedge (s \text{ AGT } o_1) \wedge (s \text{ ORNT } o_2) \wedge$
  $(s \text{ OBJ o}) \wedge (s \text{ TEMP t})]$
  $\rightarrow [(s_1 \text{ FIN t}) \wedge (s_2 \text{ STRT t})]$
  with $\langle\text{give-act}\rangle$ = give, leave, send, $\langle\text{make as a gift}\rangle$, ...          (160)

Similar axioms are obtained for classes of concepts describing an act of acquiring a possession. In that group we include find, take, and receive. It is interesting that in German juridical texts a difference is made between "*Eigentümer*" (En: "*owner*") and "*Besitzer*" (En: "*possessor*"). In this context, the

---

[29] Please note that Axiom (160) can not be interpreted within the framework of standard predicate calculus. It has rather to be taken in the sense of a logic of actions. If an act s of giving specified in the premise takes place and the situation $s_1$ holds, then $s_1$ has to be finished at the time t of the act, i.e. it has to be marked by ($s_1$ FIN t); additionally, a new situation $s_2$ = ($o_2$ POSS o) has to be created and included in the knowledge base that is characterized by ($s_2$ STRT t).

corresponding concept **Eigentümer** (En: **owner**) e who has the object o juridically at his disposal must be characterized by (e POSS o), while the concept **Besitzer** (En: **possessor**) b with whom the object o is physically located
must be characterized by (o LOC b). If this distinction is properly be taken into
account, Axiom (160) has to be modified, since the owner is not necessarily
changed by a sending act.

## 18.2.64    PRED/PREDR/PREDS: Predicative Concept Governing a Plurality

**PRED/PREDR/PREDS:**
**PRED**: $\ddot{s}o \cup \overline{so}$              with   $so = o \setminus (abs \cup re)$
**PREDR**: $\ddot{r}e \times \overline{re}$
**PREDS**: $[\ddot{s}i \cup \overline{abs}] \times [\overline{si} \cup \overline{abs}]$

**Definition:** The relationships (g PRED c) with c $\in$ so (see the definition
above), (g PREDR c) with c $\in$ re, and (g PREDS c) with c $\in$ abs, are abbreviations for the indirect specification of a predicate c that defines a plurality[30] g
by means of the relations EXT and SETOF:

- (g PRED/PREDR/PREDS c) $\leftrightarrow$ $\exists$ m (g EXT m) $\wedge$ (m SETOF c)      (161)
  The choice of PRED, PREDR, and PREDS has to be made according to the
  sort of c.

c is the predicative concept that determines the elements of the plurality g, or,
to be exact, the elements of the extensional of g.

**Mnemonics:** En: predication (Ge: Prädikation)
          (g PRED/PREDR/PREDS c) – [the plurality g is characterized
                                    by the predicate c]

**Question pattern:** What plurality is $\langle g \rangle$?

**Explanation:** The relations PRED, PREDR, and PREDS connect an entity
representing a plurality at the intensional level with a corresponding characteristic set predicate in an abbreviated form. These constructs are equivalent
to the more expressive but somewhat cumbersome representations using the
combination EXT + SETOF (see Fig. 18.36).

---

[30] To spare the term *set* for representatives of [**ETYPE** $\geq$ 1] at the preextensional level, we use
the word *plurality* as a technical term denoting collections of entities at the intensional level.

The relations PRED, PREDR, and PREDS cannot be substituted by SUB, SUBR, or SUBS, respectively, as the concepts ⟨many elephants⟩ or ⟨several revolutions⟩ show. They are not direct subconcepts of elephant or revolution, respectively (see Fig. 18.36). Otherwise, information characterizing the node elephant, for instance, would be inherited by the concept ⟨many elephants⟩ (e.g. this plurality would also possess exactly one trunk). The extensionals of the concepts ⟨many elephants⟩ and ⟨several revolutions⟩, which can be reached via the relation EXT, must themselves be connected to the concepts elephant and revolution, respectively, by means of the relation SETOF. The analogue can be said of the relations PREDR and SUBR.

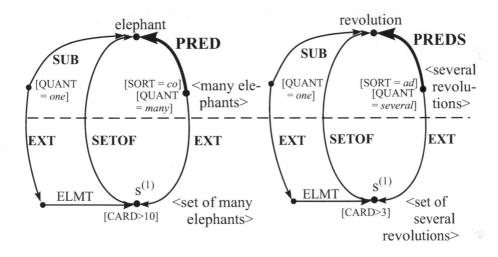

**Figure 18.36.** PRED as an abbreviation for EXT + SETOF

To simplify the meaning representations, the relation PRED0 is introduced as a superordinate relationship with regard to PRED, PREDR, and PREDS, i.e. PRED0 = PRED ∪ PREDR ∪ PREDS holds. PRED0 is important for the treatment of meaning molecules (see Chap. 12) and of pluralities defined by them, if the sort of the meaning facet to be selected cannot be derived from the context (cf. SUB0).

## 18.2.65    PROP: Relation Between Object and Property

**PROP:** $o \times p$

**Definition:** The assertion (o PROP p) establishes a connection between an object o and a property p, which, by definition, is not a relational of functional quality.

**Mnemonics:** En: property (Ge: Eigenschaft)
(o PROP p) – [o has the property p]

**Question pattern:** $\langle WH \rangle$ {[be] / [look like] / [have the property] / ... } $\langle p \rangle$?
Which property [do] $\langle o \rangle$ {possess / have / characterize / ... }?
What [be] $\langle o \rangle$ like?
What {kind / type / ... } of object [be] $\langle o \rangle$?

**Explanation:** If the property p attached to o by (o PROP p) belongs to sort [$tq$] (i.e. it is a total quality), then the interpretation of p is independent of the corresponding object o. Properties such as dead, empty, and circular can even be extensionally interpreted by assigning corresponding classes of real world entities to them (i.e. the class of dead, empty, and circular things, respectively).

We encounter another situation with properties belonging to sort $gq \subset p$ (gradable qualities). These properties (e.g. big, expensive, and fast) can be interpreted only in relation to the class of entities determined by the corresponding conceptual object k. $\langle$a large ant$\rangle$, for instance, means that the animal in question is large compared with a typical ant or within the class of ants (a large ant is a tiny animal compared to a small elephant). From this we see that there are no classes for big, expensive, fast things, respectively.

The union of the sorts [$tq$] and [$gq$] into one sort [$p$] can be justified by the observation that in a QAS both types of properties are asked for in the same way, and the answers to these questions are also produced in the same way. Moreover, the predicative use of adjectives denoting these properties is linguistically admissible in both cases (in contrast to semantically associative properties, where this is not allowed).[31]

Semantically associative properties of objects as well as operational properties have to be specified in a semantic representation by means of the function ∗PMOD (rather than PROP) because both bear a functional character.

---

[31] This aspect is also important for the generation of natural language texts from semantic representations, which is influenced by the sorts of nodes.

## 18.2.66 PROPR: Relation Between a Plurality and a Semantically Relational Property

**PROPR:** $\ddot{o} \times rq$

**Definition:** The expression (g PROPR r) is used to characterize a plurality g by means of a semantically relational quality r.[32]

**Mnemonics:** En: property, relational (Ge: relationale Eigenschaft)
  (g PROPR r) – [the plurality g is characterized by
              the relational property r]

**Question pattern:** How are the elements of ⟨g⟩ related to each other? Which properties [do] ⟨g⟩ have?

**Explanation:** We often specify properties in natural language which neither apply to a collection of elements as a whole nor to every element of the collection for itself. Upon closer semantic inspection they rather turn out to be relations between the elements of that collection. This holds regardless of the fact that the adjectives corresponding to these properties can occur in the surface structure of a sentence in attributive use as well as in predicative use. To represent these propositions semantically, the relation PROPR together with the special sort [rq] for semantically relational properties are provided. The exact interpretation of the expression (o PROPR r) heavily depends on the meaning of the property r ∈ rq.

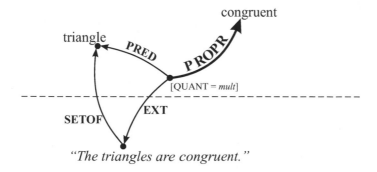

"The triangles are congruent."

**Figure 18.37.** Pluralities and relational properties

---

[32] Please recall that a **plurality** is an intensional whose counterpart at the preextensional level is a set. The sort label $\ddot{o}$ means "object whose extension is a set with [**CARD** ≥ 2]".

**Annotation:** In contrast to properties in the narrower sense [**SORT** = $p$], relational properties [**SORT** = $rq$] are not inherited by individual entities. Therefore, a formula analogous to Axiom (168) (see relation SUB) does not hold for the relation PROPR.

### 18.2.67 PURP: Relation Specifying a Purpose

**PURP:** $[si \cup o] \times [si \cup ab]$

**Definition:** The assertion (s PURP p) expresses that the situation or object s has the purpose or aim p.

**Mnemonics:** En: purpose (Ge: Zweck / Nutzen)
(s PURP p) – [s has the purpose p]

**Question pattern:** {For which purpose / To which end / Why} $\langle si \rangle$?
{For which purpose / To which end} [be] $\langle o \rangle$ {used / applied ... }?
What purpose [do] $\langle o \rangle$ serve?

**Explanation:** In German and English, the relation PURP is often described by prepositional phrases introduced by "*für*" or "*zu*" (En: "*for*"), or by infinitive constructions.

(18.163)  Ge: "*P. liegt um zu [entspannen]*$^{PURP_{arg2}}$ *auf der Terrasse.*"
En: "*P. lies on the terrace [to relax]*$^{PURP_{arg2}}$."

(18.164)  Ge: "*P. trägt einen Hut, damit [er keine Erkältung bekommt]*$^{PURP_{arg2}}$."
En: "*P. wears a hat so that [he does not catch a cold]*$^{PURP_{arg2}}$."

(18.165)  Ge: "*Deregulierung dient [der Belebung des Marktes]*$^{PURP_{arg2}}$."
En: "*Deregulation is useful for [the stimulation of the market]*$^{PURP_{arg2}}$."

(18.166)  Ge: "*P. benötigt einen Ball zum [Spielen]*$^{PURP_{arg2}}$."
En: "*P. needs a ball to [play]*$^{PURP_{arg2}}$."

The following examples illustrate the use of the relation PURP in the representation of the purpose of objects:

(18.167)  Ge: "*Das Werkzeug dient zum [Entfernen der Räder]*$^{PURP_{arg2}}$."
En: "*The tool is used for [the removal of the wheels]*$^{PURP_{arg2}}$."
or somewhat shorter:
Ge: "*Das Werkzeug zum [Entfernen der Räder]*$^{PURP_{arg2}}$."
En: "*The tool for [the removal of the wheels]*$^{PURP_{arg2}}$."

(18.168)  Ge: *"Die Sorten dienen [der Definition]*$^{PURP}{}_{arg2}$ *von Funktionen und Relations."*

(18.169)  En: *"The sorts are used for [defining functions and relations.]*$^{PURP}{}_{arg2}$*"*

    or somewhat shorter:

Ge:*"Sorten zur [Definition von Funktionen und Relations]*$^{PURP}{}_{arg2}$*."*

En: *"Sorts for [the definition of functions and relations]*$^{PURP}{}_{arg2}$*."*

Also, situations and abstract concepts can be used as a second argument of PURP. The relation BENF (*"beneficiary"* of an action) in the field of concrete objects can be seen as a counterpart of PURP in the field of situations and abstract concepts.

## 18.2.68  QMOD: Quantitative Modification

**QMOD:** $[s \cup \ddot{d}] \times m$

**Definition:** The expression (d QMOD q) is used to specify a certain amount of a substance or of a collection of objects d by modifying it with a quantity q.

**Mnemonics:** En: quantitative modification (Ge: quantitative Modifizierung)
    (d QMOD q) – [d is quantitatively determined by q]

**Question pattern:** How many $\{ \langle s \rangle\ /\ \langle \ddot{d} \rangle \} \dots$?
What amount of $\{ \langle s \rangle\ /\ \langle \ddot{d} \rangle \} \dots$?

**Explanation:** In contrast to the relation VAL, the second argument of QMOD actually adds new information, i.e. it delivers a more detailed quantitative specification of a substance or a collection which determines the amount of the entity given by the first argument. The specification of a relation VAL in an ATTR-SUB construct only explicates the value implicitly determined by this construct, whereas the information given by a QMOD relation cannot be derived from the context. In connection with substances, the specification of a QMOD relation, together with the SUB relation, selects a certain partition of the world supply of that substance (e.g. in the phrase Ge: ⟨100 Liter Wasser⟩ or En: ⟨100 liters of water⟩).[33]

    Collections modified by QMOD bear a certain "substance character" (e.g. Ge:⟨3 kg Nägel⟩ or En: ⟨3 kg of nails⟩).

---

[33] Characteristically enough, this is expressed in some languages by the so-called "genitivus partitivus".

Ge: *"100 Liter Wasser"*          En: *"3 kg Nägel"*
En: *"100 litres of water"*          En: *"3 kg of nails"*

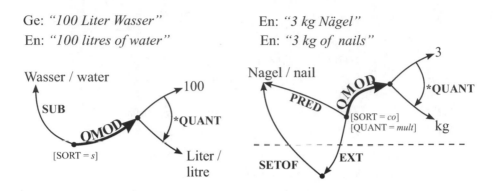

**Figure 18.38.** Quantitative modification of substances and pluralities

## 18.2.69    REAS: General Reason for a Situation

**REAS:** $([si \cup abs] \times [si \cup abs]) \cup [p \times p] \cup [aq \times aq] \cup [rq \times rq]$

**Definition:** The statement ($s_1$ REAS $s_2$) indicates a general reason or general grounds, which can be explicated either causally (CAUS), logically (IMPL), or by social norms (JUST). $s_1$ is the reason for $s_2$.

**Mnemonics:** En: reason (Ge: Grund)
        ($s_1$ REAS $s_2$) – [$s_1$ is the general reason for $s_2$]

**Question pattern:** {Why / By what reason / On what grounds} ⟨si⟩?
How can ⟨si⟩ be justified?

**Explanation:** Formally the relation REAS is the union of the relations CAUS, IMPL, and JUST.

- ($s_1$ REAS $s_2$) $\leftrightarrow_{Def}$ ($s_1$ CAUS $s_2$) $\vee$ ($s_1$ JUST $s_2$) $\vee$ ($s_1$ IMPL $s_2$)      (162)

The characteristics of the aforementioned relations and their relation to COND are represented in Fig. 18.39.

The relation REAS was introduced because it is very difficult in practically realized NLP systems (and also for human beings) to distinguish between the *"real reason"* CAUS, the *"logical reason"* IMPL, and the *"ethical or moral reason"* JUST. This distinction can in general be made only on the basis of background knowledge[34] (see also Sect. 11.2).

---

[34] The inclusion of COND in this problem area is reasonable, because conditional relationships can also be drawn upon when questions for reasons have to be answered (in the example above, *"{Why / When / . . . } will somebody be punished?"*).

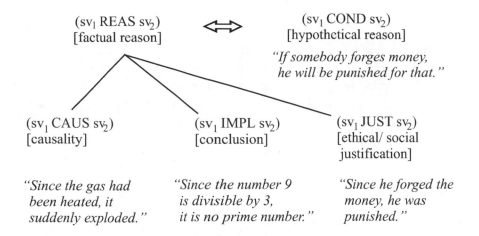

Figure 18.39. Overview of the relations representing reasons

## 18.2.70 RPRS: Representational Form or Manifestation of an Object

**RPRS:** $o \times o$

**Definition:** The expression ($o_1$ RPRS $o_2$) specifies that $o_1$ appears in the representational form or manifestation $o_2$.

**Mnemonics:** En: representative (Ge: Repräsentant)
($o_1$ RPRS $o_2$) – [$o_1$ appears in the form or gestalt $o_2$]

**Question pattern:** In what role $\langle dy \rangle$?
How [do] $\langle o \rangle$ {appear / exist / occur ... }?
{How / In what form} [be] $\langle o \rangle$ {represented / presented / shown / ... } ?

**Explanation:** The arguments of the relation RPRS can be abstract concepts or concrete objects:

(18.170) Ge: *"Die Matrix wird in [Dreiecksform]*$^{RPRS_{arg2}}$ *ausgegeben."*
En: *"The matrix is output in [a triangular form]*$^{RPRS_{arg2}}$*."*
(18.171) Ge: *"Eine Landkarte in [Mercator-Projektion]*$^{RPRS_{arg2}}$ *..."*
En: *"A map in [Mercator projection]*$^{RPRS_{arg2}}$ *..."*
(18.172) Ge: *"Das Volk als [Ankläger]*$^{RPRS_{arg2}}$ *..."*
En: *"The people as [prosecutor]*$^{RPRS_{arg2}}$ *..."*
(18.173) Ge: *"Die Neuregelung in Form [eines Gesetzes]*$^{RPRS_{arg2}}$ *..."*

En: *"The new regulations in the form of [a law]*$^{RPRS_{arg2}}$ *..."*

Also in completely described situations, the relation RPRS holds between objects, and not between the representative of the situation and a participating object. Moreover, the following examples show that the embedding of RPRS in the semantic representation of a situation is normally contextually restricted. This means that the actor in Example (18.174) does not always exist in its manifestation as Nathan but only during the performance in Berlin. The analogue holds for Example (18.175), where it is stated that carbon does not always appear as $CO_2$ but, rather, when it is absorbed by a plant (compare Figures 18.40a and 18.40b).

(18.174)  Ge: *"[Der Schauspieler]*$^{RPRS_{arg1}}$ *tritt in Berlin*
          *als [Nathan]*$^{RPRS_{arg2}}$ *auf."*
     En: *"[The actor]*$^{RPRS_{arg1}}$ *appears in Berlin as [Nathan]*$^{RPRS_{arg2}}$*."*
(18.175)  Ge: *"[Kohlenstoff]*$^{RPRS_{arg1}}$ *wird von den Pflanzen*
          *als [CO$_2$]*$^{RPRS_{arg2}}$ *aufgenommen."*
     En: *"[Carbon]*$^{RPRS_{arg1}}$ *is absorbed by plants as [CO$_2$]*$^{RPRS_{arg2}}$*."*

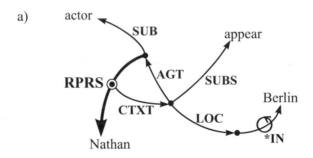

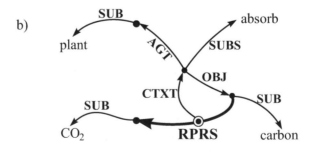

**Figure 18.40.** Contextual boundedness of the RPRS relation

## 18.2.71    RSLT: C-Role – Result

**RSLT:** $[si \cup abs] \times [o \cup si]$

**Definition:** The statement (s RSLT r) establishes a semantic connection between a situation s (typically an event) and its result r.

**Mnemonics:** En: result (Ge: Resultat)
   (s RSLT r) – [s has the result r]

**Question pattern:**
What [be] {produced / created / made / brought about / … } by … ?
Into ⟨WHA⟩ [be] {transformed / changed / … } … ?
What result [do] ⟨s⟩ have?
Where [do] ⟨s⟩ lead to?
What results from the {production / creation / … } … ?
In ⟨WHA⟩ [do] ⟨s⟩ end?

**Explanation:** The result of an event can be a material product:

(18.176) *"The firm Nikon [produces]$^{\text{RSLT}}{}_{arg1}$ [cameras]$^{\text{RSLT}}{}_{arg2}$."*

it can be also an abstract object or a situation.

(18.177) *"[The competition]$^{\text{RSLT}}{}_{arg1}$ ended in [a draw]$^{\text{RSLT}}{}_{arg2}$."*

(18.178) *"As a result of [the relief action]$^{\text{RSLT}}{}_{arg1}$, [the miners were saved]$^{\text{RSLT}}{}_{arg2}$."*

(18.179) *"[Unnecessary waiting]$^{\text{RSLT}}{}_{arg1}$ leads to [disadvantages]$^{\text{RSLT}}{}_{arg2}$."*

As a counterpart of the relation INIT the relation RSLT is often used in the semantic representation of transformation processes.

(18.180) *"The program transforms [the logical expression]$^{\text{INIT}}{}_{arg2}$ into [its Skolem normal form]$^{\text{RSLT}}{}_{arg2}$."*

If the second argument is a situation s $\in$ *si*, the following rules can be established. (These are different for temporally extended and nonextended events.)
   For temporally nonextended events v, we obtain:

- (begin(v) EQU end(v)) $\wedge$ (v RSLT s) $\rightarrow$ (s STRT v)          (163)

In this formula begin(v) and end(v) denote the temporal beginning and end of the event v, respectively. In general, the following relationship holds for situational results s $\in$ *si*:

- (v RSLT s) → (v FIN s)                                                                                    (164)

i.e. the situation v ends with the beginning of s, or the resulting situation s
begins with the end of v.

## 18.2.72    SCAR: C-Role – Carrier of a State (Passive)

**SCAR:** $[st \cup as] \times o$

**Definition:** The assertion (s SCAR o) connects a nonmental state s to an object
o which is in this state, or which carries this state without playing an active role
in it.

**Mnemonics:** En: state carrier (Ge: Zustandsträger)
        (s SCAR o) – [s has o as carrier of the state]

**Question pattern:** ⟨WH⟩ [be] in ⟨st⟩?
⟨WH⟩ [carry] ⟨st⟩?
In what state is ⟨o⟩?

**Explanation:** It is characteristic of the admissibility of the notation (s SCAR
o) that o is passively experiencing the state s (therefore, the name "*state experiencer*" is proposed). The term "*state*" has to be understood in the broadest
sense (not only in the narrower sense as a physical state).

(18.181) "[*The car*]$\mathrm{SCAR}_{arg2}$ [*weighs*]$\mathrm{SCAR}_{arg1}$ *a ton.*"
(18.182) "[*Peter*]$\mathrm{SCAR}_{arg2}$ [*sits*]$\mathrm{SCAR}_{arg1}$ *on the table.*"

The boundary between the relations SCAR and AGT is not so easy to draw (see
also the description of the relation MEXP), since the carrier of a state sometimes has to keep up this state intentionally (e.g. for states like ⟨hold on to⟩
and ⟨cling to⟩). In these cases, we propose a double characterization by AGT
and SCAR, because the tension between passively experiencing and intentionally acting can be appropriately expressed by that. The semantic difference is
illustrated by the following sentences:

(18.183) "[*The ape*]$\mathrm{AGT+SCAR}_{arg2}$ [*clings*]$\mathrm{AGT+SCAR}_{arg1}$ *to the branch.*"
(18.184) "[*The fruit*]$\mathrm{SCAR}_{arg2}$ [*is heavily hanging*]$\mathrm{SCAR}_{arg1}$ *from the*
        *branch.*"

To demonstrate what objects can be met as carriers of states, the following
examples are used:

(18.185) "[*The firm*]$\text{SCAR}_{arg2}$ *lacks a lot of money.*"

(18.186) "[*The garden*]$\text{SCAR}_{arg2}$ *is bordered by a fence.*"

(18.187) "[*The institution*]$\text{SCAR}_{arg2}$ *bears the full responsibility.*"

As a test for distinguishing SCAR from EXP, the query "*To whom does something happen?*" can be used. This question is appropriate for EXP but not for SCAR.

### 18.2.73   SETOF: Relation Between the Extensional of a Plurality and the Governing Predicative Concept

**SETOF:** $pe^{(n)} \times \bar{o}$          with $n \geq 1$ and o having [**ETYPE** = (n-1)]

**Definition:** The statement (g SETOF c) establishes the connection between a set g, i.e. an entity of the preextensional level, and a generic concept c, meaning that all elements of g are extensionals of entities which are subordinate to the concept c at the intensional level.[35]

**Mnemonics:** En: set of (Ge: Menge von)

      (g SETOF c) – [g is a collection (a set) of c]

**Question pattern:** What kinds of entities are the elements of $\langle g \rangle$?

**Explanation:** The assertion (g SETOF c) states that g is a set of c, or more formally expressed,

- (g SETOF c) $\wedge$ (x ELMT g) $\wedge$ (y EXT x) $\rightarrow$ (y SUB c)         (165)

The relation SETOF is used to characterize a set by means of a predicative concept, and not, for instance, by an enumeration of its elements (see *ITMS).

The example of Fig. 18.41 illustrates how the relations SETOF and EXT mediate between SUB at the intensional level, and SUBM or ELMT at the preextensional level.

The application of set relations in semantic representations of collective nouns is shown in Figure 18.42. The relationship between Matterhorn (a mountain) and Alps (a mountain range in Europe) can only be described adequately by including the preextensional level. In this figure, the Alps are shown as a collection (set) of mountains from which the Matterhorn is an element.

---

[35] See annotation (footnote) for EXT on page 494.

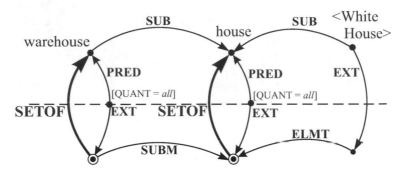

**Figure 18.41.** The relation SETOF as mediator between intensional and preextensional level

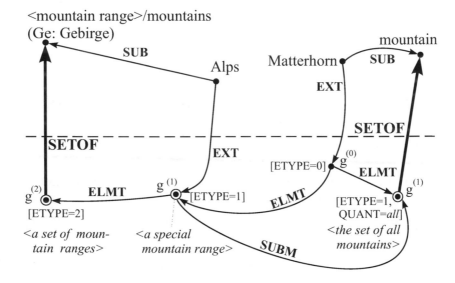

**Figure 18.42.** The connection of concepts with different ETYPE values by relations of the preextensional level

It does not hold that (**Matterhorn** SUB **Alps**). The fact that the Alps are more than a set of mountains (they are characterized by a special spatial arrangement of the mountains) is not represented at the preextensional level. This should be described additionally at the intensional level.

## 18.2.74    SITU: Situational Embedding or Abstract Location

**SITU:** $[si \cup o] \times [si \cup o]$

**Definition:** The assertion ($s_1$ SITU $s_2$) expresses the situational embedding or abstract location $s_2$ of an object or situation $s_1$.

**Mnemonics:** En: situational embedding (Ge: situative Einbettung)
     ($s_1$ SITU $s_2$) – [$s_2$ is the situational embedding or abstract location of $s_1$]

**Question pattern:** Where $\langle si \rangle$?
In what situation [be] $\langle o \rangle$ {observed / met / seen}?
{$\langle$loc-praep-a$\rangle$ $\langle$WHA$\rangle$} $\langle si \rangle$?
                    where $\langle$loc-praep-a$\rangle \in$ {at, in, on, over, ... }. [36]

**Explanation:** The relation SITU was primarily defined as the union of the relations CIRC and CTXT. But it turned out to be useful also to cover the representation of "*abstract locations*", such as ⟨on television⟩, ⟨at the wedding⟩, etc., which are very close to circumstances and contextual restrictions. Since such abstract locations can be specified for concrete objects as well as for abstract objects, the domain of the first argument of SITU has deliberately been extended to the sort *o*. With this extended definition, the meaning of expressions like ⟨the man in the play⟩ or ⟨the aria in the opera⟩ can also be represented by means of SITU without introducing a special relation LOCA for abstract locations. Because of the omission of LOCA, the following implication is valid only from left to right (and not vice versa).

- ($s_1$ CIRC $s_2$) $\vee$ ($s_1$ CTXT $s_2$) $\rightarrow$ ($s_1$ SITU $s_2$)                    (166)

The relation SITU was introduced because it is very difficult for technical NLP systems (and for human beings) to distinguish between abstract locations in the narrower sense ("*in Mary's mind*"), which sometimes are even metaphors (Ge: "*Es war ihm nicht in die Wiege gelegt.*", En: "*He was not endowed with it from birth.*"), situational embeddings or circumstances in the narrower sense ("*singing in the rain*"), and contextual restrictions ("*(only) in his imagination*"). The proper differentiation can in general only be achieved on the basis of background knowledge and exact knowledge of the dialogue situation. In order to interpret a phrase like "*the moderator on television*", one

---

[36] Please note that the range of admissible prepositions is somewhat restricted in comparison with LOC.

has to know that there are programs (talk shows, public discussions) mediated by a third person. So this phrase can possibly be read in a concrete dialogue context as *"the person who moderated the talk show"*.

The hierarchy of the relations expressing a situational embedding is shown in Fig. 18.43.

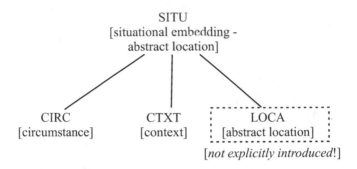

**Figure 18.43.** The generalized situational embedding

## 18.2.75    SOURC: Generalized Source or Origin

**SOURC:** $[si \cup o] \times [si \cup o \cup l]$

**Definition:** The statement (s SOURC q) expresses that the object s has the generalized source q, where s is typically an event. SOURC is defined as the union of the relations INIT, ORIG, ORIGL, ORIGM, and AVRT.

**Mnemonics:** En: source (Ge: Ursprung/Quelle)
(s SOURC q) – [s has the generalized source q]

**Question pattern:** Where [do] ⟨s⟩ {stem / come / arise ... } from?
What is the {origin / root / source ... } of ⟨s⟩?
According to the definition of SOURC, all other questions aiming at specializations of this relation are also admissible.

**Explanation:** The relation SOURC is suggested for the meaning representation of natural language sentences in cases where the available background knowledge (e.g. in the computational lexicon of an NLP system) is not sufficient for a proper differentiation between the relations INIT, ORIG, ORIGL, ORIGM, and AVRT.

**Annotation:** The relation AVRT can only under certain assumptions be seen as a specialization of SOURC. This can actually be done if the first argument is a transfer action in the broadest sense.

Example (with relation SOURC):

(18.188) "[*He withdrew*]SOURC+AVRT$_{arg1}$ *some money from* [*the bank*]SOURC+AVRT$_{arg2}$."

Counterexample (without relation SOURC):

(18.189) "[*FIFA disallowed*]$^{AVRT}{}_{arg1}$ [*the team*]$^{AVRT}{}_{arg2}$ *a title.*"

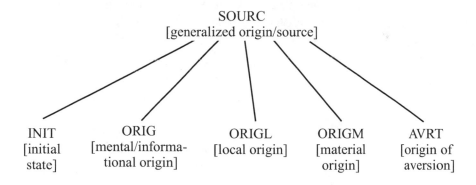

SOURC
[generalized origin/source]

| INIT | ORIG | ORIGL | ORIGM | AVRT |
|---|---|---|---|---|
| [initial state] | [mental/informa-tional origin] | [local origin] | [material origin] | [origin of aversion] |

**Figure 18.44.** Generalized source or origin

## 18.2.76  SSPE: C-Role – Entity Specifying a State

**SSPE:** $[st \cup as] \times [m \cup o \cup si]$

**Definition:** (s SSPE e) characterizes the relationship between a state s and an entity e which participates in s without being the carrier of this state. From a logical point of view, e is an essential meaning component of the predicate determining s.

**Mnemonics:** En: state specifier (Ge: Zustandsspezifikator)
    (s SSPE e) – [the state s is specified by e]

**Question pattern:** ⟨WH⟩ [characterize] ⟨st⟩?
What [do] ⟨state carrier of s⟩ {weigh / cost / ... }?

How much of some material [do] ⟨state carrier of s⟩ {contain / possess / . . . }?

**Explanation:** The expression (s SSPE e) is used to provide more details about the entity e which participates in the state s apart from the carrier of the state (see relation SCAR). Together with the concept c superordinate to s (see relation SUBS), e constitutes the logical predicate governing s.

(18.190) *"The head of the department has [the responsibility]*$^{\text{SSPE}_{arg2}}$.*"*
(18.191) *"Max weighs [30 kg]*$^{\text{SSPE}_{arg2}}$.*"*
(18.192) *"The firm lacks [sufficient money]*$^{\text{SSPE}_{arg2}}$.*"*

In the area of quantitative state specifiers, there are relationships between semantic representations containing SCAR/SSPE on the one hand and attribute-value characterizations of an object with ATTR/VAL on the other hand (see Fig. 18.45).

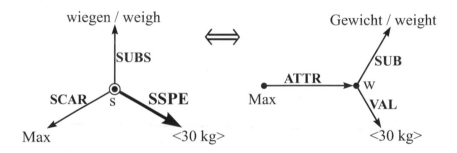

**Figure 18.45.** States and attribute-value constructs

The relationship between the representations shown in Fig. 18.45 can also be described by a corresponding meaning postulate (B-Axiom):

- (s SCAR o) ∧ (s SUBS weigh) ∧ (s SSPE q) →
  ∃w [(o ATTR w) ∧ (w SUB weight) ∧ (w VAL q)]     (167)

## 18.2.77   STRT: Relation Specifying the Temporal Beginning

**STRT:** [*si* ∪ *o* ∪ *t*] × [*t* ∪ *ta* ∪ *abs* ∪ *si*]

**Definition:** The expression (s STRT t) states that the temporal beginning of an event s or the beginning of the validity of a state of affairs s is determined by the second argument t, which can be another situation, a moment, or a period of time. If the second argument of the expression (x STRT y) denotes a situation (i.e. y ∈ *si*), then the temporal beginning of x is determined by the beginning of that time interval $t_y$ which is attached to the situation y ($t_y$ = time interval of the validity of y). In this case, the duration of y or $t_y$ must not be longer than that of situation x. The relation STRT is defined only in those cases where the first argument has a certain duration (with regard to the extension of this definition to sort *o*, see below).

**Mnemonics:** En: start (Ge: Start)
    (s STRT t) – [s starts with t / has t as temporal beginning]

**Question pattern:** Since when ⟨si⟩?
Since when [do] ⟨o⟩ {exist / be present }?
From {when on / which time } ⟨si⟩?
When [do] ⟨si⟩ {begin / start / . . . ]}

**Explanation:** Just like the meaning of the conjunction "*since*" used in the surface structure, also the relation STRT cannot be sharply defined. In general, the temporal beginning of the interval $t_y$, attached to the second argument of (x STRT y), determines the beginning of the interval $t_x$, attached to the first argument (see Sect. 7.3). The larger the period given by $t_y$, the farther the beginning of $t_x$ can be shifted within $t_y$.

    Example:

(18.193) "*Since [the 19th century]*STRT*$_{arg2}$ there have been factories.*"

does not necessarily mean "*since January 1, 1801*". As an example for a state whose temporal beginning is explicitly determined by a (relatively sharp) time moment, the following sentence is given.

(18.194) "*Peter is waiting at the railway station*
                    *since [eleven past six]*STRT*$_{arg2}$.*"

Regarding the elliptic character of phrases that seemingly introduce objects of sort *co* as a **second** argument of the relation STRT ("*Since [Potsdam]*STRT*$_{arg2}$ the Allies had . . .*"), we refer to the discussion of Example (18.11) with ANTE.

    In contrast to that, it is quite reasonable to extend the domain of the **first** argument of STRT to objects. Thus, (k STRT t) with k ∈ *o* means that t marks the temporal beginning of the existence of k ("*k exists since t*").

## 18.2.78   SUB: Subordination of Concepts Representing Objects

**SUB:** sort $\times$ $\overline{sort}$  with **sort** $\subseteq [o \setminus \{abs \cup re\}]$ as the most specific sort
which must be the same for both arguments

**Definition:** The expression ($o_1$ SUB $o_2$) specifies that the individual or generic concept $o_1$ is subordinate to the generic concept $o_2$, i.e. everything derivable for $o_2$ is also valid for $o_1$.

For concepts which can be interpreted extensionally, the assertion of ($o_1$ SUB $o_2$) means that the extension of the concept $o_1$ is contained in that of the concept $o_2$ (see Sect. 4.1 for a more detailed discussion).

The relation SUB is transitive, not reflexive, and asymmetric.

**Mnemonics:** En: subordination (Ge: Subordination / Unterordnung)
  ($o_1$ SUB $o_2$) – [$o_1$ is subordinate to the concept $o_2$]

**Question pattern:** $\langle$WH$\rangle$ [be] $\langle$o$\rangle$?
{Which / What} $\langle$o$\rangle$ [do] exist?
$\langle$WMT$\rangle$ [do] $\langle$o$\rangle$ belong?
What kind of object [be] $\langle$o$\rangle$?
{Under what concept / term} can $\langle$o$\rangle$ be subsumed?

**Explanation:** The subordination relation plays a fundamental role in the definition of concepts, where it is used to specify the **genus proximum**. SUB carries the **inheritance** of properties transferred from superordinate concepts to subordinate concepts. This inheritance relation extends within a conceptual hierarchy from a concept c at the top through every specialization of c down to the individual concepts subordinate to c. Typical axioms formally describing inheritance processes are as follows:

- ($c_1$ SUB $c_2$) $\wedge$ ($c_2$ PROP p) $\rightarrow$ ($c_1$ PROP p)  *(Transfer of properties)*  (168)
- ($o_1$ SUB $o_2$) $\wedge$ ($o_2$ ORIGM s) $\rightarrow$ ($o_1$ ORIGM s)                (169)
  *(Transfer of material origin)*
- ($o_1$ SUB $o_2$) $\wedge$ ($o_2$ ATTR $a_1$) $\rightarrow$ $\exists a_2$ ($o_1$ ATTR $a_2$) $\wedge$ ($a_2$ SUB $a_1$)    (170)
  *(Transfer of attributes)*

In this way, the relation SUB defines an **inheritance hierarchy** within the conceptual world represented in a semantic network.[37]

---

[37] The regularities expressed by axioms must be divided into expressions which have to be considered default assumptions (like the transfer of properties according to (168) or the transfer of material origin according to (169)) and expressions which are categorically valid (like the transfer of attributes (170)).

It must be stated that SUB is also used for the subordination of individual concepts under generic concepts, although a special relation (denoted by IS-A) is often proposed for that in the literature. This distinction is not necessary in MultiNet because of its clear assignment of nodes to different layers (in this case to the layers of individual and generic concepts).

### 18.2.79   SUB0: Generalized Subordination Relation

**SUB0:** $[si \cup o] \times [\overline{si} \cup \overline{o}]$

**Definition:** The assertion $(e_1 \text{ SUB0 } e_2)$ describes the most general conceptual subordination. It is defined as a union of the relations SUB, SUBS, and SUBR, i.e. the following holds:

$(e_1 \text{ SUB0 } e_2) \longleftrightarrow_{Def} (e_1 \text{ SUB } e_2) \vee (e_1 \text{ SUBS } e_2) \vee (e_1 \text{ SUBR } e_2)$    (171)

**Mnemonics:** En: (most underspecified) subordination
(Ge: (allgemeinste) Unterordnung)
$(e_1 \text{ SUB0 } e_2)$ – [between $e_1$ (subconcept) and $e_2$ (superconcept)
a generalized subordination relation holds]

**Question pattern:** To which concept [be] ⟨ent⟩ subordinate?
What superconcept(s) [do] exist for ⟨ent⟩?

**Explanation:** From the above definition, the hierarchy in Fig. 18.46 is obtained for the subordination relations.

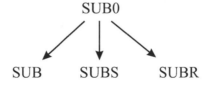

**Figure 18.46.** The hierarchy of subordination relations

The relation SUB0 is preferred for the conceptual subordination of meaning molecules (see Sect. 12.2) because, in this case, the correct selection of the proper meaning facet and, therefore, of the proper subordination relation is not possible without background knowledge (this is especially difficult for automatic NLP systems). So, it is not easy to decide without further information whether in a sentence like "*Peter likes the school.*" the facet building with

[**SORT** = *co*] (and, therefore, SUB as appropriate subordination relation) or the facet instruction with [**SORT** = *abs*] (and, therefore, SUBS as appropriate subordination relation) is meant. The analogue holds for the disambiguation of SUB and SUBR, with meaning molecules lying between sort [*co*] and sort [*re*] (see the kinship relations in Sect. 4.2, and relation ELMT).

The relation SUB0 also offers a way to deliberately postpone the decision with regard to a specific subordination relation (avoidance of disambiguation). This can be done in a later phase of language processing (i.e during inferential answer finding). In some cases, an enforced disambiguation would lead to additional and unnecessary costs without having a special effect in a QAS. The same is true for automatic translation between languages where meaning molecules are often analogously structured into meaning facets, which can be observed in English and German (compare the sentence above with the German translation "*Peter liebt die Schule.*").

## 18.2.80    SUBM/SUBME: Subsumption of Sets (Set Inclusion)

**SUBM/SUBME:** $pe^{(n)} \times pe^{(n)}$ with $n \geq 1$ ($pe^{(n)}$ is explained in Appendix A.)

**Definition:** The statement ($g_1$ SUBM $g_2$) specifies that the collection/set $g_1$ is completely contained in, but is not identical to, the collection/set $g_2$. This relation is transitive, asymmetric, and not reflexive. The reflexive relation SUBME expressing set inclusion or equality is defined analogously to SUBM.

**Mnemonics:** En: subsumption of sets (Ge: Teilmengenbeziehung)
     ($g_1$ SUBM $g_2$) – [$g_1$ is a partial set of $g_2$]

**Question pattern:** How [be] $\langle g_2 \rangle$ composed?
$\langle$WMT$\rangle$ [do] the collection $\langle g_1 \rangle$ belong?
What kind of elements [do] $\langle g_2 \rangle$ have?

**Explanation:** The relation SUBM corresponds to strict set inclusion within the framework of naive set theory. It connects entities (sets) of the preextensional level with each other. The relation SUBM can be characterized formally by the following axiom:

- ($g_1$ SUBM $g_2$) $\leftrightarrow$ ($g_1 \neq g_2$) $\wedge$ $\forall x$ [(x ELMT $g_1$) $\rightarrow$ (x ELMT $g_2$)]      (172)

An example of the cooperation of the SUBM relation at the preextensional level and the SUB relation at the intensional level can be found with SETOF.

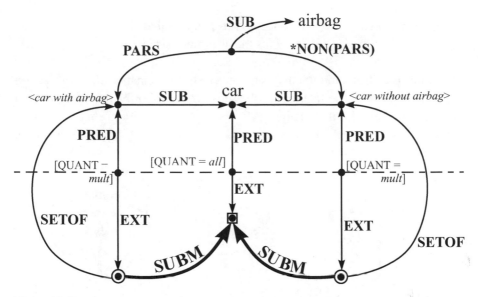

**Figure 18.47.** The subsumption of sets at the preextensional level

The use of the SUBM relation for the semantic representation of natural language expressions is illustrated by Fig. 18.47, which corresponds to the following sentence:

(18.195) "[*Some cars*]$^{\text{SUBM}_{arg1}}$ *have an airbag [some]*$^{\text{SUBM}_{arg1}}$ *not*."

### 18.2.81   SUBR: Metarelation for the Description of Relations

**SUBR:** $[si \cup re] \times [\overline{si} \cup \overline{re}]$

**Definition:** The expression (r SUBR c) is used for the subordination of relational concepts. It is especially applied to connect a relational concept r (or a situation at the metalevel) with another relational concept or an abstract situation c which determines the argument structure of r by means of the metarelations ARG1/2/3.

**Mnemonics:** En: subordination of relational concepts
        (Ge: Unterordnung von relationalen Konzepten)
    (r SUBR c) – [r is subordinate to the relational concept c]

**Question pattern:** By which concept is ⟨re⟩ dominated?
What situational concept determines the argument structure of ⟨re⟩?

**Explanation:** The relation SUBR is preferred for the semantic characterization
of verbs which describe relations in the sense of the MultiNet representational
means. Together with the relations ARG1/2/3, they provide formal constructs
at the metalevel by which the semantic primitives of MultiNet can again be
described in natural language.

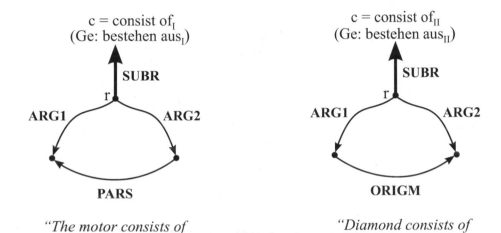

"The motor consists of
cylinder, carburetor, ..."

"Diamond consists of
carbon."

**Figure 18.48.** The argument structure of relational concepts

From the lexicographical point of view, SUBR is used to specify the argument
structure of verbs whose arguments cannot be described by C-Roles. The relation SUBR is often combined with ARG1/2/3 to represent the meaning of state
verbs obligatorily governing prepositional phrases (so-called **prepositional
verbs**) such as "*bestehen aus*" (En: "*consist of*"), "*bestehen in*" (En: "*consist
in*"), which cannot be interpreted as states in the narrower sense. The analogue
holds for the meaning representation of certain "dynamic" verbs which do not
describe events in the proper sense, such as Ge: "*beginnen/enden*" (En: "*be-
gin/end*") → STRT / FIN, Ge:"*dienen zu*" (En: "*serve as*") → PURP.
SUBR is also useful for the semantic description of concepts with sort *re*, such
as uncle or cousin. If the relational concept c in an expression (r SUBR c)
can be extensionally interpreted, then (r SUBR c) is valid if and only if the

extension $r_{EXT}$ of r is contained in the extension $c_{EXT}$ of c (for a detailed description, see Fig. 18.49).

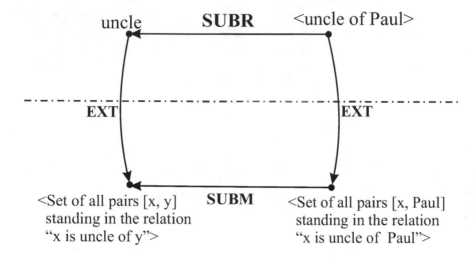

**Figure 18.49.** The extensions of relational concepts

## 18.2.82    SUBS: Subordination of Situations

**SUBS:** $[si \cup abs] \times [\overline{si} \cup \overline{abs}]$

**Definition:** The statement ($s_1$ SUBS $s_2$) characterizes the subordination of concepts which represent situations (actions, happenings, or states) where the second argument $s_2$ must always be a generic concept. The relation SUBS is transitive, asymmetric, and not reflexive.

**Mnemonics:**
En: subordination of situations (Ge: Subordination von Situationen)
    ($s_1$ SUBS $s_2$) – [the situation $s_1$ is a specialization of situation $s_2$]

**Question pattern:** What kind of situation takes place?
What does the carrier of the action $\langle si \rangle$ {do / carry out / make / … }?
By which generic {action / happening / state} is $\langle si \rangle$ dominated?
In what {state / situation} is $\langle \overline{si} \rangle$ the dominating concept?

**Explanation:** The relation SUBS is used to specify the dominating dynamic concept (in the case of events) or static concept (in the case of states) for a given situation. It establishes a corresponding hierarchy of events or states.

The inheritance of deep case relations in a hierarchy of actions is illustrated in Fig. 18.50. One can see that new and more specific valencies are added at every level of subconcepts, compared to the valency frame of the corresponding superconcepts.[38]

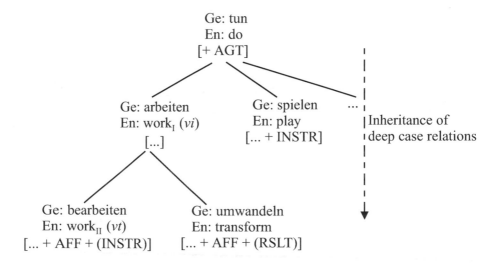

**Figure 18.50.** Detail from a SUBS hierarchy

The relation SUBS was separately introduced and distinguished from SUB because the inheritance of valency frames of actions, happenings, and states is governed by regularities other than the inheritance of properties for conceptual objects. In addition, questions for SUBS have a structure different from those for SUB. Finally, it does not seem appropriate, from a technical point of view, to attach different axioms and axiom schemata (or methods of inheritance) to a single subordination relation (because they would anyway have to be discerned in the deduction process by means of the sorts involved).

Since subordinations of concepts are frequently met in semantic representations and play an important role in logical answer finding, the differentiation into the subordination relations SUB, SUBR, and SUBS seems to be justified.

---

[38] The parentheses enclose facultative valencies (see Sect. 4.2); the dots indicate the transfer of the valency frame of the superordinate concept to its subordinate concepts.

## 18.2.83   SUBST: Relation Specifying a Substitute for an Entity

**SUBST:** $[o \times o] \cup [si \times si]$

**Definition:** The expression (x SUBST y) states that x instead of y participates in a situation, or that an object x is substituted for another object y in an event, or that a situation x holds instead of a situation y.

**Mnemonics:** En: substitute (Ge: Substitut)
   (x SUBST y) – [x is substituted for y]

**Question pattern:** Instead of ⟨WHA⟩ is ⟨x⟩ involved in the given situation? What {holds / happens / takes place / ... } instead of ⟨si⟩?
{Who / What} {appears / participates / ... } instead of ⟨o⟩?

**Explanation:** The relation (x SUBST y) allows an opposition of entities with the same sort in such a way that {a motivation / a goal / an expectation} is directed toward y, whereas x {participates / appears / holds} instead of y (depending on the sort of x).

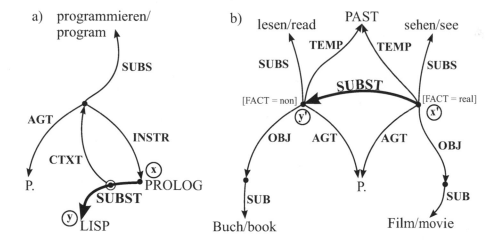

**Figure 18.51.** The elliptical character of substitutions

Examples:

(18.196)  Ge: *"P. programmiert in [PROLOG]*$^{\text{SUBST}_{arg1}}$
             *anstelle von [LISP]*$^{\text{SUBST}_{arg2}}$*."*                                    (see Fig. 18.51a)
           En: *"P. is programming in [PROLOG]*$^{\text{SUBST}_{arg1}}$
             *instead of [LISP]*$^{\text{SUBST}_{arg2}}$*."*
(18.197)  Ge: *"Anstatt [ein Buch zu lesen]*$^{\text{SUBST}_{arg1}}$*,*
             *[sah P. einen Film]*$^{\text{SUBST}_{arg2}}$*."*                                    (see Fig. 18.51b)
           En: *"Instead of [reading a book]*$^{\text{SUBST}_{arg1}}$*,*
             *[P. saw a movie]*$^{\text{SUBST}_{arg2}}$*."*

In most natural language expressions where SUBST is involved, the corresponding surface structures are elliptical constructions with two complete underlying situations x' and y', which have to be reconstructed from the sentence context, using x and y as a starting point (see Fig. 18.51a). As result, x' (P. is programming in PROLOG) is asserted and y' (P. is programming in LISP), toward which the expectations are directed, is negated.

The relation SUBST is also applied to describe the argument structure of replacement actions in the broadest sense (in this group we include exchange, substitute, replace, etc.); see Fig. 18.52. In these representations, SUBST also expresses the asymmetry between the arguments (in Fig. 18.52, x is replaced by y, and not vice versa). Another example for this is given in Part I, Fig. 5.7.

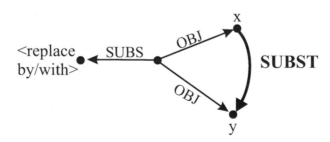

**Figure 18.52.** The semantic representation of replacements

## 18.2.84    SUPPL: Supplement Relation

**SUPPL:** $[si \cup abs] \times o$

**Definition:** The assertion (s SUPPL o) expresses that o supplements the situational concept s in the sense that o is an essential meaning component of s. In contrast to the relation OBJ, the existence or validity of o is closely tied to that of s, i.e. o is not independent of s.

**Mnemonics:** En: supplement (Ge: Supplement / Ergänzung)
(s SUPPL o) – [s is complemented by o]

**Question pattern:** $\langle$WHA$\rangle$ [do] somebody {dance / sing / play / ... }?
What action is inherently connected with $\langle$o$\rangle$?

**Explanation:** The statement (s SUPPL o) establishes an immanent connection between s and o which determines o as a logical supplement of s.
Examples:

(18.198)  Ge: (tanzen SUPPL Tanz)       En: (dance.1.1 SUPPL dance.2.1)
(18.199)  Ge: (spielen SUPPL Spiel)      En: (play SUPPL game)
(18.200)  Ge: (singen SUPPL Lied)        En: (sing SUPPL song$_1$)
   But,  Ge: (singen CHEA Gesang)    En: (sing CHEA singing/song$_2$)

This inherent connection between s and o does not mean that the object o must really be paraphrased in the surface structure of a sentence. Example:

(18.201)  *"Carreras sang before the event."* vs.
      *"Carreras sang an aria before the event."*         (see Fig. 18.53)

As the examples show, the relationships between the first and second argument must not be represented by OBJ, because a dance, a game, and a song are not independent objects of a dancing, a playing, and a singing act, respectively. Since supplements are logically implicated by the corresponding action and are not proper participants of the action, they cannot be represented by other C-Roles.

The supplement relations specified at the generic level, as in (dance.1.1 SUPPL dance.2.1), also have consequences for the inference processes in a QAS. From a special event like

(18.202)  *"They were [dancing]*$^{\text{SUPPL}_{arg1}}$ *[a tango]*$^{\text{SUPPL}_{arg2}}$.*"

one can infer the kind of supplement by means of immanent knowledge; here, a tango is a dance, or in terms of MultiNet: (tango SUB dance.2.1).

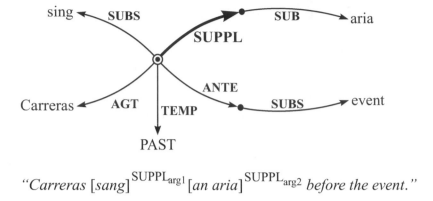

$$\text{``Carreras [sang]}^{\text{SUPPL}_{\text{arg1}}} \text{[an aria]}^{\text{SUPPL}_{\text{arg2}}} \text{ before the event.''}$$

**Figure 18.53.** The semantic representation of an intrinsic supplement

### 18.2.85   SYNO: Synonymy Relation

**SYNO:** sort × sort                with **sort** as an arbitrary, but most specific sort
                                      which must be the same for both arguments

**Definition:** The statement ($e_1$ SYNO $e_2$) connects two concepts of the same
sort which are synonymous with each other, i.e. they have the same extensional
if they are indeed extensionally interpretable. For conceptual objects, this relation corresponds to EQU (see page 491). The relation SYNO is symmetric,
reflexive, and transitive.

**Mnemonics:** En: synonym (Ge: Synonym)
        ($e_1$ SYNO $e_2$) – [$e_1$ is synonymous with $e_2$]

**Question pattern:** What has the same meaning as ⟨ent⟩?
By which concept / term can ⟨ent⟩ be substituted?

**Explanation:** Although the relation EQU is also provided by MultiNet, the
relation SYNO was introduced to emphasize the parallelism to the lexical
antonymy relation ANTO (see page 452).
    Examples:

(18.203)  En: (bachelor SYNO ⟨non-married adult man⟩)
    Ge: (Junggeselle SYNO ⟨nichtverheirateter, erwachsener Mann⟩)
    or as further German synonyms:
(18.204)  Ge: (Cousin SYNO Vetter)
(18.205)  Ge: (Rechner SYNO Computer)

(18.206)  Ge: (LKW SYNO Lastkraftwagen)

(18.207)  Ge: (bereits SYNO schon)

Synonymous concepts can be exchanged one for another in nonmodal contexts. However, this is not admissible for modal contexts! Thus, sentences like:

(18.208)  *"John knows who is the mayor of LA."* and

(18.209)  *"John knows who is the mayor of Los Angeles."*

are not synonymous, because John might not be familiar with the abbreviation LA for Los Angeles, notwithstanding the fact that (LA SYNO ⟨Los Angeles⟩) holds. Example (18.207) additionally shows that concepts which do not belong to sort *o* may also be connected by a synonymy relation.

If the differences between colloquial language and standard language are neglected or nuances between different connotations of concepts are set aside, the following pairs of concepts can also be taken as synonymous.[39]

- Ge: (Gesicht SYNO Visage)
  En: (face SYNO visage)
- Ge: (schlafen SYNO schlummern)
  En: (sleep SYNO slumber)
- Ge: (Auto SYNO Wagen)
  En: (auto SYNO car)

## 18.2.86   TEMP: Relation Specifying a Temporal Frame

**TEMP:** $[si \cup t \cup o] \times [t \cup si \cup abs \cup ta]$

**Definition:** The assertion (s TEMP t) expresses that the situation s holds within the time interval t (or, if s is an event, that it occurs within t). If the first argument is of sort *o*, then the second argument specifies the time interval or moment when o exists. It should be emphasized that t may be disconnected.[40]

---

[39] This decision depends on the application domain of the meaning representation and cannot be made absolutely. One should think of sentences like

(18.210)  *"They saw his face in the mirror."* and

(18.211)  *"They saw his visage in the mirror."*

In German, the word *"Visage"* has a derogatory connotation not present with *"Gesicht"*.

[40] In connection with temporal relations, especially with TEMP, the representatives PAST, PRES, and FUT are used to describe the underspecified past, present, and future, respectively. All three time intervals bear a deictic character and have to be resolved in a deeper semantic interpretation.

**Mnemonics:** Latin: tempus (Ge: Zeit)
    (s TEMP t) – [s holds / takes place within the time t]

**Question pattern:** When $\langle si \rangle$?
When [do] $\langle o \rangle$ {exist / live ... }?
{At which time / When} $\langle si \rangle$?
At which {day / month / year / century } $\langle si \rangle$?
What {time / hour} [do] somebody $\langle dy \rangle$?

**Explanation:** The relation TEMP (similar to CTXT, COND, MODL, etc.) has a different character than the relations describing situational knowledge. It is used in connection with situations to describe the temporal restriction of the validity of a state of affairs or to temporally restrict the course of an event or the existence of an object temporally. Examples are:

(18.212) *"Albertus Magnus [lived]*$^{\text{TEMP}_{arg1}}$
                            *[in the 13th century]*$^{\text{TEMP}_{arg2}}$*."*
(18.213) *"[Scriptures]*$^{\text{TEMP}_{arg1}}$ *from the [Middle Ages]*$^{\text{TEMP}_{arg2}}$*."*

    **Annotation:** The semantic representation of temporal adverbs like *"always"*, *"often"*, and *"sometimes"*, or similar adverbial phrases expressing repetitions of situations, have to be constructed with the layer attribute **QUANT**, which is attached to the representative of a time $t \in t$ (compare with the explanation of quantifications in Sect. 10.1). Typically, but not necessarily, the temporal extension of a situation s specified by (s TEMP t) lies in a proper subpart of the time interval t. With regard to the comparison of TEMP and DUR, see the discussion of the two relations in Sect. 7.3.

## 18.2.87   VAL: Relation Between Attribute and Value

**VAL:** $\dot{a}t \times [o \cup qn \cup p \cup fe \cup t]$

**Definition:** The statement (a VAL v) establishes a connection between an attribute that is assigned to a certain individual object o (see ATTR) and a concept v, the value of this attribute with regard to o.

**Mnemonics:** En: value (Ge: Wert)
    (a VAL v) – [the attribute a has the value v]

**Question pattern:** Which value has $\langle at \rangle$ of $\langle o \rangle$?
How many $\langle me \rangle$ [be] $\langle at \rangle$ of $\langle o \rangle$?

How $\langle gq \rangle$ [be] $\langle o \rangle$?
{In / At} which $\langle oa \rangle$ [do] $\langle si \rangle$ hold?

**Explanation:** The expression (a VAL v) is used in connection with ATTR for the specification of the value of an attribute assigned to a certain object o, i.e. it is mainly encountered in the combination (o ATTR a) $\wedge$ (a VAL v). Strictly speaking, the specification of VAL, together with its second argument v, does not yield additional or new information about the first argument (which is in contrast to QMOD); rather, it makes the value v, which is already determined by o and a, explicit. The uniqueness of values for the same object-attribute combination must be warranted by special axiom schemata.

For instance, the following expressions can be described semantically by means of VAL:

- quantitative values of operational abstract concepts
  (18.214) "*[The height of the Matterhorn]*$^{VAL_{arg1}}$" $\rightarrow$ "*4505 m*"
  (18.215) "*[The pressure in the boiler]*$^{VAL_{arg1}}$" $\rightarrow$ "*30 atm*"
- synonymous descriptions of local and temporal specifications
  (18.216) "*[The birthplace of Schiller]*$^{VAL_{arg1}}$" $\rightarrow$ "*Marbach*"
  (18.217) "*[The beginning of the French revolution]*$^{VAL_{arg1}}$" $\rightarrow$ "*1789*"
- values of nonoperational attributes
  (18.218) "*[The color of the raven]*$^{VAL_{arg1}}$" $\rightarrow$ "*black*"
  (18.219) "*[The shape of the tool]*$^{VAL_{arg1}}$" $\rightarrow$ "*cylindrical*".

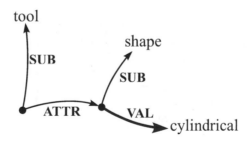

**Figure 18.54.** Example of an attribute-value assignment

The relation VAL cannot be expressed by EQU, because the arguments of VAL (as the last example clearly shows) are not equivalent concepts. In the above example, the concept **cylindrical** with [SORT = $p$] is different from $\langle$shape of a certain tool$\rangle$ with [SORT = $at$].

Figure 18.55 illustrates the possibilities provided by MultiNet to differentiate between the generic concepts **water** with the property that it boils at 100°C on the one hand, and ⟨boiling water⟩ on the other hand, together with the meaning of the sentence *"water boils at 100°C."*

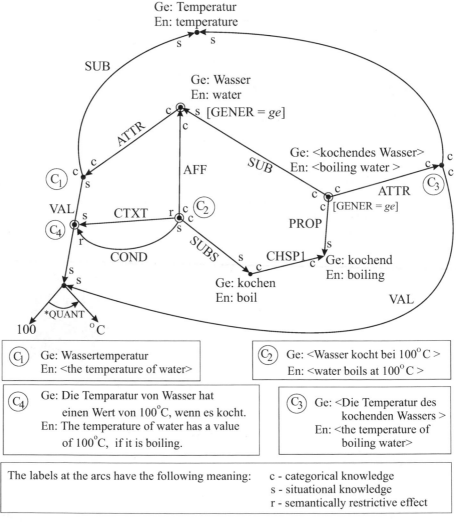

| | | | |
|---|---|---|---|
| $C_1$ | Ge: Wassertemperatur En: ⟨the temperature of water⟩ | $C_2$ | Ge: ⟨Wasser kocht bei 100°C⟩ En: ⟨water boils at 100°C⟩ |

| | | | |
|---|---|---|---|
| $C_4$ | Ge: Die Temparatur von Wasser hat einen Wert von 100°C, wenn es kocht. En: The temperature of water has a value of 100°C, if it is boiling. | $C_3$ | Ge: ⟨Die Temperatur des kochenden Wassers⟩ En: ⟨the temperature of boiling water⟩ |

The labels at the arcs have the following meaning:   c - categorical knowledge
s - situational knowledge
r - semantically restrictive effect

**Figure 18.55.** The combined application of ATTR and VAL for the characterization of generic concepts

In this example, the combination of the relations ATTR and VAL with the values of the attribute **K-TYPE** annotated at the arcs play a central role. It should also be noted that in this example the relation VAL and the situation $C_2$ are mutually restricted by a CTXT and a COND relation, respectively. (The value of the water temperature is $100^oC$ only if the water is boiling, and water is boiling only at a temperature of $100^oC$.)

## 18.2.88   VALR: Relation Between Attributes and Their Value Restriction

**VALR:** $\overline{at} \times [o \cup qn \cup p \cup fe \cup t]$

**Definition:** The expression (b VALR v) connects a generic attribute b (a concept having a functional character) with its value restriction v, i.e. a specialization subordinate to b can take only values from v or a value v' that is subordinate to v (see also Sect. 4.3.3.2).

**Mnemonics:** En: value range (Ge: Wertebereich)
(b VALR v) – [attribute b has the value restriction v]

**Question pattern:** What values can be observed with $\langle at \rangle$?
Which {attribute / attributes} can take $\langle v \rangle$ as {its / their} value?

**Explanation:** The relation VALR is the counterpart of VAL at the generic level. Together with ATTR und VAL, it plays a central role in the attribute-value characterization of objects (or, in terms of artificial intelligence, in the realization of a slot-filler mechanism). The relation VALR is used to describe the slots; see Fig. 18.56.

The descriptions of the slots by VALR are interpreted as constraints (integrity conditions) for the fillers specified by VAL. The following descriptions of value restrictions are typical:[41]

a)  an explicit enumeration of entities (Fig. 18.56a)
b)  a quantity containing a placeholder *nil* or a numeric interval instead of a concrete value (Fig. 18.56b).
c)  the specification of a superconcept as characterization of a value restriction.

---

[41] The signature of VALR also admits formal entities ([SORT = $fe$]), since strings or symbolic expressions can also occur as values or value restrictions, e.g. in the simple case of a "*name*" as an attribute, we have a series of characters (a string) as a value.

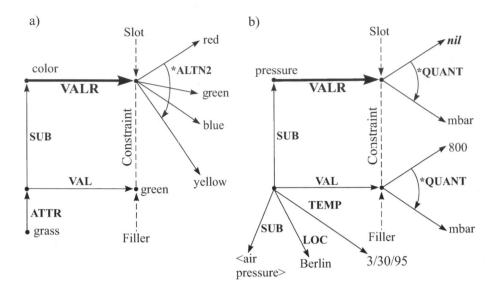

**Figure 18.56.** The specification of value restrictions

## 18.2.89   VIA: Relation Specifying a Spatial Path

**VIA:** $[d \cup dy \cup ad] \times l$

**Definition:** The assertion (s VIA w) is used for the specification of a path or way w taken by an object s $\in d$ participating in an event or of a path determining the spatial route of an event s $\in [dy \cup ad]$.

**Mnemonics:** En: via (Ge: via / über)
          (s VIA w) – [s is determined by the path w]

**Question pattern:** {Which path / Which route} is taken by ⟨o⟩?
Where [do] {somebody / something} {move / take its course}?
⟨Path-prep⟩ which ⟨o⟩ ⟨si⟩?
          with ⟨Path-prep⟩ as a preposition describing an element
          of the *FLAP-group, see function *FLP$_J$ on page 570.

**Explanation:** The following examples are typical of the description of the relation VIA in natural language:

(18.220)  Ge: *"P. fährt mit dem Zug über [München]*$^{VIA_{arg2}}$ *nach Wien."*
     En: *"P. goes by train to Vienna via [Munich]*$^{VIA_{arg2}}$.*"*

(18.221)  Ge: *"Das Flugzeug fliegt über [den Atlantik]*$^{\text{VIA}_{arg2}}$ *nach New York."*

En: *"The plane flies across [the Atlantic]*$^{\text{VIA}_{arg2}}$ *to New York."*

(18.222)  Ge: *"P. läuft entlang [des Deiches]*$^{\text{VIA}_{arg2}}$ *zum Café."*

En: *"P. walks along [the dike]*$^{\text{VIA}_{arg2}}$ *to the café."*

(18.223)  Ge: *"Der Dieb näherte sich dem Haus durch [den Garten]*$^{\text{VIA}_{arg2}}$*."*

En: *"The thief was approaching the house through [the garden]*$^{\text{VIA}_{arg2}}$*."*

(18.224)  Ge: *"Die Grenze verläuft entlang [des Flusses]*$^{\text{VIA}_{arg2}}$*."*

En: *"The border runs along [the river]*$^{\text{VIA}_{arg2}}$*."*

(18.225)  **But:**

Ge: *"Der Ballon treibt über [dem Atlantik]*$^{\text{LOC}_{arg2}}$*."*

Ge: *"The balloon drifts over [the Atlantic]*$^{\text{LOC}_{arg2}}$*."*

Analogously to the relations DIRCL and ORIGL, VIA can also be applied in an abbreviated form to objects (Ge: *"Der Zug über München"* or En: *"The train via Munich"*). The example of Fig. 18.57 shows that the specification of a spatial course is possible even if there is also a location (LOC), a local origin (ORIGL), and a local goal (DIRCL):

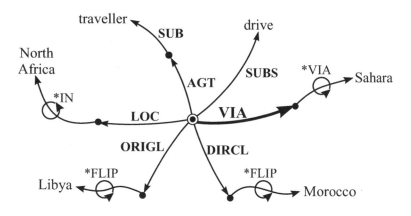

*"The traveller drives in North Africa from Libya through the Sahara to Morocco."*

**Figure 18.57.** Paths, directions and locations

The figure also demonstrates the necessity to generate locations prior to the application of local relations. The relation LOC is linked with *IN (the travel is located <u>in</u> North Africa); the locations for the relations DIRCL and ORIGL have to be generated by the underspecified functional constructs with *FLIP (see function $*FLP_J$), while the function *VIA is used to generate a path leading through the Sahara before this path can be connected to the situational node by means of VIA. This example also shows that the function *VIA as a generator of a path must not be mixed with the relation VIA connecting a situation to a location having the form of a path.

# 18.3 Functions

## 18.3.1 *ALTN1/2: Construction of Alternative Pluralities

**∗ALTN1/2:** sort × sort × ... × sort → sort        with **sort** as an arbitrary, but most specific sort

**Definition:**
The functions ∗ALTN1 and ∗ALTN2 represent strictly speaking families of functions with ∗ALTN1$_\nu$: sort$^\nu$ → sort and ∗ALTN2$_\nu$: sort$^\nu$ → sort (for $\nu \geq$ 2), which generate **alternative pluralities**, respectively. Such alternative pluralities are auxiliary constructs representing collections of entities from which at least one member (in the case of ∗ALTN1) or exactly one member (in the case of ∗ALTN2) has to be selected in order to interpret a situation comprising such a plurality as a participant.

**Mnemonics:** En: alternative (Ge: Alternative)

**Question pattern:** –

**Explanation:** In the same way as for economical reasons constituent coordinations (phrase coordinations) are not expressed in the surface structure by complete sentences but by means of elliptical constructions; the functions ∗ALTN1 and ∗ALTN2 are used as abbreviations for disjunctively conjoined events or states of affairs in the deep structure. This does not only have an economical aspect, though (see Example (18.227) and Fig. 18.58). The use of these functions is also justified by the difficulties connected with the semantic analysis of coordinative compound sentences, whose exact semantic interpretation (division into several disjunctively conjoined situations) is often not possible due to a lack of background knowledge, or because the required effort would be too much. In this sense, the *ALTN-constructs can be taken as a more compact representation of the corresponding *VEL-constructs (see Fig. 18.58).

**Annotation:** The **conjunctive** enumeration of elements is expressed by the function ∗ITMS-I.

(18.226)  Ge: "*Das Programm kann mit [Zahlen, Buchstaben oder Sonderzeichen]*∗ALTN1 *arbeiten.*"
En: "*The program can work with [numbers, letters or special characters]*∗ALTN1 ."
In this case, the "*or*" could also be interpreted as an "*and*" (→ ∗ITMS-I).

(18.227)  Ge: *"Das Medikament wird als [Flüssigkeit oder Tablette]*ALTN2*
verabreicht."*
En: *"The medicament is administered as [liquid or as tablet]*ALTN2*."*

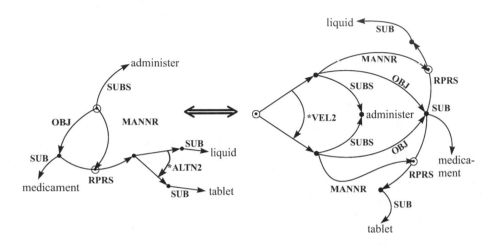

**Figure 18.58.** The resolution of an auxiliary *ALTN2 construct into two disjunctively conjoined representations

Constructs containing the functions *ALTN1 and *ALTN2 should have no place in a genuine semantic deep structure. They must be eliminated in a second interpretation step and should in particular be resolved before being used in the inference process (see Fig. 18.58). However, the admission of ALTN1/2 constructs is a real help for the syntactic-semantic analysis, and in many cases, especially when questions aim at these constructs as a unit, they can simply be returned and reformulated in the answering process without taking any pains about their deeper interpretation.

### 18.3.2  *COMP: Function for the Comparison of Properties

**\*COMP:** $gq \times [o \cup gq \cup m] \rightarrow p$

**Definition:** The function (*COMP $p_1$ c) = $p_2$ generates a new property $p_2$ by comparing the original property $p_1$ with an object c $\in$ o, with another gradable property c $\in$ gq, or with a measurement c $\in$ m. In general, $p_2$ is not gradable any more. In the typical case, where c $\in$ o, the equation (*COMP $p_1$ c) = $p_2$ expresses that property $p_2$, which is associated with the same attribute A as $p_1$, has a higher degree on a scale associated with A than property $p_1$. With regard

to the admissibility of properties or measurements in the second argument of
∗COMP, see below.

**Mnemonics:** En: comparison (Ge: Komparation)

**Question pattern:** –

**Explanation:** The function ∗COMP is used for the semantic representation
of the grammatical form **comparative**, whereby the assignment of a graded
property to an object can be made either without restriction (Example 18.228)
or with regard to a certain context (Example 18.229).

(18.228) *"The algorithm $A_1$ is [more effective]*∗COMP$_{arg1}$ *than [the
algorithm $A_2$]*∗COMP$_{arg2}$*."*      Case: a ∈ o without additional restriction

(18.229) *"A nuclear power station is [more advantageous]*∗COMP$_{arg1}$ *than
[a thermal power station]*∗COMP$_{arg2}$ *with regard to efficiency."*
Case: a ∈ o with contextual restriction (see Fig. 18.59).

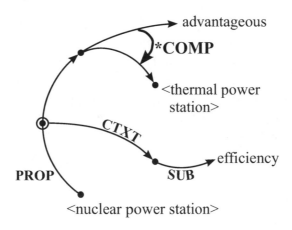

**Figure 18.59.** Contextual restriction of a comparison

The gradation of a property $p_1 \in gq$ by contrasting it with another property
$p_2 \in gq$ is needed for the direct comparison of two gradable properties and for
the semantic representation of inchoative verbs (such as Ge: *"gewinnen an"* or
En: *"gain"*) in sentences like:

(18.230)  Ge: *"Das Fahrzeug gewinnt an Geschwindigkeit."*
   En: *"The vehicle is gaining speed."*                    (see Fig. 18.60).

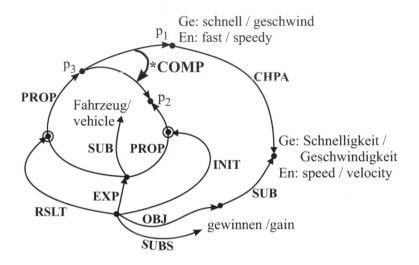

**Figure 18.60.** The growing of a property in a process

Here, the function *COMP with the second argument from *gq* is applied. The expression (*COMP $p_1$ $p_2$) = $p_3$ with $p_2 \in gq$ states that $p_3$ is a property of the same type as $p_1$ and $p_2$, but with a higher degree than that of $p_2$.

The second argument of *COMP can also be chosen from sort *m* to express the gradation of a property by comparing it with a measurement.

(18.231)  *"The tower is [higher]*COMP$_{arg1}$ than [300 m]*COMP$_{arg2}$."*

### 18.3.3  *DIFF: Set Difference

*DIFF: $pe^{(n)} \times [pe^{(n)} \cup pe^{(n-1)}] \to pe^{(n)}$          with $n \geq 1$

**Definition:** Let $(g_1 \setminus g_2) = \{el \mid (el \in g_1 \wedge \neg (el \in g_2))\}$ be the normal difference of two sets $g_1$ und $g_2$ (i.e. the set difference of two representatives at the preextensional level). Then, we define:

$$(*DIFF\ x\ y) = \begin{cases} (x \setminus y) & \text{for } x \in pe^{(n)} \text{ and } y \in pe^{(n)} \\ (x \setminus \{y\}) & \text{for } x \in pe^{(n)} \text{ and } y \in pe^{(n-1)} \end{cases}$$

**Mnemonics:** En: (set) difference – Ge: (Mengen-)Differenz

**Question pattern:** With what exception(s) does ⟨proposition p⟩ hold?

**Explanation:** The function *DIFF is used to eliminate single elements or partial sets from a set. The following holds:

- $(g_1 \text{ SUBM } g) \wedge (g_2 \text{ SUBM } g) \wedge (*\text{DIFF } g\ g_1) = g_2$
  $\rightarrow (*\text{DIFF } g\ g_2) = g_1$ ⠀⠀⠀⠀⠀⠀⠀⠀⠀⠀⠀⠀⠀⠀⠀⠀(173)

This function is used to specify exceptions. It plays a central role in the meaning representation of the prepositions "*außer*" (En: "*except for*") and "*ohne*" (En: "*without*").

⠀⠀The admission of subtracting single elements from a set by means of *DIFF is motivated by natural language phrases of the type:
(⟨plurality⟩ {without / except (for) / apart from)} ⟨individual element⟩),
as in the sentence:

(18.232) "[*<All students> except for <Peter>*]*DIFF *participated in the* game."

⠀⠀The function *DIFF can also be used to express that a set consists of the elements of two partial sets and no further elements, as shown in Fig. 18.61 (see also the example with *ITMS).

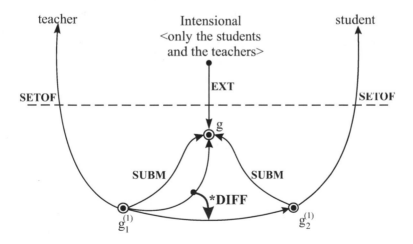

**Figure 18.61.** The partition of a set into two mutually disjoint subsets

### 18.3.4   *FLP$_J$: Functions Generating Locations

$$*\textbf{FLP}_J: co \rightarrow l \qquad\qquad \text{for } j \in [\langle\text{loc-prep}\rangle \setminus \{\text{between}\}]$$

$$\left.\begin{array}{l} d \times d \rightarrow l \\ \ddot{d} \rightarrow l \end{array}\right\} \qquad \text{for } j = \text{between}$$

**Definition:** The functions labeled *FLP$_j$ generate locations from objects. They belong to a family of similar mappings, which can be grouped into three sub-classes: *FLIP - semantic representatives of prepositions specifying the inner volume of an object or the attachment to its surface, *FLOP - semantic representatives of prepositions specifying the outer world of an object, and *FLAP - semantic representatives of prepositions specifying paths by means of given objects (see Fig. 18.62). In the case of *VIA $\in$ *FLAP, the path can also be underspecified by giving only one position on the path, as in Example (18.234) below. The use of the functions *FLAP, *FLIP, or *FLOP in a semantic representation generally denotes an underspecified location compared to the use of more specific functions subordinated to them.

Every member of the *FLP family represents the meaning of a local preposition. Except for *BETWEEN, these functions generally map elements from concrete objects [SORT = $co$] into locations [SORT = $l$]. The unary function *BETWEEN assigns a location to a collection of discrete objects, and the binary variant assigns a location to two different discrete objects. The binary function *BETWEEN is symmetric with regard to its arguments.[42]

**Mnemonics:** En: functional representation of the meaning of local prepositions – Ge: funktionale Darstellung der Bedeutung lokaler Präpositionen

**Question pattern:** A typical question for the result of the application of *FLP$_j$ is {"*Where / $\langle$loc-prep$\rangle$ $\langle$WHA$\rangle$} is x located?*" with $\langle$loc-prep$\rangle$ describing an element from *FLIP $\cup$ *FLOP; see below.

**Explanation:** The conception that local prepositions are semantically interpreted as functions generating locations from objects is cognitively supported by the observation that an utterance "*under the table*" is creating a different mental image than the utterance "*the table*". A complex example showing the

---

[42] Analogously to the relations ANLG and DISTG, a unary and a binary function is needed for the representation of the meaning spectrum of the local preposition "*between*". The first argument of the unary function must be a collection to adequately represent situations like "*Witten lies between Dortmund, Hagen and Bochum.*"

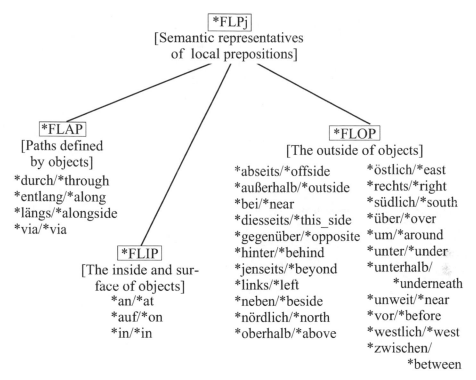

**Figure 18.62.** The hierarchy of local functions

use of these functions in combination with different local relations is given for the relation VIA.

It is convenient to derive the names of local functions from the name of the corresponding preposition by analogy and by prefixing the name of the latter with a star, i.e. we use *AT, *BETWEEN, ..., and *UNDER instead of *FLP$_{at}$, *FLP$_{between}$, and *FLP$_{under}$, respectively.[43]

Since many languages do not have special words as labels for locations (if we leave aside the local adverbs which have a referential character), the descriptions of locations in the surface structure have to be constructed grammatically by means of prepositional phrases. Analogously, the semantic representations of locations in the deep structure are generated by corresponding functions.

---

[43] Although natural language prepositions are highly ambiguous (see Sect. 12.2), there is no danger of confusion, because for every preposition from ⟨loc-prep⟩ there is only one local interpretation. In particular, there is no difference between "*directed*" and "*nondirected*" *IN in MultiNet, because directedness or non-directedness are not mirrored in the local functions, but in the relations (see Sect. 7.1).

(18.233) *"The grid is located between the anode and cathode."*

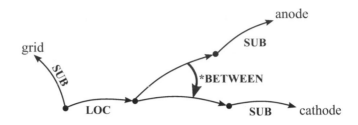

**Figure 18.63.** The representation of a binary local function

(18.234) *"Mary is flying via Singapore to Australia."*

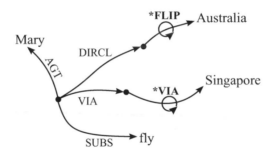

**Figure 18.64.** The representation of a path specification

## 18.3.5   *INTSC: Intersection of Sets

$*\mathbf{INTSC}$: $\mathrm{pe}^{(n)} \times \mathrm{pe}^{(n)} \to \mathrm{pe}^{(n)}$      with $n \geq 1$

$\qquad\qquad\qquad\qquad\qquad$ ($\mathrm{pe}^{(n)}$ is explained in Appendix A.)

**Definition:** The function $(*\mathrm{INTSC}\ g_1\ g_2) = g_3$ corresponds to the operation of intersection in set theory. It generates a new set $g_3 = \{\mathrm{el} \mid \mathrm{el} \in g_1 \land \mathrm{el} \in g_2\}$ from two entities $g_1$ and $g_2$ of the preextensional level which have the same order $n \geq 1$ as $g_3$.

**Mnemonics:** intersection (Ge: Durchschnitt)

**Question pattern:** –

**Explanation:** The function *INTSC plays an important role in the semantic representation of coordinations (of constituent coordinations, to be specific) describing a set whose definition expressly requires the **simultaneous** membership of its elements in two different predefined sets.

(18.235) *"The teacher asked [all students who are both amateur actors and members of the literary circle]*$^{*INTSC}$ *to take part in the performance."*

In this case, the representation of the extensional of the concept described by *"amateur actors and members of the literary circle"* is built by means of the function *INTSC, since the qualities of both groups are apparently needed in one person. This means that every participant of the performance should be a member of the collection of amateur players as well as of the literary circle.

### 18.3.6   *ITMS/*ITMS-I: Function for Enumerating Sets and Its Counterpart at the Intensional Level

**\*ITMS/\*ITMS-I:**  Functions for constructing collections of elements.
$$*ITMS: pe^{(n)} \times pe^{(n)} \times \ldots \times pe^{(n)} \to pe^{(n+1)} \quad \text{(preextensional level)}$$
$$*ITMS\text{-}I: sort \times sort \times \ldots \times sort \to \overset{..}{sort} \quad \text{(intensional level)}$$
with **sort** as an arbitrary sort common to all arguments;
in this case, the common sort needs not be most specific;
$\overset{..}{sort}$ symbolizes a plurality of entities all having the same sort

**Definition:**
The function *ITMS stands for a whole family of functions (*ITMS$_\nu$), with $\nu \in \mathcal{N} \setminus \{0,1\}$, which have different arities *ITMS$_\nu$: $[pe^{(n)}]^\nu \to pe^{(n+1)}$. Each function generates a set M from $\nu$ different entities of the same sort, where M has exactly $\nu$ entities as its elements (items). In contrast to the function *TUPL, the ordering of elements in the resulting set M is irrelevant. M is of order (n+1), compared to the order n of its elements (which corresponds to the generation of a plurality, denoted by symbol $\overset{..}{sort}$, by means of the function *ITMS-I at the intensional level); see Fig. 18.65.[44]

---

[44] So, the function *ITMS generates a set with [**ETYPE** = 1] from individual elements, a family of sets with [**ETYPE** = 2] from elementary sets, etc.

The function *ITMS-I is an abbreviation used at the intensional level to describe entities whose extension is given by a set enumerated with *ITMS at the preextensional level (see Axiom (174) and Fig. 18.66).

**Mnemonics:** En: items (Ge: (Aufzählung von) Einzelelementen)

**Question pattern:** ⟨WHT⟩ [do] ⟨g⟩ belong?

**Explanation:** The function *ITMS is employed for the explicit enumeration of finite sets and therefore belongs to the expressional means of the preextensional level.

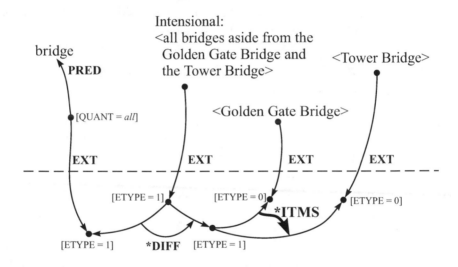

**Figure 18.65.** Combination of the functions *ITMS and *DIFF

*ITMS is often used in the semantic representations of constituent coordinations constructed with "*und*", "*sowie*", and "*sowohl ... als auch*" ... (En: "*and*" and "*as well as*"). Thus, the representation of ⟨Peter and Max⟩ in the sentence "*Peter and Max own a (certain) firm.*" has to be constructed with *ITMS-I at the intensional level and with *ITMS at the preextensional level.

The following relationship holds between *ITMS and *ITMS-I, which spares the specification of the corresponding representation at the preextensional level if that at the intensional level is already given:

- $g = (*\text{ITMS-I } a, b, \ldots, k) \leftrightarrow g_{EXT} = (*\text{ITMS } a_{EXT} \, b_{EXT} \ldots k_{EXT})$ (174)

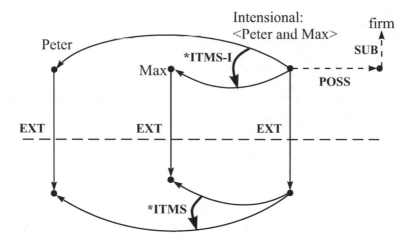

**Figure 18.66.** Representations containing the functions *ITMS-I and *ITMS at the intensional and preextensional level, respectively

### 18.3.7 ∗MODP: Function for the Modification of Properties

**∗MODP:** $[p \cup m \cup lg] \times p \to p$    with $lg$ = {very, especially, somewhat, a bit, extraordinarily ... }

**Definition:** The function $(*MODP \; x \; p_1) = p_2$ generates a new property $p_2$ modifying a given property $p_1$ by means of a quantity x, a specification of a certain degree x, or by another property x.

**Mnemonics:** En: modification of properties (Ge: Modifikation von Eigenschaften)

**Question pattern:** –

**Explanation:** The following natural language expressions can semantically be represented using the function ∗MODP:

(18.236)  Ge: *"Das Wasser ist [eisig kalt]*$^{*MODP}$*."*
    En: *"The water is [icy cold]*$^{*MODP}$*".*
(18.237)  Ge: *"Max ist [besonders freundlich]*$^{*MODP}$*."*
    En: *"Max is [especially friendly]*$^{*MODP}$*."*
(18.238)  Ge: *"Der Eiffelturm ist [300 m hoch / sehr hoch]*$^{*MODP}$*."*
    Ge: *"The Eiffel Tower is [300 m high / very high]*$^{*MODP}$*."*

It must be expressly stated that the assignment of a property p to an object o does not necessarily follow from the assignment of (∗MODP x p) to o, i.e.

- (o PROP (∗MODP x p)) ⊬ (o PROP p)                                    (175)

Thus, one cannot derive ⟨the car is long⟩ from ⟨the car is 4 m long⟩, because from two polar properties (long – short), which are values of one and the same attribute (here length), it is always the property at the positive pole or the property with the higher degree that is neutrally used to build a quantitative specification; therefore one says *"The ant is 3 mm long"*, **but not:** *"The ant is 3 mm short"*).

Properties described by compound words are often implicitly linked to relationships of association or comparison and should therefore be semantically represented with ASSOC or CORR (and not with ∗MODP):

Ge: grasgrün – *"grün wie Gras"*
En: grass green – *"green like grass"*
Ge: bleischwer – *"schwer wie Blei"*
                    En: *"heavy as lead"*
Ge: kohlrabenschwarz – *"schwarz wie Kohle bzw. wie ein Rabe"*
En: pitch-black – *"black as pitch"*
Ge: rasiermesserscharf – *"scharf wie ein Rasiermesser"*
En: ⟨razor sharp⟩ – *"sharp as a razor"*

or, still more complicated,

Ge: todkrank – *"so krank, wie einer, der dem Tod geweiht ist"* (not *"krank wie ein Toter"*)
En: ⟨fatally/terminally ill⟩ (no direct correspondence in the form of a single word) – *"ill like somebody who is doomed to death"* (not *"ill like a dead (person)"*)

By contrast, the semantic decomposition of German compound words like dunkelblau (En: dark blue) or hochmodern (En: supermodern) can be represented with ∗MODP using appropriate modifiers (first arguments of ∗MODP).

Example:          (hochmodern EQU (∗MODP überaus modern))

## 18.3.8   ∗MODQ: Function for the Modification of Quantities

∗**MODQ:** $ng \times [m \cup qf] \rightarrow [m \cup qf]$  with ng = {circa, approximately, almost, scarcely, barely, exactly, up to, over, ... }

**Definition:** The function (∗MODQ g $m_1$) = $m_2$ generates a modified quantity $m_2 \in qf$ or measurement $m_2 \in m$ by applying a graduator $g \in ng$ to a given quantity or measurement $m_1$.

**Mnemonics:** En: modification of quantity (Ge: Modifikation einer Quantität)

**Question pattern:** –

**Explanation:** The sort [$ng$] of modificators for quantities is a finite (closed) set of a few elements. They are used together with the function ∗MODQ to specify fuzzy quantities. The following relations hold:

((∗MODQ {knapp / barely} q) MIN q)
((∗MODQ {reichlich / over} q) MAJ q)

In many domains, the specifications of quantities are fuzzy, even in those cases where exact measures are involved. So, ⟨three kg of potatoes⟩ does not necessarily mean ⟨exactly 3,000 g potatoes⟩. Therefore, it is sometimes necessary to emphasize that a certain measurement is given exactly, e.g.

(∗MODQ {exakt / exactly} (∗QUANT 3,000 g))

The function ∗MODQ can also be used to modify quantificators:

(∗MODQ {fast / almost} {alle / all})

## 18.3.9   ∗MODS: Modification of a Situational Concept

∗**MODS:** $[gr \cup m] \times [si \cup ab] \rightarrow [si \cup ab]$

**Definition:** The function (∗MODS s $h_1$) = $h_2$ is used to modify a situation (mostly an action) $h_1$ and to generate a new modified situation by means of a specifier $s \in [gr \cup m]$.

**Mnemonics:** En: modification of a situation (Ge: Modifizierung einer Situation)

**Question pattern:** –

**Explanation:** The function ∗MODS is mainly used to express gradations of the intensity or extent of situations, as in:

(18.239)  Ge: "*Er [wundert sich]*∗MODS$_{arg2}$ *[sehr]*∗MODS$_{arg1}$."
   En: "*He [is wondering]*∗MODS$_{arg2}$ *[pretty much]*∗MODS$_{arg1}$."

(18.240)  Ge: "*Ein [geringes]*∗MODS$_{arg1}$ *[Erwärmen]*∗MODS$_{arg2}$ *des Materials führte bereits zu kleinen Rissen.*"

(18.241)  En: "*A [slight]*∗MODS$_{arg1}$ *[heating]*∗MODS$_{arg2}$ *of the material caused already small fissures.*"

(18.242)  Ge: "*[20%]*∗MODS$_{arg1}$ *[Preisanstieg]*∗MODS$_{arg2}$"
   En: "*[20%]*∗MODS$_{arg1}$ *[rise in price]*∗MODS$_{arg2}$"

The function ∗MODS can also be used to express certain quantitative modifications by distance, e.g.

(18.243)  Ge: "*100m-Lauf*" or "*Hundertmeterlauf*"
   $\hat{=}$ (∗MODS (∗QUANT 100 m) Lauf)
   En: "*100-m run*" or "*hundred-meter run*"
   $\hat{=}$ (∗MODS (∗QUANT 100 m) run)

The construction of terms with ∗MODS expresses that the newly generated action has a different conceptual quality than the original. This is emphasized in the last example by the nominalization "*100m-Lauf*" (En: "*100-m run*"), which describes a special concept in sports. The exact meaning of such a construct has to be defined by B-Axioms which, in this case, involve the relation LEXT.

If the quantitative specification does not generate a new concept, as in

(18.244)  Ge: "*100 m laufen*" in contrast to "*100m-Lauf*"
   En: "*run for 100 m*" in contrast to "*a 100-m run*",

the representation has to be built directly with LEXT without using ∗MODS. The characterization of situations or events by properties (qualities), i.e. by specifying a certain mode or manner, must be based on the relation MANNR.

The function ∗MODS and the relation MANNR as constructs for modifying and specifying situations are in some sense the counterpart of the function ∗PMOD and the relation PROP, respectively, in the field of object specifications by means of properties.

## 18.3.10    *NON: Family of Functions Specifying Negation

**∗NON:**

$$\begin{cases} \langle Relation \rangle \rightarrow \langle Relation \rangle \\ md \qquad\quad \rightarrow md \\ \quad\;\;\; \rightarrow \{false\} \subseteq md \end{cases}$$

**Definition:** The operator ∗NON stands for a family of three functions which generate a complementary (negated) relation from a given relation, build a negated modal term from a modality, or represent the truth value *"false"* as a zero-place function (which is viewed as a special modality).

**Mnemonics:** Latin: non (Ge: nicht)

**Question pattern:** –

**Explanation:** To explain this family of functions, an example of every application of the function ∗NON is given (see Fig. 18.67), where cases b) and c) are connected with the use of relation MODL.

It should be remembered that the negation of the facticity of a situation (which may again contain a negation) is expressed by [**FACT**=*non*] (see also Sect. 8.2 on the treatment of negation in MultiNet).

a) Negation of a relation (i.e. of a constituent); compare Fig. 8.6 of Part I:

(18.245)  Ge: *"Renate kaufte gestern in Berlin kein Fahrrad."*
En: *"Yesterday Renate bought no bicycle in Berlin."*
This does not exclude that she bought something else.

This type of negation can be defined by an axiom schema, where the metavariable ⟨REL⟩ has to be substituted by OBJ for an application to the above example:

$$(x \; (*NON \; \langle REL \rangle) \; y) \rightarrow \neg(x \; \langle REL \rangle \; y) \tag{176}$$

b) Negated modalities:

(18.246)  Ge: *"Die Tragfläche darf nicht beschädigt werden."*[45]
En: *"The wing must not be damaged."*

---

[45] The (artificial) modality **perm** ∈ *md* in Fig. 18.67b represents the class of deontic modal expressions associated with the operator of permission (Ge: *"erlaubt sein"*, *"gestattet sein"*, *"zulässig sein"*, etc.; En: *"be allowed"*, *"be permitted"*, *"be admitted"* etc.); **perm** is used as an abbreviation for *"permission"*. **possib** ∈ *md* characterizes the modality of *"possibility"*.

c) Negation of a whole situation (sentence negation; compare Fig. 8.4):

(18.247)  Ge: *"Renate kaufte gestern <u>nichts</u> in Berlin."*

En: *"Yesterday Renate bought <u>nothing</u> in Berlin."*

All three types of negation illustrated by the aforementioned examples are shown in Figures 18.67a through 18.67c.

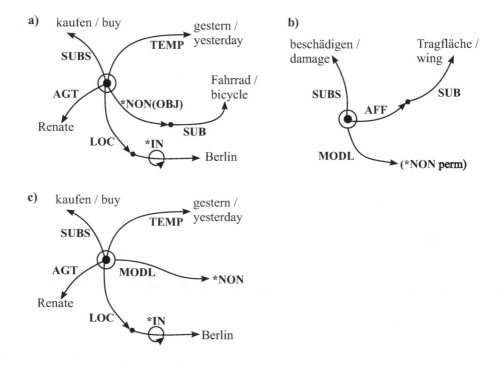

**Figure 18.67.** Different types of negation expressed with functions from the *NON family

The negations represented by the three above functions can be expressed by a single method which consequently uses only the relation MODL in connection with the zero-place function *NON and the concept of encapsulation. The application of this method is cumbersome but emphasizes the modal character of the negation in a uniform way. (It consistently employs the negator as a modal operator and permits an unlimited iteration of modal embeddings.) The representations in the following Fig. 18.68 correspond to that of Fig. 18.67. (For a better understanding see Sect. 17.3 and the convention for the graphical representation of capsules introduced in Fig. 16.3f.)

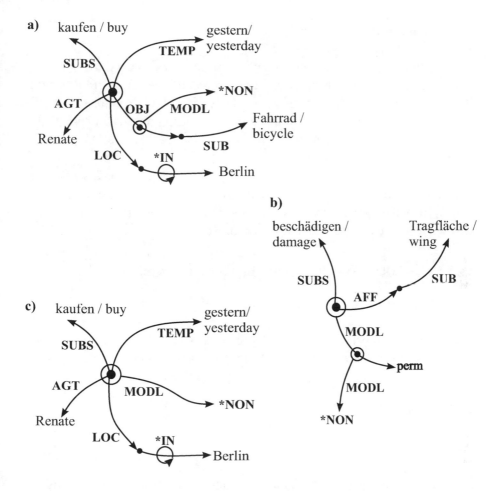

**Figure 18.68.** The standard specification of intensional negation using only MODL+*NON

## 18.3.11   *OP_J: Arithmetic Operations

$$*\text{OP}_J: qn^m \rightarrow qn \qquad \text{with } j \in \{\text{PLUS, MINUS, TIMES, DIV, POW}\}, m \geq 2$$
$$t^m \;\; \rightarrow t \qquad \text{(for time moments and intervals)}$$

**Definition:** The arithmetic operations belong to a family of functions which realize a mapping from the m-th power of sort *qn* (quantities) to *qn*. In the indicated order, they represent the operators known from arithmetic: addition, subtraction, multiplication, division, and exponentiation.

**Mnemonics:** En: (arithmetic) operation (Ge: (arithmetische) Operation)

**Question pattern:** –

**Explanation:** In MultiNet knowledge representations, the symbols for the above-mentioned operators are used, for example, for the construction of complex measurement units (m/s, $m^2$, ... ). They also play a central role in the semantic representation of natural language concepts that are explicitly or implicitly related to mathematical operations, like per, (on) average, altogether, in total, etc.

Formulas [SORT = *fe*] are generally treated in MultiNet as a whole (i.e. as an atomic entity) without considering their inner structure. Since they are subject to mathematical rather than semantic theories, formulas are not further resolved with the representational means of MultiNet.

## 18.3.12    ∗ORD: Function Defining Ordinal Numbers

∗**ORD:** *nu* → *oq*

**Definition:** The function (∗ORD n) = q generates an ordinal q from a definite natural number n. The ordinal numbers are taken as qualities (as ordering qualities, to be specific) and treated analogously to properties.

**Mnemonics:** En: order (Ge: Ordnung)

**Question pattern:** –

**Explanation:** The decision to model ordinals as properties is justified by the observation that they are analogously used in natural language. Semantically, however, they function rather as operators selecting a certain element from a collection of entities, which is the reason for assigning them a special sort (see also Fig. 18.69 and function ∗PMOD).

Figure 18.69 also shows the connection between the property of being the last member of a series, of a tuple, of an enumeration, etc. on the one hand, and cardinals and ordinals on the other hand.

Examples illustrating the attribute use of ordinals:

(18.248)  Ge: *"Der [erste]*∗ORD *August ..."*
En: *"The [first]*∗ORD *of August ..."*
(18.249)  Ge: *"Die [dritte]*∗ORD *Komponente des Vektors ..."*
En: *"The [third]*∗ORD *component of the vector ..."*

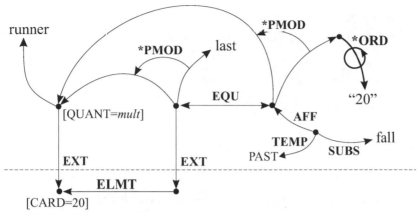

*"Twenty runners (took part in the competition).*
*The last runner fell."*

**Figure 18.69.** The character of ordinals as properties and selectors

### 18.3.13 *PMOD: Modification of Objects by Associative Properties

**\*PMOD:** $[aq \times o] \cup [oq \times (\overline{o} \cup \ddot{o})] \rightarrow o$

**Definition:** The function (\*PMOD e $o_1$) = $o_2$ combines a conceptual object $o_1$ with an associative quality (an associative property e $\in aq$) to yield a more specific concept $o_2$. This is done by associating $o_1$ with an abstract entity connected with e through the relation CHPA. \*PMOD is also used to select an element $o_2$ from a set $\ddot{o}_1$ (the extension of $o_1$) by means of the selector e (which, in this case, should be an ordinal e $\in oq$).

**Mnemonics:** En: modification by property – Ge: Modifizierung durch (funktionale) Eigenschaft

**Question pattern:** –

**Explanation:** The function \*PMOD is mainly used to deal with associative properties e $\in aq$ in contrast to the semantic representation of properties in the narrower sense, [SORT = $p$], which are treated with the PROP relation. The associative property e and the object $o_2$ form a unity from which e cannot be isolated.[46] The following implications hold:

---

[46] With regard to the use of \*PMOD in connection with ordinals, see function \*ORD.

- $o_2 = (*\text{PMOD e } o_1) \rightarrow (o_2 \text{ SUB } o_1)$        (177)
- $o_2 = (*\text{PMOD e } o_1) \wedge (\text{e CHPA ab}) \rightarrow (o_2 \text{ ASSOC ab})$        (178)

But a separate assignment of the property e to $o_2$ with the relation PROP is not entailed, and even forbidden by the signature of PROP:

- $o_2 = (*\text{PMOD e } o_1) \not\rightarrow (o_2 \text{ PROP e})$        (179)

Example:

(18.250)  Ge: *"Das [philosophische Wörterbuch]*$^{*\text{PMOD}}$*"*
       En: *"The [philosophical dictionary]*$^{*\text{PMOD}}$*"*        (see Fig. 18.70a)

The representation of this phrase has to be based on *PMOD. Here, the dictionary does **not** have the property of being philosophical.[47] But, if we take the example

(18.251)  Ge: *"Das [schwarze]*$^{\text{PROP}_{arg2}}$ *Wörterbuch"*
       En: *"The [black]*$^{\text{PROP}_{arg2}}$ *dictionary"*        (see Fig. 18.70b)

then the representation must be built by means of PROP. In this case, the dictionary actually has the property of being black.

    This consideration has consequences for the natural language generation from semantic representations. In the first case, one cannot produce from $o_2 = (*\text{PMOD philosophical dictionary})$ that *"The dictionary is philosophical"*, whereas in the second case it is allowed to reformulate from $(o_2 \text{ PROP black}) \wedge (o_2 \text{ SUB dictionary})$ that *"The dictionary is black"*.

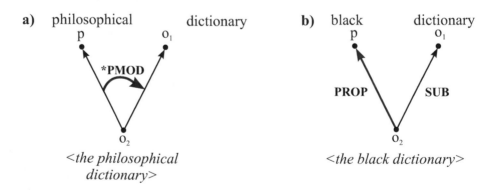

**a)** philosophical     dictionary       **b)**    black      dictionary

*&lt;the philosophical dictionary&gt;*         *&lt;the black dictionary&gt;*

**Figure 18.70.** The different representations of associative properties and ordinary properties

---

[47] In this case, the associative property philosophical is related to the abstract concept philosophy by CHPA.

## 18.3.14  *QUANT: Function Generating Quantities

**\*QUANT:** $qf \times me \to m$

**Definition:** The function (\*QUANT z e) = m generates a quantity m from a number z and a measurement unit e.

**Mnemonics:** En: quantity (Ge: Quantität)

**Question pattern:** –

**Explanation:** Measurement units can also be modified by concepts denoting containers (e.g. box, bag, mug, cup, etc.). Therefore, appositions built with these terms such as ⟨three bags of tea⟩, ⟨a cup of coffee⟩, etc. can be semantically represented with \*QUANT and QMOD.

Also, indefinite numbers (sort [*nn*]) like several, many, a few, etc. are admitted as the first argument of \*QUANT. They are used to describe fuzzy measurements (such as ⟨several kilometers⟩ and ⟨many tons⟩). On the basis of the arithmetic operations (functions \*OP$_J$) and \*QUANT, one can formulate rules for transforming measurement units into each other using convenient axioms or axiom schemata:

- ((\*QUANT z kilogram) EQU (\*QUANT (\*OP$_{TIMES}$ 1000 z) gram))

$$(180)$$

- ((\*QUANT z mile) EQU (\*QUANT(\*OP$_{TIMES}$ 1609 z) meter))   (181)

The comparison of quantities is treated semantically with the relations MIN/MAJ.

## 18.3.15  *SUPL: Function Characterizing the Superlative

**\*SUPL:** $gq \times [\bar{o} \cup \ddot{o}] \to tq$

**Definition:** The function (\*SUPL p$_1$ y) = p$_2$ generates a nongradable property p$_2$ from a generic concept or a plurality y, and a gradable property p$_1$. The resulting property p$_2$ has the highest degree within the comparison frame given by y on a scale associated with the property p$_1$.

**Mnemonics:** En: superlative (Ge: Superlativ)

**Question pattern:** –

**Explanation:** The second argument y of the function *SUPL specifies a domain (a comparison frame) on which a total ordering is defined by the gradable property $p_1$ (the first argument). The property $p_2 = (*SUPL\ p_1\ y)$ belongs to the element of the aforementioned domain marking the upper bound with regard to the ordering relation defined on y. The following implications hold:

- $(o_1$ PROP $(*SUPL\ p\ \overline{y}))$
  $\rightarrow (o_1$ SUB $\overline{y}) \wedge (o_1$ PROP p) $\hspace{3cm}$ (182)

There is also a connection between *COMP and *SUPL:

- $(o_1$ PROP $(*SUPL\ p\ y)) \wedge (o_2$ SUB y$) \wedge (o_1 \neq o_2)$
  $\rightarrow (o_1$ PROP $(*COMP\ p\ o_2))$ $\hspace{3cm}$ (183)

Including the preextensional layer, the following can be stated:

- $(o_1$ PROP $(*SUPL\ p\ \ddot{y})) \wedge (\ddot{y}$ EXT $e_1) \wedge (o_2$ EXT $e_2) \wedge$
  $(e_2$ ELMT $e_1) \wedge (o_1 \neq o_2) \rightarrow (o_1$ PROP $(*COMP\ p\ o_2))$ $\hspace{1cm}$ (184)

If the comparison frame defined by the second argument y of *SUPL cannot be determined from the context (especially during automatic analysis), as is often the case with the "absolute superlative" (or, in linguistic terms, "elative"), then the placeholder or dummy parameter *nil* must be meanwhile inserted for y. This preliminary value has to be replaced by the true comparison frame during a deeper analysis (see Sect. 6.2.3 for further details on the treatment of the superlative).

**Figure 18.71.** A preliminary (ad hoc) representation of the absolute superlative

### 18.3.16   *TUPL: Function Generating Tuples

*TUPL: sort × ... × sort → sort

**Definition:** The function *TUPL stands for a family $(TUPL_\nu)_{\nu \in N}$, $\nu > 1$, of functions with fixed arity $*TUPL_\nu: sort^\nu \to sort$, which construct a series (a tuple) from $\nu$ different entities of the same sort. The result belongs to the same sort as the arguments. It has, however, a set as its extension; in this respect it behaves similarly to pluralities or collections of elements.

**Mnemonics:** En: tuple (Ge: Tupel)

**Question pattern:** –

**Explanation:** The function *TUPL is used for an explicit enumeration of a finite number of elements. But, in contrast to *ITMS, the order of the elements in the series generated by *TUPL is significant. The function *TUPL plays a role in the meaning representation of coordinations where the order of the constituents has to be observed. It is also applied when an element-wise correlation between two collections has to be represented (see relation CORR).

(18.252) *"The components S1, S2, S3, and S4, in this succession, form a list."*

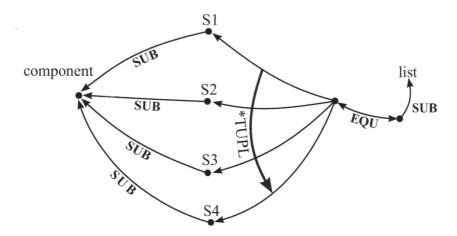

**Figure 18.72.** The representation of ordered pluralities

The function *TUPL can also be used to construct time intervals, where the starting point $t_1$ and the end point $t_2$ of the interval are combined by this function to a pair $t = (*\text{TUPL } t_1 \ t_2)$.

In contrast to *ITMS, the function *TUPL belongs to the representational means of the intensional level. Unlike *ITMS, *TUPL expresses the intensional aspect of ordering defined on a set of elements. A construct containing *TUPL at the intensional level always has an *ITMS construct at the preextensional level as its counterpart.

### 18.3.17  *UNION: Union of Sets

**\*UNION**: $\text{pe}^{(n)} \times [\text{pe}^{(n)} \cup \text{pe}^{(n-1)}] \to \text{pe}^{(n)}$     with $n \geq 1$

$$(\text{pe}^{(n)} \text{ is explained in Appendix A.})$$

**Definition:** Let $(g_1 \cup g_2) = \{\text{el} \mid (\text{el} \in g_1 \lor (\text{el} \in g_2))\}$ be the normal union of two sets $g_1$ und $g_2$. Then, we define

$$(*\text{UNION x y}) = \begin{cases} (x \cup y) & \text{for } x \in \text{pe}^{(n)} \text{ and } y \in \text{pe}^{(n)} \\ (x \cup \{y\}) & \text{for } x \in \text{pe}^{(n)} \text{ and } y \in \text{pe}^{(n-1)} \end{cases}$$

This means that we extend the ordinary definition of set union by permitting the second argument of *UNION to be a single entity with [**ETYPE**=(n-1)] if the first argument is of type [**ETYPE**=n].

**Mnemonics:** En: union (Ge: Vereinigung)

**Question pattern:** –

**Explanation:** The function *UNION is used either to combine two different sets of the same type into a resulting set, or to add a single element having type n to an already existing set of type (n+1). While the former case is illustrated in Fig. 18.73, the latter case is needed for the representation of prepositions like *"einschließlich"* (En: *"including"*), of connectors like *"und"* (En: *"and"*), or of adverbs like *"zusätzlich"* (En: *"additionally/in addition"*).

Example:

(18.253)  Ge: "[*Alle Lehrer und ein Schüler*]*UNION*

*bereiteten den Ausflug vor.*"

En: "[*All teachers and a student*]*UNION* *prepared the excursion.*"

The function $g = (*\text{UNION } g_1 \ g_2)$ plays an important role in the semantic representation of constituent coordinations where all elements of two different collections $g_1$ and $g_2$ have to be included in the plurality g described by the coordination. When representing a coordination by ∗UNION, it is not excluded by the definition of this function that the elements of g belong to both $g_1$ and $g_2$. Of course, there may be also elements of g that belong either to $g_1$ or to $g_2$.

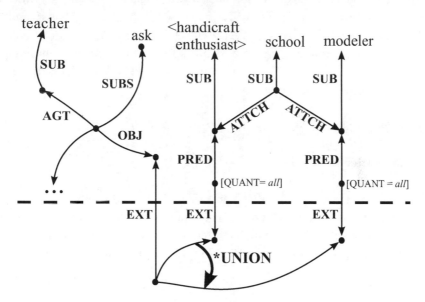

**Figure 18.73.** The union of pluralities of the same type

(18.254) *"The teacher asked [all modelers and all handicraft enthusiasts of the school]*∗UNION *(to prepare a contribution for the anniversary)."*

In this case, the representation of the extensional belonging to the concept ⟨all modelers and all handicraft enthusiasts⟩ using the function ∗UNION is appropriate because both groups normally contain members that are not elements of the other group (a representation with ∗INTSC would exclude exactly these elements).

## 18.3.18  ∗VEL1/2: Disjunctive Composition of Situations

**∗VEL1/2:** $si \times \ldots \times si \rightarrow si$

**Definition:** The functions ∗VEL1 and ∗VEL2 each represent a family of functions $(*\text{VEL1}_\nu)_{\nu \in \mathcal{N}}$ and $(*\text{VEL2}_\nu)_{\nu \in \mathcal{N}}$ with $*\text{VEL1}_\nu: si^\nu \rightarrow si$ and $*\text{VEL2}_\nu: si^\nu \rightarrow si$, $\nu \geq 2$, respectively. These functions each generate a complex real situation from alternative possibilities of realizations by combining $\nu$ situations with inclusive and exclusive OR, respectively. By default, the arguments are assumed to be hypothetical situations.

**Mnemonics:** Latin: vel (Ge: oder)

**Question pattern:** –

**Explanation:** The functions ∗VEL1 and ∗VEL2 are used for the semantic representation of coordinative sentences which are mainly built with "*or*" and "*either . . . or*", respectively, and which interconnect alternative situations. ∗VEL1 represents the inclusive OR, and ∗VEL2 represents the exclusive OR.

(18.255) *"The delegation travels either by train or by bus."*    (see Fig. 18.74)

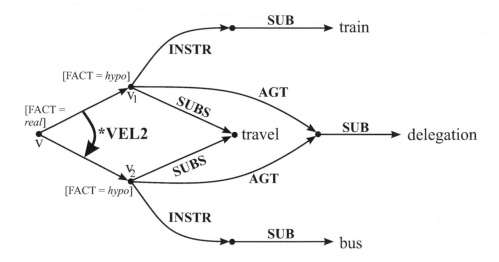

**Figure 18.74.** The representation of disjunctively conjoined situations

Since, in this case, the sentence describes two different and mutually exclusive events, a resolution of the above-mentioned sentence into two complete disjunctively connected situations is actually the adequate semantic representation. The choice of the layer attribute [**FACT** = *hypo*] as a default for the partial situations $v_1$ and $v_2$ is justified by the observation that the facticity (truth) of these situations cannot generally be decided upon without further information. In contrast, the facticity of the whole situation $v$ must be characterized by [**FACT** = *real*], since one of the alternatives specified by $*VEL1$ and $*VEL2$ must really be obtained.

**Annotation:** A corresponding construction for the logical connective AND is not explicitly provided by MultiNet since the **conjunction convention** has to be observed; it asserts that all elementary constructs of an SN have to be considered as conjunctively conjoined, as far as they are not contained in conceptual capsules linked to semantic restrictive relations.[48]

---

[48] See also the explanation of HSIT on page 497.

# Appendix A

# Table of Abbreviations

| Abbreviation | Meaning |
| --- | --- |
| AI | Artificial Intelligence |
| COLEX | Computer Lexicon of the University Hagen (predecessor of HaGenLex) |
| C-Role | Cognitive Role (of a Participant in a Situation) |
| CSN | Cognitively Oriented Semantic Networks |
| DC | Deep Case |
| DCR | Deep Case Relation |
| FOL | First Order Logic (synonym of PC1) |
| HaGenLex | Hagen German Lexicon (successor of COLEX) |
| KB | Knowledge Base |
| KRM | Knowledge Representation Model/Method |
| KRS | Knowledge Representation System |
| LoK | Logic-Oriented KRS |
| MESNET | Multilayered Extended Semantic Network (Predecessor of MultiNet) |
| MultiNet | Multilayered Extended Semantic Network (Successor of MESNET) |
| NL | Natural Language |
| NLI | Natural Language Interface |
| NLP | Natural Language Processing |
| NP | Nominal Phrase / Noun Phrase |
| PC1 | Predicate Calculus of the 1st Order (synonym of FOL) |
| PP | Prepositional Phrase |
| QAS | Question-Answering-System/Question-Answering-Game (Ge: FAS – Frage-Antwort-System/Frage-Antwort-Spiel) |
| SIN | Structured Inheritance Network |
| SN | Semantic Network |
| VP | Verb Phrase |

## Abbreviation  Meaning

| | |
|---|---|
| En: | **En**glish (Language of example sentences) |
| Fr: | **Fr**ench (Language of example sentences) |
| Ge: | **Ge**rman (Language of example sentences) |
| Ru: | **Ru**ssian (Language of example sentences) |

| | |
|---|---|
| $\dot{e}$ | Individual entity (an individual) |
| $\ddot{e}$ | Entity with a set as extensional (a plurality/a collection) |
| $\tilde{e}$ | Hypothetical entity characterized by [**FACT** = *hypo*] (This characterization has to be considered as a default which can be overwritten by additional information about the facticity of e acquired later on.) |
| e' | Real entity characterized by [**FACT** = *real*] |
| $\bar{e}$ | Generic entity characterized by [**GENER** = *ge*] |
| $e_{INT}$ | Intensional (meaning component of the entity e at the intensional level) |
| $e_{EXT}$ | Extensional (meaning component of the entity e at the preextensional level) |
| $pe^{(n)}$ | Semantic representative at the preextensional level with type of extensionality [**ETYPE** = *n*] |

| Special mark | Meaning |
|---|---|
| (??) | Used after a sentence or phrase: Indication that the sentence is not allowed or semantically defective |

# Appendix B

# Overview of the Representational Means

| Relation | Signature | Short Characteristics |
|----------|-----------|------------------------|
| AFF | $[dy \cup ad] \times [o \cup si]$ | C-Role – Affected object |
| AGT | $[si \cup abs] \times o$ | C-Role – Agent |
| ANLG/2 | $[\ddot{si} \cup \ddot{o}] \times at$ | Similarity relation between a group of entities |
| ANLG/3 | $([si \times si] \cup [o \times o]) \times at$ | Similarity relation between two entities |
| ANTE | $[t \cup ta \cup si \cup abs] \times [t \cup ta \cup si \cup abs]$ | Relation of temporal succession |
| ANTO | $sort \times sort^{*)}$ | Antonymy relation |
| ARG1/2/3 | $[re \cup si] \times ent$ | Argument specification at the metalevel |
| ASSOC | $ent \times ent$ | Relation of association |
| ATTCH | $[o \setminus at] \times [o \setminus at]$ | Attachment of objects to objects |
| ATTR | $[o \cup l \cup t] \times at$ | Specification of an attribute |
| AVRT | $[dy \cup ad] \times o$ | C-Role – Averting/Turning away from an object |
| BENF | $[si \cup o] \times [o \setminus abs]$ | C-Role – Beneficiary |
| CAUS | $[si' \cup abs'] \times [si' \cup abs']$ | Relation between cause and effect (Causality) |
| CHEA | $dy \times ad$ | Change of sorts: Event – Abstractum |
| CHPA | $[(p \cup aq) \times at] \cup [rq \times re]$ | Change of sorts: Property – Abstractum |
| CHPE | $[p \cup rq] \times [ad \cup dy]$ | Change of sorts: Property – Event |
| CHPS | $[p \cup rq] \times [as \cup st]$ | Change of sorts: Property – State |

| | | |
|---|---|---|
| CHSA | $st \times ab$ | Change of sorts: State – Abstract state |
| CHSP1/2/3 | $si \times p$ | Change of sorts: Situational concept – Property |
| CIRC | $[si \cup abs] \times [ab \cup si]$ | Relation between situation and circumstance |
| CNVRS | $sort \times sort^{*)}$ | Lexical relation between converse concepts |
| COMPL | $[p \times p] \cup [ab \times ab] \cup [si \times si]$ | Complementarity relation |
| CONC | $[si \cup abs] \times [si \cup ab]$ | Concessive relation |
| COND | $\tilde{si} \times \tilde{si}$ | Conditional relation |
| CONF | $[si \cup abs] \times [ab \cup si]$ | Reference to an external frame to which a situation conforms |
| CONTR | $[p \times p] \cup [ab \times ab] \cup [si \times si]$ | Contrary concepts |
| CORR | $sort \times sort^{*)}$ | Relation of qualitative or quantitative correspondence |
| CSTR | $[si \cup abs] \times o$ | C-Role – Causator |
| CTXT | $[si \cup abs] \times [o \cup si]$ | Relation specifying a restricting context |
| DIRCL | $[si \cup o] \times l$ | Relation specifying a local goal or a direction |
| DISTG/2 | $[\ddot{si} \cup \ddot{o}] \times at$ | Binary relation specifying a difference |
| DISTG/3 | $([si \cup si] \times [o \cup o]) \times at$ | Ternary relation specifying a difference |
| DPND | $ent_{EXT} \times ent_{EXT}$ | Dependency relation between extensionals |
| DUR | $[si \cup o] \times [t \cup si \cup abs \cup ta \cup qn]$ | Relation specifying a duration |
| ELMT | $pe^{(n)} \times pe^{(n+1)}$ with $n \geq 0$ | Element relation |
| EQU | $sort \times sort^{*)}$ | Equality/Equivalence relation |
| EXP | $[si \cup abs] \times o$ | C-Role – Experiencer |
| EXT | $ent_{INT} \times ent_{EXT}$ | Relation between intensionals and corresponding extensionals |
| FIN | $[t \cup si \cup o] \times [t \cup ta \cup abs \cup si]$ | Relation specifying the temporal end |
| GOAL | $[si \cup o] \times [si \cup o \cup l]$ | Generalized goal |
| HSIT | $si \times si$ | Relation specifying the constituents of a hypersituation |

| | | |
|---|---|---|
| IMPL | $([si \cup abs] \times [si \cup abs]) \cup$ $[p \times p] \cup [aq \times aq] \cup [rq \times rq]$ | Implication between situations |
| INIT | $[si \cup abs] \times [o \cup si]$ | Relation specifying an initial situation |
| INSTR | $[si \cup abs] \times co$ | C-Role – Instrument |
| JUST | $[si \cup abs] \times [si \cup abs]$ | Relation specifying a justification |
| LEXT | $[si \cup o] \times [l \cup m]$ | Relation specifying a local extent |
| LOC | $[o \cup si] \times l$ | Relation specifying the location of a situation |
| MAJ{E} | $qn \times qn$ | Greater-than-[or equal-to] relation between numbers or quantities |
| MANNR | $si \times [ql \cup st \cup as]$ | Relation specifying the manner of existence of a situation |
| MCONT | $[si \cup o] \times [o \cup si]$ | C-Role – Relation between a mental process and its content |
| MERO | $[[o \times o] \cup [l \times l] \cup [t \times t]$ | Meronymy relation |
| METH | $[si \cup abs] \times [dy \cup ad \cup io]$ | C-Role – Method |
| MEXP | $[si \cup abs] \times d$ | C-Role – Mental experiencer of a state |
| MIN{E} | $qn \times qn$ | Smaller-than-[or equal-to] relation between numbers or quantities |
| MODE | $[si \cup abs] \times [o \cup si \cup ql]$ | Generalized mode of an event |
| MODL | $[si \cup abs] \times md$ | Relation specifying a restricting modality |
| NAME | $ent \times fe$ | Relation specifying the name of an object |
| OBJ | $[si \cup abs] \times [o \cup si]$ | C-Role – Neutral object |
| OPPOS | $[si \cup o] \times [si \cup o]$ | C-Role – Entity being opposed by a situation |
| ORIG | $o \times [d \cup io]$ | Relation specifying an intellectual or informational source |
| ORIGL | $[o \cup si] \times l$ | Local origin |
| ORIGM | $co \times co$ | Material origin |
| ORNT | $[si \cup abs] \times o$ | C-Role – Orientation toward something |

| | | |
|---|---|---|
| PARS | $[co \times co] \cup [io \times io] \cup$ $[l \times l]$ | Part-whole relationship |
| POSS | $[co \cup io] \times [co \cup io]$ | Relation between possessor and possession |
| PRED0 | $PRED \cup PREDR \cup PREDS$ | Union of the relations representing predicative concepts |
| PRED | $\ddot{so} \cup \overline{so}$    with $so = [o \setminus (abs \cup re)]$ | Predicative concept characterizing a plurality (generically) |
| PREDR | $\ddot{re} \times \overline{re}$ | Predicative concept characterizing a plurality (relationally) |
| PREDS | $[\ddot{si} \cup \ddot{abs}] \times [\overline{si} \cup \overline{abs}]$ | Predicative concept characterizing a plurality (situationally) |
| PROP | $o \times p$ | Relation between object and property |
| PROPR | $\ddot{o} \times rq$ | Relation between a plurality and a semantic relational quality |
| PURP | $[si \cup o] \times [si \cup ab]$ | Relation specifying a purpose |
| QMOD | $[s \cup \ddot{d}] \times m$ | Relation for specifying quantitative modifications |
| REAS | $([si \cup abs] \times [si \cup abs]) \cup$ $[p \times p] \cup [aq \times aq] \cup [rq \times rq]$ | Generalized reason |
| RPRS | $o \times o$ | Appearance or manifestation of an object |
| RSLT | $[si \cup abs] \times [o \cup si]$ | C-Role – Result |
| SCAR | $[st \cup as] \times o$ | C-Role – Carrier of a state |
| SETOF | $pe^{(n)} \times \overline{o}$    with $n \geq 1$ | Relation between a set and its characterizing concept |
| SITU | $[si \cup o] \times [si \cup o]$ | Situational embedding or abstract location |
| SOURC | $[si \cup o] \times [si \cup o \cup l]$ | Generalized source |
| SSPE | $[st \cup as] \times [m \cup o \cup si]$ | C-Role – Entity specifying a state (state specifier) |
| STRT | $[si \cup o \cup t] \times [t \cup ta \cup abs \cup si]$ | Relation specifying the temporal begin |
| SUB0 | $[si \cup o] \times [\overline{si} \cup \overline{o}]$ | Generalized subordination of concepts |
| SUB | $[o \setminus \{abs \cup re\}] \times [\overline{o} \setminus \{\overline{abs \cup re}\}]$ | Relation of conceptual subordination (for objects) |
| SUBM{E} | $pe^{(n)} \times pe^{(n)}$    with $n \geq 1$ | Set inclusion |

| SUBR | $[si \cup re] \times [\overline{si} \cup \overline{re}]$ | Metarelation for the description of relations |
| SUBS | $[si \cup abs] \times [\overline{si} \cup \overline{abs}]$ | Relation of conceptual subordination (for situations) |
| SUBST | $[o \times o] \cup [si \times si]$ | Relation specifying a substitute for something |
| SUPPL | $[si \cup abs] \times o$ | Supplement relation |
| SYNO | $sort \times sort^{*)}$ | Synonymy relation |
| TEMP | $[si \cup t \cup o] \times [t \cup si \cup abs \cup ta]$ | Relation specifying the temporal embedding of a situation |
| VAL | $\dot{at} \times [o \cup qn \cup p \cup fe \cup t]$ | Relation between a specific attribute and its value |
| VALR | $\overline{at} \times [o \cup qn \cup p \cup fe \cup t]$ | Relation between a generic attribute and its value restriction |
| VIA | $[d \cup dy \cup ad] \times l$ | Relation specifying a path |

| Function | Signature | Short Characteristics |
| --- | --- | --- |
| *ALTN1/2 | $sort \times \ldots \times sort \to sort^{*)}$ | Functions generating alternative pluralities of entities |
| *COMP | $gq \times [o \cup gq \cup m] \to p$ | Function describing the comparison of properties |
| *DIFF | $pe^{(n)} \times [pe^{(n)} \cup pe^{(n-1)}] \to pe^{(n)}$   with $n \geq 1$ | Function specifying the difference of sets |
| *FLP$_J$ | $co \to l$  or $\ddot{d} \to l$  or  $d \times d \to l$ | Functions generating locations |
| *INTSC | $pe^{(n)} \times pe^{(n)} \to pe^{(n)}$   with $n \geq 1$ | Intersection of sets |
| *ITMS | $pe^{(n)} \times \ldots \times pe^{(n)} \to pe^{(n+1)}$ | Function enumerating a set |
| *ITMS-I | $sort \times \ldots \times sort \to \ddot{sort}$ | Counterpart of *ITMS at the itensional level |
| *MODP | $[p \cup m \cup lg] \times p \to p$ | Function modifying properties |
| *MODQ | $ng \times [m \cup qf] \to [m \cup qf]$ | Function modifying quantities |
| *MODS | $[gr \cup m] \times [si \cup ab] \to [si \cup ab]$ | Function modifying situations |

| *NON | $\rightarrow \{false\}$     or | Metafunction for representing |
|---|---|---|
| | $md \rightarrow md$          or | different types of negation |
| | $\langle Rel \rangle \rightarrow \langle Rel \rangle$ | |
| *OP$_J$ | $qn^m \rightarrow qn$    or | Arithmetic and other |
| | $t^m \rightarrow t$ | mathematical operations |
| *ORD | $nu \rightarrow oq$ | Function specifying |
| | | ordinal numbers |
| *PMOD | $[aq \times o \cup [oq \times \bar{o} \cup \ddot{o})] \rightarrow o$ | Modification of objects by |
| | | associative or operational |
| | | properties |
| *QUANT | $qf \times me \rightarrow m$ | Function generating quantities |
| *SUPL | $gq \times [\bar{o} \cup \ddot{o}] \rightarrow tq$ | Function describing the |
| | | superlative |
| *TUPL | $sort \times \ldots \times sort \rightarrow sort^{*)}$ | Function generating a tuple from |
| | | its components |
| *UNION | $pe^{(n)} \times [pe^{(n)} \cup pe^{(n-1)}] \rightarrow$ | Set union |
| | $pe^{(n)}$   with   $n \geq 1$ | |
| *VEL1/2 | $si \times si \times \ldots \times si \rightarrow si$ | Functions generating disjunc- |
| | | tively composed situations |

$^{*)}$ The characterization of domains by the symbol "*sort*" in the signatures means that the arguments or values classified by this label must belong to the same sort at the most specific level of specialization admissible for these arguments or values.

$\ddot{s}$ denotes sets of elements of sort s.

# Appendix C

# Semantic Templates as a Mnemonic Base for the Meaning of Relations

| Relation | Associated Pattern |
|----------|--------------------|
| (x AFF y) | [x affects / changes y] |
| (x AGT y) | [x is carried out by y] |
| (x ANLG/2 z) | [all x are similar with regard to z] |
| (x ANLG/3 y z) | [x is similar to y with regard to z] |
| (x ANTE y) | [x temporally antecedes y] |
| (x ANTO y) | [x is an antonym with regard to y] |
| (x ARG1/2/3 y) | [the relational concept x has y as 1st/2nd/3rd Argument] |
| (x ASSOC y) | [x is associated with y] |
| (x ATTCH y) | [the object x has y as an attached object] |
| (x ATTR y) | [x is characterized by the attribute y] |
| (x AVRT y) | [x is averting from y] |
| (x BENF y) | [x is destined for or beneficial to y] |
| (x CAUS y) | [x is the cause of y] |
| (x CIRC y) | [x has y as an accompanying circumstance] |
| (x CNVRS y) | [x is converse to y] |
| (x COMPL y) | [x is complementary to y] |
| (x CONC y) | [x takes place in spite of y] |
| (x COND y) | [x is a sufficient condition for y] |
| (x CONF y) | [x takes place in accordance with y] |
| (x CONTR y) | [x is contrary to y] |
| (x CORR y) | [x corresponds to y] |
| (x CSTR y) | [x has y as a causator] |
| (x CTXT y) | [x is restricted to the context y] |
| (x DIRCL y) | [x is locally directed towards y] |
| (x DISTG/2 z) | [all x differ from each other with regard to z] |
| (x DISTG/3 y z) | [x differs from y with regard to z] |
| (x DPND y) | [x depends on y] |
| (x DUR y) | [x takes place during the time y] |

| | |
|---|---|
| (x ELMT y) | [x is an element of y] |
| (x EQU y) | [x is semantically equivalent to y] |
| (x EXP y) | [x is experienced by y] |
| (x EXT y) | [x has the extension y] |
| (x FIN y) | [x is finished by y / x has y as temporal end] |
| (x GOAL y) | [x has the generalized goal y] |
| (x HSIT y) | [x comprises y as a partial situation] |
| (x IMPL y) | [x implies y] |
| (x INIT y) | [x has y as an initial situation or material] |
| (x INSTR y) | [x is carried out with the instrument y] |
| (x JUST y) | [x justifies y] |
| (x LEXT y) | [x has the local extent y] |
| (x LOC y) | [x is located at y / takes place at y] |
| (x MAJ y) | [x is greater than y] |
| (x MANNR y) | [x is carried out in the manner y] |
| (x MCONT y) | [x is characterized by the mental or informational content y] |
| (x MERO y) | [x is a (generalized) part of y] |
| (x METH y) | [x is carried out by means of method y] |
| (x MEXP y) | [x is mentally experienced by y] |
| (x MIN y) | [x is smaller than y] |
| (x MODE y) | [x is characterized by the mode y] |
| (x MODL y) | [x is modally restricted by y] |
| (x NAME y) | [x is named / called y] |
| (x OBJ y) | [the object y is (passively) participating in the situation x] |
| (x OPPOS y) | [x is opposing y] |
| (x ORIG y) | [x has the mental / informational source y] |
| (x ORIGL y) | [x originates locally from y] |
| (x ORIGM y) | [x consists of / is made of material y] |
| (x ORNT y) | [x is oriented towards y] |
| (x PARS y) | [x is part of y] |
| (x POSS y) | [x is the owner of y] |
| (x PRED y) | [the plurality x is characterized by the predicative concept y] |
| PRED{R/S/0} | analogously to PRED |
| (x PREDR y) | See PRED |
| (x PREDS y) | See PRED |
| (x PRED0 y) | See PRED |

| | |
|---|---|
| (x PROP y) | [x has the property y] |
| (x PROPR y) | [the plurality x is characterized by the relational quality y] |
| (x PURP y) | [x has the purpose y] |
| (x QMOD y) | [x is quantitatively specified by y] |
| (x REAS y) | [x is the general reason for y] |
| (x RPRS y) | [x has the form/appearance y] |
| (x RSLT y) | [x has the result y] |
| (x SCAR y) | [x has y as carrier of the state] |
| (x SETOF y) | [x is a collection of y] |
| (x SOURC y) | [x has the (generalized) source y] |
| (x SSPE y) | [the state x is specified by y] |
| (x STRT y) | [x starts with y] |
| (x SUB y) | [x is subordinate to the superconcept y] |
| (x SUB0 y) | [a generalized subordination relation exists between x (the subconcept) and y (the superconcept)] |
| (x SUBM y) | [x is a subset of y] |
| (x SUBR y) | [x is subordinate to the relational concept y] |
| (x SUBS y) | [the situation x is a specialization of the situation y] |
| (x SUBST y) | [x is a substitute for y] |
| (x SUPPL y) | [x has the conceptual supplement y] |
| (x SYNO y) | [x is synonymous to y] |
| (x TEMP y) | [x holds/takes place in the time span y or at the time moment y] |
| (x VAL y) | [the (specific) attribute x has the value y] |
| (x VALR y) | [the (generic) attribute x is characterized by the value restriction y] |
| (x VIA y) | [x is characterized by the (spatial) course or path y] |

# Characterization of Arcs with Regard to Their Knowledge Type

## (Attribute: **K-TYPE**)

The table should be read as follows:

- Let K be that arc which corresponds to the relation (R N1 N2) between the nodes N1 and N2 (R is given in the first column of the table). Then, K is assigned the knowledge type specified in the second column with regard to node N1 (i.e. with regard to the first argument of R), and K is assigned the knowledge type specified in the third column with regard to node N2 (i.e. with regard to the second argument of R).
- Thus, one and the same arc generally bears two characterizations concerning its knowledge types.
- The entries in the table have to be considered default values.

| Relation | 1st Arg. | 2nd Arg. | Mnemonics |
|---|---|---|---|
| AFF | categ | situa | C-Role – Affected object |
| AGT | categ | situa | C-Role – Agent |
| ANLG | proto | proto | Similarity relation |
| ANTE | categ | categ | Relation of temporal succession |
| ANTO | categ | categ | Antonymy relation |
| ASSOC | situa | situa | Relation of association |
| ATTCH | situa | situa | Attachment of objects to objects |
| ATTR | categ | categ | Specification of an attribute |
| AVRT | categ | situa | C-Role – Averting / Turning away |
| BENF | categ | situa | C-Role – Beneficiary |
| CAUS | situa | situa | Causality relation |
| CHEA | categ | categ | Change of sorts: Event – Abstract concept (Abstractum) |
| CHPA | categ | categ | Change of sorts: Property – Abstractum |
| CHPE | categ | categ | Change of sorts: Property – Event |
| CHPS | categ | categ | Change of sorts: Property – State |

| | | | |
|---|---|---|---|
| CHSA | categ | categ | Change of sorts: State – Abstract state |
| CHSP1/2/3 | categ | categ | Change of sorts: Situational concept – Property |
| CIRC | situa | situa | Relation between situation and circumstance |
| CNVRS | categ | categ | Lexical relation between converse concepts |
| COMPL | categ | categ | Complementarity relation |
| CONC | situa | situa | Concessive relation |
| COND | situa | restr | Conditional relation |
| CONF | situa | situa | Reference to an external frame, to which a situation conforms |
| CONTR | categ | categ | Contrary concepts |
| CORR | situa | situa | Relation of qualitative or quantitative correspondence |
| CSTR | categ | situa | C-Role – Causator |
| CTXT | restr | situa | Relation specifying a restricting context |
| DIRCL | situa | situa | Relation specifying a local goal or a direction |
| DISTG | proto | proto | Relation specifying a difference |
| DUR | categ | situa | Relation specifying a duration |
| EQU | categ | categ | Equality/Equivalence relation |
| EXP | categ | situa | C-Role – Experiencer |
| FIN | categ | situa | Relation specifying the temporal end |
| GOAL | situa | situa | Generalized goal |
| HSIT | categ | situa | Relation specifying the constituents of a hypersituation |
| IMPL | categ | categ | Implication between situations |
| INIT | categ | situa | Relation specifying an initial situation or material |
| INSTR | proto | situa | C-Role – Instrument |
| JUST | situa | situa | Relation specifying a justification |
| LEXT | situa | situa | Relation specifying a local extent |
| LOC | situa | situa | Relation specifying the location of a situation |
| MANNR | situa | situa | Relation specifying the manner of existence of a situation |

| | | | |
|---|---|---|---|
| MCONT | categ | restr | Relation between a mental process and its content |
| MERO | proto | proto | Meronymy relation |
| METH | proto | situa | C-Role – Method |
| MEXP | categ | situa | C-Role – Mental experiencer |
| MIN/MAJ | categ | categ | Smaller-than-/Greater-than-relation between numbers or quantities |
| MODE | situa | situa | Generalized mode of a situation |
| MODL | restr | situa | Relation specifying a restricting modality |
| NAME | categ | situa | Relation specifying the name of an object |
| OBJ | categ | situa | C-Role – Neutral object |
| OPPOS | categ | situa | C-Role – Entity being opposed by a situation |
| ORIG | situa | situa | Relation specifying an intellectual or informational source |
| ORIGL | situa | situa | Local origin |
| ORIGM | categ | situa | Material origin |
| ORNT | categ | situa | C-Role – Orientation towards something |
| PARS | proto | proto | Part-whole relationship |
| POSS | situa | situa | Relation between possessor and possession |
| PRED | categ | situa | Predicative concept characterizing a plurality (analogously for PREDR/PREDS/PRED0) |
| PROP | proto | situa | Relation between object and property |
| PROPR | categ | situa | Relation between a plurality and a semantic relational quality |
| PURP | situa | situa | Relation specifying a purpose |
| QMOD | categ | situa | Relation for quantitative specifications |
| REAS | situa | situa | Generalized reason |
| RPRS | situa | situa | Relation specifying the form or manifestation of an object |
| RSLT | categ | situa | C-Role – Result |
| SCAR | categ | situa | C-Role – Carrier of a state |
| SETOF | - | situa | Relation between a set and its characterizing concept |
| SOURC | situa | situa | Generalized source |

| SSPE | categ | situa | C-Role – Entity specifying a state |
|------|-------|-------|-------------------------------------|
| STRT | categ | situa | Relation specifying the temporal begin |
| SUB | categ | situa | Relation of conceptual subordination (for objects) |
| SUBR | categ | situa | Relation of conceptual subordination (for relations) |
| SUBS | categ | situa | Relation of conceptual subordination (for situations) |
| SUB0 | categ | situa | Relation of generalized conceptual subordination |
| SUBST | situa | situa | Relation specifying a substitute for something |
| SUPPL | categ | proto | Supplement relation |
| SYNO | categ | categ | Synonymy relation |
| TEMP | categ | situa | Relation specifying the temporal embedding of a situation |
| VAL | categ | situa | Relation between attribute and its value |
| VALR | categ | categ | Relation between attribute and its value restriction |
| VIA | situa | situa | Relation specifying a path |

## Remarks:

- The values of functions are always characterized by *categ* and their arguments are characterized by *situa*.
- The attribute **K-TYPE** is not relevant to relations at the preextensional level.
- Let p be a participant in a situation s described by a restricting relative clause rs. If p is the second argument of a C-role R in the representation of s, and is further described by the relative pronoun of rs, then R is characterized by *categ* with regard to its second argument p.
- On the one hand, the relations INSTR and METH immanently characterize an occurrence, which suggests a value [K-Type = *categ*] with regard to the first argument. On the other hand, the relation MODE as superordinate relation describing a generalized circumstance has to have *situa* with regard to the first argument. Because of this, a value [K-Type = *proto*] has been chosen for both, INSTR and METH, to avoid contradictions in the K-TYPE specifications.

# Appendix E

# Classes of Typical Axioms

**Preamble:**

- This appendix gives a short impression of the axiomatic apparatus standing behind the representational means of MultiNet. The axiom system is steadily extended to enrich the inferential power of the whole knowledge representation paradigm. (The following collection does not claim to be complete.)
- Constraints restricting the validity of axioms are mostly omitted in this appendix (see the corresponding remarks in the text).
- B-Axioms to be classified as default knowledge have not yet been observed.

## E.1   R-Axioms (Categorical Knowledge)

- Causality and Time
$$(x \text{ CAUS } y) \rightarrow \neg(y \text{ ANTE } x) \tag{185}$$

- Transfer of the Location from a Whole to Its Parts
$$(k_1 \text{ PARS } k_2) \wedge (k_2 \text{ LOC } l) \rightarrow (k_1 \text{ LOC } l) \tag{186}$$

- Possession of Part and Whole
$$(a \text{ POSS } b) \wedge (c \text{ PARS } b) \rightarrow (a \text{ POSS } c) \tag{187}$$

- Relationship Between Contrary Properties
$$(o \text{ PROP } p_1) \wedge (p_1 \text{ CONTR } p_2) \rightarrow \neg (o \text{ PROP } p_2) \tag{188}$$

- Complementarity of Properties
$$(p_1 \text{ COMPL } p_2) \wedge \neg(o \text{ PROP } p_1) \rightarrow (o \text{ PROP } p_2) \tag{189}$$

- Complementarity of Concepts
$$(a \text{ SUB } c_1) \wedge (c_1 \text{ COMPL } c_2) \rightarrow \neg(a \text{ SUB } c_2) \tag{190}$$

- Characterization of Semantically Associative Properties

$$o_2 = (*\text{PMOD e } o_1) \wedge (e \text{ CHPA ab}) \rightarrow (o_2 \text{ ASSOC ab}) \qquad (191)$$

- Attributes and Properties

$$(k \text{ ATTR a}) \wedge (a \text{ SUB op}) \wedge (a \text{ VAL q}) \wedge (p \text{ CHPA op}) \rightarrow$$
$$(k \text{ PROP } (*\text{MODP q p})) \qquad (192)$$

- Measurable Properties and Values of Attributes

$$(k \text{ PROP } (*\text{MODP q p})) \wedge (p \text{ CHPA op}) \rightarrow$$
$$\exists a \, [(a \text{ SUB op}) \wedge (k \text{ ATTR a}) \wedge (a \text{ VAL q})] \qquad (193)$$

- Transitivity of Comparison

$$(o_1 \text{ PROP } (*\text{COMP p } o_2)) \wedge (o_2 \text{ PROP } (*\text{COMP p } o_3)) \rightarrow$$
$$(o_1 \text{ PROP } (*\text{COMP p } o_3)) \qquad (194)$$

- The Superlative as the Highest Degree of Comparison

$$(o_1 \text{ PROP } (*\text{SUPL p y})) \wedge (o_2 \text{ SUB y}) \wedge (o_1 \neq o_2) \rightarrow$$
$$(o_1 \text{ PROP } (*\text{COMP p } o_2)) \qquad (195)$$

- Emphasizing the Similarity Between Objects Requires the Distinction in at Least One Attribute

$$(o_1 \text{ ANLG } o_2 \text{ a}) \rightarrow \exists d \, (d \neq a) \wedge (o_1 \text{ DISTG } o_2 \text{ d}) \qquad (196)$$


## E.2   R-Axioms (Default Knowledge)

- Transfer of a Material Characterization from a Whole to Its Parts

$$(k_1 \text{ PARS } k_2) \wedge (k_2 \text{ ORIGM s}) \rightarrow (k_1 \text{ ORIGM s}) \qquad (197)$$

- Inheritance of Properties

$$(o1 \text{ SUB } o2) \wedge (o2 \text{ PROP p}) \rightarrow (o1 \text{ PROP p}) \qquad (198)$$

- Inheritance of Part-Whole Relationships

$$(d1 \text{ SUB } d2) \wedge (d3 \text{ PARS } d2) \rightarrow$$
$$\exists d4 \, [(d4 \text{ SUB } d3) \wedge (d4 \text{ PARS } d1)] \qquad (199)$$

- Comparison of Properties at the Negative Pole

$$(o_1 \text{ PROP } (*\text{COMP } p_- \; o_2)) \rightarrow (o_1 \text{ PROP } p_-) \tag{200}$$

$$(o_1 \text{ PROP } (*\text{COMP } p_- \; o_2)) \rightarrow (o_2 \text{ PROP } p_-) \tag{201}$$

- Emphasizing the Difference in One Attribute (Typically) Requires
  the Similarity in Other Attributes

$$(x \text{ DISTG } y \; a_1) \rightarrow \exists a_2 \; [(a_1 \neq a_2) \wedge (x \text{ ANLG } y \; a_2)] \tag{202}$$

- Relationship Between the Values of Special Attributes
  and Corresponding Properties

$$(o_1 \text{ ATTR } o_2) \wedge (o_2 \text{ VAL } w) \wedge (w \in p) \rightarrow (o_1 \text{ PROP } w) \tag{203}$$

- Relationship Between Result and Initial Material

$$(v \text{ RSLT } d_1) \wedge (d_1 \text{ ORIGM } d_2) \rightarrow (v \text{ INIT } d_2) \tag{204}$$

# E.3 R-Axioms (Definitions of Relations)

- General Reason (Relation REAS)

$$(s_1 \text{ REAS } s_2) \leftrightarrow_{Def} (s_1 \text{CAUS } s_2) \vee (s_1 \text{ IMPL } s_2) \vee (s_1 \text{ JUST } s_2) \tag{205}$$

- Generalized Circumstances and Side Conditions
  (Relation CIRCOND)

$$(sv_1 \text{ CIRCOND } sv_2) \leftrightarrow_{Def}$$
$$(sv_1 \text{ CIRC } sv_2) \vee (sv_1 \text{ CTXT } sv_2) \vee (sv_2 \text{ COND } sv_1) \tag{206}$$

- Connection Between Inverse Relations

$$(s_1 \text{ ANTE } s_2) \leftrightarrow_{Def} (s_2 \text{ POST } s_1) \tag{207}$$

- Connection Between Binary and Ternary Analogy Relation

$$(\ddot{g} \text{ ANLG/2 } a) \leftrightarrow_{Def} \forall x \; \forall y \; [(x_{EXT} \text{ ELMT } \ddot{g}_{EXT}) \wedge$$
$$(y_{EXT} \text{ ELMT } \ddot{g}_{EXT}) \wedge (x \neq y) \rightarrow (x \text{ ANLG/3 } y \; a)] \tag{208}$$

# E.4   Axioms Concerning the Preextensional Level

- Relationship Between Conceptual Subordination and Set Relations
  $$(a \text{ SUB } b) \to (\langle \text{all } a \rangle_{EXT} \text{ SUBM } \langle \text{all } b \rangle_{EXT}) \tag{209}$$
  (if a and b are extensionally interpretable generic concepts)

- $(a \text{ SUB } b) \to (a_{EXT} \text{ ELMT } \langle \text{all } b \rangle_{EXT})$ \hfill (210)
  (extension of a – individual element; extension of b – a set)

- Relationship Between Comparison of All Elements
  of a Plurality and the Superlative
  $(o \text{ PROP } (*\text{COMP } p \ e)) \land (g \text{ PRED } c) \land [\text{QUANT}(g) = \textit{all}] \land$
  $(e_{EXT} = (*\text{DIFF } g_{EXT} \ o_{EXT})) \to (o \text{ PROP } (*\text{SUPL } p \ c ))$ \hfill (211)

- Relationship Between SETOF and SUB
  $(g \text{ SETOF } b) \land (x \text{ ELMT } g) \land (y \text{ EXT } x) \to (y \text{ SUB } b)$ \hfill (212)

- Relationship Between Sets and Their Elements
  $(g_1 \text{ SUBM } g_2) \leftrightarrow (g_1 \neq g_2) \land \forall x [(x \text{ ELMT } g_1) \to (x \text{ ELMT } g_2)]$ \hfill (213)

- Relationship Between Difference Sets
  $(g_1 \text{ SUBM } g) \land (g_2 \text{ SUBM } g) \land (*\text{DIFF } g \ g_1) = g_2$
  $\quad \to (*\text{DIFF } g \ g_2) = g_1$ \hfill (214)

# E.5   B-Axioms (Categorical Knowledge)

- Relationship Between "*give*" and "*receive*"
  $(v \text{ SUBS give.1.1}) \land (v \text{ AGT } a) \land (v \text{ OBJ } o) \land (v \text{ ORNT } d) \to$
  $\exists w (w \text{ SUBS receive.1.1}) \land (w \text{ OBJ } o) \land (w \text{ AVRT } a) \land (w \text{ EXP } d)$ (215)

- Relationship Between PARS-Relation and the Concept "*possess.1.2*"
  $(x \text{ PARS } y) \to \exists s (s \text{ SUBR possess1.2}) \land (s \text{ ARG1 } x ) \land (s \text{ ARG2 } y)$ (216)

- Composing a Name of First Name and Surname
  $(o \text{ NAME } n) \land (n = (*\text{TUPL } v \ f)) \leftrightarrow$
  $\quad\quad \exists a_1 \ \exists a_2 (o \text{ ATTR } a_1) \land (a_1 \text{ SUB } \langle \text{First Name} \rangle) \land (a_1 \text{ VAL } v) \land$
  $\quad\quad\quad (o \text{ ATTR } a_2) \land (a_2 \text{ SUB Surname}) \land (a_2 \text{ VAL } f)$ \hfill (217)

- **Possessor and Possession as Arguments of the Relation POSS**
  $\exists o$ (a SUB possessor) $\wedge$ (a ATTCH o) $\wedge$ (o SUB possession) $\wedge$
  (o EQU b) $\leftrightarrow$ (a POSS b)  (218)

- **Proportion of Weights Between Part and Whole**
  $(k_1$ PARS $k_2) \wedge (k_2$ ATTR $m_2) \wedge (m_2$ SUB weight.1.1$) \wedge (m_2$ VAL $q_2) \rightarrow$
  $\exists m_1 \exists q_1 [(k_1$ ATTR $m_1) \wedge (m_1$ SUB weight.1.1$) \wedge$
  $(m_1$ VAL $q_1) \wedge (q_1$ MIN $q_2)]$  (219)

- **Relationship Between the Concepts "*cost*" (in the sense of "*cost money*") and "*price*"**
  (z SUBS cost.2.1) $\wedge$ (z SCAR o) $\wedge$ (z SSPE v) $\rightarrow$
  $\exists a [(o$ ATTR a) $\wedge$ (a SUB price.1.1) $\wedge$ (a VAL v)]  (220)

- **Those Who Meet Each Other Are at the Same Place**
  (v SUBS meet.2.1) $\wedge$ (v EXP a) $\wedge$ (v OBJ b) $\wedge$ (v LOC l) $\rightarrow$
  (a LOC l) $\wedge$ (b LOC l)  (221)

- **Relationship Between "*send*" and "*instruct*"**
  $(s_1$ SUBS send.2.1$) \wedge (s_1$ AGT $o_1) \wedge (s_1$ OBJ $o_2) \wedge (s_1$ GOAL $o_3) \rightarrow$
  $\exists s_2 \exists s_3 [ (s_2$ SUBS instruct.2.1$) \wedge (s_2$ AGT $o_1) \wedge (s_2$ ORNT $o_2) \wedge$
  $(s_2$ MCONT $s_3) \wedge (s_3$ SUBS go.2.1 $\rangle) \wedge (s_3$ AGT $o_2)$
  $\wedge (s_3$ DIRCL $o_3)]$  (222)

- **Relationship Between the AFF-Relation and the Concept "*change*"**
  (v AFF o) $\rightarrow$ (v SUBS change.2.1)  (223)

- **Properties of an Agent**
  (e AGT o) $\rightarrow$ (e SUBS act) $\wedge$ (o PROP $\langle$capable of acting$\rangle$) $\wedge$
  $\exists s [s = (o$ PROP active)] $\wedge$ (s DUR e)  (224)

- **Relationship Between Instrument or Method and Purpose**
  $(v_1$ SUBS s) $\wedge (v_1$ AGT $k_1) \wedge [(v_1$ INSTR $k_2) \vee (v_1$ METH $k_2)] \rightarrow$
  $\exists v_2 [(v_2$ SUBS use.2.1$) \wedge (v_2$ AGT $k_1) \wedge (v_2$ OBJ $k_2) \wedge (v_2$ PURP s)]  (225)

- **Relationship Between "*weight*" (Verb) and "*weight*" (Noun)**
  (z SCAR o) $\wedge$ (z SUBS weight.2.1) $\wedge$ (z SSPE q) $\rightarrow$
  $\exists w [(o$ ATTR w) $\wedge$ (w SUB weight.1.1) $\wedge$ (w VAL q)]  (226)

- Relationship Between "*kill*" and "*cease to live*"
  $$(v\ SUBS\ kill.2.1) \wedge (v\ AFF\ a) \wedge (v\ TEMP\ t) \rightarrow$$
  $$\exists s\ [(s\ SUBS\ live.2.1) \wedge (s\ SCAR\ a) \wedge (s\ FIN\ t)] \tag{227}$$

- Transforming of Miles into Meter
  $$((*QUANT\ z\ mile.1.1)\ EQU\ (*QUANT(*OP_{TIMES}\ 1609\ z)\ meter.1.1))$$
  $$\tag{228}$$

## E.6   R-Axioms and B-Axioms (Spatio-temporal Relations)

- Mutual Exclusion of Spatial Regions
  $$(o\ LOC\ (*ABOVE\ m)) \rightarrow [\neg(o\ LOC\ (*IN\ m)) \wedge$$
  $$\neg\ (o\ LOC\ (*UNDER\ m)) \wedge \neg(o\ LOC\ (*BESIDES\ m))] \tag{229}$$

- Relationship Between Spatial Containment and the Concept "*enclose*"
  $$(y\ LOC\ (*IN\ x)) \leftrightarrow \exists z\ \exists s\ [(z\ PARS\ y) \wedge$$
  $$(s\ SUBS\ enclose.2.1) \wedge (s\ SCAR\ x) \wedge (s\ OBJ\ z)] \tag{230}$$

- Entailments Between Local Specifications
  $$(o\ LOC\ (*ABOVE\ m)) \leftrightarrow$$
  $$(o\ LOC\ (*OVER\ m)) \vee (o\ LOC\ (*AT\ m)) \tag{231}$$

- Transitivity of Local Inclusion
  $$(o\ LOC\ (*IN\ m)) \wedge (m\ LOC\ (*IN\ n)) \rightarrow (o\ LOC\ (*IN\ n)) \tag{232}$$

- Connection Between Resulting Situation and Temporal Relations
  $$(v\ RSLT\ s) \wedge (s \in si) \rightarrow (v\ FIN\ s) \wedge (v\ ANTE\ s) \tag{233}$$

- Instantaneous Event as the Begin of a Resulting Situation
  $$(v\ RSLT\ s) \wedge (s \in si) \wedge (begin(v)\ EQU\ end(v)) \rightarrow (s\ STRT\ v) \tag{234}$$

- Exclusion of Temporal Specifications
  $$(v\ TEMP\ s) \rightarrow \neg(v\ ANTE\ s) \wedge \neg(s\ ANTE\ v) \tag{235}$$

- Relationship Between Duration and Temporal Beginning and End
  $$(s\ DUR\ (*TUPL\ t_1\ t_2)) \leftrightarrow (s\ STRT\ t_1) \wedge (s\ FIN\ t_2) \tag{236}$$

# E.7 Axiom Schemata (B-Axioms)

- The Origin of an Object o from a Location l Presupposes a Movement, where o is the Agent (AGT) or the Object (OBJ) of the Motion

  $$(k \text{ ORIGL } l) \rightarrow \exists v_1 \exists v \, [(v_1 \text{ SUBS } v) \wedge (v \in \langle \text{move-act} \rangle) \wedge$$
  $$(v_1 \text{ ORIGL } l) \wedge [(v_1 \text{ AGT } k) \vee (v_1 \text{ OBJ } k)] \qquad (237)$$
  with $\langle \text{move-act} \rangle \in \{\text{move.2.1, drive.2.1, go.2.1, fly.2.1, } \dots \}$

- Transfer Acts Start New and Finish Old Relationships of Possession

  $$\exists s \, [s_1 = (o_1 \text{ POSS } o) \wedge s_2 = (o_2 \text{ POSS } o) \wedge (s \text{ SUBS } \langle \text{p-transfer-act} \rangle) \wedge$$
  $$(s \text{ AGT } o_1) \wedge (s \text{ ORNT } o_2) \wedge (s \text{ OBJ } o) \wedge (s \text{ TEMP } t)]$$
  $$\rightarrow [(s_1 \text{ FIN } t) \wedge (s_2 \text{ STRT } t)] \qquad (238)$$
  with $\langle \text{p-transfer-act} \rangle \in \{\text{give.2.1, sell.2.1, transfer.2.1, } \dots \}$

- The Possession of an Object Gives the Owner the Right of Disposal[1]

  $$(p \text{ POSS } b) \rightarrow \exists sv \, [(sv \text{ MODL perm}) \, |$$
  $$(sv \text{ SUBS } \langle \text{dispose-act} \rangle) \wedge (sv \text{ AGT } p) \wedge ((sv \text{ OBJ } b) \vee (sv \text{ AFF } b))]$$
  $$(239)$$
  with $\langle \text{dispose-act} \rangle \in \{\text{sell.2.1, lent.2.1, } \langle \text{give away} \rangle.2.1, \text{change.2.1,}$
  $$\text{destroy.2.1, } \dots \}$$

- Acts of Destruction End the Lifetime of an Object

  $$(sv \text{ SUBS } \langle \text{destr-act} \rangle) \wedge (sv \text{ AFF } o) \wedge (sv \text{ TEMP } t) \rightarrow (o \text{ FIN } t) \qquad (240)$$
  with $\langle \text{destr-act} \rangle \in \{\text{destroy.2.1, annihilate.2.1, dissect.2.1, explode.2.1,}$
  $$\text{decompose.2.1, } \dots \}$$

- Acts of Incorporation Transferring an Object Into the Agent of This Action

  $$(sv_1 \text{ SUBS } \langle \text{incorp-act} \rangle) \wedge (sv_1 \text{ AGT } a) \wedge ((sv_1 \text{ OBJ } o) \vee$$
  $$(sv_1 \text{ AFF } o)) \wedge (sv_1 \text{ TEMP } t) \rightarrow$$
  $$\exists sv_2 \, [sv_2 = (o \text{ LOC } (\text{*IN } a)) \wedge (sv_2 \text{ STRT } t)] \qquad (241)$$
  with $\langle \text{incorp-act} \rangle \in \{\text{eat.2.1, drink.2.1, swallow.2.1, inhale.2.1, } \dots \}$

---

[1] The vertical bar | in the following expression denotes a restriction (here a modal restriction) on a situation. This convention goes beyond the Predicate Calculus of First Order and causes a different treatment of the partial expressions during the phase of logical answer finding in a QAS.

# E.8   Axiom Schemata (R-Axioms)

- $(x \langle REL \rangle y) \to (x \text{ ASSOC } y)$        (Default)                                    (242)
- $(x *NON \langle REL \rangle) y \leftrightarrow \neg(x \langle REL \rangle y)$                                                    (243)

### Standard Properties of Relations

- $(x \langle REL \rangle x) \leftrightarrow \text{Reflexive} \langle REL \rangle$
- $[(x \langle REL \rangle y) \wedge (y \langle REL \rangle z) \to (x \langle REL \rangle z)] \leftrightarrow \text{Transitive} \langle REL \rangle$
- $[(x \langle REL \rangle y) \to (y \langle REL \rangle x)] \leftrightarrow \text{Symmetric} \langle REL \rangle$

| $\langle REL \rangle$ | Reflexive | Transitive | Symmetric |
|---|---|---|---|
| ANLG/3 | no | yes (restricted) | yes (1st and 2nd argument) |
| ANTE | no | yes | no |
| ANTO | no | no | yes |
| ASSOC | no | yes (restricted) | yes (restricted) |
| CAUS | no | yes | no |
| CNVRS | no | no | yes |
| COMPL | no | no | yes |
| COND | no | no | no |
| CONTR | no | no | yes |
| CORR | no | no | yes |
| DISTG/3 | no | no | yes (1st and 2nd argument) |
| EQU | yes | yes | yes |
| IMPL | yes | yes | no |
| MAJ | no | yes | no |
| MAJE | yes | yes | no |
| MIN | no | yes | no |
| MINE | yes | yes | no |
| ORIGM | no | yes (restricted) | no |
| PARS | no | yes (restricted) | no |
| SUB | no | yes | no |
| SUBM | no | yes | no |
| SUBS | no | yes | no |
| SYNO | yes | yes | yes |

# Bibliography

1. D. Abel and B. C. Ooi, editors. *Advances in Spatial Databases*, volume 692 of *LNCS*. Springer, Berlin, 1993.
2. W. Admoni. Der deutsche Sprachbau. Leningrad, 1972.
3. C. E. Alchourrón. Defeasable logics: Demarcation and affinities. In G. Crocco, L. Fariñas Del Cerro, and A. Herzig, editors, *Conditionals: from Philosophy to Computer Science*, number 5 in Studies in Logic and Computation, pages 67–102. Clarendon Press, Oxford, 1995.
4. J. F. Allen. Maintaining knowledge about temporal intervals. *Communications of the ACM*, 26(11):832–843, 1983.
5. J. Allgayer and C. Reddig. What's in a 'DET': Steps towards determiner-dependent inferencing. In K. Bläsius, U. Hedstück, and C.-R. Rollinger, editors, *Artificial Intelligence IV: Methodology, Systems, Applications*. North-Holland, Amsterdam, The Netherlands, 1990.
6. J. Allgayer and C. Reddig-Siekmann. What KL-ONE lookalikes need to cope with natural language – scope and aspect of plural noun phrases. In K. H. Bläsius, U. Hedtstück, and C.-R. Rollinger, editors, *Sorts and Types in Artificial Intelligence*, pages 240–285. Springer, Berlin, Germany, 1990.
7. J. R. Anderson and B. Fishman. The SMALLTALK programming language. *Byte*, 10(5):160–165, 1985.
8. D. Angluin and C. H. Smith. A survey of inductive inference: Theory and methods. *ACM Computing Surveys*, 15(3):238–269, 1983.
9. N. Asher and A. Lascarides. The semantics and pragmatics of presupposition. *Journal of Semantics*, 15:239–299, 1998.
10. B. T. S. Atkins and A. Zampolli, editors. *Computational Approaches to the Lexicon*. Oxford University Press, Oxford, 1994.
11. F. Baader, D. Calvanese, D. McGuinness, D. Nardi, and P. Patel-Schneider, editors. *The Description Logics Handbook*. Cambridge University Press, Cambridge, 2004.
12. F. Baader, R. Küsters, and R. Molitor. Computing least common subsumers in description logics with existential restrictions. In T. Dean, editor, *Proceedings of the 16th International Joint Conference on Artificial Intelligence (IJCAI'99)*, pages 96–101. Morgan Kaufmann, 1999.
13. C. Baker, C. Fillmore, and B. Cronin. The structure of the FrameNet data base. *Int. Journal of Lexicography*, 16(3):281–296, 2003.
14. K. Barker, T. Copeck, S. Delisle, and S. Szpakowicz. Systematic construction of a versatile case system. *Natural Language Engineering*, 3(4):279–315, 1997.
15. J. Barwise and R. Cooper. Generalized quantifiers and natural language. *Linguistics and Philosophy*, 4:159–219, 1981.
16. S. Bechhofer, I. Horrocks, C. Goble, and R. Stevens. Oiled: A reason-able ontology editor for the semantic web. In G. B. Franz Baader and T. Eiter, editors, *KI 2001: Advances in Artificial Intelligence*, pages 396–408, Vienna, Austria, 2001. Springer.
17. C. Beierle, U. Pletat, and R. Studer. Knowledge representation for natural language understanding: The $L_{LILOG}$ approach. *IEEE Transactions on Knowledge and Data Engineering*, 5(3):386–401, 1993.

18. K. Berka and L. Kreiser. *Logik-Texte – Kommentierte Auswahl zur Geschichte der modernen Logik*. Akademie-Verlag, Berlin, 3 edition, 1983.
19. W. Bibel. *Deduktion*. Oldenbourg, München, 1992.
20. M. Bierwisch. *Eine Hierarchie der syntaktisch-semantischen Merkmale*, volume V of *Studia grammatica*. Akademie-Verlag, Berlin, 1970.
21. M. Bierwisch. Semantische und konzeptuelle Repräsentation lexikalischer Einheiten. In R. Růžička and W. Motsch, editors, *Untersuchungen zur Semantik*, Studia grammatica XXII, pages 61–99. Akademie-Verlag, Berlin, 1983.
22. M. Bierwisch. On the grammar of local prepositions. In M. Bierwisch, W. Motsch, and I. Zimmermann, editors, *Syntax, Semantik und Lexikon*, volume XXIX of *Studia grammatica*, pages 1–65. Akademie-Verlag, Berlin, 1988.
23. M. Bierwisch and P. Bosch, editors. *Semantic and conceptual knowledge*, Stuttgart, 1995. Universität Stuttgart, Sonderforschungsbereich 340.
24. K. H. Bläsius and H.-J. Bürckert, editors. *Deduktionssysteme – Automatisierung des logischen Denkens*. Oldenbourg Verlag, München, 1987.
25. U. Blau. *Die dreiwertige Logik der Sprache*. Walter de Gruyter, Berlin, New York, 1978.
26. H. C. Boas. From theory to practice: Frame semantics and the design of FrameNet. In S. Langer and D. Schnorbusch, editors, *Semantik im Lexikon*, number 479 in Tübinger Beiträge zur Linguistik, pages 129–159. Narr, Tübingen, 2005.
27. D. G. Bobrow and T. Winograd. An overview of KRL. *Cognitive Science*, 1(1):3–46, 1977.
28. M. Bocheński. *Die zeitgenössischen Denkmethoden*. Franke Verlag, München, 1975.
29. R. J. Brachman. Structured inheritance networks. Technical Report No. 3742, Bolt Beranek & Newman, Cambridge, Massachusetts, 1978.
30. R. J. Brachman. On the epistemological status of semantic networks. In N. V. Findler, editor, *Associative Networks – Representation and Use of Knowledge by Computers*, pages 3–50. Academic Press, New York, 1979.
31. R. J. Brachman. What IS-A is and isn't: An analysis of taxonomic links in semantic networks. *IEEE Computer*, 16(10):30–36, 1983.
32. R. J. Brachman and H. J. Levesque, editors. *Readings in knowledge representation*. Morgan Kaufmann, Los Altos, 1985.
33. R. J. Brachman, D. McGuinness, P. Patel-Schneider, L. Resnick, and A. Borgida. Living with CLASSIC: When and how to use a KL-ONE-like language. In *Principles of Semantic Networks*, pages 401–456. Morgan Kaufmann, San Mateo, California, 1991.
34. R. J. Brachman and J. G. Schmolze. An overview of the KL-ONE knowledge representation system. *Cognitive Science*, 9(2):171–216, 1985.
35. H. Brinkmann. *Die deutsche Sprache*. Pädagogischer Verlag Schwann, Düsseldorf, 1971.
36. B. Bruce. Case systems for natural language. *Artificial Intelligence*, 6(4):327–360, 1975.
37. M. Bunge. *Kausalität, Geschichte und Probleme*. J.C.B. Mohr, Tübingen, 1987.
38. R. M. J. Byrne and P. N. Johnson-Laird. *Deduction. Essays in Cognitive Science and Psychology*. Lawrence Erlbaum, Hillsdale, 1991.
39. R. Cann, R. Kempson, and L. Marten. *The Dynamics of Language*. Elsevier, forthcoming, 2005.
40. G. N. Carlson and F. J. Pelletier, editors. *The Generic Book*. University of Chicago Press, Chicago, 1995.
41. R. Carnap. *Meaning and Necessity*. Chicago University Press, Chicago, 1947.
42. R. Carnap. *Einführung in die Pilosophie der Naturwissenschaft*. Nymphenburger, München, 1969.
43. L. Castell, M. Drieschner, and C. F. v. Weizsäcker, editors. *Quantum Theory and the Structure of Time and Space, II*. Hanser, München, 1977.
44. N. Cercone. Representing natural language in extended semantic networks. Technical Report TR75-11, Department of Computer Science, The University of Alberta, Edmonton, Canada, July 1975.

45. B. Chandrasekaran, J. R. Josephson, and V. R. Benjamins. What are ontologies, and why do we need them. *IEEE Intelligent Systems*, 14(1):20–26, 1999.
46. M. Chein and M.-L. Mugnier. Positive nested conceptual graphs. In D. Lukose, H. Delugach, M. Keeler, L. Searle, and J. Sowa, editors, *Conceptual Structures: Fulfilling Peirce's Dream (Fifth International Conference on Conceptual Structures, ICCS'97)*, number 1257 in Lecture Notes in Artificial Intelligence, pages 95–109, Berlin, 1997. Springer.
47. N. Chomsky. *Lectures on Government and Binding*. Foris, Dordrecht, The Netherlands, 1981.
48. W. F. Clocksin and C. S. Mellish. *Programming in PROLOG*. Springer, Berlin, 1981.
49. R. Conrad. *Lexikon sprachwissenschaftlicher Termini*. Bibliographisches Institut, Leipzig, 1985.
50. G. Crocco, L. Fariñas Del Cerro, and A. Herzig, editors. *Conditionals: from Philosophy to Computer Science*. Number 5 in Studies in Logic and Computation. Clarendon Press, Oxford, 1995.
51. W. R. Cyre. Executing conceptual graphs. In M.-L. Mugnier and M. Chein, editors, *Conceptual Structures: Theory, Tools and Applications (6th International Conference on Conceptual Structures, ICCS'98)*, number 1453 in Lecture Notes in Artificial Intelligence, pages 51–64, Berlin, 1998. Springer.
52. K. Dahlgren. *Naive Semantics for Natural Language Understanding*. Natural Language Processing and Machine Translation. Kluwer Academic Publishers, Boston, 1988.
53. D. Davidson. The logical form of action sentences. In N. Rescher, editor, *The Logic of Decision and Action*, pages 81–95. The University Press, Pittsburgh, 1967.
54. D. Davidson, editor. *Essays on Actions and Events*. Clarendon Press, Oxford, 2001.
55. F. M. Donini, M. Lenzerini, D. Nardi, and A. Schaerf. Reasoning in description logics. In G. Brewka, editor, *Principles of Knowledge Representation*, Studies in Logic, Language and Information, pages 193–238. CSLI Publications, 1996.
56. D. R. Dowty. On the semantic content of the notion of 'thematic role'. In G. Chierchia, B. H. Partee, and R. Turner, editors, *Properties, Types and Meaning*, volume 2: Semantic Issues, pages 69–129. Kluwer Academic Publishers, Dordrecht, The Netherlands, 1989.
57. D. R. Dowty. *Word Meaning and Montague Grammar*. Kluwer Academic Publishers, Dordrecht, The Netherlands, 1991.
58. M. Eimer. *Konzepte von Kausalität: Verursachungszusammenhänge und psychologische Begriffsbildung*. Verlag Hans Huber, Bern, 1987.
59. M. Ellsworth, K. Erk, P. Kingsbury, and S. Pado. PropBank, SALSA, and Framenet: How design determines product. In *Proceedings of LREC 04, Workshop on Building Lexical Ressources from Semantically Annotated Corpora*, Lisbon, Spain, 2004.
60. R. Evans and G. Gazdar. DATR: A language for lexical knowledge representation. Cognitive Science Research Paper CSRP 382, University of Sussex, Cognitive and Computing Sciences, Brighton, England, Nov. 1995.
61. G. Fauconnier. *Mental Spaces: Aspects of Meaning Construction in Natural Language*. Cambridge University Press, Cambridge, England, 1994.
62. J. Faye, U. Scheffler, and M. Urchs, editors. *Logic and causal reasoning*. Akademie Verlag, 1994.
63. E. Feigenbaum and J. Feldmann. *Computers and Thought*. McGraw Hill, New York, 1963.
64. C. Fellbaum, editor. *Wordnet. An Electronic Lexical Database*. MIT Press, Cambridge, Massachusetts, 1998.
65. R. Ferber. *Zenons Paradoxien der Bewegung und die Struktur von Raum und Zeit*. Number 76 in Zetemata. Beck, München, 1981.
66. C. J. Fillmore. The case for case. In E. Bach and R. Harms, editors, *Universals in Linguistic Theory*, pages 1–88. Holt, Rinehart & Winston, New York, 1968.
67. W. Flämig, editor. *Zum Konjunktiv in der deutschen Gegenwartssprache*. Akademie-Verlag, Berlin, 1959.

68. C. Fox and S. Lappin. *Foundations of Intensional Semantics*. Blackwell Publishers, Oxford, 2005. (in press).
69. C. Freksa. *Repräsentation und Verarbeitung räumlichen Wissens*. Number 245 in Informatik-Fachberichte. Springer, Berlin, 1990.
70. R. Freundlich. *Sprachtheorie*. Springer, Wien, New York, 1970.
71. D. M. Gabbay. *Fibring logics*. Clarendon Press, Oxford, 1999. Volume 38: Oxford logic guides.
72. D. M. Gabbay and H. Wansing. *What is Negation?* Kluwer, Dordrecht, 1999.
73. A. Galton, editor. *The logic of aspect*. Oxford University Press, Oxford, 1984.
74. A. Galton. Time and change for AI. In D. M. Gabbay, C. J. Hogger, and J. Robinson, editors, *Handbook of Logic in Artificial Intelligence and Logic Programming*, pages 175–240. Clarendon Press, Oxford, 1995. Volume 4: Epistemic and Temporal Reasoning.
75. P. Gärdenfors, editor. *Generalized Quantifiers. Linguistic and Logical Approaches*, volume 31 of *Studies in Linguistics and Philosophy*. D. Reidel, Dordrecht, The Netherlands, 1987.
76. M. R. Genesereth and N. J. Nilsson. *Logische Grundlagen der Künstlichen Intelligenz*. Vieweg, Braunschweig, 1989.
77. A. Gerstenkorn. *Das Modal-System im heutigen Deutsch*. Wilh. Fink, München, 1976.
78. I. Glöckner. *Fuzzy Quantifiers in Natural Language: Semantics and Computational Models*. PhD thesis, Universität Bielefeld, Technische Fakultät, Apr. 2003.
79. I. Glöckner, S. Hartrumpf, and R. Osswald. From GermaNet glosses to formal meaning postulates. In B. Fisseni, H.-C. Schmitz, B. Schröder, and P. Wagner, editors, *Sprachtechnologie, mobile Kommunikation und linguistische Ressourcen – Beiträge zur GLDV Tagung 2005 in Bonn*, pages 394–407. Peter Lang, Frankfurt am Main, 2005.
80. I. Glöckner and H. Helbig. Wissensrepräsentation und Antwortfindung mit Mehrschichtigen Erweiterten Semantischen Netzen. *Künstliche Intelligenz*, 2:49–55, 2005.
81. C. Gnörlich. *Technologische Grundlagen der Wissensverwaltung für die automatische Sprachverarbeitung*. PhD thesis, FernUniversität Hagen, Fachbereich Informatik, Hagen, Germany, 2002.
82. C. Goddard. *Semantic Analysis: A practical introduction*. Oxford University Press, Inc., New York, 1998.
83. R. Green, C. A. Bean, and S. H. Myaeng, editors. *The Semantics of Relationships*, Dordrecht, Boston, London, 2002. Kluwer Academic Publishers.
84. P. H. Grice. Logic and conversation. In P. Cole and I. Morgan, editors, *Speech Acts. Syntax and Semantics*, volume 3. Academic Press, New York, 1975.
85. B. J. Grosz and C. L. Sidner. Attention, intentions, and the structure of discourse. *Computational Linguistics*, 12(3):175–204, 1986.
86. A. Grünbaum. *Philosophical Problems of Space and Time*. Kluwer Academic Publishers, Dordrecht, The Netherlands, 1973.
87. M. Gupta et al., editors. *Approximate reasoning in expert systems*. North-Holland, Amsterdam, The Netherlands, 1985.
88. E. Hajičova. Some questions of formal models in linguistic semantics. *CTP*, pages 343–345, 1975.
89. E. Hajičová, J. Panevova, and P. Sgall. Meaning, sense and valency. *Folia linguistica*, 14:57–64, 1980.
90. E. Hajičová, B. Partee, and P. Sgall. *Topic-focus articulation, tripartite structures, and semantic content*. Kluwer, Amsterdam, The Netherlands, 1998.
91. C. Hamann. Adjectives. In A. von Stechow and D. Wunderlich, editors, *Semantik. Ein internationales Handbuch der zeitgenössichen Forschung*, pages 657–673. Walter de Gruyter, Berlin, 1991.
92. S. O. Hansson. The emperor's new clothes: Some recurring problems in the formal analysis of counterfacts. In G. Crocco, L. Fariñas Del Cerro, and A. Herzig, editors, *Conditionals:*

*from Philosophy to Computer Science*, number 5 in Studies in Logic and Computation, pages 13–31. Clarendon Press, Oxford, 1995.

93. W. Harper, R. Stalnaker, and G. Pearce, editors. *Ifs*. D. Reidel, Dordrecht, The Netherlands, 1981.

94. S. Hartrumpf. IBL: An inheritance-based lexicon formalism. AI-report 1994-05, University of Georgia, Artificial Intelligence Center, Athens, Georgia, 1994.

95. S. Hartrumpf. Hybrid disambiguation of prepositional phrase attachment and interpretation. In *Proceedings of the Joint Conference on Empirical Methods in Natural Language Processing and Very Large Corpora (EMNLP/VLC-99)*, pages 111–120, College Park, Maryland, 1999.

96. S. Hartrumpf. Partial evaluation for efficient access to inheritance lexicons. In N. Nicolov and R. Mitkov, editors, *Recent Advances in Natural Language Processing II: Selected Papers from RANLP'97*, volume 189 of *Current Issues in Linguistic Theory*, pages 57–68. John Benjamins, Amsterdam, The Netherlands, 2000.

97. S. Hartrumpf. *Hybrid Disambiguation in Natural Language Analysis*. PhD thesis, Fern-Universität Hagen, Fachbereich Informatik, Hagen, Germany, June 2002.

98. S. Hartrumpf. Question answering using sentence parsing and semantic network matching. In C. Peters and F. Borri, editors, *Results of the CLEF 2004 Cross-Language System Evaluation Campaign, Working Notes for the CLEF 2004 Workshop*, pages 385–392, Bath, England, Sept. 2004.

99. S. Hartrumpf and H. Helbig. The generation and use of layer information in multilayered extended semantic networks. In P. Sojka, I. Kopeček, and K. Pala, editors, *Proceedings of the 5th International Conference on Text, Speech and Dialogue (TSD 2002)*, Lecture Notes in Artificial Intelligence LNCS/LNAI 2448, pages 89–98, Brno, Czech Republic, Sept. 2002.

100. S. Hartrumpf, H. Helbig, and R. Osswald. The semantically based computer lexicon Ha-GenLex – Structure and technological environment. *Traitement automatique des langues*, 44(2), 2003.

101. W. Hartung. Zur Behandlung der Negation im Deutschunterricht an Ausländer. *Deutsch als Fremdsprache*, 2:19, 1966.

102. S. W. Hawking. *Eine kurze Geschichte der Zeit*. Rowohlt, Reinbek bei Hamburg, 1991.

103. I. Heim. File Change Semantics and the Familiarity Theory of Definiteness. In R. Bäuerle et al., editors, *Meaning, Use and Interpretation of Language*. de Gruyter, Berlin, 1983.

104. G. Helbig and W. Rickens. *Die Negation*. VEB Verlag Enzyklopädie, 1969.

105. G. Helbig and W. Schenkel. *Wörterbuch zur Valenz und Distribution deutscher Verben*. Niemeyer, Tübingen, 1983.

106. H. Helbig. A new method for deductive answer finding in a question-answering system. In B. Gilchrist, editor, *IFIP Congress Proceedings*, Information Processing, pages 389–393. IFIP, North-Holland, 1977.

107. H. Helbig. Natural language communication with the question answering system FAS-80. In *First International Conference on Artificial Intelligence and Information Control Systems of Robots*, Smolenice, CSSR, 1980.

108. H. Helbig. *Semantische Repräsentation von Wissen in einem Frage-Antwort-System*. Dissertation B (Habilitation), Part I+II, Akademie der Wissenschaften, Berlin, 1983.

109. H. Helbig. Natural language access to the database of the AIDOS/VS information retrieval system. In I. Plander, editor, *Artificial Intelligence and Information-Control Systems of Robots*, pages 171–174. North-Holland, Amsterdam, The Netherlands, 1984.

110. H. Helbig. Syntactic-semantic analysis of natural language by a new word-class controlled functional analysis. *Computers and Artificial Intelligence*, 5(1):53–59, 1986.

111. H. Helbig. *Künstliche Intelligenz und automatische Wissensverarbeitung*. Verlag Technik, Berlin, 2 edition, 1996.

112. H. Helbig. *Die semantische Struktur natürlicher Sprache: Wissensrepräsentation mit MultiNet*. Springer, Berlin, 2001.

113. H. Helbig. Meaning representation with multilayered extended semantic networks. In *Proceedings of the 18th Florida Artificial Intelligence Conference (FLAIRS-05)*, pages 32–37, 2005.

114. H. Helbig and C. Gnörlich. Multilayered Extended Semantic Networks as a language for meaning representation in NLP systems. In A. Gelbukh, editor, *Computational Linguistics and Intelligent Text Processing*, pages 69–85, Berlin, 2002. Springer.

115. H. Helbig, C. Gnörlich, and D. Menke. Realization of a user-friendly access to networked information retrieval systems. In *Proceedings of the AAAI Spring Symposium on Natural Language Processing for the World Wide Web*, pages 62–71, Stanford, California, 1997.

116. H. Helbig and S. Hartrumpf. Word class functions for syntactic-semantic analysis. In *Proceedings of the 2nd International Conference on Recent Advances in Natural Language Processing (RANLP'97)*, pages 312–317, Tzigov Chark, Bulgaria, Sept. 1997.

117. H. Helbig and M. Schulz. Knowledge representation with MESNET: A multilayered extended semantic network. In *Proceedings of the AAAI Spring Symposium on Ontological Engineering*, pages 64–72, Stanford, California, 1997.

118. D. H. Helman, editor. *Analogical Reasoning*. Kluwer, Dordrecht, The Netherlands, 1988.

119. G. G. Hendrix. Encoding knowledge in partitioned networks. In N. V. Findler, editor, *Associative Networks – Representation and Use of Knowledge by Computers*, pages 51–92. Academic Press, New York, 1979.

120. L. Hermodsson. Semantische Strukturen der Satzgefüge im kausalen und konditionalen Bereich. Acta universitatis upsaliensis, University of Uppsala, Uppsala, 1978.

121. A. Herskovits. *Language and Spatial Cognition*. Cambridge University Press, Cambridge, England, 1986.

122. O. Herzog and C.-R. Rollinger, editors. *Text Understanding in LILOG*. Springer, Berlin, Heidelberg, New York, 1991.

123. A. Heyting. Die formalen Regeln der intuitionistischen Logik. *Sitzungsberichte der Preußischen Akad. Wiss., Phys.-Math. Kl*, pages 42–56, 1930.

124. I. Horrocks, P. Patel-Schneider, and F. van Harmelen. From SHIQ and RDF to OWL: The making of a web ontology language. *Journal of Web Semantics*, 1(1):7–26, 2003.

125. I. Horrocks, U. Sattler, and S. Tobies. Practical reasoning for expressive description logics. In H. Ganzinger, D. McAllester, and A. Voronkov, editors, *Proc. of the 6th Int. Conference on Logic for Programming and Automated Reasoning (LPAR'99)*, number 1705 in Lecture Notes in Artificial Intelligence, pages 161–180. Springer-Verlag, 1999.

126. E. H. Hovy. Automated discourse generation using discourse structure relations. *Artificial Intelligence*, 63:341–385, 1993.

127. G. Huber. *JAVA: die Referenz*. Heise, Hannover, 1996.

128. M. A. Iris, B. E. Litowitz, and M. Evens. Problems of the part-whole relation. In M. Evens, editor, *Relational Models of the Lexicon – Representing Knowledge in Semantic Networks*, chapter 12, pages 261–288. Cambridge University Press, Cambridge, England, 1988.

129. H. O. Ismail. *Reasoning and Acting in Time*. Technical report 2001-11, Univ. at Buffalo, the State University of New York: Dpt. of Computer Science and Engineering, 2001.

130. R. Jackendoff. *Semantic Structures*. MIT Press, Cambridge, Massachusetts, 1990.

131. J. M. Janas and C. B. Schwind. Extensional Semantic Networks. In N. V. Findler, editor, *Associative Networks – Representation and Use of Knowledge by Computers*, pages 267–305. Academic Press, New York, 1979.

132. P. N. Johnson-Laird. *Mental Models: Towards a Cognitive Science of Language, Inference, and Consciousness*. Harvard University Press, Cambridge, Massachusetts, 1983.

133. W. Jung. *Grammatik der Deutschen Sprache*. Bibliographisches Institut, Leipzig, 1982.

134. H. Kamp and U. Reyle. *From Discourse to Logic: Introduction to Modeltheoretic Semantics of Natural Language, Formal Logic and Discourse Representation Theory*. Number 42 in Studies in Linguistics and Philosophy. Kluwer Academic Publishers, Dordrecht, The Netherlands, 1993.

135. I. Kant. *Kritik der reinen Vernunft*. Meiner, Hamburg, 1976.

136. R. M. Kaplan and J. W. Bresnan. Lexical-functional grammar: A formal system for grammatical representation. In J. W. Bresnan, editor, *The Mental Representation of Grammatical Relations*, pages 173–281. MIT Press, Cambridge, Massachusetts, 1982.
137. R. Kempson. *Presupposition and the Delimitation of Semantics*. Cambridge University Press, Cambridge, 1975.
138. C. Kennedy, editor. *Projecting the Adjektive*. Garland Publishing, New York, London, 1999.
139. F. Kiefer. Über Präsuppositionen. In F. Kiefer, editor, *Semantik und generative Grammatik II*. Athenäum, Frankfurt/M., 1972.
140. G. Klaus and M. Buhr, editors. *Philosophisches Wörterbuch*. VEB Bibliographisches Institut, Leipzig, 1965.
141. G. Klose, E. Lang, and T. Pirlein, editors. *Ontologie und Axiomatik der Wissensbasis von LILOG, Wissensmodellierung im IBM Deutschland LILOG-Projekt*, volume 307 of *Informatik-Fachberichte*. Springer, 1992.
142. T. Kohonen. Self-organized formation of topologically correct feature maps. *Biological Cybernetics*, 44:59–69, 1982.
143. T. Kohonen. *Self-Organization and Associative Memory*. Springer, Berlin, Heidelberg, New York, 3 edition, 1989.
144. L. Kreiser, S. Gottwald, and W. Stelzner, editors. *Nichtklassische Logik*. Akademie-Verlag, Berlin, 1988.
145. S. A. Kripke. A completeness theorem in modal logic. *Journal of Symbolic Logic*, 24:1–14, 1959.
146. S. A. Kripke. Semantic analysis of modal logic I: Normal modal and propositional calculi. *Zeitschrift für Mathematische Logik und Grundlagen der Mathematik*, 9:67–96, 1963.
147. S. A. Kripke. Naming and necessity. In D. Davidson and G. Harman, editors, *Semantics of Natural Language*, pages 252–355. D. Reidel, Dordrecht, The Netherlands, 1972.
148. C. Kunze. Semantische Relationstypen in GermaNet. In S. Langer and D. Schnorbusch, editors, *Semantik im Lexikon*, number 479 in Tübinger Beiträge zur Linguistik, pages 161–178. Narr, Tübingen, 2005.
149. C. Kunze and A. Wagner. Anwendungsperspektiven des GermaNet, eines lexikalisch-semantischen Netzes für das Deutsche. In I. Lemberg, B. Schröder, and A. Storrer, editors, *Chancen und Perspektiven computergestützter Lexikographie*, volume 107 of *Lexicographica Series Maior*, pages 229–246. Niemeyer, Tübingen, 2001.
150. G. Lakoff. Lingusitics and natural logic. *Synthese*, 22:151–271, 1970.
151. G. Lakoff. *Woman, Fire, and Dangerous Things*. University of Chicago Press, Chicago, London, 1987.
152. E. Lang. *Semantik der koordinativen Verknüpfung*, volume XIV of *Studia grammatica*. Akademie-Verlag, Berlin, 1977.
153. E. Lang. Linguistische vs. konzeptuelle Aspekte der LILOG Ontologie – Anfragen von außen. In G. Klose, E. Lang, and T. Pirlein, editors, *Ontologie und Axiomatik der Wissensbasis von LILOG*, pages 23–45. Springer, Berlin, 1992.
154. R. Langacker. *Theoretical prerequisites*, volume 1 of *Foundations of Cognitive Grammar*. Stanford University Press, Stanford, 1990.
155. R. Langacker. *Descriptive application*, volume 2 of *Foundations of Cognitive Grammar*. Stanford University Press, Stanford, 1991.
156. S. Lappin, editor. *The Handbook of Contemporary Semantic Theory*. Blackwell Publishers, Malden, Mass., 1996.
157. F. Lehmann, editor. *Semantic Networks in Artificial Intelligence*. Pergamon Press, Oxford, 1992.
158. D. B. Lenat and R. V. Guha. *Building Large Knowledge-based Systems: Representation and Inference in the Cyc Project*. Addison-Wesley, Reading, Massachusetts, 1990.

159. J. Leveling and H. Helbig. A robust natural language interface for access to bibliographic databases. In B. S. Nagib Callaos, Maurice Margenstern, editor, *Proc. of the 6th Conference on Systemics, Cybernetics and Informatics*, volume XI, pages 133–138, Orlando, Florida, July 2002. International Institute of Informatics and Systemics (IIIS).

160. B. Levin. *English Verb Classes and Alternations. A Preliminary Investigation*. University of Chicago Press, Chicago, 1993.

161. D. Lewis. General semantics. In D. Davidson and G. Herman, editors, *Semantics of Natural Language*. D. Reidel, Dordrecht, The Netherlands, 1972.

162. S. Löbner. *Wahr neben Falsch. Duale Operatoren als die Quantoren natürlicher Sprache*. Number 244 in Linguistische Arbeiten. Max Niemeyer Verlag, Tübingen, 1990.

163. S. Löbner. Polarity in natural language: Predication, quantification and negation in particular and characterizing sentences. *Linguistics and Philosophy*, 23:213–308, 2000.

164. R. Lütticke and H. Helbig. Problem solving in an interactive internet-based learning environment. In M. Auer and U. Auer, editors, *Interactive computer aided learning (ICL) 2003, International Workshop in Villach (Austria)*, Kassel, 2003. University Press.

165. R. Lütticke, C. Gnörlich, and H. Helbig. Der Einsatz eines virtuellen Labors in der Informatik-Lehre. *Softwaretechnik-Trends der GI*, 22(3):57–59, 2002.

166. R. Lütticke, C. Gnörlich, and H. Helbig. VILAB - a virtual electronic laboratory for applied computer science. In *Proceedings of the Conference Networked Learning in a Global Environment*, page 135, Canada/The Netherlands, 2002. ICSC Academic Press.

167. J. Lyons. *Introduction to Theoretical Linguistics*. Cambridge Univ. Press, Cambridge, 1971.

168. J. Lyons. *Semantics*, volume 1. Cambridge Univ. Press, Cambridge, 1977.

169. J. Lyons. *Semantics*, volume 2. Cambridge Univ. Press, Cambridge, 1977.

170. J. Mackie. *The Cement of Universe*. Oxford University Press, Oxford, 1974.

171. M. J. Maher, A. Rock, G. Antoniou, D. Billington, and T. Miller. Efficient defeasible reasoning systems. *International Journal on Artificial Intelligence Tools*, 10:483–501, 2001.

172. K. Mahesh, S. Nirenburg, J. Cowie, and D. Farwell. An assessment of Cyc for natural language processing. Technical Report MCCS-96-302, Computing Research Laboratory, New Mexico State University, New Mexico, Sept. 1996.

173. H. Mallot. Spatial cognition: Behavioral competences, neural mechanisms, and evolutionary scaling. *Kognitionswissenschaft*, 8(1):40–48, Aug. 1999.

174. W. C. Mann and S. A. Thompson. Rhetorical structure theory: Description and construction of text structures. In G. Kempen, editor, *Natural Language Generation*. Martinus Nijhoff Publishers, Dordrecht, The Netherlands, 1987.

175. W. C. Mann and S. A. Thompson. Rhetorical structure theory: Toward a functional theory of text organization. *Text*, 8(3):243–281, 1988.

176. S. Marthen. Untersuchungen zur Assimilation größerer Wissensbestände aus textueller Information. Master's thesis, FernUniversität Hagen, Hagen, Germany, Feb. 2002.

177. T. Matsui. *Bridging and Relevance*. John Benjamins, Amsterdam, The Netherlands, 2000.

178. J. McCarthy. Programs with common sense. In M. L. Minsky, editor, *Semantic Information Processing*, pages 403–418. MIT Press, Cambridge, MA, 1968.

179. J. McCarthy and P. Hayes. Some philosophical problems from the standpoint of artificial intelligence. In B. Meltzer and D. Michie, editors, *Machine Intelligence 4*, pages 463–502. University Press, Edinburgh, 1969.

180. J. McDermott. R1: A rule based configurer of computer systems. *Artificial Intelligence*, 19(1):39–88, 1982.

181. J. Mill. *A System of Logic*, volume I and II. Longmans, Green, Reader and Dyer, London, 8 edition, 1872.

182. G. A. Miller and P. N. Johnson-Laird. *Language and Perception*. Cambridge University Press, Cambridge, England, 1976.

183. M. Minsky. A framework for representing knowledge. In P. H. Winston, editor, *The Psychology of Computer Vision*, pages 211–277. McGraw-Hill, New York, 1975.

184. R. Montague. Pragmatics and intensional logic. *Semantics of Natural Language*, 1972.

185. R. Montague. *Formal Philosophy, Selected Papers of Richard Montague*. Yale Univ. Press, New Haven, 1974.

186. D. A. Moon. Object-oriented programming with FLAVORS. In N. Meyrowitz, editor, *Proceedings of the Conference on Object-Oriented Programming Systems, Languages, and Applications (OOPSLA)*, number 11 in SIGPLAN Notices, pages 1–8, New York, NY, 1986. ACM Press.

187. L. S. Murawjowa. *Die Verben der Bewegung im Russischen*. Verlag Russische Sprache, Moskau, 1978.

188. S. E. Newstead and K. Coventry. The role of context and functionality in the interpretation of quantifiers. *European Journal of Cognitive Psychology*, 12(2):243–259, 2000.

189. S. E. Newstead, P. Pollard, and D. Riezebos. The effect of set size on the interpretation of quantifiers used in rating scales. *Applied Ergonomics*, 18(3):178–182, 1987.

190. L. of Congress. *ANSI/NISO Z39.50-1995 specifies versions 2 and 3 of the Z39.50 protocol*. Z39.50 Maintenance Agency, 1995.

191. R. Osswald. *A Logic of Classification – with Applications to Linguistic Theory*. PhD thesis, FernUniversität Hagen, Fachbereich Informatik, Hagen, Germany, July 2002.

192. R. Osswald. Eine Werkbank zur Erstellung und Pflege des semantikbasierten Computerlexikons HaGenLex. In E. Buchberger, editor, *Proceedings of KONVENS 2004*, Schriftenreihe der Österreichischen Gesellschaft für Artificial Intelligence, Band 5, pages 149–152, Wien, 2004.

193. R. Osswald. Concept hierarchies from a logical point of view. In B. Ganter, R. Godin, and E. M. Nguifo, editors, *ICFCA-2005 International Conference on Formal Concept Analysis*, pages 15–30, Lens, France, 2005. IUT de Lens.

194. R. Osswald and H. Helbig. Derivational semantics in HaGenLex – an interim report. In S. Langer and D. Schnorbusch, editors, *Semantik im Lexikon*, number 479 in Tübinger Beiträge zur Linguistik, pages 87–127. Narr, Tübingen, 2005.

195. T. Parsons. Thematic relations and arguments. *Linguistic Inquiry*, 26(4):635–662, 1995.

196. G. Patzig. *Sprache und Logik*. Vandenhoek & Rupprecht, Göttingen, 1970.

197. J. Pearl. *Probabilistic Resoning in Intelligent Systems: Networks of Plausible Inference*. Morgan Kaufmann, San Mateo, Ca., 1988.

198. C. Peltason. The BACK system – An overview. *SIGART Bulletin*, 2(3):114–119, 1991.

199. J. Piaget. *The child's conception of physical causality*. Routledge and Kegan Paul, London, 1970.

200. M. Pinkal. Vagheit und Ambiguität. In A. von Stechow and D. Wunderlich, editors, *Semantik. Ein internationales Handbuch der zeitgenössichen Forschung*, pages 250–269. Walter de Gruyter, Berlin, 1991.

201. M. Pinkal. Semantikformalismen für die Sprachverarbeitung. In G. Görz, C.-R. Rollinger, and J. Schneeberger, editors, *Handbuch der Künstlichen Intelligenz*, pages 739–782. Oldenbourg, München, 2000.

202. W. Pohlers. *Proof Theory*, volume 1407 of *Lecture Notes in Mathematics*. Springer, Berlin, 1989.

203. C. Pollard and I. A. Sag. *Head-Driven Phrase Structure Grammar*. Studies in Contemporary Linguistics. University of Chicago Press, Chicago, Illinois, 1994.

204. S. Pribbenow. *Räumliche Konzepte in Wissens- und Sprachverarbeitung. Hybride Verarbeitung von Lokalisierung*. Deutscher Universitätsverlag, Wiesbaden, 1993.

205. J. Pustejovsky. The generative lexicon. *Computational Linguistics*, 17:409–441, 1991.

206. J. Pustejovsky. *The Generative Lexicon*. MIT Press, Cambridge, Massachusetts, 1995.

207. H. Putnam. *Mind, Language and Reality*, volume 2 of *Philosophical Papers*. Cambridge University Press, Cambridge, England, 1975.

208. M. R. Quillian. Semantic memory. In M. Minsky, editor, *Semantic Information Processing*, pages 227–270. MIT Press, Cambridge, Massachusetts, 1968.
209. W. Quine. *Grundzüge der Logik*. Number 65 in Suhrkamp Taschenbuch Wissenschaft. Suhrkamp, Frankfurt am Main, 1969.
210. G. Rauh. *Tiefenkasus, thematische Relationen und Thetarollen*. Gunter Narr, Tübingen, 1988.
211. H. Reichenbach. *Elements of Symbolic Logic*. Free Press, New York, 1947.
212. R. Reiter. A logic for default reasoning. *Artificial Intelligence*, 13(1/2):81–132, 1980.
213. D. Richardson. Some unsolvable problems involving elementary functions of a real variable. *Journal Symb. Logic*, 133·511, 1968.
214. J. Robinson. Kasus, Kategorie und Konfiguration. *Journal of Linguistics*, pages 51–80, 1970. Übersetzung.
215. M. Rooth. Noun phrase interpretation in Montague grammar, file change semantics and situation semantics. In Gärdenfors [75], pages 237–268.
216. D. Rumelhart, P. Lindsay, and D. Norman. A process model for longterm memory. In E. Tulving and W. Donaldson, editors, *Organization of Memory*, chapter 4, pages 198–221. Academic Press, New York, 1972.
217. D. E. Rumelhart and J. L. McClelland. *Parallel Distributed Processing: Explorations in the Microstructure of Cognition. Vol. 1: Foundations*. MIT Press, Cambridge, Massachusetts, 1986.
218. B. Russell. On the notions of cause. In *Proceedings of the Aristotelian Society*, volume 13, pages 1–26, 1913.
219. E. Sandewall. Representing natural language information in predicate calculus. In B. Meltzer and D. Michie, editors, *Machine Intelligence VI*, volume 6, pages 255–277. American Elsevier, New York, 1971.
220. R. C. Schank. Conceptual dependency: A theory of natural language understanding. *Cognitive Psychology*, 3(4):532–631, 1972.
221. R. C. Schank. Conceptual dependency theory. In R. C. Schank, editor, *Conceptual Information Processing*, chapter 3, pages 22–82. Prentice Hall, New Haven, 1975.
222. R. C. Schank and R. P. Abelson. *Scripts, plans, goals and understanding*. Erlbaum, Hillsdale, 1977.
223. R. C. Schank, C. Goldman, C. Rieger, and C. Riesbeck. MARGIE: Memory, Analysis, Response Generation and Inference on English. In *Proceedings 3rd International Joint Conference on Artificial intelligence*, 1973.
224. H. Schildt. *C++ from the ground up*. McGraw-Hill, New York, 1998.
225. L. K. Schubert. Extending the expressive power of semantic networks. Technical Report TR74-18, Department of Computer Science, The University of Alberta, Edmonton, Canada, Nov. 1974.
226. M. Schulz. On the acquisition of consistent subcategorization frames. Technical Report, FernUniversität Hagen, Hagen, 1997.
227. M. Schulz. *Eine Werkbank zur interaktiven Erstellung semantikbasierter Computerlexika*. PhD thesis, FernUniversität Hagen, Fachbereich Informatik, Hagen, Germany, Aug. 1998.
228. M. Schulz and H. Helbig. COLEX: Ein Computerlexikon für die automatische Sprachverarbeitung. Informatik-Bericht 210, FernUniversität Hagen, Hagen, Germany, Dec. 1996.
229. J. R. Searle, F. Kiefer, and M. Bierwisch. *Speech Act Theory and Pragmatics*. D. Reidel, Dordrecht, The Netherlands, 1980.
230. P. Sgall. On the notion of semantic language. In *Proceedings (COLING 76)*, 1976.
231. P. Sgall and E. Hajičová. *Topic, Focus and Generative Semantics*. Scriptor, Kronberg, Taunus, 1973.
232. G. Shafer. *The Art of Causal Conjecture*. MIT Press, Cambridge, Massachusetts, 1996.
233. S. C. Shapiro. A net structure for semantic information storage, deduction and retrieval. In *Proceedings of the Second International Joint Conference on Artificial Intelligence*, pages 512–523, Morgan Kaufmann, Los Altos, CA, 1971.

234. S. C. Shapiro. The SnePS semantic network processing system. In N. V. Findler, editor, *Associative Networks: The Representation and Use of Knowledge by Computers*, pages 179–203. Academic Press, New York, 1979.

235. S. C. Shapiro. Case studies of SNePS. *SIGART Bulletin*, 2(3):128, 1991.

236. S. C. Shapiro. Relevance logic in computer science. In A. R. Anderson, N. D. Belnap, and M. Dunn, editors, *Entailment, Volume II*, pages 553–563. Princeton University Press, Princeton, 1992.

237. S. C. Shapiro. Formalizing English. *International Journal of Expert Systems*, 9(1):151–171, 1996.

238. S. C. Shapiro. A logic of arbitrary and indefinite objects. In *Proceedings of the Ninth International Conference on Knowledge Representation and Reasoning (KR-2004)*, pages 565–575, AAAI, Menlo Park, California, 2004.

239. S. C. Shapiro and W. J. Rapaport. The SNePS family. In F. Lehmann, editor, *Semantic Networks in Artificial Intelligence*, pages 243–275. Pergamon Press, Oxford, 1992.

240. S. M. Shieber. *An Introduction to Unification-Based Approaches to Grammar*. Number 4 in CSLI Lecture Notes. Stanford University, Stanford, California, 1986.

241. J. Shoenfield. *Mathematical Logic*. Addison-Wesley, Reading, 1967.

242. D. Siefkes. Über die fruchtbare Vervielfältigung der Gedanken beim Reden. *Forschung und Lehre*, 10:551–555, 1995.

243. G. Simonet. Two FOL semantics for simple and nested conceptual graphs. In M.-L. Mugnier and M. Chein, editors, *Conceptual Structures: Theory, Tools and Applications (6th International Conference on Conceptual Structures, ICCS'98)*, number 1453 in Lecture Notes in Artificial Intelligence, pages 240–254, Berlin, 1998. Springer.

244. A. Sinowjew and H. Wessel. *Logische Sprachregeln, eine Einführung in die Logik*. VEB Deutscher Verlag der Wissenschaften, Berlin, 1975.

245. K.-E. Sommerfeldt and H. Schreiber. *Wörterbuch zur Valenz und Distribution deutscher Adjektive*. VEB Bibliographisches Institut, Leipzig, 1980.

246. K.-E. Sommerfeldt and H. Schreiber. *Wörterbuch zur Valenz und Distribution deutscher Substantive*. VEB Bibliographisches Institut, Leipzig, 1980.

247. F. Sommers. *The logic of natural language*. Clarendon Press, Oxford, 1982.

248. J. F. Sowa. *Conceptual Structures. Information Processing in Mind and Machine*. The System Programming Series. Addison-Wesley, Reading, Massachusetts, 1984.

249. J. F. Sowa. *Knowledge Representation: Logical, Philosophical, and Computational Foundations*. Brooks & Cole, Pacific Grove, 2000.

250. M. Steedman. *Surface Structure and Interpretation*, volume 30 of *Linguistic Inquiry Monographs*. MIT Press, Cambridge, Massachusetts, 1996.

251. W. Stegmüller. *Hauptströmungen der Gegenwartsphilosophie*. Kröner, Stuttgart, 1989.

252. G. Stickel. *Untersuchungen zur Negation im heutigen Deutsch*. Vieweg, Braunschweig, 1970.

253. P. Suppes. *A Probabilistic Theory of Causality*. North-Holland, Amsterdam, The Netherlands, 1970.

254. G. Takeuti. *Proof Theory*, volume 81 of *Studies in Logic and the Foundations of Mathematics*. North-Holland Publishing Company, Amsterdam, 1975.

255. W. Tepfenhart and W. Cyre, editors. *Conceptual Structures: Standards and Practices (7th International Conference on Conceptual Structures, ICCS'99)*, number 1640 in Lecture Notes in Artificial Intelligence, Berlin, 1999. Springer.

256. L. Tesnière. *Eléments de syntaxe structurale*. Klincksieck, Paris, 1959.

257. J. Thorp. *Free will: A defence against neurophysiological determinism*. Routledge & Paul, London, 1980.

258. I. Tjaden. Semantische Präpositionsinterpretation im Rahmen der Wortklassengesteuerten Analyse. Master's thesis, FernUniversität Hagen, Hagen, Germany, 1996.

259. D. S. Touretzky. *The Mathematics of Inheritance Systems*. Research Notes in Artificial Intelligence. Pitman Publishing, London, 1986.

260. W. Trilling. *Fragen zur Geschichtlichkeit Jesu.* St. Benno-Verlag GmbH, Leipzig, 3 edition, 1969.
261. E. Tulving and W. Donaldson. *Organization of Memory.* Academic Press, New York, 1972.
262. J. van Benthem. *Essays in Logical Semantics.* D. Reidel, Dordrecht, The Netherlands, 1986.
263. J. van Benthem. *The Logic of Time.* Kluwer, Dordrecht, The Netherlands, 1991.
264. E. van der Meer. Zeitkodierung in Wissenskörpern. *Zeitschrift für Psychologie*, 207(3–4):363–381, 1999.
265. Z. Vendler. *Linguistics in Philosophy.* Cornell University Press, Ithaca, New York, 1967.
266. L. Vila. A survey on temporal reasoning in artificial intelligence. *AI Communications*, 7(1):4–28, Mar. 1994.
267. N. Vilain. The restricted language architecture of a hybrid representation system. In *Proceedings of the 9th International Joint Conference on Artifical Intelligence*, pages 547–551, Los Angeles, California, 1985.
268. K. von Luck and B. Owsnicki-Klewe. KL-ONE: Eine Einführung. In P. Struß, editor, *Wissensrepräsentation*, pages 103–121. Oldenbourg, München, 1991.
269. A. von Stechow and D. Wunderlich, editors. *Semantik. Ein internationales Handbuch der zeitgenössichen Forschung.* Walter de Gruyter, Berlin, 1991.
270. G. H. von Wright. *Causality and determinism.* Number 10 in The Woodbridge Lectures. Columbia University Press, New York, 1974.
271. W. Wahlster, editor. *Verbmobil: Foundations of speech-to-speech translation.* Springer, Heidelberg, 2000.
272. W. Wahlster. SmartWeb: Mobile applications of the semantic web. In *Proc. KI 2004: Advances in Artificial Intelligence*, volume 3238 of *LNAI*, pages 50–51, Berlin, 2004. Springer.
273. G. Wahrig. *Deutsches Wörterbuch.* Bertelsmann-Lexikon-Verlag, Gütersloh, 1992.
274. D. E. Walker, editor. *Automating the lexicon: research and practice in a multilingual environment.* Oxford University Press, Oxford, 1995.
275. R. Weatherford. *The Implications of Determinism.* Routledge, London, 1991.
276. A. Wierzbicka. *Semantics: Primes and Universals.* Oxford University Press, Oxford, 1996.
277. Y. Wilks. The preference semantics family. *Computers Math. Applic.*, 23(2):205–221, 1992.
278. T. Winograd. *Language as a Cognitive Process: Volume I: Syntax.* Addison-Wesley, Reading, Massachusetts, 1983.
279. L. Wittgenstein. *Philosophische Untersuchungen.* Suhrkamp, Frankfurt, 1975.
280. S. Wolf and R. Setzer. *Wissensverarbeitung mit KEE: Einführung in die Erstellung von Expertensystemen.* Oldenbourg, München, 1991.
281. W. A. Woods. What's in a link: Foundations for semantic networks. In D. G. Bobrow and A. Collins, editors, *Representation and Understanding*, pages 35–82. Academic Press, New York, 1975.
282. W. A. Woods. Semantics and quantification in natural language question answering. In B. J. Grosz, K. Sparck-Jones, and B. L. Webber, editors, *Readings in Natural Language Processing*, pages 205–248. Morgan Kaufmann, Los Altos, California, 1986.
283. D. Wunderlich and M. Herweg. Lokale und Direktionale (Spatial and Directional Prepositions). In A. von Stechow and D. Wunderlich, editors, *Semantik. Ein internationales Handbuch der zeitgenössichen Forschung*, pages 758–785. Walter de Gruyter, Berlin, 1991.
284. A. Zell. *Simulation neuronaler Netze.* Oldenbourg, München, 1997.

# List of Figures

# Index

# Cognitive Technologies